The

Campbell Family of New York City, New York

and their ancestors

The

Campbell Family of New York City, New York

and their ancestors

© 2022 Kerry Gans

Maps: Base map © maproom.net
DNA symbol: Freepik from www.flaticon.com

To all those who came before us:
We would not be who we are without your work and sacrifice.
You are not forgotten.
– Kerry Gans

Table of Contents

PREFACE

This book is the result of twenty years of genealogical research. In addition to full source citations as endnotes after each chapter, I placed a name index to help look up individuals, and a place index that provides a good overview of where our ancestors originated and lived.

Our lineage is Irish and Scottish. Since all our immigrants were recent, the jump back to "the old country" happened quickly. For our Irish side, this means not very much information could be found, as Irish records are notoriously sparse. We fared better researching in Scotland.

Because of this disparity of information, I have chosen to discuss our Irish lineage in the first chapter, instead of starting with the Campbell name chapter. Chapter Two is the Campbell chapter, and the Scottish line runs from there.

I was able to trace our Scottish line to the Scottish Royal line, so the book includes chapters on the Scottish and English Royal connections. I deliberately kept these chapters short, as the royal lines are well-researched by experts, and if you wish to find more information it is easy for you to do on your own.

Since DNA-based genealogy has come into the mainstream, I have been able to prove parts of our line by DNA matches. Any ancestral couple that has been confirmed by DNA matches has a DNA symbol next to their names.

Please note that ages and spellings vary. I copy the data as written on the documents. They do not always add up from one document to the next. Sometimes the names are spelled differently in the same document. So do not be thrown if ages float around or names morph. It was very, very common in the time before Social Security and when many folks were illiterate.

I hope you enjoy this family history, complete with lineage trees and photos. Anyone reading this book with information to add, or evidence to prove or disprove information in this book, please contact me so we can grow our family history together!

Kerry Gans
4 August 2021

THE IRISH

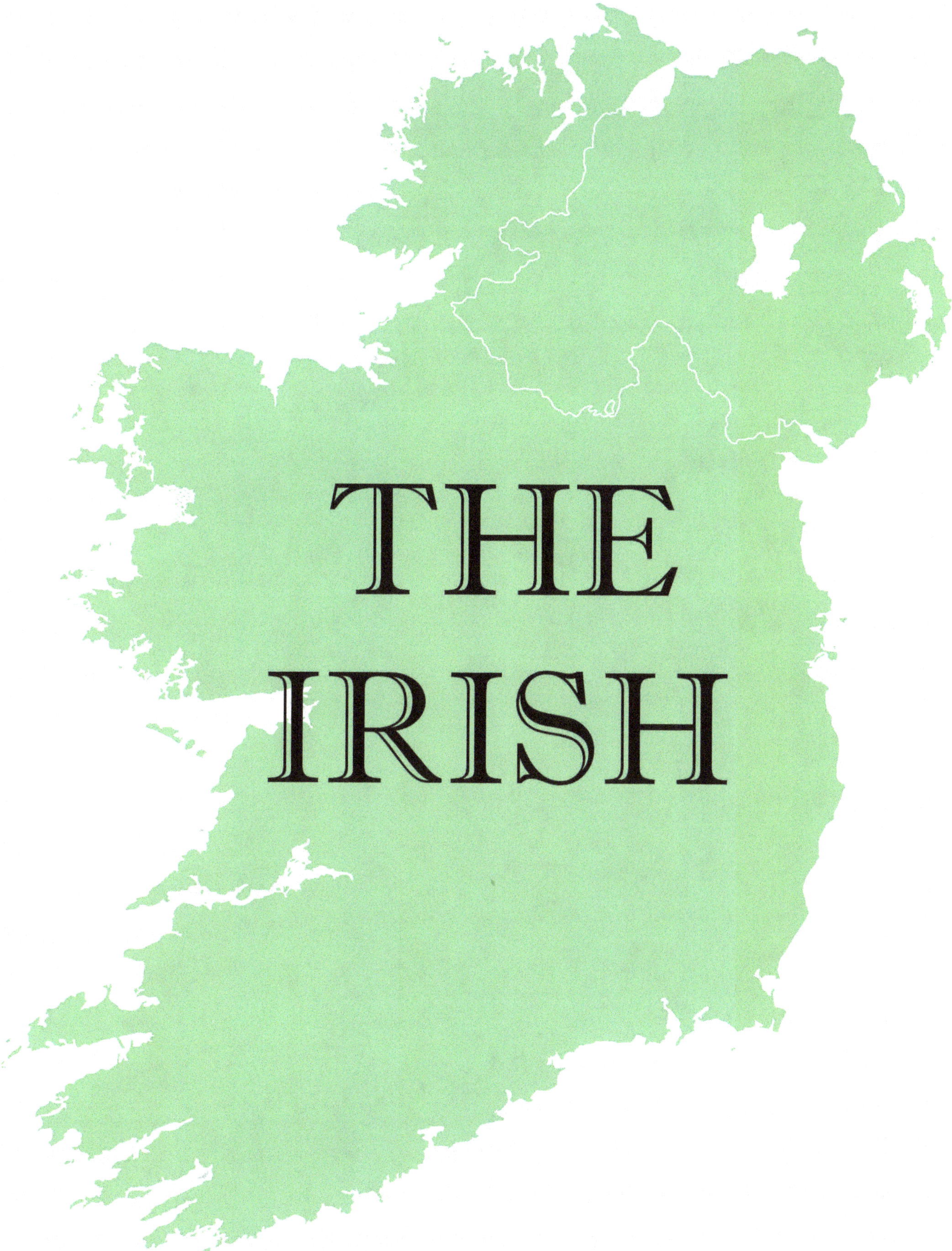

THE HAYDEN-SUTTON LINEAGE

NORTHERN
IRELAND

REPUBLIC OF
IRELAND

TIPPERARY
(HAYDEN)

CARLOW
(SUTTON)

THE SUTTON-HAYDEN LINEAGE

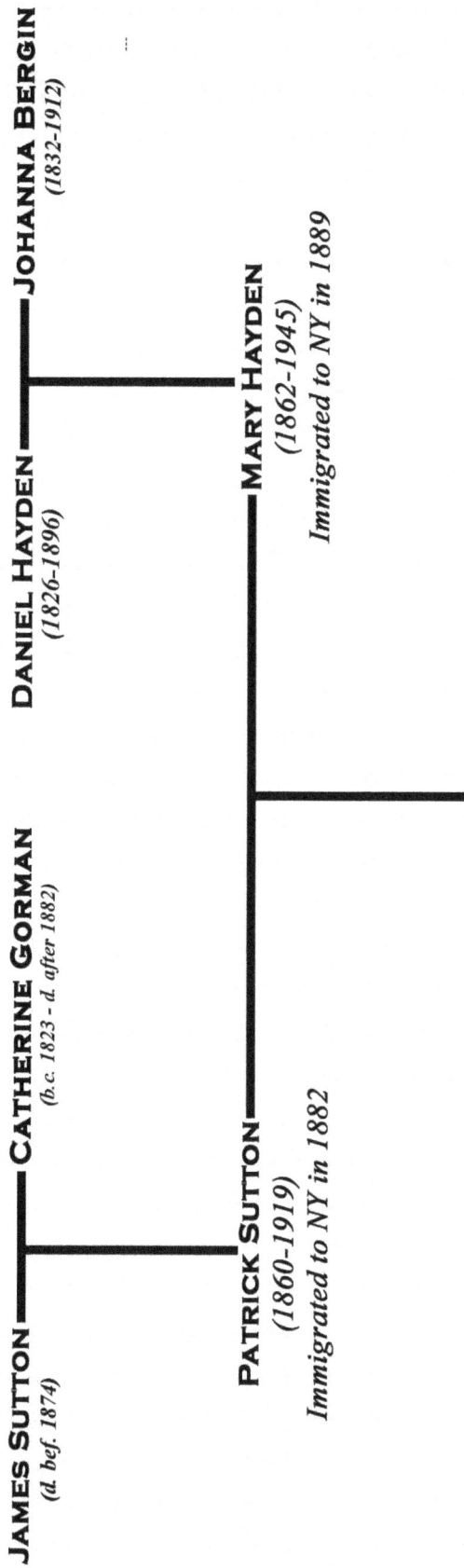

JAMES SUTTON
(d. bef. 1874)

CATHERINE GORMAN
(b.c. 1823 - d. after 1882)

DANIEL HAYDEN
(1826-1896)

JOHANNA BERGIN
(1832-1912)

PATRICK SUTTON
(1860-1919)
Immigrated to NY in 1882

MARY HAYDEN
(1862-1945)
Immigrated to NY in 1889

(continued next page)

THE SUTTON FAMILY
(colored blocks denote generations)

PATRICK SUTTON
(1860-1919)
Immigrated to NY in 1882

MARY HAYDEN
(1862-1945)
Immigrated to NY in 1889

MICHAEL MAHER

LIZZIE HAYDEN
(1883 in Ireland-1978 in NJ)
never married, no children

JAMES
(1892-1978)
first married

(1) ANNA MCNICHOLL
(1900-1922)
no children

then married

(2) KATHRYN MURRAY
(c. 1902-1984)

BARBARA SUTTON
(1935-1988)
M. THOMAS LOTH

JOHANNA
(1894-1908)
never married,
no children

NICHOLAS
(1896-1956)
maybe married,
no children

CATHERINE
(1898-1970)

married

WILLIAM LANG
(1884-1967)

WILLIAM LANG *(1923-2000)*
M. ANNE O'DONNELL (1926-2000)

ANNA
(1899-1987)

married

JOHN HACKETT
(1898 in Ireland-1953 in NY)

JACKIE HACKETT
(1928-2007)
M. PATRICIA RYAN

MAUREEN HACKETT
(1929-2017)
married, no children

ANNE HACKETT
(1931-1983)
never married, no children

KATHERINE HACKETT
(1942-1942)
never married, no children

MARGARET
(1901-1963)

married

WILLIAM WALDRON
(1905, England-1978, Ohio)

(LIVING)

WILLIAM WALDRON *(1937-2001)*

MARY
(1904-1975)

married

EDWARD CAMPBELL
(1903-1963)

see Campbell Lineage tree
for children

AGNES
(1908-1953)
never married,
no children

THE HAYDEN LINEAGE

The Hayden lineage is a bit of a mystery. The first known couple is Daniel Hayden and Judith (Johanna) Bergin (see below). While researching parents for Daniel and Johanna, I received not one, but *two* emails from people in Australia. Each traced to a Bergin family who had immigrated, but left behind a child— Johanna Bergin, the same age as our Johanna *and* from the Nenagh area of Tipperary, where our Johanna is from. I am going to include this family here as if they are ours, but we need more confirmation.

Daniel Bergin (b.c. 1806) and Margaret Russell (b.c. 1810)

Assuming that the link with Australia is correct, Daniel Bergin and Margaret Russell were our Johanna's parents. Daniel was christened 12 August 1806, and Margaret was christened 7 March 1810. They were married 20 October 1828 in Roscrea Parish, County Tipperary, with witnesses Michael Maher and Peg Cotton.[1] Margaret's parents were John Russell (a publican in Nenagh) and Elizabeth (Betty) Cleary. Daniel's parents were Daniel Bergin, farmer, and Catherine Maunsell.[2] The only Bergin in Tipperary listed in *Griffith's Valuation of 1857* was Mrs. Catherine Bergin in Nenagh, barony of Upper Ormond, parish Kilruane, townland/place name of Knockanabohilly. She rented her property from William Jackson.[3] This was perhaps Catherine Maunsell Bergin. And if our Johanna was the Johanna Bergin left behind by her parents, then she could have lived with her grandmother Catherine.

Daniel and Margaret had eight children:

- Daniel (b.c. 1828) – born in Ireland
- Mary (b.c. 1829) – born in Ireland
- *Judith/Johanna* (1832-1912) – left behind in Ireland
- Elizabeth (b. 29 April 1839)
- Margaret (Maggie) – born in Australia
- Ann – born in Australia
- John – born in Australia
- James – born in Australia

In 1839, Daniel, Margaret, and family immigrated to Sydney, New South Wales, Australia aboard the *Hero of Malown*. On the passenger list, a note stated that the Bergins had left their seven year-old daughter Johanna behind in Ireland.[4] This Bergin family were "bounty immigrants" who paid 19 pounds per adult, 10 pounds each for children Danny (11), Mary (10), and Elizabeth (1). Maggie, Ann, John, and James were born in Australia.[5]

Daniel Hayden (c. 1828-1896) and Judith (Johanna) Bergin (1832-1912)

Daniel Hayden does not appear in *Griffith's Valuation*, but he may not have had property of his own yet, as he was not married. I noticed an entry for a Martin Hayden in Nenagh, and since firstborn sons were often named for their grandfathers, I found it interesting that Daniel's firstborn son was also Martin. There were other Haydens in Nenagh at the time, but the forenames do not match any of Daniel's sons. This may not mean anything, but I wanted to note it.

Martin Hayden's info was: County Tipperary, barony of Upper Ormond, union of Nenagh, parish of Lisbunny, townland/place name Ballynalick. Martin rented land in this same place to a Thomas Hayden, likely a son. Martin rented his land from Thomas Hackett.[6] There is also a baptismal entry for a Daniel Hayden, baptized on 2 January 1829, in Eastwood, Templemore Parish. His parents were Thomas Hayden and Margaret Kinally. So perhaps Daniel was the son of Thomas, with Martin as a grandfather.[7]

In Ireland, Johanna was a common nickname for Judith (I believe they both stem from the same Gaelic name). Daniel was born about 1828,[8] and Johanna in 1832.[9] Daniel and Johanna were married 26 January 1859 in Templemore Parish (Catholic), in Tipperary, Ireland.[10] This was close to Nenagh in North Tipperary. On the marriage notes, Johanna's residence was listed as Sorrell Hill. There was a Sorrellhill House in Templemore, a landed estate owned by the Gowans.[11] That may have been where she worked/lived, as the only other Sorrell Hill I could find is a town near Wicklow, 2.5 hours away today by car. Sorrellhill House, on the other hand, was in Roscrea, where the people I believe to be Johanna's parents were married.

Also, as noted above, the only Bergin in Tipperary listed in *Griffith's Valuation of 1857* was Mrs. Catherine Bergin in Nenagh, barony of Upper Ormond, parish Kilruane, townland/place name of Knockanabohilly. There is no direct indication that this was a relative of Johanna, but this may be her widowed grandmother, who Johanna might have been living with since she was not yet married. Knockanabohilly is only about 8 km (5 miles) from Ballynalick, where Martin Hayden lived.[12] If all this speculation is correct, Daniel and Johanna would have lived close to each other for much of their lives.

Daniel and Johanna had four children:[13]

- Martin (1859-1930) – at Templemore Parish[14] – married Bridget Maher,[15] had children Daniel and Johanna.[16] He died 24 June 1930 in Athnid, Tipperary, Ireland.[17]
- *Mary* (1862-1945) – baptized 15 June 1862 at Templemore Parish[18]
- Joseph (1865-1952) – in Kilclonagh, Littleton, Tipperary[19] – married Katherine Ryan,[20] and had children Bridget, Daniel (Danny), and John (Jack) in Ireland, then immigrated to New York in 1907[21] and had Mary and Joseph (Joey) in New York.[22] He died 11 June 1952 in New York, N.Y.[23]
- Patrick (1868-1951) – in Kilclonagh, Littleton, Tipperary,[24] died 3 October 1951 in Thurles, Tipperary, Ireland at age 82. He never married.[25]

On 4 July 1883 Mary had a daughter, Elizabeth Hayden (known as Cousin Lizzie), with Michael Maher, who may have been the brother of Bridget, Martin Hayden's wife. Mary and Michael did not marry, but Elizabeth was baptized in Thurles Parish, Tipperary, Ireland.[26] In 1901, Elizabeth was living with her grandmother Johanna, and uncles Martin and Patrick.[27]

Daniel Hayden died 27 Jul 1896 in Athnid, Littleton, Tipperary, Ireland.[28]

In 1901, Johanna (67) lived in Athnid More, Rahelty, Tipperary, Ireland, with sons Martin (38) and Patrick (30). Martin was married to Bridget (24), and they had a son, Daniel (8 months). Also living there was Eliza Hayden (18), listed as Johanna's daughter, but in reality, her granddaughter.[29]

In 1911, Johanna (90) still lived in Athnid More, Rahelty, Tipperary, Ireland, with sons Patrick (39) and Martin (48). Martin's wife Bridget (31) and children Daniel (10) and Johanna (8) were also there.[30]

Johanna Bergin Hayden died 23 June 1912, in Thurles, Littleton, Tipperary, Ireland.[31]

Mary Hayden, born 14 June 1862 in Ireland,[32] immigrated to New York City on the ship *Brittanic*, arriving 8 June 1889.[33] She was listed as 20. There she met and married **Patrick Sutton** (see *Sutton Lineage* below).

THE SUTTON LINEAGE

James Sutton (d. before 1874) and Catherine Gorman (c. 1823-after 1882)

James Sutton married Catherine Gorman 15 March 1844 in Borris Roman Catholic Parish, County Carlow, Ireland. The witnesses to the marriage were Thomas McCabe and Mary Gorman. Mary was likely related to Catherine, perhaps a sister.[34]

James and Catherine had six children:

- John (1)[35] (1846-before 1856)
- Nicholas Gorman[36] (1850-1893) – married Annie Cuttle, had children Mary (b. 1879), James Emmett (c. 1883-1886), Catherine (Kate) (1884-1948), and Gilbert (1886-1938)
- Mary[37] (b. 1853)
- John J. (2)[38] (1856-between 1900-1910) – married Annie Byrnes, had no children
- *Patrick*[39] (1859-1919) – married Mary Hayden (see *Hayden Lineage* above)
- Anne[40] (1861-1925) – immigrated to America and died while living with her brother John

In 1846, James and family lived in Newtown, St. Mullins Parish, County Carlow, Ireland.[41]

In 1852, James' family lived in Newtown on Lot 4e, a basic laborer's cabin valued at 5 shillings (the cheapest valuation). They rented from Michael Breen, and James' name was misspelled as "Sutley".[42]

In 1857, they still lived on Lot 4e, but this time they rented from Peter Breen. The house was still valued at 5 shillings, but they added a garden, which contained 25 perches of land. This was less than a quarter of an acre. The garden was valued at 3 shillings, giving a total valuation of 8 shillings. Peter Breen was replaced later as immediate lessor or landlord by John Kavanagh.[43]

In 1874, Lot 4e was rented to Widow Sutton, so James had died by this time. The garden was now a "small" garden unworthy of valuation, so the valuation of the house was once again 5 shillings.[44]

In 1878, the updated valuation notes that Lot 4e had been demolished. No more notations of Widow Sutton or Patrick were found in subsequent valuations.[45]

The three sons of James and Catherine emigrated from Ireland to New York City, New York, USA. Nicholas arrived sometime before 1879, since his first known child was born in New York in that year. Nicholas and his wife Annie Cuttle Sutton had four* known children:[46]

- Mary[47] (b. 1879)
- James Emmett[48] (c. 1882-1886)
- Catherine (Kate)[49] (1884-1948) – she married Stanley B. Moles. Oddly, in her marriage and death records, she listed her birth year as 1894 – unlikely since her father died in February of 1893[50][51]

- Gilbert (1886-1938)

*There is a birth record for an unnamed daughter born 27 October 1883.[52] This is not Catherine. James was three when he died and was likely born in 1882. Therefore, this unknown daughter would fit between James and Catherine.

On the 1880 New York census, Nicholas was listed as a stable man living at 230 East 46th Street, New York (Manhattan - District 546). With him were wife Annie (25) and daughter Mary (1).[53] In the 1888 NYC Directory, he was listed as a driver living at 312 E. 46th.[54] In the 1891 NYC Directory, he was a porter living at 233 East 46th Street.[55]

Nicholas died 21 February 1893 and was buried in Calvary Cemetery.[56] His baptism date was 28 May 1850. Patt Gorman and Bridget Fenlon were the sponsors on his baptismal record. Patt was no doubt a relation to Catherine – brother, perhaps.[57]

Nicholas' wife Annie's death date is unknown. I found a record for an Annie Sutton who died in 1887, but she is buried in Greenwood Cemetery.[58] Nicholas, their son James Emmett, as well as Nicholas' brothers John and Patrick and their families, are all in Calvary Cemetery, so it would seem unlikely that she would be elsewhere. So while the date fits, more research is needed.

After Nicholas' and Annie's deaths, their three children went to live with Nicholas' brother John and his wife, Annie.[59]

John was baptized 20 January 1856. John Doyle and Catherine Doyle were the sponsors on his baptismal record.[60] His wife Annie Byrnes (daughter of Patrick Byrnes and Mary Grennan) was born in July 1863,[61] and they married 23 June 1889 in New York City.[62] They had no known children. According to the 1900 census, John immigrated in 1880 and Annie immigrated in 1883.[63]

Later censuses show John's immigration as 1881. They also tell a strange story about his naturalization. The 1900 census shows him as naturalized, the 1910 and 1920 censuses show him as not yet naturalized but having papers of intention submitted, and the 1930 and 1940 censuses show him as still an alien.

On the 1900 census, John was listed as a day laborer. The family lived in a rented house at 200 46th Street, New York. The household consisted of John (38) and wife Annie (36) with John's nieces and nephews (Nicholas' children), Mary (21), Kate (15), and Gilbert (14). Also living there were two boarders: Edward Hogan (24) and Thomas McGuire (30), both from Ireland.[64]

In 1905, the family was at 771 Third Ave. John (45) lived there with wife Anna (40), and nieces Mary (26) (spelled Mannie on the form) and Kate (20). There was also a grand-niece, Annie (4) but no indication of who she belongs to. I am guessing Mary, as Kate would have been only 16 at her birth, and Gilbert (not shown on this census) would have been only 15 at her birth (and 19 on this census). The nieces worked as salespeople, and John was a laborer. All the Suttons were shown as U.S. citizens on this census. There was also a boarder, James Collins (30) from Ireland.[65]

In 1910, the family was at 766 Third Ave. John (53) lived here with wife Anna (45), nephew Gilbert J. Sutton (24), and Anna M. Sutton (10). Anna M. was listed as John's daughter, however, his wife Anna was listed as having no children. I believe her to be the same Anna who was the grand-niece on the 1905

4

census—she'd be the right age. John was listed as a state guard for the express industry. He was also listed as having filed papers to be naturalized. Also with them was a lodger, Mitchell Callun (23) from Ireland.[66]

Anna M. Sutton died at age 17 in 1918. She was buried in Calvary Cemetery in the same plot as John and Annie and Gilbert would be. On the stone she was listed as "grand-niece." [67]

In 1920, they were still at 766 Third Ave. John (58) lived there with wife Annie (53) and nephew Gilbert (33), who was erroneously listed as son. John was retired and Gilbert was a city clerk. John's citizenship status was listed as "Pa," meaning he had filed papers to become a U.S. citizen.[68]

On 24 March 1925, John's sister Annie Sutton died at John's residence of 766 Third Ave. It is unknown when she came to America. She was also buried in the plot with John's family at Calvary Cemetery.[69]

In 1930, John (65), Annie (61) and nephew Gilbert (44) lived at 308 Willis Ave. Gilbert was a clerk with the U.S. Finance Dept. John worked in the stables. Annie and John were Aliens (not naturalized). [70]

Gilbert J. Sutton died 16 November 1938, and is buried in the plot of John Sutton in Calvary Cemetery.[71] At this point, John's sister Annie, grand-niece Anna M., and Gilbert were buried there.

In 1940, John (80) and Annie (73) still lived at 308 Willis Ave. Neither worked outside the home. They were both listed as Aliens (not naturalized.)[72]

John Sutton died in May 1941, and Annie died 1 Sept 1946. Both are buried in John's plot in Calvary Cemetery.[73]

While we know that the Sutton siblings' father, James, died in Ireland before 1874, what happened to their mother Catherine is unclear. The youngest son, Patrick (our ancestor), came to America 24 May 1882 on the ship *Italy*.[74] With him on the manifest is a woman named Catherine Sutton. Her age is not quite right, but it could be his mother. I have found no further information on this woman beyond the immigration record.

Patrick Sutton (1859–1919) and Mary Hayden (1862–1945)

Patrick Sutton was baptized 21 August 1859. James Fenlon and Maria Breen/Brien were the sponsors on his baptismal record.[75] Patrick's parents lived and worked on the Breen farm in Newtown, St. Mullins Parish, County Carlow, Ireland.

Patrick arrived in New York on 24 May 1882. He came on the ship *Italy*, possibly with his mother, Catherine.[76]

From 1889-1895, Patrick lived at 337 East 47th Street in New York City.[77] He married **Mary Hayden** 1 May 1892 at St. Joseph's Parish, 371 6th Ave., Manhattan, New York City. Patrick's brother and his wife, Nicholas J. Sutton and Annie Sutton, were witnesses.[78]

Patrick and Mary had eight children:[79] [80]

- James (1892-1978) – married Anna H. McNicholl, then married Kathryn C. Murray [81]
- Johanna (1894-1908) [82]
- Nicholas (1896-1956) [83]
- Catherine (1898-1970) – married William E. Lang [84]
- Anna (1899-1987) – married John Hackett, had John, Anne, Maureen, and Katherine.[85]
- Margaret/Marguerite (1901-1963) – married William Waldron [86]
- **Mary Margaret** (1904-1975) [87] – married Edward Alexander Campbell (see *Campbell Lineage*)
- Agnes (1908-1953)[88]

In 1896 and 1897, Patrick and family lived at 329 East 23rd Street, Manhattan.[89]

In 1900, Patrick (40) and Mary (32) lived at 321 East 46th Street, Manhattan. With them were children James (7), Johanna (6), Nicholas (4), Catherine (2) and Annie (6 months). Patrick worked as a baggage man for the railroad. This census indicates he was naturalized.[90]

In 1910, the family still lived at 321 East 46th Street. Along with Patrick (50) and Mary (42) were children James (erroneously listed as Joseph) (17), Nicholas (14), Katherine (12), Anna (10), Margaret (9), Mary (6) and Agnes (2). Johanna had died in 1908. Patrick worked as a baggage man for the railroad, and James was working as a clerk in a hotel.[91]

Patrick Sutton died 11 March 1919 in Bellevue Hospital. The cause of his death is listed as chronic pulmonary tuberculosis. The family lived at 335 52nd Street, Manhattan. He was 59 years old at the time of his death and was buried at (2nd) Calvary Cemetery in Section 55, Range 4, Plot B, Grave 17.[92] [93]

During World War I, Patrick and Mary's son Nicholas Sutton went to Canada to enlist. It is noted in his Canadian records that he had astigmatism in his right eye and a detached retina (caused by being hit with a stone in 1904) in his left eye.[94]

Nicholas' Canadian attestation was made 31 May 1918. He swore that he was born in Toronto, Canada, which seems unlikely. He also said he was born in 1895, instead of 1896. After enlisting, he arrived in England 15 July 1918, was transferred from the Quebec Canadian Reserve unit he came with to the 42nd Battalion (the Black Watch), which then went to France on 31 Oct 1918. They—or at least, he—returned to England 7 Feb 1919, and went back to Canada in March 1919.[95] On 8 March 1919, Nicholas was on the ship *Adriatic*, travelling with the battalion from Bramshott, England, to "Montreal or West." This particular leg was from Nova Scotia.[96] His regimental number was 3085292. His discharge certificate says he enlisted in the 20th Can Reserve Que Rgt on 31 May 1918, and served in the 42nd Bn, RHC. Private Nicholas John Sutton was discharged "due to general demobilization" on 11 March 1919. [97]

In 1920, Mary (55) and family lived at 335 52nd Street in Manhattan. All the children still lived at home: James (27), Nicholas (23), Catherine (22), Anna (20), Margaret (18), Mary (15), and Agnes (11). All the children except Agnes were working, and mother Mary was at home. All the children were employed as "clerks": James in theatrical, Nicholas in a syrup factory, Catherine, Anna, Margaret and Mary in department stores.[98]

In 1930, Mary (67) and family lived at 401 145th Street, east of Willis Ave. in the Bronx. It seems to have been an apartment house, as many other families are listed at the same address. Children Nicholas (33), Margaret (29) and Agnes (22) all lived with her. Nicholas is listed as married (date of marriage about 1922), although there is no wife in evidence. Family lore says he married when he was in the Canadian military, although that would have been in 1918 or 1919, not 1922. Nicholas worked as an elevator operator, Margaret was a floor lady in Macy's, and Agnes was a cashier in Bloomingdales.[99]

In 1940, Mary lived at 31-58 36th Street in Queens. Mary (77) lived with children Nicholas (43) and Agnes (32). The census said she had lived at that address since at least 1935. They rented for $38 a month. Nicholas was in elevator construction in the building trade and making $1250 a year, and Agnes was a cashier at a department store.[100]

Mary Hayden Sutton died 15 October 1945 in Manhattan at age 83. She lived at 248-10 Depew in Little Neck, the residence of her daughter Mary Sutton Campbell, where she had resided for about a year before her death. She died of cancer, and she was buried in (2nd) Calvary Cemetery on Long Island on 18 October 1945, in Section 55, Range 4, Plot B, Grave 17, along with husband Patrick and daughter Agnes.[101] [102]

Mary Margaret Sutton married ***Edward Alexander Campbell*** on 22 February 1927[103]. For an accounting of her life with Edward, see the *Campbell Lineage* chapter.

---

[1] *Daniel Bergin & Margaret Russell.* North Tipperary Genealogy & Heritage Services, *Roscrea Roman Catholic Parish*, accessed on Roots Ireland (formerly Irish History Foundation). http://www.rootsireland.ie/

[2] *Bergin family to Australia.* Ancestry.com, New South Wales, Australia, Assisted Immigrant Passenger Lists, 1828-1896 [database on-line]. State Records Authority of New South Wales; Kingswood New South Wales, Australia; Entitlement certificates of persons on bounty ships; Series: 5314; Reel: 1302. Vessel: Hero of Malown.

[3] *Catherine Maunsell Bergin.* Griffith's Valuation, the Valuation Office of Ireland, 1857.

[4] *Bergin family to Australia.* Ancestry.com, New South Wales, Australia, Assisted Immigrant Passenger Lists, 1828-1896 [database on-line]. State Records Authority of New South Wales; Kingswood New South Wales, Australia; Entitlement certificates of persons on bounty ships; Series: 5314; Reel: 1302. Vessel: Hero of Malown.

[5] *Bergin family in Australia.* Genealogy.com forums, separately from both Alvie Bergin (jmschy@bigpond.com) and Joy Prouse (joyprouse@hotmail.com)

[6] *Martin Hayden.* Griffith's Valuation, the Valuation Office of Ireland, 1857.

[7] *Daniel Hayden*, baptism, Templemore Parish, County Tipperary, Ireland.

[8] *Daniel Hayden* death certificate. https://civilrecords.irishgenealogy.ie/churchrecords/images/deaths_returns/deaths_1896/05890/4670967.pdf.

[9] *Johanna Bergin Hayden.* Death Record. *RootsIreland.ie,* http://ifhf.rootsireland.ie/view_detail.php?recordid=629798&type=dcv&recordCentre=tipperarynorth&page=1.

[10] *Daniel Hayden & Johanna Bergin.* North Tipperary Genealogy & Heritage Services, *Templemore Roman Catholic Parish*, Ref No 284/08 - Tipperary North Family History Research Center; Diocese of Cashel and Emly. Marriages, July 1858 to May 1859, Microfilm 02492 / 03 | Page 154.

[11] *Johanna Bergin, Sorrell Hill.* http://landedestates.nuigalway.ie/LandedEstates/jsp/property-show.jsp?id=4788

[12] *Catherine Maunsell Bergin.* Griffith's Valuation, the Valuation Office of Ireland, 1857.

[13] *Johanna Bergin.* North Tipperary Genealogy & Heritage Services, *Templemore Roman Catholic Parish,* Ref No 284/08 - Tipperary North Family History Research Center.

[14] *Martin Hayden.* Church Records from Ireland, Ref No 284/08 - Tipperary North Family History Research Center; Templemore; County of Tipperary; Diocese of Cashel and Emly. Baptisms, Oct. 1859 to Dec. 1859, Microfilm 02492 / 03 | Page 54.

[15] *Martin Hayden & Bridget Maher.* Marriage record. *RootsIreland.ie,* http://ifhf.rootsireland.ie/view_detail.php?recordid=586051&type=mcv&recordCentre=tipperarynorth&page=1.

[16] *Johanna Hayden.* Birth Records, *RootsIreland.ie,* http://ifhf.rootsireland.ie/view_detail.php?recordid=636710&type=bcv&recordCentre=tipperarynorth&page=1.

[17] *Martin Hayden.* Death Record. *Irishgenealogy.ie,* https://civilrecords.irishgenealogy.ie/churchrecords/images/deaths_returns/deaths_1930/04917/4334641.pdf

[18] *Mary Hayden.* Church Records from Ireland, Ref No 284/08 - Tipperary North Family History Research Center; County of Tipperary; Diocese of Cashel and Emly. Baptisms, Apr. 1862 to June 1862, Microfilm 02492 / 03 | Page 66.

[19] *Joseph Hayden.* Church Records from Ireland, Ref No 284/08 - Tipperary North Family History Research Center.

[20] *Joseph Hayden & Katherine Ryan.* Marriage Record. *Irishgenealogy.ie,* https://civilrecords.irishgenealogy.ie/churchrecords/details-civil/3e23c72290799

[21] *Joseph Hayden*. Ancestry.com. *Passenger Lists, Year: 1907*; Arrival: New York, New York; Microfilm Serial: T715, 1897-1957; Microfilm Roll: Roll 0924; Line: 1; Page Number: 124.

[22] *Joseph Hayden*. Ancestry.com. *1920 United States Census*, Year: 1920; Census Place: Manhattan Assembly District 1, New York, New York; Roll: T625_1185; Page: 10B; Enumeration District: 95.

[23] *Joseph Hayden*. Research/Tree of, madeinthe80s2003 on Ancestry. https://www.ancestry.com/family-tree/person/tree/10868120/person/-565509746/facts.

[24] *Patrick Hayden*. Church Records from Ireland, Ref No 284/08 - Tipperary North Family History Research Center.

[25] *Patrick Hayden*. Death Certificate, *Irishgenealogy.ie*, https://civilrecords.irishgenealogy.ie/churchrecords/images/deaths_returns/deaths_1951/04496/4181405.pdf.

[26] *Elizabeth Hayden*. Baptismal record. *RootsIreland.ie*, http://ifhf.rootsireland.ie/view_detail.php?recordid=1823641&type=bch&recordCentre=tipperarynorth&page=1.

[27] *Elizabeth Hayden*. Ancestry.com. *Web: Ireland, Census, 1901* [database on-line]. Provo, UT, USA: Ancestry.com Operations, Inc., 2013.

[28] *Daniel Hayden*. Death Certificate, *Irishgenealogy.ie*, https://civilrecords.irishgenealogy.ie/churchrecords/images/deaths_returns/deaths_1896/05890/4670967.pdf.

[29] *Johanna Bergin Hayden*. *1901 Ireland Census*, Ancestry.com. Web: Ireland, Census, 1901 [database on-line]. Provo, UT, USA: Ancestry.com Operations, Inc., 2013. Original data: Census of Ireland 1901/1911. The National Archives of Ireland. http://www.census.nationalarchives.ie/search/: accessed 20 July 2018.

[30] *Johanna Bergin Hayden*. *1911 Ireland Census*, Ancestry.com. Web: Ireland, Census, 1911 [database on-line]. Provo, UT, USA. Original data: Census of Ireland 1901/1911. The National Archives of Ireland. http://www.census.nationalarchives.ie/search/: accessed 20-07-18.

[31] *Johanna Bergin Hayden*. Death Record. *RootsIreland.ie*, http://ifhf.rootsireland.ie/view_detail.php?recordid=629798&type=dcv&recordCentre=tipperarynorth&page=1.

[32] *Mary Hayden*. Church Records from Ireland, Ref No 284/08 - Tipperary North Family History Research Center; County of Tipperary; Diocese of Cashel and Emly. Baptisms, Apr. 1862 to June 1862, Microfilm 02492 / 03 | Page 66.

[33] *Mary Hayden*. Passenger Lists, Ship: Britannic, pg 12, line 703; Year: 1889; Arrival: New York, United States; Microfilm Serial: M237; Microfilm Roll: 534; Line: 29; List Number: 747.

[34] *James Sutton & Catherine Gorman*. Borris (Ireland) Parish records. Borris; Counties of Wexford, Carlow; Diocese of Kildare and Leighlin. Marriages, Mar. 1844 to May 1844, Microfilm 04196 / 03 | Page 213.

[35] *John Sutton*. St. Mullins (Ireland) Parish records. St. Mullins; Counties of Carlow, Wexford; Diocese of Kildare and Leighlin. Baptisms, July 1846 to Sep. 1846, Microfilm 04196 / 09 | Page 75.

[36] *Nicholas Gorman Sutton*. St. Mullins (Ireland) Parish records. St. Mullins; Counties of Carlow, Wexford; Diocese of Kildare and Leighlin. Baptisms, Apr. 1850 to Aug. 1850; Microfilm 04196 / 09 | Page 90.

[37] *Mary Sutton*. St. Mullins (Ireland) Parish records. St. Mullins; Counties of Carlow, Wexford; Diocese of Kildare and Leighlin. Baptisms, Jan. 1853 to Apr. 1853, Microfilm 04196 / 09 | Page 96.

[38] *John J. Sutton*. St. Mullins Parish (Ireland) records. St. Mullins; Counties of Carlow, Wexford; Diocese of Kildare and Leighlin. Baptisms, Jan. 1856 to June 1856, Microfilm 04196 / 09 | Page 103.

[39] *Patrick Sutton*. St. Mullins Parish (Ireland) records. St. Mullins; Counties of Carlow, Wexford; Diocese of Kildare and Leighlin. Baptisms, July 1859 to Nov. 1859, Microfilm 04196 / 09 | Page 112.

[40] *Anne Sutton*. St. Mullins (Ireland) Parish records. St. Mullins; Counties of Carlow, Wexford; Diocese of Kildare and Leighlin. Baptisms, Nov. 1861 to Mar. 1862, Microfilm 04196 / 09 | Page 120.

[41] *John Sutton*. St. Mullins (Ireland) Parish records. St. Mullins; Counties of Carlow, Wexford; Diocese of Kildare and Leighlin. Baptisms, July 1846 to Sep. 1846, Microfilm 04196 / 09 | Page 75.

[42] *James Sutton*. Giffith's Primary Valuation, Year: 1852, Valuation Office of Ireland, Co. Carlow, Barony of St. Mullins (Lower), Parish of St. Mullins, Union of New Ross, Electoral Division of Tinnahinch, p 884.

[43] *James Sutton*. Giffith's Primary Valuation (1st revision), Year: 1857, Valuation Office of Ireland, Co. Carlow, Barony of St. Mullins (Lower), Parish of St. Mullins, Union of New Ross, Electoral Division of Tinnahinch.

[44] *Catherine Gorman Sutton*. Giffith's Primary Valuation (2nd revision), Year: 1874, Valuation Office of Ireland, Co. Carlow, Barony of St. Mullins (Lower), Parish of St. Mullins, Union of New Ross, Electoral Division of Tinnahinch.

[45] *Catherine Gorman Sutton*. Giffith's Primary Valuation (3rd revision), Year: 1878, Valuation Office of Ireland, Co. Carlow, Barony of St. Mullins (Lower), Parish of St. Mullins, Union of New Ross, Electoral Division of Tinnahinch, p 85.

[46] *Nicholas Sutton*. 1900 United States Census, Year: 1900; Census Place: Manhattan, New York, New York; Roll: 1107; Page: 15A; Enumeration District: 0585; FHL microfilm: 1241107.

[47] *Mary Sutton*. 1880 United States Census, Year: 1880; Census Place: New York City, New York, New York; Roll: 893; Family History Film: 1254893; Page: 113B; Enumeration District: 546; Image: 0229.

[48] *James Emmett Sutton*. FamilySearch.org (LDS records), "New York, New York City Municipal Deaths, 1795-1949," database, FamilySearch (https://familysearch.org/ark:/61903/1:1:2WJR-HGX : accessed 28 April 2016), James Emmett Sutton, 31 Jan 1886; citing Death, Manhattan, New York, New York, United States, New York.

[49] *Catherine Sutton*. 1900 United States Census, Year: 1900; Census Place: Manhattan, New York, New York; Roll: 1107; Page: 15A; Enumeration District: 0585; FHL microfilm: 1241107.

[50] *Catherine Sutton Moles*. FamilySearch.org (LDS records), "New York, New York City Municipal Deaths, 1795-1949," database, FamilySearch (https://familysearch.org/ark:/61903/1:1:2W2V-X5N : accessed 28 April 2016), Anne Cuttle in entry for Catherine Moles, 26 May 1948; citing Death, Brooklyn, Kings, New York.

[51] *Catherine Sutton Moles*. FamilySearch.org (LDS records), "New York, New York City Municipal Deaths, 1795-1949," database, FamilySearch (https://familysearch.org/ark:/61903/1:1:2W2V-X5N : accessed 28 April 2016), Anne Cuttle in entry for Catherine Moles, 26 May 1948; citing Death, Brooklyn, Kings, New York.

[52] *Unnamed daughter Sutton*. FamilySearch.org (LDS records), "New York, New York City Births, 1846-1909," database, FamilySearch (https://familysearch.org/ark:/61903/1:1:2WDC-RT3 : accessed 28 April 2016), Annie Cuttle Sutton in entry for Sutton, 27 Oct 1883; citing Birth, Manhattan, New York, New York.

[53] *Nicholas Sutton*. 1880 United States Census, Year: 1880; Census Place: New York City, New York, New York; Roll: 893; Family History Film: 1254893; Page: 113B; Enumeration District: 546; Image: 0229.

[54] *Nicholas Sutton*. New York City Directory. Year: 1888. Ancestry.com. *U.S. City Directories, 1822-1995* [database on-line]. Provo, UT, USA: Ancestry.com Operations, Inc., 2011.

[55] *Nicholas Sutton*. New York City Directory, Year: 1891. Ancestry.com. U.S. City Directories, 1822-1995 [database on-line]. Provo, UT, USA: Ancestry.com Operations, Inc., 2011.

[56] *Nicholas Gorman Sutton*. Death Certificate, New York City Deaths, 1892-1902; Deaths Reported in January-February-March, 1893; Certificate #: 6351.

[57] *Nicholas Gorman Sutton*. St. Mullins Parish (Ireland) records. St. Mullins; Counties of Carlow, Wexford; Diocese of Kildare and Leighlin. Baptisms, Apr. 1850 to Aug. 1850; Microfilm 04196 / 09 | Page 90.

[58] *Annie Sutton*. Find A Grave.com, http://www.findagrave.com/cgi-bin/fg.cgi?page=gr&GRid=58043208.

[59] *John Sutton*. 1900 United States Census, Year: 1900; Census Place: Manhattan, New York, New York; Roll: 1107; Page: 15A; Enumeration District: 0585; FHL microfilm: 1241107.

[60] *John J. Sutton*. St. Mullins (Ireland) Parish records. St. Mullins; Counties of Carlow, Wexford; Diocese of Kildare and Leighlin. Baptisms, Jan. 1856 to June 1856, Microfilm 04196 / 09 | Page 103.

[61] *Annie Byrnes*. FamilySearch.org (LDS records), "BillionGraves Index," database, FamilySearch (https://familysearch.org/ark:/61903/1:1:KF6Y-4VD : accessed 28 April 2016), Gilbert J. Sutton, died Nov 1938; citing BillionGraves (http://www.billiongraves.com : 2012), Burial at Calvary Cemetery, Woodside, New York.

[62] *John Sutton & Annie Byrnes*. FamilySearch.org (LDS records), "New York, New York City Marriage Records, 1829-1940," database, FamilySearch (https://familysearch.org/ark:/61903/1:1:249H-63C : accessed 28 April 2016), John Sutton and Annie Byrnes, 23 Jun 1889; citing Marriage, Manhattan, New York, New York.

[63] *John Sutton*. 1900 United States Census, Year: 1900; Census Place: Manhattan, New York, New York; Roll: 1107; Page: 15A; Enumeration District: 0585; FHL microfilm: 1241107.

[64] *John Sutton*. 1900 United States Census, Year: 1900; Census Place: Manhattan, New York, New York; Roll: 1107; Page: 15A; Enumeration District: 0585; FHL microfilm: 1241107.

[65] *John Sutton*. New York State Archives; Albany, New York; State Population Census Schedules, 1905; Election District: A.D. 22 E.D. 15; City: Manhattan; County: New York; Page: 31; digital images.

[66] *John Sutton*. 1910 United States Census, Year: 1910; Census Place: Manhattan Ward 19, New York, New York; Roll: T624_1042; Page: 2A; Enumeration District: 0497; FHL microfilm: 1375055.

[67] *Anna M. Sutton*. FamilySearch.org (LDS records), "BillionGraves Index," database, FamilySearch (https://familysearch.org/ark:/61903/1:1:KF6Y-4VD : accessed 28 April 2016), Gilbert J. Sutton, died Nov 1938; citing BillionGraves (http://www.billiongraves.com : 2012), Burial at Calvary Cemetery, Woodside, New York.

[68] *John Sutton*. 1920 United States Census, Year: 1920; Census Place: Manhattan Assembly District 12, New York, New York; Roll: T625_1207; Page: 6A; Enumeration District: 913; Image: 852.

[69] *Annie Sutton*. FamilySearch.org (LDS records), "New York, New York City Municipal Deaths, 1795-1949," database, FamilySearch (https://familysearch.org/ark:/61903/1:1:2WBQ-32V : accessed 28 April 2016), Annie Sutton, 24 Mar 1925; citing Death, Manhattan, New York, New York, United States.

[70] *John Sutton*. 1930 United States Census, Year: 1930; Census Place: Bronx, Bronx, New York; Roll: 1463; Page: 11B; Enumeration District: 0970; Image: 471.0; FHL microfilm: 2341198.

[71] *Gilbert J. Sutton*. Ancestry.com, Ancestry.com. New York, New York, Death Index, 1862-1948 [database on-line]. Provo, UT, USA: Ancestry.com Operations, Inc., 2014.

[72] *John Sutton*. 1940 United States Census, Year: 1940; Census Place: New York, Bronx, New York; Roll: T627_2462; Page: 10B; Enumeration District: 3-75.

[73] *John Sutton & Annie Byrnes Sutton*. FamilySearch.org (LDS records), "BillionGraves Index," database, FamilySearch (https://familysearch.org/ark:/61903/1:1:KF6Y-4VD : accessed 28 April 2016), Gilbert J. Sutton, died Nov 1938; citing BillionGraves (http://www.billiongraves.com : 2012), Burial at Calvary Cemetery, Woodside, New York.

[74] *Patrick Sutton*. Ancestry.com. New York, Passenger and Immigration Lists, 1820-1850, Year: 1882; Arrival: New York, New York; Microfilm Serial: M237, 1820-1897; Microfilm Roll: Roll 452; Line: 49; List Number: 691.

[75] *Patrick Sutton*. St. Mullins (Ireland) Parish records. St. Mullins; Counties of Carlow, Wexford; Diocese of Kildare and Leighlin. Baptisms, July 1859 to Nov. 1859, Microfilm 04196 / 09 | Page 112.

[76] *Patrick Sutton*. Ancestry.com. New York, Passenger and Immigration Lists, 1820-1850. Year: 1882; Arrival: New York, New York; Microfilm Serial: M237, 1820-1897; Microfilm Roll: Roll 452; Line: 50; List Number: 691.

[77] *Patrick Sutton*. 1889-1895 New York City Directories.

[78] *Patrick Sutton & Mary Hayden*. Certified copy of the marriage of Patrick Sutton and Mary Hayden from St. Joseph's Church in Greenwich Village. Obtained 7 February 2020.

[79] *Patrick Sutton & Mary Hayden.* 1900 United States Census, Year: 1900; Census Place: Manhattan, New York, New York; Roll: 1107; Page: 13A; Enumeration District: 0589; FHL microfilm: 1241107.

[80] *Patrick Sutton & Mary Hayden.* 1910 United States Census, Year: 1910; Census Place: Manhattan Ward 19, New York, New York; Roll: T624_1041; Page: 5B; Enumeration District: 1103; ; FHL microfilm: 1375054.

[81] *James Sutton.* Personal information: (This person experienced or had direct knowledge of the event in question.) Dolores Campbell Penders, daughter of Edward Alexander Campbell & Mary Margaret Sutton.

[82] *Johanna A. Sutton.* Death Certificate, "New York, New York City Municipal Deaths, 1795-1949," database, FamilySearch (https://familysearch.org/ark:/61903/1:1:2W9Z-9HJ : accessed 9 April 2016), Johanna A. Sutton, 28 Sep 1908; citing Death, Manhattan, New York, New York, United States, New York.

[83] *Nicholas Sutton.* Social Security Death Index, Ancestry.com. U.S., Social Security Applications and Claims Index, 1936-2007 [database online]. Provo, UT, USA: Ancestry.com Operations, Inc., 2015.

[84] *Catherine Sutton.* Personal information: (This person experienced or had direct knowledge of the event in question.) Dolores Campbell Penders, daughter of Edward Alexander Campbell & Mary Margaret Sutton.

[85] *Anna Sutton.* Personal information: (This person experienced or had direct knowledge of the event in question.) Dolores Campbell Penders, daughter of Edward Alexander Campbell & Mary Margaret Sutton.

[86] *Margaret Sutton.* Personal information: (This person experienced or had direct knowledge of the event in question.) Dolores Campbell Penders, daughter of Edward Alexander Campbell & Mary Margaret Sutton.

[87] *Mary Sutton Campbell.* Death Certificate, Mary Sutton Campbell, PA Dept of Health; Registered # 8687775.

[88] *Agnes Sutton,* dates from the Mass Card from her funeral.

[89] *Patrick Sutton.* 1896-1897 New York City Directories.

[90] *Patrick Sutton family.* 1900 US Census New York, 1900 US Census New York, Year: 1900; Census Place: Manhattan, New York, New York; Roll: 1107; Page: 13A; Enumeration District: 0589; FHL microfilm: 1241107.

[91] *Patrick Sutton family.* 1910 United States Census, Year: 1910; Census Place: Manhattan Ward 19, New York, New York; Roll: T624_1041; Page: 5B; Enumeration District: 1103; ; FHL microfilm: 1375054

[92] *Patrick Sutton.* Death Certificate, Patrick Sutton, NYC Dept of Health; Registered # 9959.

[93] *Patrick Sutton.* Cemetery Records, (2nd) Calvary Cemetery, 49-02 Laurel Hill Blvd., Woodside, NY 11377.

[94] *Nicholas J. Sutton.* Fold3.com, Canada, Soldiers of the First World War, 1914-1918. Compiled Service Record. https://www.fold3.com/image/666520919?terms=nicholas,john,sutton

[95] *Nicholas J. Sutton.* Fold3.com, Canada, Soldiers of the First World War, 1914-1918. Compiled Service Record. https://www.fold3.com/image/666520919?terms=nicholas,john,sutton

[96] *Nicholas J. Sutton.* "Canada Passenger Lists, 1881-1922," database with images, FamilySearch (https://familysearch.org/ark:/61903/1:1:2H22-7YJ : accessed 29 April 2016), Nicholas John Sutton, Mar 1919; citing Immigration, Halifax, Nova Scotia, Canada, T-14794, Library and Archives Canada, Ottawa, Ontario.

[97] *Nicholas J. Sutton.* Fold3.com, Canada, Soldiers of the First World War, 1914-1918. https://www.fold3.com/image/666520933.

[98] *Mary Hayden Sutton family.* 1920 US Census New York, Year: 1920; Census Place: Manhattan Assembly District 14, New York, New York; Roll: T625_1210; Page: 3B; Enumeration District: 980; Image: 40.

[99] *Mary Hayden Sutton family.* 1930 US Census New York, Year: 1930; Census Place: Bronx, Bronx, New York; Roll: 1463; Page: 14A; Enumeration District: 32; Image: 1144.0; FHL microfilm: 2341198.

[100] *Mary Hayden Sutton family.* 1940 US Census, Year: 1940; Census Place: New York, Queens, New York; Roll: T627_2721; Page: 3B; Enumeration District: 41-99.

[101] *Mary Hayden Sutton.* Death Certificate, Mary Hayden Sutton, NYC Dept of Health, Certificate # 7999.

[102] *Mary Hayden Sutton.* Cemetery Records, (2nd) Calvary Cemetery, 49-02 Laurel Hill Blvd., Woodside, NY 11377.

[103] *Edward Campbell & Mary Sutton.* Marriage License of Edward Campbell and Mary Sutton, County of New York City, New York, Registered # 3605; Feb 8, 1927

THE HAYDEN-SUTTON FAMILY

MARY HAYDEN SUTTON
& PATRICK SUTTON
Location: New York City
Date: Unknown

MARY HAYDEN SUTTON
Location: New York City, Date: Unknown

MARY MARGARET SUTTON
graduation from elementary school
Location: New York City, Date: 1919

THE HAYDEN-SUTTON FAMILY

AGNES, ANNA, & MARY SUTTON
Location: New York
Date: 1914

NICHOLAS SUTTON
Canadian Army
Location: Unknown, Date: 1918

MARY MARGARET SUTTON
Location: New York, Date: 1919

AGNES SUTTON
Location: New York, Date: 1923

THE HAYDEN-SUTTON FAMILY

GROOM: JAMES SUTTON *(left)*
BRIDE: ANNA MCNICHOLL
BEST MAN: NICHOLAS SUTTON
OTHERS: ANNA'S SISTER MAY AND HER DAUGHTER
Location: Manhattan, NYC
Date: 5 Aug 1922

BRIDE: ANNA SUTTON
GROOM: JOHN HACKETT *(right)*
ATTENDANTS: MARY SUTTON & EDWARD CAMPBELL
Location: New York City, NY
Date: 1926

The Hayden-Sutton Family

Nana Sutton, Family & Friends
Location: New York, Date: Dec 1941

MARY HAYDEN SUTTON

DOLORES CAMPBELL

DONALD & BOBBY CAMPBELL

BOBBY CAMPBELL

MAUREEN HACKETT

JACKIE HACKETT

DOLORES CAMPBELL

DONALD CAMPBELL

MARY HAYDEN SUTTON

ANNIE HACKETT

BARBARA SUTTON

MARY WALDRON

BILLY WALDRON

EDWARD CAMPBELL

Nana & Grandkids
Location: 248-10 DePew Ave, Little Neck, NY, Date: 14 June 1944

THE HAYDEN-SUTTON FAMILY

ANNA SUTTON HACKETT

JACKIE HACKETT

AGNES SUTTON

ANNE HACKETT

MARY SUTTON CAMPBELL

BILLY LANG

EDWARD CAMPBELL, SR.

*Location:
248-10 DePew Ave.,
Little Neck, New York
Date: June 1950*

*Dolores
Campbell's
Graduation*

CATHERINE SUTTON LANG

DOLORES CAMPBELL

THE HAYDEN-SUTTON FAMILY

JOHN HACKETT, JACKIE
HACKETT, ANNA SUTTON
HACKETT & ANNE HACKETT
Location: New York
Date: c. 1950

EDWARD CAMPBELL
& CATHERINE SUTTON LANG

EDWARD CAMPBELL, SR.
& WILLIAM "WILLIE" LANG

Location: New York
Date: 9 April 1950 (Easter)

ANNE O'DONNELL LANG
& WILLIAM "BILLY" LANG

THE HAYDEN-SUTTON FAMILY

Location: Dolores Campbell's bridal shower, Albertson, New York, Date: 1952

LIZZIE HAYDEN   **MARY SUTTON CAMPBELL**   **AGNES SUTTON**

CATHERINE SUTTON LANG   **MARGARET/MARGUERITE SUTTON WALDRON**   **ANNA SUTTON HACKETT**

THE HAYDEN-SUTTON FAMILY

MARY HAYDEN SUTTON
Location: 248-10 DePew Ave,
Little Neck, NY
Her 82nd birthday
Date: 14 June 1944

MARY SUTTON CAMPBELL, LIZZIE
HAYDEN, MARYANN CAMPBELL
Location: College Point, Queens, NYC, New York
Date: c. 1966

DOLORES CAMPBELL, MARY HAYDEN SUTTON,
MARY SUTTON CAMPBELL, DONALD CAMPBELL
Location: New York
Date Dec 1941

SUTTON CEMETERY

CALVARY CEMETERY
Woodside, New York

PATRICK'S SISTER ANNIE, BROTHER JOHN AND HIS WIFE ANNA,
BROTHER NICHOLAS, MOST OF NICHOLAS' CHILDREN (JAMES, KATE,
& GILBERT), AND ONE OF NICHOLAS' GRANDCHILDREN (ANNA
MARIE) ARE ALSO BURIED IN CALVARY CEMETERY, BUT I DO NOT
HAVE PHOTOS OF THEIR HEADSTONES.

THE
SCOTTISH

The Campbell Lineage

DURNESS
(BIRTHPLACE OF
HUGH CAMPBELL, B. 1821)

PULROSSIE
(BIRTHPLACE OF DONALD CAMPBELL,
IMMIGRANT TO THE USA)

DUFFUS
(DEATH PLACE OF
HUGH CAMPBELL, B. 1821)

SCOTLAND

AYRSHIRE
(BIRTHPLACE OF OUR FIRST
KNOWN CAMPBELL ANCESTOR,
HUGH CAMPBELL, B.C. 1787)

THE CAMPBELL LINEAGE

HUGH CAMPBELL
(b. 1787)

MARY MACKAY
(1785-1867)
(see MacKay Lineage)

HUGH CAMPBELL
(1821-1905)

ANN MCINTOSH
(1818-1904)
(see McIntosh Lineage)

DONALD MCINTOSH CAMPBELL
(1860-1945)
Immigrated to NY 1886

ISABELLA MORRISON
(1864-1907)
Immigrated to NY 1882
(see Morrison Lineage)

(continued on next page)

THE CAMPBELL FAMILY
(colored blocks denote generations)

ISABELLA MORRISON
(1864-1907)
Immigrated to NY in 1882

DONALD CAMPBELL
(1860-1945)
Immigrated to NY in 1886

LILY DAVY

MARY CAMPBELL
(1919-2010)
never married, no children

EDWARD
(1903-1963)
married
MARY SUTTON
(1904-1975)

WILLIAM
(1900-1930)
married Paula Memminger:
no children

GRACE
(1897-1920)
married Henry Rochel,
no children

JOHN
(1895-1895)
never married,
no children

MARGARET
(1891-1894)
never married,
no children

CAROLINE
(1889-1922)
married
DANIEL VETTER
(1887-1961)

ANNIE
(1887-1959)
married
ROLAND HASSENTEUFEL
(1885-1945)

BELLA
(1885-1896)
never married,
no children

DOLORES CAMPBELL
M. EDWARD PENDERS

DONALD EDWARD CAMPBELL
M. ANDREE FORTIER

ROBERT CAMPBELL
M. GRACE BABKOWSKA

EDWARD CAMPBELL
M. (1) ANASTASIA PLANK
M. (2) SONJA SCHULTZ

(LIVING)

ISABELLE (BELLA) VETTER *(1911-1990)*
M. HENRY ORLANDI *(1906-1970)*

DOROTHY (DOTTIE) VETTER *(1918-1996)*
M. PAUL HOUCK SR. *(1911-1987)*

CHARLES HASSENTEUFEL
(1909-1955) M. EDNA MASON

GEORGE HASSENTEUFEL
(1911-1984)
M. ALMA DOUGHERTY

ROLAND HASSENTEUFEL, JR.
(1913-1941)
never married, no children

MAE HASSENTEUFEL
(1915-2001)
M. ROBERT LOCKWOOD

WILLIAM HASSENTEUFEL
(1917-1941)
never married, no children

THE CAMPBELL LINEAGE

~ *Hugh Campbell (b.1786) and Mary MacKay (1785-1867)* ~
(see MacKay Lineage)

Hugh Campbell was born around 1786,[1] although where remains a mystery. His oldest child's birth record stated that he was "from the shire of Ayr."[2] There was also family lore that claimed he was from the Borders, or southern Scotland.

Investigation by Scottish genealogist Bruce Durie pointed to Hugh originating in Stevenson, Ayrshire. On first inspection, we found two Hugh Campbells born at the right time (c.1786)—one the son of John Campbell and Isobel Boyd, the other the son of John Campbell and Grizel Boyd. We were unsure if this John Campbell was married twice, playing away from home, or if there were actually two separate John Campbells.[3]

Hugh Campbell, son of John Campbell, rope maker, and Isabel Boyd, was born September 2, 1787, and baptized on September5.[4]
Hugh Campbell, son of John Campbell, rope maker, and Grizel Boyd, was born August 28, 1792, and baptized on August 29.[5]

A local census from 1819 clarified the issue somewhat. John Campbell and Isobel Boyd were still married, so this John could not have also married Grizel Boyd. Also, John and Isobel's son Hugh still resided in Stevenson, was married, and had children. So he was not our Hugh Campbell.[6]

So what of Grizel Boyd Campbell's son Hugh? Grizel was found on that same 1819 local census, listed as living with a Hugh Campbell. Unfortunately, there was no indication of age or of relationship between the two. The way the form was filled out, it seemed to indicate that Grizel was the wife of this Hugh, rather than the mother. Yet the baptismal record clearly states that the father of her Hugh was John Campbell. On an 1822 version of that census, Grizel was found but not with Hugh. In 1836, neither was found.[7]

The above origins are still speculation. What is known is that at some point in his life, our Hugh relocated to the Sarsgrum, Durness, Sutherland area. He married Mary MacKay (born 1785, Reay, Durness, Scotland) (see *MacKay Lineage*) on 10 February 1809 in Eriboll, Sutherland.[8] They had ten children, some of whom emigrated to Canada and Australia:

- Jean[9] (b. 1810) – married John McDonald, emigrated to Australia
- Hughina[10] (b. 1811) – married James Mathew, emigrated to Australia
- Georgina[11] (1813-1874) – married John McKay[12]
- Barbara[13] (1815-1897) – married William Weir[14]
- Mary[15] (1817-1885) – married Thomas Campbell[16]
- Robert[17] (1819-1908) – married Mary Weir[18]
- *Hugh*[19] (1821-1905) – married Ann McIntosh[20] (see *McIntosh Lineage*)
- Margaret[21] (1823-1902) – married William Miller[22]
- Thomas[23] (b. 1826) – married Elizabeth Ross, emigrated to Canada
- Magdaline[24] (1829-1908)[25] – married George Henry Robson, emigrated to Australia

His marriage record in 1809[26] said that Hugh was a shepherd. We next see him on the 1841 census. Please note that in the 1841 census, all ages except for those under 10 were rounded to the nearest ten. In 1841, Hugh (50) was plying his trade in Sarsgrum, Durness, Sutherland, a town in the Scottish Highlands, located on the east side of the Kyle of Durness, about 3 miles southwest of Durness itself. His household consisted of wife Mary (50), children Barbara (20) and Robert (30). There were also two grandchildren, Alexander McDonald (5), and Georgina Campbell (2). There was no indication who these children belonged to, but since eldest daughter Jean married a John McDonald, this was probably her son. As to young Georgina, we can only speculate that Robert might have been her father. Hugh's mother-in-law, Barbara Morison MacKay (70), also lived there, as well as two laborers, John Mather (30) and Edward McCallum (40).[27]

It is unclear when Hugh Campbell died. My information indicated a death between 1841 and 1851, but no death or burial record had been found for Hugh.

In 1851, Mary (62) was the head of the household in Sarsgrum. The transcription of the 1851 census listed Mary as married, but on examining the actual page it seemed clear that she was marked as a widow and the transcription was in error. She watched over son Thomas (28), his daughter Georgina (4 – not the same Georgina as ten years before), and her grandson Alexander McDonald (15), who in this census was listed as a girl, Alexandra, but I do not know which is correct. Mary's mother Barbara Morison Mackay was still going strong at 88.[28]

In 1861, Hugh was definitely deceased. Mary (73), was listed as the "widow of the late manager" (presumably farm manager). She lived in Laggburg, Durness, Sutherland, with a 15-year-old servant Barbara McCullock.[29]

Mary MacKay Campbell died 6 November 1867, in a town called Inshoir, in Durness, Sutherland. Her grandson John Weir was the informant.[30] There is no burial information for her. The most likely place of burial for Mary and Hugh is Balnakeil Cemetery, Durness, but no records have been found.

Young **Hugh Campbell** is our line.

Hugh Campbell (1821-1905) and Ann McIntosh (1818-1904)
(see McIntosh Lineage)

Hugh Campbell was born 23 April 1821, the seventh child and second son of Hugh Campbell and Mary MacKay.[31] He and his brothers and sisters grew up in Sarsgrum, Durness, Sutherland.

Like his father Hugh before him, young Hugh became a shepherd in the Sarsgrum area. In 1841, he was living in the town of Rispond, 5 miles east of Durness on the chilly north Atlantic coast. His household consisted of himself and two younger sisters, Margaret and Magdalene.[32] Much of the rest of his family still lived in Sarsgrum with his parents.

Hugh's living arrangements changed on 27 August 1841, when he married Ann McIntosh.[33] He was 20, she 23, when they married in Eriboll, Scotland.

Ann's parents were shepherd John McIntosh and his wife Mary Oag MacKenzie (see *McIntosh Lineage*). Ann was born in 1818 in Strathbeg, Sutherland.[34]

After their marriage, Hugh and Ann had at least six children:[35] [36]

- John (b. c. 1843)[37]
- James (b.c. 1849)[38] – emigrated to the Falkland Islands, married Elizabeth Fell
- Hugh (b. c. 1853)[39]
- Thomas (b. c. 1855)[40]
- William (b. c. 1857)[41]
- **Donald McIntosh**[42] (1860-1945) – emigrated to America, married Isabella Morrison, (see *Morrison Lineage*) then Lily Davy

Hugh and family had wanderlust in their genes, as evidenced by a number of his siblings emigrating to Canada and Australia. Hugh didn't leave Scotland, but he moved frequently.

In 1851, Hugh (28) and Ann (30) lived in Scourie More, a town on the western coast on Eddrachillis Bay. At this time, they had son John (8), and Hugh's sister Magdalene (26) was visiting them.[43] Their son James (3) was living with Ann's parents John and Mary McIntosh in Durness, Sutherland.[44]

In January of 1860, they lived in Pulrossie, a town on the Dornoch Firth on the eastern coast, a full 63 miles from Scourie More, and about 7 miles west from Dornoch itself. Here they had the last of their children, Donald McIntosh Campbell, born in "the Red House" in Pulrossie on 28 January 1860.[45] [46] He joined older brothers John, James, Hugh, Thomas and William. There were 10 years between John and James, and four years between James and Hugh, so it was possible that there were other children who died in the interim.

The 1861 census found the family in the town of Eiden, located in Rogart, about 12 miles northwest of Dornoch, but inland from the coast. Oldest son John had left the nest, but the other sons were still too young: Hugh was 8, Thomas was 6, William was 4, and Donald was almost 2.[47] Son James (12) lived on a nearby farm, working as a shepherd boy.[48]

In 1871, Hugh and Ann, both about 50 years old, had moved again. All of their previous homes had been in their native Sutherland, but now they moved to county Moray, near the Moray Firth. They lived in Little Plewland, in Drainie parish. Hugh (18), William (14) and Donald (11) still lived at home, but Thomas (16) had gone off to seek his fortune elsewhere.[49] Son James was not found on the 1871 Scotland census, but he married Elizabeth Fell in 1877 in the Falkland Islands, so possibly he had already moved there.

In 1881, Hugh (60) and Ann (59) lived in the town of Easter Burnsides, still in Drainie parish of Moray. Sons Hugh (28), William (24) and Donald (21) still lived at home, although they were all working now. Young Hugh was a coachman, William was a shepherd like his father and grandfather, and Donald was a carpenter. There was also a granddaughter Mary (age 5) in the house, but there is no indication who the father was.

Eldest son John (38) was married to Mary A., and they lived in Kirkton Farr in Farr, Sutherland, at Ishlamby (Shepherd House). John was a shepherd, and the couple had one child, Jane A., who was only a year old. Also living with them was 12-year-old Mary J. McBeth, listed as a servant but whose occupation was listed as "scholar." and 22-year-old Alexander Munro, a boarder who was also a shepherd.[50]

By 1891, Hugh and Ann's nest was empty—so empty, in fact, that even the elder Hugh (70) was missing! He had not died, so it is unknown where he was at this time. There was a Hugh Campbell, living alone, working as an agricultural laborer up in the Tongue area, whose birth date fits with ours, but there is no way to know for certain if that was him. Ann (69) lived in Duffus in Moray, with granddaughter Mary, who was 15 and working as a domestic servant.[51]

Eldest son John (45) had settled in as a shepherd in Badanloch, Kildonan, Sutherland. He lived with wife Mary Ann (40), and children Jane Ann (17) who was still in school, Mary E. (8), Hughina (5), and Isabella (3). Missing was son Robert, who should have been about 10, as he is 19 on the 1901 census.[52]

Hugh the younger (38) lived in Duffus, at Burnside House, working as a domestic coachman.[53] Donald (31) had emigrated to New York, USA (more on him below). There was no sign of Thomas (36) or William (24) – or rather, there were too many Thomas and William Campbells to know which were the correct ones.

In 1901 Hugh and Ann lived in Duffus, Moray. Hugh, at age 80, had finally retired. Hughina Campbell (16), daughter of their son John, lived with them, and worked as a domestic servant.[54]

Son John (53) lived on Balinroich Farm in Fearn, Ross and Cromarty with his family – wife Mary Ann (50), children Robert (19), Bella (13), Mary E. (10), and Maggie (6). Robert was a shepherd's assistant.[55]

There was a Hugh Campbell (48) employed to care for horses (as a hostler) at the Atholl Arms Hotel in Blair Atholl, Perthshire who could have been our Hugh, given his previous employment as a coachman.[56]

Again, there were so many Thomases and Williams on the 1901 census, there was no way to tell which, if any, was the correct one. None have the proper birthplace and birth date match, so it was impossible to trace them.

Ann McIntosh Campbell died of cardiac disease at age 86 on 5 July 1904 in Gallowhill, Duffus.[57] Hugh Campbell died of morbus cordis (heart disease) aged 84 on 19 May 1905, also in Gallowhill, Duffus.[58] Their son Hugh was the informant for both of them.

Donald Campbell (1860-1945) and Isabella Morrison (1862-1907)
(see Morrison Lineage)

Donald McIntosh Campbell, as mentioned above, was born in Pulrossie, Creich, Sutherland, Scotland on 28 January 1860.[59] He lived with his parents for his entire life in Scotland, and became a carpenter in his adult life.

In 1886, Donald (24) left Scotland for New York City, New York in America, arriving May 3. He came aboard shipmaster John Wilson's *SS Ethiopia*, ports of departure Glasgow, Scotland, and Moville, Ireland. His occupation is listed as a joiner,[60] which is another term for a carpenter, particularly a cabinetmaker. This is also a term used in shipbuilding, and in later years Donald worked in the shipbuilding industry.

Isabella Morrison, daughter of John (III) Morrison and Isabella Rankin Wood, was born in Gamrie, Banff, Scotland, on 18 August 1864 [61] (see *Morrison Lineage*). She immigrated to New York City on 18 April 1882 aboard the ship *Italy*.[62]

On 24 March 1888, Donald (36) petitioned to become a citizen of the United States,[63] and on 7 July 1897, he was naturalized by the Supreme Court of New York County. At that time, Donald and family lived at

732 Amsterdam Ave. in New York City. His witness was Neil MacKay of 255 West 24th Street, New York City Both were carpenters. [64]

Donald Campbell and Isabella Morrison's marriage took place 28 December 1886, in Manhattan, New York.[65] They were married by a clergyman named John L. Peck, at the John Street Methodist Episcopal Church (now the John Street United Methodist Church) at 44 John Street in New York City. They had eight children:

- Bella[66] (1885-1896)
- Annie[67] (1887-1959) – married Rolland Hassenteufel[68]
- Caroline[69][70] (1889-1922) – married Daniel Vetter[71][72]
- Marguerite/Margaret[73] (1891-1894)
- John H.[74] (October 1895-Nov 1895)
- Grace E.[75][76] (1897-1920) – married Henry J. Rochel[77]
- William[78][79] (1900-1930) – married Pauline Menninger[80]
- *Edward Alexander[81]* (1903-1963) – married Mary Sutton (see *Hayden-Sutton Lineage*)

In 1900, Donald (39) and family lived in Manhattan, New York, at 53 West 98th Street. With him were wife Isabella Morrison Campbell (36), and children Annie (14), Caroline (10), Grace (4), and William (4 months). The census said they had seven children total, but only four were living. Family lore says the other three children died in a diphtheria outbreak.[82]

In 1903, Donald and family lived at 131 Elm Street, New York City, New York.[83]

On May 17, 1907, Isabella Morrison Campbell died at age 42 of arterial sclerosis with cerebral thrombosis and paralysis.[84] She was buried in St. Michael's Cemetery in Section H, Lot 5518, on May 19.[85] Also in this plot are seven other family members: Marguerite, John H., Bella, Grace, Caroline, William, and Caroline's husband, Daniel Vetter.

Isabella left behind Donald and her five surviving children – the youngest, Edward (more on him below), was only four.

In 1910, Donald lived at 967 Lawncrest in Queens, New York City. He was a 47-year-old widower and still a carpenter, presently in the building industry. Daughter Caroline (20) ran the household for him, and cared for younger siblings Grace (12), William (10), and Edward (6). Daughter Annie (24) had left the nest.[86]

Leaving his younger children with his daughter Caroline in New York City, Donald remarried in Buffalo, New York. His second wife was an Englishwoman named Lily Davy. They married 25 Nov 1918, and their daughter Mary was born 8 Feb 1919.[87]

By 1920, Donald (55) lived in a rented house in Buffalo, New York, with his second wife Lily (42) and daughter Mary L. Campbell (1). Lily had immigrated in 1909. Donald was a shipbuilder with Ferguson's company in Buffalo.[88]

Caroline Campbell (30) had married, and in 1920 lived in Queens with husband Daniel Vetter (31), daughters Isabella Vetter (8) and Dorothy Vetter (1), and her brothers William (19) and Edward (16). Her sister Grace had died on 22 August 1920.[89] Daniel Vetter was an electrician, and both the Campbell brothers were listed as electricians as well, no doubt working with their brother-in-law.[90]

In 1930, Donald (65) and Lily (52) were at 65 16th Street in Buffalo. He owned that house and was worth $4,000. Young Mary was 11, and Lily's mother, Mary J. Davy (75), had immigrated in 1910 and was living with them. Donald was a carpenter in the building trade.[91]

In 1940, Donald (80) was still at 65 16th Street in Buffalo with second wife Lily (62), daughter Mary (21), and mother-in-law Mary Jane Davy (85).[92]

Donald McIntosh Campbell died on June 5, 1945, in Buffalo, New York. He died of coronary thrombosis and was buried in White Chapel Memorial Park in Buffalo on June 7, 1945.[93]

Edward Alexander Campbell (1903-1963) and Mary Margaret Sutton (1904-1975)
(see Sutton-Hayden Lineage)

Born June 8, 1903, Edward Alexander Campbell was the youngest child of Donald Campbell and Isabella Morrison Campbell.[94] Edward was only four when his mother died, and lived most of his life in the care of elder sister Caroline while his father worked.[95] Once his father remarried, Edward lived full time with his sister and her husband Daniel.[96]

On December 23, 1924, Edward (24) was baptized at the Church of the Holy Cross at 329 West 42nd Street in New York.[97]

On February 22, 1927, Edward (24) married Mary Sutton (22)[98] Mary was born 21 March 1904, daughter of Irish immigrants Patrick Sutton and Mary Hayden Sutton[99] (see *Hayden-Sutton Lineage*). Edward worked as an electrician, but was handy in many areas, and lived at 30-05 30th, Astoria, Queens New York.[100]

They had five children:[101] [102] [103]

- Dolores (1928-2020)[104] – married Edward Penders
- Donald Edward (1931-1972) – married Andrée Fortier
- Robert (1933-1981)[105] – married Grace Babkowska
- Edward (1937-1994)[106] – married first Anastasia Plank, then Sonja Schultz
- *(Living)*

In 1930, the small family lived at 2352 31st Road in Queens, New York. Edward (26) was an electrician with a contractor, and Mary (25) was at home with 1-year-old Dolores.[107]

In 1940, Edward (37) lived with his wife Mary (36) and children Dolores (11), Donald (8), Robert (7), and Edward (2) at 3524 94th Street. They had lived at this address in 1935 as well.[108]

Edward Alexander Campbell died at age 60 on November 6, 1963 of a glioblastoma of the brain (brain tumor) in Great Neck, New York.[109] His wife Mary Sutton Campbell died at age 71 on September 21, 1975 in Norristown, Pennsylvania, of metastatic carcinoma originating in the breast.[110] Both were buried in St. Charles/Resurrection Cemetery in Farmingdale, New York in Section 30, Row Q, Grave 194.[111]

Campbell Lineage

[1] *Hugh Campbell & Mary Mackay*, 1841 Scotland Census, Parish: Durness; ED: 2; Page: 2; Line: 1230; Year: 1841.

[2] *Jean Campbell*, Scotland Old Parish Records, O.P.R. Births 048/ 0010 0112, Durness, accessed 30 May 2008 from http://www.scotlandspeople.gov.uk.

[3] *John Campbell*, Dr. Bruce Durie research. Bruce Durie is a professional Scottish genealogist.

[4] *Hugh Campbell son of Isobel Boyd*, Scotland Old Parish Records, O.P.R. Births 615/ 0010 0138, Stevenston, accessed 30 May 2008 from www.scotlandspeople.gov.uk.

[5] *Hugh Campbell son of Grizel Boyd*, Scotland Old Parish Records, O.P.R. Births 615/ 0010 0159, Stevenston, accessed 30 May 2008 from www.scotlandspeople.gov.uk.

[6] *Hugh Campbell son of Isobel Boyd*, Inhabitants *of Stevenston and Saltcoats from Dr. Landsborough, 1819 1822, and 1836.* Informal census compiled by the local minister.

[7] *Hugh Campbell son of Grizel Boyd*, Inhabitants *of Stevenston and Saltcoats from Dr. Landsborough, 1819 1822, and 1836.* Informal census compiled by the local minister.

[8] *Hugh Campbell & Mary Mackay*, Scotland Old Parish Records, O.P.R. Marriages 048/ 0010 0141, Durness, accessed 07/04/2008 from http://www.scotlandspeople.gov.uk.

[9] *Jean Campbell*, Scotland Old Parish Records, O.P.R. Births 048/ 0010 0112, Durness, accessed 30 May 2008 from http://www.scotlandspeople.gov.uk.

[10] *Hughina Campbell*, Scotland Old Parish Records, O.P.R. Births 048/ 0010 0114, Durness, accessed 30 May 2008 from www.scotlandspeople.gov.uk.

[11] *Georgina Campbell*, Scotland Old Parish Records, O.P.R. Births 048/ 0010 0115, Durness, accessed 30 May 2008 from http://www.scotlandspeople.gov.uk

[12] *Georgina Campbell Mackay*, Scotland Death Register, 1874, (Statutory registers Deaths 048/ 10) 1874. ScotlandsPeople.gov.uk, accessed 12 Feb 2021.

[13] *Barbara Campbell*, Scotland Old Parish Records, O.P.R. Births 048/ 0010 0116, Durness, accessed 30 May 2008 from http://www.scotlandspeople.gov.uk.

[14] *Barbara Campbell Weir*, Scotland Death Register, 1897, Delting, Scotland Statutory Deaths, 002/ 11. Accessed 14 July 2019, Scotland's People.

[15] *Mary Campbell*, Scotland Old Parish Records, O.P.R. Births 048/ 0010 0118, Durness, accessed 30 May 2008 from www.scotlandspeople.gov.uk.

[16] *Mary Campbell Campbell*, Scotland Death Register, Scotland's People. 1885 (Statutory registers Deaths 043/ 18). ScotlandsPeople.gov.uk. Accessed 25 May 2019.

[17] *Robert Campbell*, Scotland Old Parish Records, O.P.R. Births 048/ 0010 0119, Durness, accessed 30 May 2008 from www.scotlandspeople.gov.uk.

[18] *Robert Campbell*, Scotland Death Register, 1908, (Statutory registers Deaths 036/ 3). ScotlandsPeople.gov.uk, accessed 12 Feb 2021.

[19] *Hugh Campbell*, Scotland Old Parish Records, O.P.R. Births 048/ 0020 0004, Durness, accessed 07/04/2008 from http://www.scotlandspeople.gov.uk.

[20] *Hugh Campbell*, Scotland Death Register. Year: 1905; Deaths 132/2 13; District of Duffus, County of Elgin. ScotlandsPeople.gov.uk, accessed 17 March 2017.

[21] *Margaret Campbell*, Scotland Old Parish Records, O.P.R. Births 048/ 0020 0005, Durness, accessed 30 May 2008 from www.scotlandspeople.gov.uk.

[22] *Margaret Campbell Miller*, Scotland Death Register, 1902, (Statutory registers Deaths 002/ 1). ScotlandsPeople.gov.uk, accessed 11 Feb 2021.

[23] *Thomas Campbell*, Charmaine Langford Research. Charmaine Langford is a descendant of Magdaline Campbell.

[24] *Magdalene Campbell*, Scotland Old Parish Records, O.P.R. Births 048/ 0020 0008, Durness, accessed 30 May 2008 from www.scotlandspeople.gov.uk.

[25] *Magdalene Campbell Robson*, Death Certificate, 1901, New South Wales, Australia.

[26] *Hugh Campbell & Mary Mackay*, Scotland Old Parish Records, O.P.R. Marriages 048/ 0010 0141, Durness, accessed 07/04/2008 from http://www.scotlandspeople.gov.uk.

[27] *Hugh Campbell & Mary Mackay Campbell*, 1841 Scotland Census, Parish: Durness; ED: 2; Page: 2; Line: 1230; Year: 1841.

[28] *Mary Mackay Campbell*, 1851 Scotland Census, Parish: Durness; ED: 6; Page: 2; Line: 16; Roll: CSSCT1851_11; Year: 1851.

[29] *Mary Mackay Campbell*, 1861 Scotland Census, Parish: Durness; ED: 2; Page: 1; Line: 1; Roll: CSSCT1861_7.

[30] *Mary Mackay Campbell*, Scotland Statutory Records Index, Durness Parish, County of Sutherland, year 1867, p. 6, Statutory Deaths 048/00 0016, accessed 8 June 2008 from www.scotlandspeople.gov.uk.

[31] *Hugh Campbell*, Scotland Old Parish Records, O.P.R. Births 048/ 0020 0004, Durness, accessed 07/04/2008 from http://www.scotlandspeople.gov.uk.

[32] *Hugh Campbell*, 1841 Scotland Census, Parish: Durness; ED: 4; Page: 10; Line: 1030; Year: 1841.

[33] *Hugh Campbell & Ann McIntosh*, Scotland Old Parish Records, O.P.R. Marriages 048/ 0020 0031, Durness, accessed 07/04/2016 from http://www.scotlandspeople.gov.uk.

[34] *Ann McIntosh*, Scotland Old Parish Records, Ann McIntosh, O.P.R. Births 048/ 10 162, Durness, accessed 17 Mar 2017 from www.scotlandspeople.gov.uk.

[35] *Hugh Campbell & Ann McIntosh Campbell*, 1851 Scotland Census, Parish: Eddrachillis; ED: 2; Page: 20; Line: 7; Roll: CSSCT1851_12; Year: 1851.

[36] *Hugh Campbell & Ann McIntosh Campbell*, 1861 Scotland Census, Parish: Rogart; ED: 1; Page: 14; Line: 10; Roll: CSSCT1861_7.

[37] *John Campbell*, 1851 Scotland Census, Parish: Eddrachillis; ED: 2; Page: 20; Line: 7; Roll: CSSCT1851_12; Year: 1851.

[38] *James Campbell*, 1851 Scotland Census, Parish: Durness; ED: 1; Page: 3; Line: 12; Roll: CSSCT1851_11; Year: 1851.

[39] *Hugh Campbell*, 1861 Scotland Census, Parish: Rogart; ED: 1; Page: 14; Line: 10; Roll: CSSCT1861_7.

[40] *Thomas Campbell*, 1861 Scotland Census, Parish: Rogart; ED: 1; Page: 14; Line: 10; Roll: CSSCT1861_7.

[41] *William Campbell*, 1861 Scotland Census, Parish: Rogart; ED: 1; Page: 14; Line: 10; Roll: CSSCT1861_7.

[42] *Donald McIntosh Campbell*, Birth certificate. In possession of Kerry Gans Douglas.

[43] *Hugh Campbell & Ann McIntosh Campbell*, 1851 Scotland Census, Parish: Eddrachillis; ED: 2; Page: 20; Line: 7; Roll: CSSCT1851_12; Year: 1851.

[44] *James Campbell*, 1851 Scotland Census, Parish: Durness; ED: 1; Page: 3; Line: 12; Roll: CSSCT1851_11; Year: 1851.

[45] *Donald McIntosh Campbell*, Birth certificate. In possession of Kerry Gans Douglas.

[46] *Donald McIntosh Campbell*, Scotland Statutory Records Index, Statutory Births 046/01 0005, accessed 07/04/2008 from www.scotlandspeople.gov.uk.

[47] *Hugh Campbell & Ann McIntosh Campbell*, 1861 Scotland Census, Parish: Rogart; ED: 1; Page: 14; Line: 10; Roll: CSSCT1861_7.

[48] *James Campbell*, 1861 Scotland Census, Parish: Rogart; ED: 1; Page: 5; Line: 18; Roll: CSSCT1861_7.

[49] *Hugh Campbell & Ann McIntosh Campbell*, 1871 Scotland Census, Parish: Drainie; ED: 6; Page: 11; Line: 10; Roll: CSSCT1871_24.

[50] *John Campbell*, 1881 Scotland Census, Parish: Farr; ED: 7; Page: 3; Line: 10; Roll: cssct1881_13

[51] *Hugh Campbell & Ann McIntosh Campbell*, 1891 Scotland Census, Parish: Duffus; ED: 7; Page: 5; Line: 1; Roll: CSSCT1891_37.

[52] *John Campbell*, 1891 Scotland Census, Parish: Kildonan; ED: 7; Page: 1; Line: 18; Roll: CSSCT1891_14.

[53] *Hugh Campbell*, 1891 Scotland Census, Parish: Duffus; ED: 7; Page: 3; Line: 9; Roll: CSSCT1891_37.

[54] *Hugh Campbell & Ann McIntosh Campbell*, 1901 Scotland Census, Parish: Duffus; ED: 4; Page: 2; Line: 6; Roll: CSSCT1901_39.

[55] *John Campbell*, 1901 Scotland Census, Parish: Fearn; ED: 3; Page: 6; Line: 1; Roll: CSSCT1901_17.

[56] *Hugh Campbell*, 1901 Scotland Census, Parish: Blair Atholl; ED: 7; Page: 9; Line: 13; Roll: CSSCT1901_116.

[57] *Ann McIntosh Campbell*, Scotland Death Register, Year: 1904; Death Record 131/2 16; District of Duffus, County of Elgin.

[58] *Hugh Campbell*, Scotland Death Register, Year: 1905; Deaths 132/2 13; District of Duffus, County of Elgin

[59] *Donald McIntosh Campbell*, Birth Certificate, In possession of Kerry Gans Douglas.

[60] *Donald Campbell*, Passenger Lists, Year: 1886; Arrival: New York, New York; Microfilm Serial: M237, 1820-1897; Microfilm Roll: Roll 494; Line: 40; List Number: 480 accessed on Ancestry.com.

[61] *Isabella Morrison*, Scotland Statutory Records Index, Statutory Births 155/00 0081, Parish: Gamrie; County: Banff; p 27; entry 81 for the year 1864. Accessed 19 May 2008 from www.scotlandspeople.gov.uk

[62] *Isabella Morrison*, Castle Garden Immigration Records, http://www.castlegarden.org/quick_search_detail.php?p_id=1665957.

[63] *Donald Campbell*, Naturalization Papers, Court of Common Pleas, New York, New York. Copies in possession of Kerry Gans Douglas.

[64] *Donald Campbell*, Naturalization Papers, National Archives and Records Administration (NARA); Washington, D.C; Soundex Index to Petitions for Naturalizations Filed in Federal, State, and Local Courts in New York City, 1792-1906 (M1674); Microfilm Serial: M1674; Microfilm Roll: 42 accessed on Ancestry.com.

[65] *Donald Campbell & Isabella Morrison*, Marriage License, "New York, Marriages, 1686-1980," index, FamilySearch (https://familysearch.org/pal:/MM9.1.1/F6QP-BS9 : accessed 16 Nov 2012), 28 Dec 1886; citing reference, FHL microfilm 1570941.

[66] *Isabella Campbell*, Cemetery Records & Tombstone, St. Michael's Cemetery, 7202 Astoria Blvd., East Elmhurst, NY 11370.

[67] *Annie Campbell*, 1900 United States Census, Year: 1900; Census Place: Manhattan, New York, New York; Roll: 1105; Page: 7A; Enumeration District: 0533; FHL microfilm: 1241105.

[68] *Annie Campbell & Rolland Hassenteufel*, Marriage. Dolores Campbell Penders, daughter of Edward Alexander Campbell. (This person experienced or had direct knowledge of the event in question.)

[69] *Caroline Campbell*, 1900 United States Census, Year: 1900; Census Place: Manhattan, New York, New York; Roll: 1105; Page: 7A; Enumeration District: 0533; FHL microfilm: 1241105.

[70] *Caroline Campbell Vetter*, Cemetery Records & Tombstone, St. Michael's Cemetery, 7202 Astoria Blvd., East Elmhurst, NY 11370.

[71] *Caroline Campbell & Daniel Vetter*, Marriage. Dolores Campbell Penders, daughter of Edward Alexander Campbell. (This person experienced or had direct knowledge of the event in question.)

[72] *Caroline Campbell Vetter & Daniel Vetter*, 1920 US Census, Year: 1920; Census Place: Queens Assembly District 4, Queens, New York; Roll: T625_1233; Page: 12B; Enumeration District: 237; Image: 356.

[73] *Marguerite Campbell*, Cemetery Records & Tombstone, St. Michael's Cemetery, 7202 Astoria Blvd., East Elmhurst, NY 11370.

[74] *John H. Campbell*, Cemetery Records & Tombstone, St. Michael's Cemetery, 7202 Astoria Blvd., East Elmhurst, NY 11370.

[75] *Grace E. Campbell*, 1900 United States Census, Year: 1900; Census Place: Manhattan, New York, New York; Roll: 1105; Page: 7A; Enumeration District: 0533; FHL microfilm: 1241105.

[76] *Grace E. Campbell Rochel*, Cemetery Records & Tombstone, St. Michael's Cemetery, 7202 Astoria Blvd., East Elmhurst, NY 11370.

[77] *Grace Campbell & Henry J. Rochel*, marriage. Grace Campbell, Death Certificate, Department of Health of NYC, registered # 3680.

[78] *William Campbell*, 1900 United States Census, Year: 1900; Census Place: Manhattan, New York, New York; Roll: 1105; Page: 7A; Enumeration District: 0533; FHL microfilm: 1241105.

[79] *William Campbell*, Cemetery Records & Tombstone, St. Michael's Cemetery, 7202 Astoria Blvd., East Elmhurst, NY 11370.

[80] *William Campbell & Pauline Menninger*, marriage. Dolores Campbell Penders, daughter of Edward Alexander Campbell. (This person experienced or had direct knowledge of the event in question.)

[81] *Edward Alexander Campbell*, Birth Certificate, City of New York Health Department, Borough of Queens, #C308; Certificate # 1636.

[82] *Donald Campbell & Isabella Morrison Campbell*, 1900 United States Census, Year: 1900; Census Place: Manhattan, New York, New York; Roll: 1105; Page: 7A; Enumeration District: 0533; FHL microfilm: 1241105.

[83] *Edward Alexander Campbell*, Birth Certificate, City of New York Health Department, Borough of Queens, #C308; Certificate # 1636, Edward Alexander Campbell.

[84] *Isabella Morrison Campbell*, Death Certificate, NY Dept of Health, Certificate No 1438.

[85] *Isabella Morrison Campbell*, Cemetery Records & Tombstone, St. Michael's Cemetery, 7202 Astoria Blvd., East Elmhurst, NY 11370.

[86] *Donald Campbell*, 1910 United States Census, Year: 1910; Census Place: Queens Ward 1, Queens, New York; Roll: T624_1064; Page: 4B; Enumeration District: 1165; ; FHL microfilm: 1375077.

[87] *Mary Campbell*, birth. Mary Campbell, daughter of Donald McIntosh Campbell and Lily Davy, told Kerry Gans Douglas. (This person experienced or had direct knowledge of the event in question.)

[88] *Donald Campbell & Lily Davy Campbell*, 1920 US Census, Year: 1920; Census Place: Buffalo Ward 24, Erie, New York; Roll: T625_1108; Page: 5A; Enumeration District: 238; Image: 351.

[89] *Grace Campbell Rochel*, Death Certificate, Department of Health of NYC, registered # 3680.

[90] *Edward Campbell*, 1920 US Census, Year: 1920; Census Place: Queens Assembly District 4, Queens, New York; Roll: T625_1233; Page: 12B; Enumeration District: 237; Image: 356.

[91] *Donald Campbell & Lily Davy Campbell*, 1930 US Census, Year: 1930; Census Place: Buffalo, Erie, New York; Roll: 1433; Page: 18B; Enumeration District: 309; Image: 387.0; FHL microfilm: 2341168.

[92] *Donald Campbell & Lily Davy Campbell*, 1940 US Census, Year: 1940; Census Place: Buffalo, Erie, New York; Roll: T627_2839; Page: 7B; Enumeration District: 64-534.

[93] *Donald Campbell*, Death Certificate, NY Dept of Health, Reg. # 32480-3263.

[94] *Edward Alexander Campbell*, Birth Certificate, City of New York Health Department, Borough of Queens, #C308; Certificate # 1636.

[95] *Edward Campbell*, 1910 United States Census, Year: 1910; Census Place: Queens Ward 1, Queens, New York; Roll: T624_1064; Page: 4B; Enumeration District: 1165; ; FHL microfilm: 1375077.

[96] *Edward Campbell*, 1920 US Census, Year: 1920; Census Place: Queens Assembly District 4, Queens, New York; Roll: T625_1233; Page: 12B; Enumeration District: 237; Image: 356.

[97] *Edward Campbell*, Baptismal certificate, issued Jan 21, 1927 from the Church of the Holy Cross, 329 West 42nd Street, New York, New York.

[98] *Edward Campbell & Mary Sutton*, Marriage License, County of New York City, New York, Registered # 3605; Feb 8, 1927.

[99] *Mary Sutton*, Birth Certificate, NY Dept of Health; Certificate # 14796.

[100] *Edward Campbell & Mary Sutton*, Marriage License, County of New York City, New York, Registered # 3605; Feb 8, 1927.

[101] *Edward Campbell & Mary Sutton Campbell*, 1930 US Census, Year: 1930; Census Place: Queens, Queens, New York; Roll: 1583; Page: 4B; Enumeration District: 26; Image: 80.0; FHL microfilm: 2341318.

[102] *Edward Campbell & Mary Sutton Campbell*, 1940 US Census, Year: 1940; Census Place: New York, Queens, New York; Roll: T627_2733; Page: 7B; Enumeration District: 41-635.

[103] *Edward Campbell & Mary Sutton Campbell*, Dolores Campbell Penders and Maryann Campbell Gans, daughters of Edward Campbell and Mary Sutton Campbell, told Kerry Gans Douglas. (This person experienced or had direct knowledge of the event in question.)

[104] *Dolores Campbell Penders*, Kerry Gans Douglas attended the funeral of Dolores Campbell Penders. (This person experienced or had direct knowledge of the event in question.)

[105] *Robert Campbell*, Cemetery Records, St. Charles Cemetery, 2015 Wellwood Ave, Farmingdale, NY 11735.

[106] *Edward Campbell*, Cemetery Records, St. Charles Cemetery, 2015 Wellwood Ave, Farmingdale, NY 11735.

[107] *Edward Campbell & Mary Sutton Campbell*, 1930 US Census, Year: 1930; Census Place: Queens, Queens, New York; Roll: 1583; Page: 4B; Enumeration District: 26; Image: 80.0; FHL microfilm: 2341318.

[108] *Edward Campbell & Mary Sutton Campbell*, 1940 US Census, Year: 1940; Census Place: New York, Queens, New York; Roll: T627_2733; Page: 7B; Enumeration District: 41-635.

[109] *Edward Campbell*, Death Certificate, NY Dept of Health District # 2951; Registered # 84723 506.

[110] *Mary Sutton Campbell*, Death Certificate, PA Dept of Health; Registered # 8687775.

[111] *Edward Campbell & Mary Sutton Campbell*, Cemetery Records, St. Charles Cemetery, 2015 Wellwood Ave, Farmingdale, NY 11735.

SARSGRUM, DURNESS, SCOTLAND

Sarsgrum was a farm where Hugh Campbell of Ayr worked as a shepherd in 1841 and perhaps before/after. These photos were sent to me by an email contact back in 2009.

CAMPBELL FAMILY

HUGH CAMPBELL & ANN MCINTOSH CAMPBELL
Location: Scotland
Date: unknown
Dog: unknown

DONALD CAMPBELL (1860-1945)
Location: Glasgow, Date: c. 1886

DONALD CAMPBELL & 2ND WIFE LILY DAVY
Location: Buffalo, NY, Date: unknown

CHILDREN OF DONALD CAMPBELL & ISABELLA MORRISON

EDWARD, CAROLINE, GRACE, ANNIE, & WILLIAM
Location: New York City, Date: c. 1907

DONALD (FATHER), WILLIAM, EDWARD & GRACE
Location: New York, Date: 1909

CAMPBELL FAMILY

EDWARD CAMPBELL
Location: NY, Date: c. 1905

**DOLORES CAMPBELL,
MACDOUGAL THE DOG,
MARY CAMPBELL**
Location: Buffalo, NY, Date 1930

*Mary was Donald's daughter with
2nd wife Lily Davy*

**EDWARD & WILLIAM
CAMPBELL**
*Location: NY,
Date c. 1911*

**WILLIAM CAMPBELL &
ANNIE CAMPBELL
HASSENTEUFEL**
(siblings)
Location: NY, Date: 1925

**DANIEL VETTER &
CAROLINE CAMPBELL VETTER**
Location: New York, Date: unknown

**HENRY ROCHEL &
GRACE CAMPBELL ROCHEL**
Location: New York, Date: 1920

Campbell Family

Edward Campbell
Location: NY, Date: c. 1917

**Pauline Menninger Campbell
& William Campbell**
Location: NY, Date: 1925

**The Hassenteufel/Hassen Family
Back: Charlie, Annie Campbell, Roland, Sr.
Front: May, William, Roland, Jr.**
Location: New york, Date: 1925

CAMPBELL FAMILY

**HENRY ROCHEL &
GRACE CAMPBELL ROCHEL**
Location: NY, Date: 1920

**EDWARD & BILL
CAMPBELL**
*Location: NY,
Date: c. 1920*

**MARY CAMPBELL
& DOTTIE VETTER**
Location: NY, Date: 1922

**MARY SUTTON CAMPBELL, GEORGE HASSEN/HASSENTEUFEL,
PAULINE MENNINGER CAMPBELL, CHARLIE HASSEN/HASSENTEUFEL**
Location: NY, Date: c. 1930

CAMPBELL FAMILY

ISABELLA "BELLA" VETTER ORLANDI, EDWARD CAMPBELL SR., & CAROLINE HOUCK
Location: New York
Date: 1950

Bella & Dottie Vetter were Edward Campbell's nieces, daughters of his sister Caroline Campbell & her husband Daniel Vetter.

MARYANN CAMPBELL, CAROLINE & VIRGINIA "GINNY" HOUCK
Location: Sunken Meadow Beach, NY
Date: 1951

DOROTHY "DOTTIE" VETTER HOUCK
Location: New York
Date: 1952

Dottie was sister to Bella, daughter of Caroline Campbell Vetter, and mother of Caroline & Ginny Houck

EDWARD CAMPBELL & MARY SUTTON

Location: New York
Date: 1925

Location: New York
Date: September 1926

South Brother Island, NY
Date: July 1924

Location, Niagra Falls
Honeymoon
Date: February 1927

Location:
Slattery's Store,
Mountain View, NJ
Date: 1931
With children Donald
& Dolores

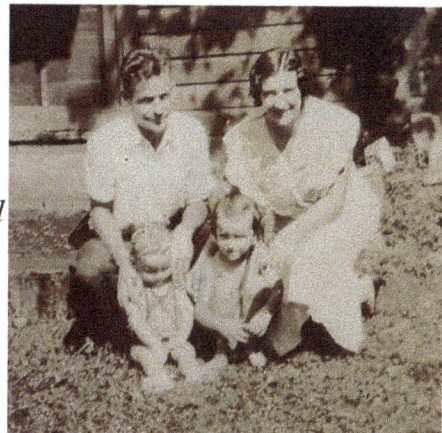

Location: New York
Date: c. 1928

EDWARD CAMPBELL & MARY SUTTON

Location: New York
Date: 1937

Location: 248-10 DePew Ave.,
Little Neck, NY
Date: June 1947

Location: 248-10 DePew Ave.,
Little Neck, NY
Bobby's graduation
Date: June 1947

Location: 248-10 DePew Ave.,
Little Neck, NY
Maryann's christening
Date: Aug 1947

EDWARD CAMPBELL & MARY SUTTON

Location: Canoe Club, South Brother Island in the East River, NYC
Date: 1924

17 May 1942

Location:
248-10 DePew Ave.,
Little Neck, N.Y.

1948

Location: Daughter Dolores' Wedding, Douglaston, NY
Date: 7 June 1952

EDWARD CAMPBELL & MARY SUTTON

Location: 26 Highland Ave., Great Neck, NY
Maryann's 4th birthday
Date: 1951

Location: 26 Highland Ave., Great Neck, NY
Maryann's graduation
Date 1964

Location: St. Aloysius Church, Great Neck, NY
Maryann's wedding
Date: October 1969

Location: 26 Highland Ave., Great Neck, NY
with granddaughter Kerry
Date: c. 1973

American Martyrs Church, Monroeville, PA
grandson D.J.'s christenng
Date: June 1970

CHILDREN OF
EDWARD CAMPBELL & MARY SUTTON

DOLORES, DONALD, & BOBBY CAMPBELL
Location: New York, Date: 1937

BOBBY & EDWARD CAMPBELL
Location: New York, Date: 1938

FRONT: EDWARD, MARY, EDWARD JR., BOBBY (GRADUATE)
BACK: DONALD & DOLORES
Location: 248-10 DePew Ave, Little Neck, NY, Date: 1947

CHILDREN OF
EDWARD CAMPBELL & MARY SUTTON

**BOBBY, DONALD,
EDWARD, DOLORES**
Date: October 1942

**DONALD,
MARYANN, BOBBY**
Date: Aug 1948

**DOLORES, DONALD,
EDWARD, BOBBY**
Date: 1945

*Location for all but the graduation:
248-10 DePew Ave., Little Neck, NY*

**DOLORES, MARYANN (& TEDDY)
& EDWARD**
Date: Aug 1948

**BOBBY, DONALD, EDWARD SR.,
DOLORES, MARYANN, MARY, EDWARD**
Location: 26 Highland Place, Great Neck, NY
Date: June 1951

**MARYANN, EDWARD SR., DOLORES,
MARY, EDWARD, DONALD, BOBBY**
Date: Feb 1949

CHILDREN OF
EDWARD CAMPBELL & MARY SUTTON

EDWARD, BOBBY, ED PENDERS, DOLORES, MARY, EDWARD SR., DONALD, MARYANN
Location: Dolores' Wedding, Douglaston, NY
Date: 7 June 1952

ED PENDERS, BOBBY, EDWARD, EDWARD SR., DONALD, ANDREE FORTIER, MARY, MARYANN, DOLORES
Location: Donald's Wedding, Montreal, Canada
Date: 7 June 1955

DONALD, DOLORES, EDWARD, MARYANN, BOBBY
Location: 26 Highland Place, Great Neck, NY
Date: 14 April 1968

CAMPBELL CEMETERIES

ST. MICHAEL'S CEMETERY
East Elmhurst, NY

Here lies Isabella Morrison Campbell and all of her children except Annie and Edward.
Photos courtey of the cemetery.

CAMPBELL CEMETERIES

St. Charles Cemetery
Farmingdale, NY

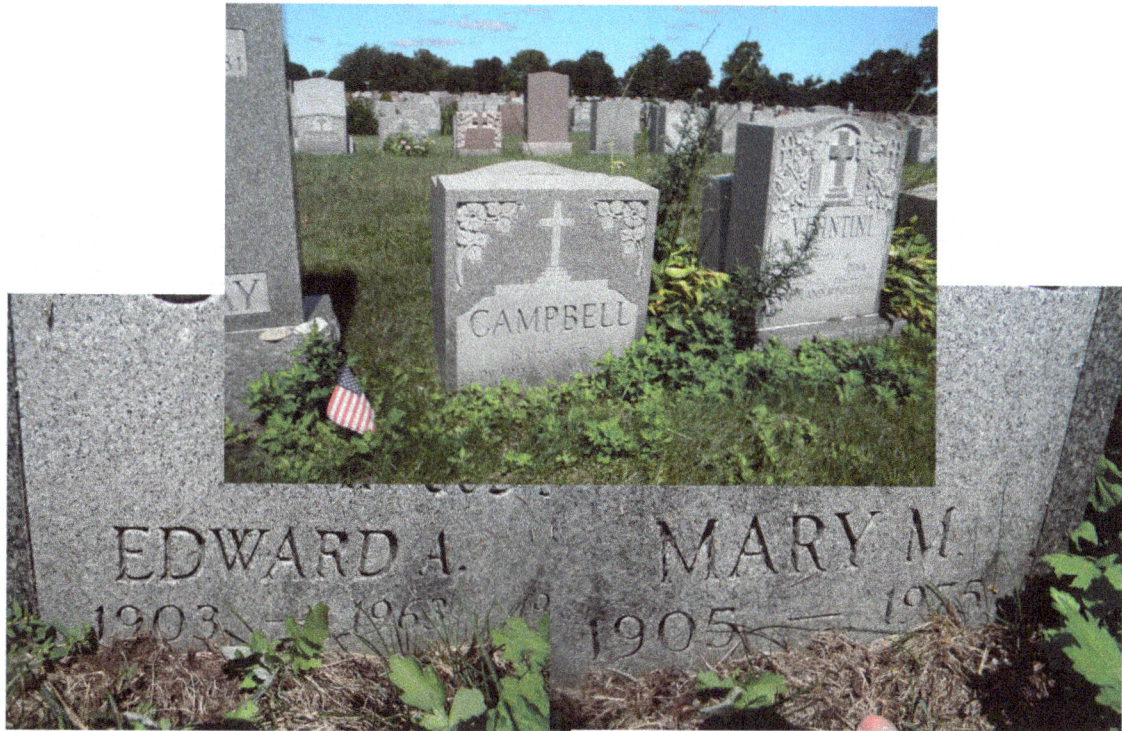

EDWARD A.
1903 — 1963

MARY M.
1905 — 1955

CAMPBELL

BELOVED HUSBAND
ROBERT P.
1933 — 1981

BELOVED HUSBAND
AND FATHER
EDWARD J.
1937 — 1994

ALWAYS IN OUR HEARTS

Original Stone

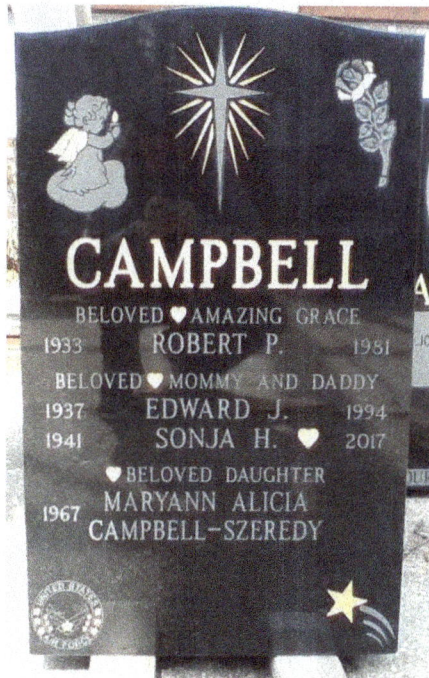

CAMPBELL

BELOVED ♥ AMAZING GRACE
1933   ROBERT P.   1981
BELOVED ♥ MOMMY AND DADDY
1937   EDWARD J.   1994
1941   SONJA H. ♥   2017
♥ BELOVED DAUGHTER
1967   MARYANN ALICIA
CAMPBELL-SZEREDY

New Stone, 2019

THE MORRISON LINEAGE

GAMRIE, GLENQUITHLE,
BLACKHILLOCKS, KING
EDWARD & NEW BYTH

SCOTLAND

THE MORRISON-IRONSIDE LINEAGE

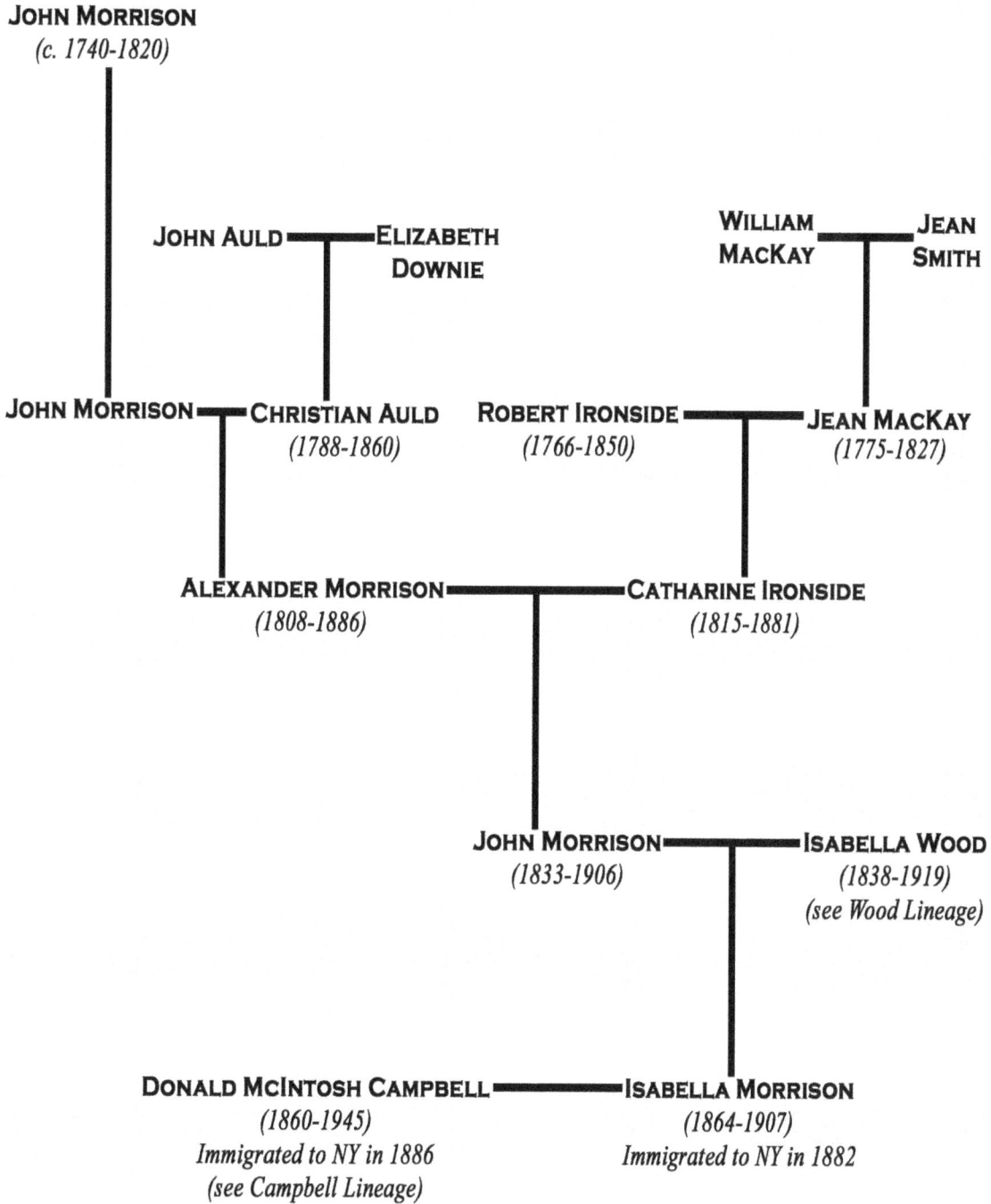

JOHN MORRISON
(c. 1740-1820)

JOHN AULD ━ **ELIZABETH DOWNIE**

WILLIAM MACKAY ━ **JEAN SMITH**

JOHN MORRISON ━ **CHRISTIAN AULD**
(1788-1860)

ROBERT IRONSIDE
(1766-1850)
━ **JEAN MACKAY**
(1775-1827)

ALEXANDER MORRISON
(1808-1886)
━ **CATHARINE IRONSIDE**
(1815-1881)

JOHN MORRISON
(1833-1906)
━ **ISABELLA WOOD**
(1838-1919)
(see Wood Lineage)

DONALD MCINTOSH CAMPBELL
(1860-1945)
Immigrated to NY in 1886
(see Campbell Lineage)
━ **ISABELLA MORRISON**
(1864-1907)
Immigrated to NY in 1882

THE MORRISON LINEAGE

John (I) Morrison (1740-1820)

John (I) Morrison was born around 1740. He died in January of 1820, at age 80. At the time of his death, he lived in Glenquithle, Aberdour (Aberdeen), Aberdeenshire, Scotland. Glenquithle was a family farm. He was buried 22 January 1820 in the churchyard of Gamrie, Banff.[1] Although this is not definitively our John, he lived and died on the same farm our ancestor farmed, so it is likely to be our line.

His wife is unknown, but he had at least one son, *John (II)Morrison*.

John (II) Morrison and Christian Auld (1788-1860)

It is unknown when John (II) Morrison was born (or when he died).Since his first known child was born in 1808, he was possibly born around 1788.

Christian Auld, daughter of John Auld and Elizabeth Downie, was born 3 June 1788 in Clechden, Gamrie, Banffshire, Scotland.[2] John and Christian were not married, and apparently did not stay together after their son was born, as she lived with her sister in later censuses.

Christian and John had one known son: *Alexander Morrison* (1808-1886).[3]

Eight years later, in 1816, John had an illegitimate daughter, Elspet Morrison, by a woman named Elspet Ross. At that time, he was a farmer in Glenquithle, Aberdour (Aberdeen), Aberdeenshire, Scotland.[4] In 1825, he and Elspet Ross had another illegitimate child, this one a boy, George Morrison.[5]

In 1841, Christian (53) was living in the village of New Aberdour, Aberdour, in Aberdeenshire, and working as a farm laborer. She lived with a 70-year-old woman named Isabella Simpson.[6]

In 1851, Christian (63) was living in Cushnie, Gamrie, Banffshire, with her sisters Margaret and Mary. Her occupation was listed as a pauper (farm servant).[7]

Christian Auld died 7 August 1860, in Cushnie, Gamrie, Banffshire at age 72, of a disease of the spine of several years duration, and was buried in the Gamrie churchyard.[8]

It is unknown when John (II) Morrison died, but I found a death certificate from the website Scotland's People with a John Morrison who died in 1860 in Banffshire. This could be our John. The certificate stated that he was married, although I have not found if our John ever married—only 3 illegitimate children. This record listed his parents as John Morrison and Isabella Badenach. The informant on this death was a James Morrison, his son. I have no knowledge of our John having a son James, so this record needs more research to confirm or disprove.[9]

John and Christian's son *Alexander* married Catharine Ironside in 1833.

Alexander Morrison (b.c. 1808-1886) and Catharine Ironside (1815-1881)
(*see Ironside Lineage*)

Alexander Morrison was born about 1808 in Gamrie parish, Banffshire, Scotland, based on his recorded age at his death.[10] [11] On 27 June 1833, he married Catharine Ironside (see *Ironside Lineage*) in Aberdour (Aberdeen), Aberdeenshire.[12] Catharine was born 8 March 1815, in Baggriehill, Gamrie, Banffshire, and baptized 16 March 1815.[13]

Alexander and Catharine had eight children:

- *John* (1833–1906) – married Isabella Rankin Wood [14] [15] (see *Wood Lineage*)
- Alexander (1836-1913) – married Mary Clark [16] [17]
- Isabella (b. 1838) [18]
- Catherine (1840-1875) [19] [20]
- George (1844-1933) – married Jessie Angus [21] [22]
- William Willox (1847-1902) [23] [24]
- James (b. 1851) [25]
- Ann B. (b. 1854) [26]

Alexander spent his entire life as a farmer or farm laborer. In 1841, at age 30, he was a farmer at Glenquithle, Aberdeen. You will note that this is the same farm his grandfather was associated with. His household included wife Catharine (25) and children John (7), Alexander (4), Isabella (3) and Catherine (1). John was the only one not born in Aberdeen. Some farm servants also lived with them – Rebecca Aden, age 12, John Donald, 15, Anne Ranken, 15, and Garden Wales, 25.[27]

In 1851, the family still lived in Glenquithle, and Alexander (43) was a farmer of 65 acres. Wife Catharine (35) and children John (17), Alexander (15), Isabella (13) and James (6 months) lived with him. They had a servant, 17-year-old Jean Jamieson.[28] I don't know where Catherine (11) has gone—she seems young to be out as a servant, but we have a 12-year-old servant on the 1841 census above. I will also note that both George and William Willox should be on this census and are not, because they were visiting Ann Bruce (59), in Glenquithe, Aberdour, Aberdeen, Scotland. Who is Ann Bruce? Since in 1854 Alexander and Catherine name their new daughter Ann Bruce Morrison, there is obviously a connection.[29]

In 1861, Alexander (52) had moved from his 65-acre farm in Aberdeen to Pratston Hill, in Gamrie, Banffshire. He worked as a general laborer. His household was smaller—only wife Catharine (46), Isabella (23), James (10) and Ann B. (7) lived with him.[30]

In 1861, the missing William Willox was working as a cattle boy at Newton of Melrose, Gamrie, Banffshire. William W. Morrison was 14, and lived with James Bremner (43), his wife Rachel (32), their children Barbara (10), Ann (7), and Margaret (10 months), and servants George Murdoch (ploughman, aged 50) and Barbara Donaldson (18).[31] There were many George Morrisons, with no way of knowing which was correct.

In 1871, Alexander (63) lived in Torhead, Gamrie, Banffshire, still working as a general laborer. Wife Catharine (56) was still by his side, and daughter Catherine (31) reappeared. Also living with them was granddaughter Charlotte Morrison (7), but there was no indication as to whom she belongs.[32]

In 1881, Alexander (73) and Catharine (66) had youngest Ann B. (27) living at home, but she worked as a domestic servant in the area. They lived at Hill of Troup, Gamrie, Banffshire, with Alexander as a general laborer.[33]

Catharine Ironside Morrison (66) died 1 November 1881, at Torhead, Troup, Gamrie, Banffshire, of paralysis she had for 2 years. Her husband was the informant.[34] She was buried in the Kirkyard of St. John's in Gamrie.[35]

Alexander Morrison (78) died 2 June 1886 in Touchar, Monquhitter, Aberdeen, at the home of his son George. He died of chronic prostatic inflammation and senile debility. His son George was the informant.[36] He was also buried at the Kirkyard of St. John's in Gamrie.[37]

Alexander and Catharine's son **John Morrison** married Isabella Wood in 1858.

🧬 *John (III) Morrison (1833-1909) and Isabella Rankin Wood (1838-1919)* 🧬
(see Wood Lineage)

John (III) Morrison was born in Gamrie, Banffshire, Scotland on 5 September 1833.[38] John married Isabella Rankin Wood on 20 February 1858 in Gamrie, Banffshire[39] Isabella was the daughter of Alexander Wood and Elizabeth Gibb (see the *Wood Lineage*), and was born 18 January 1838.[40]

John and Isabella had ten children:[41] [42] [43]

- Catherine (b. 1858)
- Alexander (1) (b. 1859) died soon after birth
- Alexander (2) (b. 1862)
- *Isabella* (1864-1907) – married Donald Campbell [44] [45] (see *Campbell Lineage*)
- John (b. 1866)
- Caroline Cruden (b. 1869)
- Elizabeth Jane (b. 1872)
- Annie (b. 1874)
- Maggie (b. 1874)
- William (b. 1878)

At the time of their marriage (1858), John lived in Black Hillocks, Gamrie. Black Hillocks was another family farm, next door to Glenquithle.[46] John's maternal grandfather, Robert Ironside, owned the farm in 1841, and it seems to have passed to John between then and 1858.

In 1861, Isabella Wood Morrison (22) and her family were living with her father Alexander Wood (60) in Black Hillocks, Gamrie, Banffshire. Alexander was an agricultural laborer. Isabella and John's children Alexander (1) and Catherine (3) lived there, too, but John was not listed on the census, likely living on another farm working.[47]

A likely candidate was John Morrison (20) living not too far away in Daups, also in Gamrie, Banffshire. He was an agricultural laborer on a 71-acre farm owned by 40-year-old Alexander Robertson. Also living there was another servant, Martha Grant (20), and the rest of the Robertson family: wife Margaret (28) and children Alexander (8), Elizabeth (5), Margaret (3), and George (1).[48]

In 1871, Isabella Wood Morrison (32) was still living with her father Alexander Wood (70) in Black Hillocks, Gamrie, Banffshire. He was still an agricultural laborer. Again, John was not listed as living there, but the kids were there: Alexander (9), Isabella (6), John (4), and Caroline (1). I was unable to locate John on any other census.[49]

In 1881, Isabella Wood Morrison (43) lived on a farm in Middleton Hill, Gamrie, Banffshire. Alexander Wood was 81 at this time and listed as a crofter of 7 ½ arable acres. John was still not listed on the census, but there were three more children in the family. Alexander (19), Isabella (16) and John (14) were gone. To take their places were twin girls Ann and Margaret (6), and William (3).[50]

In 1881, John (47) was living at Crossbrae, Turriff, Aberdeenshire. He was a farm servant on the 130-acre farm of John Sim (58). Also living there were servants Sophia Alexander (15), James Burnet (17), Elizabeth Clark (48), and Thomas Rennie (18), as well as John Sim's niece, Elizabeth Sim (13).[51]

In 1881, the daughter Isabella Morrison was 16, and working as a domestic servant in Dundee, Fofarshire. She resided in the Honeyman household at 21 Airlie Place. The household consisted of Walter Honeyman (32), an accountant, his wife Jessie (28), his mother Janet (74), and Walter and Jessie's children, William (2) and Arthur (8 months).[52]

In 1891, Isabella Wood Morrison was living at Middleton Hill, Gamrie, Banffshire. She was listed as a crofter's wife, and the head of the household. In the household were her children Bessie (19) and William (11), and a granddaughter, Annabella Morrison (1). Annabella was the illegitimate daughter of Isabella and John's daughter Caroline.[53]

In 1891, John (57) was in Holm, King Edward, Aberdeenshire. He was working as a farm servant for 54-year-old Alexander Forbes. The only other servant was James Ross (19). The rest of the household was the large Forbes family: mother Jane Forbes (88), wife Elsie Forbes (49), and children Mary (18), Elizabeth (16), William (13), Andrew (12), Elsie (8), Charles (6), and Alexina (3).[54]

In 1901, Isabella Wood Morrison (62) was living at Square, King Edward parish, Aberdeenshire. She was listed as a farm servant's wife, so John was still alive, although again not living with her. The only other person in the household was granddaughter Annabella (11), who was in school.[55]

In 1901, John (67) was living on Little Byth Farm in Aberdour (Aberdeen), Aberdeenshire. He was a farm servant but specified as a horseman. George Donald (53) owned the farm; also living there were servants Mary Anderson (32), John Barbar (30), Bella Cowie (25), and John Grant (24).[56]

John (III) Morrison worked as a farm servant until the end of his days. He died 10 July 1906, while living in Square, New Byth, King Edward, Aberdeenshire. His wife, Isabella, reported the death. His cause of death was carcinoma ventriculi (stomach cancer). They said he had had it for two years.[57]

Isabella Rankin Wood Morrison stayed in New Byth until her death, 21 October 1919. She died of heart disease. Her son Alexander reported her death, and she was listed as living on Main Street in New Byth.[58]

Young **Isabella Morrison** immigrated to New York City on 18 April 1882 aboard the ship *Italy*.[59] I consider this a highly probable date for Isabella's immigration. She appeared in Scotland on the 1881 census[60], and married in New York in 1886. The only three records indicating any Isabella Morrison immigrating in that timeframe were for women ages 2, 20, and 27. Our Isabella would have been 18, but ages on immigration documents are notoriously inaccurate, so the age of 20 seems likely. She was listed as a servant/gentleman's servant, which fits with her occupation in 1881 as a house servant, and her purported tenure as a servant at Skibo Castle.

In New York, she married **Donald McIntosh Campbell** on 28 December 1886. For further information about her life with Donald in the United States, go to the *Campbell Lineage*.

[1] Scotland Old Parish Records, *John (I) Morrison*, O.P.R. Deaths 169/00 0030 0006 ABERDOUR (ABERDEEN), accessed 17 April 2016 from www.scotlandspeople.gov.uk

[2] Scotland Old Parish Records, *Christian Auld*, O.P.R. Births 155/00 0020 0371 GAMRIE AND MACDUFF, accessed 17 April 2016 from www.scotlandspeople.gov.uk.

[3] Scotland Statutory Records Index, *Alexander Morrison*, Statutory Deaths 223/00 0025, accessed 16 April 2016 on www.scotlandspeople.gov.uk.

[4] Scotland Old Parish Records, *Elspet Morrison*, O.P.R. Births 169/00 0020 0163 ABERDOUR (ABERDEEN), accessed 17 April 2016 from www.scotlandspeople.gov.uk.

[5] Scotland Old Parish Records, 02/02/1825 *George Morison* (Old Parish Registers Births 155/ 30 28 Gamrie and Macduff) Page 28 of 770, Scotland's People website.

[6] *Christian Auld*, 1841 Scotland Census, Parish: Aberlour; ED: 2; Page: 3; Line: 1360; Year: 1841.

[7] *Christian Auld*, 1851 Scotland Census, Parish: Gamrie; ED: 4A; Page: 8; Line: 15; Roll: CSSCT1851_34; Year: 1851.

[8] Scotland Statutory Records Index, *Christian Auld*, Statutory Deaths 155/00 0034, accessed 17 April 2016 from www.scotlandspeople.gov.uk.

[9] Scotland Death Register, 1860, *John Morrison* (Statutory registers Deaths 147/1120). ScotlandsPeople.gov.uk, accessed 11 Feb 2017.

[10] Scotland Statutory Records Index, *Alexander Morrison*, Statutory Deaths 223/00 0025, accessed 16 April 2016 on www.scotlandspeople.gov.uk.

[11] Cemetery Records. The Kirkyard at St. John's, Parish of Gamrie. Tombstone inscription: "Inscription on stone:- In memory of *ALEXANDER MORRISON*, farmer, West Glenquithle, Auchmedden, who died 2nd June 1886. aged 79; also his wife *CATHERINE IRONSIDE* who died 1st November 1881, aged 66. Their son WILLIAM WILLOX, who died 9th March 1902, aged 64; their daughter CATHERINE who died 29th October 1875, aged 34."

[12] Scotland Old Parish Records, *Alexander Morrison and Catherine Ironside*, O.P.R. Marriages 169/ 0030 0239 Aberdour (Aberdeen), accessed 27 July 2008 from www.scotlandspeople.gov.uk.

[13] Scotland Old Parish Records, *Catherine Ironside*, O.P.R. Births 155/ 0020 0324 Gamrie and Macduff, accessed 27 July 2008 on www.scotlandspeople.gov.uk.

[14] Scotland Old Parish Records, *John (III) Morrison*, O.P.R. Births 155/ 0030 0074 Gamrie and Macduff, accessed 20 May 2008 from www.scotlandspeople.gov.uk.

[15] Scotland Statutory Records Index, *John (III) Morrison*, Statutory Deaths 210/A2 0016, accessed 28 July 2008 from www.scotlandspeople.gov.uk.

[16] Scotland Old Parish Records, 1836 *Alexander Morrison*,169/30 182, Aberdour. ScotlandsPeople.gov.uk.

[17] Scotland Death Register, 1913, *Alexander Morrison* (Statutory Registers Deaths 678/ 9), ScotlandsPeople.gov.uk.

[18] *Alexander Morrison & Catherine Ironside Morrison*, 1841 Scotland Census, Parish: Aberlour; ED: 1; Page: 16; Line: 730; Year: 1841.

[19] *Alexander Morrison & Catherine Ironside Morrison*, 1841 Scotland Census, Parish: Aberlour; ED: 1; Page: 16; Line: 730; Year: 1841.

[20] Cemetery Records. The Kirkyard at St. John's, Parish of Gamrie. Tombstone inscription: "Inscription on stone:- In memory of *ALEXANDER MORRISON*, farmer, West Glenquithle, Auchmedden, who died 2nd June 1886. aged 79; also his wife *CATHERINE IRONSIDE* who died 1st November 1881, aged 66. Their son WILLIAM WILLOX, who died 9th March 1902, aged 64; their daughter CATHERINE who died 29th October 1875, aged 34."

[21] Scotland Old Parish Records, 1844, *George Morison* (OPR 169/30 182), SctotlandsPeople.gov.uk

[22] Scotland Death Register, 1933, *George Morrison* (Statutory Registers Deaths 184/ 3). ScotlandsPeople.gov.uk.

[23] *Alexander Morrison & Catherine Ironside Morrison*, 1851 Scotland Census, Parish: Aberdour; ED: 1; Page: 18; Line: 9; Roll: CSSCT1851_42; Year: 1851.

[24] Cemetery Records. The Kirkyard at St. John's, Parish of Gamrie. Tombstone inscription: "Inscription on stone:- In memory of *ALEXANDER MORRISON*, farmer, West Glenquithle, Auchmedden, who died 2nd June 1886. aged 79; also his wife *CATHERINE IRONSIDE* who died 1st November 1881, aged 66. Their son WILLIAM WILLOX, who died 9th March 1902, aged 64; their daughter CATHERINE who died 29th October 1875, aged 34."

[25] *Alexander Morrison & Catherine Ironside Morrison*, 1851 Scotland Census, Parish: Aberdour; ED: 1; Page: 17; Line: 19; Roll: CSSCT1851_42; Year: 1851.

[26] *Alexander Morrison & Catherine Ironside Morrison*, 1861 Scotland Census, Parish: Gamrie; ED: 3; Page: 14; Line: 11; Roll: CSSCT1861_22.

[27] *Alexander Morrison & Catherine Ironside Morrison*, 1841 Scotland Census, Parish: Aberlour; ED: 1; Page: 16; Line: 730; Year: 1841.

[28] *Alexander Morrison & Catherine Ironside Morrison*, 1851 Scotland Census, Parish: Aberdour; ED: 1; Page: 17; Line: 19; Roll: CSSCT1851_42; Year: 1851.

[29] *Alexander Morrison & Catherine Ironside Morrison*, 1851 Scotland Census, Parish: Aberdour; ED: 1; Page: 18; Line: 9; Roll: CSSCT1851_42; Year: 1851.

[30] *Alexander Morrison & Catherine Ironside Morrison*, 1861 Scotland Census, Parish: Gamrie; ED: 3; Page: 14; Line: 11; Roll: CSSCT1861_22.

[31] *William Willox Morrison*, 1861 Scotland Census, Parish: Gamrie; ED: 8; Page: 8; Line: 15; Roll: CSSCT1861_22.

[32] *Alexander Morrison & Catherine Ironside Morrison*, 1871 Scotland Census, Parish: Gamrie; ED: 3; Page: 12; Line: 1; Roll: CSSCT1871_28.

[33] *Alexander Morrison & Catherine Ironside Morrison*, 1881 Scotland Census, Parish: Gamrie; ED: 3; Page: 7; Line: 7; Roll: cssct1881_45.

[34] Scotland Statutory Records Index, *Catherine Ironside Morrison*, Statutory Deaths 155/0A 0042, accessed 16 April 2016 from www.scotlandspeople.gov.uk.

[35] Cemetery Records. The Kirkyard at St. John's, Parish of Gamrie. Tombstone inscription: "Inscription on stone:- In memory of *ALEXANDER MORRISON*, farmer, West Glenquithle, Auchmedden, who died 2nd June 1886. aged 79; also his wife *CATHERINE IRONSIDE* who died 1st November 1881, aged 66. Their son WILLIAM WILLOX, who died 9th March 1902, aged 64; their daughter CATHERINE who died 29th October 1875, aged 34."

[36] Scotland Statutory Records Index, *Alexander Morrison*, Statutory Deaths 223/00 0025, accessed 16 April 2016 on www.scotlandspeople.gov.uk.

[37] Cemetery Records. The Kirkyard at St. John's, Parish of Gamrie. Tombstone inscription: "Inscription on stone:- In memory of *ALEXANDER MORRISON*, farmer, West Glenquithle, Auchmedden, who died 2nd June 1886. aged 79; also his wife *CATHERINE IRONSIDE* who died 1st November 1881, aged 66. Their son WILLIAM WILLOX, who died 9th March 1902, aged 64; their daughter CATHERINE who died 29th October 1875, aged 34."

[38] Scotland Old Parish Records, *John (III) Morrison*, O.P.R. Births 155/ 0030 0074 Gamrie and Macduff, accessed 20 May 2008 from www.scotlandspeople.gov.uk.

[39] Scotland Statutory Records Index, *John (III) Morrison and Isabella Wood*, Statutory Marriages 155/00 0001 accessed 19 May 2008 from www.scotlandspeople.gov.uk.

[40] Scotland Old Parish Records, *Isabella Wood*, O.P.R. Births 155/ 0030 0097 Gamrie and Macduff, accessed 23 May 2008 from www.scotlandspeople.gov.uk.

[41] *John (III) Morrison & Isabella Rankin Wood*, 1861 Scotland Census, Parish: Gamrie; ED: 3; Page: 10; Line: 10; Roll: CSSCT1861_22.

[42] *John (III) Morrison & Isabella Rankin Wood*, 1871 Scotland Census, Parish: Gamrie; ED: 3; Page: 15; Line: 19; Roll: CSSCT1871_28.

[43] *John (III) Morrison & Isabella Rankin Wood*, 1881 Scotland Census, Parish: Gamrie; ED: 3; Page: 5; Line: 7; Roll: cssct1881_45.

[44] *Isabella Morrison*, Scotland Statutory Records Index, Statutory Births 155/00 0081, Parish: Gamrie; County: Banff; p 27; entry 81 for the year 1864. Accessed 19 May 2008 from www.scotlandspeople.gov.uk

[45] Death Certificate of *Isabella Morrison Campbell*, NY Dept of Health, Certificate No 1438.

[46] Scotland Statutory Records Index, *John (III) Morrison and Isabella Wood*, Statutory Marriages 155/00 0001 accessed 19 May 2008 from www.scotlandspeople.gov.uk.

[47] *John (III) Morrison & Isabella Rankin Wood*, 1861 Scotland Census, Parish: Gamrie; ED: 3; Page: 10; Line: 10; Roll: CSSCT1861_22.

[48] *John (III) Morrison & Isabella Rankin Wood*, 1861 Scotland Census, Parish: Gamrie; ED: 3; Line: 13; Year: 1861.

[49] *John (III) Morrison & Isabella Rankin Wood*, 1871 Scotland Census, Parish: Gamrie; ED: 3; Page: 15; Line: 19; Roll: CSSCT1871_28.

[50] *John (III) Morrison & Isabella Rankin Wood*, 1881 Scotland Census, Parish: Gamrie; ED: 3; Page: 5; Line: 7; Roll: cssct1881_45.

[51] *John (III) Morrison & Isabella Rankin Wood*, 1881 Scotland Census, Parish: Turriff; ED: 5; Line: 18; Year: 1881.

[52] *Isabella Morrison*, 1881 Scotland Census, FHL Film 0203479 GRO Ref Vol 282-1 EnumDist 15, Pg. 7.

[53] *John (III) Morrison & Isabella Rankin Wood*, 1891 Scotland Census, Parish: Gamrie; ED: 3; Page: 1; Line: 4; Roll: CSSCT1891_43.

[54] *John (III) Morrison & Isabella Rankin Wood*, 1891 Scotland Census, Parish: King Edward; ED: 3; Line: 13; Year: 1891.

[55] *John (III) Morrison & Isabella Rankin Wood*, 1901 Scotland Census, Parish: King Edward; ED: 5; Page: 15; Line: 7; Roll: CSSCT1901_70.

[56] *John (III) Morrison & Isabella Rankin Wood*, 1901 Scotland Census, Parish: Aberdour; ED: 3; Line: 8; Year: 1901.

[57] Scotland Statutory Records Index, *John (III) Morrison*, Statutory Deaths 210/A2 0016, accessed 28 July 2008 from www.scotlandspeople.gov.uk.

[58] Scotland Statutory Records Index, *Isabella Wood Morrison*, Statutory Deaths 210/A2 0017, accessed 28 July 2008 from www.scotlandspeople.gov.uk.

[59] *Isabella Morrison*, Castle Garden Immigration Records, http://www.castlegarden.org/quick_search_detail.php?p_id=1665957.

[60] *Isabella Morrison*, 1881 Scotland Census, FHL Film 0203479 GRO Ref Vol 282-1 EnumDist 15, Pg. 7.

MORRISON FAMILY

ISABELLA MORRISON
(1864-1907)
Date of photo unknown

This is the only photo we have from the Morrison Family.
Isabella had 8 siblings, but I believe all stayed in Scotland.

THE
McIntosh
Lineage

DURNESS, SUTHERLAND
(BIRTHPLACE OF ANN McINTOSH)

ASSYNT, SUTHERLAND
(BIRTHPLACE OF JOHN McINTOSH)

SCOTLAND

The McIntosh Lineage

John McIntosh —— Ann McLeod

Donald MacKenzie —— Isabella MacKay

John McIntosh
(1792-1869)

Mary MacKenzie
(1791-1878)

Ann McIntosh
(1818-1904)
married Hugh Campbell
(see Campbell Lineage)

THE MCINTOSH LINEAGE

John McIntosh (c. 1792-1869) and Mary Oag MacKenzie (c. 1791-1878)

John McIntosh was born about 1792, in Assynt, Sutherland,[1] to parents John McIntosh and Ann McLeod.[2] Mary Oag MacKenzie was born about 1791 in Durness, Sutherland,[3] to parents Donald MacKenzie and Isabella MacKay.[4]

John and Mary married on 7 June 1817 in Strathbeg, Durness, Sutherland, and John was listed as a shepherd.[5]

John and Mary had at least five children:

- *Ann*[6] (1818-1904) – married Hugh Campbell (see *Campbell Lineage*)
- Isabella[7] (b. 1825) – married Donald MacKay
- Elizabeth[8] (b.c. 1826)
- John[9] (b.c. 1828)
- Mary[10] (b. 1833)

In 1851, John (61) and Mary (60) lived in Badrociumher, Strathmore, Sutherland, where John was a shepherd. In their house were their children John (23) and Elizabeth (26), and grandson James Campbell (3) (see *Campbell Lineage*). Mary's sister Effie MacKenzie also lived with them. She was listed as being aged 10, but should have been more like age 56, as she was aged 66 in the 1861 census.[11]

In 1861, the family was in Casheldhu, Durness, Sutherland. John (70) was listed as a former shepherd. He lived with wife Mary (68), his children John (31) and Elizabeth (33), sister-in-law Effy McKenzie (66), and a boarder, Harry Munro (22). John the younger was a shepherd, Effy was a pauper, formerly domestic servant, Harry was an assistant shepherd, and Elizabeth and Mary had no occupation listed.[12]

John McIntosh died 11 January 1869 in Durness, Sutherland.[13]

In 1871, widowed Mary (80) lived in Eriboll House, Durness, Sutherland. Her children John (40), Elizabeth (46) and Mary (36) all lived there. Three grandchildren also lived with them: John (7) and Mary (3) McIntosh, daughter Mary's children, and John McKay (8), daughter Isabella's son. There was also a boarder, Robert Gunn. John and Robert were shepherds.[14]

Mary MacKenzie McIntosh died on 16 May 1878 in Durness, Sutherland.[15]

John and Mary's daughter *Ann* married *Hugh Campbell*, so go to the *Campbell Lineage* chapter for details of her life.

---

[1] *John McIntosh*, 1861 Scotland Census, Parish: Durness; ED: 6; Page: 2; Line: 12; Roll: CSSCT1861_7.
[2] *John McIntosh*, Scotland Death Register, 1869 (Statutory registers of Deaths 048/ 3). Scotland's People. Accessed at 02 January 2020 00:42.
[3] *Mary Mackenzie*, 1861 Scotland Census, Parish: Durness; ED: 6; Page: 2; Line: 12; Roll: CSSCT1861_7.
[4] *Mary MacKenzie McIntosh*, Scotland Death Register, 1878 (Statutory registers of Deaths 048/ 4). Scotland's People. Accessed at 02 January 2020 04:50.
[5] *John McIntosh & Mary MacKenzie*, Research of Robert Barton, Strathbeg History, www.countysutherland.co.uk

[6] *Ann McIntosh*, Scotland Old Parish Records, Ann McIntosh, O.P.R. Births 048/ 10 162, Durness, accessed 17 Mar 2017 from www.scotlandspeople.gov.uk.

[7] *Isabella McIntosh*, Ancestry.com, Scotland, Select Births and Baptisms, 1564-1950 [database on-line]. Provo, UT, USA: Ancestry.com Operations, Inc., 2014.

[8] *Elizabeth McIntosh*, 1861 Scotland Census, Parish: Durness; ED: 6; Page: 2; Line: 12; Roll: CSSCT1861_7.

[9] *John McIntosh*, 1861 Scotland Census, Parish: Durness; ED: 6; Page: 2; Line: 12; Roll: CSSCT1861_7.

[10] *Mary McIntosh*, Ancestry.com, Scotland, Select Births and Baptisms, 1564-1950 [database on-line]. Provo, UT, USA: Ancestry.com Operations, Inc., 2014.

[11] *John and Mary McIntosh and family*, 1851 Scotland Census, Parish: Durness; ED: 1; Page: 3; Line: 12; Roll: CSSCT1851_11; Year: 1851.

[12] *John and Mary McIntosh and family*, 1861 Scotland Census, Parish: Durness; ED: 6; Page: 2; Line: 12; Roll: CSSCT1861_7.

[13] *John McIntosh*, Scotland Death Register, 1869 (Statutory registers of Deaths 048/ 3). Scotland's People. Accessed at 02 January 2020 00:42.

[14] *Mary McIntosh and family*, 1871 Scotland Census, Parish: Durness; ED: 6; Page: 5; Line: 14; Roll: CSSCT1871_9.

[15] *Mary MacKenzie McIntosh*, Scotland Death Register, 1878 (Statutory registers of Deaths 048/ 4). Scotland's People. Accessed at 02 January 2020 04:50.

THE MACKAY LINEAGE

STRATHNAVER
(THE LAND OF MACKAY)

SCOTLAND

MacKay Lineage

EARL MALCOLM MacEth
m. Gille Adoman,
sister of Lord of the Isles

GORMFLAITH MacEth
m. Harold Maddadson
(See Norwegian Lineage)

DONALD MacEth

KENNETH MacEth

IYE MacEth

IYE MOR MacKay
m. dau. of Walter De Baltroddie,
Bishop of Caithness

DONALD MacKay
m. dau. of Iye MacNeil of Gigha

IYE MacKay

DONALD MacKay

ANGUS MacKay
m. dau. of Torquil MacLeod of Isle of Lewis

ANGUS DU MacKay
m. (1) Elizabeth MacDonald,
grandau. of Robert II Stewart
m. (2) dau. of Alexander MacDonald,
great-granddau. of Robert II Stewart
(see MacDonald Lineage)

NEIL VASS MacKay
m. Elizabeth Munro

ANGUS ROY MacKay
m. dau. of Kenneth MacKenzie

IYE ROY DU MacKay
m. dau. of Norman O'Beolan

DONALD MacKay
m. Helen Sinclair
(see Sinclair Lineage)

IYE DU MacKay
m. Helen MacLeod,
his first cousin via
dau. of Iye Roy Du MacKay
m. Christian Sinclair

(Aberach Line)

IAN ABERACH MacKay
m. Unknown MacIntosh

WILLIAM DU ABERACH MacKay
m. dau. of Hector Roy MacKenzie

WILLIAM ABERACH MacKay
m. dau. of Thomas Murray

JOHN WILLIAMSON MacKay
m. dau of Donald MacKay

NEIL MacEAN MacWILLIAM MacKay

(Scoury Line)

DONALD BALLOCH MacKay
m. Euphemia Munro

DONALD MacKay
m. Christian Munro

WILLIAM MacKay
m. Elizabeth Corbet

HUISTEAN DU MacKay
m. Jane Gordon

(Strathy Line)

JOHN MacKay OF STRATHY
m. Agnes Sinclair,
great-granddau. of James V Stewart
(see Stewart Lineage)

JANET MacKay
m. Hector Munro

HECTOR MUNRO

BARBARA MacKay

JOHN MacKay OF SKERRAY

HECTOR MacKay

MARGARET MUNRO

DONALD MacKay
m. Esther Gunn

HECTOR MacKay

HUGH MacKay
m. Barbara Morrison

MARY MacKay

HUGH CAMPBELL
(see Campbell Lineage)

THE MACKAY CLAN

The MacKay genealogy starts way back in the mists of time. As with any timeline that begins so far back, it is best to take unsupported family history with a grain of salt. Tales become embellished over time, and there is no person immune to the "wishful thinking" syndrome of using vague evidence to place an ancestor into a genealogical relationship that is erroneous just because we wish that connection existed.

Most of the information in this chapter comes from the tome *The Book of MacKay*, which traces the family history out of the mists of time into the 1700s. Because I believe the writer tried his best to be as factual as possible, I have used this book as my guide. I note where information has come from other sources.

In the beginning …

The traditional lineage of Clan MacKay goes something like this:

The murky progenitor of the family was an Earl of Moray called Heth/Eth/Aodh.[1] All these names are variations of the same Gaelic name. He married a daughter of Lulach, King of Scotland. Lulach was a king of the Line of Moray—a royal lineage long in opposition to the stronger Line of Atholl, who usually occupied the throne (see *MacAlpin Dynasty*).[2]

Earl Eth and his unnamed wife had at least one son, ***Angus MacEth***.[3] Angus was born in 1097 in Stranith, East Lothian, Scotland.[4]

Earl Eth died around 1103[5].

Angus became Earl. The Earls of Moray had long been a strong and formidable force—Moray was a quasi-independent state within Scotland at times. Angus was the grandson of a King of Scotland, so he felt that he was a rightful heir to the throne. Thus, he eventually rebelled against the kings of Scotland, dying in 1130 at Strathcathro in a failed uprising against King David I (see *MacAlpin Dynasty*).[6] [7]

With him was his son ***Malcolm MacEth***. There is some confusion whether Malcolm MacEth was Angus' son or brother. *The Book of MacKay* says Malcolm was Angus' son,[8] so I will use that information since we have no evidence proving either side conclusively.

Whichever the true line, Malcolm MacEth escaped the disastrous uprising in 1130 against David I, and fled to the Western Isles, where he married a sister of Somerled, King of Argyll and the Isles (see *MacDonald Lineage*).[9] [10] Malcolm continued the guerilla warfare until 1137, when he was captured at Galloway and imprisoned in Roxburgh Castle.[11] [12]

Malcolm and his wife had 2 known children:

- ***Donald*** [13] (d. after 1156)
- Gormflaith[14] – married Harold Maddadson, 18th Jarl of Orkney and Shetland, 5th Earl of Caithness and Sutherland[15] (see *Norwegian Lineage*)

With Malcolm imprisoned, his brother-in-law Somerled, powerful King of the Isles, backed Donald MacEth in an uprising against Scotland's King Malcolm IV. Malcolm IV captured Malcolm MacEth's son

Donald in 1156 at Withorn in Galloway and imprisoned him with his father.[16][17] Nothing more was heard of Donald.

Tradition holds that Malcolm IV then released Malcolm MacEth after some sort of treaty was reached, and made him Earl of Ross in return for peace. Here, too, the accounts differ, with one source saying Malcolm MacEth rose up again and was killed in 1160, and with another saying that the real Malcolm MacEth lived in peace the rest of his life, and an imposter from the Isles claiming to be "the Earl of Moray" waged a war and was killed in 1160. Either way, Malcolm MacEth was no longer a factor in the struggle.[18]

Kenneth MacEth,[19] who is generally accepted as Donald MacEth's son, but may possibly be a younger son of Malcolm MacEth, rose against Alexander II in 1214 in conjunction with Donald Bane MacWilliam, and was killed in the fighting, beheaded by Ferchar Macantagart, the future Earl of Ross.[20] This uprising was finally put down in 1223.[21]

All of the above is the MacKay lore. In 2007, Alasdair Ross published a study of the contemporary reports and found compelling evidence that the Malcolm who fought with Angus MacEth and Malcolm MacEth, Earl of Ross, were in fact two separate people.

There was strong evidence that Malcolm, ally of Angus, was not, in fact, Angus MacKay's son. Near-contemporary reports name Malcolm as an illegitimate son of King Alexander I of Scotland, and an ally of Angus, rather than a direct relation.[22] Alasdair Ross' essay laid out convincing evidence that Malcolm was Alexander's son, which would make Donald the grandson of Alexander I. Further investigation showed a probable link to a man named Adam, killed by King William, who was possibly Donald's son and father of Kenneth.[23] Researcher Richard Oram also says that the Malcolm who fought with Angus was not a MacEth, but was the illegitimate son of Alexander I. He says there was a Malcolm MacEth who was a rebel, but not until the 1160s.[24]

Given Ross' evidence and Oram's corroboration, it is very likely that our "Malcolm MacEth" is not a MacEth at all, and therefore has no place in this lineage. But I included the stories above because they are traditionally attributed to the dark beginnings of the MacKay clan.

What this means genealogically is that after Angus MacEth there is a gap of 3-4 generations in time before we get to the first authenticated MacKay, Iye MacEth, purported to be Kenneth's son or grandson.

A word about the MacKay migration and name

So, how did the Moray-based MacEth clan end up in Strathnaver (now called The Land of MacKay), which was part of Caithness at that time? They began as the ancient Clan Morgan, from Moray and Buchan, with the "mor" coming from the Gaelic meaning "sea" or "sea bright." When the Moraymen kept rising, David I and then Malcolm IV, cleared Moray of all the dissidents. The MacEth clan moved to Strathnaver, a part of Caithness, which was ruled by Norwegian Earl of Caithness, Harold Maddadson, who was married to Malcolm MacEth's daughter, Gormflaith. They settled there, holding their lands by force against the local families.[25]

The next question is, "How did we get from MacEth to MacKay as a surname?" There are several ways this could have happened. Gaelic is a convoluted language, and there are multiple spellings of the same name. The MacEths descended from the Earl Eth of Moray. Eth can also be spelled Aodh or Aed, and the most common English spelling of Aodh is Iye. Thus, "MacEth" could have been spelled MacAoidh or MacIye.

Alternately, the first MacEth descendant to settle permanently in Strathnaver was Iye MacEth. His sons would have then been MacIye, which is easily morphed to MacKay.[26]

Iye MacEth, 1st Chief of Strathnaver[27]
(b.c. 1210)

Iye MacEth was born about 1210, but whether he was the son or nephew (or neither) of Kenneth MacEth is uncertain. Either way, he was purported to be the great-grandson of Malcolm MacEth. However, as we have seen above, we cannot know if he descended from Malcolm, son of Alexander, or the actual Malcolm MacEth, Earl of Ross—or neither. Regardless, Iye is the first of the MacKay line we can prove. With his son Iye Mor, the surname morphed from MacEth to MacKay, and the clan took root.

He survived through the iron-fisted reign of Alexander II. When Alexander II died, and his very young son Alexander III was in his long minority rule, the central government lost much of its control in the Highland area, and Iye MacEth was able to establish himself and his family in the Strathnaver area.

Iye had three known children:
- *Iye Mor* – succeeded as chief of the MacKay clan.
- Morgan
- Martin – said to have settled in Galloway, which was another area under Norse rule, and therefore favorable to the rebel elements of the MacEth line. It was where Donald MacEth was captured.

Iye Mor MacKay, 2nd Chief of Strathnaver
(married c. 1263)

Iye Mor MacKay became chamberlain to the Bishop of Caithness, Walter de Baltrodi. Walter de Baltrodi was confirmed as Bishop of Caithness by Pope Urban IV in 1263. As both son-in-law and chamberlain of the Bishop, Iye Mor gathered a great deal of power to himself, including 12 davochs of land in Durness,[28] the best grass and pastureland in North Scotland.

Around 1263, Farquhar Macintagart, Earl of Ross, harassed the western isles, especially Skye. He was vicious, burning villages, sacking churches, ripping open pregnant women and spearing infants. Hakon, King of Norway, who owned the western isles, protested to King Alexander III of Scotland, but Alexander did nothing. In response, Hakon sailed to the isles in 1263 to rectify the situation. In the end, Hakon sailed away, defeated by the weather, and rounded Cape Wrath. When he anchored in Loch Eriboll, some of his men went ashore to restock, and the Durness men attacked them. Since Iye Mor was a leading person in Durness, and his duties would have included protecting the bishop's lands around Loch Eriboll, it is likely that he would have taken part in the raid on the Norsemen. This helped solidify the MacKay footing in Strathnaver. Later that year, Alexander III purchased the western isles from Norway, bringing peace.[29]

Iye Mor MacKay died around 1300 and had only one known child, son *Donald*.[30]

Donald MacKay, 3rd Chief of Strathnaver
(c. 1270-1330)

Donald MacKay was born sometime after 1263 when his parents married, but before 1270.[31] He married a daughter of Iye MacNeil, son of Neil of Gigha, an island close to Kintyre, between the coast and the isle of Islay. Donald was chief from 1300 through his death in 1330.[32]

Donald's life spanned the struggle for Scottish independence under William Wallace and Robert Bruce, but we have no information to confirm what role, if any, he and his Strathnaver MacKays played in the fight. There is little doubt that the Argyle MacKays were present at the Battle of Bannockburn, under the command of Angus Óg of the Isles (see *MacDonald Lineage*). Since Donald's wife's relatives would have been fighting, and the MacKays were always fighters for freedom, it was likely they were in the fray, but there is no chronicle of it.[33]

Donald MacKay and his wife had one known son, *Iye*.[34]

Iye MacKay, 4th Chief of Strathnaver
(chief from 1330-1370)

The main conflict of Iye MacKay's time was a long and bloody feud with the family of the Earls of Sutherland. While the main source of the conflict has been lost in time, it was likely over land. The Earl of Sutherland was given a charter of Earldom in Sutherland by King David I of Scotland (see *MacAlpin Dynasty*), because the Earl had married David's sister. Iye owned many lands at the time, and some of them fell under the new Earldom of Sutherland. Iye refused to acknowledge the Earl as his feudal overlord, and sought to have arbitration of the matter.[35]

In 1370, Iye, his son and heir Donald, the Earl of Sutherland and his brother Nicholas, and other arbiters, most likely the Lord of the Isles, the Earl of Ross, and the Earl of Buchan, met at Dingwall Castle. The arbitration went Iye's way, and just as he seemed about to win his claim, Nicholas Sutherland rose in the middle of the night and killed Iye and Donald while they slept. He then fled.[36]

So it was that the fourth chief and his heir died in the same night, leaving the chiefdom to pass to Donald's son Angus.

Iye MacKay had three known children:[37]

- *Donald* – died with him at Dingwall Castle.
- Farquhar – a physician to King Robert II Stewart, and a favorite of the King's son, the Earl of Buchan. He obtained by royal charter the lands of Melness and Hope, and other lands in Durness in 1379, and the islands around Strathnaver in 1386.
- Mariota – the handfast wife of the Earl of Buchan. They had children: Alexander, Earl of Mar; Andrew; Walter; James; Duncan; and Margaret, who married Robert, the Earl of Sutherland.

Donald MacKay, the Younger of Strathnaver[38]
(killed 1370)

Donald MacKay was murdered by Nicholas Sutherland at Dingwall Castle in 1370, along with his father. Donald had four known sons:

- *Angus* – succeeded as chief
- Huistean Du – tutor to his nephew Angus Du (Angus' son)
- Martin – settled in Galloway (perhaps conflated with Martin, son of Iye MacEth, above)
- Neil – settled in Creich and had three sons, Thomas, Morgan, and Neil

Angus MacKay, 5th Chief of Strathnaver[39]
(chief from 1370-1403)

Angus MacKay, having lost his father and grandfather to the murderous Nicholas Sutherland, kept the blood feud raging between the two families. Earl William, brother of Nicholas, died in 1370, the same year as the murders, and may very well have been a victim of the feud. The feud quieted somewhat during the reign of Earl Robert of Sutherland, who married Angus' cousin Margaret, but it simmered nonetheless.

In 1391, the MacKays joined Duncan Stewart, son of the Earl of Buchan and relation of the MacKay clan, when he invaded the Braes of Angus. His Highland troops destroyed an army of mail-clad eastern gentry, so fierce was their fighting.[40]

Angus married the daughter of Torquil MacLeod of the Isle of Lewis, and later, Margaret MacNicol. Torquil MacLeod also owned property and a castle in Assynt, on the west coast of Sutherland. Angus and Torquil's daughter had at least two sons:[41]

- *Angus Du* – succeeded his father.
- Rorie Gald, or Rorie the Islander – called that because he was fostered by maternal relatives on Lewis. Rorie died in a battle near Dingwall in 1411.

Angus MacKay died in 1403, passing the torch to his son *Angus Du*.[42]

Angus Du MacKay, 6th Chief of Strathnaver[43]
(chief from 1403-1433)

Angus Du MacKay became chief upon the death of his father in 1403. He was still quite young, and was tutored by his uncle, Huistean Du. Huistean Du somehow offended Angus Du's mother, and in 1406 her brother Malcolm, son of Torquil MacLeod, invaded Strathnaver, laying waste to it and the neighboring land of Brae-Chat. Making his way back to Lewis with much loot, MacLeod was overtaken by the MacKays at Tuiteam Tarvach, in Strathoikel. Malcolm MacLeod was killed, and his army defeated. The battle is known as La Tuiteam Tarvach, or the Day of Great Slaughter.[44]

Donald, Lord of the Isles, tried to claim the vacant Earldom of Ross. His claim was legal, but he was opposed by the Buchans, and because of Angus Du's relationship with the Earl of Mar, Angus Du got involved on Buchan's side. When Donald of the Isles marched on Dingwall Castle in 1411, Angus Du, with

3,000 men, tried to bar the way. Angus Du was overpowered and captured, [45] and his brother Rorie Gald was killed. Angus Du was sent as prisoner to a castle on the west coast, and Donald was finally stopped at Harlaw. [46] [47] [48]

After the war Donald and Angus Du made their peace. Donald gave Angus Du the hand of his sister Elizabeth (sometimes seen as Margaret), in marriage. Elizabeth was the daughter of John MacDonald (see *MacDonald Lineage*) and his wife Margaret Stewart, daughter of King Robert II Stewart of Scotland (see *Stewart Dynasty*). [49] [50] Soon after Angus Du and Elizabeth had their son Neil Vass, Donald gave Angus Du lands of Strathhalladale, Creich, and others. [51] Angus Du later gave this land to another branch of the MacKay family, to bring the family closer together.

Angus Du continued the blood feud with the Sutherlands by raiding Moray and Caithness, both of which were held by heirs of Nicholas Sutherland, the murderer of Dingwall. He fought a battle with the men of Caithness in 1426 at Harpsdale Hill, two miles south of Halkirk. [52]

In 1427, King James I Stewart (see *Stewart Dynasty*) came north to Inverness. He had been imprisoned in England until 1424, and when he returned, he disliked the disorder in his kingdom, and came to the Highlands to reclaim his authority. James I held a Parliament in Inverness and he summoned the Highland chiefs as members. However, when they appeared, he clapped them in irons, including Angus Du, Alexander MacDonald, Lord of the Isles. [53] James I soon released Angus Du, but he required that Angus Du's son Neil Vass be left as a hostage to assure his loyalty. Neil was sent to the Bass Rock for a time. This heavy-handed action instilled resentment in the Highland chiefs, leading to James I's murder in Perth ten years later. [54]

Angus Du was a powerful chieftain, mostly because of his large and sprawling family, who could rally to arms quickly. His cousin Thomas Neilson, whom he had chartered lands to earlier, was a vital part of that power, and his death in 1430, and the division of his lands, badly weakened Angus Du.

Angus Du's enemies in Sutherland and Caithness decided to take advantage of Angus Du's weakness, and in 1433 they invaded Strathnaver.

Angus Du was further weakened by his eldest son Neil Vass still being hostage to James I. The invasion was therefore met by Angus Du's younger son, Ian Aberach. Ian was Neil's half-brother, son of Angus Du and his second wife, a daughter of Alexander MacDonald, Lord of the Isles. [55] Ian was fostered by maternal relatives in Lochaber, which gave rise to his name, Ian Aberach, John the Lochaber man.

Ian and his forces met the invasion at Drum nan Coup, at the head of a pass north of Ben Loyal, within two miles of Castle Varrich, the MacKay stronghold. Angus Du, helpless with ill health, was carried onto the field of battle in a litter. The enemy, hearing this, believed that they would have an easy time of overpowering the young Ian. The MacKays stood firm however, and eventually put the invaders to flight, killing them in great numbers. [56]

Although they gained the victory, Angus Du MacKay was slain by an enemy arrow.

Angus Du had five sons:[57]

- *Neil Vass* – by his first wife, who succeeded his father.
- *Ian Aberach* – by his second wife. His lineage will figure into our line again later, and we will detail it separately.
- Roderick
- William
- Angus

Neil Vass MacKay, 7th Chief of Strathnaver
(chief from 1433-1450)

Neil Vass MacKay was born c. 1413.[58] Neil, as he was known before his imprisonment, was only 14 years old when sent to Bass prison in exchange for his father.[59] When his father Angus Du was killed in 1433, Neil became the chief, but he was still imprisoned at Bass (a castle on Bass Island in the Firth of Forth). It wasn't until 1436 that he was able, with the help of a kinswoman, to escape Bass prison. It was because of his imprisonment at Bass that he gained his nickname, Neil Vass.[60]

For the three years of his chiefdom that he was in prison, the clan was run by Ian Aberach, the hero of Drum nan Coup. He was the target of numerous assassination attempts by the Sutherland men seeking revenge, and often slept the night in "a most inaccessible rocky fastness, near Castle Varrich, called to this day Leabaidh Ian Aberich, that is John of Lochaber's bed."[61] While Neil Vass was still away, Ian Aberach led his MacKays into a battle with the men of Caithness, with whom they had the ongoing feud mentioned above. He met them at Tom an Dris, on the river Hallandale. Ian won the bloody battle handily, with much slaughter. To this day, human bones wash out of the ground in storms.[62]

When Neil Vass appeared in 1436 to claim his chiefdom, things could have gotten bloody. Ian was a popular chief, proven in battle, while Neil hadn't been seen since 1427 – almost a decade before. But Ian Aberach was a man of honor, and he stepped aside to give the chiefdom to its rightful heir – showing the valor and chivalry that were to come to epitomize the Aberach MacKays. Neil Vass, grateful for his half-brother's unselfishness, bestowed upon him numerous lands in Strathnaver, although the descendants of Ian Aberach would be stripped of this land in the future due to lack of written charter of ownership.[63]

Once Neil Vass was back in charge, another clash with the Caithness men arose. Since Neil Vass had no military experience, it is almost certain that the captain of this expedition was Ian Aberach. The MacKays were once again victorious, with Ian trapping the Caithness men in a clever looping tactic. The battle of Ruaig Shansiad, Sandside Chase is still spoken of today, and the bones of the dead can still be dug out of the soil.[64]

Neil Vass MacKay married a daughter of George (some sources say Hugh) Munro of Fowlis and his wife, a daughter of Ross of Balnagown (some say Margaret Sutherland of Duffus). Neil and his wife Elizabeth had two sons and a daughter:[65]

- *Angus Roy* – succeeded his father
- John Roy – had a son William Roy
- Elizabeth – married John MacGillion of Lochbuy, chief of the MacLean clan

35

Angus Roy MacKay, 8th Chief of Strathnaver[66]
(chief from 1460-1486)

During Angus Roy MacKay's time, the Sutherland-MacKay feud abated to the extent that one of his daughters married a Sutherland man. Without the Sutherlands to go to war with, the MacKays turned their weapons elsewhere.

Around 1478, the Clan Keith was moving into Caithness, and ran afoul of the powerful Clan Gunn. The Keiths asked the MacKays for their help in pressing their claim. The Keiths and Angus Roy's forces met the Gunns on Tannach Moor, near Wick. There was great slaughter on both sides, and the Gunns were overwhelmed and defeated. Soon thereafter, the Keiths massacred the chief Gunn and his sons in the chapel of St. Tyer near Wick.[67]

A feud between the MacKays and the Rosses of Balnagown broke out. It lasted a long time, and much blood was shed. This feud, like most, was probably over land, as some of the lands once owned by Thomas Neilson MacKay were owned by the Rosses, and the MacKays had never let go of their claim to those forfeited lands.[68]

While Angus Roy raided into Ross with much success early on, he tried it one too many times. About 1486, he was overpowered near the church of Tabert. He fled into the church for refuge, but the Rosses set fire to the church and burnt him to death. At the time, the central Scottish government was in turmoil, with James III under siege by his nobles and his own son, the future king James IV (see *Stewart Dynasty*). This is probably why no action was ever taken against the Rosses for their sacrilege of killing a man in a church.[69]

Angus Roy MacKay married a daughter of Chief Kenneth MacKenzie of Kintail and Lady Agnes Frazer, who was the daughter of Chief Hugh Frazer and Margaret Lyon. Angus Roy and his wife had at least five children:[70]

- *Iye Roy* – succeeded his father
- John Riavach – died at Flodden in 1513
- Neil Naverach – married a daughter of Hutcheon Sutherland of Croystoun and had a son, John
- A daughter who married Hector MacKenzie of Auchterned near Dingwall, son of Hector Roy of Gairloch
- A daughter who married Sutherland of Dirot

Iye Roy MacKay, 9th Chief of Strathnaver[71]
(chief from 1486-1517)

The MacKays did not take kindly to Angus Roy being killed, and in a church no less. On 11 July 1487, the MacKays marched into Ross under the leadership of Angus Roy's second son John Riavich, and William Du mac Ean Aberich (Ian Aberach's son and then-current chief of the Aberach clan).[72]

They met the Rosses at Aldicharrish and demolished them, killing Alexander Ross and 17 other landed gentlemen, as well as many foot soldiers. The MacKays then burned and looted their way out of Ross, unopposed. The Scottish central government turned a blind eye to this raid, since they had not stepped in to reconcile the murder of Angus Roy, and so this raid was considered justified under the code of law at the time.[73]

Iye Roy MacKay was one of the first MacKays to have grasped that written charters were needed to secure land—force of arms was no longer enough. In due course, he received acknowledgement of his rights to many lands in Strathnaver, as well as putting "on the books" the charter of land granted to his family by Donald, Lord of the Isles in 1415. This did not keep the government from ignoring his rights to those lands from Donald and claiming some of those lands for the Crown.[74]

The MacKays apparently raided the Rosses again in 1493, with the same success as before. This time, however, the Rosses took them to court, and in 1501 the court deemed that the MacKays should pay a substantial amount in reparations. It is unknown if the MacKays paid any of it.[75]

In 1494, John Riavich MacKay was pardoned for his actions in Ross by the government, but it is clear that more blood was shed after that time, because Iye Roy and David Ross were called before the Earl of Argyle on 4 October 1496, and formally "reconciled," vowing to shed no more blood.[76]

Iye Roy worked for King James IV as a chief to help keep the peace in the north. In return, James IV recognized his rights to Strathnaver lands, and granted him other lands in reward for his services.[77]

In 1499, Iye Roy was asked to find and arrest Sutherland of Dirlot, who was fleeing after murdering his relative. Although Dirlot was a nephew of Iye Roy, his uncle arrested him and delivered him to the government. In return, James IV, on 4 November 1499, gave Iye Roy vast lands previously held by Dirlot, in Strathnaver, Sutherland, and Caithness.[78]

Iye Roy also proved his loyalty to King James IV by helping to quell the revolts in the Hebrides Islands in 1503, 1505, and 1506. In 1505, Parliament found Torquil MacLeod of the Isle of Lewis guilty of treason, and called for his capture. Iye Roy and others, after battering Stornoway Castle with artillery, took MacLeod prisoner in 1506.[79] This resulted in Iye Roy being granted even more land from the King.[80]

In 1511, Iye Roy and his son secured even more ancestral land, buying the lands of Melness and Hope from the heir of Farquhar MacKay, Robert II's physician.[81]

King James IV decided to invade England, and the MacKays went with him. The invasion resulted in the disaster at Flodden in 1513. Iye Roy lived, but his brother John Riavich, as well as the Bishop of Caithness and the Earl of Caithness (see *Sinclair Lineage*) all perished, as did King James IV himself along with innumerable others.[82]

After King James IV died at Flodden, the Hebrides Islands, under the leadership of Donald Galda, revolted again. They were somewhat subdued in 1515, but in 1517 things flared up again, and the government asked Iye Roy and other Highland chiefs for help. What exactly happened was not known, but Donald Galda died shortly thereafter.[83]

The long-standing feud with the Sutherlands came to a temporary truce when Iye Roy and Adam Gordon, Earl of Sutherland, signed a bond of friendship on 31 July 1517.[84]

Iye Roy married a "celebrated beauty," a daughter of Norman O'Beolan, son of Patrick O'Beolan of Carloway in Lewis. The O'Beolans were the descendants of a well-known priestly family of Applecross, whose progenitor was St. Maolrubha. This marriage was not recognized by canon law, which would have made all of Iye Roy's children illegitimate, and therefore unable to inherit.[85]

But once again, Iye Roy showed his grasp of the laws, and on 8 August 1511, he had obtained from King James IV a precept of legitimation for his two surviving sons, John and Donald. Iye Roy and his wife had five children: [86]

- John – succeeded his father in 1517
- *Donald* – succeeded his brother John in 1529
- Angus – died fighting the Rosses near Tain, before 1511
- A daughter who married Hugh MacLeod of Assynt and had children Neil and Helen. *Helen MacLeod* married her first cousin *Iye Du MacKay* of Strathnaver
- A daughter, who married Alexander Sutherland, son of Earl John of Sutherland, by his second marriage

Iye Roy MacKay died toward the end of 1517.[87]

Donald MacKay, 11th Chief of Strathnaver[88]
(chief from 1529-1550)

Donald MacKay's brother John, the 10th Chief of Strathnaver, died in 1529 with no children. Donald, as Iye Roy's next oldest son, took over as Chief.

At about the time of Donald's succession, he assisted the Forbes clan in a feud with the Seatons of Aberdeenshire. This raid resulted in the death of Alexander Seaton of Meldrum, and Donald and others were brought before the court to answer for it. As a result, some of his lands were apparently forfeited to his enemies the Sutherlands. However, on 26 July 1536, Donald obtained a pardon for himself and his Strathnaver clansmen. [89]

Donald seemed to have gained the favor of King James V (see *Stewart Dynasty*). He accompanied the king on a voyage around the north of Scotland in May 1539. He returned to court with the king, and on 18 December 1539, obtained a charter for his ancestral lands from the king himself. These lands included Farr, Armadale, Straye, Rynewe, Kynnald, Golspie, Dirlot, Cattack, Broynach, Kilchalumkill in Strabrora, Davach Lochnaver, Davach Eriboll, lands in Stromay, the mill of Kinald, part of the island of Sanday, and the lands of Melness and Hope. He stayed in Stirling for about a year, obtaining other lands in Durness from the Bishop of Caithness.[90]

In 1542, Donald secured to his clan the lands of Strathnaver and a portion in Moray that had been held from him as punishment for his 1529 raid against the Seatons. Once released from the Sutherlands, he had them back securely and with no strings attached.[91]

Toward the close of 1542, King James V gathered his army to go to war with England. Donald and his son Iye Du, as well as a number of their clansmen, answered the muster at Lauder. Because the king opposed the Reformation, he was unpopular. Many people did not show up, and those who did had little enthusiasm for the endeavor. This lackluster army was routed at Solway Moss, and many of the leading men were taken back to England as prisoners, including Iye Du MacKay.[92]

Donald returned to Edinburgh with James V, where, on 28 November 1542, the king granted him lands forfeited from some of the northern nobles who didn't fight. James V died a few days later, leaving his infant daughter, Mary, Queen of Scots, in a troubled and corrupt minority.[93]

In England, at the instigation of King Henry VIII, Iye Du and some of the other captives began promoting the cause of marrying the young Mary, Queen of Scots to the Prince of Wales. The Bishop of Caithness, Robert Stuart, came to England to speak to his brother, the Earl of Lennox (one of Iye Du's faction) about this scheme. When he left, he left his lands protected by the Earl of Caithness (see *Sinclair Lineage*) and Donald MacKay. Donald went into Sutherland and left his kinsmen at Skibo Castle to protect Robert's lands there.[94]

On 28 April 1549, the Bishop of Caithness brought together the Earls of Caithness and Sutherland, and Donald MacKay, and all four swore a bond of friendship and defense. So, the long-standing feud between the MacKays and Sutherlands seemed to be reconciled at last.[95]

The MacKay feud with the Rosses of Balnagown (who had burned Angus Roy in the church) still went on however, with another bloody raid into Ross in 1550.[96]

Donald MacKay married Helen Sinclair, daughter of Alexander Sinclair of Stempster, second son of William Sinclair, Earl of Caithness (see the *Sinclair Lineage*).[97] They had one son and two daughters: [98]

- *Iye Du* – succeeded his father
- A daughter who married *John Williamson Aberach MacKay*, 4th chief of the Aberach clan
- Florence – married Neil MacLeod of Assynt

Iye Du MacKay, 12th Chief of Strathnaver[99]
(chief from 1550-1572)

Iye Du MacKay was at Solway Moss with his father, and taken hostage by King Henry VIII. Henry VIII took good care of his Scottish prisoners, treating them well, trying to promote a marriage between Mary, Queen of Scots and Edward, Prince of Wales. If his prisoners agreed to push for this union in Scotland, they would be allowed to go back to Scotland with no ransom—under the condition that they would return if they were not successful in getting agreement to this proposal. Iye Du supported this marriage, although there is no way to know if he really thought it was a good idea, or if he just wanted the freedom that came with it.[100]

Iye Du was a man of his word. He returned to Scotland in the spring of 1543 to push this proposal, but when he and his compatriots failed, they returned to England as they had promised.[101] In 1544, on Glasgow Muir, Iye Du and his faction attacked the ruling governor of Scotland (remember, Queen Mary was still a child), and were roundly defeated. Iye Du returned to England after this failure, and remained there for another three years in the military service of England.[102] On 10 March 1554, Iye Du got a pardon for his part in the Glasgow affair.[103]

In 1546, there was another battle between Iye Du's faction and the Scottish government, which the Scots lost. In 1548, Iye Du was present at the capture and fortification of Haddington, again on the English side. It must be understood that at this point, the wars were not just over if Mary would marry Edward. These were also religious wars, with the English-supported faction pressing for Protestant Reformation, while the

Scottish government supported the Roman Catholic Church. So while Iye Du (given his family's history) would not have wanted Scotland to lose her independence to England (which the marriage would inevitably accomplish), it may be that he was an ardent Protestant, and that was the real driving force behind his support of the English cause.[104]

Because of Iye Du's affiliation with the English against the Scottish government, he was in a precarious position when his father died in 1550. He had made deadly enemies of the Sutherlands and Lord Huntly, who were favorites of the government, and Huntly especially used this favor to ruthlessly wrest land from nobles in the north and exterminate those who stood in his way. When Donald MacKay died in 1550, Huntly and his allies declared that Donald had been illegitimate – conveniently overlooking the decree of legitimacy that his father, Iye Roy, had obtained from James IV in 1511. As a result, Iye Du was disinherited from his lands.[105]

In 1552, the Queen mother summoned Iye Du and several of his allies to come to Inverness, but Iye Du knew if he appeared he would be thrown in prison, so he and his allies stayed away. A similar summons came in 1553, and again he declined. In 1554, the Earl of Sutherland was commissioned to capture Iye Du MacKay, and to this end he raised an army and a fleet, and besieged the MacKay stronghold of Borve Castle on a promontory of the Aird of Farr. Iye Du slipped from the siege and gathered a troop of Aberach MacKays, and struck in Sutherland, setting the land ablaze in retaliation.[106] Still, after a long and bloody siege, Borve Castle fell, and Iye Du was captured and imprisoned in Dumbarton Castle from 1 February to 20 October 1555.

For capturing Iye Du, the Earl of Sutherland was granted the MacKay lands in stewardship and a yearly pension of 1,000 merks. At that moment, the ancient feud between the Sutherlands and MacKays seemed to have been won by the Sutherlands.[107]

In 1562, Queen Mary made a circuit of her northern territories. When Mary arrived at Inverness on 5 October 1562, she pardoned Iye Du for fighting on the English side. No doubt this was done in gratitude for the northern clans' support for her against Lord Huntly, and because Iye Du was an enemy of Huntly of old, and therefore an ally. Indeed, when Huntly was "put to the horn" on 17 October, the clans at feud with Huntly, namely the MacIntoshes, MacKays, and Forbeses, were given free hand to apprehend him dead or alive. Huntly was slain at the Battle of Corrichie.[108]

In the political upheaval that followed, with Queen Mary making disastrous decisions as to husbands and allies, the MacKay's Strathnaver lands passed in succession to Darnley, Earl of Ross, then George Gordon, Earl of Huntly, then to Alexander Gordon, Earl of Sutherland. All of this happened in spite of the records proving that Donald MacKay had been legitimized, and his lands were properly chartered (deeded), and many of the lands Donald held were *not* inherited from his father, but were chartered to him directly, making his illegitimacy a null point anyway.[109]

Is it any wonder that Iye Du was an angry man when he heard all of the above? In 1567, he swept into Sutherland and wasted the barony of Skibo and set the town of Dornoch on fire, and later Strathflete also felt his wrath.[110]

This might have brought Iye Du even more problems, but the political times were changing. Queen Mary had fallen into disgrace, and MacKay's ally, the Earl of Moray, was regent. Even though Moray was assassinated, Huntly, who held power then, deemed it prudent to make peace with MacKay. On 29 July 1570, Iye Du signed an agreement between himself, the Earl of Huntly and the Earl of Sutherland. Huntly returned all of Iye Du's Strathnaver lands for the sum of 3,000 merks. However, Huntly still held the feudal superiority of the lands, which was a bitter pill for Iye Du to swallow.[111]

In 1570, when Iye Du was about 70 years old, he and about 20 other men were crossing the Crask in the dead of winter and were overtaken by a snowstorm. About 18 of his people died, and only two or three survived.[112]

Meantime, the MacKay alliance with the Earls of Caithness—at this time George Sinclair, 4th Earl of Caithness (see *Sinclair Lineage*)—was still strong. When Huntly and Sutherland assailed the Forbes clan in Aberdeen in 1571-2, Caithness and MacKay wreaked havoc in Sutherland, driving the Sutherland allies to flee.[113] [114]

Iye Du had married twice. His first wife, Helen MacLeod, was his first cousin. Her father, Hugh MacLeod of Assynt, had married a daughter of Iye Roy MacKay. Because Iye Du and Helen did not get papal dispensation for the marriage, his children from this marriage were not allowed to succeed to the chieftainship of Strathnaver. They had two sons:[115]

- John Beg – killed in a skirmish at Balnakeil, Durness in 1579
- ***Donald Balloch*** – founded the Scoury MacKays, and who will figure into our lineage again later

Iye Du MacKay's second wife was Christian Sinclair. In their marriage record, she is listed as a "cousin" to George Sinclair, Earl of Caithness (see *Sinclair Lineage*).[116] Her father is variously listed as John, William, David or George Sinclair of Dun, (a "natural" or illegitimate son of John Sinclair, 3rd Earl of Caithness), and Margaret Calder. This means Iye Du and Christian were second cousins, but this was acceptable in the eyes of the church. They had five children:[117]

- ***Huistean Du*** – succeeded from his father
- William of Bighouse – founded the Bighouse branch of MacKays
- Eleanor – married Donald Bane MacLeod of Assynt
- Jane – married Alexander Sutherland of Berridale
- Barbara – married Alexander MacDavid, chief of the clan of Gunn

Huistean Du MacKay, 13th Chief of Strathnaver[118]
(chief 1572-1614)

Huistean Du MacKay was born in 1561,[119] and was only 11 years old when his father died. While there were some MacKays who believed that the elder sons from the first (non-canon) marriage should succeed Iye Du, Huistean Du was eventually accepted. When he finally came of age, Huistean bestowed some land on Donald Balloch, thus making the peace with him.

Scotland itself was in upheaval during this time. Mary, Queen of Scots was imprisoned in England, and eventually beheaded in 1587. Her son, James VI, was a minor used by one faction and another, a mere pawn in the turbulent times. In MacKay Country, Alexander, Earl of Sutherland, and George Sinclair, 4th Earl of Caithness (see *Sinclair Lineage*) waged a deadly feud with each other.[120] The young Huistean Du was between them, weakened by being the head of a divided clan.

While Huistean Du was a minor, he lived with George Sinclair, 4th Earl of Caithness, thus binding the two families close.[121] The Strathnaver MacKays were led, in the meantime, by John Mor MacKay, who had also led them during Iye Du's imprisonment in Dumbarton. But Earl George Sinclair found John Mor to be too independent, not pliant enough to the Earl's wishes. So, Earl George had him put to death. John Beg, Huistean Du's oldest half-brother, took the leadership after that, but Earl George didn't care for him, either. Earl George took care of John Beg by going to the Aberach MacKays and claiming that John Beg was being unfaithful to Huistean Du. In 1579, the Aberach MacKays and the MacLeods of Assynt attacked John Beg and his Gunn Clan supporters at Balnakiel, Durness, killing John Beg and many others.[122] Earl George's interference had effectively split the strong MacKay clan into two factions, against each other instead of together. The Aberach MacKays and the Gunns waged a bloody feud between them for many years after.[123]

Huistean Du came to power on his eighteenth birthday, and he faced the above division in his clan. Unable to reconcile them, he was forced to choose between them. Unfortunately, he chose the side opposed to the Aberach MacKays, in spite of the fact that the division had come because the Aberach MacKays were defending him from the alleged unfaithfulness. It is hard to know if Huistean Du had been aware of that fact, however, because he had been living with Earl George at his castle, and quite probably only knew whatever version of the truth Earl George chose to tell him. If only Huistean Du had settled land upon his Aberach relatives, as he did on John Beg's brother Donald Balloch MacKay, his life might have been very different.[124]

The consequences of Huistean Du's choice were immediate: The powerful Aberach MacKays changed sides and joined Alexander Gordon, the Earl of Sutherland, the MacKay's ancient enemy, strengthening Sutherland's hand considerably. Earl Alexander also gained power over the MacKays by receiving the feudal overlordship of the Strathnaver lands from Earl George Huntly, who held them from the agreement with Iye Du.[125]

But Sutherland did not stop there. He knew that so long as MacKay and the Earl of Caithness stood together, Sutherland did not have a prayer of beating them. So when George, 4th Earl of Caithness died, Earl Alexander saw his chance. He quickly went to the new earl, George Sinclair, 5th Earl of Caithness, proposing that a sister of Earl Huntly be married to Earl George. He also resigned the feudal lordship of Strathnaver to the crown, only to have it conferred on his son and heir via royal charter, creating Lord Strathnaver.[126]

George, 5th Earl of Caithness, was not a very wise or strong earl. His two allies were the MacKays and the Gunns, and he should have recognized that without them he would be at the mercy of Sutherland and Huntly. However, when those two devious earls invited Earl George to a meeting and proposed that if he were to exterminate the Gunns, he would be given a bond of friendship between the three and the hand of Huntly's sister, Earl George said yes.[127]

In 1586, the extermination got underway. A force divided into two parties—one from Sutherland, one from Caithness—surrounded the Gunns, who retreated into Strathnaver trying to avoid conflict since they were outnumbered. Then a strange thing happened, which threw a wrench into the Earls' plan.[128]

William "Bighouse" MacKay had just raided some MacLeods and was heading home, driving some "lifted" cattle before him. His party stumbled upon the Sutherland party, and the two began skirmishing over the loot, in a battle later called La Tom Fraoich, or the Day of the Heather-Brush. The MacKays made off with the loot.[129]

In the night, however, the MacKays came across the Gunns, retreating from the Caithness force near Altgawn. They decided to fight alongside their long-time allies against the faithless aggression of the Caithness men. The Caithness men were surprised by the combined force, and their leader, Henry Sinclair (cousin of Earl George) and scores of his men were killed. The Sutherland force, discovering the defeat, quietly retreated back to Sutherland.[130]

At this same time, Huistean Du was at Earl George's castle, trying to shore up the weak alliance. When the news of the battle reached them, Huistean Du prudently fled for home. Caithness and Sutherland eventually ran the Gunns out of Strathnaver into Ross, where the Aberach MacKays finally defeated them. That one branch of MacKays would defend the Gunns and the other oppose them, shows how divided the clan was at this time.[131]

Eventually, the Earls of Caithness and Sutherland fell out, and Caithness decided to invade Sutherland. Huistean Du accompanied Caithness as his ally, apparently forgiving him his treatment of the Gunns. In March of 1587, the two forces met near Helmsdale. The Earl of Sutherland sent two secret envoys behind Caithness lines—one to Huistean Du, one to the Earl of Caithness. Both envoys wanted the other party to defect. Huistean Du said no. Earl George said yes. As soon as Huistean Du learned that Earl George had turned on him, he and his men went back to Strathnaver.[132]

Now Huistean Du was in a hard spot. His allies, the Gunns, were gone, his own clan was sharply divided, and his other ally Earl George had proved to be no ally at all. So Huistean Du was left to make his own peace with Alexander, Earl of Sutherland.

Earl Alexander offered these terms: Huistean Du owed him 50,000 Scots pounds in back feudal dues, but he would forgive him the debt and give him his daughter's hand in marriage (Huistean Du had divorced his first wife[133]), if Huistean Du would recognize Sutherland's feudal superiority. Huistean Du agreed. He married Lady Jane Gordon in December 1589, but never really reconciled himself to his vassalage to his father-in-law.[134] All this came about if you will recall, because the legal charters giving the Strathnaver lands to the MacKays had been illegally ignored after Donald MacKay's death.

With the MacKays and Gunns now on the Sutherland side of the fence, the weak willed 5th Earl of Caithness paid dearly. Sutherland and his allies poured into Caithness, and when they couldn't take Girnigoe Castle, they wasted the town of Wick in what has become known as La na Creich Mor, The Day of the Great Spoil (February 1589).[135] In June, James Sinclair of Murkle (see *Sinclair Lineage*) raided into Sutherland, but was met and defeated by Huistean Du in the heights of Brora.[136] In 1590, Earl George himself attacked Sutherland, and Huistean Du took men into Caithness and spoiled it to the gates of Thurso.[137]

Huistean Du was not all secure, though. In Strathnaver, a bloody feud between the Aberach MacKays and the other MacKays was raging, although there are no details as to what caused this latest flare up. Suffice it to say that it suited the Sutherland family and their advancement to keep the MacKays divided.

The hostility between Caithness, Sutherland, and the MacKays became so aggressive following the sack of Wick that the Privy Council called all three in front of them on 25 July 1595, and ordered them to keep the peace.[138] In 1601, the Earl of Caithness purported to want to hunt in Reay Forest, but he collected such a large "hunting" party that Huistean Du became suspicious. Huistean Du and his allies met them at the border of the forest. The Caithness men had no desire to fight, so they fled without drawing a sword. To mark this bloodless triumph, Huistean Du and his allies erected heap of stones on the shoulder of Ben Griam and called it Carn Teichidh, the Cairn of Flight.[139] [140] The Earl of Caithness tried the same stunt again in 1607, with no success.[141]

Huistean Du was sometimes called upon to supply men and arms to fight for King James VI, as were all the nobles of the time. One such instance came on 31 January 1602, when he was asked to raise a levy of 100 men to assist Queen Elizabeth of England in putting down an Irish rebellion.[142]

In 1608, King James VI called upon Huistean Du to help subdue the Isle of Lewis. Huistean Du and those who owned land along the coast were also ordered not to allow any of the rebels to settle in their lands. On 26 March 1609, Huistean Du and others were found guilty of not giving sufficient assistance to the government in the Lewis affair. Although Huistean Du (who did not bother to show up for the proceeding) was found to be a rebel, he doesn't seem to have actually suffered by it at all.[143]

As we have seen, Huistean Du MacKay married twice:

His first wife, Lady Elizabeth Sinclair, was the daughter of George Sinclair, 4th Earl of Caithness (see *Sinclair Lineage*). They had one daughter, Christina, who married John MacIntosh of Dalzell.[144]

His second wife, Lady Jane Gordon, was the eldest daughter of Alexander Gordon, Earl of Sutherland. They had four children:[145]

- Donald – became chief, and was made 1st Lord of Reay
- *John* – progenitor of the Strathy MacKays
- Annas – married John Sinclair of Brims, Caithness
- Mary – married Hector Munro, then married her cousin Alexander Gunn of Killearnan

Huistean Du MacKay died at Tongue on 2 September 1614.[146]

Here we leave the main branch of the Strathnaver MacKays. Our lineage runs through Huistean Du's second son John, and his Strathy MacKays. The Scoury MacKays and the Aberach MacKays will also appear again.

John MacKay, 1st Chief of Strathy[147]
(chief from 1626-1645)

John MacKay of Strathy, the second son of Huistean Du, was given land by his brother, Donald, 1st Lord of Reay. On 23 September 1626, he was given the lands of Dilred, Cattack, Dalmore, Knockdhu, Daluachrach, and Dalreith,[148] as well as the lands of Strathy, Armadale, Portskerray and Glen of Kinloch-Strathy, with fishing rights of the river on 2 May 1631.[149]

In 1618, John had married Agnes Sinclair, daughter of Sir James Sinclair of Murkle and Lady Elizabeth Stewart (see *Sinclair Lineage* and *Stewart Dynasty*). They had five children:[150] [151] [152]

- Hugh of Strathy – succeeded John as chief of Strathy
- *John of Skerray*
- James of Kirtomy

- Elizabeth – married Patrick Sinclair, eldest son of John Sinclair of Brims
- Jane – married William MacKay, 3rd Chief of the Bighouse MacKays

John MacKay of Strathy died at Dilred Castle in 1645.[153]

John MacKay, 1st of Skerray[154]

The second son of John MacKay of Strathy, John MacKay of Skerray did not succeed to the chieftainship. John MacKay of Skerray was captured at Balveny Castle in 1649, along with John MacKay, 2nd Lord of Reay.[155] This was the year Charles I was beheaded, so the fracas at Balveny Castle was probably part of the ensuing upheaval. After his release (date unknown), John obtained the town and lands of Skerray-Horisdale, port and strath thereof, on 28 November 1659, thus becoming John of Skerray. These lands were given to him in wadset, which means the conveyance of lands in payment of a debt.[156]

John lived through the beheading of Charles I, the Cromwell wars, and the Restoration of the monarchy with Charles II. Other than the above capture at Balveny Castle, it is unknown if he took any active part in the struggles. Since others at the castle were Royalist, it is probable that he also was a Royalist sympathizer.

John was appointed Commissioner of Supply for the shire of Sutherland in 1685, and again in 1690.[157]

John married Margaret, daughter of Hector Munro of Eriboll. They had four children:[158]

- John – died without children before 1679
- *Hector* – succeeded his father
- Donald – a notary public who married a different Margaret Munro
- Hugh of Cairnloch

It is unknown when John MacKay of Skerray died, but he was alive in 1709.[159]

Hector MacKay, 2nd of Skerray[160]

Little is known about him. He inherited Skerray because his elder brother predeceased their father.[161]

Hector MacKay of Skerray married Barbara MacKay, daughter of Captain William MacKay of Borely (see *Scoury MacKays* below). Hector and Barbara had six children:[162]

- *Donald* – succeeded his father
- John of Clashneach – factor for the 3rd Lord of Reay. Married the daughter of William MacKay of Strathan-Melness (an Aberach MacKay line)
- Angus – tacksman of Kinloch
- George
- Barbara – married John Munro of Skinit
- Ann – married Angus MacKay of Rennivie (a Bighouse MacKay line)

Donald MacKay, 3rd of Skerray[163]

Donald MacKay of Skerray inherited the wadset of Skerray from his father, but he resigned it to his relative, the 3rd Lord of Reay on 17 May 1723.[164] His wife is sometimes said to be Esther Gunn, daughter of the chief of the Gunns, Donald Gunn, but other sources say her name was unknown.

The couple had at least two children:[165]

- **Hector**
- A daughter who married John MacKay of Moudale (an Aberach MacKay line)

Hector MacKay[166]

Hector MacKay's wife is unknown, but he had at least one son: **Hugh MacKay**.

Hugh MacKay
(b. 1750)

Hugh MacKay was born in 1750 in Eddrachillis, Sutherland, Scotland. On his marriage record and on two of his children's birth records, his alias was MacAchin mac Dhoilic Achin Skerray – translated as son of Hector, son of Donald, son of Hector of Skerray.

On 13 February 1782, Hugh married Barbara Morison in Eriboll, Sutherland. They had children:[167]

- Margaret
- George
- **Mary (1785-1867)** – married Hugh Campbell (see *Campbell Lineage*)
- Donald (b. 1786)
- Unknown (b. 1787)
- Alexander (b. 1789)
- Barbara (b. 1793)

It is unknown when Hugh MacKay died, but it was before 1841, because at that time his widow Barbara was living with her daughter Mary's family.[168] Barbara, born 1766 in Eddrachillis, died on 12 July 1860 in Kinlochbervie, Sutherland, Scotland, and was buried at Oldshoremore Burial Grounds.[169]

Their daughter **Mary MacKay** married **Hugh Campbell** on 10 Feb 1809 in Eriboll. For their lives together, go to the *Campbell Lineage* chapter.

Please see next page to read about the *Scoury MacKays* and the *Aberach MacKays*.

THE SCOURY MACKAYS

The Scoury MacKays (modern spelling: Scourie) were founded by Donald Balloch MacKay, son of Iye Du MacKay of Strathnaver and his first wife, Helen MacLeod of Assynt. Since Iye Du and Helen were first cousins, Donald Balloch was not allowed to inherit the Strathnaver chieftainship. His younger half-brother, Huistean Du, the chief of Strathnaver, settled lands upon Donald Balloch, and the new line was born.

Donald Balloch MacKay, 1st of Scoury[170]

In 1590, Donald Balloch (this means "Donald of the Spot," probably referring to a birthmark) MacKay commanded a large force of archers at the Battle of Clynetradwell near Brora, assisting the 5th Earl of Caithness. Three times he regained control of his archers as they were thrown into confusion, and eventually won the day. [171]

On 31 December 1605, he received lands from his half-brother Huistean Du, namely the lands of Kinlochbervie, Scouriemore, Scouriebeg, and Eriboll.[172] On 26 February 1606, Donald gave his wife sasine (passed the land to her) in life rent (she gets the benefits for life but cannot dispose of the land herself) and to son Neil in feu (he was the administrator and feudal holder) of all his lands.[173]

Donald married Euphemia, daughter of Hugh Munro of Assynt, Ross. They had eight children:[174]

- Neil – succeeded his father but resigned the chieftainship to his brother Hugh
- Hugh, 2nd of Scoury
- ***Donald of Borley***
- Captain William – fought in the Thirty Years' War
- Margaret – married Alexander Sutherland of Kilphedder
- Janet – married William Mor, son of Neil MacEan Mac William, chief of the Aberach MacKays
- Christian – married Murdo, the eldest son of Neil MacEan Mac William, chief of the Aberach MacKays
- Ann – married John Tarrel of Strathflete

Donald Balloch MacKay died around 1620.[175]

Donald MacKay of Borley[176]

Donald MacKay of Borley was the third son of Donald Balloch. He lived for some time in Iddenmore in Durness. He was a prominent Royalist during the civil war and was with the Lord Reay at the Balveny Castle affair in 1649.[177]

He married Christian Munro, daughter of Reverend Robert Munro of Creich, Sutherland. They had four children:[178]

- ***William***
- Angus
- Major Iye of Keoldale
- Donald

Captain William MacKay of Borley

William MacKay of Borley, like his father, was a zealous Royalist. He led a company of MacKays at the Battle of Worcester on 3 September 1651, where Cromwell defeated the Scots and Royalists. He was appointed Commissioner of Supply for Sutherland in 1685 and 1691. Either there was more than one Commissioner of Supply at a time, or some data is incorrect, as these are also the dates when John MacKay of Skerray was Commissioner of Supply in Sutherland.[179] He also had sasine of life rent in Skerray.[180]

William MacKay of Borley married Elizabeth, daughter of Alexander Corbet of Arkboll, Ross and had eight children:[181]

- Captain Hugh
- Donald
- Reverend John of Lairg
- Elizabeth – married three times: Charles MacKay of the Sandwood MacKays, Robert Neilson Aberach MacKay of the Aberach MacKays, and John Grey of Rhine, Rogart
- *Barbara* – married *Hector MacKay, 2nd of Skerray*, as seen above
- Christina – married Hugh Munro of Achany
- Isobell – married John MacKay of the Melness MacKays
- Jane – married Murdo MacKay, son of Robert, son of Murdo Neilson, the Aberach MacKay chieftain

Please see next page for the *Aberach MacKay Lineage.*

THE ABERACH MACKAYS

The Aberach MacKay clan motto is "Bi Tren," Gaelic for "Be Valiant." This was later Latinized for Lord Reay into "Manu Forti," meaning "with a strong hand."

Ian Aberach MacKay, 1st of Achness

If you have read the above biographies of Angus Du MacKay and Neil Vass MacKay, you will remember that Ian Aberach MacKay gallantly led the MacKay clan in many battles during the failing health of his father and the imprisonment of his half-brother. In thanks, Neil Vass conferred lands upon him.[182]

The seat of the Aberach MacKays was at Achness, about two miles below Loch Naver, on the east side of the river. Their traditional burial place was at Gnubeg, on an eminence close to the northern shore of Loch Naver, in a special part of the cemetery walled off from the rest.[183]

Ian Aberach MacKay married a daughter of MacIntosh of MacIntosh, and had two sons:[184]

- *William Du* – succeeded his father
- John

William Du Aberach MacKay, 2nd of Achness

William Du Aberach MacKay played a part at the Battle of Aldicharrish in 1487, fighting alongside his cousin MacIntosh of MacIntosh. He likely witnessed at the Cathedral Church of Dornoch on 2 April 1497, the Precept of King James IV (see *Stewart Dynasty*) to Iye MacKay of Strathnaver.[185]

He married a daughter of Hector Roy MacKenzie of Gairloch by his wife, a daughter of Ranald MacRanald of Moidart. They had two known sons:[186]

- *William*
- Donald – killed at Loch Salchie with his brother in 1517

William MacKay, 3rd of Achness

William MacKay was killed in 1517 at Loch Salchie, between Loch Shin and Oikel, fighting against the Murrays, who were probably in league with the Rosses, with whom the MacKays had a longstanding feud.[187]

William married a daughter of Thomas Murray of Tullibardine. They had at least six sons:[188]

- Thomas
- *John*
- Gavin
- Alexander
- Murdo
- Neil – placed in charge of Skibo Castle by the MacKays during the upheaval of 1545

John Williamson Aberach MacKay, 4th of Achness

John Williamson Aberach MacKay and nine others were summoned to appear before the Lords of Justice in Inverness in 1538 for allegedly harboring rebels. Nothing appears to have come of that accusation.[189]

John married a daughter of Donald MacKay of Strathnaver and Helen Sinclair. They had a son and a daughter:[190]

- ***Neil MacEan MacWilliam***
- Margaret – married William Sutherland

Neil MacEan MacWilliam Aberach MacKay, 5th of Achness

Neil MacEan MacWilliam Aberach MacKay witnessed the sasine to his cousin, Iye Du of Strathnaver on 20 April 1571.[191] He also witnessed the grant for the charter which Iye Du obtained. Neil and Iye Du were fast friends and allies, but the affairs of 1579 drove a wedge between Neil and Iye Du's son Huistean Du, as mentioned above.[192]

The same 1579 affairs caused a long and bloody feud with the Gunn clan, including a fierce clash at Beallach Vigais, about the middle of Strath Halladale on the west side of the river.

Neil married a daughter of Hector Munro of Contalich, and had the following:[193]

- Murdo – married Christian MacKay, daughter of Donald Balloch MacKay of Scoury
- William Mor – married Janet MacKay, daughter of Donald Balloch MacKay of Scoury
- Robert
- Neil
- ***Janet, who married Hector Munro of Eriboll, Chief of the Munros. They had son Hector Munro, who had a daughter Margaret Munro, who married John MacKay, 1st of Skerray.***

This ends our MacKay lineage. As seen above, **Mary MacKay,** daughter of **Hugh MacKay of the Skerray line**, married **Hugh Campbell**, so to continue on, please see the *Campbell Lineage* chapter.

---

[1] Angus MacKay, *The Book of MacKay* (Edinburgh: Norman MacLeod, 1906), p. 21.

[2] E. William Robertson, *Scotland Under Her Early Kings: A History of the Kingdom to the Close of the 13th Century, Part One* (Edinburgh: Edmonston and Douglas, 1862), p. 189.

[3] Angus MacKay, *The Book of MacKay* (Edinburgh: Norman MacLeod, 1906), p. 22.

[4] E. William Robertson, *Scotland Under Her Early Kings: A History of the Kingdom to the Close of the 13th Century, Part One* (Edinburgh: Edmonston and Douglas, 1862), p. 189.

[5] E. William Robertson, *Scotland Under Her Early Kings: A History of the Kingdom to the Close of the 13th Century, Part One* (Edinburgh: Edmonston and Douglas, 1862), p. 190.

[6] Angus MacKay, *The Book of MacKay* (Edinburgh: Norman MacLeod, 1906), p. 22.

[7] E. William Robertson, *Scotland Under Her Early Kings: A History of the Kingdom to the Close of the 13th Century, Part One* (Edinburgh: Edmonston and Douglas, 1862), p. 190.

[8] Angus MacKay, *The Book of MacKay* (Edinburgh: Norman MacLeod, 1906), p. 22.

[9] Raymond Campbell Paterson, *The Lords of the Isles: A History of Clan Donald* (Birlinn Limited, Edinburgh, 2001), p. 5.

[10] E. William Robertson, *Scotland Under Her Early Kings: A History of the Kingdom to the Close of the 13th Century, Part One* (Edinburgh: Edmonston and Douglas, 1862), p. 189.

[11] Angus MacKay, *The Book of MacKay* (Edinburgh: Norman MacLeod, 1906), p. 22.

[12] E. William Robertson, *Scotland Under Her Early Kings: A History of the Kingdom to the Close of the 13th Century, Part One* (Edinburgh: Edmonston and Douglas, 1862), p. 190.

[13] Angus MacKay, *The Book of MacKay* (Edinburgh: Norman MacLeod, 1906), p. 23, 27.

[14] Angus MacKay, *The Book of MacKay* (Edinburgh: Norman MacLeod, 1906), p. 24, 27.

[15] James Grey, *Sutherland & Caithness in Saga-Time, or, The Jarls & The Freskyns* (Oliver & Boyd, Edinburgh, 1922), p. 45.

[16] Angus MacKay, *The Book of MacKay* (Edinburgh: Norman MacLeod, 1906), p. 23.

[17] E. William Robertson, *Scotland Under Her Early Kings: A History of the Kingdom to the Close of the 13th Century, Part One* (Edinburgh: Edmonston and Douglas, 1862), p. 350.

[18] Angus MacKay, *The Book of MacKay* (Edinburgh: Norman MacLeod, 1906), p. 26, 27.

[19] Angus MacKay, *The Book of MacKay* (Edinburgh: Norman MacLeod, 1906), p. 26, 27.

[20] Angus MacKay, *The Book of MacKay* (Edinburgh: Norman MacLeod, 1906), p. 26.

[21] E. William Robertson, *Scotland Under Her Early Kings: A History of the Kingdom to the Close of the Thirteenth Century, Part Two* (Edinburgh: Edmonston and Douglas, 1862), p. 4.

[22] Alasdair Ross, *The Identity of the Prisoner of Roxburgh Castle* (in S. Arbuthnot & K Hollo (eds.), Kaarina, Fil súil nglais – A grey eye looks back: A Festschrift in Honour of Colm Ó Baoill, (Ceann Drochaid, 2007)), p. 276.

[23] Alasdair Ross, *The Identity of the Prisoner of Roxburgh Castle* (in S. Arbuthnot & K Hollo (eds.), Kaarina, Fil súil nglais – A grey eye looks back: A Festschrift in Honour of Colm Ó Baoill, (Ceann Drochaid, 2007)), p. 282.

[24] Richard Oram (Ed.), *The Kings and Queens of Scotland* (Tempus Publishing Ltd., Stroud, Gloucestershire, England, 2001), p. 67.

[25] Angus MacKay, *The Book of MacKay* (Edinburgh: Norman MacLeod, 1906), p. 15.

[26] Angus MacKay, *The Book of MacKay* (Edinburgh: Norman MacLeod, 1906), p. 7.

[27] Angus MacKay, *The Book of MacKay* (Edinburgh: Norman MacLeod, 1906), p. 35.

[28] James Grey, *Sutherland & Caithness in Saga-Time, or, The Jarls & The Freskyns* (Oliver & Boyd, Edinburgh, 1922), p. 68.

[29] Angus MacKay, *The Book of MacKay* (Edinburgh: Norman MacLeod, 1906), p. 37-40.

[30] Angus MacKay, *The Book of MacKay* (Edinburgh: Norman MacLeod, 1906), p. 41.

[31] Angus MacKay, *The Book of MacKay* (Edinburgh: Norman MacLeod, 1906), p. 41.

[32] Angus MacKay, *The Book of MacKay* (Edinburgh: Norman MacLeod, 1906), p. 43.

[33] Angus MacKay, *The Book of MacKay* (Edinburgh: Norman MacLeod, 1906), p. 41-43.

[34] Angus MacKay, *The Book of MacKay* (Edinburgh: Norman MacLeod, 1906), p. 44.

[35] Angus MacKay, *The Book of MacKay* (Edinburgh: Norman MacLeod, 1906), p. 44-49.

[36] Angus MacKay, *The Book of MacKay* (Edinburgh: Norman MacLeod, 1906), p. 44.

[37] Angus MacKay, *The Book of MacKay* (Edinburgh: Norman MacLeod, 1906), p. 44-49.

[38] Angus MacKay, *The Book of MacKay* (Edinburgh: Norman MacLeod, 1906), p. 50.

[39] Angus MacKay, *The Book of MacKay* (Edinburgh: Norman MacLeod, 1906), p. 50.

[40] Angus MacKay, *The Book of MacKay* (Edinburgh: Norman MacLeod, 1906), p. 52-53.

[41] Angus MacKay, *The Book of MacKay* (Edinburgh: Norman MacLeod, 1906), p. 53.

[42] Angus MacKay, *The Book of MacKay* (Edinburgh: Norman MacLeod, 1906), p. 52.

[43] Angus MacKay, *The Book of MacKay* (Edinburgh: Norman MacLeod, 1906), p. 53.

[44] Angus MacKay, *The Book of MacKay* (Edinburgh: Norman MacLeod, 1906), p. 54.

[45] Ronald Williams, *The Lords of the Isles: The Clan Donald and the Early Kingdom of the Scots* (Chatto & Windus - The Hogarth Press, London, 1984), p. 187.

[46] Angus MacKay, *The Book of MacKay* (Edinburgh: Norman MacLeod, 1906), p. 55.

[47] Fitzroy Maclean, *A Concise History of Scotland* (First published 1970. This version published 2002. Thames & Hudson Ltd., London), p. 52.

[48] Raymond Campbell Paterson, *The Lords of the Isles: A History of Clan Donald* (Birlinn Limited, Edinburgh, 2001), p. 34.

[49] Angus MacKay, *The Book of MacKay* (Edinburgh: Norman MacLeod, 1906), p. 55, 61.

[50] Ronald Williams, *The Lords of the Isles: The Clan Donald and the Early Kingdom of the Scots* (Chatto & Windus - The Hogarth Press, London, 1984), p. 166.

[51] Angus MacKay, *The Book of MacKay* (Edinburgh: Norman MacLeod, 1906), p. 55.

[52] Angus MacKay, *The Book of MacKay* (Edinburgh: Norman MacLeod, 1906), p. 56.

[53] Ronald Williams, *The Lords of the Isles: The Clan Donald and the Early Kingdom of the Scots* (Chatto & Windus - The Hogarth Press, London, 1984), p. 197.

[54] Angus MacKay, *The Book of MacKay* (Edinburgh: Norman MacLeod, 1906), p. 57.

[55] Angus MacKay, *The Book of MacKay* (Edinburgh: Norman MacLeod, 1906), p. 59, 61.

[56] Angus MacKay, *The Book of MacKay* (Edinburgh: Norman MacLeod, 1906), p. 59.

[57] Angus MacKay, *The Book of MacKay* (Edinburgh: Norman MacLeod, 1906), p. 54-62.

[58] Angus MacKay, *The Book of MacKay* (Edinburgh: Norman MacLeod, 1906), p. 65.

[59] Angus MacKay, *The Book of MacKay* (Edinburgh: Norman MacLeod, 1906), p. 57.

[60] Angus MacKay, *The Book of MacKay* (Edinburgh: Norman MacLeod, 1906), p. 65.

[61] Angus MacKay, *The Book of MacKay* (Edinburgh: Norman MacLeod, 1906), p. 64.

[62] Angus MacKay, *The Book of MacKay* (Edinburgh: Norman MacLeod, 1906), p. 63-66.

[63] Angus MacKay, *The Book of MacKay* (Edinburgh: Norman MacLeod, 1906), p. 63-66.

[64] Angus MacKay, *The Book of MacKay* (Edinburgh: Norman MacLeod, 1906), p. 65.

[65] Angus MacKay, *The Book of MacKay* (Edinburgh: Norman MacLeod, 1906), p. 66.

[66] Angus MacKay, *The Book of MacKay* (Edinburgh: Norman MacLeod, 1906), p. 66.
[67] Angus MacKay, *The Book of MacKay* (Edinburgh: Norman MacLeod, 1906), p. 68.
[68] Angus MacKay, *The Book of MacKay* (Edinburgh: Norman MacLeod, 1906), p. 68.
[69] Angus MacKay, *The Book of MacKay* (Edinburgh: Norman MacLeod, 1906), p. 68.
[70] Angus MacKay, *The Book of MacKay* (Edinburgh: Norman MacLeod, 1906), p. 69.
[71] Angus MacKay, *The Book of MacKay* (Edinburgh: Norman MacLeod, 1906), p. 69.
[72] Angus MacKay, *The Book of MacKay* (Edinburgh: Norman MacLeod, 1906), p. 70.
[73] Angus MacKay, *The Book of MacKay* (Edinburgh: Norman MacLeod, 1906), p. 70.
[74] Angus MacKay, *The Book of MacKay* (Edinburgh: Norman MacLeod, 1906), p. 72.
[75] Angus MacKay, *The Book of MacKay* (Edinburgh: Norman MacLeod, 1906), p. 74.
[76] Angus MacKay, *The Book of MacKay* (Edinburgh: Norman MacLeod, 1906), p. 73.
[77] Angus MacKay, *The Book of MacKay* (Edinburgh: Norman MacLeod, 1906), p. 71.
[78] Angus MacKay, *The Book of MacKay* (Edinburgh: Norman MacLeod, 1906), p. 74.
[79] Angus MacKay, *The Book of MacKay* (Edinburgh: Norman MacLeod, 1906), p. 75.
[80] Angus MacKay, *The Book of MacKay* (Edinburgh: Norman MacLeod, 1906), p. 72.
[81] Angus MacKay, *The Book of MacKay* (Edinburgh: Norman MacLeod, 1906), p. 76.
[82] Angus MacKay, *The Book of MacKay* (Edinburgh: Norman MacLeod, 1906), p. 76.
[83] Angus MacKay, *The Book of MacKay* (Edinburgh: Norman MacLeod, 1906), p. 77.
[84] Angus MacKay, *The Book of MacKay* (Edinburgh: Norman MacLeod, 1906), p. 77.
[85] Angus MacKay, *The Book of MacKay* (Edinburgh: Norman MacLeod, 1906), p. 77.
[86] Angus MacKay, *The Book of MacKay* (Edinburgh: Norman MacLeod, 1906), p. 78.
[87] Angus MacKay, *The Book of MacKay* (Edinburgh: Norman MacLeod, 1906), p. 77.
[88] Angus MacKay, *The Book of MacKay* (Edinburgh: Norman MacLeod, 1906), p. 78.
[89] Angus MacKay, *The Book of MacKay* (Edinburgh: Norman MacLeod, 1906), p. 86.
[90] Angus MacKay, *The Book of MacKay* (Edinburgh: Norman MacLeod, 1906), p. 88.
[91] Angus MacKay, *The Book of MacKay* (Edinburgh: Norman MacLeod, 1906), p. 89-90.
[92] Angus MacKay, *The Book of MacKay* (Edinburgh: Norman MacLeod, 1906), p. 90.
[93] Angus MacKay, *The Book of MacKay* (Edinburgh: Norman MacLeod, 1906), p. 90.
[94] Angus MacKay, *The Book of MacKay* (Edinburgh: Norman MacLeod, 1906), p. 86-93.
[95] Angus MacKay, *The Book of MacKay* (Edinburgh: Norman MacLeod, 1906), p. 91-92.
[96] Angus MacKay, *The Book of MacKay* (Edinburgh: Norman MacLeod, 1906), p. 93.
[97] Darryl Lundy (compiler), *The Peerage.com* (http://thepeerage.com/index.htm), http://thepeerage.com/p19800.htm#i197995.
[98] Angus MacKay, *The Book of MacKay* (Edinburgh: Norman MacLeod, 1906), p. 93.
[99] Angus MacKay, *The Book of MacKay* (Edinburgh: Norman MacLeod, 1906), p. 93.
[100] Angus MacKay, *The Book of MacKay* (Edinburgh: Norman MacLeod, 1906), p. 94.
[101] Angus MacKay, *The Book of MacKay* (Edinburgh: Norman MacLeod, 1906), p. 95.
[102] Angus MacKay, *The Book of MacKay* (Edinburgh: Norman MacLeod, 1906), p. 95.
[103] Angus MacKay, *The Book of MacKay* (Edinburgh: Norman MacLeod, 1906), p. 95.
[104] Angus MacKay, *The Book of MacKay* (Edinburgh: Norman MacLeod, 1906), p. 95.
[105] Angus MacKay, *The Book of MacKay* (Edinburgh: Norman MacLeod, 1906), p. 98.
[106] Angus MacKay, *The Book of MacKay* (Edinburgh: Norman MacLeod, 1906), p. 98.
[107] Angus MacKay, *The Book of MacKay* (Edinburgh: Norman MacLeod, 1906), p. 98.
[108] Angus MacKay, *The Book of MacKay* (Edinburgh: Norman MacLeod, 1906), p. 100.
[109] Angus MacKay, *The Book of MacKay* (Edinburgh: Norman MacLeod, 1906), p. 101.
[110] Angus MacKay, *The Book of MacKay* (Edinburgh: Norman MacLeod, 1906), p. 102.
[111] Angus MacKay, *The Book of MacKay* (Edinburgh: Norman MacLeod, 1906), p. 103.
[112] Angus MacKay, *The Book of MacKay* (Edinburgh: Norman MacLeod, 1906), p. 104-105.
[113] Angus MacKay, *The Book of MacKay* (Edinburgh: Norman MacLeod, 1906), p. 104-105.
[114] Roland William Saint-Clair, *Saint-Clairs of the Isles: A History of the Sea-Kings of Orkney and their Scottish Successors of the Sirname Sinclair* (Auckland, New Zealand, H. Brett, General Printer and Publisher, Shortland and Fort Streets 1898), p. 193.
[115] Angus MacKay, *The Book of MacKay* (Edinburgh: Norman MacLeod, 1906), p. 78, 105-106.
[116] Roland William Saint-Clair, *Saint-Clairs of the Isles: A History of the Sea-Kings of Orkney and their Scottish Successors of the Sirname Sinclair* (Auckland, New Zealand, H. Brett, General Printer and Publisher, Shortland and Fort Streets 1898), p. 193.
[117] Angus MacKay, *The Book of MacKay* (Edinburgh: Norman MacLeod, 1906), p. 106.
[118] Angus MacKay, *The Book of MacKay* (Edinburgh: Norman MacLeod, 1906), p. 106.
[119] Angus MacKay, *The Book of MacKay* (Edinburgh: Norman MacLeod, 1906), p. 107.
[120] Roland William Saint-Clair, *Saint-Clairs of the Isles: A History of the Sea-Kings of Orkney and their Scottish Successors of the Sirname Sinclair* (Auckland, New Zealand, H. Brett, General Printer and Publisher, Shortland and Fort Streets 1898), p. 193.
[121] Angus MacKay, *The Book of MacKay* (Edinburgh: Norman MacLeod, 1906), p. 107-108.
[122] Roland William Saint-Clair, *Saint-Clairs of the Isles: A History of the Sea-Kings of Orkney and their Scottish Successors of the Sirname Sinclair* (Auckland, New Zealand, H. Brett, General Printer and Publisher, Shortland and Fort Streets 1898), p. 193.
[123] Angus MacKay, *The Book of MacKay* (Edinburgh: Norman MacLeod, 1906), p. 108.

[124] Angus MacKay, *The Book of MacKay* (Edinburgh: Norman MacLeod, 1906), p. 109.
[125] Angus MacKay, *The Book of MacKay* (Edinburgh: Norman MacLeod, 1906), p. 109.
[126] Angus MacKay, *The Book of MacKay* (Edinburgh: Norman MacLeod, 1906), p. 109-110.
[127] Angus MacKay, *The Book of MacKay* (Edinburgh: Norman MacLeod, 1906), p. 109-110.
[128] Angus MacKay, *The Book of MacKay* (Edinburgh: Norman MacLeod, 1906), p. 111-112.
[129] Angus MacKay, *The Book of MacKay* (Edinburgh: Norman MacLeod, 1906), p. 111-112.
[130] Angus MacKay, *The Book of MacKay* (Edinburgh: Norman MacLeod, 1906), p. 111-112.
[131] Angus MacKay, *The Book of MacKay* (Edinburgh: Norman MacLeod, 1906), p. 111-112.
[132] Angus MacKay, *The Book of MacKay* (Edinburgh: Norman MacLeod, 1906), p. 113-114.
[133] Angus MacKay, *The Book of MacKay* (Edinburgh: Norman MacLeod, 1906), p. 114.
[134] Angus MacKay, *The Book of MacKay* (Edinburgh: Norman MacLeod, 1906), p. 114-115.
[135] Angus MacKay, *The Book of MacKay* (Edinburgh: Norman MacLeod, 1906), p. 115-116.
[136] Angus MacKay, *The Book of MacKay* (Edinburgh: Norman MacLeod, 1906), p. 116.
[137] Angus MacKay, *The Book of MacKay* (Edinburgh: Norman MacLeod, 1906), p. 116.
[138] Angus MacKay, *The Book of MacKay* (Edinburgh: Norman MacLeod, 1906), p. 119.
[139] Angus MacKay, *The Book of MacKay* (Edinburgh: Norman MacLeod, 1906), p. 119-120.
[140] Vance Sinclair, *The History of Clan Sinclair: Viking Raider, Templar Knight, Highland Warrior* (England: Vance Sinclair, 2018), p. 82.
[141] Angus MacKay, *The Book of MacKay* (Edinburgh: Norman MacLeod, 1906), p. 120.
[142] Angus MacKay, *The Book of MacKay* (Edinburgh: Norman MacLeod, 1906), p. 120-121.
[143] Angus MacKay, *The Book of MacKay* (Edinburgh: Norman MacLeod, 1906), p. 120-121.
[144] Angus MacKay, *The Book of MacKay* (Edinburgh: Norman MacLeod, 1906), p. 115.
[145] Angus MacKay, *The Book of MacKay* (Edinburgh: Norman MacLeod, 1906), p. 123.
[146] Angus MacKay, *The Book of MacKay* (Edinburgh: Norman MacLeod, 1906), p. 123.
[147] Angus MacKay, *The Book of MacKay* (Edinburgh: Norman MacLeod, 1906), p. 123.
[148] Angus MacKay, *The Book of MacKay* (Edinburgh: Norman MacLeod, 1906), p. 310.
[149] Angus MacKay, *The Book of MacKay* (Edinburgh: Norman MacLeod, 1906), p. 311.
[150] Angus MacKay, *The Book of MacKay* (Edinburgh: Norman MacLeod, 1906), p. 311.
[151] Charles Mosley, ed, *Burke's Peerage & Baronetage, 106th Edition* (Routledge; Slp edition (May 1, 1999), 2 volumes).
[152] Darryl Lundy (compiler), *The Peerage.com* (http://thepeerage.com/index.htm), http://thepeerage.com/p19856.htm#i198553.
[153] Angus MacKay, *The Book of MacKay* (Edinburgh: Norman MacLeod, 1906), p. 311.
[154] Angus MacKay, *The Book of MacKay* (Edinburgh: Norman MacLeod, 1906), p. 311.
[155] Angus MacKay, *The Book of MacKay* (Edinburgh: Norman MacLeod, 1906), p. 314.
[156] Angus MacKay, *The Book of MacKay* (Edinburgh: Norman MacLeod, 1906), p. 314.
[157] Angus MacKay, *The Book of MacKay* (Edinburgh: Norman MacLeod, 1906), p. 314.
[158] Angus MacKay, *The Book of MacKay* (Edinburgh: Norman MacLeod, 1906), p. 314.
[159] Angus MacKay, *The Book of MacKay* (Edinburgh: Norman MacLeod, 1906), p. 314.
[160] Angus MacKay, *The Book of MacKay* (Edinburgh: Norman MacLeod, 1906), p. 314.
[161] Angus MacKay, *The Book of MacKay* (Edinburgh: Norman MacLeod, 1906), p. 315.
[162] Angus MacKay, *The Book of MacKay* (Edinburgh: Norman MacLeod, 1906), p. 292, 315.
[163] Angus MacKay, *The Book of MacKay* (Edinburgh: Norman MacLeod, 1906), p. 315.
[164] Angus MacKay, *The Book of MacKay* (Edinburgh: Norman MacLeod, 1906), p. 315.
[165] Angus MacKay, *The Book of MacKay* (Edinburgh: Norman MacLeod, 1906), p. 315-316.
[166] Angus MacKay, *The Book of MacKay* (Edinburgh: Norman MacLeod, 1906), p. 316.
[167] Scotland Old Parish Records, Hugh MacKay and Barbara Morrison, O.P.R. Marriages 048/ 0010 0127, Durness, accessed 10 June 2008 from www.scotlandspeople.gov.uk.
[168] 1841 Scotland Census, Parish: Durness; ED: 2; Page: 2; Line: 1470; Year: 1841.
[169] Scotland Statutory Records Index, Barbara Morrison MacKay, District: Kinlochbervie; County: Sutherland; Entry # 9; p. (illegible) Statutory Deaths 049/02 0009, accessed 8 July 2012 from www.scotlandspeople.gov.uk.
[170] Angus MacKay, *The Book of MacKay* (Edinburgh: Norman MacLeod, 1906), p. 78, 106.
[171] Angus MacKay, *The Book of MacKay* (Edinburgh: Norman MacLeod, 1906), p. 286.
[172] Angus MacKay, *The Book of MacKay* (Edinburgh: Norman MacLeod, 1906), p. 287.
[173] Angus MacKay, *The Book of MacKay* (Edinburgh: Norman MacLeod, 1906), p. 287.
[174] Angus MacKay, *The Book of MacKay* (Edinburgh: Norman MacLeod, 1906), p. 287.
[175] Angus MacKay, *The Book of MacKay* (Edinburgh: Norman MacLeod, 1906), p. 287.
[176] Angus MacKay, *The Book of MacKay* (Edinburgh: Norman MacLeod, 1906), p. 288.
[177] Angus MacKay, *The Book of MacKay* (Edinburgh: Norman MacLeod, 1906), p. 292.
[178] Angus MacKay, *The Book of MacKay* (Edinburgh: Norman MacLeod, 1906), p. 292.
[179] Angus MacKay, *The Book of MacKay* (Edinburgh: Norman MacLeod, 1906), p. 292.
[180] Angus MacKay, *The Book of MacKay* (Edinburgh: Norman MacLeod, 1906), p. 315.
[181] Angus MacKay, *The Book of MacKay* (Edinburgh: Norman MacLeod, 1906), p. 292.
[182] Angus MacKay, *The Book of MacKay* (Edinburgh: Norman MacLeod, 1906), p. 66.
[183] Angus MacKay, *The Book of MacKay* (Edinburgh: Norman MacLeod, 1906), p. 242-269.

[184] Angus MacKay, *The Book of MacKay* (Edinburgh: Norman MacLeod, 1906), p. 244.

[185] Angus MacKay, *The Book of MacKay* (Edinburgh: Norman MacLeod, 1906), p. 244.

[186] Angus MacKay, *The Book of MacKay* (Edinburgh: Norman MacLeod, 1906), p. 244.

[187] Angus MacKay, *The Book of MacKay* (Edinburgh: Norman MacLeod, 1906), p. 244-245.

[188] Angus MacKay, *The Book of MacKay* (Edinburgh: Norman MacLeod, 1906), p. 244-245.

[189] Angus MacKay, *The Book of MacKay* (Edinburgh: Norman MacLeod, 1906), p. 245.

[190] Angus MacKay, *The Book of MacKay* (Edinburgh: Norman MacLeod, 1906), p. 245.

[191] Angus MacKay, *The Book of MacKay* (Edinburgh: Norman MacLeod, 1906), p. 246.

[192] Angus MacKay, *The Book of MacKay* (Edinburgh: Norman MacLeod, 1906), p. 108.

[193] Angus MacKay, *The Book of MacKay* (Edinburgh: Norman MacLeod, 1906), p. 246.

THE
IRONSIDE
LINEAGE

GAMRIE,
BANFFSHIRE

SCOTLAND

THE IRONSIDE LINEAGE

(tree is combined with Morrison tree)

Robert Ironside (1766-1850) and Jean MacKay (1775-1827)

Robert Ironside was born around 1766.[1] Jean MacKay, daughter of William MacKay (possible son of Hugh MacKay and Jannet Massie) and Jean Smith, was born 7 June 1775, in Baggriehill, parish of Gamrie, Banffshire, Scotland and baptized 11 June 1775.[2]

Robert and Jean married 25 August 1798 in Gamrie, Banff,[3] and had eight known children:[4]

- William (1799-1857)
- Jean [5] (1801-1883)
- Margaret (1804-1888) – married Joseph Barclay in 1828
- Ann (1807-1891) – married George Milne in 1835
- James (b. 1810)
- Barbara (1812-1898) – had a son with Alexander Smith in 1834
- *Catherine (1815-1881)* – married Alexander Morrison
- Robert [6] (1818-1900) – married Margaret Morrison in 1841

Jean MacKay Ironside died 4 October 1827 in Black Hillocks, Gamrie, Banffshire. Her death entry listed her as Jean MacKay, not Jean Ironside, but the age (51) was correct and Black Hillocks was the Ironside family farm.[7]

On the 1841 Scottish census, the family lived in Black Hillocks, Gamrie, Banff. Robert was 70, and a farmer. Living with him were daughter Jean (35) and son Robert Junior (20), who was an agricultural laborer, and Robert's wife, Margaret (20). There was also Alexander Smith, aged 7, the out-of-wedlock son of Robert's daughter Barbara Ironside and Alexander Smith.[8]

Robert Ironside died 3 August 1850 in Black Hillocks, the family farm.[9] His age at death, 84, puts his birth around 1766. This is at odds with his age on the 1841 census, but we know that they rounded ages on that census, so they are not accurate. I did find a baptism record for a Robert Ironside on 28 February 1766 in Darnabo, Fyvie, Turriff, Aberdeenshire, with a father of William Ironside, so that could be our Robert.[10]

Catherine Ironside married Alexander Morrison in 1833. See the *Morrison Lineage* chapter for their lives.

---

[1] *Robert Ironside*, 1841 Scotland Census, Parish: Gamrie; ED: 1; Page: 4; Line: 1350; Year: 1841.

[2] Scotland Old Parish Records, *Jean MacKay*, O.P.R. Births 155/00 0020 0106 GAMRIE AND MACDUFF, accessed 15 April 2016 from www. scotlandspeople.gov.uk

[3] Scotland Old Parish Records, *Robert Ironside and Jean MacKay*, O.P.R. Marriages 155/00 0010 0329 GAMRIE AND MACDUFF, accessed 15 April 2016 from www.scotlanspeople.gov.uk.

[4] GenesReunited website. Research from Kenny Malley and Catherine Milne Scott. Accessed January 2009 from www.genesreunited.co.uk

[5] *Robert Ironside*, 1841 Scotland Census, Parish: Gamrie; ED: 1; Page: 4; Line: 1350; Year: 1841.

[6] *Robert Ironside*, 1841 Scotland Census, Parish: Gamrie; ED: 1; Page: 4; Line: 1350; Year: 1841.

[7] Scotland Old Parish Records, 04/10/1827, *Jean McKay* (Old Parish Registers Deaths 155/ 40 18 Gamrie and Macduff) Page 18 of 64. ScotlandsPeople.gov.uk, accessed 13 Feb 2021.

[8] *Robert Ironside*, 1841 Scotland Census, Parish: Gamrie; ED: 1; Page: 4; Line: 1350; Year: 1841.

[9] Scotland Old Parish Records, 03/08/1850, *Robert Ironside* (Old Parish Registers Deaths 155/ 40 56 Gamrie and Macduff) Page 56 of 64. ScotlandsPeople.gov.uk, accessed 13 Feb 2021.

[10] Scotland Old Parish Records, 28/02/1766, *Robert Ironside* (Old Parish Registers Births 197/ 20 5 Fyvie) Page 5 of 205. ScotlandsPeople.gov.uk, accessed 13 Feb 2021.

THE
WOOD
LINEAGE

GAMRIE,
BANFFSHIRE

SCOTLAND

THE WOOD LINEAGE

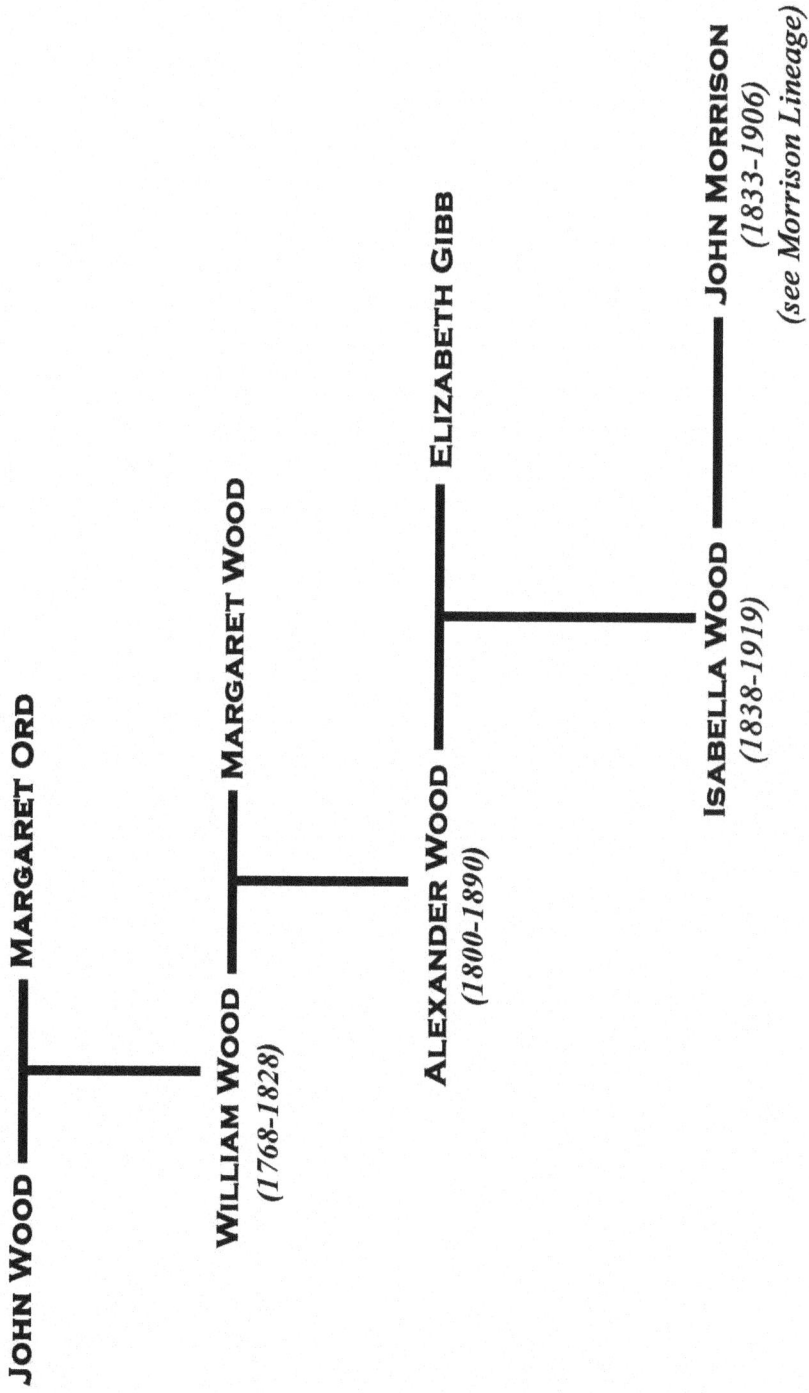

JOHN WOOD ——— **MARGARET ORD**

WILLIAM WOOD ——— **MARGARET WOOD**
(1768-1828)

ALEXANDER WOOD ——— **ELIZABETH GIBB**
(1800-1890)

ISABELLA WOOD ——— **JOHN MORRISON**
(1838-1919)   *(1833-1906)*
(see Morrison Lineage)

THE WOOD LINEAGE

John Wood and Margaret Ord

I found no records of this couple themselves—no marriage, no births. Their earliest known child was born in 1758, so they likely married a year or so before, making their estimated births around 1737. The Scottish Old Parish Records (OPR) revealed at least 8 children for them:

- Margaret (b. 1758)[1]
- Anne (b. 1759)[2]
- John (1761[3]-1842[4]) – married first Isobel Rankin[5], second Anne Morrison[6]
- Peter (b. 1762)[7]
- James (b. 1764)[8]
- Christian (b. 1766)[9]
- *William* (1768[10]-1828[11]) – married Margaret Wood[12]
- George (b. 1771)[13]

All the children were baptized in the parish of Gamrie and Macduff in Banffshire.

William Wood (1768-1828) and Margaret Wood

William Wood was born on 9 May 1768 in Seatown, Crovie, Gamrie and Macduff, Banffshire. [14] William Wood and Margaret Wood (yes, that was her maiden name) married on 24 November 1790, in Crovie, Gamrie and MacDuff, Banffshire. [15] They had 5 known children:

- John (b. 1791)[16]
- William (b. 1794)[17]
- George (b. 1796)[18]
- Peter (b. 1798)[19]
- *Alexander* (1800[20]-1890[21]) – married Elizabeth Gibb

William Wood died on 9 March 1828 in Netenshars, Gamrie and Macduff, Banffshire. [22] I have no information on Margaret Wood's birth or death, as the name was quite common and there were too many to choose from.

Alexander Wood (1800-1890) and Elizabeth Gibb

Alexander Wood was born 2 November 1800 in Gamrie, Banffshire, and baptized 16 November 1800.[23]

Alexander married Elizabeth Gibb sometime before 1826,[24] and they had at least 4 children:

- Jane (b. 1826) [25] – married Alexander Morrison[26]
- John (b. 1830) [27] – lived in New Pitsligo in 1890 [28]
- William (b.1832)[29]
- *Isabella Rankin* [30] (1838-1919)[31] – married John Morrison[32]

I wondered about Isabella's middle name. Rankin sounds like a surname, and surnames were sometimes used as middle names – they were often the mother's maiden name. But Isabella's mother's maiden name was Gibb. However, Isabella's father Alexander had an uncle, John Wood, whose first wife was Isobel Rankin. Isobel Rankin died around 1802, when Alexander was only about 2 years old, so why he would choose to name his daughter after an aunt he would not remember, I do not know, but it appears that he did.

In 1841, Alexander (41) was a single father to Jane (15) and Isabella (3). Elizabeth Gibb Wood did not appear on any of the census forms with her husband or children, so I believe she died after 1838 and before 1841. Alexander lived in Middleton, Gamrie, Banffshire, and worked as an agricultural laborer.[33]

John survived to adulthood but I do not know about William. The boys should have been about eleven and nine in 1841. Also in Middleton, working as an agricultural laborer, was a 10-year-old John Wood.[34] In Knowhead, Gamrie, Banffshire, there was a William Wood, age 8.[35]

Another possibility was found on the 1841 census of Auchterless, Aberdeenshire. On the Anderson farm, there were three young boys named Wood—Robert (15), Alexander (13), and John (12).[36] It was common after a mother died for the father to either remarry or send his children elsewhere. Since all three boys were old enough to work, Alexander possibly sent them as a unit to work, keeping the girls at home to care for him and the house. If this is correct, then Robert and Alexander were also children of Alexander Wood and Elizabeth Gibb. We do have a DNA match through an Alexander Wood of this age who immigrated to Ontario, Canada, so this is a likely hypothesis.

In 1851, Alexander (51) lived in Powie's Den, Gamrie, Banffshire, still working as an agricultural laborer. Young Isabella (13) still lived with him, but Jane had married.[37]

Alexander Wood died "of old age" on 29 January 1890, at the age of 89, in Black Hillocks, Gamrie, Banffshire.[38]

Isabella Rankin Wood married **John (III) Morrison** 20 February 1858. Since she lived with her father, Alexander, even after her marriage (in fact, until his death), we will pick up his lifeline—and hers—in the *Morrison Lineage* pages.

---

[1] *Margaret Wood*, Scotland Old Parish Records, 1758, O.P.R. Births 155/20 6, Gamrie and Macduff. ScotlandsPeople.gov.uk, accessed 21 Feb 2021.

[2] *Anne Wood*, Scotland Old Parish Records, 1759, O.P.R. Births 155/20 12, Gamrie and Macduff. ScotlandsPeople.gov.uk, accessed 21 Feb 2021.

[3] *John Wood*, Scotland Old Parish Records, 05/04/1761 (Old Parish Registers Births 155/ 20 21 Gamrie and Macduff) Page 21 of 573. Scotland's People, accessed 30 May 2019.

[4] *John Wood*, Scotland Old Parish Records, 1842, (OPR Deaths 155/40 45 Gamrie and Macduff). ScotlandsPeople.gov.uk, accessed 12 Feb 2021.

[5] *John Wood*, Scotland Old Parish Records, 28/06/1788, (Old Parish Registers Marriages 155/ 10 246 Gamrie and Macduff) Page 246 of 384. ScotlandsPeople.gov.uk, accessed 30 May 2019.

[6] *John Wood*, Scotland Old Parish Records, 25/12/1805 (Old Parish Registers Marriages 155/ 10 351 Gamrie and Macduff) Page 351 of 384. Scotland's People accessed 30 May 2019.

[7] *Peter Wood*, Scotland Old Parish Records, 1762, O.P.R. Births 155/20 29, Gamrie and Macduff. ScotlandsPeople.gov.uk, accessed 21 Feb 2021.

[8] *James Wood*, Scotland Old Parish Records, 1764, OPR Births 155/20 39, Gamrie and Macduff. ScotlandsPeople.gov.uk, accessed 12 Feb 2021.

[9] *Christian Wood*, Scotland Old Parish Records, 1766, O.P.R. Births 155/20 48, Gamrie and Macduff. ScotlandsPeople.gov.uk, accessed 21 Feb 2021.

[10] *William Wood*, Scotland Old Parish Records, 16/05/1768 (Old Parish Registers Births 155/ 20 59 Gamrie and Macduff) Page 59 of 573. Scotland's People, accessed 30 May 2019.

[11] *William Wood*, Scotland Old Parish Records, 09/03/1828 (Old Parish Registers Deaths 155/ 40 21 Gamrie and Macduff) Page 21 of 64. Scotland's People, accessed 30 May 2019.

[12] *William Wood*, Scotland Old Parish Records, 24/11/1790 (Old Parish Registers Marriages 155/ 10 248 Gamrie and Macduff) Page 248 of 384. Scotland's People, accessed 30 May 2019.

[13] *George Wood*, Scotland Old Parish Records, 1771, O.P.R. Births 155/20 80, Gamrie and Macduff. ScotlandsPeople.gov.uk, accessed 21 Feb 2021.

[14] *William Wood*, Scotland Old Parish Records, 16/05/1768 (Old Parish Registers Births 155/ 20 59 Gamrie and Macduff) Page 59 of 573. Scotland's People, accessed 30 May 2019.

[15] *William Wood*, Scotland Old Parish Records, 24/11/1790 (Old Parish Registers Marriages 155/ 10 248 Gamrie and Macduff) Page 248 of 384. Scotland's People, accessed 30 May 2019.

[16] *John Wood*, Scotland Old Parish Records, 21/08/1791 (Old Parish Registers Births 155/ 20 207 Gamrie and Macduff). Scotland's People, accessed 30 May 2019.

[17] *William Wood*, Scotland Old Parish Records, 13/03/1794 (Old Parish Registers Births 155/ 20 218 Gamrie and Macduff). Scotland's People, accessed 21 Feb 2021.

[18] Scotland Old Parish Records, 16/06/1796 WOOD, GEORGE (Old Parish Registers Births 155/ 20 226 Gamrie and Macduff). Scotland's People, accessed 21 Feb 2021.

[19] *Peter Wood*, Scotland Old Parish Records, 21/06/1798 (Old Parish Registers Births 155/ 20 237 Gamrie and Macduff). Scotland's People, accessed 21 Feb 2021.

[20] *Alexander Wood*, Scotland Old Parish Records, O.P.R. Births 155/ 0020 0250 Gamrie and Macduff, accessed 27 July 2008 on www.scotlandspeople.gov.uk.

[21] *Alexander Wood*, Scotland Statutory Records Index, Statutory Deaths 155/A1 0003 accessed 15 April 2016 on www.scotlandspeople.gov.uk.

[22] *William Wood*, Scotland Old Parish Records, 09/03/1828 (Old Parish Registers Deaths 155/ 40 21 Gamrie and Macduff) Page 21 of 64. Scotland's People, accessed 30 May 2019.

[23] *Alexander Wood*, Scotland Old Parish Records, O.P.R. Births 155/ 0020 0250 Gamrie and Macduff, accessed 27 July 2008 on www.scotlandspeople.gov.uk.

[24] *Alexander Wood*, Scotland Old Parish Records, O.P.R. Births 155/ 0020 0250 Gamrie and Macduff, accessed 27 July 2008 on www.scotlandspeople.gov.uk.

[25] *Jane Wood*, 1841 Scotland Census, Parish: Gamrie; ED: 2; Page: 2; Line: 350; Year: 1841.

[26] *Jane Wood & Alexander Morrison*, Ancestry.com, Scotland, Select Marriages, 1561-1910 [database on-line]. Provo, UT, USA: Ancestry.com Operations, Inc., 2014.

[27] *John Wood*, FamilySearch.org (LDS records), "Scotland Births and Baptisms, 1564-1950," database, FamilySearch (https://familysearch.org/ark:/61903/1:1:XY64-FXN : accessed 16 April 2016), 04 Jun 1830; citing GAMRIE,BANFF,SCOTLAND, reference ; FHL microfilm 990,994.

[28] *Alexander Wood*, Scotland Statutory Records Index, Statutory Deaths 155/A1 0003 accessed 15 April 2016 on www.scotlandspeople.gov.uk.

[29] *William Wood*, FamilySearch.org (LDS records), "Scotland Births and Baptisms, 1564-1950," database, FamilySearch (https://familysearch.org/ark:/61903/1:1:XY64-5FJ : accessed 16 April 2016), 30 Jun 1832; citing GAMRIE,BANFF,SCOTLAND, reference ; FHL microfilm 990,994.

[30] *Isabella Rankin Wood*, 1841 Scotland Census, Parish: Gamrie; ED: 2; Page: 2; Line: 350; Year: 1841.

[31] *Isabella Rankin Wood Morrison*, Scotland Statutory Records Index, Statutory Deaths 210/A2 0017, accessed 28 July 2008 from www.scotlandspeople.gov.uk.

[32] *Isabella Wood & John Morrison*, Scotland Statutory Records Index, Statutory Marriages 155/00 0001 accessed 19 May 2008 from www.scotlandspeople.gov.uk.

[33] *Alexander Wood*, 1841 Scotland Census, Parish: Gamrie; ED: 2; Page: 2; Line: 350; Year: 1841.

[34] *John Wood*, 1841 Scotland Census, Parish: Gamrie; ED: 2; Page: 1; Line: 1080; Year: 1841.

[35] *William Wood*, 1841 Scotland Census, Parish: Gamrie; ED: 3; Page: 12; Line: 867; Year: 1841.

[36] *Robert, Alexander, & John Wood*, 1841 Scotland Census, Parish: Auchterless; ED: 5; Page: 4; Line: 1050; Year: 1841.

[37] *Alexander Wood*, 1851 Scotland Census, Parish: Gamrie; ED: 2A; Page: 1; Line: 3; Roll: CSSCT1851_34; Year: 1851.

[38] *Alexander Wood*, Scotland Statutory Records Index, Statutory Deaths 155/A1 0003 accessed 15 April 2016 on www.scotlandspeople.gov.uk.

THE NOBILITY

MacDonald:
The Lords of
the Isles

The Lordship of the Isles
(at its greatest extent)

SCOTLAND

MacDonald Lineage:
The Lords of the Isles

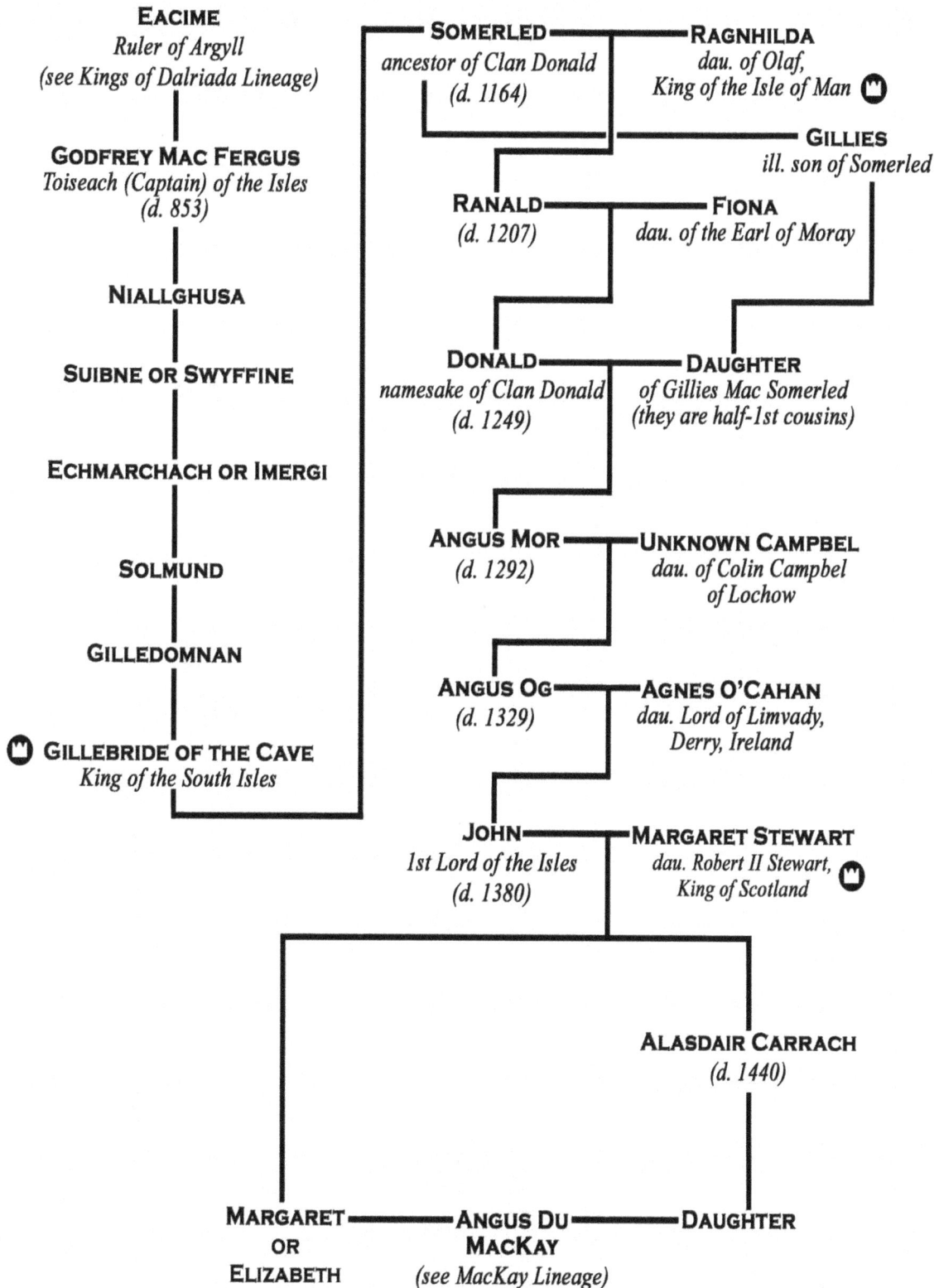

EACIME
Ruler of Argyll
(see Kings of Dalriada Lineage)

SOMERLED
ancestor of Clan Donald
(d. 1164)

RAGNHILDA
dau. of Olaf,
King of the Isle of Man ♛

GODFREY MAC FERGUS
Toiseach (Captain) of the Isles
(d. 853)

GILLIES
ill. son of Somerled

NIALLGHUSA

RANALD
(d. 1207)

FIONA
dau. of the Earl of Moray

SUIBNE OR SWYFFINE

ECHMARCHACH OR IMERGI

DONALD
namesake of Clan Donald
(d. 1249)

DAUGHTER
of Gillies Mac Somerled
(they are half-1st cousins)

SOLMUND

ANGUS MOR
(d. 1292)

UNKNOWN CAMPBEL
dau. of Colin Campbel
of Lochow

GILLEDOMNAN

♛ **GILLEBRIDE OF THE CAVE**
King of the South Isles

ANGUS OG
(d. 1329)

AGNES O'CAHAN
dau. Lord of Limvady,
Derry, Ireland

JOHN
1st Lord of the Isles
(d. 1380)

MARGARET STEWART
dau. Robert II Stewart,
King of Scotland ♛

ALASDAIR CARRACH
(d. 1440)

MARGARET
OR
ELIZABETH

ANGUS DU
MACKAY
(see MacKay Lineage)

DAUGHTER

MACDONALD: THE LORDS OF THE ISLES

I have included the MacDonalds in the nobility even though none of them never held an actual title from the Scottish government until very late in their lineage, beyond where our line diverges. However, throughout most of our MacDonald lineage they reigned as the "Lords of the Isles," a virtually independent kingdom nominally under the overlordship of Norway and later of Scotland.

The Lords of the Isles trace their ancestry back to Conn of the Hundred Battles, High King in Tara (Ireland) in the 3rd century.[1] This lineage, more tradition and legend than provable fact, is recounted in the *Kings of Dalriada* section of this book.

From Eacime, last of the Dalriadic royal line, the lineage enters the chaotic Viking period, and records and names of the Clan Donald ancestors are more a matter of faith than proof. Nevertheless, the Viking era lineage reads like this:[2]

Godfrey mac Fergus – Toiseach (Captain) of the Isles, d. 853
Niallghusa
Suibne or Swyffine
Echmarcach or Imergi
Solmund
Gilledomnan – married a daughter of Sigurd, 11th Jarl of Orkney and Shetland (see *Norwegian Lineage*)
Gillebride – King of the South Isles
Somerled – first historic ancestor of Clan Donald

Godfrey mac Fergus was likely not the son of Eacime as is usually claimed, but more likely the son of Fergus, King of Oriel, in Ireland. There is evidence that in 835, Kenneth MacAlpin (see *MacAlpin Dynasty*) called upon his Irish allies for help against the invading Norse. Godfrey and his force answered the call – the last time in history that the Irish would answer the call of their Scottish cousins – and gained some sort of foothold in the Isles.[3]

Godfrey held his position as chief of the Innse Gall (Islands of the Strangers) in the Isles until his death in 853.[4] Although he was Gaelic, his name was Norse, suggesting that even at that early date there was a mixing of the Gaelic and Norse cultures. His immediate successors could not hold out against the Vikings, but the Viking culture never dominated the Isles the way it did in Orkney and Shetland.

Somerled was the first historic ancestor of Clan Donald whom we have a great deal of information about. His father, Gillebride, and his grandfather, Gilledomnan, were also documented, but lost their holdings in the Isles during the vicious Viking era to King Magnus Barelegs of Norway in his raids of 1098. His grandfather, Gilledomnan, is often equated with Earl Gilli who married the daughter of Sigurd, 11th Jarl of Orkney and Shetland, but there is some doubt that they are the same person.[5]

Somerled MacGillebride
(d. 1164)

Somerled's name was Norse, meaning "Summer Sailor," but he was undeniably a Gael, presented as seventh in the male line from Godfrey, Toiseach (Captain) of the Isles, who died in 853.[6]

Whatever Somerled's true descent, the other chieftains acknowledged Somerled's descent from Clan Colla (Dalriada's roots), and Norse accounts speak of him as one of the old house of Dalriada.[7]

Somerled's father, Gillebride, was dispossessed of his Isles holdings by the Vikings and found refuge with his kin in Ireland. He brought a fighting force back to Scotland to try to regain his patrimony, but apparently was unsuccessful, since in 1130 he was living with his son in a cave in Morvern. Apparently he had no followers and no prospects—thus his nickname, Gillebride of the Cave.[8] Gillebride may also have supported the last Celtic King of Scotland, Donald Ban, who was overthrown. This may also have stymied Gillebride's fortunes.[9] Somerled was likely born between 1100 and 1110.

Somerled's fortunes changed when the leader of the local clan, MacInnes, was killed by the Danes. Internal rivalries prevented the clan from choosing a leader from among themselves (Gaels elected their leaders; it was not always from father to son). The clan knew of Somerled, and knew that as a descendant of Clan Colla, he would be acceptable to the warriors.[10]

The people found him fishing in a stream and asked him to lead them. Somerled said if he caught the big salmon he was after, he would take it as a positive sign. He caught it and said he had to take it back to his father, and that he would meet the clan the next day. In the meantime, he ordered them to light multiple campfires that night, to give the impression of a large war band.[11]

The next day, Somerled realized the Danish force was much larger than his, so he had his men march past the same hill three times, wearing three different sets of clothes, thus making the Danes think they were a large force. The Danes tried to flee but were routed.[12]

Somerled also took control of Argyll and the old Dalriadic patrimony, which some would say was his by right. Under him, a new Gaelic pride began to rise. By the 1140s, Somerled established himself in Lorn, Kintyre, and Knapdale.[13]

Somerled wanted to marry Ragnhilda, the daughter of King Olaf of the Isle of Man. Olaf was very powerful, ruling all the southern islands, and he didn't want this upstart Gael marrying his daughter.[14]

Olaf went on a raid to the island of Skye. Somerled offered to assist in the raid if Olaf would let him marry Ragnhilda. Olaf refused, and demanded Somerled's ships by feudal right, as he was Somerled's nominal overlord. Somerled joined him with two galleys.[15]

In the night, Somerled's friend Maurice MacNeil swam under Olaf's boat and bored holes, which he then sealed with tallow. The next day, in open waters the tallow melted, and Olaf's ship started taking on water. Olaf asked Somerled for help, and Somerled refused—unless Olaf let him marry his daughter. Olaf agreed, and Somerled had MacNeil fix the boat with the pegs they had prepared for that very purpose.[16]

Somerled married Ragnhilda in 1140.[17]

Somerled had many sons. Before he married Ragnhilda, he had four sons by three different women.

By a first marriage he had:[18]
- Somerled the Younger
- Gilliecolum, who died with his father, Somerled, in 1164

He also had two "natural" sons: [19]
- Gillies, by a woman of the Bisset family from the Glens of Antrim
- Gall "the Foreigner" MacSgillin, by a Lowland woman

With his wife Ragnhilda, he had five children:[20]
- ***Ranald***
- Dugall – founder of the MacDougalls of Lorne
- Angus
- Olaf – probably died as a child, as nothing but his name remains
- Beatrice – first Prioress of Iona

Somerled, not content with his mainland possessions, positioned himself at the center of the Celtic-Norse world, with diplomatic, political, and marital ties to Ireland, Man, Galloway, Moray, and Norway. Since his father had been King of the Southern Isles, he likely felt they were his by right. But island supremacy demanded a fleet, so Somerled secretly began building ships, utilizing technical improvements that made them superior to the Viking longships. By 1158, Somerled had 53 ships, and by 1164 he had 160.[21]

Somerled's principal fortress was Casteall Claidh (the Castle of the Trench), built circa 1154 on Fraoch Island overlooking the Sound of Islay. It was reportedly the first castle in the Hebrides to follow the square design of Norman keeps.[22]

In 1153, King Olaf of Man was killed, and his son Godfrey (Godred) took over. Godfrey was a tyrant, and his people hated him. There was a conspiracy to put Dugall, son of Somerled and Ragnhilda (and therefore Olaf's grandson) on the throne.[23][24]

Godfrey did not approve of this, and he and Somerled met in a sea battle off the west coast of Islay on Epiphany, 6 January 1156. They fought a pitched battle all through the night. The actual date of the night battle was probably 12 January, which was the night of the full moon. Somerled won the lengthy battle. However, he had suffered so many losses that he could not follow up the victory.[25][26] Somerled and Godfrey agreed to split the islands between them. Godfrey got the Isles of Man and Skye, and all the Hebrides north of Ardnamurchan, and Somerled got all the islands south of Ardnamurchan, including Mull, Jura, Islay, and the rich peninsula of Kintyre.[27][28]

In 1158, Somerled displaced Godfrey and conquered Man, with much destruction. After this victory, Somerled held vast lands: the Isles of Man, Mull, Coll, Tiree, Colonsay, Islay, Gigha, and the lesser isles, and the mainland areas of Kintyre, Knapdale, Lorne, and Argyll. The Isles he held as a vassal of the Norwegian king. The mainland areas he held by sword, as he had no official grant of them from the Scottish kings.[29][30]

Somerled pursued a deliberately Celtic (Gaelic) policy. At this time, the Scottish kings were bringing in the Norman influences from England, and the native Gaels were becoming sidelined by Normans, Flemish, and other foreign courtiers. After David I's father, Malcolm III, died, there had been a Gaelic uprising wanting to place Malcolm's brother Donald Ban on the throne. Somerled's father likely supported Donald Ban in this failed uprising, so it is hardly surprising that Somerled also supported Gaelic pride and nationalism. This policy brought him into direct conflict with Scottish kings David I and Malcolm IV.[31]

If you have already read the *MacKay Lineage* chapter, or the *MacAlpin Dynasty* chapter, then you are familiar with the next part of the story.

In Moray, Lulach, claimant of the throne, had a daughter who married Aed, the Bishop of Dunkeld and Earl of Moray. They had children Angus and Malcolm MacEth, who rose in revolt against David I. Angus was killed, but Malcolm escaped to the Highlands, and allied himself with Somerled. They sealed their alliance when Malcolm married Somerled's sister sometime before 1134.[32][33][34][35]

Malcolm was captured, but Somerled continued his support of the family, backing his nephew Donald MacEth until Donald's 1156 capture and imprisonment in Roxburgh Castle.[36]

When King David I died, King Malcolm IV was still a child, and his councilors convinced him that Somerled was a continuing threat to his realm. Malcolm sent Gilchrist, Earl of Angus, to subdue Somerled. They fought to a standstill, and Somerled and Malcolm eventually signed a treaty, one of the terms being the release of Malcolm and Donald MacEth from Roxburgh, which happened in 1157.[37][38]

In 1164, the FitzAlans (later the Stewarts) had pushed their power to the shores of the Firth of Clyde, which threatened Somerled, and prompted him into a preemptive strike.

Somerled sailed up the Clyde to Greenock with 160 ships, and advanced upon Renfrew with men from Kintyre, Argyll, the Hebrides, and even Vikings from Dublin. Walter FitzAlan, first hereditary High Steward of Scotland (see *Stewart Lineage*), tried to negotiate with him. Walter wanted the islands of Arran and Bute for himself, and King Malcolm wanted Kintyre and Argyll back. Malcolm did admit that the Isles were Somerled's by right of his wife. Somerled was the first of his line to be referred to in contemporary annals as ri Innse Gall—"King of the Isles."[39]

Somerled replied that he was resolved to "lose all or keep all."[40]

Somerled and his son Gilliecolum (Gille Brigte) were killed in the ensuing battle. All contemporary sources say he was killed in the battle, although a different version of his death was circulated years later.[41]

Just for good measure, here is the disputed version of his death:

Malcolm hesitated to attack, for he had no malice toward Somerled. However, the nobles wanted to get rid of him, so they persuaded Somerled's page to stab Somerled and his son Gilliecolum to death in the night. When the Gaels saw their leader dead, they returned to their ships and went home. Malcolm had Somerled's body buried at Iona, perhaps in tacit recognition of his rights to the Isles.[42][43]

Walter FitzAlan probably obtained his rights to the Isle of Bute at this time, although it was disputed by Somerled's family for generations to come.

Even after Malcolm won the day, Somerled's sons still divided up not just the Isles, but the mainland areas, too. Only Somerled's sons by Ragnhilda could inherit the Isles, so his other sons had to split the mainland.[44] Our line follows **Ranald**, eldest son of Somerled and Ragnhilda.

Ranald MacSomerled of Islay
(d. 1207)

Ranald (sometimes Reginald) inherited Islay, Kintyre, and all the Isles south of Ardnamurchan, except for Man, which reverted back to the Norse King Ragnvald, who was the overlord of the Northern Hebrides.[45]

The brothers (Dugall, Angus, and Ranald) did not get along, to the point where Angus and Ranald actually went to war. In 1192, Ranald was defeated by Angus in battle.[46] [47]

Unlike his father, Ranald was a pacifist, and a deeply religious man.[48] He was Roman Catholic, and founded a number of monasteries. He restored the abbey church on Iona and established a Benedictine community of monks there. In 1203, he also established a Benedictine convent there, with his sister Beatrice, as the first Prioress.[49]

His greatest contribution was the building of the Cistercian Abbey of Saddell in Kintyre. Ranald traveled to Rome, and returned with consecrated dust to scatter on the foundation of the abbey.[50] He also patronized the abbey of Paisley, which was a bit odd because Paisley was located outside of Isle dominion.[51]

He married Fiona, the daughter of the Earl of Moray, and they had three sons:[52]

- ***Donald***
- Ruairi (Rory)
- Angus

Ranald and his brothers Angus and Dugall were rarely united, and this infighting would have been disastrous if the kings of Scotland had chosen to move against them at this time. Luckily, they did not, being distracted by problems with England.[53]

Ranald is said to have died in 1207, and was buried at Iona.[54] But the actual date of his death is uncertain—it could have been as early as the battle with Angus in 1192, or as late as 1227.[55]

His son Donald got southern Kintyre, Islay, and the south Isles. Ruairi got Garmoran after his uncle Angus MacSomerled, along with all of Angus' sons, was killed in 1210.[56] Ruairi also got northern Kintyre and Ugadale outright but inherited the Isles of Arran and Bute along with a dispute.[57] As mentioned above, the Stewarts had their eye on those isles. They were possessed by Somerled's son Angus, who was killed in 1210, along with all of his sons and heirs. However, Alexander Stewart had married Jane, daughter of James, son of Angus MacSomerled, and therefore she was the lone heiress of the Angus lands—including Arran and Bute. So, the Stewarts claimed that they, not Ruairi, should own Arran and Bute.[58]

But we follow ***Donald***'s adventures in our line.

Donald of the Isles
(d. 1249)

Donald, unlike his father, but like his grandfather, Somerled, was warlike. In 1211, Donald allied with his brother Ruairi and Thomas of Galloway and raided Ireland with 76 galleys. Together, they plundered Derry and the peninsula of Innisowen.[59]

Donald married the daughter of Gillies MacSomerled, Somerled's illegitimate son. That made Gillies Donald's half-uncle, and Donald's wife was therefore his half-first cousin.[60] Donald and Gillies eventually quarreled, and Donald killed Callum Alin, Gillies' son and Donald's brother-in-law. Donald then incited the MacNeils of Lennox to expel Gillies from his lands in Kintyre.[61]

With his wife, Donald had two sons: [62] [63]

- ***Angus Mor***
- Alasdair (There is some dispute if this son existed, since the name Alasdair/Alexander was not used among Gaels at this time.)

He possibly also had a natural son:[64]

- Murchad

At some point after Donald inherited Ranald's lands, Donald and his uncle Dugall MacSomerled went to Norway, where Donald was formally granted his rights to the Isles by King Magnus. Later, Donald and Dugall quarreled, probably because of an ongoing dispute in Mull, and Donald killed Dugall.[65]

In 1214, Alexander II came to the Scottish throne. Donald and Ruairi aided the rebel MacEths, and may have given the MacKays refuge in Ugadale. [66]

Alexander II sent an envoy to Donald, demanding that Donald repudiate his ties to the Norwegian king and acknowledge the sovereignty of the Scottish crown. Donald said no, that he held the Isles of the King of Norway. The envoy said that Alexander would give the Isles to whomever he wished, and Donald would have no say.[67] Donald replied that since his ancestor King Olaf had taken and held the Isles by conquest, Donald technically didn't owe allegiance to anybody. When this line of reasoning failed, Donald surprised and killed the envoy and his men the next day at dawn.[68]

This set off a disastrous chain of events. In 1221, King Alexander invaded MacDonald lands, expelling Ruairi from Arran, and driving another man, named Somerled, from Kintyre. Alexander established a number of his own people in the captured areas.[69] Most notably, from both historical and personal genealogical viewpoints, was the installation of a knight of Strathclyde descent: Colin Wry-mouth or Cambeul. Colin Campbell married the heiress of Duncan mac Duibhne, the Irish chieftain of Lochow, and built his castle of Innis Chonnel on an island in Loch Awe, in Argyll.[70]

In retaliation, King Hakon of Norway instituted a raid in which they wrested Bute from the Stewarts in three days of fighting.[71] King Hakon appointed Ewan of Lorne the overlord of the Norwegian territories in the Hebrides,[72] but later Ewan seized the Isle of Man for himself. Hakon had Donald and Ruairi (Ewan's cousins) drive him out again. While Ruairi was away doing this, the Stewarts took Bute back from him.[73]

Donald, in his later years, went to Rome to atone for his sins—and, some say, to get a writ from the Pope saying that he had the rights to the Isles and the mainland areas of Argyll and Kintyre. He was a generous benefactor of Saddell Abbey and the Iona monasteries, and may have joined the brotherhood of Paisely Abbey, like his father.[74]

Donald died at Skipness circa 1249, and was buried on Iona. His son, ***Angus Mor***, inherited his lands.[75]

Angus Mor of the Isles
(d. 1292)

Although Donald of the Isles was the founder of the surname "MacDonald," that surname did not come into common use until the 16th century. Donald and his immediate descendants used "of the Isles."[76]

Angus Mor of the Isles came to power around 1249. King Hakon of Norway and King Alexander III of Scotland were having a tug of war over the Isles—which the MacDonalds felt belonged to neither king, but to them. When Hakon came to Scotland in 1261 to challenge Scottish King Alexander, he expected all the clans of the Isles to rally to his cause. Most did, but Angus Mor and his cousin Ewen of Lorne did not.[77][78] Given that Hakon had run Ewen out of Man a few years earlier, his recalcitrance was understandable.

Angus Mor, however, had his own reasons for holding back. He didn't like the interference of sovereignty of any kind. No doubt he would have preferred to remain a vassal of Norway, since they were farther away and this made him virtually autonomous, but he hoped he could stay neutral and come out of the fight with his lands intact.[79]

King Hakon didn't like being snubbed by his subjects. He sent men to attack their lands until they submitted. Eventually, Angus submitted to Hakon on the Isle of Gigha, and surrendered his Islay lands to him. Hakon restored them, but taxed Kintyre 100 cows as punishment.[80][81]

Angus' uncle Ruairi attacked Rothesay Castle on Bute, which was a Stewart castle, and won it back for himself. Angus joined Hakon at the peace talks with Alexander, but they dragged on and on, so Hakon sent Angus foraging up Loch Long for supplies. Angus and his men landed 60 ships at Arrochar[82][83] and hauled the galleys overland to Loch Lamond to plunder there, and in Lennox and Stirling. He was away on this mission when the actual fight between Hakon and Alexander broke out, and so was not part of the Norwegian defeat.[84][85]

In 1266, Norway ceded the Hebrides to Scotland, and Angus and the other island clans had a new master – King Alexander III of Scotland.[86] Alexander granted amnesty to all the clan chiefs who fought for Hakon, since he understood that they owed Hakon allegiance. Those who submitted to Alexander were not only pardoned, but were confirmed in their existing possessions, as was Angus Mor.[87]

Angus' uncle Ruairi didn't fare as well. Alexander gave the northern isles of Lewis and Skye to Ferchar Macantagart, Earl of Ross, thus depriving Ruairi of some of his holdings. In return, Ruairi was given Uist, Barra, Eigg, and Rhum. However, Ruairi lost forever his prizes of Arran and Bute, which were given permanently to the High Stewards of Scotland.[88]

Angus was a powerful man in the new Scotland. He, Colin Campbell, and other western chiefs, represented the western lands in the 1284 Parliament that regulated the succession when all of Alexander III's children predeceased him.[89] When Alexander III died, and then his granddaughter and heir the Maid of Norway died, the Great Cause was upon them.[90]

In 1286, Angus Mor had entered into the Turnberry Band, allying himself with Robert de Brus (grandfather of the future Robert I the Bruce) (see *De Brus Lineage*) and other nobles, including James Stewart, High Steward of Scotland. This Band chiefly dealt with Irish affairs.[91]

In 1288, the Cause was hotly contested between Robert de Brus and John Balliol, who was strongly supported by his relatives, the Comyns.[92] Angus Mor and his son Alasdair Óg entered into a bond of association to further the Brus claim (see *De Brus Lineage*).[93][94]

In 1291, the Cause was put to King Edward I of England (see *Continental Dynasty*) for arbitration. Like all the nobles present at the debate in Berwick, Angus Mor swore allegiance to Edward as his overlord, but Angus continued to back the Brus claim.[95][96]

When John Balliol was crowned, Angus was not happy. In Feb 1293 King John Balliol summoned Angus to appear before him to pay homage, and Angus ignored him.[97][98]

Angus married a daughter of Sir Colin Campbell of Lochow, which is ironic considering that the Campbells and the MacDonalds were to become bitter enemies. But Angus married Campbell's daughter, and by her had at least three sons:[99]

- Alasdair Óg (this is the first authentic record of Alexander being used in the West)
- *Angus Óg*
- Iain (John) Sprangach (Bold John)

Some historians also name a fourth son, Duncan.[100]

Angus Mor died circa 1300. Alasdair got Islay and Argyll. Angus Óg got Kintyre and Mull, although the Lorne clan claimed Mull as its own. John got Ardnamurchan.[101]

With the Balliol-Bruce conflict and the Wars of Scottish Independence brewing, it was then that *Angus Óg* and his MacDonalds entered onto the national stage.

Angus Óg of the Isles
(d. 1329)

Angus Óg was the younger brother, so his brother, Alasdair, was head of the clan until his death passed the chieftainship to Angus Óg.[102] Angus Óg was still powerful in his own right, with the lands of Kintyre and Mull to his name, as well as ships under his command.[103]

In 1301, Angus had been the Admiral of the Western Isles in service to the English king, Edward I, but since that time he had removed himself from politics, keeping neutral. But he was soon to be on the front lines of the struggle for Scottish independence.[104][105]

In 1306, things were bad for Robert the Bruce (see the *Stewart Dynasty*). He had just crowned himself king of Scotland and lost his first battle at Methven. Fleeing for his life—a fugitive in his own country—and hiding from his own people as well as the English, he turned to his escape of last resort, Angus Óg of the Isles.[106][107]

Robert remembered that Angus Mor had supported his grandfather's claim, and was hoping that Angus Óg would support him. But even this hope was a slim one, because Angus Óg himself was in a precarious position in 1306.[108][109]

At that time, Angus Óg held Kintyre and Mull, but he was in dispute over Mull with John of Lorne, who also was a strong Comyn supporter and rabidly anti-Bruce. To make things more difficult, Angus Óg's brother, Alasdair, head of the MacDonald clan, had married a Lorne girl, which allied him with the Comyn faction against Bruce. So Angus Óg was himself surrounded by Comyn supporters, and Bruce's flight to him was hardly a sure path to safety.[110]

But Sir Neil Campbell of Lochow secured ships for Bruce, and the king sailed to Angus Óg at Saddell Castle. Angus Óg welcomed them, and immediately moved Bruce to the fortress of Dunavertie at the tip of Kintyre for safety. Still not feeling that Bruce was secure, Angus Óg moved Bruce to the island of Rathlin off the Antrim coast of Ireland. Dunavertie was besieged just a few days after the move was made. [111] [112]

While Robert the Bruce rested up on Rathlin, John of Lorne made a move in his personal war with Angus Óg over Mull. John sent the three MacLean brothers to make his case. They killed Angus Óg's steward, and kidnapped Angus Óg. John wasn't as grateful as the brothers thought he should be, so Angus Óg said if they'd switch sides, he would reward them well. They freed him, and he kept his word. He rewarded them richly, and the MacLeans became staunch allies of his.[113]

In 1307, Robert the Bruce returned to the mainland with ships and an army of Islemen, courtesy of Angus Óg. Angus Óg may have been present at the defeat of Thomas and Alexander Bruce at Loch Ryan. He escaped, but the Bruce brothers were hanged.[114] [115]

Angus' brother, Alasdair, fought against Bruce, but Alasdair was captured and imprisoned, and presumably died in Dundonald Castle in Ayrshire. Angus Óg became the chief of Clan Donald, and from then on the Islemen fought only for Bruce.[116] While most accept the 1308 date as the transfer of power, author Raymond Campbell Paterson makes a strong case for it being much earlier—in 1299.[117]

Angus Óg played a vital role in the Battle of Bannockburn, when the outnumbered Bruce army defeated the army of King Edward II of England (see *Continental Dynasty*), effectively ending the First War for Scottish Independence. On June 24, 1314, Angus' men were stationed on the right, under Bruce's command. Bruce's army was largely Celtic, including Angus' Islemen. It is said that when Angus arrived with his troops, Robert the Bruce said to him, "My hope is constant in thee." The Battle of Bannockburn saw the rout of the 25,000-man English army on the constricted, marshy field of Bannockburn. King Edward II barely escaped the field.[118] [119]

As a reward, in 1315, Bruce bestowed upon Angus Óg the ancient Clan Donald lands of Islay, Mull, Jura, Coll, Tiree, Colonsay, Morvern, Ardnamurchan and Glencoe, along with part of the Lochaber lands taken from the Comyns. The MacRuairis were given Lorne, Garmoran, the northern isles, and the rest of Lochaber.[120] However, Bruce convinced Angus to give up the lands of Knapdale and the Kintyre peninsula (which passed to Robert Stewart, the future Robert II) (see *Stewart Dynasty*), because of their strategic importance, as well as Argyll, which passed to Neil Campbell of Lochaw.[121]

King Robert I the Bruce was forever grateful to his faithful ally Angus Óg, but he was always aware that Angus had joined him as an ally, not a subject or servant, and of the great power of the Isles. It is said that he left instructions for his successors to never let the Hebrides be under the rule of one man and to always deal justly with the Isles.[122]

Robert I died at Cardross in June 1329, and Angus Óg died not long after at Finlaggan in Islay. Angus Óg was buried at Iona, and his tombstone reads, "Hic jacet corpus Angus filii Domini Angus de Ila."[123] The date of Angus' death is disputed, and he may have died as early as 1318.

By a handfast marriage to a daughter of Dugall MacEanruig, he had a son:[124]

- Iain Fraoch

Angus Óg had married Agnes O'Cahan, the daughter of the Irish Lord of Limavady, who ruled in Derry, Ireland. By her, he had: [125]

- *John of Islay* – the first Lord of the Isles

John of Islay, 1ˢᵗ Lord of the Isles
(d. 1380)

John of Islay was the first, and possibly most astute, of the four official Lords of the Isles.

John came to power soon after Robert I the Bruce's death. If you have read the *Stewart Dynasty* chapter, then you already know that this was a time of great turmoil. David II Bruce, the rightful king of Scotland, was a child, and Edward Balliol, son of deposed Scottish King John Balliol claimed the crown for himself, with English backing.[126]

John of Islay, in spite of his father's unwavering loyalty to Robert the Bruce, decided to support Edward Balliol.[127] [128] This may seem faithless of him, but there were reasons—primarily that the MacDonalds always put their interests ahead of those of Scotland, because they always felt that they were apart from, and equal to, Scotland. John backed Balliol mostly because the acting Regent of Scotland, the Earl of Mar, refused to confirm John in his inheritance, even though Angus Óg clearly had held his lands from Robert I.[129] When Edward Balliol promised (and did) confirm him in his lands, and in the wake of the Scottish disaster at the Battle of Halidon Hill in 1333, John went with the winning side.[130]

On 12 December 1335, John and Balliol entered into a treaty of alliance at Perth. In September 1336, John was granted Knapdale and Kintyre (held by the Stewarts). He added the Isles of Skye and Lewis (held by the Earl of Ross) once Balliol declared those lands forfeit. Finally, John also gained as a new charter for all of his other lands.[131]

John, however, knew the real power behind Balliol was King Edward III of England (see *Continental Dynasty*), and he made sure to keep a constant and cordial relationship with the king, although John never played any active role in moving against Edward's enemies in Scotland.[132]

When David II came back to power in Scotland in 1341, he forfeited John's lands. John ignored the forfeiture, and his power was never challenged in the Isles. John was safe in ignoring his king; David was powerless to enforce the forfeit order, since he was still at odds with England. David needed John's active help, or at least his neutrality, so that David could invade England. David made peace with John and confirmed him in all of his territory—but not the Stewart's Knapdale and Kintyre, or the Earl of Ross' Skye and Lewis.[133] [134]

John was already pretty well set, but then his father-in-law (possibly brother-in-law), Ranald MacRuairi died with no male heirs, and all of his lands passed to his daughter Amie MacRuairi. Although Amie and John were third cousins, they had obtained a papal dispensation to marry.[135] [136]

They had at least four children:[137]

- John (d. before 1369)
- Ranald
- Godfrey
- Mary – married Lachlan MacLean of Duart

Through his wife, John inherited Garmoran, Uist, Eigg, Barra, Rhum, and the rest of Lochaber. The Scottish government, perhaps still remembering Robert I's admonition not to let the Isles be controlled by one man, was reluctant to confirm so much land to one person. This reluctance flipped John back to the Balliol side of the ongoing conflict.[138] [139]

Robert Stewart became the Regent of Scotland (see *Stewart Dynasty*) after David's capture at Neville's Cross, and John was left unconfirmed in his lands—but also unmolested. In a 1353 treaty, John of Islay obtained control as overlord of most of John of Lorne's lands—lands which eventually passed to the Stewarts and then the Campbells. It was in this 1353 treaty that John of Islay first used the title "Lord of the Isles."[140]

There is a disputed story that John went to France with a Scottish force in 1354 to fight for King John, and that our John was captured by the English Black Prince at Poitiers in September 1356, then held in England until December 1357, when he was ransomed. His cordial relations with King Edward III were not renewed after this.[141] This legend has been well refuted as a misreading of the names of the captured—a Sir John de Isle was taken prisoner. Also, it was impossible for John of Islay to be both a prisoner of the English and an ally of the English at the Treaty of Berwick in the same year.

In 1360 John was the Governor of Edinburgh Castle. When Robert Stewart and his son rebelled against David II in 1363 and Robert was jailed, David made John Seneschal of Scotland. In 1366, John was sent to Flanders to negotiate a wool monopoly with the Flemings.[142]

However, discontent grew against David and his oppressive taxes, and John and some of the other magnates rebelled. David released Robert Stewart to curb the rebellion, and Robert brought John into line in 1369, in a surprisingly easy manner.[143] [144]

Actually, it was not so surprising, because by 1369, Robert Stewart and John of Islay were firm allies. John had married Robert's daughter Margaret in 1358, after divorcing his first wife Amie.[145] [146] Possibly, Amie had died by this time, since there is no record of the marriage being annulled. John's marriage to Margaret was a wise move on John's part—David still had no heir, which meant Robert was likely to become king someday. Also, Margaret was the heiress to lands John coveted—Knapdale and Kintyre.[147] [148]

In 1371, the new King Robert II Stewart confirmed John in all of his lands, including granting him Knapdale and Kintyre, providing that the lands devolved to Margaret's eldest son when John died.[149] [150] Amie and her sons were taken care of to their satisfaction, while ensuring that John and Margaret's eldest son, Donald, would be John's heir.[151]

John and Margaret had at least six children:

- Donald, 2nd Lord of the Isles (d. 1422)
- John Mor "The Tanister" (d. 1472)
- *Alasdair Carrach of Keppoch*
- Hugh
- *Margaret/Elizabeth* – married *Angus Du MacKay,* 6th Chief of Strathnaver
- Agnes – married Sir John Montgomery of Ardrossen

In 1380, John of Islay was taken ill of a flux (an excessive flow of fluid, such as a hemorrhage or diarrhea) at Ardgour, taken to Ardtornish, and died there three days later. He was buried at Icolkille.[152] Another source says he died in 1387 and was buried at Iona.[153]

His heir, Donald, was still a minor, but John's eldest son by Amie honored his agreement with his father and was a good regent for Donald's vast holdings.[154]

Donald inherited huge amounts of land. On the mainland, he held Lochaber, Gormoran, Morvern, Knapdale and Kintyre. In the islands, he held Islay, Gigha, Mull, Colonsay, Jura, Scarba, Tiree, Eigg, Rhum, Lewis, Harris, the Uists, Benbecula, and Barra.[155]

However, we do not follow Donald, 2nd Lord of the Isles. Our line passes through John's daughter *Margaret/Elizabeth*, who married *Angus Du MacKay*, 6th Chief of Strathnaver, sometime before October of 1415. For that story, go to the *MacKay Lineage* chapter.

Alasdair Carrach MacDonald of Keppoch

Alasdair was a son of John, a brother to the Margaret who married Angus Du MacKay of Strathnaver. In the *Book of MacKay*, it is said that after Margaret died, Angus married a daughter of Alasdair Carrach of Keppoch, Margaret's brother. In other words, Angus married his first wife's niece, which is why his second sons were considered illegitimate by the church—the laws of sanguinity.

I have found no mention of this marriage in the two MacDonald books I read, but just in case Alasdair is, in fact, our ancestor, here is a little information on his life.

When John died, Alasdair inherited part of Mull and lands in Lochaber beyond the Lochy in Mamore and Glen Spean.[156]

When the 3rd Lord of the Isles, Alexander, was imprisoned, the Earl of Mar invaded MacDonald lands. Alasdair fought for Alexander alongside Donald Balloch MacDonald, one of the clans' greatest warriors. At the Battle of Inverlochy, Alasdair's 220 archers helped the MacDonalds win the day.[157][158]

In retaliation, King James I (see *Stewart Dynasty*) took Alasdair's lands in Lochaber and gave them to the Mackintosh clan. The MacDonalds of Keppoch ignored the orders of the king and continued to hold the land by sword-right (meaning they would only leave by force of arms), creating a feud between the Keppoch MacDonalds and the Clan Chattan that lasted for 200 years.[159][160]

Alasdair Carrach of Keppoch was one of the four "great men" of Clan Donald who served on the Council of the Lordship of the Isles, which met at Finlaggan Castle in Islay.[161]

His descendants were the Clan MacDonald of Keppoch,[162] although our line (possibly) goes through his unnamed daughter who (possibly) married Angus Du MacKay of Strathnaver. To further muddy the issue, Raymond Campbell Paterson claims that John's son was Alexander (Alasdair), FATHER of Alasdair Carrach, with whom he is often confused. If this is true, then the woman who married Angus Du MacKay would not have been Alasdair Carrach's daughter, but his sister, daughter of Alasdair the Elder.

[1] Ronald Williams, *The Lords of the Isles: The Clan Donald and the Early Kingdom of the Scots* (Chatto & Windus - The Hogarth Press, London, 1984) p. 63.

[2] Ronald Williams, *The Lords of the Isles: The Clan Donald and the Early Kingdom of the Scots* (Chatto & Windus - The Hogarth Press, London, 1984) p. 63.

[3] Ronald Williams, *The Lords of the Isles: The Clan Donald and the Early Kingdom of the Scots* (Chatto & Windus - The Hogarth Press, London, 1984) p. 112.

[4] Ronald Williams, *The Lords of the Isles: The Clan Donald and the Early Kingdom of the Scots* (Chatto & Windus - The Hogarth Press, London, 1984) p. 112.

[5] Ronald Williams, *The Lords of the Isles: The Clan Donald and the Early Kingdom of the Scots* (Chatto & Windus - The Hogarth Press, London, 1984) p. 112.

[6] Ronald Williams, *The Lords of the Isles: The Clan Donald and the Early Kingdom of the Scots* (Chatto & Windus - The Hogarth Press, London, 1984) p. 63, 115.

[7] Ronald Williams, *The Lords of the Isles: The Clan Donald and the Early Kingdom of the Scots* (Chatto & Windus - The Hogarth Press, London, 1984) p. 112.

[8] Ronald Williams, *The Lords of the Isles: The Clan Donald and the Early Kingdom of the Scots* (Chatto & Windus - The Hogarth Press, London, 1984) p. 113.

[9] Ronald Williams, *The Lords of the Isles: The Clan Donald and the Early Kingdom of the Scots* (Chatto & Windus - The Hogarth Press, London, 1984) p. 119.

[10] Ronald Williams, *The Lords of the Isles: The Clan Donald and the Early Kingdom of the Scots* (Chatto & Windus - The Hogarth Press, London, 1984) p. 114.

[11] Ronald Williams, *The Lords of the Isles: The Clan Donald and the Early Kingdom of the Scots* (Chatto & Windus - The Hogarth Press, London, 1984) p. 114.

[12] Ronald Williams, *The Lords of the Isles: The Clan Donald and the Early Kingdom of the Scots* (Chatto & Windus - The Hogarth Press, London, 1984) p. 114.

[13] Ronald Williams, *The Lords of the Isles: The Clan Donald and the Early Kingdom of the Scots* (Chatto & Windus - The Hogarth Press, London, 1984), p. 115-116.

[14] Ronald Williams, *The Lords of the Isles: The Clan Donald and the Early Kingdom of the Scots* (Chatto & Windus - The Hogarth Press, London, 1984) p. 115-116.

[15] Ronald Williams, *The Lords of the Isles: The Clan Donald and the Early Kingdom of the Scots* (Chatto & Windus - The Hogarth Press, London, 1984) p. 115-116.

[16] Ronald Williams, *The Lords of the Isles: The Clan Donald and the Early Kingdom of the Scots* (Chatto & Windus - The Hogarth Press, London, 1984) p. 116.

[17] Ronald Williams, *The Lords of the Isles: The Clan Donald and the Early Kingdom of the Scots* (Chatto & Windus - The Hogarth Press, London, 1984) p. 116.

[18] Ronald Williams, *The Lords of the Isles: The Clan Donald and the Early Kingdom of the Scots* (Chatto & Windus - The Hogarth Press, London, 1984) p. 125.

[19] Ronald Williams, *The Lords of the Isles: The Clan Donald and the Early Kingdom of the Scots* (Chatto & Windus - The Hogarth Press, London, 1984) p. 125.

[20] Ronald Williams, *The Lords of the Isles: The Clan Donald and the Early Kingdom of the Scots* (Chatto & Windus - The Hogarth Press, London, 1984) p. 125.

[21] Ronald Williams, *The Lords of the Isles: The Clan Donald and the Early Kingdom of the Scots* (Chatto & Windus - The Hogarth Press, London, 1984) p. 117.

[22] Ronald Williams, *The Lords of the Isles: The Clan Donald and the Early Kingdom of the Scots* (Chatto & Windus - The Hogarth Press, London, 1984) p. 117.

[23] Ronald Williams, *The Lords of the Isles: The Clan Donald and the Early Kingdom of the Scots* (Chatto & Windus - The Hogarth Press, London, 1984) p. 117.

[24] Raymond Campbell Paterson, *The Lords of the Isles: A History of Clan Donald* (Birlinn Limited, Edinburgh, 2001), p. 6-7.

[25] Ronald Williams, *The Lords of the Isles: The Clan Donald and the Early Kingdom of the Scots* (Chatto & Windus - The Hogarth Press, London, 1984) p. 117.

[26] Raymond Campbell Paterson, *The Lords of the Isles: A History of Clan Donald* (Birlinn Limited, Edinburgh, 2001), p. 6-7.

[27] Ronald Williams, *The Lords of the Isles: The Clan Donald and the Early Kingdom of the Scots* (Chatto & Windus - The Hogarth Press, London, 1984) p. 118.

[28] Raymond Campbell Paterson, *The Lords of the Isles: A History of Clan Donald* (Birlinn Limited, Edinburgh, 2001), p. 7.

[29] Ronald Williams, *The Lords of the Isles: The Clan Donald and the Early Kingdom of the Scots* (Chatto & Windus - The Hogarth Press, London, 1984) p. 118.

[30] Raymond Campbell Paterson, *The Lords of the Isles: A History of Clan Donald* (Birlinn Limited, Edinburgh, 2001), p. 7.

[31] Ronald Williams, *The Lords of the Isles: The Clan Donald and the Early Kingdom of the Scots* (Chatto & Windus - The Hogarth Press, London, 1984) p. 119-20.

[32] Ronald Williams, *The Lords of the Isles: The Clan Donald and the Early Kingdom of the Scots* (Chatto & Windus - The Hogarth Press, London, 1984) p. 121.

[33] Raymond Campbell Paterson, *The Lords of the Isles: A History of Clan Donald* (Birlinn Limited, Edinburgh, 2001), p. 5.

[34] E. William Robertson, *Scotland Under Her Early Kings: A History of the Kingdom to the Close of the 13th Century, Part One* (Edinburgh: Edmonston and Douglas, 1862), p. 345.

[35] Angus MacKay, *The Book of MacKay* (Edinburgh: Norman MacLeod, 1906), p. 22.

[36] Ronald Williams, *The Lords of the Isles: The Clan Donald and the Early Kingdom of the Scots* (Chatto & Windus - The Hogarth Press, London, 1984) p. 121.

[37] Ronald Williams, *The Lords of the Isles: The Clan Donald and the Early Kingdom of the Scots* (Chatto & Windus - The Hogarth Press, London, 1984) p. 122.

[38] Raymond Campbell Paterson, *The Lords of the Isles: A History of Clan Donald* (Birlinn Limited, Edinburgh, 2001), p. 8.

[39] Ronald Williams, *The Lords of the Isles: The Clan Donald and the Early Kingdom of the Scots* (Chatto & Windus - The Hogarth Press, London, 1984) p. 123.

[40] Ronald Williams, *The Lords of the Isles: The Clan Donald and the Early Kingdom of the Scots* (Chatto & Windus - The Hogarth Press, London, 1984) p. 123.

[41] Raymond Campbell Paterson, *The Lords of the Isles: A History of Clan Donald* (Birlinn Limited, Edinburgh, 2001), p. 9-10.

[42] Ronald Williams, *The Lords of the Isles: The Clan Donald and the Early Kingdom of the Scots* (Chatto & Windus - The Hogarth Press, London, 1984) p. 123.

[43] Raymond Campbell Paterson, *The Lords of the Isles: A History of Clan Donald* (Birlinn Limited, Edinburgh, 2001), p. 9-10.

[44] Ronald Williams, *The Lords of the Isles: The Clan Donald and the Early Kingdom of the Scots* (Chatto & Windus - The Hogarth Press, London, 1984) p. 125.

[45] Ronald Williams, *The Lords of the Isles: The Clan Donald and the Early Kingdom of the Scots* (Chatto & Windus - The Hogarth Press, London, 1984) p. 127.

[46] Ronald Williams, *The Lords of the Isles: The Clan Donald and the Early Kingdom of the Scots* (Chatto & Windus - The Hogarth Press, London, 1984) p. 127.

[47] Raymond Campbell Paterson, *The Lords of the Isles: A History of Clan Donald* (Birlinn Limited, Edinburgh, 2001), p. 11.

[48] Ronald Williams, *The Lords of the Isles: The Clan Donald and the Early Kingdom of the Scots* (Chatto & Windus - The Hogarth Press, London, 1984) p. 127.

[49] Ronald Williams, *The Lords of the Isles: The Clan Donald and the Early Kingdom of the Scots* (Chatto & Windus - The Hogarth Press, London, 1984) p. 128.

[50] Ronald Williams, *The Lords of the Isles: The Clan Donald and the Early Kingdom of the Scots* (Chatto & Windus - The Hogarth Press, London, 1984) p. 128.

[51] Ronald Williams, *The Lords of the Isles: The Clan Donald and the Early Kingdom of the Scots* (Chatto & Windus - The Hogarth Press, London, 1984) p. 129.

[52] Ronald Williams, *The Lords of the Isles: The Clan Donald and the Early Kingdom of the Scots* (Chatto & Windus - The Hogarth Press, London, 1984) p. 129.

[53] Ronald Williams, *The Lords of the Isles: The Clan Donald and the Early Kingdom of the Scots* (Chatto & Windus - The Hogarth Press, London, 1984) p. 130.

[54] Ronald Williams, *The Lords of the Isles: The Clan Donald and the Early Kingdom of the Scots* (Chatto & Windus - The Hogarth Press, London, 1984) p. 132.

[55] Raymond Campbell Paterson, *The Lords of the Isles: A History of Clan Donald* (Birlinn Limited, Edinburgh, 2001), p. 11-12.

[56] Ronald Williams, *The Lords of the Isles: The Clan Donald and the Early Kingdom of the Scots* (Chatto & Windus - The Hogarth Press, London, 1984) p. 127.

[57] Ronald Williams, *The Lords of the Isles: The Clan Donald and the Early Kingdom of the Scots* (Chatto & Windus - The Hogarth Press, London, 1984) p. 132.

[58] Ronald Williams, *The Lords of the Isles: The Clan Donald and the Early Kingdom of the Scots* (Chatto & Windus - The Hogarth Press, London, 1984) p. 127.

[59] Ronald Williams, *The Lords of the Isles: The Clan Donald and the Early Kingdom of the Scots* (Chatto & Windus - The Hogarth Press, London, 1984) p. 132.

[60] Ronald Williams, *The Lords of the Isles: The Clan Donald and the Early Kingdom of the Scots* (Chatto & Windus - The Hogarth Press, London, 1984), p. 126, 132.

[61] Ronald Williams, *The Lords of the Isles: The Clan Donald and the Early Kingdom of the Scots* (Chatto & Windus - The Hogarth Press, London, 1984) p. 132-3

[62] Ronald Williams, *The Lords of the Isles: The Clan Donald and the Early Kingdom of the Scots* (Chatto & Windus - The Hogarth Press, London, 1984) p. 133.

[63] Raymond Campbell Paterson, *The Lords of the Isles: A History of Clan Donald* (Birlinn Limited, Edinburgh, 2001), p. 12.

[64] Ronald Williams, *The Lords of the Isles: The Clan Donald and the Early Kingdom of the Scots* (Chatto & Windus - The Hogarth Press, London, 1984) p. 133.

[65] Ronald Williams, *The Lords of the Isles: The Clan Donald and the Early Kingdom of the Scots* (Chatto & Windus - The Hogarth Press, London, 1984) p. 133.

[66] Ronald Williams, *The Lords of the Isles: The Clan Donald and the Early Kingdom of the Scots* (Chatto & Windus - The Hogarth Press, London, 1984) p. 133.

[67] Ronald Williams, *The Lords of the Isles: The Clan Donald and the Early Kingdom of the Scots* (Chatto & Windus - The Hogarth Press, London, 1984) p. 133.

[68] Ronald Williams, *The Lords of the Isles: The Clan Donald and the Early Kingdom of the Scots* (Chatto & Windus - The Hogarth Press, London, 1984) p. 134.

[69] Raymond Campbell Paterson, *The Lords of the Isles: A History of Clan Donald* (Birlinn Limited, Edinburgh, 2001), p. 12.

[70] Ronald Williams, *The Lords of the Isles: The Clan Donald and the Early Kingdom of the Scots* (Chatto & Windus - The Hogarth Press, London, 1984) p. 134.

[71] Ronald Williams, *The Lords of the Isles: The Clan Donald and the Early Kingdom of the Scots* (Chatto & Windus - The Hogarth Press, London, 1984) p. 136.

[72] Ronald Williams, *The Lords of the Isles: The Clan Donald and the Early Kingdom of the Scots* (Chatto & Windus - The Hogarth Press, London, 1984) p. 136.

[73] Ronald Williams, *The Lords of the Isles: The Clan Donald and the Early Kingdom of the Scots* (Chatto & Windus - The Hogarth Press, London, 1984) p. 137.

[74] Ronald Williams, *The Lords of the Isles: The Clan Donald and the Early Kingdom of the Scots* (Chatto & Windus - The Hogarth Press, London, 1984) p. 137.

[75] Ronald Williams, *The Lords of the Isles: The Clan Donald and the Early Kingdom of the Scots* (Chatto & Windus - The Hogarth Press, London, 1984) p. 137.

[76] Ronald Williams, *The Lords of the Isles: The Clan Donald and the Early Kingdom of the Scots* (Chatto & Windus - The Hogarth Press, London, 1984) p. 132.

[77] Ronald Williams, *The Lords of the Isles: The Clan Donald and the Early Kingdom of the Scots* (Chatto & Windus - The Hogarth Press, London, 1984) p. 138.

[78] Raymond Campbell Paterson, *The Lords of the Isles: A History of Clan Donald* (Birlinn Limited, Edinburgh, 2001), p. 15.

[79] Ronald Williams, *The Lords of the Isles: The Clan Donald and the Early Kingdom of the Scots* (Chatto & Windus - The Hogarth Press, London, 1984) p. 138.

[80] Ronald Williams, *The Lords of the Isles: The Clan Donald and the Early Kingdom of the Scots* (Chatto & Windus - The Hogarth Press, London, 1984) p. 139.

[81] Raymond Campbell Paterson, *The Lords of the Isles: A History of Clan Donald* (Birlinn Limited, Edinburgh, 2001), p. 15.

[82] Ronald Williams, *The Lords of the Isles: The Clan Donald and the Early Kingdom of the Scots* (Chatto & Windus - The Hogarth Press, London, 1984) p. 139.

[83] Raymond Campbell Paterson, *The Lords of the Isles: A History of Clan Donald* (Birlinn Limited, Edinburgh, 2001), p. 15.

[84] Ronald Williams, *The Lords of the Isles: The Clan Donald and the Early Kingdom of the Scots* (Chatto & Windus - The Hogarth Press, London, 1984) p. 140.

[85] Raymond Campbell Paterson, *The Lords of the Isles: A History of Clan Donald* (Birlinn Limited, Edinburgh, 2001), p. 15.

[86] Ronald Williams, *The Lords of the Isles: The Clan Donald and the Early Kingdom of the Scots* (Chatto & Windus - The Hogarth Press, London, 1984) p. 140.

[87] Ronald Williams, *The Lords of the Isles: The Clan Donald and the Early Kingdom of the Scots* (Chatto & Windus - The Hogarth Press, London, 1984) p. 141.

[88] Ronald Williams, *The Lords of the Isles: The Clan Donald and the Early Kingdom of the Scots* (Chatto & Windus - The Hogarth Press, London, 1984) p. 141.

[89] Raymond Campbell Paterson, *The Lords of the Isles: A History of Clan Donald* (Birlinn Limited, Edinburgh, 2001), p. 16.

[90] Ronald Williams, *The Lords of the Isles: The Clan Donald and the Early Kingdom of the Scots* (Chatto & Windus - The Hogarth Press, London, 1984) p. 141.

[91] Raymond Campbell Paterson, *The Lords of the Isles: A History of Clan Donald* (Birlinn Limited, Edinburgh, 2001), p. 17.

[92] Ronald Williams, *The Lords of the Isles: The Clan Donald and the Early Kingdom of the Scots* (Chatto & Windus - The Hogarth Press, London, 1984) p. 145.

[93] Ronald Williams, *The Lords of the Isles: The Clan Donald and the Early Kingdom of the Scots* (Chatto & Windus - The Hogarth Press, London, 1984) p. 149.

[94] Raymond Campbell Paterson, *The Lords of the Isles: A History of Clan Donald* (Birlinn Limited, Edinburgh, 2001), p. 17.

[95] Ronald Williams, *The Lords of the Isles: The Clan Donald and the Early Kingdom of the Scots* (Chatto & Windus - The Hogarth Press, London, 1984) p. 149.

[96] Raymond Campbell Paterson, *The Lords of the Isles: A History of Clan Donald* (Birlinn Limited, Edinburgh, 2001), p. 18.

[97] Ronald Williams, *The Lords of the Isles: The Clan Donald and the Early Kingdom of the Scots* (Chatto & Windus - The Hogarth Press, London, 1984) p. 149.

[98] Raymond Campbell Paterson, *The Lords of the Isles: A History of Clan Donald* (Birlinn Limited, Edinburgh, 2001), p. 17-8.
[99] Ronald Williams, *The Lords of the Isles: The Clan Donald and the Early Kingdom of the Scots* (Chatto & Windus - The Hogarth Press, London, 1984) p. 149.
[100] Ronald Williams, *The Lords of the Isles: The Clan Donald and the Early Kingdom of the Scots* (Chatto & Windus - The Hogarth Press, London, 1984) p. 149.
[101] Ronald Williams, *The Lords of the Isles: The Clan Donald and the Early Kingdom of the Scots* (Chatto & Windus - The Hogarth Press, London, 1984) p. 149.
[102] Raymond Campbell Paterson, *The Lords of the Isles: A History of Clan Donald* (Birlinn Limited, Edinburgh, 2001), p. 20.
[103] Ronald Williams, *The Lords of the Isles: The Clan Donald and the Early Kingdom of the Scots* (Chatto & Windus - The Hogarth Press, London, 1984), p. 149.
[104] Ronald Williams, *The Lords of the Isles: The Clan Donald and the Early Kingdom of the Scots* (Chatto & Windus - The Hogarth Press, London, 1984) p. 153.
[105] Raymond Campbell Paterson, *The Lords of the Isles: A History of Clan Donald* (Birlinn Limited, Edinburgh, 2001), p. 20.
[106] Ronald Williams, *The Lords of the Isles: The Clan Donald and the Early Kingdom of the Scots* (Chatto & Windus - The Hogarth Press, London, 1984) p. 154.
[107] Raymond Campbell Paterson, *The Lords of the Isles: A History of Clan Donald* (Birlinn Limited, Edinburgh, 2001), p. 21.
[108] Ronald Williams, *The Lords of the Isles: The Clan Donald and the Early Kingdom of the Scots* (Chatto & Windus - The Hogarth Press, London, 1984) p. 154.
[109] Raymond Campbell Paterson, *The Lords of the Isles: A History of Clan Donald* (Birlinn Limited, Edinburgh, 2001), p. 21.
[110] Ronald Williams, *The Lords of the Isles: The Clan Donald and the Early Kingdom of the Scots* (Chatto & Windus - The Hogarth Press, London, 1984) p. 154.
[111] Ronald Williams, *The Lords of the Isles: The Clan Donald and the Early Kingdom of the Scots* (Chatto & Windus - The Hogarth Press, London, 1984) p. 154.
[112] Raymond Campbell Paterson, *The Lords of the Isles: A History of Clan Donald* (Birlinn Limited, Edinburgh, 2001), p. 21.
[113] Ronald Williams, *The Lords of the Isles: The Clan Donald and the Early Kingdom of the Scots* (Chatto & Windus - The Hogarth Press, London, 1984) p. 155.
[114] Ronald Williams, *The Lords of the Isles: The Clan Donald and the Early Kingdom of the Scots* (Chatto & Windus - The Hogarth Press, London, 1984) p. 155.
[115] Raymond Campbell Paterson, *The Lords of the Isles: A History of Clan Donald* (Birlinn Limited, Edinburgh, 2001), p. 21.
[116] Ronald Williams, *The Lords of the Isles: The Clan Donald and the Early Kingdom of the Scots* (Chatto & Windus - The Hogarth Press, London, 1984) p. 157.
[117] Raymond Campbell Paterson, *The Lords of the Isles: A History of Clan Donald* (Birlinn Limited, Edinburgh, 2001), p. 20.
[118] Ronald Williams, *The Lords of the Isles: The Clan Donald and the Early Kingdom of the Scots* (Chatto & Windus - The Hogarth Press, London, 1984) p. 158-61.
[119] Raymond Campbell Paterson, *The Lords of the Isles: A History of Clan Donald* (Birlinn Limited, Edinburgh, 2001), p. 22.
[120] Ronald Williams, *The Lords of the Isles: The Clan Donald and the Early Kingdom of the Scots* (Chatto & Windus - The Hogarth Press, London, 1984) p. 161.
[121] Ronald Williams, *The Lords of the Isles: The Clan Donald and the Early Kingdom of the Scots* (Chatto & Windus - The Hogarth Press, London, 1984) p. 162.
[122] Ronald Williams, *The Lords of the Isles: The Clan Donald and the Early Kingdom of the Scots* (Chatto & Windus - The Hogarth Press, London, 1984) p. 162.
[123] Ronald Williams, *The Lords of the Isles: The Clan Donald and the Early Kingdom of the Scots* (Chatto & Windus - The Hogarth Press, London, 1984) p. 169.
[124] Ronald Williams, *The Lords of the Isles: The Clan Donald and the Early Kingdom of the Scots* (Chatto & Windus - The Hogarth Press, London, 1984) p. 170.
[125] Ronald Williams, *The Lords of the Isles: The Clan Donald and the Early Kingdom of the Scots* (Chatto & Windus - The Hogarth Press, London, 1984) p. 169-70.
[126] Ronald Williams, *The Lords of the Isles: The Clan Donald and the Early Kingdom of the Scots* (Chatto & Windus - The Hogarth Press, London, 1984) p. 170.
[127] Ronald Williams, *The Lords of the Isles: The Clan Donald and the Early Kingdom of the Scots* (Chatto & Windus - The Hogarth Press, London, 1984) p. 170.
[128] Raymond Campbell Paterson, *The Lords of the Isles: A History of Clan Donald* (Birlinn Limited, Edinburgh, 2001), p. 25.
[129] Ronald Williams, *The Lords of the Isles: The Clan Donald and the Early Kingdom of the Scots* (Chatto & Windus - The Hogarth Press, London, 1984) p. 171.
[130] Raymond Campbell Paterson, *The Lords of the Isles: A History of Clan Donald* (Birlinn Limited, Edinburgh, 2001), p. 25.
[131] Ronald Williams, *The Lords of the Isles: The Clan Donald and the Early Kingdom of the Scots* (Chatto & Windus - The Hogarth Press, London, 1984) p. 171.
[132] Ronald Williams, *The Lords of the Isles: The Clan Donald and the Early Kingdom of the Scots* (Chatto & Windus - The Hogarth Press, London, 1984) p. 172-3.
[133] Ronald Williams, *The Lords of the Isles: The Clan Donald and the Early Kingdom of the Scots* (Chatto & Windus - The Hogarth Press, London, 1984) p. 173.
[134] Raymond Campbell Paterson, *The Lords of the Isles: A History of Clan Donald* (Birlinn Limited, Edinburgh, 2001), p. 26.

[135] Ronald Williams, *The Lords of the Isles: The Clan Donald and the Early Kingdom of the Scots* (Chatto & Windus - The Hogarth Press, London, 1984) p. 174.

[136] Raymond Campbell Paterson, *The Lords of the Isles: A History of Clan Donald* (Birlinn Limited, Edinburgh, 2001), p. 26.

[137] Ronald Williams, *The Lords of the Isles: The Clan Donald and the Early Kingdom of the Scots* (Chatto & Windus - The Hogarth Press, London, 1984) p. 166, 180.

[138] Ronald Williams, *The Lords of the Isles: The Clan Donald and the Early Kingdom of the Scots* (Chatto & Windus - The Hogarth Press, London, 1984) p. 174.

[139] Raymond Campbell Paterson, *The Lords of the Isles: A History of Clan Donald* (Birlinn Limited, Edinburgh, 2001), p. 26.

[140] Ronald Williams, *The Lords of the Isles: The Clan Donald and the Early Kingdom of the Scots* (Chatto & Windus - The Hogarth Press, London, 1984) p. 174-5.

[141] Ronald Williams, *The Lords of the Isles: The Clan Donald and the Early Kingdom of the Scots* (Chatto & Windus - The Hogarth Press, London, 1984) p. 175.

[142] Ronald Williams, *The Lords of the Isles: The Clan Donald and the Early Kingdom of the Scots* (Chatto & Windus - The Hogarth Press, London, 1984) p. 176.

[143] Ronald Williams, *The Lords of the Isles: The Clan Donald and the Early Kingdom of the Scots* (Chatto & Windus - The Hogarth Press, London, 1984) p. 176.

[144] Raymond Campbell Paterson, *The Lords of the Isles: A History of Clan Donald* (Birlinn Limited, Edinburgh, 2001), p. 27.

[145] Ronald Williams, *The Lords of the Isles: The Clan Donald and the Early Kingdom of the Scots* (Chatto & Windus - The Hogarth Press, London, 1984) p. 176.

[146] Raymond Campbell Paterson, *The Lords of the Isles: A History of Clan Donald* (Birlinn Limited, Edinburgh, 2001), p. 27-8.

[147] Ronald Williams, *The Lords of the Isles: The Clan Donald and the Early Kingdom of the Scots* (Chatto & Windus - The Hogarth Press, London, 1984) p. 177.

[148] Raymond Campbell Paterson, *The Lords of the Isles: A History of Clan Donald* (Birlinn Limited, Edinburgh, 2001), p. 27-8.

[149] Ronald Williams, *The Lords of the Isles: The Clan Donald and the Early Kingdom of the Scots* (Chatto & Windus - The Hogarth Press, London, 1984) p. 178.

[150] Raymond Campbell Paterson, *The Lords of the Isles: A History of Clan Donald* (Birlinn Limited, Edinburgh, 2001), p. 27-8

[151] Ronald Williams, *The Lords of the Isles: The Clan Donald and the Early Kingdom of the Scots* (Chatto & Windus - The Hogarth Press, London, 1984) p. 177.

[152] Ronald Williams, *The Lords of the Isles: The Clan Donald and the Early Kingdom of the Scots* (Chatto & Windus - The Hogarth Press, London, 1984) p. 178.

[153] Raymond Campbell Paterson, *The Lords of the Isles: A History of Clan Donald* (Birlinn Limited, Edinburgh, 2001), p. 27-8.

[154] Ronald Williams, *The Lords of the Isles: The Clan Donald and the Early Kingdom of the Scots* (Chatto & Windus - The Hogarth Press, London, 1984) p. 178.

[155] Ronald Williams, *The Lords of the Isles: The Clan Donald and the Early Kingdom of the Scots* (Chatto & Windus - The Hogarth Press, London, 1984) p. 178.

[156] Ronald Williams, *The Lords of the Isles: The Clan Donald and the Early Kingdom of the Scots* (Chatto & Windus - The Hogarth Press, London, 1984) p. 182.

[157] Ronald Williams, *The Lords of the Isles: The Clan Donald and the Early Kingdom of the Scots* (Chatto & Windus - The Hogarth Press, London, 1984) p. 200-1.

[158] Raymond Campbell Paterson, *The Lords of the Isles: A History of Clan Donald* (Birlinn Limited, Edinburgh, 2001), p. 43-4.

[159] Ronald Williams, *The Lords of the Isles: The Clan Donald and the Early Kingdom of the Scots* (Chatto & Windus - The Hogarth Press, London, 1984) p. 202.

[160] Raymond Campbell Paterson, *The Lords of the Isles: A History of Clan Donald* (Birlinn Limited, Edinburgh, 2001), p. 44.

[161] Ronald Williams, *The Lords of the Isles: The Clan Donald and the Early Kingdom of the Scots* (Chatto & Windus - The Hogarth Press, London, 1984) p. 209.

[162] Ronald Williams, *The Lords of the Isles: The Clan Donald and the Early Kingdom of the Scots* (Chatto & Windus - The Hogarth Press, London, 1984) p. 182.

THE NORWEGIANS:
THE JARLS OF ORKNEY &
THE EARLS OF CAITHNESS

SHETLAND & ORKNEY
OWNED BY NORWAY

HISTORIC CAITHNESS,
OWNED BY SCOTLAND
(MODERN SUTHERLAND &
CAITHNESS COUNTIES)

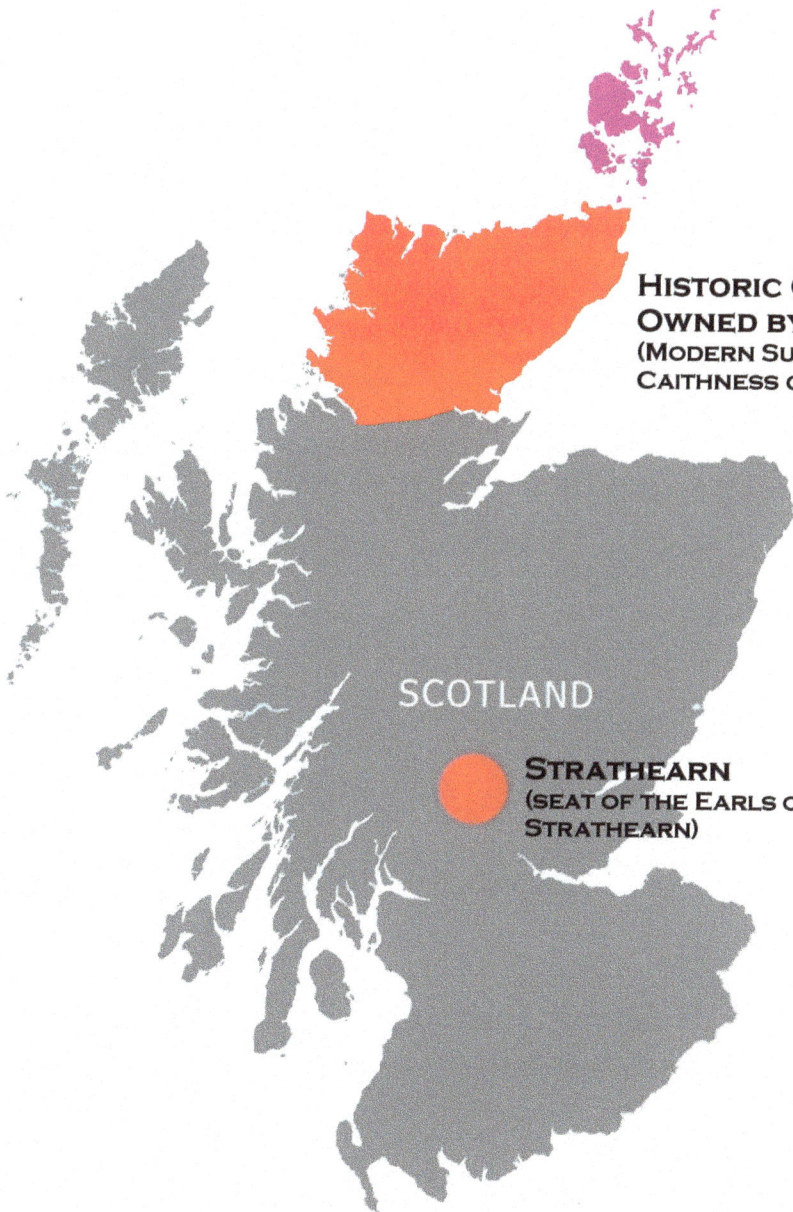

SCOTLAND

STRATHEARN
(SEAT OF THE EARLS OF
STRATHEARN)

THE JARLS OF ORKNEY & THE EARLS OF CAITHNESS (NORWEGIAN LINEAGE)

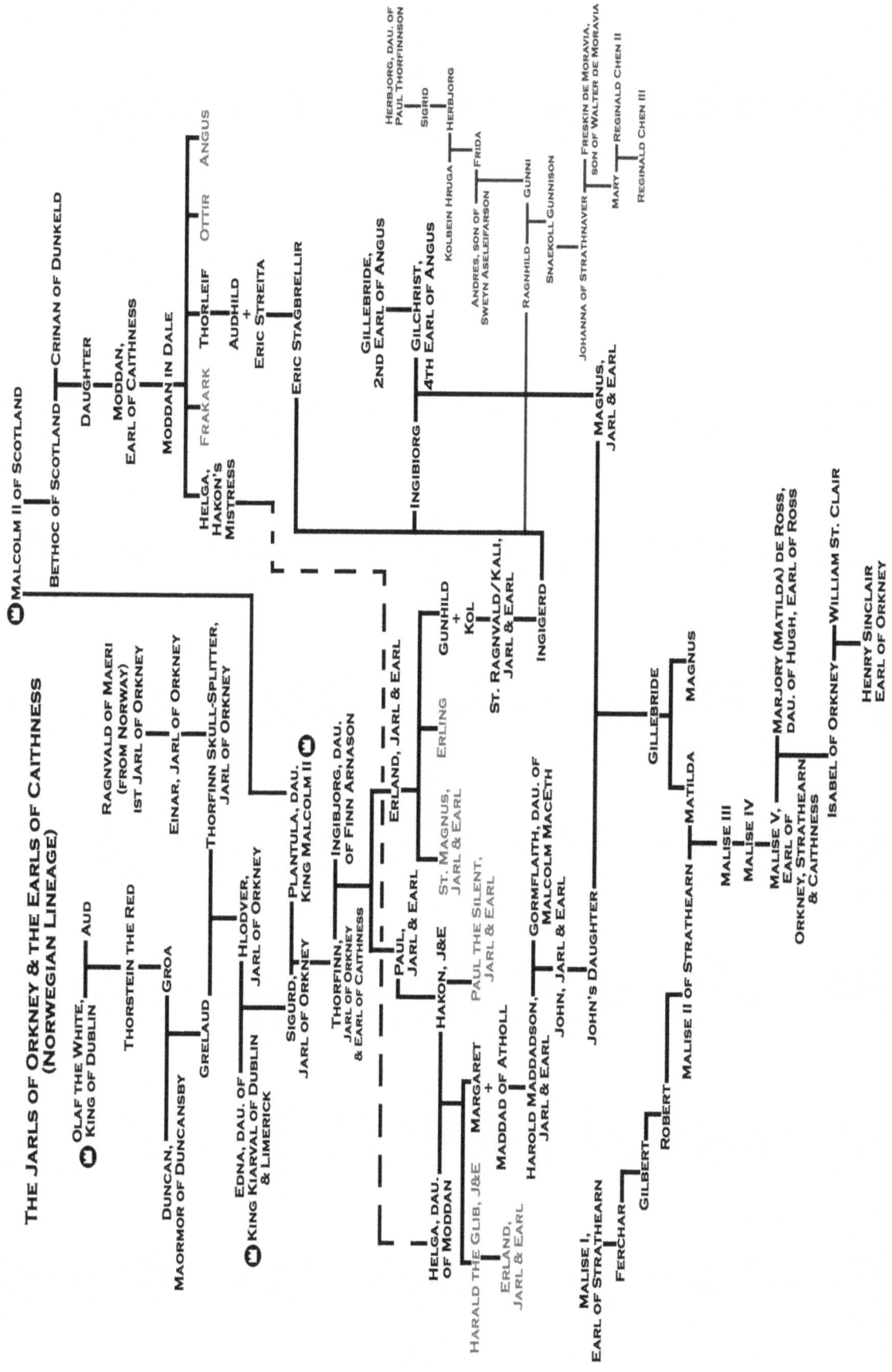

MALCOLM II OF SCOTLAND

BETHOC OF SCOTLAND — CRINAN OF DUNKELD

DAUGHTER

MODDAN, EARL OF CAITHNESS

MODDAN IN DALE

FRAKARK — THORLEIF — OTTIR — ANGUS

AUDHILD + ERIC STREITA

HELGA, HAKON'S MISTRESS

ERIC STAGBRELLIR

GILLEBRIDE, 2ND EARL OF ANGUS

GILCHRIST, 4TH EARL OF ANGUS

INGIBIORG

HERBJORG, DAU. OF PAUL THORFINNSON

SIGRID

KOLBEIN HRUGA — HERBJORG

ANDRES, SON OF SWEYN ASELEIFARSON — FRIDA

GUNNI

RAGNHILD — SNAEKOLL GUNNISON

JOHANNA OF STRATHNAVER

FRESKIN DE MORAVIA, SON OF WALTER DE MORAVIA

MARY — REGINALD CHEN II

REGINALD CHEN III

MAGNUS, JARL & EARL

OLAF THE WHITE, KING OF DUBLIN — AUD

THORSTEIN THE RED

RAGNVALD OF MAERI (FROM NORWAY) 1ST JARL OF ORKNEY

DUNCAN, MAORMOR OF DUNCANSBY

GROA

GRELAUD

EINAR, JARL OF ORKNEY

THORFINN SKULL-SPLITTER, JARL OF ORKNEY

HLODVER, JARL OF ORKNEY

EDNA, DAU. OF KING KIARVAL OF DUBLIN & LIMERICK

SIGURD, JARL OF ORKNEY

PLANTULA, DAU. KING MALCOLM II

INGIBJORG, DAU. OF FINN ARNASON

THORFINN, JARL OF ORKNEY & EARL OF CAITHNESS

ERLAND, JARL & EARL

GUNHILD + KOL

ST. RAGNVALD/KALI, JARL & EARL

INGIGERD

ERLING

PAUL, JARL & EARL

ST. MAGNUS, JARL & EARL

HAKON, J&E

PAUL THE SILENT, JARL & EARL

MARGARET + MADDAD OF ATHOLL

HELGA, DAU. OF MODDAN

HARALD THE GLIB, J&E

ERLAND, JARL & EARL

HAROLD MADDADSON, JARL & EARL

GORMFLAITH, DAU. OF MALCOLM MACETH

JOHN, JARL & EARL

JOHN'S DAUGHTER

GILLEBRIDE

MAGNUS

MALISE I, EARL OF STRATHEARN

FERCHAR

GILBERT

ROBERT

MALISE II OF STRATHEARN

MALISE OF STRATHEARN — MATILDA

MALISE III

MALISE IV

MALISE V, EARL OF ORKNEY, STRATHEARN & CAITHNESS

MARJORY (MATILDA) DE ROSS, DAU. OF HUGH, EARL OF ROSS

ISABEL OF ORKNEY — WILLIAM ST. CLAIR

HENRY SINCLAIR EARL OF ORKNEY

NORWEGIANS: THE JARLS OF ORKNEY & THE EARLS OF CAITHNESS

With genealogy that reaches as far back as 870 A.D., we must allow for embellishment and error. But it is fun stuff and there is always truth somewhere in the mists. Many of the sources I used pull information from the same Norse sagas. However, different interpretations sometimes have different dates attached and even different relationships (such as someone being cited as a sister vs. a daughter). Since *Sutherland and Caithness in Saga-Time* was a work devoted to the Sagas in particular, I chose to use James Gray's translation as the authoritative one. Dates in parentheses are dates they held power, not birth or death dates.

The Norwegian lineage was often convoluted—many people claimed the earldoms, and one family married into another then they fell out, then they married again. … In the end, the Earldoms of Orkney and Caithness ended up in our *Sinclair Lineage*, which is in another chapter. "Jarl" is Norse for "earl."

The lineage tree on the previous page has one branch and a few names that are printed in a lighter gray. This branch (Ragnhild and Gunni) and names are not in our direct line, but they do figure into the story, and this will help place them in the family.

It is worth noting that although this is the Norse lineage, many of the jarls we will see are only partly Norse. Once the full-blooded Norsemen got to Scotland, they usually married Gaelic women.[1] So the actual ratio of Norse blood versus Gaelic blood fluctuates wildly from one generation to the next.

The Orkney and Shetland Islands are easily found on a map. The area known as "Caithness" is a little more confusing, as it was on the Scottish mainland. It encompassed all of the modern counties of Caithness and Sutherland, and perhaps the northern part of modern Ross and Cromarty county.[2] This area extends across the entire North Atlantic coast, down the eastern coast to include Dornoch Firth, and down the western coast to Eddrachillis Bay, and possibly farther. We see much of this same area in the *MacKay Lineage* chapter and the *Sinclair Lineage* chapter.

Our Norse saga starts in the 870s. Norway, Sweden, and Denmark were consolidating, becoming feudal monarchies. Viking warriors rebelled against the feudal rules, refusing to become subservient to any overlord. They ran to the Scottish islands and Ireland to maintain their liberty.[3]

In 872, Harald Harfagr, King of Norway, brought a fleet to the Orkney and Shetland Islands, intending to once and for all crush a group of rebellious Vikings hiding there.[4] With him was his good friend Ragnvald, Jarl of Maeri. Ragnvald's son Ivar was killed in the fighting, even though King Harald was successful. To make up for this loss, King Harald made Ragnvald Jarl of Orkney and the Shetland.[5]

Ragnvald of Maeri, 1st Jarl of Orkney and Shetland

Ragnvald of Maeri didn't want to go to Orkney, since he already held the Jarldom of Maeri in Norway, and was settled there with his family. So, he gave the jarldom to his brother Sigurd.[6]

Sigurd (2nd Jarl of Orkney) allied with Thorstein the Red and they invaded mainland Scotland, conquering all of Caithness and Sutherland. King Constantine I of Scotland (see *MacAlpin Dynasty*) signed over these lands to Thorstein, but then betrayed the treaty and killed Thorstein.[7][8]

Sigurd's reign ended in 890, after a victory over Scottish Mormaer (earl) Malbride the Buck-Tooth. Sigurd killed Malbride, and hung the man's head off his saddle horn as a trophy. Malbride's bucktooth supposedly chafed his leg as he rode; the cut became infected, and he died. [9] His son Guthorm (3rd Jarl of Orkney) ruled for one winter, then died, and the jarldom reverted back to Ragnvald and his sons.[10] [11] [12]

Ragnvald had five sons, the eldest killed on Orkney with King Harald. His remaining children were Hallad, Thorir, Hrollaug (this may have been Rollo, later 1st Duke of Normandy) and *Einar*. Ragnvald sent Hallad (4th Jarl of Orkney) to Orkney, but he returned when things got too rough for him there.[13] [14] [15]

Ragnvald's youngest son, Einar, who was the son of a slave woman and therefore not fully Norse, volunteered to go. Einar, who was purportedly quite ugly, said to his father, "If you let me go, you'll never have to see my face again." Ragnvald supposedly replied, "Go, and don't come back."[16] [17] [18]

In 891, Einar successfully subdued Orkney in the name of Norway.[19] [20] He had a decent relationship with the people on the Scottish mainland, because he taught the people of Turfness, county Moray, how to use peat for fuel, and is often called Torf-Einar.[21]

Ragnvald of Maeri was murdered by two of King Harald Harfagr's sons between 891 and 900. [22] [23]

Einar Ragnvaldsson, 5th Jarl of Orkney and Shetland (891-920)

Einar Ragnvaldsson claimed his jarldom in Orkney in 891. He cleared the pirate Vikings from his islands, and subdued all resistance.[24]

After his father's murder, Einar returned to Norway to avenge his death. However, one of the murderers, Halfdan Halegg (Long-shanks) fled from Norway to Orkney, and usurped Orkney in Einar's absence. Einar returned in force and defeated Halfdan in North Ronaldsay Firth. Halfdan tried to escape by hiding among the fugitives, but Einar spied him and killed him using the torturous "spread-eagle" or "blood-eagle" death.[25] [26] [27]

In 900, King Harald came to Orkney to avenge his son's ignominious death. However, he was satisfied with the payment of 60 marks of gold to atone for the death, because Einar was provoked by the murder of his father, who had also been King Harald's friend.[28] [29]

Einar was a successful jarl, and he died "in bed" (a disdainful euphemism for any death not in battle) in 920.[30]

Einar had three sons: Arnkell, Erland, and *Thorfinn Hausa-Kliufr (Skull-Splitter)*. Arnkell and Erland joined the expedition of Eric Bloodaxe to England, and were killed there, leaving Thorfinn to claim the jarldom.[31] [32] [33]

Thorfinn Skull-Splitter Einarson, 6th Jarl of Orkney and Shetland (920-963)

Thorfinn Skull-Splitter Einarson married Grelaud, daughter of Groa and Duncan, Mormaor of Caithness, Scotland.[34] Groa herself was the daughter of Thorstein the Red, who was killed in 875 by King Constantine I, son of Kenneth MacAlpin, (see *MacAlpin Dynasty*). Thorstein was a Viking from Ireland, son of King

Olaf "the White" Hvitr of Dublin, and Aud.[35] Olaf the White was the son of King Lochlann or Ingiald of Norway, and he later married an Irish princess and a daughter of Kenneth MacAlpin, King of Alba (Scotland), in order to secure his positions.[36] Aud "the Deep-Minded" was the daughter of Ketil Flatnose, a Norse earl of the northern isles, who refused to pay taxes to the Norwegian king and was ran away to Iceland.[37] Thorfinn's marriage to Grelaud brought a great deal of mainland territories into Thorfinn's holdings.[38]

Thorfinn was a great chief and fighter, although (despite his name) he preferred peace. He also "died in bed" in 963 and is buried at Hoxa, Mound's Isthmus on South Ronaldsay.[39]

Thorfinn had five sons: Arnfinn, Havard, *Hlodver*, Ljotr and Skuli. Three of the sons had the misfortune of marrying Ragnhild, daughter of Eric Bloodaxe. Arnfinn and Havard were both murdered at Ragnhild's instigation, and she finally married Ljotr.[40] [41] [42]

Son Skuli decided that, rather than fight his brother Lotjr (who was the current, 9th jarl, after Arnfinn the 7th and Havard the 8th) for Orkney, he would claim their mainland lands in Caithness legally. Skuli went to the Scottish court, and made his case. The king created him Earl of Caithness, and sent Skuli off to claim it by force from his brother.[43] [44]

He squared off against his brother Ljotr and was killed by Ljotr. Ljotr died of wounds after the Battle of Skitten Moor.[45] [46] That left Hlodver as the last son standing, and he inherited the Jarldom of Orkney.[47]

Hlodver Thorfinnson, 10th Jarl of Orkney and Shetland (963-980)

Hlodver Thorfinnson escaped the wiles of evil Ragnhild and married Edna, the daughter of Kiarval, King of the Hy Ivar of Dublin and Limerick.[48] He was a peaceful jarl, and died in bed in 980. He was buried at Hofn, probably Huna, in Caithness, near John O'Groats (the northeastern-most town on the tip of mainland Scotland).[49]

His son *Sigurd the Stout* took over the jarldom.[50] [51]

Sigurd Hlodverson, 11th Jarl of Orkney and Shetland (980 – 1014)

Sigurd Hlodverson was not satisfied with just having the Orkneys and Shetland, and he claimed all Caithness through the blood of Duncan, his great-grandfather. Sigurd was, in fact, two-thirds Gaelic.[52]

His claim to Caithness was not well received. Two Celtic chiefs, Crinan of Dunkeld and Maelsnechtan of Moray, opposed him. They met in the Battle of Dungal's Noep, and Sigurd was victorious, although he had such great losses that he retreated to Orkney.[53] [54]

While most of mainland Scotland was Christian (or at least nominally so), the Norse Orkneys were still pagan Odinists. As Sigurd returned from the Dungal's Noep battle, King Olaf Tryggvison of Norway captured him. King Olaf told him that Sigurd would convert to Christianity or die. Sigurd and the Orkneys converted on the spot.[55] To keep Sigurd honest in his loyalty to the Norwegian king and to Christianity, King Olaf took Sigurd's son Hundi as a hostage, and Hundi later died in captivity.[56] [57]

Sigurd then deserted the Norse cause for the Scots side. He assisted King Malcolm II (see *MacAlpin Dynasty*) in subduing Moray. [58] [59] Malcolm II was grateful for his help, and Sigurd married Malcolm's daughter, Plantula, as his second wife in 1007. [60] [61] [62]

Sigurd also tried to exert his authority over the Western Isles by appointing his son-in-law Gilli (or Gilledomnan) as their governor. Gilledomnan is said to be the grandfather of Somerled of the Isles (see *MacDonald Lineage*).[63]

Sigurd was famous for his Raven banner,[64] which was made by his Irish mother, Edna. Another version of the legend has the banner being made by a seeress Audna at Skida Myre.[65] Both versions claimed that the banner was enchanted, and would bring victory to the host that followed it, but death to the individual who carried it. [66] [67]

Sigurd became embroiled in an Irish dispute because of his blood relation to the Kings of Dublin. The dispute was between the heathen king of Dublin, Sigtrigg Silkbeard, and the Christian king, Brian Boru. Sigurd, though a convert to Christianity, sided with the Dublin king.[68] On 23 April 1014, the two sides met at Clontarf. During the battle, Sigurd's Raven banner-carrier fell, and Sigurd himself took it up. Sigurd Hlodverson died on the battlefield, killed by Murchad, son of Brian Boru, High King of Erin. [69] [70] [71]

Thorfinn Sigurdson, 13th Jarl of Orkney and Shetland, and 1st Earl of Caithness (1014-1057)

Thorfinn Sigurdson, born 1008, was the son of Sigurd and Plantula.[72] [73] Although he was a Norse earl, by blood Thorfinn was mostly Gaelic.[74]

When Sigurd died in 1014, Thorfinn was six years old. He was not Sigurd's only son—Sigurd had three older sons by his first wife. Somerled, Brusi, and Einar (12th co-jarls of Orkney) claimed the Orkney Islands, splitting them between them.[75] King Malcolm II of Scotland (see *MacAlpin Dynasty*) immediately created Thorfinn as Earl of Caithness, so that Malcolm could secure the north of Scotland to the crown.[76] Remember, Thorfinn is Malcolm's grandson, and some say that he was raised at the court of his grandfather. [77] [78]

Thorfinn established himself at Duncansby in Caithness, on the shore of the Pentland Firth. Duncansby was also the seat of Thorfinn's great-great-grandfather Duncan. He spent much of his youth trying to consolidate the Orkneys and Shetland into his rule, much assisted in his quest by his grandfather Malcolm II.[79] When his brother Somerled died, Thorfinn inherited his third of Orkney.[80]

When Thorfinn came of age, he went to his brothers and demanded this third of the Orkneys as his by right. Brusi and Einar agreed to this.[81] Then Einar killed a Norse subject, angering King Olaf of Norway. Thorfinn and Einar traveled to Norway, but Einar remained in disgrace, while Thorfinn became a favorite of the king, which angered Einar.[82]

Thorfinn's friend Thorkel tried to make peace between the brothers, but Einar planned three ambushes on Thorkel. Thorkel survived them all, and then killed Einar at Thorkel's hall in Sandvik, in Deerness, Kirkwall. Thorkel ran to King Olaf, who welcomed him gratefully.[83]

Upon Einar's death, Brusi and Thorfinn disputed over his portion of Orkney. King Olaf the Stout of Norway decided that Einar's portion should go to Brusi, leaving Thorfinn with his original third.[84] [85]

In 1028, Brusi complained that Thorfinn wasn't paying enough toward the upkeep of defense of the islands. Thorfinn replied that he would pay more if Brusi gave him Einar's share, which Brusi did. When Brusi died in 1031, Thorfinn finally gained all of Orkney for himself as the 13th Jarl.[86][87]

Things went awry for Thorfinn after Malcolm II's murder in 1034. Malcolm's grandson, Thorfinn's cousin, King Duncan (see *MacAlpin Dynasty*) demanded a feudal tribute from him. Thorfinn refused, saying that Malcolm had given him Caithness, and that he owed Duncan nothing.[88][89]

Duncan declared Thorfinn's earldom forfeit, and created his own nephew, Moddan, as Earl of Caithness.[90] This was the beginning of the confusion and conflict over the various claims on the earldom in the future.[91][92]

Moddan took an army to Caithness to drive Thorfinn out of his earldom. Thorfinn had superior manpower, and crushed Moddan. Thorfinn then ravaged the neighboring counties of Sutherland and Ross, then returned to Caithness to man his longboats.[93][94][95]

Moddan raised a second army, and he marched toward Caithness again. King Duncan followed by sea with an eleven-ship fleet. Duncan and Thorfinn clashed off the Mull of Deerness in the Mainland (the biggest island) of Orkney, with stiff hand-to-hand combat. Thorfinn drove Duncan back to Moray, which Thorfinn also ravaged.[96][97][98]

Thorfinn sent his friend Thorkel to Thurso in Caithness, where Moddan was hiding. Thorkel set fire to Moddan's house, which killed him. He returned to Thorfinn in Moray.[99][100] King Duncan raised another army and attacked. The armies clashed near Burghead at Standing Stone in Duffus on 14 August 1040. Thorfinn won, and Duncan was killed shortly thereafter by Macbeth's men in a smithy about two miles from Elgin.[101][102][103]

Macbeth became King of Scotland, and he left Thorfinn in peace in the north. Note that Macbeth was also Thorfinn's cousin, the son of another daughter of Malcolm II.[104][105] These three cousins, who were supposed to have been bound by blood, instead fractured Scotland in their struggle for power. Some allege that Thorfinn and Macbeth had a secret alliance to destroy Duncan, since there was peace between the two once Macbeth came to the throne, but there has never been proof of this.[106][107]

In 1044, Thorfinn married Ingibjorg, Finn Aranson's daughter. Finn Aranson was the Jarl of Holland.[108]

Thorfinn's nephew Ragnvald Burison was granted his father's two shares of Orkney and Shetland by King Magnus the Good of Norway, and at first Thorfinn, busy elsewhere, acquiesced.[109]

After eight years co-ruling, Thorfinn wanted a larger share of the islands because he needed more money to support his fighting men. Ragnvald fought, allied with Thorfinn's relative Kalf Arnason. Kalf and Thorfinn met in battle in Pentland Firth off Rattar Brough, east of Dunnet Head. Thorfinn barely escaped the sea battle, but persuaded Kalf to join his side. Together, they defeated Ragnvald, who ran to Norway.[110][111]

In 1046, Ragnvald returned and cornered Thorfinn on Mainland of Orkney. He set fire to Thorfinn's hall at Orphir, trapping him inside. Thorfinn ripped a panel out of the back of the house. He and his wife rowed across the Pentland Firth to Caithness and hid among friends. Thorfinn allowed everyone in Orkney to believe he was dead.[112][113]

At Yuletide, Thorfinn returned and surrounded the house where Ragnvald was. Ragnvald escaped by leaping through his besiegers while disguised as a priest. Ragnvald rescued his dog, too, but the little lapdog barked when in hiding. Thorkel found and killed him. Thorfinn annihilated all but one man and sent him back to Norway to tell the tale.[114][115]

Finally, Thorfinn ruled as the sole Jarl of Orkney and Shetland, and the sole Earl of Caithness, with tributary lands in Ross, the Western Isles, Galloway, and Ireland.[116]

The last period of his life was more peaceful. Around 1047, he visited King Magnus in Norway, and befriended Harald Hardrada, the king's successor.[117] Thorfinn then visited King Sweyn of Denmark and Henry III, Emperor of Germany. In 1050 he went to Rome, visiting the Pope and getting Thorolf appointed as Bishop of Orkney. His cousin King Macbeth of Scotland possibly accompanied him to Rome.[118][119]

Thorfinn returned to his hall in Birsay on Mainland Island in Orkney. He lived his last years in peace, and he built Christchurch, a minster at Birsay.[120]

Thorfinn Sigurdson died "of a sickness" in 1057 or 1058, and his widow Ingibjorg married King Malcolm III of Scotland in 1059 (see *MacAlpin Dynasty*).[121]

Paul and Erland Thorfinnson, 14th Jarls of Orkney and Shetland, and 2nd Earls of Caithness (1057-1098)

Paul and Erland Thorfinnson, the sons of Thorfinn and Ingibjorg, were particularly pacific jarls. They held the jarldom jointly and divided up the lands. Neither Paul nor Erland spent much time in Caithness. Although they still held the title, they let the power go to the Gaelic Mormaers, especially the family of Moddan, who we met earlier.[122]

Their mother's marriage to Malcolm III strengthened Scotland's hold on Caithness and Sutherland, as well as Scotland's connection to Orkney and Shetland, because the brothers were now the king's stepsons as well as Earls of Caithness. They also had a half-brother, Duncan, who was Malcolm III's eldest son. Whatever the other benefits of Ingibjorg's remarriage, it brought peace to the north of Scotland for the next 30 years.[123]

The only time the brothers left Orkney was to accompany Norwegian King Harald Hardrada Sigurdson and his son Prince Olaf to attack England.[124] Harald was killed, his army defeated by King Harold Godwinson of England at Stamford Bridge in September 1066, just three days before William the Conqueror landed. The brothers and Prince Olaf were taken prisoner, and later released.[125]

Paul and Erland ruled harmoniously until their sons fell out with each other and drew their fathers into the mess. Paul's son Hakon argued with Erland's sons Magnus and Erling. Erland sent Hakon off to Norway in 1090.[126]

In 1098, King Magnus Barefoot deposed Paul and Erland Thorfinnson and sent them to Norway, where they died soon after.[127] He made his son Sigurd the jarl, but Sigurd eventually left to assume the throne when his father was killed in Ireland. The jarldom reverted to Paul and Erland's heirs.[128]

Now things started to get messy with the jarldom and earldom. Obviously either Paul or Erland predeceased the other. If the surviving brother had claimed the entirety of Orkney, then the jarldom would have probably passed down in a single line. Since this did not happen, the jarldom was left up in the air for the acrimonious cousins to fight over.

Because there were so many co-jarls, I have grouped them together, so you may see several of the same number. Only when a jarl managed to hold Orkney for an extended time without a co-ruler did I advance the numbers. Other writers use different numbering systems.

Hakon Paulson, 15th Jarl of Orkney and Shetland, and 3rd Earl of Caithness
(1105 – 1123)
St. Magnus Erlandson, 15th Jarl of Orkney and Shetland, and 3rd Earl of Caithness
(1103 – 1116)

Paul's son Hakon, who had been run out of Orkney in 1090, went to Norway. King Magnus decided to raid the Hebrides, and he took Hakon Paulson, as well as Erland's sons Magnus and Erling. During this campaign, young Magnus Erlandson decided that he could no longer stand to take the lives of people he had no quarrel with. So, he abandoned the fight and went to the Scottish court.[129] In 1103, Magnus was created Earl of Caithness by the Scottish King. However, since Orkney was under Norwegian rule, he got no help for his claim there from Scotland.[130]

After King Magnus of Norway's death in 1105, Hakon returned to Orkney with the title of Jarl of Orkney, and seized all of the islands, including Magnus' share.[131] Since Erling was heard from no more, he probably was killed on the expedition to the Hebrides.[132]

Magnus came to Orkney to claim his portion, and Hakon said he would give Magnus his proper share only if Magnus got a grant of it from the Norwegian king. Magnus laid his case before King Eystein of Norway, who gave him his grant in 1106.[133] The cousins managed to live peacefully for a while, even joining forces against a common enemy when Dufnjal and Thorbjorn landed at Burrafirth in Unst in Shetland. In 1107, Magnus married, but it was commonly said that he and his wife lived together "as maidens." In any event, the two had no offspring.[134]

In 1111, Magnus went to visit Henry I of England (see *Continental Dynasty*), and while he was gone, Hakon seized all of Orkney and Caithness. When Magnus returned to reclaim his lands, a battle was averted by "the good men" of Orkney. A compromise was reached, and the cousins split Orkney, Shetland, and Caithness equally.[135]

About five years later, the cousins argued again, and again urged by the "good men," were to make another compromise. They agreed to meet in Egilsay, each bringing two ships of men with them. Magnus arrived with his two ships, as agreed, but Hakon brought seven or eight ships, holding all hostage and claiming that only one of them could leave alive. Under Hakon's orders, Hakon's cook murdered Magnus Erlandson on 16 April 1116.[136] [137]

Hakon then went to Magnus' mother, Thora's, house. Thora had been preparing a feast in celebration of the reconciliation. Hakon told her Magnus was dead and ate the feast. Thora asked for her son's body, and Hakon granted it. She buried Magnus at Christ's Kirk in Birsay. Twenty-one years later, on 13 December 1137, Jarl Magnus' relics were moved to St. Magnus' Cathedral in Kirkwall.[138]

Hakon then went to Rome and Jerusalem,[139] where he apparently was transformed, because he came back and was a good ruler from then on. He built the round church at Orphir on Mainland, Orkney, which was the only Templar Church in Scotland.[140]

While Magnus had no children, Hakon had at least four. By his lawful wife, he had Paul Hakonson, known as Paul the Silent. By his mistress, Helga, he had Harald Hakonson, known as Harald the Glib,[141] and two daughters, Ingibiorg and Margaret. Ingibiorg married Olaf Bitling, King of the Sudreys (Isle of Man, the Hebrides, and islands in the Firth of Clyde), and their offspring will enter into the story briefly later.

A word about Helga the mistress. Remember Moddan, King Duncan's nephew who was named Earl of Caithness but then was killed by Thorfinn Sigurdson's men? He had left a son, known as Moddan in Dale. The Moddan family had gained much of their power back in the quiet rule of Paul and Erland. Helga, Hakon's mistress, was one of Moddan in Dale's daughters. This was one point where the blood of the Norse jarls and the blood of the Gaelic claimant to Caithness came together.[142]

In 1123, Hakon Paulson died, and his sons Paul the Silent (Umalgi) and Harald the Glib (Slettmali) inherited the jarldom and the earldom.[143]

Paul Umalgi (the Silent) Hakonson, 16th Jarl of Orkney and Shetland, and 4th Earl of Caithness (1123-1138)
Harald Slettmali (the Glib) Hakonson, 16th Jarl of Orkney and Shetland, and 4th Earl of Caithness (1123-1125)
Ragnvald Kolson, 17th Jarl of Orkney and Shetland (1116-1158)
Harold Maddadson, 18th Jarl of Orkney and Shetland, and 5th Earl of Caithness (1138-1206)

After Hakon's death in 1123, his two sons took over the jarldom.[144] Paul Hakonson lived mainly in Orkney, and Harald Hakonson lived mostly in Caithness. King David I of Scotland (see *MacAlpin Dynasty*) made Harald the Earl of Caithness, and Harald shared Orkney with Paul.[145]

Harald was much more sympathetic to Scotland, largely because of his Gaelic mother, Helga, Moddan in Dale's daughter. He spent much of his time in North Kildonan in Caithness, where his mother lived. Helga lived with her widowed sister, Frakark. Audhild, daughter of another sister Thorleif, and Helga's daughter Margaret, another of Hakon's illegitimate children, also lived with them.[146]

Frakark and Helga decided that Harald should have all of Orkney, and that Paul should be killed. They made a poisoned shirt for Paul, but before they gave it to him, Harald somehow put it on and he died, leaving an infant son, Erland Haraldson.[147] This unexpected turn of events left all of Orkney and Caithness in Paul's hands, and created mortal enemies of Paul and Frakark.[148]

In the meantime, there was a boy named Kali Kolson growing up in Agdir, Norway. Whereas both Harald the Glib and Paul the Silent were from the line of Paul Thorfinnson, Kali descended from the line of Erland Thorfinnson, Paul's brother. St. Magnus, as we saw, was Erland's son, and he died without children. But Erland also had a daughter, Magnus' sister, Gunhild. She married Kol, a Norseman, and they had a son, Kali.[149] Kali was very talented, and well educated—he could read and write.[150]

At 15 years old, Kali went to Grimsby (near Hull in England) to trade, and met a young man named Harald Gillikrist. They became friends, and Harald confided that he was a son of the late King Magnus Barelegs. He asked Kali if the current king, Sigurd, who was Harald's half-brother, would receive him well if Harald came to court. Kali encouraged him to go.[151]

Kali returned to Bergen, Norway in 1116, about the same time his uncle Magnus was murdered by Hakon in Orkney. Upon Magnus' death, King Sigurd made Kali Jarl of Orkney for Magnus' share of the islands. King Sigurd also changed his name, creating him Jarl Ragnvald, supposedly because of a striking resemblance to the early Ragnvald, the founder of the lineage.[152]

But Paul did not want to give up half of Orkney. He point-blank refused Ragnvald's claim, so Ragnvald needed to use force or guile to get it. Ragnvald allied himself with Frakark. Frakark, never having forgiven Paul for Harald's death, was more than happy to oblige, but she had an ulterior motive. Margaret, Harald's sister, had married Maddad, Earl of Atholl, and they had an infant son, Harold Maddadson. Ragnvald promised Frakark that if they won, she could have Paul's half of Orkney for Harold.[153] [154]

Before the battle for Orkney, several other events happened. In 1126, King Harald of Norway (the one young Kali had befriended) reconfirmed his right to half of the Orkney jarldom. In 1135, Ragnvald fought on Harald's side at Floruvoe, in a civil war between Harald and his nephew Magnus.[155]

But by 1136, fresh from his victory with King Harald, Ragnvald turned his attention back to his jarldom. Frakark and Ragnvald, in two separate fleets, invaded Orkney and Shetland. Paul defeated Frakark's fleet in Orkney, and Ragnvald's fleet in Yell Sound in Shetland. Ragnvald and his men managed to escape to Norway.[156]

A man named Olaf Hrolfson, father of Gunni and Sweyn Asleifarson, allied with Paul. Frakark's grandson, Olvir Rosta, burned him alive in his house, which understandably created a mortal enemy of Sweyn.[157]

Sweyn Asleifarson appeared again when Ragnvald landed at Westray. This time Ragnvald defeated Paul's forces, and then he allied himself with Sweyn. Sweyn kidnapped Jarl Paul when he was hunting otters near Westness on the Orkney isle of Rousay. Sweyn took Paul to Paul's half-sister Margaret, who somehow forced him to abdicate in favor of her five-year-old son, Harold Maddadson. Harold was then sole Earl of Caithness. Paul Hakonson then vanished from history, leaving no children. Some theories say he lived out the rest of his life quietly, others say Margaret imprisoned and killed him.[158] [159]

Now that Paul was gone, Ragnvald had time for peaceful endeavors, and built the Cathedral of St. Magnus in Kirkwall.[160] Ragnvald seemed to have been a reasonable man, and when in 1137 Bishop John of Glasgow and Bishop William the Old of Egilsay approached him with the proposition that Harold Maddadson should also have half of Orkney because of Paul's abdication, Ragnvald agreed. The people of Orkney ratified the decision. Harold arrived in 1139, and his tutor was Thorbiorn Klerk, one of Frakark's grandsons and brother-in-law to Sweyn Asleifarson. [161] [162]

According to the laws of the day, when someone was murdered, the family of the killer could pay the family of the victim a weregeld, a monetary atonement for the death. If the family of the victim accepted the money, then all was forgiven, and they could not take blood revenge against the killer or his family. Sweyn had accepted weregeld from Ottir of Thurso, Frakark's brother, for the death of his father and so the death should have been forgiven.[163] But Sweyn would not let it go, and he cornered Frakark in her house, burning her alive. Thus ended the life of one of the most powerful female figures in this male-dominated time of history.[164]

In 1148, Ragnvald and 15-year-old Harold Maddadson went to visit King Ingi in Norway. While there, Ragnvald met Eindridi, who persuaded him to undertake a voyage to Constantinople (Micklegarth). Ragnvald and Harold were wrecked in *The Help* and *The Arrow*, respectively, at Gulberwick on the Shetland coast. All aboard were saved.[165]

In 1150, they made a second try, but this time Eindridi wrecked off the coast of Shetland.[166]

In 1151, Ragnvald finally succeeded, while Harold decided to stay behind to keep an eye on the jarldom. Ragnvald sailed away. They touched upon France, then went to Bilbao in Spain. He sailed around Galicia, then passed through the Straits of Gibraltar, where they were deserted by Eindridi. Ragnvald was not shaken. He sailed along the Barbary Coast, captured the Saracen ship *Dromund*, burned her, and sold the prisoners in Barbary, although he let the prince go free. He passed Crete, landed at Acre, and bathed in the Jordan on St. Lawrence Day, 10 August 1152.[167] He visited Jerusalem, and then finally made it to Constantinople, where he was warmly received despite the efforts of Eindridi (who arrived first) to discredit him. After some time there, he returned to Bulgaria and Apulia and Rome, then overland to Denmark and Norway in 1153.[168] [169]

Ragnvald Kolson, 17ᵗʰ Jarl of Orkney and Shetland
(1116-1158)
Harold Maddadson, 18ᵗʰ Jarl of Orkney and Shetland, and 5ᵗʰ Earl of Caithness
(1138-1206)
Erland Haraldson, 18ᵗʰ Jarl of Orkney and Shetland, and 5ᵗʰ Earl of Caithness
(1153-1156)

As you can see from the headings of this and the last section (and the next), the jarldom and earldom have gotten confusing. This arose from so many people having half-shares of the two earldoms at different times. Basically, there were three competing factions for the land: the two Norse lines of Thorfinn's sons, Paul and Erland, and the Gaelic Moddan line, established by Duncan I when he gave his nephew the Earldom of Caithness.

Paul Thorfinnson's line was represented by Harold Maddadson. This also represented the Moddan line, because Harold's grandmother Helga was a Moddan daughter. Erland Thorfinnson's line was held by Ragnvald Kolson, son of Gunhild, Erland's daughter.

When we left the story, Ragnvald was in Norway in 1153, after a two-year journey through the Mediterranean. But time had not stood still in Orkney while he was gone.

Perhaps doubting Harold Maddadson's loyalty to Norway, King Eystein of Norway seized him and made him swear allegiance to Norway in 1153. Harold, 20 years old at the time, did so, and was released upon payment of three gold marks in ransom.[170] Harold's father, Maddad, died, and his mother, Margaret, came to Orkney, where she had a child by Gunni, Sweyn's brother.[171]

In the meantime, Erland, Harald the Glib's son and Harold Maddadson's cousin, came of age and went to the Scottish court. King Malcom granted him half of the Earldom of Caithness, which didn't sit well with Harold, who had been the sole earl until then.[172] [173]

As a result, when Erland Haraldson came to Harold to demand half of Orkney as well, Harold refused. He told Erland that he would only give him half of Orkney if King Eystein of Norway granted it to him.[174] Much to Harold's dismay, Erland returned with the news that Eystein had granted him half of Orkney—*Harold's* half! Eystein wanted Ragnvald to keep his half, so divested Harold of his. The Orkney people agreed to this as well.[175] [176]

Harold tried and failed to regain the Orkneys by force, then turned to plundering with his mother's new husband, Erland the Young.[177]

This was the situation that Ragnvald returned to, in 1153.[178] Harold, for some, reason harbored ill feelings for Ragnvald, but he tried, unsuccessfully, to get him on his side. Harold tried, also unsuccessfully, to kill Erland and Sweyn in Shetland.[179]

In 1154, Ragnvald's only child, a daughter Ingigerd, married Eric Stagbrellir. Eric was the son of Eric Streita and Audhild, daughter of Thorleif, who was a sister of Frakark and Helga, and another daughter of Moddan in Dale. This meant the Moddan line and the line of Erland Thorfinnson had merged.[180]

While at his daughter's wedding, Ragnvald heard that Harold Maddadson was nearby. Eric Stagbrellir was Harold's second cousin, so he tried to reconcile Harold and Ragnvald. The two finally were reconciled 25 September 1154.[181]

In 1156, they allied against Erland and Sweyn. Erland and Sweyn's forces got the upper hand at Orphir in Orkney, but Ragnvald and Harold escaped across the Pentland Firth to Caithness, since Harold was still earl of half of Caithness. Later on, after Sweyn had left on other business, Ragnvald and Harold returned and killed a drunken Erland Haraldson off Durnsey near Finstown.[182] [183]

Erland, who had the rights of his jarldom and earldom, also held Moddan lands left to him by Earl Ottir of Thurso, who was his grandmother's brother. Since Erland had no children, his Moddan lands, as well as rights to claim the jarldom and earldom, would have most likely devolved to Eric Stagbrellir, his second cousin.[184]

In 1158, Ragnvald and Harold went red deer and reindeer hunting in Caithness, which they did every year. On 20 August 1158, at a homestead called Force, Ragnvald Kolson was assassinated by Thorbiorn Klerk,[185] who was Frakark's grandson and Harold Maddadson's tutor as a child. Although his motive was not stated, one can guess that he wanted to get all of Orkney and Caithness for Harold, much as his grandmother Frakark had desired for her son. The proof may be in the aftermath, for Harold refused to pursue Thorbiorn as he fled.[186] However, there were some of Ragnvald's entourage without ulterior motives, and they chased Thorbiorn, and he was killed. Ragnvald was buried in the choir of St. Magnus Cathedral.[187] [188]

In 1192, Ragnvald was canonized as St. Ragnvald, with full papal sanctions.[189] [190]

Ragnvald's death changed the standings of the ongoing quarrel over claims to the jarldom and earldom. As we have seen, Ragnvald had only one daughter, Ingigerd, who married Eric Stagbrellir of the Moddan family. This meant that all of Ragnvald's claims to the Jarldom of Orkney (he never held the title of Earl of Caithness), as well as all his lands in Caithness, Sutherland, and the hill country in Halkirk, Lathern, and Strathnaver, would pass to Eric Stagbrellir and his heirs. As we have also seen, Eric was the inheritor of the

Moddan lands of Erland Haraldson as well. So two people had claims to the lands on Orkney and Caithness: Harold Maddadson (the combined lines of Paul Thorfinnson and Moddan), and Eric Stagbrellir (the combined lines of Erland Thorfinnson and Moddan).

Harold Maddadson, 18th Jarl of Orkney and Shetland, and 5th Earl of Caithness (1138-1206)
Harald the Young (Ungi) Stagbrellir, 18th Jarl of Orkney and Shetland, and 5th Earl of Caithness (1158-1198)
King Ragnvald Gudrodson of the Sudreys, 5th Earl of Caithness (1198-1201)

Upon Ragnvald's death in 1158, Harold Maddadson got his wish and became sole jarl of Orkney and Shetland and sole earl of Caithness. He was 25 years old.[191] [192]

Harold married twice. His first wife was Afreka, daughter of Duncan, Earl of Fife. With her, he had Henry, Hakon, Helena, and Margaret.[193] Later in his life he "put her away" and married Gormflaith MacEth.[194] With her, he had sons Thorfinn, David, and John[195], and daughters Gunnhilda, Herborga, and Langlif.[196]

Since Harold was now the sole jarl and earl, this would have seemed to put an end to the conflicting claims to the titles and lands, but that was not the case, because as noted above, there was still Eric Stagbrellir.

Eric Stagbrellir and Ingigerd Ragnvaldsdottir married in 1154 and had six children: Harald Ungi (the Young), Magnus, Ragnvald, and daughters Ingibiorg, Elin, and Ragnhild. Eric himself never made a claim for any of Ragnvald's lands after the jarl was killed in 1158,[197] and it is unknown when he died. But when Eric died, the inheritance would pass to each of his sons in turn, and, if those lines failed, then to the oldest sons of the daughters. Eric and Ingigerd's eldest son, Harald Ungi Stagbrellir, did make a claim upon his grandfather's titles, however, so the confusion over the claims continued.

In 1196, Harald Ungi gained a grant of half of Orkney from the Norwegian king, and half of Caithness from the Scottish king. A word about the scope of Caithness at this point.[198]

Caithness, as defined previously, was all of modern-day Caithness and Sutherland, and probably part or all of Ross and Comarty. Also in 1196, a man named Hugo Freskyn (also called Hugo de Moravia), part of a powerful Gaelic family close to the kings of Scotland, was granted a large amount of land in what is now Sutherland. In particular, it was the modern-day parishes of Creich, Dornoch, Rogart, Golspie, Clyne, Loth, and most of Kildonan and Lairg. These lands were therefore no longer part of the Earldom of Caithness (they eventually became an earldom in themselves in 1237, when the first Earl of Sutherland was created by Alexander II).[199]

So, the half of Caithness that Harald Ungi received was half minus the Freskyn lands, so it was a smaller share than before, although still vast. Harold Maddadson, angered at having to share yet again, did not take this news well.[200]

Things came to a head in 1196.[201] This was the year that Hugo Freskyn was granted his lands, and the year Harald Ungi claimed his rights as well, because it was in 1196 that Harold Maddadson's power was at its lowest ebb. In 1195, Harold had been stripped of Shetland by Norwegian King Sverri.[202] [203] That was probably part of the reason Harold Maddadson reacted so badly to Harald Ungi's grant of Caithness lands.

Harold's second wife, as stated above, was Gormflaith MacEth. Gormflaith was the daughter of Malcolm MacEth, a one-time Momaer (Earl) of Moray and persistent rebel against the Scottish kings. Malcolm MacEth had claimed rights to the Scottish throne through a female line, and he was a constant source of strife and warfare until his imprisonment.[204]

Gormflaith seemed to have also taken up the rebel banner, as did her brother, who had continued the fight after Malcolm's imprisonment. Gormflaith, married to a powerful jarl and earl in Harold Maddadson, convinced him that he should conquer Ross and Moray, which she believed were hers by birthright.[205] [206]

So, Harold and his eldest son by Gormflaith, Thorfinn, went to war, and they met the army of Scottish King William I the Lion in Caithness. William defeated Thorfinn and destroyed Harold's castle in Thurso. [207] Harold submitted, and promised to meet William in Nairn, and to bring his son Thorfinn and others to serve as hostages to ensure his loyalty in the future.[208] [209]

However, Harold arrived at Nairn alone. He begged to keep Thorfinn, and send his other sons in his place, but William threw Harold in jail until Thorfinn showed up to take his place. William declared all of Harold's holdings in Caithness forfeit for his rebellion, and it was at this point that Hugo Freskyn got his Sutherland grants, and Harald Ungi was given his grant of half of Caithness.[210] Harald Ungi didn't have it easy, though—he could only have his lands if he could take them by conquest.[211]

Harald Ungi failed to take Orkney and Caithness. In a battle in 1198 near Wick in Caithness, Harald Ungi Stagbrellir was killed.[212] [213]

With Harald Ungi gone, Harold Maddadson tried to make terms with William I, but William stipulated that if Harold wanted Caithness back, he had to "put away" Gormflaith and get back with Afreka. Harold refused to do this. He still held Caithness by force of arms, having defeated Harald Ungi, although he had no legal title to it anymore.[214] [215]

William I called upon King Ragnvald Gudrodson, the Viking King of the Sudreys and Man. King Ragnvald had a right to Caithness, because he was the great-grandson of Hakon, via his oldest daughter Ingibjorg.[216] [217] King Ragnvald was successful, driving Harold out of Caithness near Achness, when Harold returned to Orkney. King Ragnvald returned to Man, leaving six stewards in charge of Caithness.[218] [219]

In 1201, Harold Maddadson murdered one of the stewards and returned with force to Thurso to punish the Caithness people. Bishop John interceded, and Harold mutilated him, nearly blinding and muting him, but John recovered. Harold then drove out the rest of the stewards.[220] [221]

King William I punished Harold by having Harold's son Thorfinn (who was his hostage) blinded, and so mutilated that he died. William collected an army, but Harold evaded him and went to England to try to negotiate with King John (see *Continental Dynasty*).[222] [223]

Later in 1201, Harold got his Caithness earldom back through the intercession of Bishop Rogers of St. Andrews. Harold paid King Ragnvald 2,000 pounds in silver to buy it back.[224] In 1202, Harold got the earldom back from William with a fine of every fourth penny the people of Caithness possessed.[225]

In 1206, Harold Maddadson's long reign came to an end at age 73.[226] His son David succeeded him to the jarldom and earldom.[227]

David Haroldson, 19th Jarl of Orkney and 6th Earl of Caithness
(1206-1214)
John Haroldson, 19th Jarl of Orkney and 6th Earl of Caithness
(1206-1231)

Some sources claim David and John Haroldson split Orkney and Caithness, while brother Heinrek tried unsuccessfully to establish himself in Ross. Others have David succeeding as sole heir, then John upon David's death. Either way, David died without children in 1214, and John became sole Jarl of Orkney and Earl of Caithness.[228] [229]

King William I of Scotland was unsure of John's loyalty, given his father's history. On 1 August 1214, William took John's daughter as a hostage. John's son Harald remained with John.[230] [231]

In 1218, John went to Norway to witness a successful ordeal by King Hakon's (then a boy) mother to prove he was the lawful son of the late King Hakon Sverrison, and thus entitled to the crown.[232]

In 1222, when John returned, the people of Caithness met at his house to demand that he relieve them of the oppressive tithes demanded by Bishop Adam of Caithness. John refused to intervene, and either suggested or refused to oppose their attack on Bishop Adam in his house near Brawl Castle, where John lived.[233]

When the mob arrived at Bishop Adam's house, some attempt at reconciliation was made. Earl John was sent for, but he refused to come and intervene. After that, some men grabbed the bishop, threw him into the house, and burned him alive.[234]

King Alexander II marched to Caithness and punished the people involved. He made John's lands forfeit for his refusal to get involved, but he gave them back to John that year at Yuletide.[235]

A word about John's Caithness earldom. Above, we mentioned that Hugo Freskyn was granted the Sutherland parishes in 1196, but Harold Maddadson still held the rest of the Caithness lands. John's Caithness holdings were much smaller. Along with not having Shetland and the Freskyn lands, he also did not hold the vast land of Strathnaver. Strathnaver stretched from the modern border with Caithness in the east, to the western edge of Scotland, all the way north to the Atlantic. Strathnaver may have been the half of the larger Caithness that Harald Ungi was granted by William I. Western Strathnaver was held by force of arms by the MacKay clan, and the eastern part was insecurely held by the Moddan family, represented at that time by Eric Stagbrellir's youngest daughter, Ragnhild's, husband Gunni, and their son Snaekoll Gunnison. So, Earl John's Caithness very closely mirrored the lands of modern Caithness.[236]

In 1223, John went to Bergen in Norway with Bishop Bjarni of Orkney to consider the rival claims of King Hakon and Jarl Skuli to the crown. In 1224, he returned to Bergen with his son Harald, to leave Harald as a hostage for his loyalty.[237] John had already given up his daughter to the Scottish king to pledge his loyalty to him. John was obviously torn between two masters, as many of his predecessors had been. It was clear that John favored Norway over Scotland. He would need to choose a side, because a war for the Hebrides Islands was looming between the two countries.

Unfortunately, when Harald was released in 1226, he drowned on the return voyage home.[238] This did not shake John's loyalty to Norway. In 1228, he sent presents to Norway and received a longship and other gifts in return.[239]

In 1230, John aided King Olaf of Man, a friend of the Norse king, by giving him a longship, *The Ox*, to enable him to return from Norway to Man. Later that same year, John aided a Norse expedition which had attacked the Southern Hebrides by harboring its ships in Orkney on their way back to Norway.[240]

In 1231, Snaekoll Gunnison, St. Ragnvald's great-grandson via Ragnhild Stagbrellir, went to Earl John and demanded his share of Orkney. Snaekoll marched to Thurso to enforce his claim, but John refused any lands in Orkney, and was unwilling to give Snaekoll his rights in Caithness.[241]

At Thurso, Snaekoll's men overheard that John was planning to kill them, and they moved first. They killed John Haroldson in the cellar of his lodgings, inflicting nine wounds. They crossed to Orkney and dug in at the castle of Cobbie Row on the Viera and outlasted a winter-long siege. The men of Orkney decided that all questions arising out of Earl John's death would be decided by King Hakon in Bergen.[242]

In 1232, the parties went to Bergen, and King Hakon punished Snaekoll's side, some with death, some with imprisonment. Snaekoll was kept alive and lived a long time in Norway. Tradition holds that Snaekoll, deprived of his rights in Norwegian Orkney by King Hakon, returned to Scottish Caithness very late in his life.[243]

So, with Snaekoll away in Norway for many years, and John's only heir a nameless daughter held hostage by the Scottish crown, what happened to Caithness and Orkney?

The Earls of Angus
(1233-1321)

After John's death, Caithness was taken over by the Scottish crown, and eventually divided up amongst three viable claimants.[244]

First was Earl John's nameless daughter, who was entitled to all of Orkney and John's quarter-part of Caithness, called North Caithness at this time.[245]

Next was Johanna of Strathnaver, a woman of mysterious origin who was probably Snaekoll Gunnison's daughter. As such, she would have been entitled to half of Caithness, in addition to the other sizeable Moddan lands she held in her own right.[246]

The other quarter of Caithness, as well as the title Earl of Caithness, would have gone to the third claimant—Magnus, the son of the Earl of Angus. Magnus' mother was either Ingibiorg or Elin Stagbrellir, Ragnhild's older sister. (Ragnhild was Snaekoll's mother.) Ingibiorg/Elin married Gilchrist, 4th Earl of Angus, and had Magnus. Since Magnus was an heir of the elder sister, he would get not only the part of Caithness called South Caithness, but the title as well.[247]

In a twist of fate, Magnus married John's daughter, thus inheriting Orkney, John's North Caithness and his mother's South Caithness, leaving him as the 7th Earl of half of Caithness, and 20th Jarl of Orkney.[248] The part of historic Caithness known as Sutherland was removed from Magnus' earldom and given to the family of Freskyn de Moravia, and William de Moravia was raised to the 1st Earl of Sutherland in 1237. William was the uncle of Freskyn de Moravia, Lord of Duffus, who later married Johanna of Strathnaver (above, inheritor of the other half of Caithness).[249]

Magnus died in 1239, and Gillebride, probably his son but possibly his younger brother, inherited the Earldoms as 21st Jarl of Orkney, 8th Earl of Caithness. Gillebride had at least two children, his son Magnus and his daughter Matilda. *Matilda* married Malise II, Earl of Strathearn.[250]

The Earls of Strathearn

When Matilda married Malise II, Earl of Strathearn, we leave the direct line of the jarldom and earldom behind. We will join it again some 60 years from here, with their great-grandson, Malise V. Until that time, the earldom follows Matilda's brother, Magnus', heirs. When that line runs out, it comes down hers.

But let us turn our attention to the Earl of Strathearn line. The Strathearn Earls were not Norse—they were a powerful native Gaelic family. Strathearn was located in the county Perth, and was the valley of the river Earn, beginning from Loch Earn. It contained the towns of St. Fillans, Comrie, Crieff, Muthill, Braco, Auchterarder, and Dunning.

Our story begins with the earliest recorded (there were no doubt powerful rulers of this family prior to him) Earl of Strathearn, Malise I. Malise was the Anglicanized version of the Gaelic Maol Íosa, meaning "tonsured devotee of Jesus." Note that the dates in parentheses are dates they held the earldom, not necessarily birth and death dates.

Malise I, Earl of Strathearn
(c. 1115-c. 1153)

Malise I was one of the witnesses to Alexander III's charter for the founding of the Priory of Scone in 1115.[251]

As a proud Gaelic Scot, he had little to do with the new Scotto-Norman court surrounding the kings of Scotland. He did assist King David I (see *MacAlpin Dynasty*) with his invasion of England at the Battle of the Standard/the Battle of Northallerton.[252][253]

Contemporary historians say that a great deal of tension arose before the battle, as native Gaels and imported Anglo-Norman troops argued over pride of place in the battle lines. Supposedly, Malise reprimanded David I for failing to appreciate the loyalty of native Scots, and reminded him of the traditional precedence the Gaelic fighters enjoyed in the royal army.[254][255] David I caved to the demands of his Gaelic chiefs, and sent in the lightly armed and not-at-all armored Gaels in the forefront. Predictably, the Gaels were decimated, causing the Battle of the Standard to become a rout by the English. This moment could be seen as a symbolic victory of the new Anglo-Norman chivalry over native Gaelic traditions.[256]

After the Battle of the Standard, Malise was required to give a hostage—possibly his son *Fearchar*. Status as a royal hostage was both honorable and dangerous. There was honor because only the sons of the most prestigious nobles were acceptable, but also dangerous because an angry king often took out his displeasure on the hostages, threatening or harming or even killing them. So, when David I chose Malise I to send one of his sons, it signaled that David acknowledged Malise's status as an influential nobleman, but it also showed he was displeased with Malise I at the time.[257]

Fearchar, Earl of Strathearn
(c.1153-1171)

It is unknown when Malise I died, but Fearchar had the earldom in 1153, as he was most likely one of the nobles at the inauguration of Malcolm IV. He also disdained the Scotto-Norman court. He was the most important native Scottish noble of his day.[258]

When King Malcolm IV joined English King Henry II's (see *Continental Dynasty*) expedition to Toulese, as if Malcolm were no more than a feudal tributary, Fearchar led the Revolt of the Earls in 1160 to protest. Malcolm took no retribution against Fearchar or the other five earls involved, so perhaps he thought they were justified.[259] [260]

Fearchar married Ethne, and they had three sons: *Gillebride* (or Gilbert), Malise, and Christian.[261]

Fearchar died in 1171, and his son Gillebride succeeded him.[262] [263]

Gillebride, Earl of Strathearn
(1171-1223)

Gillebride succeeded to the title in 1171.[264] Unlike his ancestors, he was active in the Scottish courts, appearing there often, especially during William I's reign.[265] He even served as Justiciar of Scotia, the most senior legal officer in Scotland.[266]

Gillebride accompanied William in his struggles against Harold Maddadson (see above) in 1196. When William was captured at Alnwick by the English, Gillebride was one of the nobles who joined his king as a prisoner at Falaise.[267] [268]

In 1213, he acted as an arbiter over the succession of the Earldom of Menteith, which was immediately to the west of his own Strathearn.[269] In 1214, he was present at the coronation of Alexander II at Scone, and at the memorial ceremonies marking the death of William I.[270] [271]

Later, Gillebride withdrew into his own territories, rising to duty only in the surrounding area. This could have had something to do with the death of his eldest son, but it could also have been a sign of the ongoing tension between the ancient Gaelic rulers and the new Anglo-Norman court. He and his family, before and after him, tried very hard to ensure the survival of native forms of lordship in an age when those traditions were under attack by the new feudal ideals of the royal court and foreign settlers.[272]

The Strathearn Earls apparently held their lands with no feudal ties to the crown—in other words, they did not owe knights to fight or other tributes of the sort. Still, the crown tried to create this feudal tie with them. In 1187, William I gave lands confiscated from northern rebels to loyal noblemen. Gillebride was granted Kinveachy in Inverness, and Madderty.[273] These were held with very light ties (only one knight was required as tribute), but they were ties nonetheless. Gillebride eventually alienated both of those lands, and busied himself with only his own Strathearn territory.[274]

In 1223, Gillebride died. He had married twice: to Maud d'Aubigny and to Iseulte de Kinbuck. Between the two of them, he had seven sons and three daughters. The sons were: Gilchrist, William, Fearchar, **Robert**, Fergus, Malise, and Gillebride of Glencarny. The daughters were: Maud, who married Malcolm I, Earl of Fife, Cecilia, who married Walter Ruthven, and Ethne, who married David de le Haye.[275] [276]

Robert, Earl of Strathearn
(1223-1245)

Robert was Gillebride's fourth son, but he was the oldest surviving son, so he inherited the title in 1223.[277] Not much is known about him.[278]

He did go to York in 1237 as part of the delegation who negotiated the Treaty of York between King Alexander II of Scotland and King Henry III of England (see *Continental Dynasty*). This treaty, among other things, set the southern boundary of Scotland at its present location.[279] [280]

Robert died in 1245, leaving five children, three sons and two daughters. The sons were: *Malise II*, Aodh, and Gilbert. The daughters were: Annabella, who first married Sir John de Restalrig, then Sir Patrick Graham of Kincardin, and Maria.[281] [282]

Malise II, Earl of Strathearn
(1245-1271)

Malise II inherited the title in 1245, upon the death of his father.[283] He reached outside his small kingdom, inviting French-speaking and English settlers into his holdings and into his entourage. He was quite the diplomat, able to retain the favor of both the Scottish and English kings. He also managed to steer a middle course through the turmoil of the Comyn-Durward rivalry that haunted the Scottish court in the 13th century.[284]

Malise II was present at York for the renewal of peace with England, and at Scone in 1249 for the coronation of young Alexander III.[285] His relationship with King Henry III of England (see *Continental Dynasty*) was such that Malise II was one of the nobles Henry picked to rule Scotland during Alexander's long minority. He was also mentioned in connection with arrangements made for the birth of the queen's first child.[286]

He married four times, and here is where we join the stories of the Norse earls above.

His first wife was Marjory de Muschamp, with whom he had daughters Muriel and Maria. His second wife was Matilda, daughter of Gillebride, Jarl of Orkney and Earl of Caithness,[287] with whom he had the rest of his children: *Malise III*, Robert, and Cecelia. His third wife was Emma, and fourth was Maria, daughter of Ewen MacDougall.[288]

Malise II died in 1271.[289]

Malise III, Earl of Strathearn
(1271-1317)

Malise III took over his father's earldom in 1271.[290]

He helped keep Scotland stable after Alexander III's death in 1286 by raising a levy in 1287 to assist in upholding the peace.[291]

Malise III married Agnes Comyn, daughter of Alexander Comyn, the Earl of Buchan, in a marriage arranged by his father, Malise II.[292] They had four children: *Malise IV*, Gilbert, Robert, and Maud, who married Sir Robert de Thony.[293]

His marriage into the powerful Comyn family put him on the Balliol side of the conflict with Bruce for the Scottish crown. After the Maid of Norway's death in 1290, two men contended for the crown – John de Balliol, and Robert (V) de Brus (grandfather of future King Robert I) (see *De Brus Lineage*). They agreed to hold an election in front of Scottish auditors, presided over by Edward I of England (see *Continental Dynasty*). Malise III was one of the Scottish auditors who would decide the crown.[294] A decision was reached 17 Nov 1292, in favor of John. He was crowned 30 Nov 1292 at Scone.

At these 1292 deliberations, Edward I demanded that all present recognize him as the Lord Paramount (feudal overlord) of Scotland. Malise, and all the others, pledged their allegiance to Edward.[295] [296]

This pledge greatly undermined King John's ability to rule, and in July 1295, the Parliament at Stirling took control of the government away from King John and put it in the hands of a council. Malise III was a member of that governing council, and therefore was involved with the treaty with France, which came to be known as the Auld Alliance.[297]

This treaty with France provoked an invasion by Edward I of England. Malise III joined the Scottish forces in 1296, ravaging Carlisle and its environs. England won, and King John Balliol was forced to abdicate, fleeing to France. Malise III and others re-pledged their loyalty to Edward I in August 1296, but Edward didn't trust him and required two of his sons to stay in England to ensure his loyalty.[298] [299]

Hostages notwithstanding, in 1297, Malise III joined "Braveheart" William Wallace's uprising in the First War of Scottish Independence. This uprising was said to be on behalf of exiled King John Balliol. Malise III tried to play both sides of the fence. During the 1297 uprising, he acted as an agent of Edward I of England, capturing MacDuff and his sons, but then joining Wallace in a raid into English Northumberland. Once again, Edward I forgave him because of earlier assistance Malise III had provided for him.[300]

Malise III, like many other earls, was torn between two bad choices once Robert I Bruce (see *Stewart Dynasty*) took the throne in 1306. Malise III, married into the Balliol faction, was a supporter of the legitimate king, John Balliol – but that meant siding with England against his fellow Scots. But to support Bruce, he would have to support an essential usurper over the rightful Balliol king. A usurper vs. England – which was the lesser of two evils?[301]

As a result, neither side trusted Malise III. Bruce's forces besieged him at his stronghold in Kenmore, and then Edward I imprisoned him in England until 1310. He still held his title but had lost effective control of his lands. His son Malise IV—a fierce Bruce supporter—ran them.[302]

After Malise III's release, he was still loyal to England, although now the king was Edward II, and assisted Edward II (see *Continental Dynasty*) in holding Perth in 1313. He was captured there by his own son, Malise IV, who persuaded Robert I of Scotland to spare his life.[303] [304]

Malise III died in 1317.[305]

Malise IV, Earl of Strathearn
(1317-1329)

Malise IV was born around 1272,[306] and gained the earldom in 1317. Although his father, Malise III, had been a traitor to Bruce, and his earldom subject to forfeiture because of that, Malise IV's unswerving loyalty to Robert I Bruce (see *Stewart Dynasty*) saved his lands, and Malise IV was allowed to inherit the earldom without penalty.[307]

He was an ardent supporter of Robert the Bruce in the Scottish Wars of Independence. He fought on the Scottish side, and against his own father (who supported the English). At Perth, he captured his father, and persuaded Robert the Bruce to spare his life.[308] He continued to be a close friend of the royal court throughout Robert I's reign.[309] He even survived, unscathed, the condemnation of his own mother, Agnes, who was still an agent of the English as they tried to restore the Balliol monarchy in 1320.[310][311] Malise was one of the earls who signed the famed 1320 Declaration of Arbroath to the Pope, a letter signed by most of the Scottish nobility declaring their independence from England and King Robert I Bruce as their rightful sovereign.[312]

He married twice. His first wife is unknown, but author Roland William Saint-Clair and others suspect she might have been a daughter of Magnus, Earl of Orkney, who died without sons. This could be how the Orkney earldom passed to Malise (aside from his claim through his grandmother). The uncertainty of Earl Magnus' death date means the Orkney earldom may have passed briefly to Malise IV around 1321, before passing to his son Malise V upon his own death in 1329.[313]

Malise's second wife was Johanna Meneith, daughter of Sir John Meneith.[314] They had at least one son, *Malise V*, (who may have been the son of the first wife mentioned above) and a daughter Maria, who married Sir John de Moravia of Drumsagard. Maria and John had Maurice de Moravia, who inherited the Earldom of Strathearn after Malise V died.[315]

Malise IV died in 1329, the same year as Robert I Bruce.[316]

Malise V, Earl of Strathearn,
13th Earl of Caithness, 26th Jarl of Orkney
(1329-1350)

Malise V gained the Strathearn earldom upon his father's death in 1329. After many years of the Jarldom of Orkney and Earldom of Caithness passing through a different lineage, and possibly briefly through his father, they came to Malise V in 1329. His claim to the earldoms came through his great-grandmother Matilda of Orkney, who married Malise II.[317]

After Robert I Bruce's death, the Balliol faction, with English help, tried to put Edward Balliol (King John's son) on the throne. Malise V, torn between his father's loyalty to the Bruce cause and his familial obligation to the Balliol cause, chose to side with Balliol.[318]

He fought alongside Edward Balliol and the English forces at the Battle of Halidon Hill July 19, 1333.[319] The Scots lost this battle disastrously, and many of their high-ranking noblemen died there. Edward Balliol did take the throne then, although precariously.

Because of his participation at Halidon Hill, Malise V was not safe in his Strathearn lands, and fled to his northern estates (most likely in his Earldom of Caithness) in 1334. At some point, he signed over his Strathearn earldom to Edward Balliol. Malise V fully expected that once Balliol was on the throne, he would get his earldom back. That did not happen. [320] [321]

At a Parliament in Holyrood in 1334, where most of the nobles "disinherited" by Robert I for supporting the Balliol cause in 1313 were reinstated, Malise V was left out in the cold. He was, for some unknown reason—perhaps because of his father's loyalty to Bruce—branded a traitor to the new Balliol crown, and his earldom given to John de Warrene, English Earl of Surrey and Edward Balliol's grandfather. [322]

Malise V spent the rest of his life trying to get back his earldom. Even when King David II Bruce gained the throne, he was not successful. David II was willing to let his support of Balliol pass with leniency (David let him keep his life and his Orkney and Caithness holdings), but didn't return Strathearn to Malise. It was finally given to Maurice de Moravia, Malise V's nephew, and then to Robert Stewart (see *Stewart Dynasty*). [323]

Malise continued to hold the Jarldom of Orkney and the Earldom of Caithness. Malise married twice. His second wife was Marjory, daughter of Hugh (Aodh), 4th Earl of Ross. They had four daughters:

- Maud – married Weland de Ard
- *Isabel* – married William St. Clair/Sinclair (see *Sinclair Lineage*)
- Agneta (Agnes) – married Erngisl Suneson
- Euphemiz (Euphemia) – did not marry. [324]

Since he had no male heirs, in 1344 Malise made special provisions that the Earldom of Caithness would go through Isabel. Her line did not, however, claim it until her great-grandson William (see *Sinclair Lineage*), as the kings ignored the provisions made by her father and passed it to others first. [325] Malise V died in 1350, although his power as Earl of Strathearn effectively ended in 1333. [326]

After his death, Agnes' husband became 27th Jarl of Orkney. Grandson Alexander de Ard became 14th Earl of Caithness. [327]

Malise's grandson Henry St. Clair/Sinclair (see *Sinclair Lineage*) became 1st Earl of Orkney in 1379, with the blessing of the Norwegian king. Although Norway had recognized the jarls after John Haraldson, the 19th jarl died in 1231, the Norwegian king re-created the earldom at #1 for Henry Sinclair. Although the Norwegian crown held the Orkney Islands until 1468, the control had gone to the Scottish nobles. [328]

Henry 1st Earl's son, Henry, became the 2nd Earl of Orkney circa 1404. Malise V's great-great-grandson (Henry the younger's son) William Sinclair, inherited both the 3rd Earl of Orkney (c. 1420) and 1st Earl of Caithness (1455) titles. In 1470 (two years after Norway ceded the Islands to Scotland), the Scottish crown asked William to give Orkney to them, and he did, retaining the title Earl of Caithness. Note that William was considered the 1st Earl of Caithness, as the title had lapsed and been recreated for him. [329]

This brings the complicated saga of the Norse jarls and earls to an end, and meets up with the *Sinclair Lineage*, which is in another chapter.

As a footnote, although the Hebrides Islands were ceded to Scotland in 1266, the Orkney and Shetland Islands remained in Norway's hands until 1468, when they came to Scotland as part of the dowry for Princess Margaret, wife of King James III of Scotland. The islands were given as collateral for Margaret's actual dowry of 58,000 florins, which was never paid. Norway had tried to make payment and reclaim the islands on several occasions, as late as the reign of Charles II (circa 1660s). [330]

Although Scotland annexed Orkney and Shetland to itself in 1470, it took a long time for Norse laws, customs, and languages to die out in Orkney, and even longer in Shetland.[331]

---

[1] James Gray, *Sutherland & Caithness in Saga-Time, or, The Jarls & The Freskyns* (Oliver & Boyd, Edinburgh, 1922), p. 15.

[2] James Gray, *Sutherland & Caithness in Saga-Time, or, The Jarls & The Freskyns* (Oliver & Boyd, Edinburgh, 1922), p. 11-12.

[3] James Gray, *Sutherland & Caithness in Saga-Time, or, The Jarls & The Freskyns* (Oliver & Boyd, Edinburgh, 1922), p. 17-18.

[4] Ronald Williams, *The Lords of the Isles: The Clan Donald and the Early Kingdom of the Scots* (Chatto & Windus - The Hogarth Press, London, 1984), p. 78, 81.

[5] James Gray, *Sutherland & Caithness in Saga-Time, or, The Jarls & The Freskyns* (Oliver & Boyd, Edinburgh, 1922), p. 18.

[6] James Gray, *Sutherland & Caithness in Saga-Time, or, The Jarls & The Freskyns* (Oliver & Boyd, Edinburgh, 1922), p. 18

[7] James Gray, *Sutherland & Caithness in Saga-Time, or, The Jarls & The Freskyns* (Oliver & Boyd, Edinburgh, 1922), p. 18, 19.

[8] Ronald Williams, *The Lords of the Isles: The Clan Donald and the Early Kingdom of the Scots* (Chatto & Windus - The Hogarth Press, London, 1984), p. 78.

[9] James Gray, *Sutherland & Caithness in Saga-Time, or, The Jarls & The Freskyns* (Oliver & Boyd, Edinburgh, 1922), p. 18, 19.

[10] James Gray, *Sutherland & Caithness in Saga-Time, or, The Jarls & The Freskyns* (Oliver & Boyd, Edinburgh, 1922), p. 19.

[11] E. William Robertson, *Scotland Under Her Early Kings: A History of the Kingdom to the Close of the 13th Century, Part One* (Edinburgh: Edmonston and Douglas, 1862), p. 80.

[12] Ronald Williams, *The Lords of the Isles: The Clan Donald and the Early Kingdom of the Scots* (Chatto & Windus - The Hogarth Press, London, 1984), p. 81.

[13] James Gray, *Sutherland & Caithness in Saga-Time, or, The Jarls & The Freskyns* (Oliver & Boyd, Edinburgh, 1922), p. 19.

[14] E. William Robertson, *Scotland Under Her Early Kings: A History of the Kingdom to the Close of the 13th Century, Part One* (Edinburgh: Edmonston and Douglas, 1862), p. 80.

[15] Ronald Williams, *The Lords of the Isles: The Clan Donald and the Early Kingdom of the Scots* (Chatto & Windus - The Hogarth Press, London, 1984), p. 81.

[16] James Gray, *Sutherland & Caithness in Saga-Time, or, The Jarls & The Freskyns* (Oliver & Boyd, Edinburgh, 1922), p. 19.

[17] E. William Robertson, *Scotland Under Her Early Kings: A History of the Kingdom to the Close of the 13th Century, Part One* (Edinburgh: Edmonston and Douglas, 1862), p. 80.

[18] Ronald Williams, *The Lords of the Isles: The Clan Donald and the Early Kingdom of the Scots* (Chatto & Windus - The Hogarth Press, London, 1984), p. 81.

[19] E. William Robertson, *Scotland Under Her Early Kings: A History of the Kingdom to the Close of the 13th Century, Part One* (Edinburgh: Edmonston and Douglas, 1862), p. 80.

[20] Ronald Williams, *The Lords of the Isles: The Clan Donald and the Early Kingdom of the Scots* (Chatto & Windus - The Hogarth Press, London, 1984), p. 78, 81.

[21] James Gray, *Sutherland & Caithness in Saga-Time, or, The Jarls & The Freskyns* (Oliver & Boyd, Edinburgh, 1922), p. 19.

[22] James Gray, *Sutherland & Caithness in Saga-Time, or, The Jarls & The Freskyns* (Oliver & Boyd, Edinburgh, 1922), p. 19.

[23] Ronald Williams, *The Lords of the Isles: The Clan Donald and the Early Kingdom of the Scots* (Chatto & Windus - The Hogarth Press, London, 1984), p. 81.

[24] James Gray, *Sutherland & Caithness in Saga-Time, or, The Jarls & The Freskyns* (Oliver & Boyd, Edinburgh, 1922), p. 19.

[25] E. William Robertson, *Scotland Under Her Early Kings: A History of the Kingdom to the Close of the 13th Century, Part One* (Edinburgh: Edmonston and Douglas, 1862), p. 81.

[26] James Gray, *Sutherland & Caithness in Saga-Time, or, The Jarls & The Freskyns* (Oliver & Boyd, Edinburgh, 1922), p. 19.

[27] Ronald Williams, *The Lords of the Isles: The Clan Donald and the Early Kingdom of the Scots* (Chatto & Windus - The Hogarth Press, London, 1984), p. 81.

[28] E. William Robertson, *Scotland Under Her Early Kings: A History of the Kingdom to the Close of the 13th Century, Part One* (Edinburgh: Edmonston and Douglas, 1862), p. 81.

[29] Ronald Williams, *The Lords of the Isles: The Clan Donald and the Early Kingdom of the Scots* (Chatto & Windus - The Hogarth Press, London, 1984), p. 81.

[30] James Gray, *Sutherland & Caithness in Saga-Time, or, The Jarls & The Freskyns* (Oliver & Boyd, Edinburgh, 1922), p. 20.

[31] E. William Robertson, *Scotland Under Her Early Kings: A History of the Kingdom to the Close of the 13th Century, Part One* (Edinburgh: Edmonston and Douglas, 1862), p. 82.

[32] James Gray, *Sutherland & Caithness in Saga-Time, or, The Jarls & The Freskyns* (Oliver & Boyd, Edinburgh, 1922), p. 20.

[33] Ronald Williams, *The Lords of the Isles: The Clan Donald and the Early Kingdom of the Scots* (Chatto & Windus - The Hogarth Press, London, 1984), p. 81.

[34] E. William Robertson, *Scotland Under Her Early Kings: A History of the Kingdom to the Close of the 13th Century, Part One* (Edinburgh: Edmonston and Douglas, 1862), p. 82.

[35] James Gray, *Sutherland & Caithness in Saga-Time, or, The Jarls & The Freskyns* (Oliver & Boyd, Edinburgh, 1922), p. 20.

[36] Ronald Williams, *The Lords of the Isles: The Clan Donald and the Early Kingdom of the Scots* (Chatto & Windus - The Hogarth Press, London, 1984) p. 73.

[37] Ronald Williams, *The Lords of the Isles: The Clan Donald and the Early Kingdom of the Scots* (Chatto & Windus - The Hogarth Press, London, 1984), p. 78.

[38] James Gray, *Sutherland & Caithness in Saga-Time, or, The Jarls & The Freskyns* (Oliver & Boyd, Edinburgh, 1922), p. 20.

[39] James Gray, *Sutherland & Caithness in Saga-Time, or, The Jarls & The Freskyns* (Oliver & Boyd, Edinburgh, 1922), p. 20.

[40] E. William Robertson, *Scotland Under Her Early Kings: A History of the Kingdom to the Close of the 13th Century, Part One* (Edinburgh: Edmonston and Douglas, 1862), p. 83.

[41] James Gray, *Sutherland & Caithness in Saga-Time, or, The Jarls & The Freskyns* (Oliver & Boyd, Edinburgh, 1922), p. 20.

[42] Ronald Williams, *The Lords of the Isles: The Clan Donald and the Early Kingdom of the Scots* (Chatto & Windus - The Hogarth Press, London, 1984), p. 81.

[43] E. William Robertson, *Scotland Under Her Early Kings: A History of the Kingdom to the Close of the 13th Century, Part One* (Edinburgh: Edmonston and Douglas, 1862), p. 83.

[44] James Gray, *Sutherland & Caithness in Saga-Time, or, The Jarls & The Freskyns* (Oliver & Boyd, Edinburgh, 1922), p. 20.

[45] E. William Robertson, *Scotland Under Her Early Kings: A History of the Kingdom to the Close of the 13th Century, Part One* (Edinburgh: Edmonston and Douglas, 1862), p. 84.

[46] James Gray, *Sutherland & Caithness in Saga-Time, or, The Jarls & The Freskyns* (Oliver & Boyd, Edinburgh, 1922), p. 20.

[47] James Gray, *Sutherland & Caithness in Saga-Time, or, The Jarls & The Freskyns* (Oliver & Boyd, Edinburgh, 1922), p. 21.

[48] E. William Robertson, *Scotland Under Her Early Kings: A History of the Kingdom to the Close of the 13th Century, Part One* (Edinburgh: Edmonston and Douglas, 1862), p. 84.

[49] James Gray, *Sutherland & Caithness in Saga-Time, or, The Jarls & The Freskyns* (Oliver & Boyd, Edinburgh, 1922), p. 21.

[50] E. William Robertson, *Scotland Under Her Early Kings: A History of the Kingdom to the Close of the 13th Century, Part One* (Edinburgh: Edmonston and Douglas, 1862), p. 84.

[51] James Gray, *Sutherland & Caithness in Saga-Time, or, The Jarls & The Freskyns* (Oliver & Boyd, Edinburgh, 1922), p. 21.

[52] James Gray, *Sutherland & Caithness in Saga-Time, or, The Jarls & The Freskyns* (Oliver & Boyd, Edinburgh, 1922), p. 21.

[53] E. William Robertson, *Scotland Under Her Early Kings: A History of the Kingdom to the Close of the 13th Century, Part One* (Edinburgh: Edmonston and Douglas, 1862), p. 85.

[54] James Gray, *Sutherland & Caithness in Saga-Time, or, The Jarls & The Freskyns* (Oliver & Boyd, Edinburgh, 1922), p. 21.

[55] Ronald Williams, *The Lords of the Isles: The Clan Donald and the Early Kingdom of the Scots* (Chatto & Windus - The Hogarth Press, London, 1984), p. 82.

[56] E. William Robertson, *Scotland Under Her Early Kings: A History of the Kingdom to the Close of the 13th Century, Part One* (Edinburgh: Edmonston and Douglas, 1862), p. 86.

[57] James Gray, *Sutherland & Caithness in Saga-Time, or, The Jarls & The Freskyns* (Oliver & Boyd, Edinburgh, 1922), p. 21.

[58] E. William Robertson, *Scotland Under Her Early Kings: A History of the Kingdom to the Close of the 13th Century, Part One* (Edinburgh: Edmonston and Douglas, 1862), p. 94.

[59] James Gray, *Sutherland & Caithness in Saga-Time, or, The Jarls & The Freskyns* (Oliver & Boyd, Edinburgh, 1922), p. 21, 26.

[60] E. William Robertson, *Scotland Under Her Early Kings: A History of the Kingdom to the Close of the 13th Century, Part One* (Edinburgh: Edmonston and Douglas, 1862), p. 111.

[61] James Gray, *Sutherland & Caithness in Saga-Time, or, The Jarls & The Freskyns* (Oliver & Boyd, Edinburgh, 1922), p. 21, 27.

[62] Ronald Williams, *The Lords of the Isles: The Clan Donald and the Early Kingdom of the Scots* (Chatto & Windus - The Hogarth Press, London, 1984), p. 59.

[63] Ronald Williams, *The Lords of the Isles: The Clan Donald and the Early Kingdom of the Scots* (Chatto & Windus - The Hogarth Press, London, 1984), p. 82.

[64] Ronald Williams, *The Lords of the Isles: The Clan Donald and the Early Kingdom of the Scots* (Chatto & Windus - The Hogarth Press, London, 1984), p. 83.

[65] Ronald Williams, *The Lords of the Isles: The Clan Donald and the Early Kingdom of the Scots* (Chatto & Windus - The Hogarth Press, London, 1984), p. 89.

[66] E. William Robertson, *Scotland Under Her Early Kings: A History of the Kingdom to the Close of the 13th Century, Part One* (Edinburgh: Edmonston and Douglas, 1862), p. 94.

[67] James Gray, *Sutherland & Caithness in Saga-Time, or, The Jarls & The Freskyns* (Oliver & Boyd, Edinburgh, 1922), p. 21.

[68] Ronald Williams, *The Lords of the Isles: The Clan Donald and the Early Kingdom of the Scots* (Chatto & Windus - The Hogarth Press, London, 1984), p. 88.

[69] E. William Robertson, *Scotland Under Her Early Kings: A History of the Kingdom to the Close of the 13th Century, Part One* (Edinburgh: Edmonston and Douglas, 1862), p. 94.

[70] James Gray, *Sutherland & Caithness in Saga-Time, or, The Jarls & The Freskyns* (Oliver & Boyd, Edinburgh, 1922), p. 22.

[71] Ronald Williams, *The Lords of the Isles: The Clan Donald and the Early Kingdom of the Scots* (Chatto & Windus - The Hogarth Press, London, 1984), p. 94.

[72] James Gray, *Sutherland & Caithness in Saga-Time, or, The Jarls & The Freskyns* (Oliver & Boyd, Edinburgh, 1922), p. 27, 31.

[73] Ronald Williams, *The Lords of the Isles: The Clan Donald and the Early Kingdom of the Scots* (Chatto & Windus - The Hogarth Press, London, 1984), p. 97.

[74] James Gray, *Sutherland & Caithness in Saga-Time, or, The Jarls & The Freskyns* (Oliver & Boyd, Edinburgh, 1922), p. 28.

[75] Ronald Williams, *The Lords of the Isles: The Clan Donald and the Early Kingdom of the Scots* (Chatto & Windus - The Hogarth Press, London, 1984), p. 97.

[76] James Gray, *Sutherland & Caithness in Saga-Time, or, The Jarls & The Freskyns* (Oliver & Boyd, Edinburgh, 1922), p. 27.

[77] E. William Robertson, *Scotland Under Her Early Kings: A History of the Kingdom to the Close of the 13th Century, Part One* (Edinburgh: Edmonston and Douglas, 1862), p. 95, 111-112.

[78] Ronald Williams, *The Lords of the Isles: The Clan Donald and the Early Kingdom of the Scots* (Chatto & Windus - The Hogarth Press, London, 1984), p. 97.

[79] James Gray, *Sutherland & Caithness in Saga-Time, or, The Jarls & The Freskyns* (Oliver & Boyd, Edinburgh, 1922), p. 27.

[80] E. William Robertson, *Scotland Under Her Early Kings: A History of the Kingdom to the Close of the 13th Century, Part One* (Edinburgh: Edmonston and Douglas, 1862), p. 112.

[81] E. William Robertson, *Scotland Under Her Early Kings: A History of the Kingdom to the Close of the 13th Century, Part One* (Edinburgh: Edmonston and Douglas, 1862), p. 112.

[82] James Gray, *Sutherland & Caithness in Saga-Time, or, The Jarls & The Freskyns* (Oliver & Boyd, Edinburgh, 1922), p. 28.

[83] James Gray, *Sutherland & Caithness in Saga-Time, or, The Jarls & The Freskyns* (Oliver & Boyd, Edinburgh, 1922), p. 28.

[84] E. William Robertson, *Scotland Under Her Early Kings: A History of the Kingdom to the Close of the 13th Century, Part One* (Edinburgh: Edmonston and Douglas, 1862), p. 112.

[85] Ronald Williams, *The Lords of the Isles: The Clan Donald and the Early Kingdom of the Scots* (Chatto & Windus - The Hogarth Press, London, 1984), p. 97.

[86] E. William Robertson, *Scotland Under Her Early Kings: A History of the Kingdom to the Close of the 13th Century, Part One* (Edinburgh: Edmonston and Douglas, 1862), p. 113.

[87] James Gray, *Sutherland & Caithness in Saga-Time, or, The Jarls & The Freskyns* (Oliver & Boyd, Edinburgh, 1922), p. 28.

[88] E. William Robertson, *Scotland Under Her Early Kings: A History of the Kingdom to the Close of the 13th Century, Part One* (Edinburgh: Edmonston and Douglas, 1862), p. 114.

[89] Ronald Williams, *The Lords of the Isles: The Clan Donald and the Early Kingdom of the Scots* (Chatto & Windus - The Hogarth Press, London, 1984), p. 98.

[90] Ronald Williams, *The Lords of the Isles: The Clan Donald and the Early Kingdom of the Scots* (Chatto & Windus - The Hogarth Press, London, 1984), p. 98.

[91] E. William Robertson, *Scotland Under Her Early Kings: A History of the Kingdom to the Close of the 13th Century, Part One* (Edinburgh: Edmonston and Douglas, 1862), p. 114.

[92] James Gray, *Sutherland & Caithness in Saga-Time, or, The Jarls & The Freskyns* (Oliver & Boyd, Edinburgh, 1922), p. 28.

[93] E. William Robertson, *Scotland Under Her Early Kings: A History of the Kingdom to the Close of the 13th Century, Part One* (Edinburgh: Edmonston and Douglas, 1862), p. 114.

[94] James Gray, *Sutherland & Caithness in Saga-Time, or, The Jarls & The Freskyns* (Oliver & Boyd, Edinburgh, 1922), p. 29.

[95] Ronald Williams, *The Lords of the Isles: The Clan Donald and the Early Kingdom of the Scots* (Chatto & Windus - The Hogarth Press, London, 1984), p. 98.

[96] E. William Robertson, *Scotland Under Her Early Kings: A History of the Kingdom to the Close of the 13th Century, Part One* (Edinburgh: Edmonston and Douglas, 1862), p. 114.

[97] James Gray, *Sutherland & Caithness in Saga-Time, or, The Jarls & The Freskyns* (Oliver & Boyd, Edinburgh, 1922), p. 29.

[98] Ronald Williams, *The Lords of the Isles: The Clan Donald and the Early Kingdom of the Scots* (Chatto & Windus - The Hogarth Press, London, 1984), p. 98.

[99] E. William Robertson, *Scotland Under Her Early Kings: A History of the Kingdom to the Close of the 13th Century, Part One* (Edinburgh: Edmonston and Douglas, 1862), p. 114-115.

[100] Ronald Williams, *The Lords of the Isles: The Clan Donald and the Early Kingdom of the Scots* (Chatto & Windus - The Hogarth Press, London, 1984), p. 99.

[101] E. William Robertson, *Scotland Under Her Early Kings: A History of the Kingdom to the Close of the 13th Century, Part One* (Edinburgh: Edmonston and Douglas, 1862), p. 116.

[102] James Gray, *Sutherland & Caithness in Saga-Time, or, The Jarls & The Freskyns* (Oliver & Boyd, Edinburgh, 1922), p. 29.

[103] Ronald Williams, *The Lords of the Isles: The Clan Donald and the Early Kingdom of the Scots* (Chatto & Windus - The Hogarth Press, London, 1984), p. 100.

[104] James Gray, *Sutherland & Caithness in Saga-Time, or, The Jarls & The Freskyns* (Oliver & Boyd, Edinburgh, 1922), p. 29-30.

[105] Ronald Williams, *The Lords of the Isles: The Clan Donald and the Early Kingdom of the Scots* (Chatto & Windus - The Hogarth Press, London, 1984), p. 82.

[106] E. William Robertson, *Scotland Under Her Early Kings: A History of the Kingdom to the Close of the 13th Century, Part One* (Edinburgh: Edmonston and Douglas, 1862), p. 116.

[107] Ronald Williams, *The Lords of the Isles: The Clan Donald and the Early Kingdom of the Scots* (Chatto & Windus - The Hogarth Press, London, 1984), p. 100.

[108] James Gray, *Sutherland & Caithness in Saga-Time, or, The Jarls & The Freskyns* (Oliver & Boyd, Edinburgh, 1922), p. 30, 32.

[109] Ronald Williams, *The Lords of the Isles: The Clan Donald and the Early Kingdom of the Scots* (Chatto & Windus - The Hogarth Press, London, 1984), p. 100.

[110] James Gray, *Sutherland & Caithness in Saga-Time, or, The Jarls & The Freskyns* (Oliver & Boyd, Edinburgh, 1922), p. 30.

[111] Ronald Williams, *The Lords of the Isles: The Clan Donald and the Early Kingdom of the Scots* (Chatto & Windus - The Hogarth Press, London, 1984), p. 101.

[112] James Gray, *Sutherland & Caithness in Saga-Time, or, The Jarls & The Freskyns* (Oliver & Boyd, Edinburgh, 1922), p. 30.

[113] Ronald Williams, *The Lords of the Isles: The Clan Donald and the Early Kingdom of the Scots* (Chatto & Windus - The Hogarth Press, London, 1984), p. 101.

[114] James Gray, *Sutherland & Caithness in Saga-Time, or, The Jarls & The Freskyns* (Oliver & Boyd, Edinburgh, 1922), p. 30-31.

[115] Ronald Williams, *The Lords of the Isles: The Clan Donald and the Early Kingdom of the Scots* (Chatto & Windus - The Hogarth Press, London, 1984), p. 101-2.

[116] James Gray, *Sutherland & Caithness in Saga-Time, or, The Jarls & The Freskyns* (Oliver & Boyd, Edinburgh, 1922), p. 31.

[117] Ronald Williams, *The Lords of the Isles: The Clan Donald and the Early Kingdom of the Scots* (Chatto & Windus - The Hogarth Press, London, 1984), p. 102.

[118] James Gray, *Sutherland & Caithness in Saga-Time, or, The Jarls & The Freskyns* (Oliver & Boyd, Edinburgh, 1922), p. 31.

[119] Ronald Williams, *The Lords of the Isles: The Clan Donald and the Early Kingdom of the Scots* (Chatto & Windus - The Hogarth Press, London, 1984), p. 102.

[120] Ronald Williams, *The Lords of the Isles: The Clan Donald and the Early Kingdom of the Scots* (Chatto & Windus - The Hogarth Press, London, 1984), p. 102.

[121] James Gray, *Sutherland & Caithness in Saga-Time, or, The Jarls & The Freskyns* (Oliver & Boyd, Edinburgh, 1922), p. 31-32.

[122] James Gray, *Sutherland & Caithness in Saga-Time, or, The Jarls & The Freskyns* (Oliver & Boyd, Edinburgh, 1922), p. 32.

[123] James Gray, *Sutherland & Caithness in Saga-Time, or, The Jarls & The Freskyns* (Oliver & Boyd, Edinburgh, 1922), p. 32.

[124] Ronald Williams, *The Lords of the Isles: The Clan Donald and the Early Kingdom of the Scots* (Chatto & Windus - The Hogarth Press, London, 1984), p. 104.

[125] James Gray, *Sutherland & Caithness in Saga-Time, or, The Jarls & The Freskyns* (Oliver & Boyd, Edinburgh, 1922), p. 33.

[126] James Gray, *Sutherland & Caithness in Saga-Time, or, The Jarls & The Freskyns* (Oliver & Boyd, Edinburgh, 1922), p. 33.

[127] E. William Robertson, *Scotland Under Her Early Kings: A History of the Kingdom to the Close of the 13th Century, Part One* (Edinburgh: Edmonston and Douglas, 1862), p. 165.

[128] James Gray, *Sutherland & Caithness in Saga-Time, or, The Jarls & The Freskyns* (Oliver & Boyd, Edinburgh, 1922), p. 33.

[129] E. William Robertson, *Scotland Under Her Early Kings: A History of the Kingdom to the Close of the 13th Century, Part One* (Edinburgh: Edmonston and Douglas, 1862), p. 400.

[130] James Gray, *Sutherland & Caithness in Saga-Time, or, The Jarls & The Freskyns* (Oliver & Boyd, Edinburgh, 1922), p. 33.

[131] James Gray, *Sutherland & Caithness in Saga-Time, or, The Jarls & The Freskyns* (Oliver & Boyd, Edinburgh, 1922), p. 33.

[132] E. William Robertson, *Scotland Under Her Early Kings: A History of the Kingdom to the Close of the 13th Century, Part One* (Edinburgh: Edmonston and Douglas, 1862), p. 400.

[133] E. William Robertson, *Scotland Under Her Early Kings: A History of the Kingdom to the Close of the 13th Century, Part One* (Edinburgh: Edmonston and Douglas, 1862), p. 401.

[134] James Gray, *Sutherland & Caithness in Saga-Time, or, The Jarls & The Freskyns* (Oliver & Boyd, Edinburgh, 1922), p. 33.

[135] James Gray, *Sutherland & Caithness in Saga-Time, or, The Jarls & The Freskyns* (Oliver & Boyd, Edinburgh, 1922), p. 33-34.

[136] E. William Robertson, *Scotland Under Her Early Kings: A History of the Kingdom to the Close of the 13th Century, Part One* (Edinburgh: Edmonston and Douglas, 1862), p. 401.

[137] James Gray, *Sutherland & Caithness in Saga-Time, or, The Jarls & The Freskyns* (Oliver & Boyd, Edinburgh, 1922), p. 34.

[138] James Gray, *Sutherland & Caithness in Saga-Time, or, The Jarls & The Freskyns* (Oliver & Boyd, Edinburgh, 1922), p. 34.

[139] E. William Robertson, *Scotland Under Her Early Kings: A History of the Kingdom to the Close of the 13th Century, Part One* (Edinburgh: Edmonston and Douglas, 1862), p. 401.

[140] James Gray, *Sutherland & Caithness in Saga-Time, or, The Jarls & The Freskyns* (Oliver & Boyd, Edinburgh, 1922), p. 34.

[141] E. William Robertson, *Scotland Under Her Early Kings: A History of the Kingdom to the Close of the 13th Century, Part One* (Edinburgh: Edmonston and Douglas, 1862), p. 401.

[142] James Gray, *Sutherland & Caithness in Saga-Time, or, The Jarls & The Freskyns* (Oliver & Boyd, Edinburgh, 1922), p. 35.

[143] James Gray, *Sutherland & Caithness in Saga-Time, or, The Jarls & The Freskyns* (Oliver & Boyd, Edinburgh, 1922), p. 37.

[144] E. William Robertson, *Scotland Under Her Early Kings: A History of the Kingdom to the Close of the 13th Century, Part One* (Edinburgh: Edmonston and Douglas, 1862), p. 401.

[145] James Gray, *Sutherland & Caithness in Saga-Time, or, The Jarls & The Freskyns* (Oliver & Boyd, Edinburgh, 1922), p. 37.

[146] James Gray, *Sutherland & Caithness in Saga-Time, or, The Jarls & The Freskyns* (Oliver & Boyd, Edinburgh, 1922), p. 37.

[147] E. William Robertson, *Scotland Under Her Early Kings: A History of the Kingdom to the Close of the 13th Century, Part One* (Edinburgh: Edmonston and Douglas, 1862), p. 402.

[148] James Gray, *Sutherland & Caithness in Saga-Time, or, The Jarls & The Freskyns* (Oliver & Boyd, Edinburgh, 1922), p. 37-38.

[149] E. William Robertson, *Scotland Under Her Early Kings: A History of the Kingdom to the Close of the 13th Century, Part One* (Edinburgh: Edmonston and Douglas, 1862), p. 402.

[150] James Gray, *Sutherland & Caithness in Saga-Time, or, The Jarls & The Freskyns* (Oliver & Boyd, Edinburgh, 1922), p. 38-39.

[151] James Gray, *Sutherland & Caithness in Saga-Time, or, The Jarls & The Freskyns* (Oliver & Boyd, Edinburgh, 1922), p. 39.

[152] James Gray, *Sutherland & Caithness in Saga-Time, or, The Jarls & The Freskyns* (Oliver & Boyd, Edinburgh, 1922), p. 39.

[153] E. William Robertson, *Scotland Under Her Early Kings: A History of the Kingdom to the Close of the 13th Century, Part One* (Edinburgh: Edmonston and Douglas, 1862), p. 403.

[154] James Gray, *Sutherland & Caithness in Saga-Time, or, The Jarls & The Freskyns* (Oliver & Boyd, Edinburgh, 1922), p. 39.

[155] James Gray, *Sutherland & Caithness in Saga-Time, or, The Jarls & The Freskyns* (Oliver & Boyd, Edinburgh, 1922), p. 39.

[156] James Gray, *Sutherland & Caithness in Saga-Time, or, The Jarls & The Freskyns* (Oliver & Boyd, Edinburgh, 1922), p. 39.

[157] James Gray, *Sutherland & Caithness in Saga-Time, or, The Jarls & The Freskyns* (Oliver & Boyd, Edinburgh, 1922), p. 39.

[158] E. William Robertson, *Scotland Under Her Early Kings: A History of the Kingdom to the Close of the 13th Century, Part One* (Edinburgh: Edmonston and Douglas, 1862), p. 403-404.

[159] James Gray, *Sutherland & Caithness in Saga-Time, or, The Jarls & The Freskyns* (Oliver & Boyd, Edinburgh, 1922), p. 39-40.

[160] E. William Robertson, *Scotland Under Her Early Kings: A History of the Kingdom to the Close of the 13th Century, Part One* (Edinburgh: Edmonston and Douglas, 1862), p. 403.

[161] James Gray, *Sutherland & Caithness in Saga-Time, or, The Jarls & The Freskyns* (Oliver & Boyd, Edinburgh, 1922), p. 40.

[162] E. William Robertson, *Scotland Under Her Early Kings: A History of the Kingdom to the Close of the 13th Century, Part One* (Edinburgh: Edmonston and Douglas, 1862), p. 404.

[163] James Gray, *Sutherland & Caithness in Saga-Time, or, The Jarls & The Freskyns* (Oliver & Boyd, Edinburgh, 1922), p. 41.

[164] James Gray, *Sutherland & Caithness in Saga-Time, or, The Jarls & The Freskyns* (Oliver & Boyd, Edinburgh, 1922), p. 40.

[165] James Gray, *Sutherland & Caithness in Saga-Time, or, The Jarls & The Freskyns* (Oliver & Boyd, Edinburgh, 1922), p. 41.

[166] James Gray, *Sutherland & Caithness in Saga-Time, or, The Jarls & The Freskyns* (Oliver & Boyd, Edinburgh, 1922), p. 41.

[167] James Gray, *Sutherland & Caithness in Saga-Time, or, The Jarls & The Freskyns* (Oliver & Boyd, Edinburgh, 1922), p. 41.

[168] E. William Robertson, *Scotland Under Her Early Kings: A History of the Kingdom to the Close of the 13th Century, Part One* (Edinburgh: Edmonston and Douglas, 1862), p. 405.

[169] James Gray, *Sutherland & Caithness in Saga-Time, or, The Jarls & The Freskyns* (Oliver & Boyd, Edinburgh, 1922), p. 41-42.

[170] E. William Robertson, *Scotland Under Her Early Kings: A History of the Kingdom to the Close of the 13th Century, Part One* (Edinburgh: Edmonston and Douglas, 1862), p. 405.

[171] James Gray, *Sutherland & Caithness in Saga-Time, or, The Jarls & The Freskyns* (Oliver & Boyd, Edinburgh, 1922), p. 42.

[172] E. William Robertson, *Scotland Under Her Early Kings: A History of the Kingdom to the Close of the 13th Century, Part One* (Edinburgh: Edmonston and Douglas, 1862), p. 406.

[173] James Gray, *Sutherland & Caithness in Saga-Time, or, The Jarls & The Freskyns* (Oliver & Boyd, Edinburgh, 1922), p. 42.

[174] E. William Robertson, *Scotland Under Her Early Kings: A History of the Kingdom to the Close of the 13th Century, Part One* (Edinburgh: Edmonston and Douglas, 1862), p. 406.

[175] E. William Robertson, *Scotland Under Her Early Kings: A History of the Kingdom to the Close of the 13th Century, Part One* (Edinburgh: Edmonston and Douglas, 1862), p. 407.

[176] James Gray, *Sutherland & Caithness in Saga-Time, or, The Jarls & The Freskyns* (Oliver & Boyd, Edinburgh, 1922), p. 42.

[177] James Gray, *Sutherland & Caithness in Saga-Time, or, The Jarls & The Freskyns* (Oliver & Boyd, Edinburgh, 1922), p. 42.

[178] E. William Robertson, *Scotland Under Her Early Kings: A History of the Kingdom to the Close of the 13th Century, Part One* (Edinburgh: Edmonston and Douglas, 1862), p. 407.

[179] James Gray, *Sutherland & Caithness in Saga-Time, or, The Jarls & The Freskyns* (Oliver & Boyd, Edinburgh, 1922), p. 42.

[180] James Gray, *Sutherland & Caithness in Saga-Time, or, The Jarls & The Freskyns* (Oliver & Boyd, Edinburgh, 1922), p. 42.

[181] James Gray, *Sutherland & Caithness in Saga-Time, or, The Jarls & The Freskyns* (Oliver & Boyd, Edinburgh, 1922), p. 42-43.

[182] E. William Robertson, *Scotland Under Her Early Kings: A History of the Kingdom to the Close of the 13th Century, Part One* (Edinburgh: Edmonston and Douglas, 1862), p. 407.

[183] James Gray, *Sutherland & Caithness in Saga-Time, or, The Jarls & The Freskyns* (Oliver & Boyd, Edinburgh, 1922), p. 43.

[184] James Gray, *Sutherland & Caithness in Saga-Time, or, The Jarls & The Freskyns* (Oliver & Boyd, Edinburgh, 1922), p. 43.

[185] E. William Robertson, *Scotland Under Her Early Kings: A History of the Kingdom to the Close of the 13th Century, Part One* (Edinburgh: Edmonston and Douglas, 1862), p. 407.

[186] James Gray, *Sutherland & Caithness in Saga-Time, or, The Jarls & The Freskyns* (Oliver & Boyd, Edinburgh, 1922), p. 43.

[187] E. William Robertson, *Scotland Under Her Early Kings: A History of the Kingdom to the Close of the 13th Century, Part One* (Edinburgh: Edmonston and Douglas, 1862), p. 407.

[188] James Gray, *Sutherland & Caithness in Saga-Time, or, The Jarls & The Freskyns* (Oliver & Boyd, Edinburgh, 1922), p. 44.

[189] E. William Robertson, *Scotland Under Her Early Kings: A History of the Kingdom to the Close of the 13th Century, Part One* (Edinburgh: Edmonston and Douglas, 1862), p. 407.

[190] James Gray, *Sutherland & Caithness in Saga-Time, or, The Jarls & The Freskyns* (Oliver & Boyd, Edinburgh, 1922), p. 44.

[191] E. William Robertson, *Scotland Under Her Early Kings: A History of the Kingdom to the Close of the 13th Century, Part One* (Edinburgh: Edmonston and Douglas, 1862), p. 407.

[192] James Gray, *Sutherland & Caithness in Saga-Time, or, The Jarls & The Freskyns* (Oliver & Boyd, Edinburgh, 1922), p. 44.

[193] James Gray, *Sutherland & Caithness in Saga-Time, or, The Jarls & The Freskyns* (Oliver & Boyd, Edinburgh, 1922), p. 44-45.

[194] Angus MacKay, *The Book of MacKay* (Edinburgh: Norman MacLeod, 1906), p. 24, 27.

[195] E. William Robertson, *Scotland Under Her Early Kings: A History of the Kingdom to the Close of the 13th Century, Part One* (Edinburgh: Edmonston and Douglas, 1862), p. 409.

[196] James Gray, *Sutherland & Caithness in Saga-Time, or, The Jarls & The Freskyns* (Oliver & Boyd, Edinburgh, 1922), p. 45.

[197] James Gray, *Sutherland & Caithness in Saga-Time, or, The Jarls & The Freskyns* (Oliver & Boyd, Edinburgh, 1922), p. 50.

[198] James Gray, *Sutherland & Caithness in Saga-Time, or, The Jarls & The Freskyns* (Oliver & Boyd, Edinburgh, 1922), p. 50-51.

[199] James Gray, *Sutherland & Caithness in Saga-Time, or, The Jarls & The Freskyns* (Oliver & Boyd, Edinburgh, 1922), p. 50.

[200] James Gray, *Sutherland & Caithness in Saga-Time, or, The Jarls & The Freskyns* (Oliver & Boyd, Edinburgh, 1922), p. 50-51.

[201] E. William Robertson, *Scotland Under Her Early Kings: A History of the Kingdom to the Close of the 13th Century, Part One* (Edinburgh: Edmonston and Douglas, 1862), p. 409.

[202] E. William Robertson, *Scotland Under Her Early Kings: A History of the Kingdom to the Close of the 13th Century, Part One* (Edinburgh: Edmonston and Douglas, 1862), p. 432.

[203] James Gray, *Sutherland & Caithness in Saga-Time, or, The Jarls & The Freskyns* (Oliver & Boyd, Edinburgh, 1922), p. 53.

[204] James Gray, *Sutherland & Caithness in Saga-Time, or, The Jarls & The Freskyns* (Oliver & Boyd, Edinburgh, 1922), p. 49.

[205] E. William Robertson, *Scotland Under Her Early Kings: A History of the Kingdom to the Close of the 13th Century, Part One* (Edinburgh: Edmonston and Douglas, 1862), p. 409.

[206] James Gray, *Sutherland & Caithness in Saga-Time, or, The Jarls & The Freskyns* (Oliver & Boyd, Edinburgh, 1922), p. 49.

[207] E. William Robertson, *Scotland Under Her Early Kings: A History of the Kingdom to the Close of the 13th Century, Part One* (Edinburgh: Edmonston and Douglas, 1862), p. 409.

[208] E. William Robertson, *Scotland Under Her Early Kings: A History of the Kingdom to the Close of the 13th Century, Part One* (Edinburgh: Edmonston and Douglas, 1862), p. 410.

[209] James Gray, *Sutherland & Caithness in Saga-Time, or, The Jarls & The Freskyns* (Oliver & Boyd, Edinburgh, 1922), p. 51.

[210] E. William Robertson, *Scotland Under Her Early Kings: A History of the Kingdom to the Close of the 13th Century, Part One* (Edinburgh: Edmonston and Douglas, 1862), p. 410-411.

[211] James Gray, *Sutherland & Caithness in Saga-Time, or, The Jarls & The Freskyns* (Oliver & Boyd, Edinburgh, 1922), p. 51.

[212] E. William Robertson, *Scotland Under Her Early Kings: A History of the Kingdom to the Close of the 13th Century, Part One* (Edinburgh: Edmonston and Douglas, 1862), p. 412.

[213] James Gray, *Sutherland & Caithness in Saga-Time, or, The Jarls & The Freskyns* (Oliver & Boyd, Edinburgh, 1922), p. 51.

[214] E. William Robertson, *Scotland Under Her Early Kings: A History of the Kingdom to the Close of the 13th Century, Part One* (Edinburgh: Edmonston and Douglas, 1862), p. 412.

[215] James Gray, *Sutherland & Caithness in Saga-Time, or, The Jarls & The Freskyns* (Oliver & Boyd, Edinburgh, 1922), p. 51-52.

[216] E. William Robertson, *Scotland Under Her Early Kings: A History of the Kingdom to the Close of the 13th Century, Part One* (Edinburgh: Edmonston and Douglas, 1862), p. 412.

[217] James Gray, *Sutherland & Caithness in Saga-Time, or, The Jarls & The Freskyns* (Oliver & Boyd, Edinburgh, 1922), p. 52.

[218] E. William Robertson, *Scotland Under Her Early Kings: A History of the Kingdom to the Close of the 13th Century, Part One* (Edinburgh: Edmonston and Douglas, 1862), p. 413.

[219] James Gray, *Sutherland & Caithness in Saga-Time, or, The Jarls & The Freskyns* (Oliver & Boyd, Edinburgh, 1922), p. 52.

[220] E. William Robertson, *Scotland Under Her Early Kings: A History of the Kingdom to the Close of the 13th Century, Part One* (Edinburgh: Edmonston and Douglas, 1862), p. 413.

[221] James Gray, *Sutherland & Caithness in Saga-Time, or, The Jarls & The Freskyns* (Oliver & Boyd, Edinburgh, 1922), p. 52.

[222] E. William Robertson, *Scotland Under Her Early Kings: A History of the Kingdom to the Close of the 13th Century, Part One* (Edinburgh: Edmonston and Douglas, 1862), p. 413.

[223] James Gray, *Sutherland & Caithness in Saga-Time, or, The Jarls & The Freskyns* (Oliver & Boyd, Edinburgh, 1922), p. 52-53.

[224] E. William Robertson, *Scotland Under Her Early Kings: A History of the Kingdom to the Close of the 13th Century, Part One* (Edinburgh: Edmonston and Douglas, 1862), p. 413.

[225] James Gray, *Sutherland & Caithness in Saga-Time, or, The Jarls & The Freskyns* (Oliver & Boyd, Edinburgh, 1922), p. 53.

[226] E. William Robertson, *Scotland Under Her Early Kings: A History of the Kingdom to the Close of the 13th Century, Part One* (Edinburgh: Edmonston and Douglas, 1862), p. 405.

[227] James Gray, *Sutherland & Caithness in Saga-Time, or, The Jarls & The Freskyns* (Oliver & Boyd, Edinburgh, 1922), p. 53.

[228] E. William Robertson, *Scotland Under Her Early Kings: A History of the Kingdom to the Close of the 13th Century, Part One* (Edinburgh: Edmonston and Douglas, 1862), p. 432.

[229] James Gray, *Sutherland & Caithness in Saga-Time, or, The Jarls & The Freskyns* (Oliver & Boyd, Edinburgh, 1922), p. 55.

[230] E. William Robertson, *Scotland Under Her Early Kings: A History of the Kingdom to the Close of the 13th Century, Part One* (Edinburgh: Edmonston and Douglas, 1862), p. 432.

[231] James Gray, *Sutherland & Caithness in Saga-Time, or, The Jarls & The Freskyns* (Oliver & Boyd, Edinburgh, 1922), p. 55.

[232] James Gray, *Sutherland & Caithness in Saga-Time, or, The Jarls & The Freskyns* (Oliver & Boyd, Edinburgh, 1922), p. 55.

[233] James Gray, *Sutherland & Caithness in Saga-Time, or, The Jarls & The Freskyns* (Oliver & Boyd, Edinburgh, 1922), p. 55.

[234] James Gray, *Sutherland & Caithness in Saga-Time, or, The Jarls & The Freskyns* (Oliver & Boyd, Edinburgh, 1922), p. 55.

[235] James Gray, *Sutherland & Caithness in Saga-Time, or, The Jarls & The Freskyns* (Oliver & Boyd, Edinburgh, 1922), p. 56.

[236] James Gray, *Sutherland & Caithness in Saga-Time, or, The Jarls & The Freskyns* (Oliver & Boyd, Edinburgh, 1922), p. 56.

[237] James Gray, *Sutherland & Caithness in Saga-Time, or, The Jarls & The Freskyns* (Oliver & Boyd, Edinburgh, 1922), p. 56.

[238] James Gray, *Sutherland & Caithness in Saga-Time, or, The Jarls & The Freskyns* (Oliver & Boyd, Edinburgh, 1922), p. 56.

[239] James Gray, *Sutherland & Caithness in Saga-Time, or, The Jarls & The Freskyns* (Oliver & Boyd, Edinburgh, 1922), p. 57.

[240] James Gray, *Sutherland & Caithness in Saga-Time, or, The Jarls & The Freskyns* (Oliver & Boyd, Edinburgh, 1922), p. 57.

[241] James Gray, *Sutherland & Caithness in Saga-Time, or, The Jarls & The Freskyns* (Oliver & Boyd, Edinburgh, 1922), p. 57.

[242] James Gray, *Sutherland & Caithness in Saga-Time, or, The Jarls & The Freskyns* (Oliver & Boyd, Edinburgh, 1922), p. 57.

[243] James Gray, *Sutherland & Caithness in Saga-Time, or, The Jarls & The Freskyns* (Oliver & Boyd, Edinburgh, 1922), p. 57-58.

[244] James Gray, *Sutherland & Caithness in Saga-Time, or, The Jarls & The Freskyns* (Oliver & Boyd, Edinburgh, 1922), p. 60.

[245] James Gray, *Sutherland & Caithness in Saga-Time, or, The Jarls & The Freskyns* (Oliver & Boyd, Edinburgh, 1922), p. 60.

[246] James Gray, *Sutherland & Caithness in Saga-Time, or, The Jarls & The Freskyns* (Oliver & Boyd, Edinburgh, 1922), p. 61.

[247] James Gray, *Sutherland & Caithness in Saga-Time, or, The Jarls & The Freskyns* (Oliver & Boyd, Edinburgh, 1922), p. 60.

[248] James Gray, *Sutherland & Caithness in Saga-Time, or, The Jarls & The Freskyns* (Oliver & Boyd, Edinburgh, 1922), p. 60.

[249] James Gray, *Sutherland & Caithness in Saga-Time, or, The Jarls & The Freskyns* (Oliver & Boyd, Edinburgh, 1922), p. 68.

[250] James Gray, *Sutherland & Caithness in Saga-Time, or, The Jarls & The Freskyns* (Oliver & Boyd, Edinburgh, 1922), p. 65.

[251] Roland William Saint-Clair, *Saint-Clairs of the Isles: A History of the Sea-Kings of Orkney and their Scottish Successors of the Sirname Sinclair* (Auckland, New Zealand, H. Brett, General Printer and Publisher, Shortland and Fort Streets 1898), p. 435.

[252] Cynthia J. Neville, *Native Lordship in Medieval Scotland: The Earldoms of Strathearn & Lennox, c. 1140-1365* (Four Courts Press, Portland & Dublin, 2005), p. 17.

[253] Roland William Saint-Clair, *Saint-Clairs of the Isles: A History of the Sea-Kings of Orkney and their Scottish Successors of the Sirname Sinclair* (Auckland, New Zealand, H. Brett, General Printer and Publisher, Shortland and Fort Streets 1898), p. 435.

[254] Cynthia J. Neville, *Native Lordship in Medieval Scotland: The Earldoms of Strathearn & Lennox, c. 1140-1365* (Four Courts Press, Portland & Dublin, 2005), p. 18.

[255] Roland William Saint-Clair, *Saint-Clairs of the Isles: A History of the Sea-Kings of Orkney and their Scottish Successors of the Sirname Sinclair* (Auckland, New Zealand, H. Brett, General Printer and Publisher, Shortland and Fort Streets 1898), p. 435.

[256] Cynthia J. Neville, *Native Lordship in Medieval Scotland: The Earldoms of Strathearn & Lennox, c. 1140-1365* (Four Courts Press, Portland & Dublin, 2005), p. 18.

[257] Cynthia J. Neville, *Native Lordship in Medieval Scotland: The Earldoms of Strathearn & Lennox, c. 1140-1365* (Four Courts Press, Portland & Dublin, 2005), p. 19.

[258] Cynthia J. Neville, *Native Lordship in Medieval Scotland: The Earldoms of Strathearn & Lennox, c. 1140-1365* (Four Courts Press, Portland & Dublin, 2005), p. 17.

[259] Cynthia J. Neville, *Native Lordship in Medieval Scotland: The Earldoms of Strathearn & Lennox, c. 1140-1365* (Four Courts Press, Portland & Dublin, 2005), p. 18-19.

[260] Roland William Saint-Clair, *Saint-Clairs of the Isles: A History of the Sea-Kings of Orkney and their Scottish Successors of the Sirname Sinclair* (Auckland, New Zealand, H. Brett, General Printer and Publisher, Shortland and Fort Streets 1898), p. 435-436.

[261] Cynthia J. Neville, *Native Lordship in Medieval Scotland: The Earldoms of Strathearn & Lennox, c. 1140-1365* (Four Courts Press, Portland & Dublin, 2005), p. 11.

[262] Cynthia J. Neville, *Native Lordship in Medieval Scotland: The Earldoms of Strathearn & Lennox, c. 1140-1365* (Four Courts Press, Portland & Dublin, 2005), p. 11.

[263] Roland William Saint-Clair, *Saint-Clairs of the Isles: A History of the Sea-Kings of Orkney and their Scottish Successors of the Sirname Sinclair* (Auckland, New Zealand, H. Brett, General Printer and Publisher, Shortland and Fort Streets 1898), p. 435.

[264] Roland William Saint-Clair, *Saint-Clairs of the Isles: A History of the Sea-Kings of Orkney and their Scottish Successors of the Sirname Sinclair* (Auckland, New Zealand, H. Brett, General Printer and Publisher, Shortland and Fort Streets 1898), p. 436.

[265] Cynthia J. Neville, *Native Lordship in Medieval Scotland: The Earldoms of Strathearn & Lennox, c. 1140-1365* (Four Courts Press, Portland & Dublin, 2005), p. 19.

[266] Cynthia J. Neville, *Native Lordship in Medieval Scotland: The Earldoms of Strathearn & Lennox, c. 1140-1365* (Four Courts Press, Portland & Dublin, 2005), p. 20.

[267] Cynthia J. Neville, *Native Lordship in Medieval Scotland: The Earldoms of Strathearn & Lennox, c. 1140-1365* (Four Courts Press, Portland & Dublin, 2005), p. 20.

[268] Roland William Saint-Clair, *Saint-Clairs of the Isles: A History of the Sea-Kings of Orkney and their Scottish Successors of the Sirname Sinclair* (Auckland, New Zealand, H. Brett, General Printer and Publisher, Shortland and Fort Streets 1898), p. 436.

[269] Cynthia J. Neville, *Native Lordship in Medieval Scotland: The Earldoms of Strathearn & Lennox, c. 1140-1365* (Four Courts Press, Portland & Dublin, 2005), p. 20-21.

[270] Cynthia J. Neville, *Native Lordship in Medieval Scotland: The Earldoms of Strathearn & Lennox, c. 1140-1365* (Four Courts Press, Portland & Dublin, 2005), p. 20.

[271] Roland William Saint-Clair, *Saint-Clairs of the Isles: A History of the Sea-Kings of Orkney and their Scottish Successors of the Sirname Sinclair* (Auckland, New Zealand, H. Brett, General Printer and Publisher, Shortland and Fort Streets 1898), p. 436.

[272] Cynthia J. Neville, *Native Lordship in Medieval Scotland: The Earldoms of Strathearn & Lennox, c. 1140-1365* (Four Courts Press, Portland & Dublin, 2005), p. 21.

[273] Roland William Saint-Clair, *Saint-Clairs of the Isles: A History of the Sea-Kings of Orkney and their Scottish Successors of the Sirname Sinclair* (Auckland, New Zealand, H. Brett, General Printer and Publisher, Shortland and Fort Streets 1898), p. 436.

[274] Cynthia J. Neville, *Native Lordship in Medieval Scotland: The Earldoms of Strathearn & Lennox, c. 1140-1365* (Four Courts Press, Portland & Dublin, 2005), p. 23.

[275] Roland William Saint-Clair, *Saint-Clairs of the Isles: A History of the Sea-Kings of Orkney and their Scottish Successors of the Sirname Sinclair* (Auckland, New Zealand, H. Brett, General Printer and Publisher, Shortland and Fort Streets 1898), p. 436.

[276] Cynthia J. Neville, *Native Lordship in Medieval Scotland: The Earldoms of Strathearn & Lennox, c. 1140-1365* (Four Courts Press, Portland & Dublin, 2005), p. 11.

[277] Roland William Saint-Clair, *Saint-Clairs of the Isles: A History of the Sea-Kings of Orkney and their Scottish Successors of the Sirname Sinclair* (Auckland, New Zealand, H. Brett, General Printer and Publisher, Shortland and Fort Streets 1898), p. 436.

[278] Cynthia J. Neville, *Native Lordship in Medieval Scotland: The Earldoms of Strathearn & Lennox, c. 1140-1365* (Four Courts Press, Portland & Dublin, 2005), p. 23.

[279] Cynthia J. Neville, *Native Lordship in Medieval Scotland: The Earldoms of Strathearn & Lennox, c. 1140-1365* (Four Courts Press, Portland & Dublin, 2005), p. 23.

[280] Roland William Saint-Clair, *Saint-Clairs of the Isles: A History of the Sea-Kings of Orkney and their Scottish Successors of the Sirname Sinclair* (Auckland, New Zealand, H. Brett, General Printer and Publisher, Shortland and Fort Streets 1898), p. 436.

[281] Cynthia J. Neville, *Native Lordship in Medieval Scotland: The Earldoms of Strathearn & Lennox, c. 1140-1365* (Four Courts Press, Portland & Dublin, 2005), p. 11.

[282] Roland William Saint-Clair, *Saint-Clairs of the Isles: A History of the Sea-Kings of Orkney and their Scottish Successors of the Sirname Sinclair* (Auckland, New Zealand, H. Brett, General Printer and Publisher, Shortland and Fort Streets 1898), p. 436.

[283] Cynthia J. Neville, *Native Lordship in Medieval Scotland: The Earldoms of Strathearn & Lennox, c. 1140-1365* (Four Courts Press, Portland & Dublin, 2005), p. 23.

[284] Cynthia J. Neville, *Native Lordship in Medieval Scotland: The Earldoms of Strathearn & Lennox, c. 1140-1365* (Four Courts Press, Portland & Dublin, 2005), p. 24-25.

[285] Roland William Saint-Clair, *Saint-Clairs of the Isles: A History of the Sea-Kings of Orkney and their Scottish Successors of the Sirname Sinclair* (Auckland, New Zealand, H. Brett, General Printer and Publisher, Shortland and Fort Streets 1898), p. 437.

[286] Cynthia J. Neville, *Native Lordship in Medieval Scotland: The Earldoms of Strathearn & Lennox, c. 1140-1365* (Four Courts Press, Portland & Dublin, 2005), p. 24.

[287] James Gray, *Sutherland & Caithness in Saga-Time, or, The Jarls & The Freskyns* (Oliver & Boyd, Edinburgh, 1922), p. 65.

[288] Cynthia J. Neville, *Native Lordship in Medieval Scotland: The Earldoms of Strathearn & Lennox, c. 1140-1365* (Four Courts Press, Portland & Dublin, 2005), p. 11.

[289] Cynthia J. Neville, *Native Lordship in Medieval Scotland: The Earldoms of Strathearn & Lennox, c. 1140-1365* (Four Courts Press, Portland & Dublin, 2005), p. 11.

[290] Cynthia J. Neville, *Native Lordship in Medieval Scotland: The Earldoms of Strathearn & Lennox, c. 1140-1365* (Four Courts Press, Portland & Dublin, 2005), p. 11.

[291] Cynthia J. Neville, *Native Lordship in Medieval Scotland: The Earldoms of Strathearn & Lennox, c. 1140-1365* (Four Courts Press, Portland & Dublin, 2005), p. 31.

[292] Cynthia J. Neville, *Native Lordship in Medieval Scotland: The Earldoms of Strathearn & Lennox, c. 1140-1365* (Four Courts Press, Portland & Dublin, 2005), p. 11, 25.

[293] Cynthia J. Neville, *Native Lordship in Medieval Scotland: The Earldoms of Strathearn & Lennox, c. 1140-1365* (Four Courts Press, Portland & Dublin, 2005), p. 11.

[294] Cynthia J. Neville, *Native Lordship in Medieval Scotland: The Earldoms of Strathearn & Lennox, c. 1140-1365* (Four Courts Press, Portland & Dublin, 2005), p. 31-2.

[295] Cynthia J. Neville, *Native Lordship in Medieval Scotland: The Earldoms of Strathearn & Lennox, c. 1140-1365* (Four Courts Press, Portland & Dublin, 2005), p. 32.

[296] Roland William Saint-Clair, *Saint-Clairs of the Isles: A History of the Sea-Kings of Orkney and their Scottish Successors of the Sirname Sinclair* (Auckland, New Zealand, H. Brett, General Printer and Publisher, Shortland and Fort Streets 1898), p. 437.

[297] Cynthia J. Neville, *Native Lordship in Medieval Scotland: The Earldoms of Strathearn & Lennox, c. 1140-1365* (Four Courts Press, Portland & Dublin, 2005), p. 32.

[298] Cynthia J. Neville, *Native Lordship in Medieval Scotland: The Earldoms of Strathearn & Lennox, c. 1140-1365* (Four Courts Press, Portland & Dublin, 2005), p. 32.

[299] Roland William Saint-Clair, *Saint-Clairs of the Isles: A History of the Sea-Kings of Orkney and their Scottish Successors of the Sirname Sinclair* (Auckland, New Zealand, H. Brett, General Printer and Publisher, Shortland and Fort Streets 1898), p. 438.

[300] Cynthia J. Neville, *Native Lordship in Medieval Scotland: The Earldoms of Strathearn & Lennox, c. 1140-1365* (Four Courts Press, Portland & Dublin, 2005), p. 32.

[301] Cynthia J. Neville, *Native Lordship in Medieval Scotland: The Earldoms of Strathearn & Lennox, c. 1140-1365* (Four Courts Press, Portland & Dublin, 2005), p. 33.

[302] Cynthia J. Neville, *Native Lordship in Medieval Scotland: The Earldoms of Strathearn & Lennox, c. 1140-1365* (Four Courts Press, Portland & Dublin, 2005), p. 33.

[303] Cynthia J. Neville, *Native Lordship in Medieval Scotland: The Earldoms of Strathearn & Lennox, c. 1140-1365* (Four Courts Press, Portland & Dublin, 2005), p. 33.

[304] Roland William Saint-Clair, *Saint-Clairs of the Isles: A History of the Sea-Kings of Orkney and their Scottish Successors of the Sirname Sinclair* (Auckland, New Zealand, H. Brett, General Printer and Publisher, Shortland and Fort Streets 1898), p. 438.

[305] Cynthia J. Neville, *Native Lordship in Medieval Scotland: The Earldoms of Strathearn & Lennox, c. 1140-1365* (Four Courts Press, Portland & Dublin, 2005), p. 11.

[306] Roland William Saint-Clair, *Saint-Clairs of the Isles: A History of the Sea-Kings of Orkney and their Scottish Successors of the Sirname Sinclair* (Auckland, New Zealand, H. Brett, General Printer and Publisher, Shortland and Fort Streets 1898), p. 439.

[307] Cynthia J. Neville, *Native Lordship in Medieval Scotland: The Earldoms of Strathearn & Lennox, c. 1140-1365* (Four Courts Press, Portland & Dublin, 2005), p. 33.

[308] Cynthia J. Neville, *Native Lordship in Medieval Scotland: The Earldoms of Strathearn & Lennox, c. 1140-1365* (Four Courts Press, Portland & Dublin, 2005), p. 33.

[309] Cynthia J. Neville, *Native Lordship in Medieval Scotland: The Earldoms of Strathearn & Lennox, c. 1140-1365* (Four Courts Press, Portland & Dublin, 2005), p. 34.

[310] Roland William Saint-Clair, *Saint-Clairs of the Isles: A History of the Sea-Kings of Orkney and their Scottish Successors of the Sirname Sinclair* (Auckland, New Zealand, H. Brett, General Printer and Publisher, Shortland and Fort Streets 1898), p. 439.

311 Cynthia J. Neville, *Native Lordship in Medieval Scotland: The Earldoms of Strathearn & Lennox, c. 1140-1365* (Four Courts Press, Portland & Dublin, 2005), p. 35.
312 Roland William Saint-Clair, *Saint-Clairs of the Isles: A History of the Sea-Kings of Orkney and their Scottish Successors of the Sirname Sinclair* (Auckland, New Zealand, H. Brett, General Printer and Publisher, Shortland and Fort Streets 1898), p. 439.
313 Roland William Saint-Clair, *Saint-Clairs of the Isles: A History of the Sea-Kings of Orkney and their Scottish Successors of the Sirname Sinclair* (Auckland, New Zealand, H. Brett, General Printer and Publisher, Shortland and Fort Streets 1898), p. 86.
314 Cynthia J. Neville, *Native Lordship in Medieval Scotland: The Earldoms of Strathearn & Lennox, c. 1140-1365* (Four Courts Press, Portland & Dublin, 2005), p. 35.
315 Cynthia J. Neville, *Native Lordship in Medieval Scotland: The Earldoms of Strathearn & Lennox, c. 1140-1365* (Four Courts Press, Portland & Dublin, 2005), p. 11.
316 Cynthia J. Neville, *Native Lordship in Medieval Scotland: The Earldoms of Strathearn & Lennox, c. 1140-1365* (Four Courts Press, Portland & Dublin, 2005), p. 35.
317 Cynthia J. Neville, *Native Lordship in Medieval Scotland: The Earldoms of Strathearn & Lennox, c. 1140-1365* (Four Courts Press, Portland & Dublin, 2005), p. 35.
318 Cynthia J. Neville, *Native Lordship in Medieval Scotland: The Earldoms of Strathearn & Lennox, c. 1140-1365* (Four Courts Press, Portland & Dublin, 2005), p. 35.
319 Cynthia J. Neville, *Native Lordship in Medieval Scotland: The Earldoms of Strathearn & Lennox, c. 1140-1365* (Four Courts Press, Portland & Dublin, 2005), p. 35.
320 Cynthia J. Neville, *Native Lordship in Medieval Scotland: The Earldoms of Strathearn & Lennox, c. 1140-1365* (Four Courts Press, Portland & Dublin, 2005), p. 35.
321 Roland William Saint-Clair, *Saint-Clairs of the Isles: A History of the Sea-Kings of Orkney and their Scottish Successors of the Sirname Sinclair* (Auckland, New Zealand, H. Brett, General Printer and Publisher, Shortland and Fort Streets 1898), p. 439.
322 Cynthia J. Neville, *Native Lordship in Medieval Scotland: The Earldoms of Strathearn & Lennox, c. 1140-1365* (Four Courts Press, Portland & Dublin, 2005), p. 35.
323 Cynthia J. Neville, *Native Lordship in Medieval Scotland: The Earldoms of Strathearn & Lennox, c. 1140-1365* (Four Courts Press, Portland & Dublin, 2005), p. 36.
324 Cynthia J. Neville, *Native Lordship in Medieval Scotland: The Earldoms of Strathearn & Lennox, c. 1140-1365* (Four Courts Press, Portland & Dublin, 2005), p. 11.
325 Roland William Saint-Clair, *Saint-Clairs of the Isles: A History of the Sea-Kings of Orkney and their Scottish Successors of the Sirname Sinclair* (Auckland, New Zealand, H. Brett, General Printer and Publisher, Shortland and Fort Streets 1898), p. 439.
326 Cynthia J. Neville, *Native Lordship in Medieval Scotland: The Earldoms of Strathearn & Lennox, c. 1140-1365* (Four Courts Press, Portland & Dublin, 2005), p. 36.
327 Roland William Saint-Clair, *Saint-Clairs of the Isles: A History of the Sea-Kings of Orkney and their Scottish Successors of the Sirname Sinclair* (Auckland, New Zealand, H. Brett, General Printer and Publisher, Shortland and Fort Streets 1898), p. 184.
328 Roland William Saint-Clair, *Saint-Clairs of the Isles: A History of the Sea-Kings of Orkney and their Scottish Successors of the Sirname Sinclair* (Auckland, New Zealand, H. Brett, General Printer and Publisher, Shortland and Fort Streets 1898), p. 96.
329 Roland William Saint-Clair, *Saint-Clairs of the Isles: A History of the Sea-Kings of Orkney and their Scottish Successors of the Sirname Sinclair* (Auckland, New Zealand, H. Brett, General Printer and Publisher, Shortland and Fort Streets 1898), p. 106,113, 121, 185.
330 James Gray, *Sutherland & Caithness in Saga-Time, or, The Jarls & The Freskyns* (Oliver & Boyd, Edinburgh, 1922), p. 71.
331 James Gray, *Sutherland & Caithness in Saga-Time, or, The Jarls & The Freskyns* (Oliver & Boyd, Edinburgh, 1922), p. 71.

Sinclair: The Earls of Orkney & Caithness

Earldom of
Orkney & Shetland

Earldom of Caithness

SCOTLAND

Barony of Roslin

THE SINCLAIR LINEAGE

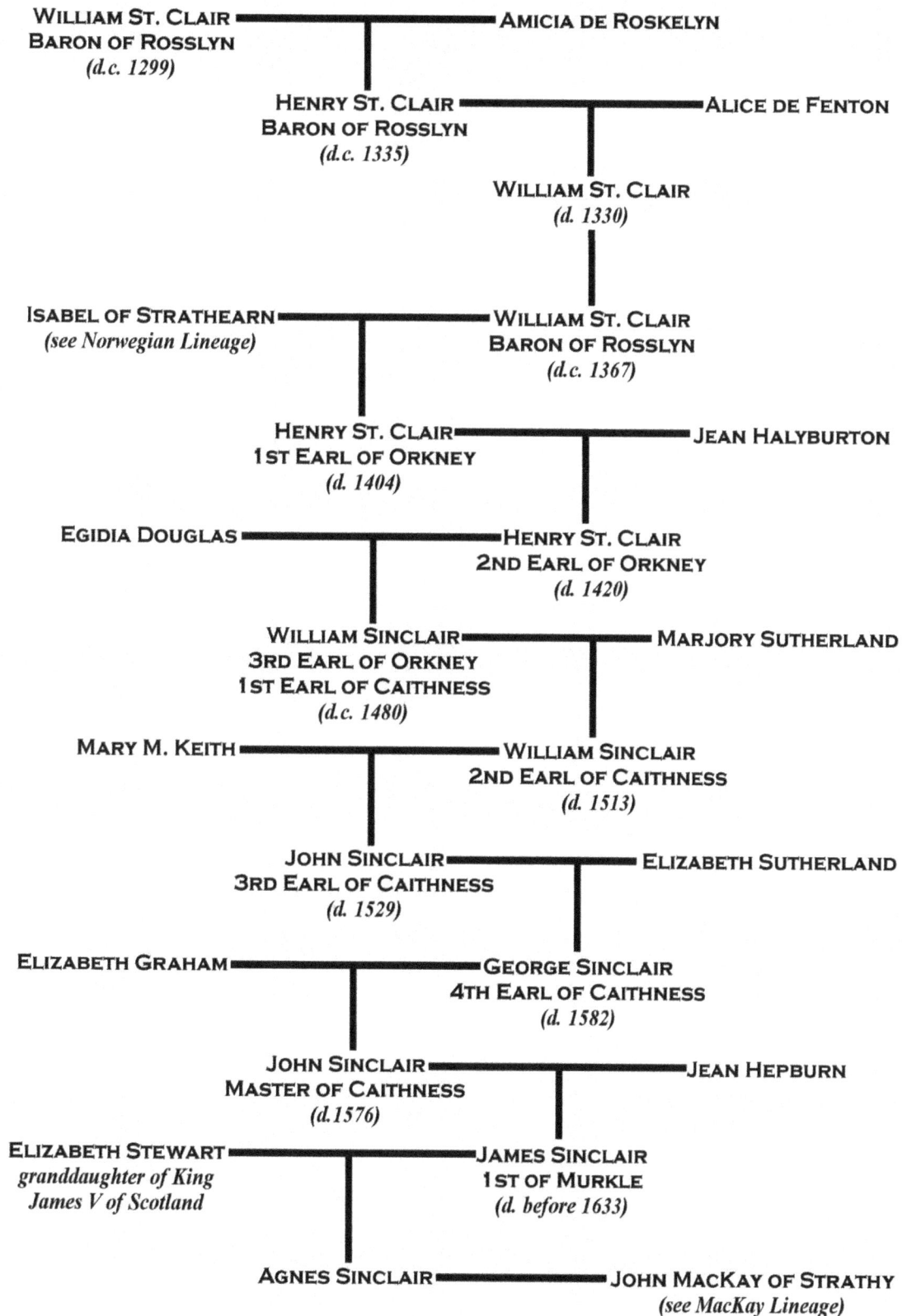

WILLIAM ST. CLAIR
BARON OF ROSSLYN
(d.c. 1299) ━━━━━━━ AMICIA DE ROSKELYN

HENRY ST. CLAIR
BARON OF ROSSLYN
(d.c. 1335) ━━━━━━━ ALICE DE FENTON

WILLIAM ST. CLAIR
(d. 1330)

ISABEL OF STRATHEARN
(see Norwegian Lineage) ━━━━━━━ WILLIAM ST. CLAIR
BARON OF ROSSLYN
(d.c. 1367)

HENRY ST. CLAIR
1ST EARL OF ORKNEY
(d. 1404) ━━━━━━━ JEAN HALYBURTON

EGIDIA DOUGLAS ━━━━━━━ HENRY ST. CLAIR
2ND EARL OF ORKNEY
(d. 1420)

WILLIAM SINCLAIR
3RD EARL OF ORKNEY
1ST EARL OF CAITHNESS
(d.c. 1480) ━━━━━━━ MARJORY SUTHERLAND

MARY M. KEITH ━━━━━━━ WILLIAM SINCLAIR
2ND EARL OF CAITHNESS
(d. 1513)

JOHN SINCLAIR
3RD EARL OF CAITHNESS
(d. 1529) ━━━━━━━ ELIZABETH SUTHERLAND

ELIZABETH GRAHAM ━━━━━━━ GEORGE SINCLAIR
4TH EARL OF CAITHNESS
(d. 1582)

JOHN SINCLAIR
MASTER OF CAITHNESS
(d.1576) ━━━━━━━ JEAN HEPBURN

ELIZABETH STEWART
*granddaughter of King
James V of Scotland* ━━━━━━━ JAMES SINCLAIR
1ST OF MURKLE
(d. before 1633)

AGNES SINCLAIR ━━━━━━━ JOHN MACKAY OF STRATHY
(see MacKay Lineage)

ST. CLAIR/SINCLAIR:
THE EARLS OF ORKNEY AND CAITHNESS

The name Sinclair derives from Saint-Clair. The original St. Clairs were from Normandy, France, where there are several places called Saint-Clair. The first known St. Clairs in Britain arrived as soldiers with William the Conqueror in 1066. These St. Clairs claim a descent from Rollo/Hrolf, the Norse 1st Duke of Normandy, (see *Continental Dynasty*), who was supposedly the son of Ragnvald, 1st Jarl of Orkney (see *Norwegian Lineage*).[1]

As early as 1160, there was a different line of St. Clairs in Herdmanston, Scotland. However, this lineage and our St. Clairs have no known connection until a marriage over a hundred years later.[2] Our St. Clair line shows up in the Barony of Rosslyn/Roslin. The origin of the Barons of Rosslyn is murky. The traditional lineage has Sinclairs all the way back to 1069, at the time of King Malcolm III Canmore of Scotland. The "traditional" first Baron of Rosslyn was William, and the Barony was handed down through the family in unbroken succession through Henry, Henry, William, Henry, and William.[3] Only at this point do contemporary records begin to show the true lay of the land, with yet another William St. Clair.

The dates in parentheses are dates the respective barons held their offices, not birth and death, and the Roman numerals in parentheses after names are inserted by me for clarity, not numerals they themselves used during their lifetimes.

William (I) St. Clair, Baron of Rosslyn
(1280-1299)

There are two distinct schools of thought on William (I) St. Clair's origin. Author Vance Sinclair has him as the son of the 6th Baron of Rosslyn, also named William. Vance Sinclair says he married Jane Halyburton, daughter of Lord Dirletone, but this is at odds with other sources. A Jean Halyburton, daughter of Sir William, Lord of Dirletoun, *did* marry a Sinclair, but it was Henry Sinclair, the 1st Earl of Orkney some 100 years later.[4]

Others claim this William St. Clair came from France and married Amicia de Roskelyn, daughter of Henry de Roskelyn, the then-current Baron of Rosslyn, and inherited the Barony upon that Henry's death.[5]

Given the prevalence of Henrys in the "traditional" St. Clair Rosslyn lineage above, there could be an argument made that both stories are correct. Perhaps there was a line of Sinclair Barons from 1069, and this William was a later immigrant from Normandy who married his distant cousin. But this is all speculation on my part.

William (I) was generally accepted to be the second son of Robert de St. Clair in Normandy and his wife Eleanor de Dreux, the daughter of Robert, Earl of Druex, and his wife, Joland of Coucy.[6] As a second son, he would not inherit much, so he went to Scotland to seek his fortune.

Why Scotland? Through his grandmother Joland, he was related to Scotland's king, Alexander III, so he felt his prospects there might be good.[7] William soon became a favorite of the king, and began to make a name for himself. He held various sheriff posts between 1264 and 1266, namely in Haddington, Linlithgow, and Edinburgh. He served as the High-sheriff of Edinburgh in 1278. He was also made

Panetarius of Scotland, which meant he was responsible for overseeing the provisions for the palace and royal family.[8]

As a mark of his favor in court, William was appointed guardian to Alexander III's son, Prince Alexander, from 1279-1281. It was during those years, in 1280, that William obtained the lands of Innerleith and was granted the Barony of Rosslyn, which his family was to hold for hundreds of years, I think even to the present day.[9]

By 1284, all of Alexander III's children had died, and there was no direct heir to the throne. William sat in the Parliament at Scone that decided what the succession should be if Alexander should die childless, in an effort to avoid a bloody struggle for power. They decided that Alexander's granddaughter, Margaret of Norway, would succeed him.[10]

In 1285, Alexander chose a new wife, Yoland de Dreux from France. William, kin to both Alexander and Yoland, was chosen to go to France to escort her back to England. Because Alexander and Yoland were childless in 1286 when Alexander died, the throne was open for Margaret of Norway, who was only about seven years old.[11]

King Edward I of England (see *Continental Dynasty*) was always looking for ways to subjugate Scotland, and he suggested a marriage between Margaret of Norway and his own son, Edward II. In 1290, as Margaret made her way from Norway to Scotland, William was one of the nobles who signed the letter of Birgham, which agreed to this proposal. Unfortunately, young Margaret never made it to Scotland, dying in the Orkney islands.[12]

Edward I overplayed his hand, thinking he had more support in Scotland than he did, and demanded that Scotland turn over all her fortresses and castles to him, seeing as the throne was vacant and no one was in charge. William and other fortress holders flatly refused. Edward backed down, biding his time.[13]

Edward did not have long to wait. In 1292 he was asked to decide which of multiple claimants to the throne should be crowned king. The two main contenders were John Balliol and Robert de Brus (ancestor of future King Robert I Bruce—see *De Brus Lineage*). William supported Balliol, who was Edward's choice in the end. Balliol, however, swore fealty to Edward, making all of Scotland a fief of England. All the nobles present swore fealty to Edward, since their king had.[14]

The Scots really didn't like being under England's thumb, so they rebelled. Edward invaded in 1296, and William was part of the defense of Dunbar castle. The castle fell to Edward due to lack of resources, and William was taken in chains to the Tower of London. On 7 April 1299, William's widow, Amicia, living by the King's leave in Edinburgh, was given a two-year protective order. It is therefore assumed William had died prior to this date, probably still a captive in the Tower of London.[15]

William (I) St. Clair married Amicia de Roskelyn, the daughter of the previous Baron of Rosslyn, Henry de Roskelyn. They had children:[16]

- *Henry* – next Baron of Rosslyn
- William – Bishop of Dunkeld
- Annabel – married Sir David Wemyss

Henry (I) St. Clair, Baron of Rosslyn
(1299-1335)

Henry (I) St. Clair was with his father when they both swore fealty to Edward I of England in 1292, and at Dunbar when they rebelled against Edward. Henry, too, was captured, and imprisoned in England in St. Briavel's castle. On 7 April 1299, he was exchanged and ransomed, and so regained his freedom.[17][18]

Henry was rewarded for his loyalty to King Robert I Bruce (see *Stewart Dynasty*) by being made sheriff of Lanark in 1305, witnessing a charter in 1314, and having King Robert I raise Henry's Pentland Moor lands to the status of free hunting.[19] It was also likely that Henry and his men were with Robert the Bruce at Bannockburn.[20]

In 1320, Henry was Panetarius of Scotland, an office he inherited from his father. The office did not pass to Henry's children, but to John Comyn, and then on to other families.[21]

Also in 1320, Henry was one of the nobles who signed the Declaration of Arbroath, the Scottish declaration to the Pope of their independence from England and of Robert I Bruce as rightful king.[22][23]

By 1321, Henry was Ballius of Caithness, meaning he was basically the governor of that large area in the north of Scotland, again showing he was trusted by the king.[24]

Henry (I) St. Clair's death date is a bit murky. The last time he appeared on paperwork was 1335, when he and his wife forfeited a third of their barony lands. He married Alice de Fenton, and they had children:[25]

- *William (II), the Younger* – killed in 1330 on Crusade. William and his brother accompanied the heart of Robert I Bruce on Crusade, and were killed in Spain.[26]
- John – killed in 1330 on Crusade

William (II) the Younger's wife was unknown, but his children were:[27]

- *William (III)* – inherited Barony of Rosslyn
- Margaret – married first Thomas Stewart, 2nd Earl of Angus, second William St. Clair of Herdmanston, the first known connection between these families
- Thomas – Ballius of Orkney
- John

William (III) St. Clair, Baron of Rosslyn
(c.1335-1367)

William (III) St. Clair was still a minor when he inherited the barony from his grandfather. In 1358, King David granted William lands in Merton and Merchamyston, and then William went to war on the Continent. However, since he was mentioned in several charters from 1362-1367, he returned safely from that adventure. His sons were likely still minors when he died, which would explain his brother being named Ballius of Orkney rather than his heir Henry, and why almost a decade elapsed between William's disappearance from the records and his son Henry stepping into the Earldom of Orkney.[28]

William (III) St. Clair married Isabel of Strathearn (see *Norwegian Lineage*), a marriage which would bring the St. Clairs much power and land. They had children:[29]

- *Henry (II)* – became 1st Earl of Orkney as well as Lord of Rosslyn
- Margaret
- David of Newburgh

Henry (II) St. Clair, 1st Earl of Orkney, Lord of Rosslyn (1379-1404)

By right of his mother, Isabel of Strathearn, Henry (II) St. Clair inherited the Earldom of Orkney. The earldom had been carried by other male lines of the family, but when those lines failed, it traced back through Isabella (see *Norwegian Lineage*).

In 1379, he and his cousins Alexander de Ard, Earl of Caithness, and Sir Malise Sperra, Lord of Skaldale, traveled to Norway to let the king rule on who should become Earl of Orkney, as they each thought they should. The king gave the earldom to Henry, as well as returning to the earldom the Lordship of Shetland, which had been forfeited back in 1195.[30][31]

The terms of Henry's investiture in the Orkney earldom were strict: he owed men to the King of Norway when called, and he couldn't build castles, go to war, enter into agreements with the bishop, nor give away any of his rights without the king's consent. He had to answer for his whole administration, and upon his death the earldom would revert back to the Norwegian king. The king would then dole it out to whomever they chose—sons of the earl were not guaranteed a succession. As part of the agreement, Malise Sperra resigned all claims to the earldom for himself and his heirs.[32]

After 1380, Henry ignored the terms of his investiture and began to build a castle at Kirkwall. In 1388, Henry was in Norway, doing duty to the Norwegian crown. He was there as Councillor of State, and acknowledged Eric of Pomerania as the rightful king of Norway. In 1389, Henry and his cousin Malise Sperra were at the accession of King Eric.[33][34]

Later in 1389, Malise Sperra tried to take land in the Shetland Islands by force; he refused to submit to court rulings, and was killed in the ensuing fighting.[35][36]

In 1393, Henry subdued more trouble in the Shetlands, and built a fort there. He left his admiral, Sir Nicolo Zeno, a native of Venice, in charge. Nicolo went voyaging in June of 1393, and found Greenland. However, he fell ill there, returned home, and died.[37][38]

Back in Rosslyn, 13 May 1396, Henry's daughter Elizabeth and her husband Sir John de Drummond of Cargyll (brother to King Robert II's wife, Annabell) renounced any claim for themselves or their heirs to any part of the Orkneys, leaving those rights to Henry and his male issue.[39]

Henry St. Clair, Earl of Orkney, is often credited with a great voyage all the way to North America, discovering Nova Scotia and leaving a settlement there and on the North American mainland in Rhode Island.[40] The memoirs of his own admiral, though, told a different story. An Orkney native who had been missing for 26 years, he arrived back and told a tale of lands far away, usually assumed to be North America. Around 1396 or a little after, this inspired Henry to try to get there himself, but bad weather hindered him, and he ended up landing on Greenland. His admiral said Henry and a band of men stayed for a year before coming home. Henry was said to have explored both coasts of Greenland while he was there.[41]

Henry appeared on a charter dated 24 Jan 1404, wherein King Robert III of Scotland (see *Stewart Dynasty*) freed the Earl of Orkney (no other title given) of his Castle Guard due for the Baronies of Rosline, Pentland, Pentland Moor, Colsland, Merton, and Mertonehall, all in the viscounty or sheriffship of Edinburgh.[42]

The earl's date of death was sometime in 1404, while defending his islands from southern invaders. As there was an English record of an attempted invasion of Orkney at this time, it is usually assumed the invaders were this English fleet.[43]

Henry (II) St. Clair married multiple times. He was said to have married Florentina, Princess of Denmark in 1363, by whom he had no children. He was known to have married Jean Halyburton, daughter of Sir William Halyburton of Direltoun. With Jean, he had four sons and nine daughters:[44] [45]

- ***Henry (III)*** – succeeded as 2nd Earl of Orkney, married Egida Douglas
- John – married Ingeberg, daughter of King Waldemar of Denmark
- James
- Walter

Henry (II) was also said to have married Elizabeth of Strathearn, by whom he had Margaret, who married James of Craigie, Lord of Hupe. Henry had a bevy of other children attributed to him, mothers unknown:[46]

- William
- Thomas
- Marjory – married Sir David Menzies of Wemyss
- Jean – married Sir John Forrester, Laird of Corstorphine
- Mary – married Sir Thomas Somerville of Carnwath, Laird Sommervaill
- Elizabeth – married Sir John Drummond of Cargyll

And these daughters, names and mothers unknown, were also supposed to be his:[47]

- Daughter 1 – married the Laird of Dalhousie
- Daughter 2 – married Sandilands, Laird of Calder
- Daughter 3 – married Hay, Earl of Errol
- Daughter 4 – married Tweedie, Laird of Drummelzier
- Daughter 5 – married Cockburne, Laird of Stirling
- Daughter 6 – married Heron, Laird of Mareton/Merton

After Henry (II)'s death, his son ***Henry (III) St. Clair*** inherited the Earldom.

Henry (III) St. Clair, 2nd Earl of Orkney, Baron of Rosslyn
(1404-1420)

Henry (III) St. Clair became the 2nd Earl of Orkney upon his father's death in 1404. Very soon after, he was made a guardian of Prince James, son of King Robert III of Scotland (see *Stewart Dynasty*). Robert III was locked in a struggle with his own brother, Robert, for the throne. Realizing that his brother might try to harm his son, Robert III asked Henry to take James to France for safekeeping. Henry tried, but he and the young prince were captured by the English on 30 March 1405 at Flamborough, England. Henry was released soon after the capture, but James was held captive for many years.[48 49]

Upon his marriage to Egidia (Jill) Douglas, Henry gained much land, since she was Sir William Douglas of Nithsdale's only heir and William had been murdered in 1390.[50] The lands Henry got were: the Lordship of Nithsdale, the Wardonrie of the Three Marches between Berwick and Whithorne, with the Baronies of Hectford, Harbertshire, Grameshaw, Kirktone, Cavers, Roxborough, and the Sheriffship of Nithsdale, with the town of Dumfries.[51]

On 12 September 1410, Henry gave his brother John a charter for the lands of Sunellis, Hope, and Loganhouse in Pentland Moor, near Edinburgh.[52]

Scotland and France had a long-standing alliance against the English, and in 1412 Henry and Archibald Douglas went to France to help the French king fight off an English invasion.[53 54]

Henry needed help governing the far-flung Orkneys, particularly in the troublesome Shetlands, so in 1418 Henry sent his brother John to Norway, where John swore fealty to King Eric for the king's lands in Shetland. John would administer them in accordance with the ancient Norwegian laws, and upon John's death they would revert to the Norwegian crown.[55 56]

The last paperwork Henry appeared on was on 23 November 1419, when Henry signed an indenture with Adam of Dalkel of the Buthagh. Adam was married to Sabey Menzies, who may have been Henry's niece.[57]

Henry (III) St Clair died 1 February 1420.[58] He had married Egidia Douglas and they had two children:[59]

- Beatrix – married James "the Gross" Douglas, 7th Earl of Douglas, 1st Earl of Avondale
- *William (IV)* – Henry's successor

William (IV) Sinclair, 3rd Earl of Orkney, 1st Earl of Caithness, Baron of Rosslyn
(1420-1476)

William (IV) Sinclair took the title of Earl of Orkney upon his father's death in 1420. Shortly after, on 31 May 1421, he was one of five earls among the 20 hostages offered to free King James I of Scotland (see *Stewart Dynasty*) from English captivity. This offer was rejected, so he never went into captivity.[60]

William, like his father, paid scant attention to making friends with his Norse overlord or keeping up his obligations to him. This got him in trouble with Norway, and King Eric of Norway placed Orkney in trust of the Bishop of Orkney, Thomas de Tulloch, for one year. After the Bishop, King Eric entrusted the Isles to David Menzies of Wemyss, William's uncle by marriage to his aunt Jean. David was an awful, tyrannical governor, and in 1426 the Islanders lodged a complaint with King Eric. With David Menzies ousted,

Bishop Thomas de Tulloch took over again for the next seven years, until William received his formal investiture. William took the title when his father died, but was a minor and not invested until reaching adulthood.[61]

In 1423, when King James I returned to Scotland, William was among the earls who met him. Twenty-eight hostages were chosen at that time, but William was not among them.[62]

On 12 Aug 1434, William finally made his formal application to King Eric for investiture of the earldom, and was granted such, with terms much like those given to his grandfather Earl Henry.[63] He was also invested with keeping the castle of Kirkwall for the Norwegian king, which, ironically, Henry had built in violation of the terms set for him.[64]

In 1436, William was Admiral of Scotland. In this role, he escorted Princess Margaret of Scotland to France to marry the Dauphin (later King Louis XI).[65][66]

After the death of Norway's King Eric, William needed to reaffirm his investiture with Eric's successor. To that end, he traveled to Norway and on 25 April 1448 he gave his oath of allegiance to King Christian I.[67]

William was the Baron of Rosslyn who built the now-famous Chapel of Rosslyn (photos can be found online).[68] William obtained the founding charter for the collegiate chapel in 1446, but building commenced in 1456, after all the craftsmen's houses were built.[69]

On 28 Aug 1455, William was created the 1st Earl of Caithness. If you have read the *Norwegian Lineage* chapter, you know there were Earls of Caithness prior to William, however it was not unusual for earldoms to be "recreated" after difficult or confusing successions, so his was started over at #1. William was the hereditary rights-holder of this earldom as the heir male of Malise V of Strathearn, who had held the title before him. Malise (who had no sons) had made special provisions that the Caithness earldom be passed to his daughter Isabel of Strathearn, William's great-grandmother. However, the Crown ignored Isabel's rights to Caithness, and granted it to another line, Alexander de Ard. Alexander died childless, and the earldom passed through four other men who died childless, and was then restored to the rightful line in William Sinclair.[70]

And so William (IV) Sinclair became a very powerful man, holding both the Earldoms of Orkney (via Norway) and Caithness (via Scotland). Only his great-great-grandfather, Malise V, had held similar power in feudal Scotland. Given his power, in 1460 William was one of the six governors appointed to rule during the minority of James III.[71]

King James III of Scotland (see *Stewart Dynasty*) eventually married Princess Margaret of Norway. On 8 September 1468, her father, King Christian I, used Orkney and Shetland as a promise to pay 58,000 florins for Margaret's dowry. This signing over to Scotland was never meant to be permanent, and is still argued to this day.[72] In 1470, James III asked William to resign his Earldom of Orkney to the crown. William did, receiving in exchange Ravenscraig Castle, Fife, and its lands.[73]

In 1476, William (IV) resigned the Earldom of Caithness in favor of his third son, William (V) (reserving a life rent), and resigned the Rosslyn estate in favor of his second son, Oliver. His first son (by another wife) was also named William, but this William was considered a wastrel and was therefore disinherited by his father.[74]

William (IV) Sinclair died sometime around 1480[75]. He had married three times, first to Margaret Douglas, daughter of Archibald Douglas, 4th Earl of Douglas, and they had:[76] [77] [78]

- Katherine – married Alexander Stewart, Duke of Albany
- William "the Wastrel" – later Lord Sinclair

William (IV) married second, Marjory Sutherland, by whom he had:[79] [80] [81]

- Sir Oliver – next Baron of Rosslyn
- *William (V)* – next Earl of Caithness
- John – Bishop nominate of Caithness
- Sir David of Swynbrocht
- Alexander
- George
- Robert
- Arthur
- Eleanor
- Elizabeth – married Sir John Houston
- Margaret – Sir David Boswell of Balmuto and Glasmouth
- Euphemia
- Marjory – married Andrew Leslie, Master of Rothes
- Marietta

William (IV) Sinclair also married Janet Yeman, with whom he had no children.[82]

William (V) Sinclair, 2nd Earl of Caithness (1476-1513)

William (V) Sinclair took over from his father in 1476,[83] [84] and became involved early on in government machinations. King James III of Scotland (see *Stewart Dynasty*) was an unpopular king because he played favorites, and many of his favorites were men of the arts; and because of this there was a strong suspicion of homosexuality. This became a festering sore point among the nobles, and in 1482 the storm broke at Lauder. At the Lauder Bridge, William and a group of other nobles surprised James III and hung a number of his favorites.[85]

James III managed to keep his throne, but by 1488 his own son, the future James IV, was trying to depose him. This time William sided with the rightful king, but William missed the decisive battle at Sauchieburn, arriving too late to participate. King James III died in the battle or soon after, and King James IV came to the throne.[86]

William built the Sinclair's Caithness stronghold of Girnigoe Castle between 1476 and 1479, consolidating their power as new earls, whose family was not native to the area.[87]

There was a story of bad blood between William and his father-in-law, Sir Gilbert/William Keith of Inverugie. As William was returning from a hunt, his father-in-law, angry over some dispute, shot him with an arrow. It lodged in the back of his neck, but William managed to ride home to Girnigoe Castle, not badly wounded.[88] [89]

116

In 1505, William sat on the Scottish Parliament.[90] [91]

William married Mary M. Keith, daughter of Sir Gilbert/William Keith of Inverugie. The couple had:[92] [93] [94]

- *John* – 3rd Earl of Caithness
- Alexander of Stemster and Dunbeath

He also fathered a natural son, William Sinclair.

William (V) Sinclair died 9 September 1513, at the bloody battle of Flodden, where the loss of King James IV (see *Stewart Dynasty*) and a large portion of the nobility led to a governmental crisis in Scotland.[95] [96]

John Sinclair, 3rd Earl of Caithness
(1513-1529)

John Sinclair became earl upon his father's death at Flodden. He was more insular than his father, or perhaps the governmental tumult following losing so many nobles and the king made him wish to stay on the sidelines. His main issues were with his neighbor, the Earl of Sutherland.[97]

Around 1514, perhaps because of unrest due to the Flodden disaster, Adam, Earl of Sutherland, a neighbor of Caithness, entered into a bond of friendship and alliance with John for their mutual protection. To secure this, he gave John some land in Strathully. John took the land, but allied himself with Sutherland's foes. This did not promote good will between the two men.[98]

After being at odds for some ten years, especially about the Strathully lands Sutherland gave John in return for help that never came, Adam of Sutherland and John went to the Bishop of Aberdeen, who pronounced his decision. They lived peacefully afterward.[99]

John decided to help his cousin William Lord Sinclair regain the Orkney Islands from the Scottish Crown. The Islanders fought behind their current governor, James Sinclair (another relative). James was victorious and Earl John and many of his followers were killed on 18 May 1529.[100] [101]

John Sinclair married Elizabeth Sutherland, daughter of William Sutherland of Duffus and Janet Innes. John and Elizabeth had:[102] [103] [104]

- William – died 1527
- *George* – successor to the earldom

John Sinclair also had a natural son, David, who was Bailie of the Bishop of Caithness.[105] [106]

George Sinclair, 4th Earl of Caithness
(1529-1582)

George Sinclair inherited the earldom when his father was killed in 1529, but it was not until 1555 that records show his name. His time as earl spanned 53 years, at a time when the average life expectancy was 40 (skewed because of high infant and child mortality), so likely he was a minor when he inherited.

In July 1555, along with John, Earl of Sutherland, George met with Queen Mary to settle matters in the northern part of the country. He was supposed to bring his countrymen with him, but did not, and therefore spent time in prison in Inverness, Aberdeen, and Edinburgh until he paid a substantial sum of money for his release.[107]

George was involved with the intrigues that surrounded Mary, Queen of Scots, during her entire reign. In 1560, he attended a secret meeting of the Catholic Party. At this meeting, they agreed to send an envoy to France to offer Scotland's service and refresh their attachment.[108]

Most likely at the behest of the Earl of Sutherland, in 1561 a group of men murdered several people in Caithness with whom they had a grudge. George responded by banishing them and taking their castle. They attacked again, but the Earl of Sutherland convinced Queen Mary to pardon them. George was furious with Sutherland's interference, and this formed the basis for a (new) long antipathy between the Earls of Sutherland and Caithness.[109]

On 15 May 1565, George attended the convention of Scottish nobility at Stirling to discuss the marriage prospects of Queen Mary. She announced her intent to marry Henry Stuart, Lord Darnley, and all approved.[110]

George was made Justiciar of the North of Scotland on 17 April 1566. His jurisdiction encompassed all of Caithness and Sutherland, and included the power to banish and kill, and to pardon any crime except treason. This post was one his ancestors had held, so this was a renewal of his hereditary rights.[111]

In 1567, George sent his ally Iye Du MacKay (see *MacKay Lineage*) to attack Sutherland's lands. He captured Skibo and the young Earl of Sutherland was carried back to Girnigoe Castle, where George forced him (at 15 years of age), to marry his daughter Barbara (then 32). It came to light that Barbara and Iye Du had an "undue intimacy" which was later grounds for divorce. Sutherland escaped George in 1569.[112] [113]

Also in 1567, George continued his governmental intrigues. As chancellor of the jury trial of James Hepburn, Earl of Bothwell, for murdering Darnley, he and the jury acquitted Bothwell and cleared the way for him to marry the newly widowed Queen Mary, which Bothwell immediately did.[114] [115]

In 1570, the Murrays and Sutherlands of Duffus got into a feud, and George took the Sutherlands' side. He sent his son John and Iye Du MacKay to settle the matter. John destroyed the Murrays' town, including burning the Cathedral and attacking the castle. The Murrays gave up and came to terms, for which they gave hostages. When John returned to George with the hostages, George didn't agree to the terms and killed all the hostages. John was furious, and went to live with Iye Du MacKay.[116] [117]

Two years later, in 1572, George heard that John and Iye Du Mackay might be plotting against him, so he reached out to John repeatedly saying he wanted to make peace. Eventually John and Iye Du came to

Girnigoe Castle, but Iye Du sensed something amiss and fled. John could not escape, and was thrown in prison by his father. John died of starvation and torture in 1576.[118] [119]

George married Elizabeth Graham, daughter of William Graham, Earl of Montrose, and Lady Janet Keith. George and Elizabeth had:[120] [121]

- *John, Master of Caithness* – died in 1576 in his father's dungeon
- William of Mey, ancestor of the Sinclairs of Ulbster – strangled by his brother John
- George of Mey – inherited the title "of Mey" upon brother William's death
- Barbara – married Alexander, Earl of Sutherland, divorced 1573
- Elizabeth – married first Alexander Sutherland of Duffus, second Huistean du MacKay of Strathnaver (see *MacKay Lineage*)
- Margaret – married William Sutherland of Duffus
- A second Barbara – married Alexander Innes of Innes[122]
- Agnes – married Andrew Hay, Earl of Erroll

Another daughter, Janet, who married Robert Munro of Fowlis, is also sometimes attributed to George.

George Sinclair died 9 September 1582, and was buried in Rosslyn Chapel. In his will, all his money went to son George of Mey, but the earldom title and land went to John's son George.[123]

Sir John Sinclair, Master of Caithness

John Sinclair, who died before his father, never became earl, but his son did. John had seen to that on 2 October 1525, when John obtained a charter from Queen Mary that gave the earldom as a male fee to himself and his male heirs. This is why his son George inherited the earldom upon his father George's death, instead of John's surviving brother, George of Mey.[124] [125]

As we have seen, when Earl George killed the hostages during the Murray conflict, John left to live with Iye Du MacKay. This in turn led to John being imprisoned in his father's castle dungeon. John at one point plotted an escape, but it was discovered and reported by his brother William, and foiled by the execution of John's accomplice. William came to visit John in jail, they argued, and John crushed the life out of William in spite of being in chains. Their father was displeased, and John was starved and tortured until he died. The exact manner of his death is disputed, but that it was torturous is agreed upon by all chroniclers.[126] [127]

John was married to Jean Hepburn, daughter of Patrick Hepburn, 3rd Earl of Bothwell, and Agnes Sinclair (daughter of William "the Wastrel," son of William (IV) 3rd Earl of Caithness). John and Jean divorced in 1575, but they had children:[128] [129]

- Agnes
- George – 5th Earl of Caithness
- *James* – 1st of Murkle
- John – 1st of Greenland and Ratter

John Sinclair also had two natural sons, David and Henry.[130]

Our line departs from the earls, and follows James Sinclair, 1st of Murkle, from whom we gain our royal blood.

James Sinclair, 1st of Murkle

James Sinclair of Murkle was the second son of John. He was frequently enumerated as a Suitor of Court.[131] His vast land holdings centered on Murkle in Caithness, east of Thurso.[132]

In June 1589, James raided into Sutherland territory at the behest of his brother George, 5th Earl of Caithness. He plundered Strathullie and burned Criboll. A MacKay contingent engaged them at Bora, and James was repelled by Huistean du MacKay (see *MacKay Lineage*).[133] [134]

James fell out with his powerful brother George in 1592. George was protecting Francis Stewart, Earl of Bothwell, who was their half-brother through their mother, from the wrath of King James VI. Francis and George had a fight, and George decided to curry favor with the king by intending to turn Francis over to him. James found out and warned Francis, who fled to Naples. George, furious at this betrayal, banished James for life—or, as it turned out, until 1594, when James returned with his brother's forgiveness.[135]

In 1623, Earl George had run up huge debts and otherwise put himself on the wrong side of the king, and he was ordered to be apprehended under a commission of fire and sword, which was granted to his long-time enemy Robert Gordon, the Earl of Sutherland. Gordon amassed an army with George's son William at its head to capture George. (William had spent five years in prison for his father's debts, and was not pleased.) George escaped to Orkney, and gave his permission to his followers to submit to William and Sutherland rather than defy the king's orders. James and his son James were among those who swore allegiance to the king. William took over as Earl of Caithness, and his father, George, was eventually allowed back after paying a hefty fine.[136]

James Sinclair, 1st of Murkle married Elizabeth Stewart, daughter of Robert Stewart, Earl of Orkney, who was a natural son of King James V of Scotland. James and Elizabeth had:[137] [138] [139]

- Sir James – his successor to Murkle
- Francis
- *Agnes* – married John MacKay of Dirlot and Strathy (see *MacKay Lineage*)[140]

James Sinclair of Murkle died before 5 June 1633, on which date a document involving James' sons James and Francis identified their father as "the late James Sinclair of Murkle."[141]

Here we leave the Sinclair line and follow *Agnes* to the *MacKay Lineage*. It is through Agnes' mother that we gain our royal blood. Agnes and *John MacKay* are the fourth great-grandparents of *Mary MacKay*, wife of *Hugh Campbell of Ayr*.

---

[1] Vance Sinclair, *The History of Clan Sinclair: Viking Raider, Templar Knight, Highland Warrior* (England: Vance Sinclair, 2018), p. 6-9.

[2] Roland William Saint-Clair, *Saint-Clairs of the Isles: A History of the Sea-Kings of Orkney and their Scottish Successors of the Sirname Sinclair* (Auckland, New Zealand, H. Brett, General Printer and Publisher, Shortland and Fort Streets 1898), p. 278.

[3] Vance Sinclair, *The History of Clan Sinclair: Viking Raider, Templar Knight, Highland Warrior* (England: Vance Sinclair, 2018), p. 10-15.

[4] Vance Sinclair, *The History of Clan Sinclair: Viking Raider, Templar Knight, Highland Warrior* (England: Vance Sinclair, 2018), p. 15.

[5] Roland William Saint-Clair, *Saint-Clairs of the Isles: A History of the Sea-Kings of Orkney and their Scottish Successors of the Sirname Sinclair* (Auckland, New Zealand, H. Brett, General Printer and Publisher, Shortland and Fort Streets 1898), p. 282.

[6] Roland William Saint-Clair, *Saint-Clairs of the Isles: A History of the Sea-Kings of Orkney and their Scottish Successors of the Sirname Sinclair* (Auckland, New Zealand, H. Brett, General Printer and Publisher, Shortland and Fort Streets 1898), p. 279.

[7] Roland William Saint-Clair, *Saint-Clairs of the Isles: A History of the Sea-Kings of Orkney and their Scottish Successors of the Sirname Sinclair* (Auckland, New Zealand, H. Brett, General Printer and Publisher, Shortland and Fort Streets 1898), p. 280.

[8] Roland William Saint-Clair, *Saint-Clairs of the Isles: A History of the Sea-Kings of Orkney and their Scottish Successors of the Sirname Sinclair* (Auckland, New Zealand, H. Brett, General Printer and Publisher, Shortland and Fort Streets 1898), p. 279.

[9] Roland William Saint-Clair, *Saint-Clairs of the Isles: A History of the Sea-Kings of Orkney and their Scottish Successors of the Sirname Sinclair* (Auckland, New Zealand, H. Brett, General Printer and Publisher, Shortland and Fort Streets 1898), p. 279-280.

[10] Roland William Saint-Clair, *Saint-Clairs of the Isles: A History of the Sea-Kings of Orkney and their Scottish Successors of the Sirname Sinclair* (Auckland, New Zealand, H. Brett, General Printer and Publisher, Shortland and Fort Streets 1898), p. 280.

[11] Roland William Saint-Clair, *Saint-Clairs of the Isles: A History of the Sea-Kings of Orkney and their Scottish Successors of the Sirname Sinclair* (Auckland, New Zealand, H. Brett, General Printer and Publisher, Shortland and Fort Streets 1898), p. 280.

[12] Roland William Saint-Clair, *Saint-Clairs of the Isles: A History of the Sea-Kings of Orkney and their Scottish Successors of the Sirname Sinclair* (Auckland, New Zealand, H. Brett, General Printer and Publisher, Shortland and Fort Streets 1898), p. 280.

[13] Roland William Saint-Clair, *Saint-Clairs of the Isles: A History of the Sea-Kings of Orkney and their Scottish Successors of the Sirname Sinclair* (Auckland, New Zealand, H. Brett, General Printer and Publisher, Shortland and Fort Streets 1898), p. 281.

[14] Roland William Saint-Clair, *Saint-Clairs of the Isles: A History of the Sea-Kings of Orkney and their Scottish Successors of the Sirname Sinclair* (Auckland, New Zealand, H. Brett, General Printer and Publisher, Shortland and Fort Streets 1898), p. 281.

[15] Roland William Saint-Clair, *Saint-Clairs of the Isles: A History of the Sea-Kings of Orkney and their Scottish Successors of the Sirname Sinclair* (Auckland, New Zealand, H. Brett, General Printer and Publisher, Shortland and Fort Streets 1898), p. 281-282.

[16] Roland William Saint-Clair, *Saint-Clairs of the Isles: A History of the Sea-Kings of Orkney and their Scottish Successors of the Sirname Sinclair* (Auckland, New Zealand, H. Brett, General Printer and Publisher, Shortland and Fort Streets 1898), p. 282.

[17] Roland William Saint-Clair, *Saint-Clairs of the Isles: A History of the Sea-Kings of Orkney and their Scottish Successors of the Sirname Sinclair* (Auckland, New Zealand, H. Brett, General Printer and Publisher, Shortland and Fort Streets 1898), p. 282-283.

[18] Vance Sinclair, *The History of Clan Sinclair: Viking Raider, Templar Knight, Highland Warrior* (England: Vance Sinclair, 2018), p. 18.

[19] Roland William Saint-Clair, *Saint-Clairs of the Isles: A History of the Sea-Kings of Orkney and their Scottish Successors of the Sirname Sinclair* (Auckland, New Zealand, H. Brett, General Printer and Publisher, Shortland and Fort Streets 1898), p. 283.

[20] Vance Sinclair, *The History of Clan Sinclair: Viking Raider, Templar Knight, Highland Warrior* (England: Vance Sinclair, 2018), p. 21-22.

[21] Roland William Saint-Clair, *Saint-Clairs of the Isles: A History of the Sea-Kings of Orkney and their Scottish Successors of the Sirname Sinclair* (Auckland, New Zealand, H. Brett, General Printer and Publisher, Shortland and Fort Streets 1898), p. 283.

[22] Roland William Saint-Clair, *Saint-Clairs of the Isles: A History of the Sea-Kings of Orkney and their Scottish Successors of the Sirname Sinclair* (Auckland, New Zealand, H. Brett, General Printer and Publisher, Shortland and Fort Streets 1898), p. 283.

[23] Vance Sinclair, *The History of Clan Sinclair: Viking Raider, Templar Knight, Highland Warrior* (England: Vance Sinclair, 2018), p. 23.

[24] Roland William Saint-Clair, *Saint-Clairs of the Isles: A History of the Sea-Kings of Orkney and their Scottish Successors of the Sirname Sinclair* (Auckland, New Zealand, H. Brett, General Printer and Publisher, Shortland and Fort Streets 1898), p. 283.

[25] Roland William Saint-Clair, *Saint-Clairs of the Isles: A History of the Sea-Kings of Orkney and their Scottish Successors of the Sirname Sinclair* (Auckland, New Zealand, H. Brett, General Printer and Publisher, Shortland and Fort Streets 1898), p. 283.

[26] Roland William Saint-Clair, *Saint-Clairs of the Isles: A History of the Sea-Kings of Orkney and their Scottish Successors of the Sirname Sinclair* (Auckland, New Zealand, H. Brett, General Printer and Publisher, Shortland and Fort Streets 1898), p. 284.

[27] Roland William Saint-Clair, *Saint-Clairs of the Isles: A History of the Sea-Kings of Orkney and their Scottish Successors of the Sirname Sinclair* (Auckland, New Zealand, H. Brett, General Printer and Publisher, Shortland and Fort Streets 1898), p. 284.

[28] Roland William Saint-Clair, *Saint-Clairs of the Isles: A History of the Sea-Kings of Orkney and their Scottish Successors of the Sirname Sinclair* (Auckland, New Zealand, H. Brett, General Printer and Publisher, Shortland and Fort Streets 1898), p. 284-285.

[29] Roland William Saint-Clair, *Saint-Clairs of the Isles: A History of the Sea-Kings of Orkney and their Scottish Successors of the Sirname Sinclair* (Auckland, New Zealand, H. Brett, General Printer and Publisher, Shortland and Fort Streets 1898), p. 285.

[30] Roland William Saint-Clair, *Saint-Clairs of the Isles: A History of the Sea-Kings of Orkney and their Scottish Successors of the Sirname Sinclair* (Auckland, New Zealand, H. Brett, General Printer and Publisher, Shortland and Fort Streets 1898), p. 96.

[31] Vance Sinclair, *The History of Clan Sinclair: Viking Raider, Templar Knight, Highland Warrior* (England: Vance Sinclair, 2018), p. 29.

[32] Roland William Saint-Clair, *Saint-Clairs of the Isles: A History of the Sea-Kings of Orkney and their Scottish Successors of the Sirname Sinclair* (Auckland, New Zealand, H. Brett, General Printer and Publisher, Shortland and Fort Streets 1898), p. 97.

[33] Roland William Saint-Clair, *Saint-Clairs of the Isles: A History of the Sea-Kings of Orkney and their Scottish Successors of the Sirname Sinclair* (Auckland, New Zealand, H. Brett, General Printer and Publisher, Shortland and Fort Streets 1898), p. 98.

[34] Vance Sinclair, *The History of Clan Sinclair: Viking Raider, Templar Knight, Highland Warrior* (England: Vance Sinclair, 2018), p. 30.

[35] Roland William Saint-Clair, *Saint-Clairs of the Isles: A History of the Sea-Kings of Orkney and their Scottish Successors of the Sirname Sinclair* (Auckland, New Zealand, H. Brett, General Printer and Publisher, Shortland and Fort Streets 1898), p. 98.

[36] Vance Sinclair, *The History of Clan Sinclair: Viking Raider, Templar Knight, Highland Warrior* (England: Vance Sinclair, 2018), p. 31.

[37] Roland William Saint-Clair, *Saint-Clairs of the Isles: A History of the Sea-Kings of Orkney and their Scottish Successors of the Sirname Sinclair* (Auckland, New Zealand, H. Brett, General Printer and Publisher, Shortland and Fort Streets 1898), p. 100.

[38] Vance Sinclair, *The History of Clan Sinclair: Viking Raider, Templar Knight, Highland Warrior* (England: Vance Sinclair, 2018), p. 31-32.

[39] Roland William Saint-Clair, *Saint-Clairs of the Isles: A History of the Sea-Kings of Orkney and their Scottish Successors of the Sirname Sinclair* (Auckland, New Zealand, H. Brett, General Printer and Publisher, Shortland and Fort Streets 1898), p. 100.

[40] Vance Sinclair, *The History of Clan Sinclair: Viking Raider, Templar Knight, Highland Warrior* (England: Vance Sinclair, 2018), p. 33-35.

[41] Roland William Saint-Clair, *Saint-Clairs of the Isles: A History of the Sea-Kings of Orkney and their Scottish Successors of the Sirname Sinclair* (Auckland, New Zealand, H. Brett, General Printer and Publisher, Shortland and Fort Streets 1898), p. 100-101.

[42] Roland William Saint-Clair, *Saint-Clairs of the Isles: A History of the Sea-Kings of Orkney and their Scottish Successors of the Sirname Sinclair* (Auckland, New Zealand, H. Brett, General Printer and Publisher, Shortland and Fort Streets 1898), p. 100.

[43] Roland William Saint-Clair, *Saint-Clairs of the Isles: A History of the Sea-Kings of Orkney and their Scottish Successors of the Sirname Sinclair* (Auckland, New Zealand, H. Brett, General Printer and Publisher, Shortland and Fort Streets 1898), p. 102.

[44] Roland William Saint-Clair, *Saint-Clairs of the Isles: A History of the Sea-Kings of Orkney and their Scottish Successors of the Sirname Sinclair* (Auckland, New Zealand, H. Brett, General Printer and Publisher, Shortland and Fort Streets 1898), p. 102.

[45] Vance Sinclair, *The History of Clan Sinclair: Viking Raider, Templar Knight, Highland Warrior* (England: Vance Sinclair, 2018), p. 28.

[46] Roland William Saint-Clair, *Saint-Clairs of the Isles: A History of the Sea-Kings of Orkney and their Scottish Successors of the Sirname Sinclair* (Auckland, New Zealand, H. Brett, General Printer and Publisher, Shortland and Fort Streets 1898), p. 102.

[47] Roland William Saint-Clair, *Saint-Clairs of the Isles: A History of the Sea-Kings of Orkney and their Scottish Successors of the Sirname Sinclair* (Auckland, New Zealand, H. Brett, General Printer and Publisher, Shortland and Fort Streets 1898), p. 102.

[48] Roland William Saint-Clair, *Saint-Clairs of the Isles: A History of the Sea-Kings of Orkney and their Scottish Successors of the Sirname Sinclair* (Auckland, New Zealand, H. Brett, General Printer and Publisher, Shortland and Fort Streets 1898), p. 106.

[49] Vance Sinclair, *The History of Clan Sinclair: Viking Raider, Templar Knight, Highland Warrior* (England: Vance Sinclair, 2018), p. 36.

[50] Roland William Saint-Clair, *Saint-Clairs of the Isles: A History of the Sea-Kings of Orkney and their Scottish Successors of the Sirname Sinclair* (Auckland, New Zealand, H. Brett, General Printer and Publisher, Shortland and Fort Streets 1898), p. 104.

[51] Roland William Saint-Clair, *Saint-Clairs of the Isles: A History of the Sea-Kings of Orkney and their Scottish Successors of the Sirname Sinclair* (Auckland, New Zealand, H. Brett, General Printer and Publisher, Shortland and Fort Streets 1898), p. 104.

[52] Roland William Saint-Clair, *Saint-Clairs of the Isles: A History of the Sea-Kings of Orkney and their Scottish Successors of the Sirname Sinclair* (Auckland, New Zealand, H. Brett, General Printer and Publisher, Shortland and Fort Streets 1898), p. 110-111.

[53] Roland William Saint-Clair, *Saint-Clairs of the Isles: A History of the Sea-Kings of Orkney and their Scottish Successors of the Sirname Sinclair* (Auckland, New Zealand, H. Brett, General Printer and Publisher, Shortland and Fort Streets 1898), p. 108.

[54] Vance Sinclair, *The History of Clan Sinclair: Viking Raider, Templar Knight, Highland Warrior* (England: Vance Sinclair, 2018), p. 38.

[55] Roland William Saint-Clair, *Saint-Clairs of the Isles: A History of the Sea-Kings of Orkney and their Scottish Successors of the Sirname Sinclair* (Auckland, New Zealand, H. Brett, General Printer and Publisher, Shortland and Fort Streets 1898), p. 108-109.

[56] Vance Sinclair, *The History of Clan Sinclair: Viking Raider, Templar Knight, Highland Warrior* (England: Vance Sinclair, 2018), p. 36.

[57] Roland William Saint-Clair, *Saint-Clairs of the Isles: A History of the Sea-Kings of Orkney and their Scottish Successors of the Sirname Sinclair* (Auckland, New Zealand, H. Brett, General Printer and Publisher, Shortland and Fort Streets 1898), p. 109.

[58] Roland William Saint-Clair, *Saint-Clairs of the Isles: A History of the Sea-Kings of Orkney and their Scottish Successors of the Sirname Sinclair* (Auckland, New Zealand, H. Brett, General Printer and Publisher, Shortland and Fort Streets 1898), p. 108, 110.

[59] Roland William Saint-Clair, *Saint-Clairs of the Isles: A History of the Sea-Kings of Orkney and their Scottish Successors of the Sirname Sinclair* (Auckland, New Zealand, H. Brett, General Printer and Publisher, Shortland and Fort Streets 1898), p. 103-104, 108.

[60] Roland William Saint-Clair, *Saint-Clairs of the Isles: A History of the Sea-Kings of Orkney and their Scottish Successors of the Sirname Sinclair* (Auckland, New Zealand, H. Brett, General Printer and Publisher, Shortland and Fort Streets 1898), p. 113.

[61] Roland William Saint-Clair, *Saint-Clairs of the Isles: A History of the Sea-Kings of Orkney and their Scottish Successors of the Sirname Sinclair* (Auckland, New Zealand, H. Brett, General Printer and Publisher, Shortland and Fort Streets 1898), p. 114.

[62] Roland William Saint-Clair, *Saint-Clairs of the Isles: A History of the Sea-Kings of Orkney and their Scottish Successors of the Sirname Sinclair* (Auckland, New Zealand, H. Brett, General Printer and Publisher, Shortland and Fort Streets 1898), p. 113.

[63] Vance Sinclair, *The History of Clan Sinclair: Viking Raider, Templar Knight, Highland Warrior* (England: Vance Sinclair, 2018), p. 44.

[64] Roland William Saint-Clair, *Saint-Clairs of the Isles: A History of the Sea-Kings of Orkney and their Scottish Successors of the Sirname Sinclair* (Auckland, New Zealand, H. Brett, General Printer and Publisher, Shortland and Fort Streets 1898), p. 115.

[65] Roland William Saint-Clair, *Saint-Clairs of the Isles: A History of the Sea-Kings of Orkney and their Scottish Successors of the Sirname Sinclair* (Auckland, New Zealand, H. Brett, General Printer and Publisher, Shortland and Fort Streets 1898), p. 116.

[66] Vance Sinclair, *The History of Clan Sinclair: Viking Raider, Templar Knight, Highland Warrior* (England: Vance Sinclair, 2018), p. 44.

[67] Roland William Saint-Clair, *Saint-Clairs of the Isles: A History of the Sea-Kings of Orkney and their Scottish Successors of the Sirname Sinclair* (Auckland, New Zealand, H. Brett, General Printer and Publisher, Shortland and Fort Streets 1898), p. 120-121.

[68] Vance Sinclair, *The History of Clan Sinclair: Viking Raider, Templar Knight, Highland Warrior* (England: Vance Sinclair, 2018), p. 47.

[69] Roland William Saint-Clair, *Saint-Clairs of the Isles: A History of the Sea-Kings of Orkney and their Scottish Successors of the Sirname Sinclair* (Auckland, New Zealand, H. Brett, General Printer and Publisher, Shortland and Fort Streets 1898), p. 121.

[70] Roland William Saint-Clair, *Saint-Clairs of the Isles: A History of the Sea-Kings of Orkney and their Scottish Successors of the Sirname Sinclair* (Auckland, New Zealand, H. Brett, General Printer and Publisher, Shortland and Fort Streets 1898), p. 121, 185.

[71] Roland William Saint-Clair, *Saint-Clairs of the Isles: A History of the Sea-Kings of Orkney and their Scottish Successors of the Sirname Sinclair* (Auckland, New Zealand, H. Brett, General Printer and Publisher, Shortland and Fort Streets 1898), p. 122.

[72] Roland William Saint-Clair, *Saint-Clairs of the Isles: A History of the Sea-Kings of Orkney and their Scottish Successors of the Sirname Sinclair* (Auckland, New Zealand, H. Brett, General Printer and Publisher, Shortland and Fort Streets 1898), p. 123.

[73] Roland William Saint-Clair, *Saint-Clairs of the Isles: A History of the Sea-Kings of Orkney and their Scottish Successors of the Sirname Sinclair* (Auckland, New Zealand, H. Brett, General Printer and Publisher, Shortland and Fort Streets 1898), p. 124.

[74] Roland William Saint-Clair, *Saint-Clairs of the Isles: A History of the Sea-Kings of Orkney and their Scottish Successors of the Sirname Sinclair* (Auckland, New Zealand, H. Brett, General Printer and Publisher, Shortland and Fort Streets 1898), p. 124.

[75] Roland William Saint-Clair, *Saint-Clairs of the Isles: A History of the Sea-Kings of Orkney and their Scottish Successors of the Sirname Sinclair* (Auckland, New Zealand, H. Brett, General Printer and Publisher, Shortland and Fort Streets 1898), p. 125.

[76] Roland William Saint-Clair, *Saint-Clairs of the Isles: A History of the Sea-Kings of Orkney and their Scottish Successors of the Sirname Sinclair* (Auckland, New Zealand, H. Brett, General Printer and Publisher, Shortland and Fort Streets 1898), p. 126.

[77] John Henderson, *Caithness Family History* (Edinburgh: David Douglas, 1884), p. 2.

[78] Vance Sinclair, *The History of Clan Sinclair: Viking Raider, Templar Knight, Highland Warrior* (England: Vance Sinclair, 2018), p. 44.

[79] Roland William Saint-Clair, *Saint-Clairs of the Isles: A History of the Sea-Kings of Orkney and their Scottish Successors of the Sirname Sinclair* (Auckland, New Zealand, H. Brett, General Printer and Publisher, Shortland and Fort Streets 1898), p. 126.

[80] John Henderson, *Caithness Family History* (Edinburgh: David Douglas, 1884), p. 2.

[81] Vance Sinclair, *The History of Clan Sinclair: Viking Raider, Templar Knight, Highland Warrior* (England: Vance Sinclair, 2018), p. 45.

[82] Roland William Saint-Clair, *Saint-Clairs of the Isles: A History of the Sea-Kings of Orkney and their Scottish Successors of the Sirname Sinclair* (Auckland, New Zealand, H. Brett, General Printer and Publisher, Shortland and Fort Streets 1898), p. 126.

[83] John Henderson, *Caithness Family History* (Edinburgh: David Douglas, 1884), p. 4.

[84] Vance Sinclair, *The History of Clan Sinclair: Viking Raider, Templar Knight, Highland Warrior* (England: Vance Sinclair, 2018), p. 48.

[85] Roland William Saint-Clair, *Saint-Clairs of the Isles: A History of the Sea-Kings of Orkney and their Scottish Successors of the Sirname Sinclair* (Auckland, New Zealand, H. Brett, General Printer and Publisher, Shortland and Fort Streets 1898), p. 186-187.

[86] Roland William Saint-Clair, *Saint-Clairs of the Isles: A History of the Sea-Kings of Orkney and their Scottish Successors of the Sirname Sinclair* (Auckland, New Zealand, H. Brett, General Printer and Publisher, Shortland and Fort Streets 1898), p. 187.

[87] Vance Sinclair, *The History of Clan Sinclair: Viking Raider, Templar Knight, Highland Warrior* (England: Vance Sinclair, 2018), p. 70.

[88] Roland William Saint-Clair, *Saint-Clairs of the Isles: A History of the Sea-Kings of Orkney and their Scottish Successors of the Sirname Sinclair* (Auckland, New Zealand, H. Brett, General Printer and Publisher, Shortland and Fort Streets 1898), p. 188-189.

[89] Vance Sinclair, *The History of Clan Sinclair: Viking Raider, Templar Knight, Highland Warrior* (England: Vance Sinclair, 2018), p. 71.

[90] Roland William Saint-Clair, *Saint-Clairs of the Isles: A History of the Sea-Kings of Orkney and their Scottish Successors of the Sirname Sinclair* (Auckland, New Zealand, H. Brett, General Printer and Publisher, Shortland and Fort Streets 1898), p. 189.

[91] John Henderson, *Caithness Family History* (Edinburgh: David Douglas, 1884), p. 4.

[92] Roland William Saint-Clair, *Saint-Clairs of the Isles: A History of the Sea-Kings of Orkney and their Scottish Successors of the Sirname Sinclair* (Auckland, New Zealand, H. Brett, General Printer and Publisher, Shortland and Fort Streets 1898), p. 189.

[93] John Henderson, *Caithness Family History* (Edinburgh: David Douglas, 1884), p. 4.

[94] Vance Sinclair, *The History of Clan Sinclair: Viking Raider, Templar Knight, Highland Warrior* (England: Vance Sinclair, 2018), p. 71.

[95] Roland William Saint-Clair, *Saint-Clairs of the Isles: A History of the Sea-Kings of Orkney and their Scottish Successors of the Sirname Sinclair* (Auckland, New Zealand, H. Brett, General Printer and Publisher, Shortland and Fort Streets 1898), p. 189.

[96] John Henderson, *Caithness Family History* (Edinburgh: David Douglas, 1884), p. 4.

[97] Vance Sinclair, *The History of Clan Sinclair: Viking Raider, Templar Knight, Highland Warrior* (England: Vance Sinclair, 2018), p. 72.

[98] Roland William Saint-Clair, *Saint-Clairs of the Isles: A History of the Sea-Kings of Orkney and their Scottish Successors of the Sirname Sinclair* (Auckland, New Zealand, H. Brett, General Printer and Publisher, Shortland and Fort Streets 1898), p. 189.

[99] Roland William Saint-Clair, *Saint-Clairs of the Isles: A History of the Sea-Kings of Orkney and their Scottish Successors of the Sirname Sinclair* (Auckland, New Zealand, H. Brett, General Printer and Publisher, Shortland and Fort Streets 1898), p. 190.

[100] Roland William Saint-Clair, *Saint-Clairs of the Isles: A History of the Sea-Kings of Orkney and their Scottish Successors of the Sirname Sinclair* (Auckland, New Zealand, H. Brett, General Printer and Publisher, Shortland and Fort Streets 1898), p. 190.

[101] Vance Sinclair, *The History of Clan Sinclair: Viking Raider, Templar Knight, Highland Warrior* (England: Vance Sinclair, 2018), p. 72.

[102] Roland William Saint-Clair, *Saint-Clairs of the Isles: A History of the Sea-Kings of Orkney and their Scottish Successors of the Sirname Sinclair* (Auckland, New Zealand, H. Brett, General Printer and Publisher, Shortland and Fort Streets 1898), p. 190.

[103] John Henderson, *Caithness Family History* (Edinburgh: David Douglas, 1884), p. 5.

[104] Vance Sinclair, *The History of Clan Sinclair: Viking Raider, Templar Knight, Highland Warrior* (England: Vance Sinclair, 2018), p. 72.

[105] Roland William Saint-Clair, *Saint-Clairs of the Isles: A History of the Sea-Kings of Orkney and their Scottish Successors of the Sirname Sinclair* (Auckland, New Zealand, H. Brett, General Printer and Publisher, Shortland and Fort Streets 1898), p. 190.

[106] Vance Sinclair, *The History of Clan Sinclair: Viking Raider, Templar Knight, Highland Warrior* (England: Vance Sinclair, 2018), p. 72.

[107] Roland William Saint-Clair, *Saint-Clairs of the Isles: A History of the Sea-Kings of Orkney and their Scottish Successors of the Sirname Sinclair* (Auckland, New Zealand, H. Brett, General Printer and Publisher, Shortland and Fort Streets 1898), p. 191.

[108] Roland William Saint-Clair, *Saint-Clairs of the Isles: A History of the Sea-Kings of Orkney and their Scottish Successors of the Sirname Sinclair* (Auckland, New Zealand, H. Brett, General Printer and Publisher, Shortland and Fort Streets 1898), p. 191.

[109] Roland William Saint-Clair, *Saint-Clairs of the Isles: A History of the Sea-Kings of Orkney and their Scottish Successors of the Sirname Sinclair* (Auckland, New Zealand, H. Brett, General Printer and Publisher, Shortland and Fort Streets 1898), p. 191.

[110] Roland William Saint-Clair, *Saint-Clairs of the Isles: A History of the Sea-Kings of Orkney and their Scottish Successors of the Sirname Sinclair* (Auckland, New Zealand, H. Brett, General Printer and Publisher, Shortland and Fort Streets 1898), p. 191.

[111] Roland William Saint-Clair, *Saint-Clairs of the Isles: A History of the Sea-Kings of Orkney and their Scottish Successors of the Sirname Sinclair* (Auckland, New Zealand, H. Brett, General Printer and Publisher, Shortland and Fort Streets 1898), p. 191.

[112] Roland William Saint-Clair, *Saint-Clairs of the Isles: A History of the Sea-Kings of Orkney and their Scottish Successors of the Sirname Sinclair* (Auckland, New Zealand, H. Brett, General Printer and Publisher, Shortland and Fort Streets 1898), p. 192.

[113] Vance Sinclair, *The History of Clan Sinclair: Viking Raider, Templar Knight, Highland Warrior* (England: Vance Sinclair, 2018), p. 76.

[114] Roland William Saint-Clair, *Saint-Clairs of the Isles: A History of the Sea-Kings of Orkney and their Scottish Successors of the Sirname Sinclair* (Auckland, New Zealand, H. Brett, General Printer and Publisher, Shortland and Fort Streets 1898), p. 191.

[115] Vance Sinclair, *The History of Clan Sinclair: Viking Raider, Templar Knight, Highland Warrior* (England: Vance Sinclair, 2018), p. 75.

[116] Roland William Saint-Clair, *Saint-Clairs of the Isles: A History of the Sea-Kings of Orkney and their Scottish Successors of the Sirname Sinclair* (Auckland, New Zealand, H. Brett, General Printer and Publisher, Shortland and Fort Streets 1898), p. 192.

[117] Vance Sinclair, *The History of Clan Sinclair: Viking Raider, Templar Knight, Highland Warrior* (England: Vance Sinclair, 2018), p. 76-77.

[118] Roland William Saint-Clair, *Saint-Clairs of the Isles: A History of the Sea-Kings of Orkney and their Scottish Successors of the Sirname Sinclair* (Auckland, New Zealand, H. Brett, General Printer and Publisher, Shortland and Fort Streets 1898), p. 193.

[119] Vance Sinclair, *The History of Clan Sinclair: Viking Raider, Templar Knight, Highland Warrior* (England: Vance Sinclair, 2018), p. 76-77.

[120] Roland William Saint-Clair, *Saint-Clairs of the Isles: A History of the Sea-Kings of Orkney and their Scottish Successors of the Sirname Sinclair* (Auckland, New Zealand, H. Brett, General Printer and Publisher, Shortland and Fort Streets 1898), p. 192.

[121] Vance Sinclair, *The History of Clan Sinclair: Viking Raider, Templar Knight, Highland Warrior* (England: Vance Sinclair, 2018), p. 79.

[122] John Henderson, *Caithness Family History* (Edinburgh: David Douglas, 1884), p. 6.

[123] Roland William Saint-Clair, *Saint-Clairs of the Isles: A History of the Sea-Kings of Orkney and their Scottish Successors of the Sirname Sinclair* (Auckland, New Zealand, H. Brett, General Printer and Publisher, Shortland and Fort Streets 1898), p. 193-194.

[124] Roland William Saint-Clair, *Saint-Clairs of the Isles: A History of the Sea-Kings of Orkney and their Scottish Successors of the Sirname Sinclair* (Auckland, New Zealand, H. Brett, General Printer and Publisher, Shortland and Fort Streets 1898), p. 194.

[125] John Henderson, *Caithness Family History* (Edinburgh: David Douglas, 1884), p. 6.

[126] Roland William Saint-Clair, *Saint-Clairs of the Isles: A History of the Sea-Kings of Orkney and their Scottish Successors of the Sirname Sinclair* (Auckland, New Zealand, H. Brett, General Printer and Publisher, Shortland and Fort Streets 1898), p. 192-193, 195.

[127] Vance Sinclair, *The History of Clan Sinclair: Viking Raider, Templar Knight, Highland Warrior* (England: Vance Sinclair, 2018), p. 77.

[128] Roland William Saint-Clair, *Saint-Clairs of the Isles: A History of the Sea-Kings of Orkney and their Scottish Successors of the Sirname Sinclair* (Auckland, New Zealand, H. Brett, General Printer and Publisher, Shortland and Fort Streets 1898), p. 195.

[129] John Henderson, *Caithness Family History* (Edinburgh: David Douglas, 1884), p. 6.

[130] Roland William Saint-Clair, *Saint-Clairs of the Isles: A History of the Sea-Kings of Orkney and their Scottish Successors of the Sirname Sinclair* (Auckland, New Zealand, H. Brett, General Printer and Publisher, Shortland and Fort Streets 1898), p. 195.

[131] Roland William Saint-Clair, *Saint-Clairs of the Isles: A History of the Sea-Kings of Orkney and their Scottish Successors of the Sirname Sinclair* (Auckland, New Zealand, H. Brett, General Printer and Publisher, Shortland and Fort Streets 1898), p. 222.

[132] John Henderson, *Caithness Family History* (Edinburgh: David Douglas, 1884), p. 24.

[133] Angus MacKay, *The Book of MacKay* (Edinburgh: Norman MacLeod, 1906), p. 116.

[134] Vance Sinclair, *The History of Clan Sinclair: Viking Raider, Templar Knight, Highland Warrior* (England: Vance Sinclair, 2018), p. 81.

[135] Vance Sinclair, *The History of Clan Sinclair: Viking Raider, Templar Knight, Highland Warrior* (England: Vance Sinclair, 2018), p. 82.

[136] Vance Sinclair, *The History of Clan Sinclair: Viking Raider, Templar Knight, Highland Warrior* (England: Vance Sinclair, 2018), p. 87.

[137] Roland William Saint-Clair, *Saint-Clairs of the Isles: A History of the Sea-Kings of Orkney and their Scottish Successors of the Sirname Sinclair* (Auckland, New Zealand, H. Brett, General Printer and Publisher, Shortland and Fort Streets 1898), p. 222.

[138] Orkney Family History Society, (Orkney Library and Archives; 44 Junction Rd., Kirkwall, Orkney, KW15 1AG, Scotland, UK), from Assistant Archivist Sarah Maclean.

[139] John Henderson, *Caithness Family History* (Edinburgh: David Douglas, 1884), p. 24.

[140] John Henderson, *Caithness Family History* (Edinburgh: David Douglas, 1884), p. 24.

[141] National Records of Scotland, Papers of the Sutherland family of Forse, Sutherland, reference GD139/133. http://catalogue.nrscotland.gov.uk/nrsonlinecatalogue/details.aspx?reference=GD139%2f133&st=1&tc=y&tl=n&tn=n&tp=n&k=Francis+Sinclair&ko=p&r=&ro=s&df=&dt=1670&di=n

DE BRUS:
THE LORDS
OF ANNANDALE

SCOTLAND

ANNANDALE

DE BRUS
YORKSHIRE HOLDINGS

ENGLAND

THE BRUS LINEAGE -
THE LORDS OF ANNANDALE

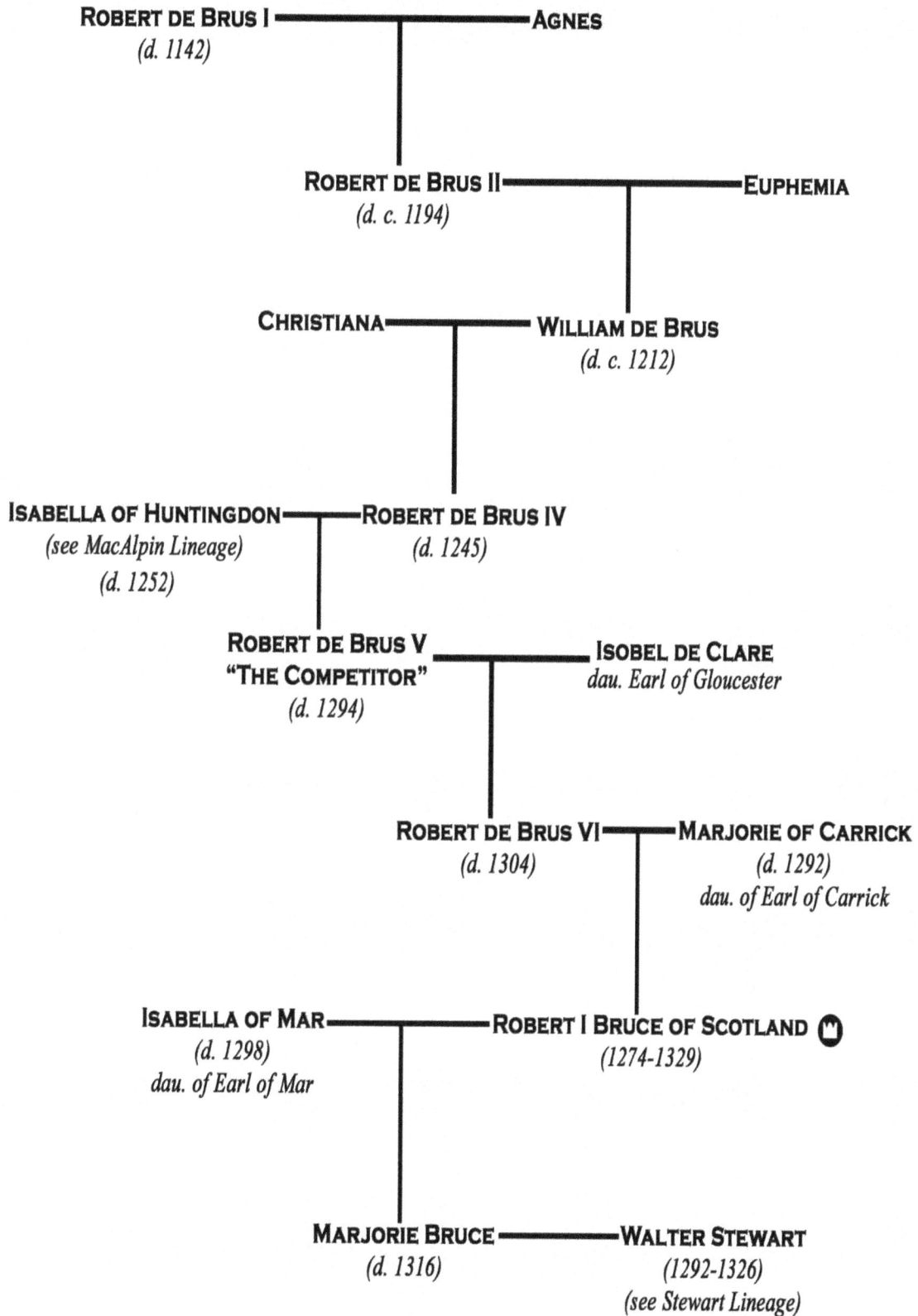

ROBERT DE BRUS I —————— **AGNES**
(d. 1142)

ROBERT DE BRUS II —————— **EUPHEMIA**
(d. c. 1194)

CHRISTIANA —————— **WILLIAM DE BRUS**
(d. c. 1212)

ISABELLA OF HUNTINGDON —————— **ROBERT DE BRUS IV**
(see MacAlpin Lineage) *(d. 1245)*
(d. 1252)

ROBERT DE BRUS V —————— **ISOBEL DE CLARE**
"THE COMPETITOR" *dau. Earl of Gloucester*
(d. 1294)

ROBERT DE BRUS VI —————— **MARJORIE OF CARRICK**
(d. 1304) *(d. 1292)*
dau. of Earl of Carrick

ISABELLA OF MAR —————— **ROBERT I BRUCE OF SCOTLAND** ♔
(d. 1298) *(1274-1329)*
dau. of Earl of Mar

MARJORIE BRUCE —————— **WALTER STEWART**
(d. 1316) *(1292-1326)*
(see Stewart Lineage)

THE DE BRUS LINEAGE

The Brus family was of Norman origins, and they became one of the major cross-border baronial families of England-Scotland. One thing that must be remembered about all the cross-border barons is that they always put their own interests first when deciding which king to support. They were loyal only to their own ambitions and territories. There is a certain irony, and circular history, in the Brus family. Robert de Brus I was the first major cross-border baron. Six generations later, King Robert I the Bruce of Scotland outlawed cross-border baronies in the 1328 Treaty of Edinburgh.[1]

The Brus family came from the Cotentin peninsula in western Normandy, between Cherbourgh and Valognes,[2] near the town of Brix—which is often styled "Bruis." Their origins are unknown, but there was an Adam de Brus who established both a castle and church in Brix, and the priory of La Luthumiére in the early 12th century. Although unclear exactly how the first Robert de Brus was related to this Adam, there was no doubt he was—the name Adam passed down through many generations of the English Brus family, and Robert owned some land in Normandy that had been part of Adam's original vassalage.[3]

Robert de Brus
(d. 1094)

There is some confusion over who was the first de Brus in England. One researcher, A.F. Murison, says the original Robert de Brus was the leader of the Brus (from Brix) contingent in William the Conqueror's army. This elder Robert died in 1094 in Cleveland, England, after having amassed 40,000 acres, consisting of 43 manors in the East and West Ridings of Yorkshire, and 51 in the North Riding of Yorkshire and in Durham. The main manor was Skelton in Cleveland.[4] This Robert was not a cross-border baron, as he only held lands in England. If this Robert is the original immigrant, then the Robert below would be Robert II, not Robert I, and everyone following would advance one number, making King Robert the Bruce the 8th Robert de Brus. But as there is dispute, I have chosen to start numbering with the first Lord of Annandale, below.

Robert (I) de Brus, Lord of Annandale
(d. 1142)

Another researcher, Ruth M. Blakely, put this Robert, the first Lord of Annandale, as the original immigrant, coming over with King Henry I of England (see *Continental Dynasty*) when he claimed the throne. Before coming to the English throne, Henry had been Count of Cotentin (where the Brus lands were located) since 1088, and he had a large Norman following.[5]

By 1103, Robert (I) de Brus had acquired at least some of the estates in his Yorkshire fief. He got the lands when Henry redistributed confiscated lands to loyal nobles like Brus.[6] Henry I had gained the throne of England over his elder brother Robert, who had been absent on Crusade at the time of their eldest brother William II's death. Upon his return, there was a war for the throne between the brothers, which Henry won.

Robert de Brus gained from this upheaval, and settled his first home base in Eskdale, at Castleton near Danby. He later moved to Castle Skelton. Robert may also have had the support of Hugh d'Avranches, Earl of Chester, who was one of Henry's most influential advisors. Robert received manors in Cleveland from Hugh prior to Hugh's death in July 1101. Robert may have been a companion of Hugh's as early as 1086, and may have known the Count of Avranches in Normandy, since his lands lay close to the Brus holdings there.[7]

Robert (I) never served Henry as a civil servant in any formal administrative or judicial capacity.[8] Nevertheless, prior to 1119, Henry had granted Robert lands in Hartness, north of the Tees river, to help defend the border and to extend Norman power into a poorly-controlled area.[9] Also by 1119, Robert had acquired a substantial group of manors in Langbaurgh, likely through marriage.[10]

Very little is known about his wife, Agnes, but documents indicate that she was an heiress to some lands in her own right, and it could have been the Langbaurgh lands.[11]

However he acquired all his lands, by 1120 Robert was the dominant baron in Cleveland, and his Langbaurgh lands totaled more than the lands owned by the four other tenants-in-chief put together![12]

As noted in the *MacAlpin Dynasty* chapter, David, youngest son of King Malcolm III of Scotland, was supposed to inherit the throne when his older brother Edgar died childless and named him heir. But instead, his brother Alexander took over, and gave David the kingdom of Strathclyde as compensation. When David went to claim Strathclyde (which is on the English border), King Henry I chose Robert as one of the English barons who accompanied David (who was also the English Earl of Huntingdon) into Scotland.[13]

David established himself in Strathclyde, and gave these Anglo-Norman barons lands in his new kingdom. Robert was the only substantial tenant-in-chief of Henry to accompany David—all the rest were lesser nobles or younger sons of nobles. David granted Robert the estate of Annandale, which was a strategic region along the border.[14][15]

Although Robert was much older and more experienced than David, the two appeared to have been close, with Robert acting as a mentor to David. A formal relationship may have existed between the two before the grant of Annandale. There is some evidence that Henry might have granted David lands in Normandy, and David might have been overlord of Brus lands in Normandy as early as 1108.[16]

When David became King of Scotland in 1124, he did not appoint Robert to a royal household post. This was most likely because Robert was essentially independent of David, since Robert had such major holdings in England as a tenant-in-chief of Henry. Robert may have personally been close with David, but he always saw himself as English, with Henry as his overlord and his Yorkshire holdings as his base.[17]

When King Stephen usurped the English throne after Henry's death in 1135, Robert accepted him. He accompanied Stephen during his tour of the north of England, and the siege of Exeter in the summer of 1136.[18]

This put Robert in direct opposition to David I of Scotland, who supported Henry's daughter Matilda (see *Continental Dynasty*) for the throne. The two met on the battlefield at the Battle of Northallerton (the Battle of the Standard) in August of 1138. Robert met with David before the battle, and tried to get him to withdraw, but failed to do so, and returned to Stephen's army.[19] Robert was older by this time, perhaps nearly 70.[20]

In the Battle of Northallerton, Robert (I) and his eldest son Adam fought for Stephen, while Robert's younger son Robert (II) fought on the Scottish side, which lost badly. It seems likely that David would have forfeited Robert's Annandale lands for siding with the English. However, Robert may have made his peace with David after the Stephen-Matilda war was over,[21] or he had renounced Annandale to his younger son Robert (II) prior to the battle, since the younger Robert (II) did inherit all those lands.[22]

Robert (I) and Agnes had four children: [23] [24]

- Adam – inherited the English lands and became Lord of Skelton
- *Robert (II)* – inherited Scottish lands, and became Lord of Annandale
- Agatha – married Ralph FitzRibald of Middleham
- Hugh

Robert (I) de Brus died in the spring of 1141 or 1142,[25] and his death split his holdings in two. His eldest son Adam inherited his Yorkshire lands, while Robert (II), who already held the lands of Annandale, remained in possession of them, and also held the Hartness estates with his brother Adam as his overlord.[26] This made sense, as at this time Hartness was in Northumberland, which was controlled by Henry, Earl of Huntingdon (King David's son) (see *MacAlpin Dynasty*), and was therefore more politically Scottish, rather than English.[27]

Robert (II) de Brus, Lord of Annandale
(d. c. 1194)

Our earliest glimpse of Robert (II) de Brus of Annandale was at the 1138 Battle of Northallerton, where he fought with King David I of Scotland against King Stephen of England and his own father. He may have been a minor at this time, because after being captured in the Scottish defeat, he was released into the keeping of his mother, Agnes.[28]

His father, Robert (I), would have probably lost Annandale when he fought against David. However, Robert (II) had possession of them later, so perhaps the forfeited lands were ceded to Robert (II) in 1139, at the Treaty of Durham.[29] [30] Robert (II) had been loyal to David, so there was no point in punishing him. Young Robert may also have been a companion of Earl Henry of Huntingdon (King David's son), and was in David's care at the time of Northallerton, which explains his fighting on the Scottish side.[31]

Sometime before 1152, Robert married Euphemia, the niece of William of Aumule. Her parents are unknown. They had three sons:[32]

- Robert (III) – who predeceased his father in 1191
- *William* – who succeeded as Lord of Annandale
- Bernard

In 1157, King Malcolm IV inherited the throne in Scotland, and Northumbria returned to English control. This meant that Robert's Hartness estates were once more English, which meant he now had the divided loyalty of all cross-border lords.[33]

This became problematic during the war between Scotland's William the Lion and England's Henry II (see *Continental Dynasty*). Robert sided with Henry II, and forfeited his Annandale lands and his castle of Lochmaben. It may seem that Robert had more ties to Scotland than England, but Robert did have more lands in England than just the Hartness estates, plus he had family ties to William of Aumule, who sided with Henry II.[34]

Also, Robert was not intimate with the Scottish kings after David died. He did accompany Malcolm IV to Toulouse in 1159 to fight for Henry's cause, but he was not a regular in Malcolm's court. Robert possibly saw the Scottish kings as vassals of the English kings, which would have made William's uprising a rebellion, and therefore Robert's allegiance went to the higher overlord—the English king.[35]

After King William's capture at Alnwick, Annandale was most likely attacked in the uprising of Gilbert and Uchtred, sons of Fergus, the last king of Galloway. It was at this time that Castle Annan was destroyed and abandoned, and the permanent move to Castle Lochmaben occurred.[36]

After William was released by Henry II, he returned to the Scottish throne. However, William had been forced to concede that Henry was his feudal overlord, and therefore William had to give back the lands he had taken from the barons loyal to Henry. Thus, Robert got Annandale back.[37]

William did not trust Robert (II), but tried to bind him to the Scottish crown by marrying Robert's eldest son Robert (III) to William's illegitimate daughter Isabel. Even before the problems of 1174, Robert (II) had grown increasingly detached from the Scottish court. He only signed three of King William's surviving charters; he was never given a royal office; he was not recorded to have played any significant role in Scottish affairs; and he was the only major landholder in Scotland who was *not* given additional lands in Lothian from King William. Perhaps William felt that Robert was becoming too powerful in the region, and did not want him to bypass William and go directly to Henry II with any political or property issues.

Robert (II) de Brus died in or before 1194, possibly in 1189,[38] and his second son, **William,** succeeded to the Lordship of Annandale, since Robert's eldest son had died in 1191.

William de Brus, Lord of Annandale
(d. 1215)

During William de Brus's lordship the Scottish Brus interest in England weakened. William never answered calls to arms from the English King, John (see *Continental Dynasty*), preferring to pay the fines instead. He paid his fines promptly to avoid having to owe anything to the English king. At the Treaty of Norham, he was the first Brus lord to stand with the Scottish king in a major confrontation with England. He also took no part in the upheaval of the Northern English barons versus the king.[39]

The lands of Hartness had originally been held by the Scottish branch as tenants of the English branch, who held it of the English king. Things got confused during a prolonged fight between the Crown and the Bishop of Durham over which one of them was the overlord of the area where Hartness lay. During this time, sometimes dues (scutage) were demanded from the Scottish branch, sometimes the English, and in the end it seemed that the Bishop of Durham claimed that the Scottish branch owed fealty to him, bypassing the English branch altogether.[40]

Since this meant a loss of rent and land to the English de Bruses, in 1199 Peter de Brus took William to court to get it settled. The case dragged on for a number of years, but was finally settled by 1201 in the Crown court. The outcome was an affirmation of the original setup of Scottish Brus holding Hartness of the English Brus, with the difference being that the English branch now held Hartness of the Bishop, not directly from the king.[41]

The Treaty of Norham between England's King John and Scotland's King William the Lion averted a war but laid crushing terms on Scotland. One of the terms was that a number of Scottish nobles had to send hostages to John's court as surety against misbehavior by King William. William sent one of his younger sons, William or John, in company of their kinsman Peter I de Brus of Skelton.[42]

This was also when King William attempted to bind the Brus family closer to him with a proposed marriage of William's son Robert (IV) with David, Earl of Huntingdon's, daughter Isabella (King William's niece) (see *MacAlpin Dynasty*). King William knew his rule was shaken and needed to bolster his power in the southwest of Scotland, which was both vulnerable and prone to fits of independence fever. This was also when King William married his brother David's daughter Margaret to the Lord of Galloway, William de Brus' neighbor.[43]

William married Christiana and had three sons:[44]

- ***Robert (IV)*** – Lord of Annandale
- John
- William

William de Brus died in 1215.[45]

Robert (IV) de Brus, Lord of Annandale
(d. 1245)

Although Robert (IV) de Brus had no substantial landed interest in England, he did have some sort of contact with King John (see *Continental Dynasty*). On 5 May 1215 he was paid 30 marks from the English Exchequer—at the same time as Alan of Galloway, who had provided men for John's army in the struggle leading up to the signing of the Magna Carta. Although it was unknown how, Robert was involved in some way that required payment for his service.[46]

Whether or not Robert was on John's side for the signing of the Magna Carta, he quickly made use of the clause allowing restoration of property rights. He was granted the manor of Elton which had been vacated by the tenant who chose to return to Normandy and was his because it had originally been granted to the tenant by Robert's father, William. He was also granted the rights to hold a market and fair at Hartelpool, a right his father had had but which had been suspended due to political turmoil in the see of Durham, where Hartelpool was located. Three years later, however, the market and fair rights were still unenforced by Robert.[47]

If he had ever been on King John of England's side, by summer of 1216 he was clearly supporting King Alexander II of Scotland. While Alexander marched into England to join the invading French Prince Louis, Robert was part of a Scottish force in Cumberland to support the rebels there.[48]

His kinsman Peter I de Brus of Skelton, a prominent rebel Yorkshire leader, likely had paid homage to Alexander II in January 1216 with other northern English nobles. If he had, this marked the first and last time the two branches of the Brus family supported a Scottish king against an English king.[49]

In June 1221, King Alexander II of Scotland married Joan, the sister of King Henry III of England (see *Continental Dynasty*). Robert (IV) accompanied him south to York and back home again. It is likely that Robert's kinsman, Peter I de Brus would have been among the Northern lords who also joined in the entourage at King Henry's request.[50]

Robert (IV) de Brus married Isabella of Huntingdon, daughter of David, Earl of Huntingdon (see *MacAlpin Dynasty*), and had:[51] [52] [53]

- ***Robert (V)*** – Lord of Annandale
- Bernard

It is through his wife Isabella that the de Brus family later claimed the throne of Scotland.[54]

Although his death date is traditionally 1245,[55] evidence shows that this was too late. In 1237, when his wife inherited English lands upon her brother's death, Robert was not named in the inheritance papers, as were the spouses of the other sisters who were co-heiresses. This was almost certain proof that he was dead by then. He may even have been dead as early as Sept. 1230, because a grant of rights to people in his Hartness lands in that year were confirmed in 1234 to Peter de Brus of Skelton, "saving Robert de Brus' heirs." Had he been alive, the confirmation would likely have been to him directly, rather than his kinsman, who acted as regent for Robert's children when they were minors.[56]

Robert (V) "the Competitor" de Brus, Lord of Annandale (1210-1292)

Robert (V) de Brus was born in 1210.[57] [58] He would have succeeded to the Lordship of Annandale upon his father's death, the date of which is uncertain. It also seems that he was a minor at the time of his father's death, which would account for Peter de Brus of Skelton's involvement in certain transactions in English Hartness on his behalf. But in 1242, Robert (V), clearly in command of his inheritance then, reached an agreement with the prior of Guisborough over rights in the manor of Castle Eden.[59] [60]

Legend says King Alexander II of Scotland had named this Robert his heir in case he died childless. However, Alexander II married a second time, in 1239, and Alexander III was born in 1241. While there is some doubt that Alexander II ever formally named Robert (V) his successor, in 1237, upon Robert's uncle, John's death, Robert was Alexander's closest male relative who was not an infant. Once Alexander III was born, and the male Comyn children (closer kin to the king than Robert) came of age, Robert's position of importance decreased accordingly.[61] [62]

In 1244, Robert (V) married Isobel de Clare, daughter of Gilbert de Clare, Earl of Gloucester and Hertford, and they had sons:[63] [64]

- ***Robert (VI)*** – Lord of Annandale
- Richard – predeceased his father on 12 October 1287 in Gascony, France, and left no heirs[65]

Upon his mother Isabella's death in 1252, Robert received 10 knight's fees in England—her share of the Earldom of Huntingdon. Additional lands in Chester and Essex brought him up to about 40 knight's fees, and Robert (V) became a major tenant-in-chief in England, bringing with it all the headaches of a cross-border baron.[66] [67]

In Aug 1255, since King Alexander III was still a minor, Robert was one of 15 regents for the young monarch. He was in favor of creating an English alliance, and cemented Alexander's marriage to Margaret, daughter of King Henry III (see *Continental Dynasty*). Robert also distrusted the Comyn faction, although this rivalry was not to flare up fully and bloodily for many years to come. He was also appointed Sheriff of Cumberland and Governor of Carlisle Castle at the same time.[68] [69]

When a new council to oversee Scotland was made in 1258, Robert was not asked to be on it. This was largely due to problems with the accounts of Carlisle Castle and perhaps even because he was seen as a possible threat to the royal dynasty. At any rate, he was out of favor with both the English King Henry III and Alexander III of Scotland, and played no major role in Scottish politics until after Alexander and his daughter's deaths.[70]

Wanting to build up his English strength, on 28 Jan 1262 Robert entered King Henry III's service. For this he was given 50 pounds a year so long as he remained in it. There is evidence that Robert frequently went back and forth between England and Scotland, as he had interests in both countries, and that at least once King Henry used him as an envoy.[71]

He fought in 1264 at Lewes with Henry III (see *Continental Dynasty*) against a rebellious noble, de Montfort, and with the English against the Northern barons. He was captured, and his son Robert (VI) , barely 21, had to negotiate his ransom.[72] [73]

In May 1266, Robert (V) arrived to help relieve Kenilworth. In November, he persuaded King Henry to make a land grant in Newcastle to the friars of the Penance of Jesus Christ. He was granted the stewardship of the Castle Carlisle for 16 months, and was frequently in the king's court as his signature on many charters attests.[74]

In 1268, in the king's favor, Robert was given many of the lands that had been forfeited by the rebel barons. Some of these he allowed the barons or their heirs to purchase back, thus raising a good deal of capital.[75] He was also made Chief Justice of England, although upon King Edward I's (see *Continental Dynasty*) succession (1272), he was not reappointed.[76]

Robert's sons Robert (VI) and Richard embarked on Crusade to Israel in August of 1270 with Prince Edward, while Robert (V) followed with Prince Edmund the following spring.[77] Robert and Prince Edmund returned by way of Clairvaux in the autumn of 1272.[78]

After his first wife died, on 3 May 1273 Robert married Christina of Ireby, who was an heiress and twice-widowed. While this marriage brought him much material gain, it was not nearly as prestigious as his first. His son Robert (VI) did not seem to approve, as he tried to disinherit his step-mother after his father's death—a claim which Christina successfully refuted.[79]

Although still in favor with the English King Edward I (see *Continental Dynasty*), Robert concentrated mainly on his northern lands after his marriage. His sons administered the family's Midland and Southern lands and fulfilled any military service due.[80]

In the Scone Parliament of 5 Feb 1283, Robert was one of the Lords who recognized the right of Margaret of Norway, Alexander III's granddaughter, to succeed to the throne if Alexander died without a child.[81]

Alexander III's sudden death in 1285 made Robert think he might have a chance to gain the throne himself. In order to achieve the crown, he had to fight off a possible posthumous child of Alexander (they were not sure if his queen was pregnant), the very young Margaret, Maid of Norway (Alexander III's grandchild), the very elderly Dervorguilla (granddaughter by an elder daughter of David, Earl of Huntingdon), and her son John de Balliol. Robert (a grandson of Earl David by a younger daughter) had to first make the case that a female could not inherit the throne, then that a grandson of an elder daughter should be overlooked in favor of the son of a younger daughter, and that no other male-lineage relative could be found. He had a tough case to make.[82] [83]

Still, he tried to make it. On 20 Sep 1286, Robert and thirteen other Scottish nobles met at Turnberry Castle, Carrick, Scotland. This meeting was to sign a pact to support Robert in his desire for the throne against John Balliol and the Comyns, who also wanted the throne. The wording of the pact was vague, and suggested, rather than an immediate open bid for the throne at that time, that Robert was laying the groundwork for support in the future should he need it. Of the barons who signed, a few were close enough to King Edward I to make it likely that Edward not only knew about the pact, but approved.[84] [85]

In October 1290, the death of young Queen Margaret of Norway, while on her way from Norway to take her throne in Scotland, put Robert's ambitions in play again.[86] The decision of succession, known as "The Great Cause" was to be settled in Northumberland, England, at Norham Castle. King Edward I of England (see *Continental Dynasty*) would make the final decision as he was overlord of both England and Scotland. Robert's many legal arguments fell flat, and Edward chose the more pliant John Balliol. When it was clear Robert would need to take the throne by force, he knew he was too old and resigned his claims in favor of his son Robert, Earl of Carrick.[87] [88] [89] In November of 1292, Robert (V) left the Norham meeting and retired to Lochmaben Castle.[90]

Although defeated in his bid for the throne, Robert remained defiant to the end. In January 1294, he secured the Bishopric of Galloway for his protégé. The bishopric of Galloway was normally a Balliol patronage, so Robert's securing it for his clerk and protégé Thomas of Kirkcudbright was a small victory.[91]

Robert (V) de Brus died 31 March 1295 at Lochmaben Castle, Dumfries, Scotland at age 85.[92] [93] He was the last de Brus to be buried at Guisborough Priory, Hartness, Yorkshire, England, a long-time Brus patronage and family foundation.[94]

Robert (VI) de Brus, Lord of Annandale, Earl of Carrick
(1253-1304)

Robert (VI) de Brus was born in 1253.[95] At age 15, in 1268, Robert was granted lands taken from the rebel barons, in reward for his loyalty to the King of England. Some of these he sold back to the baron's families for substantial sums.[96]

As mentioned above, in 1270 he went on Crusade to Israel with Prince Edward. He and his brother Richard left with Edward in August, while their father left with Prince Edmund the following spring.[97] [98]

In October 1271, Robert signed a land transaction in England, and so must have returned to England by this time.[99] Shortly after his return from the Crusades, Robert married Marjorie of Carrick. Legend has it that Marjorie was the aggressor in the marriage, literally kidnapping Robert until he agreed to marry her—much to the displeasure of the King of England. Robert profited much from the marriage in both land and stature—he became an Earl of Carrick, since Marjorie was the heiress of the Carrick Earldom.[100]

Although Robert was Earl of Carrick, he still spent a great deal of time administering the family's English lands. He was a frequent visitor at King Edward I's court, although it was his younger brother Richard who made a career of being in Edward's service.[101]

Although not often in King Alexander III of Scotland's court, Robert was trusted as an envoy to King Edward I of England (see *Continental Dynasty*), possibly because of his close relationship with the English king. He was sent as an envoy in 1277, and again in 1278 as he was Alexander's mouthpiece when Alexander needed to swear fealty to King Edward.[102]

In 1283, Robert (VI) was appointed Sheriff of Cumberland and Castellan of Carlisle. He was appointed over the protests of the local knights, who had to accept him as he had the king's backing. He was not very good at this, though, and in 1285 he was relieved of duty and fined 15 pounds when he failed to present his accounts as sheriff.[103]

Robert sided with King Edward I of England, instead of Scottish King John de Balliol in the Wars of Scottish Independence, 1292-1296. As a result, his Annandale lands were given to the Comyns, and Robert's son was stripped of the Earldom of Carrick.[104][105]

King Edward appointed Robert as the Governor of Carlisle Castle from 1295-1297. He held Carlisle against Balliol in 1296, and William Wallace in 1297.[106][107]

After Scottish King John de Balliol was defeated at Dunbar on 27 April 1296, Robert asked Edward I to make good on his promise to give the throne to Robert's father if Balliol failed. Edward refused.[108][109]

In September 1296, Robert (VI) de Brus got his Annandale lands back. With Scotland still in turmoil, he retired to his English estates to find some peace.[110] He died on his way back to Annandale, around Easter of 1304, in Cumberland, England. He is buried in Holmcultram Abbey in Cumberland (now Cumbria), England.[111][112]

In his marriage to Marjorie of Carrick, he had:

- *Robert (VII)* – King of Scotland, Robert I Bruce
- Edward
- Neil
- Thomas
- Alexander
- Isabel – married King Eric II of Norway
- Maud/Matilda – married Hugh MacWilliam, Earl of Ross
- Christina – married first Grantney, 7th Earl of Mar, then Christopher de Seton
- Mary – married Sir Neil Campbell

For the rise of *Robert (VII) de Brus*, Lord of Annandale, to *King Robert I Bruce of Scotland*, see the *Stewart Dynasty* chapter.

[1] Ruth M. Blakely, *The Brus Family in England and Scotland, 1100-1295* (Boydell Press, Woodbridge, 2005), p. 2.
[2] A.F. Murison, *King Robert the Bruce* (Edinburgh, Oliphant, Anderson & Ferrier, 1899), p. 11.
[3] Ruth M. Blakely, *The Brus Family in England and Scotland, 1100-1295* (Boydell Press, Woodbridge, 2005), p. 5.
[4] A.F. Murison, *King Robert the Bruce* (Edinburgh, Oliphant, Anderson & Ferrier, 1899), p. 12.
[5] Ruth M. Blakely, *The Brus Family in England and Scotland, 1100-1295* (Boydell Press, Woodbridge, 2005), p. 8, 12.
[6] Ruth M. Blakely, *The Brus Family in England and Scotland, 1100-1295* (Boydell Press, Woodbridge, 2005), p. 9.
[7] Ruth M. Blakely, *The Brus Family in England and Scotland, 1100-1295* (Boydell Press, Woodbridge, 2005), p. 10, 13-14.
[8] Ruth M. Blakely, *The Brus Family in England and Scotland, 1100-1295* (Boydell Press, Woodbridge, 2005), p. 11.
[9] Ruth M. Blakely, *The Brus Family in England and Scotland, 1100-1295* (Boydell Press, Woodbridge, 2005), p. 17.
[10] Ruth M. Blakely, *The Brus Family in England and Scotland, 1100-1295* (Boydell Press, Woodbridge, 2005), p. 15.

[11] Ruth M. Blakely, *The Brus Family in England and Scotland, 1100-1295* (Boydell Press, Woodbridge, 2005), p. 16.
[12] Ruth M. Blakely, *The Brus Family in England and Scotland, 1100-1295* (Boydell Press, Woodbridge, 2005), p. 17.
[13] Ruth M. Blakely, *The Brus Family in England and Scotland, 1100-1295* (Boydell Press, Woodbridge, 2005), p. 19.
[14] Ruth M. Blakely, *The Brus Family in England and Scotland, 1100-1295* (Boydell Press, Woodbridge, 2005), p. 19-21.
[15] A.F. Murison, *King Robert the Bruce* (Edinburgh, Oliphant, Anderson & Ferrier, 1899), p. 12.
[16] Ruth M. Blakely, *The Brus Family in England and Scotland, 1100-1295* (Boydell Press, Woodbridge, 2005), p. 21, 23.
[17] Ruth M. Blakely, *The Brus Family in England and Scotland, 1100-1295* (Boydell Press, Woodbridge, 2005), p. 24, 26.
[18] Ruth M. Blakely, *The Brus Family in England and Scotland, 1100-1295* (Boydell Press, Woodbridge, 2005), p. 28.
[19] A.F. Murison, *King Robert the Bruce* (Edinburgh, Oliphant, Anderson & Ferrier, 1899), p. 12.
[20] Ruth M. Blakely, *The Brus Family in England and Scotland, 1100-1295* (Boydell Press, Woodbridge, 2005), p. 28-29.
[21] Ruth M. Blakely, *The Brus Family in England and Scotland, 1100-1295* (Boydell Press, Woodbridge, 2005), p. 28-29.
[22] A.F. Murison, *King Robert the Bruce* (Edinburgh, Oliphant, Anderson & Ferrier, 1899), p. 12.
[23] Ruth M. Blakely, *The Brus Family in England and Scotland, 1100-1295* (Boydell Press, Woodbridge, 2005), p. 28-29.
[24] A.F. Murison, *King Robert the Bruce* (Edinburgh, Oliphant, Anderson & Ferrier, 1899), p. 12.
[25] A.F. Murison, *King Robert the Bruce* (Edinburgh, Oliphant, Anderson & Ferrier, 1899), p. 12.
[26] A.F. Murison, *King Robert the Bruce* (Edinburgh, Oliphant, Anderson & Ferrier, 1899), p. 12.
[27] Ruth M. Blakely, *The Brus Family in England and Scotland, 1100-1295* (Boydell Press, Woodbridge, 2005), p. 32-33.
[28] Ruth M. Blakely, *The Brus Family in England and Scotland, 1100-1295* (Boydell Press, Woodbridge, 2005), p. 29.
[29] Ruth M. Blakely, *The Brus Family in England and Scotland, 1100-1295* (Boydell Press, Woodbridge, 2005), p. 29.
[30] A.F. Murison, *King Robert the Bruce* (Edinburgh, Oliphant, Anderson & Ferrier, 1899), p. 12.
[31] Ruth M. Blakely, *The Brus Family in England and Scotland, 1100-1295* (Boydell Press, Woodbridge, 2005), p. 30.
[32] Ruth M. Blakely, *The Brus Family in England and Scotland, 1100-1295* (Boydell Press, Woodbridge, 2005), p. 36.
[33] Ruth M. Blakely, *The Brus Family in England and Scotland, 1100-1295* (Boydell Press, Woodbridge, 2005), p. 36.
[34] Ruth M. Blakely, *The Brus Family in England and Scotland, 1100-1295* (Boydell Press, Woodbridge, 2005), p. 36-37.
[35] Ruth M. Blakely, *The Brus Family in England and Scotland, 1100-1295* (Boydell Press, Woodbridge, 2005), p. 37-38.
[36] Ruth M. Blakely, *The Brus Family in England and Scotland, 1100-1295* (Boydell Press, Woodbridge, 2005), p. 39.
[37] Ruth M. Blakely, *The Brus Family in England and Scotland, 1100-1295* (Boydell Press, Woodbridge, 2005), p. 40.
[38] A.F. Murison, *King Robert the Bruce* (Edinburgh, Oliphant, Anderson & Ferrier, 1899), p. 12.
[39] Ruth M. Blakely, *The Brus Family in England and Scotland, 1100-1295* (Boydell Press, Woodbridge, 2005), p. 51-52.
[40] Ruth M. Blakely, *The Brus Family in England and Scotland, 1100-1295* (Boydell Press, Woodbridge, 2005), p. 51-52.
[41] Ruth M. Blakely, *The Brus Family in England and Scotland, 1100-1295* (Boydell Press, Woodbridge, 2005), p. 51-52.
[42] Ruth M. Blakely, *The Brus Family in England and Scotland, 1100-1295* (Boydell Press, Woodbridge, 2005), p. 67-68.
[43] Ruth M. Blakely, *The Brus Family in England and Scotland, 1100-1295* (Boydell Press, Woodbridge, 2005), p. 67-68.
[44] Ruth M. Blakely, *The Brus Family in England and Scotland, 1100-1295* (Boydell Press, Woodbridge, 2005), p. ix.
[45] A.F. Murison, *King Robert the Bruce* (Edinburgh, Oliphant, Anderson & Ferrier, 1899), p. 12.
[46] Ruth M. Blakely, *The Brus Family in England and Scotland, 1100-1295* (Boydell Press, Woodbridge, 2005), p. 70.
[47] Ruth M. Blakely, *The Brus Family in England and Scotland, 1100-1295* (Boydell Press, Woodbridge, 2005), p. 71.
[48] Ruth M. Blakely, *The Brus Family in England and Scotland, 1100-1295* (Boydell Press, Woodbridge, 2005), p. 71.
[49] Ruth M. Blakely, *The Brus Family in England and Scotland, 1100-1295* (Boydell Press, Woodbridge, 2005), p. 71.
[50] Ruth M. Blakely, *The Brus Family in England and Scotland, 1100-1295* (Boydell Press, Woodbridge, 2005), p. 59-60, 71.
[51] Ruth M. Blakely, *The Brus Family in England and Scotland, 1100-1295* (Boydell Press, Woodbridge, 2005), p. 67.
[52] E. William Robertson, *Scotland Under Her Early Kings: A History of the Kingdom to the Close of the Thirteenth Century, Part Two* (Edinburgh: Edmonston and Douglas, 1862), p. 10.
[53] John Cannon & Ralph Griffiths, *The Oxford Illustrated History of the British Monarchy* (2000 edition, Oxford University Press), Geneaolgies of Royal Lines Appendix.
[54] A.F. Murison, *King Robert the Bruce* (Edinburgh, Oliphant, Anderson & Ferrier, 1899), p. 12.
[55] A.F. Murison, *King Robert the Bruce* (Edinburgh, Oliphant, Anderson & Ferrier, 1899), p. 12.
[56] Ruth M. Blakely, *The Brus Family in England and Scotland, 1100-1295* (Boydell Press, Woodbridge, 2005), p. 72.
[57] Richard Oram (Ed.), *The Kings and Queens of Scotland* (Tempus Publishing Ltd., Stroud, Gloucestershire, England, 2001), p. 117.
[58] A.F. Murison, *King Robert the Bruce* (Edinburgh, Oliphant, Anderson & Ferrier, 1899), p. 12.
[59] A.F. Murison, *King Robert the Bruce* (Edinburgh, Oliphant, Anderson & Ferrier, 1899), p. 12.
[60] Ruth M. Blakely, *The Brus Family in England and Scotland, 1100-1295* (Boydell Press, Woodbridge, 2005), p. 75.
[61] A.F. Murison, *King Robert the Bruce* (Edinburgh, Oliphant, Anderson & Ferrier, 1899), p. 13.
[62] Ruth M. Blakely, *The Brus Family in England and Scotland, 1100-1295* (Boydell Press, Woodbridge, 2005), p. 75.
[63] Ruth M. Blakely, *The Brus Family in England and Scotland, 1100-1295* (Boydell Press, Woodbridge, 2005), p. 73, 77.
[64] A.F. Murison, *King Robert the Bruce* (Edinburgh, Oliphant, Anderson & Ferrier, 1899), p. 12.
[65] Ruth M. Blakely, *The Brus Family in England and Scotland, 1100-1295* (Boydell Press, Woodbridge, 2005), p. ix, 86.
[66] A.F. Murison, *King Robert the Bruce* (Edinburgh, Oliphant, Anderson & Ferrier, 1899), p. 12, 13.
[67] Ruth M. Blakely, *The Brus Family in England and Scotland, 1100-1295* (Boydell Press, Woodbridge, 2005), p. 76-77.
[68] A.F. Murison, *King Robert the Bruce* (Edinburgh, Oliphant, Anderson & Ferrier, 1899), p. 13.
[69] Ruth M. Blakely, *The Brus Family in England and Scotland, 1100-1295* (Boydell Press, Woodbridge, 2005), p. 77.
[70] Ruth M. Blakely, *The Brus Family in England and Scotland, 1100-1295* (Boydell Press, Woodbridge, 2005), p. 78.

[71] Ruth M. Blakely, *The Brus Family in England and Scotland, 1100-1295* (Boydell Press, Woodbridge, 2005), p. 78-9.

[72] A.F. Murison, *King Robert the Bruce* (Edinburgh, Oliphant, Anderson & Ferrier, 1899), p. 13.

[73] Ruth M. Blakely, *The Brus Family in England and Scotland, 1100-1295* (Boydell Press, Woodbridge, 2005), p. 80.

[74] Ruth M. Blakely, *The Brus Family in England and Scotland, 1100-1295* (Boydell Press, Woodbridge, 2005), p. 81.

[75] Ruth M. Blakely, *The Brus Family in England and Scotland, 1100-1295* (Boydell Press, Woodbridge, 2005), p. 81.

[76] A.F. Murison, *King Robert the Bruce* (Edinburgh, Oliphant, Anderson & Ferrier, 1899), p. 13.

[77] Ruth M. Blakely, *The Brus Family in England and Scotland, 1100-1295* (Boydell Press, Woodbridge, 2005), p. 81.

[78] Ruth M. Blakely, *The Brus Family in England and Scotland, 1100-1295* (Boydell Press, Woodbridge, 2005), p. 82.

[79] Ruth M. Blakely, *The Brus Family in England and Scotland, 1100-1295* (Boydell Press, Woodbridge, 2005), p. 82-3.

[80] Ruth M. Blakely, *The Brus Family in England and Scotland, 1100-1295* (Boydell Press, Woodbridge, 2005), p. 82-3.

[81] A.F. Murison, *King Robert the Bruce* (Edinburgh, Oliphant, Anderson & Ferrier, 1899), p. 13.

[82] Ruth M. Blakely, *The Brus Family in England and Scotland, 1100-1295* (Boydell Press, Woodbridge, 2005), p. 85.

[83] A.F. Murison, *King Robert the Bruce* (Edinburgh, Oliphant, Anderson & Ferrier, 1899), p. 13.

[84] A.F. Murison, *King Robert the Bruce* (Edinburgh, Oliphant, Anderson & Ferrier, 1899), p. 13.

[85] Ruth M. Blakely, *The Brus Family in England and Scotland, 1100-1295* (Boydell Press, Woodbridge, 2005), p. 86.

[86] A.F. Murison, *King Robert the Bruce* (Edinburgh, Oliphant, Anderson & Ferrier, 1899), p. 14.

[87] Fitzroy Maclean, *A Concise History of Scotland* (First published 1970. This version published 2002. Thames & Hudson Ltd., London), p. 35.

[88] A.F. Murison, *King Robert the Bruce* (Edinburgh, Oliphant, Anderson & Ferrier, 1899), p. 15.

[89] Ruth M. Blakely, *The Brus Family in England and Scotland, 1100-1295* (Boydell Press, Woodbridge, 2005), p. 87-88.

[90] A.F. Murison, *King Robert the Bruce* (Edinburgh, Oliphant, Anderson & Ferrier, 1899), p. 15.

[91] Ruth M. Blakely, *The Brus Family in England and Scotland, 1100-1295* (Boydell Press, Woodbridge, 2005), p. 88.

[92] Richard Oram (Ed.), *The Kings and Queens of Scotland* (Tempus Publishing Ltd., Stroud, Gloucestershire, England, 2001), p. 117.

[93] A.F. Murison, *King Robert the Bruce* (Edinburgh, Oliphant, Anderson & Ferrier, 1899), p. 15.

[94] Ruth M. Blakely, *The Brus Family in England and Scotland, 1100-1295* (Boydell Press, Woodbridge, 2005), p. 3, 88, 179.

[95] A.F. Murison, *King Robert the Bruce* (Edinburgh, Oliphant, Anderson & Ferrier, 1899), p. 15.

[96] Ruth M. Blakely, *The Brus Family in England and Scotland, 1100-1295* (Boydell Press, Woodbridge, 2005), p. 81.

[97] A.F. Murison, *King Robert the Bruce* (Edinburgh, Oliphant, Anderson & Ferrier, 1899), p. 15.

[98] Ruth M. Blakely, *The Brus Family in England and Scotland, 1100-1295* (Boydell Press, Woodbridge, 2005), p. 81.

[99] Ruth M. Blakely, *The Brus Family in England and Scotland, 1100-1295* (Boydell Press, Woodbridge, 2005), p. 82.

[100] Ruth M. Blakely, *The Brus Family in England and Scotland, 1100-1295* (Boydell Press, Woodbridge, 2005), p. 82-3.

[101] Ruth M. Blakely, *The Brus Family in England and Scotland, 1100-1295* (Boydell Press, Woodbridge, 2005), p. 84.

[102] Ruth M. Blakely, *The Brus Family in England and Scotland, 1100-1295* (Boydell Press, Woodbridge, 2005), p. 84.

[103] Ruth M. Blakely, *The Brus Family in England and Scotland, 1100-1295* (Boydell Press, Woodbridge, 2005), p. 84.

[104] A.F. Murison, *King Robert the Bruce* (Edinburgh, Oliphant, Anderson & Ferrier, 1899), p. 17.

[105] Fitzroy Maclean, *A Concise History of Scotland* (First published 1970. This version, 2002. Thames & Hudson Ltd., London), p. 36.

[106] A.F. Murison, *King Robert the Bruce* (Edinburgh, Oliphant, Anderson & Ferrier, 1899), p. 16.

[107] Ronald Williams, *The Lords of the Isles: The Clan Donald and the Early Kingdom of the Scots* (Chatto & Windus - The Hogarth Press, London, 1984), p. 146, 148.

[108] A.F. Murison, *King Robert the Bruce* (Edinburgh, Oliphant, Anderson & Ferrier, 1899), p. 16, 17.

[109] Fitzroy Maclean, *A Concise History of Scotland* (First published 1970. This version, 2002. Thames & Hudson Ltd., London), p. 36.

[110] A.F. Murison, *King Robert the Bruce* (Edinburgh, Oliphant, Anderson & Ferrier, 1899), p. 17.

[111] A.F. Murison, *King Robert the Bruce* (Edinburgh, Oliphant, Anderson & Ferrier, 1899), p. 17.

[112] Ruth M. Blakely, *The Brus Family in England and Scotland, 1100-1295* (Boydell Press, Woodbridge, 2005), p. 179.

STEWART:
HIGH STEWARDS
OF SCOTLAND

SCOTLAND

STEWART LANDS
(RENFREW, ISLES OF
ARRAN & BUTE)

THE STEWART LINEAGE

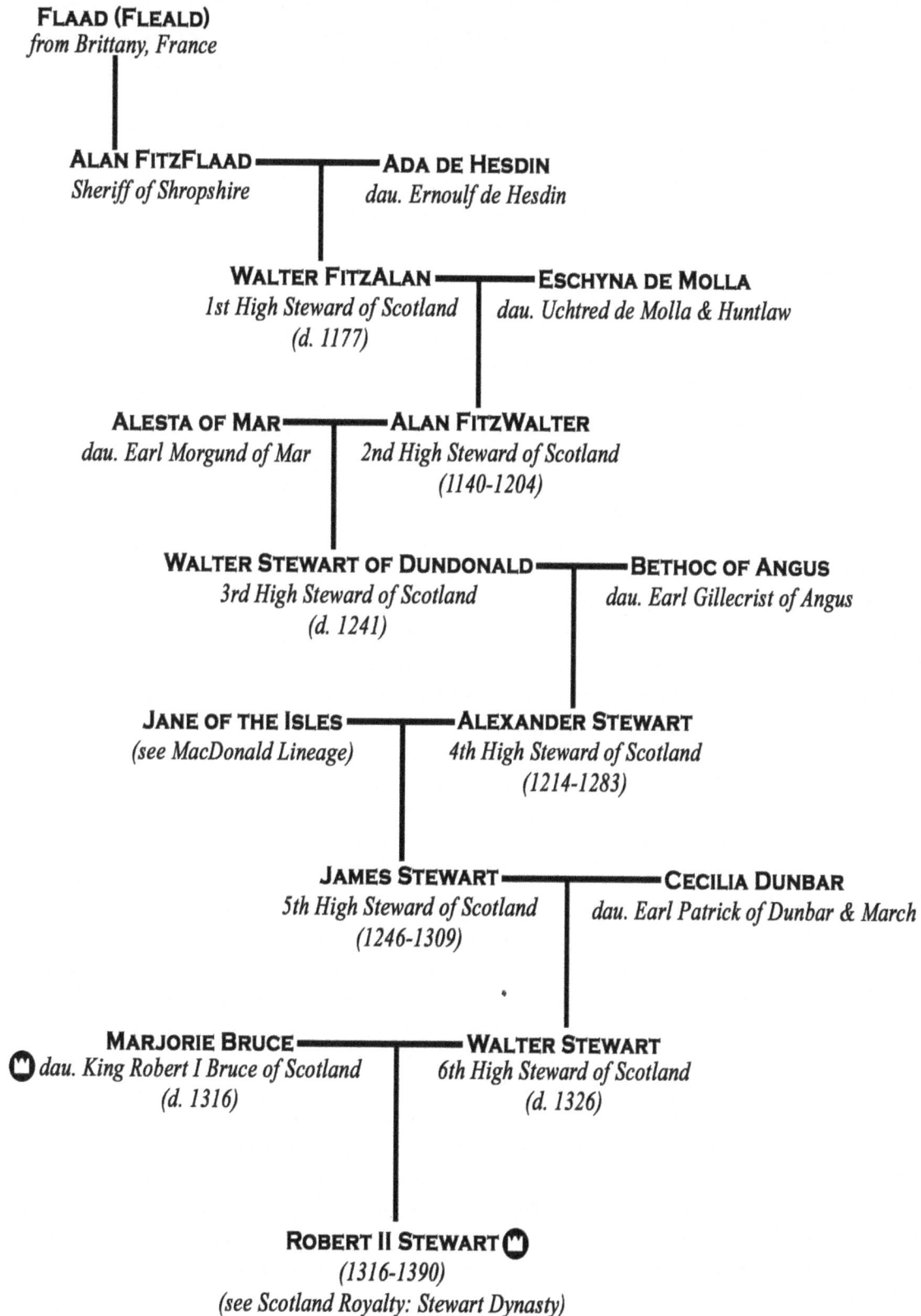

FLAAD (FLEALD)
from Brittany, France

ALAN FITZFLAAD —————— **ADA DE HESDIN**
Sheriff of Shropshire *dau. Ernoulf de Hesdin*

WALTER FITZALAN —————— **ESCHYNA DE MOLLA**
1st High Steward of Scotland *dau. Uchtred de Molla & Huntlaw*
(d. 1177)

ALESTA OF MAR —————— **ALAN FITZWALTER**
dau. Earl Morgund of Mar *2nd High Steward of Scotland*
(1140-1204)

WALTER STEWART OF DUNDONALD —————— **BETHOC OF ANGUS**
3rd High Steward of Scotland *dau. Earl Gillecrist of Angus*
(d. 1241)

JANE OF THE ISLES —————— **ALEXANDER STEWART**
(see MacDonald Lineage) *4th High Steward of Scotland*
(1214-1283)

JAMES STEWART —————— **CECILIA DUNBAR**
5th High Steward of Scotland *dau. Earl Patrick of Dunbar & March*
(1246-1309)

MARJORIE BRUCE —————— **WALTER STEWART**
dau. King Robert I Bruce of Scotland *6th High Steward of Scotland*
(d. 1316) *(d. 1326)*

ROBERT II STEWART
(1316-1390)
(see Scotland Royalty: Stewart Dynasty)

THE STEWART LINEAGE

The Stewart lineage originated in the Celtic duchy of Brittany in France. They came over to England in the early days of the Norman conquest, around the reign of Henry I.

Flaad FitzAlain

Flaad was also variously spelled Fléald or Flahault. He was from a city in Brittany called Dol, located in the Breton Marches, looking toward St. Michel across sea and quicksand.

His elder brother Alan FitzAlain was a vassal of, and possibly kinsman of, the Count of Dol. Alan was a Crusader under Geoffrey of Boulogne. Their father was Alain, dapifer (steward) of the Archbishop of Dol.[1] Alan FitzAlain inherited the office of dapifer. [2]

Some accounts say Flaad went to England, gaining a lordship on the March of Wales.[3] [4] However, there is no documentation placing him in England at all.[5] Instead, the original immigrant to England seems to have been his son, *Alan FitzFlaad*.

Alan FitzFlaad

Alan FitzFlaad was given lands in the Welsh Marches by King Henry I of England (see *Continental Dynasty*), as well as being made Sheriff of Shropshire.[6] Alan likely was among the Bretons who fought under Henry I at Mont Saint-Michel in Brittany, and this was perhaps how he gained the favor of the English monarch.[7]

His wife was Ada/Avelina de Hesdin, daughter of Ernoulf de Hesdin.[8] They had three sons:

- Jourdain/Jordan – inherited the Brittany lands and also the office of dapifer of Dol, which implies that his great-uncle Alan FitzAlain had no heirs[9]
- William – inherited the English lands and founded the house of the FitzAlan Earls of Arundel
- *Walter* – went to southern Scotland and joined the principality of Prince David (later King David I of Scotland)[10]

Alan FitzFlaad is often credited with another son, Simon, who was probably illegitimate.[11]

Walter FitzAlan, First High Steward of Scotland
(d. 1177)

Walter FitzAlan went into Scotland to make his fortune, since, as the youngest son, he had no chance of inheriting anything in England. Luck was with him, for young Prince David (see *MacAlpin Dynasty*) liked him, and when he became king he gave Walter the lands of Renfrew and Kyle, and appointed him the first High Steward, the chief officer of the Royal Household.[12] [13]

Walter outlived David by 19 years, and saw the reign of Malcolm IV and the breaking of the Princes of Galloway. He commanded the fight at Renfrew when Somerled was killed in 1164 (see *MacDonald Lineage*). He outlived Malcolm IV, and saw in William I.

Walter died in 1177[14] and was buried in Paisley Abbey, which he had founded.[15]

Walter FitzAlan married Eschyna de Molla, daughter of Uchtred de Molla and Huntlaw, and they had a son, *Alan FitzWalter*.[16]

Alan FitzWalter, 2ⁿᵈ High Steward of Scotland
(d. 1204)

Alan inherited Walter's lands, and also his title of High Steward of Scotland. He went with Richard the Lionhearted on the Second Crusade, but he returned unscathed.[17]

Alan married Alesta of Mar, the daughter of Morgan, Earl of Mar. They had at least one son, *Walter*.[18]

Alan FitzWalter died in 1204.[19]

Walter Stewart, 3ʳᵈ High Steward of Scotland
(d. 1241)

Walter was the first to use the name Stewart as his surname. King Alexander II made Walter Justiciar of Scotland as well as High Steward.[20]

Walter was present in 1238 when Alexander made Robert (V) de Brus of Annandale (see *De Brus Lineage*) his heir when the king's first wife, Joan, died childless. Alexander also gave Walter charge of the retinue to bring Alexander's second wife, Marie, from France.[21]

Walter married Bethoc, daughter of Gillecrist, Earl of Angus. They had at least four children:[22]

- John – died on Crusade under St. Louis at Damietta
- *Alexander* – inherited High Steward office
- Walter – married the co-heiress of Menteith. He eventually inherited the entire earldom of Menteith, and founded the first cadet branch of Stewarts
- Margaret – married Neil, Earl of Carrick. Their daughter, *Marjorie*, married *Robert (VI) de Brus*, and was the mother of *King Robert I the Bruce* (see *De Brus Lineage*).

Walter Stewart died in 1241.[23]

Alexander Stewart, 4ᵗʰ High Steward of Scotland
(d. 1283)

Alexander Stewart was one of the Guardians during King Alexander III's minority. During the minority, two factions fought for supremacy—the Bruce and Durward faction versus the Comyn and Queen Marie faction. Alexander Stewart helped to guide the country through those turbulent times.[24]

He married Jane of the Isles, daughter of James MacAngus of the Isles, thus gaining lands that let him control the Firth of Clyde.[25][26]

Alexander was the first Stewart to lay claim to the Isles of Arran and Bute. This put the Stewarts and the MacDonalds (see *MacDonald Lineage*) in a long-lasting feud over the rights to those islands. Alexander claimed them by right of his wife, Jane, the heiress to James MacAngus, son of Angus MacSomerled, son of Somerled, the original "owner" of the islands.[27]

Alexander took a leading part in the victory at Largs over the Norwegian King Hakon, which broke the Norwegian claim to the islands for good.[28]

Alexander and Jane had three children: .[29] [30] [31]

- ***James*** – born c. 1246
- Sir John Stewart of Bonkyll, d. 1298
- Elizabeth – married Sir William Douglas

Alexander Stewart died in 1283.[32]

James Stewart, 5th High Steward of Scotland
(1246-1309)

James Stewart became High Steward in 1283, at age 40. In 1286, he met at the de Brus stronghold of Turnberry with a group of nobles who wanted to put aside the claims of the three-year-old Maid of Norway in favor of Robert (V) de Brus of Annandale (see *De Brus Lineage*). Nothing came of it.[33]

James was one of the six Guardians to govern during the expected minority of Margaret, the Maid of Scotland. He refused to consider the joining of the Crowns of Scotland and England by her marriage to the English heir. When she died, he resumed backing de Brus.[34] In 1288, he entered into an association with Angus Mor of the Isles and his son Alasdair Óg (see *MacDonald Lineage*) to forward the de Brus claims.[35]

When King John Balliol was at war with King Edward I (see *Continental Dynasty*), James put aside his personal feelings and held Roxburgh Castle against Edward's invasion. He surrendered on terms when Balliol's cause seemed lost after the defeat of Dunbar.[36]

However, he was the first noble to show signs of national feeling. During the popular risings of the following year, he joined William Wallace and the Bishops of Glasgow and Moray, in coordinating the small local uprisings into national ones.[37] [38]

James was one of the chief men among the southern leaders whose bickering nearly wrecked the early resistance, and surrendered with them at Irvine in 1297. He then took up arms with William Wallace, and fought at the victory of Stirling Bridge. He also saw the disaster at Falkirk, where his brother John died.[39]

In 1306, at age 60, he joined King Robert I Bruce's army (see *Stewart Dynasty*), and was present at Robert I's first Parliament at St. Andrews.[40]

James married a woman who has been alternately identified as the sister of the Earl of Ulster or Cecilia Dunbar, daughter of Patrick Dunbar, the 7th Earl of Dunbar. They had one son, ***Walter Stewart***.[41]

James Stewart died in 1309.[42]

Sir Walter Stewart, 6th High Steward of Scotland
(1292-1326)

Walter Stewart was born in 1292, and was a child through most of the wars.[43] At age 22, as a squire, he led the men of his family's lands to the muster at Bannockburn. He was his cousin, Douglas', lieutenant in command of the center during the battle. Walter was knighted on the field before the battle.[44]

In 1316, he escorted Marjorie Bruce, daughter of King Robert the Bruce (see *Stewart Dynasty*), home from England, where she had been imprisoned for eight years. With her consent, the Parliament of Ayr postponed her rights to the throne in favor of Edward Bruce, Robert's brother, and his heirs. Marjorie Bruce and Walter Stewart married in 1318. Less than a year later, Marjorie died, leaving the newborn ***Robert***.[45] [46] [47] Researcher Richard Oram has the dates a bit different: Marjorie and Walter married April of 1315, Robert born in 1316, and Marjorie died in 1317. [48]

In 1318, Walter took the great fortress at Berwick after a three-week siege, and Edward II (see *Continental Dynasty*) was unable to recapture it. This was also the year Edward Bruce died in Ireland, making Walter's baby, Robert Stewart (see *Stewart Dynasty*), the heir to the throne of Scotland.[49]

Walter was a great soldier. At age 26, he was made governor of Berwick, a dangerous post near the English border. He defended it brilliantly the next year when it was under siege, by sallying out the burning Mary-port.[50]

On 9 April 1327, Walter Stewart died of a fever at the age of 34, survived by his eleven-year-old son ***Robert***.[51] [52]

Young Robert Stewart later became ***King Robert II of Scotland***. For his adventures, see the *Stewart Dynasty* chapter.

---

[1] Caroline Bingham, *Kings and Queens of Scotland* (orig. published 1976, Taplinger Publishing Co. this edition, 1985, Dorset Press), p. 55.
[2] J. Horace Round, *Studies of Peerage and Family History* (Westminster, Archibald Constable and Company Ltd., 1901), p. 123-124.
[3] Caroline Bingham, *Kings and Queens of Scotland* (orig. published 1976, Taplinger Publishing Co. this edition, 1985, Dorset Press), p. 55.
[4] Agnes Mure MacKenzie, *The Rise of the Stewarts* (Oliver & Boyd, Ltd, Edinburgh. Originally printed 1935, this printing 1957.), p. 7.
[5] J. Horace Round, *Studies of Peerage and Family History* (Westminster, Archibald Constable and Company Ltd., 1901), p. 116.
[6] Agnes Mure MacKenzie, *The Rise of the Stewarts* (Oliver & Boyd, Ltd, Edinburgh. Originally printed 1935, this printing 1957.), p. 7.
[7] J. Horace Round, *Studies of Peerage and Family History* (Westminster, Archibald Constable and Company Ltd., 1901), p. 124.
[8] J. Horace Round, *Studies of Peerage and Family History* (Westminster, Archibald Constable and Company Ltd., 1901), p. 116.
[9] J. Horace Round, *Studies of Peerage and Family History* (Westminster, Archibald Constable and Company Ltd., 1901), p. 126-127.
[10] Agnes Mure MacKenzie, *The Rise of the Stewarts* (Oliver & Boyd, Ltd, Edinburgh. Originally printed 1935, this printing 1957.), p 9.
[11] J. Horace Round, *Studies of Peerage and Family History* (Westminster, Archibald Constable and Company Ltd., 1901), p. 125.
[12] Caroline Bingham, *Kings and Queens of Scotland* (orig. published 1976, Taplinger Publishing Co. this edition, 1985, Dorset Press), p. 55.
[13] Agnes Mure MacKenzie, *The Rise of the Stewarts* (Oliver & Boyd, Ltd, Edinburgh. Originally printed 1935, this printing 1957.), p. 9.
[14] J. Horace Round, *Studies of Peerage and Family History* (Westminster, Archibald Constable and Company Ltd., 1901), p. 128-129.
[15] Agnes Mure MacKenzie, *The Rise of the Stewarts* (Oliver & Boyd, Ltd, Edinburgh. Originally printed 1935, this printing 1957.), p. 9.
[16] Agnes Mure MacKenzie, *The Rise of the Stewarts* (Oliver & Boyd, Ltd, Edinburgh. Originally printed 1935, this printing 1957.), p. 9.
[17] Agnes Mure MacKenzie, *The Rise of the Stewarts* (Oliver & Boyd, Ltd, Edinburgh. Originally printed 1935, this printing 1957.), p.9.
[18] Agnes Mure MacKenzie, *The Rise of the Stewarts* (Oliver & Boyd, Ltd, Edinburgh. Originally printed 1935, this printing 1957.), p. 9.
[19] Agnes Mure MacKenzie, *The Rise of the Stewarts* (Oliver & Boyd, Ltd, Edinburgh. Originally printed 1935, this printing 1957.), p. 10.
[20] Agnes Mure MacKenzie, *The Rise of the Stewarts* (Oliver & Boyd, Ltd, Edinburgh. Originally printed 1935, this printing 1957.), p. 10.
[21] Agnes Mure MacKenzie, *The Rise of the Stewarts* (Oliver & Boyd, Ltd, Edinburgh. Originally printed 1935, this printing 1957.), p. 10.
[22] Agnes Mure MacKenzie, *The Rise of the Stewarts* (Oliver & Boyd, Ltd, Edinburgh. Originally printed 1935, this printing 1957.),p.10, 12.
[23] Agnes Mure MacKenzie, *The Rise of the Stewarts* (Oliver & Boyd, Ltd, Edinburgh. Originally printed 1935, this printing 1957.), p. 10.
[24] Agnes Mure MacKenzie, *The Rise of the Stewarts* (Oliver & Boyd, Ltd, Edinburgh. Originally printed 1935, this printing 1957.), p. 12.
[25] Ronald Williams, *The Lords of the Isles: The Clan Donald and the Early Kingdom of the Scots* (Chatto & Windus - The Hogarth Press, London, 1984), p. 127.

[26] Raymond Campbell Paterson, *The Lords of the Isles: A History of Clan Donald* (Birlinn Limited, Edinburgh, 2001), p. 11.

[27] Ronald Williams, *The Lords of the Isles: The Clan Donald and the Early Kingdom of the Scots* (Chatto & Windus - The Hogarth Press, London, 1984) p. 127.

[28] Agnes Mure MacKenzie, *The Rise of the Stewarts* (Oliver & Boyd, Ltd, Edinburgh. Originally printed 1935, this printing 1957.), p. 12.

[29] Ronald Williams, *The Lords of the Isles: The Clan Donald and the Early Kingdom of the Scots* (Chatto & Windus - The Hogarth Press, London, 1984), p. 127.

[30] Raymond Campbell Paterson, *The Lords of the Isles: A History of Clan Donald* (Birlinn Limited, Edinburgh, 2001), p. 11.

[31] Agnes Mure MacKenzie, *The Rise of the Stewarts* (Oliver & Boyd, Ltd, Edinburgh. Originally printed 1935, this printing 1957.), p. 13-14.

[32] Agnes Mure MacKenzie, *The Rise of the Stewarts* (Oliver & Boyd, Ltd, Edinburgh. Originally printed 1935, this printing 1957.), p. 12.

[33] Agnes Mure MacKenzie, *The Rise of the Stewarts* (Oliver & Boyd, Ltd, Edinburgh. Originally printed 1935, this printing 1957.)p. 12.

[34] Agnes Mure MacKenzie, *The Rise of the Stewarts* (Oliver & Boyd, Ltd, Edinburgh. Originally printed 1935, this printing 1957.), p. 13.

[35] Ronald Williams, *The Lords of the Isles: The Clan Donald and the Early Kingdom of the Scots* (Chatto & Windus - The Hogarth Press, London, 1984) p. 149.

[36] Agnes Mure MacKenzie, *The Rise of the Stewarts* (Oliver & Boyd, Ltd, Edinburgh. Originally printed 1935, this printing 1957.), p. 13.

[37] Ronald Williams, *The Lords of the Isles: The Clan Donald and the Early Kingdom of the Scots* (Chatto & Windus - The Hogarth Press, London, 1984) p. 147.

[38] Agnes Mure MacKenzie, *The Rise of the Stewarts* (Oliver & Boyd, Ltd, Edinburgh. Originally printed 1935, this printing 1957.), p. 13.

[39] Agnes Mure MacKenzie, *The Rise of the Stewarts* (Oliver & Boyd, Ltd, Edinburgh. Originally printed 1935, this printing 1957.), p. 13.

[40] Agnes Mure MacKenzie, *The Rise of the Stewarts* (Oliver & Boyd, Ltd, Edinburgh. Originally printed 1935, this printing 1957.), p. 14.

[41] Agnes Mure MacKenzie, *The Rise of the Stewarts* (Oliver & Boyd, Ltd, Edinburgh. Originally printed 1935, this printing 1957.), p. 14.

[42] Agnes Mure MacKenzie, *The Rise of the Stewarts* (Oliver & Boyd, Ltd, Edinburgh. Originally printed 1935, this printing 1957.), p. 14.

[43] Agnes Mure MacKenzie, *The Rise of the Stewarts* (Oliver & Boyd, Ltd, Edinburgh. Originally printed 1935, this printing 1957.), p. 14.

[44] Agnes Mure MacKenzie, *The Rise of the Stewarts* (Oliver & Boyd, Ltd, Edinburgh. Originally printed 1935, this printing 1957.), p. 15.

[45] Agnes Mure MacKenzie, *The Rise of the Stewarts* (Oliver & Boyd, Ltd, Edinburgh. Originally printed 1935, this printing 1957.), p. 15.

[46] Fitzroy Maclean, *A Concise History of Scotland* (First published 1970. This version published 2002. Thames & Hudson Ltd., London), p. 45.

[47] John Cannon & Ralph Griffiths, *The Oxford Illustrated History of the British Monarchy* (2000 edition, Oxford University Press), Geneaolgies of Royal Lines Appendix.

[48] Richard Oram (Ed.), *The Kings and Queens of Scotland* (Tempus Publishing Ltd., Stroud, Gloucestershire, England, 2001), p. 142.

[49] Agnes Mure MacKenzie, *The Rise of the Stewarts* (Oliver & Boyd, Ltd, Edinburgh. Originally printed 1935, this printing 1957.), p. 15.

[50] Agnes Mure MacKenzie, *The Rise of the Stewarts* (Oliver & Boyd, Ltd, Edinburgh. Originally printed 1935, this printing 1957.), p. 15.

[51] John Cannon & Ralph Griffiths, *The Oxford Illustrated History of the British Monarchy* (2000 edition, Oxford University Press), Geneaolgies of Royal Lines Appendix.

[52] Agnes Mure MacKenzie, *The Rise of the Stewarts* (Oliver & Boyd, Ltd, Edinburgh. Originally printed 1935, this printing 1957.), p. 16.

SCOTTISH ROYALTY

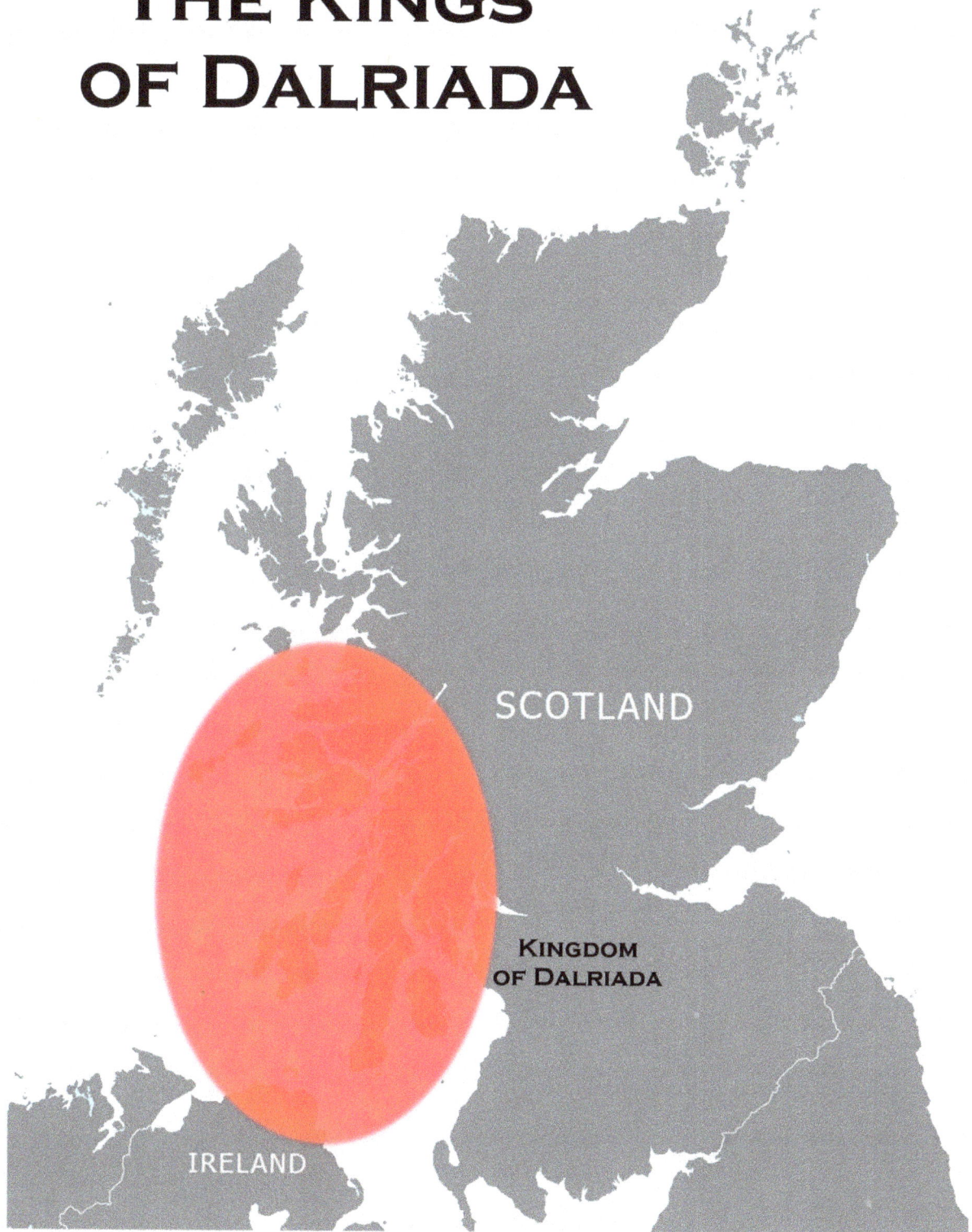

THE KINGS OF DALRIADA

SCOTLAND

KINGDOM OF DALRIADA

IRELAND

THE KINGS OF DALRIADA

(ancestors of both Scottish Kings and MacDonald Clan)

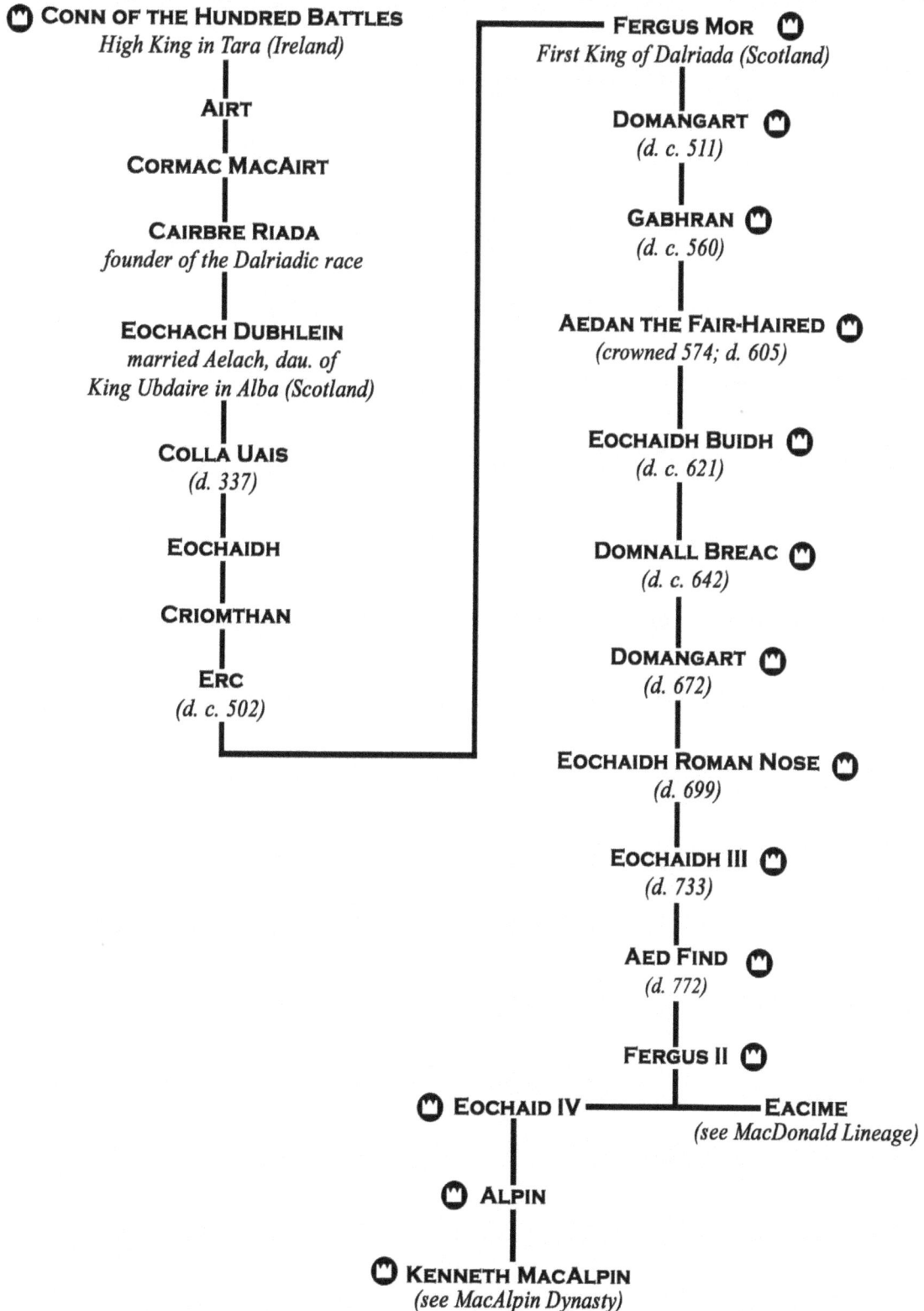

CONN OF THE HUNDRED BATTLES
High King in Tara (Ireland)

AIRT

CORMAC MACAIRT

CAIRBRE RIADA
founder of the Dalriadic race

EOCHACH DUBHLEIN
*married Aelach, dau. of
King Ubdaire in Alba (Scotland)*

COLLA UAIS
(d. 337)

EOCHAIDH

CRIOMTHAN

ERC
(d. c. 502)

FERGUS MOR
First King of Dalriada (Scotland)

DOMANGART
(d. c. 511)

GABHRAN
(d. c. 560)

AEDAN THE FAIR-HAIRED
(crowned 574; d. 605)

EOCHAIDH BUIDH
(d. c. 621)

DOMNALL BREAC
(d. c. 642)

DOMANGART
(d. 672)

EOCHAIDH ROMAN NOSE
(d. 699)

EOCHAIDH III
(d. 733)

AED FIND
(d. 772)

FERGUS II

EOCHAID IV —————— **EACIME**
(see MacDonald Lineage)

ALPIN

KENNETH MACALPIN
(see MacAlpin Dynasty)

THE KINGS OF DALRIADA

The Romans came early to Scotland, in 81 A.D., to be exact. The Romans stayed mostly in the southern part of the island, but the Pictish tribes in the north raided the Roman territory. So the Romans built Hadrian's Wall, running from the Solway to the Tyne, in 121 A.D. This proved insufficient, so the Romans built another wall farther north, the Antonine Wall, from the Forth to the Clyde, in 141 A.D.[1] By 208 A.D., the Romans had retreated south back behind Hadrian's Wall.[2][3][4]

In 350 A.D., the northern tribes were still coming past the walls, and then Saxons started invading from the North Sea. It was too much for the Romans, who faced other troubles closer to home, and they left by 430 A.D.[5]

After they left anarchy ruled, and Teutonic invaders took over most of England, driving the native Bretons into Wales, Cornwall, Cumbria, and Strathclyde.[6][7] Jutes, Saxons, and Frisians landed on the southeast coasts, while Angle tribes landed further north, a group of them landing in the 6th century in Northumbria in southern Scotland between the Tyne and Hadrian's Wall.[8]

And so ancient Scotland was inhabited by four cultures: the Picts, in the east from Caithness to the Forth, who were a Celtic race that came from Europe in the first millennium B.C.; the Bretons of Strathclyde, dominating from the Clyde to the Solway into Cumbria, another Celtic race with a kindred tongue to the Picts; and in the east, south of the Forth and into Northumbria, lived the Anglo-Saxons, a Teutonic race from the Rhine region of Europe. Throughout the 3rd and 4th centuries, the fourth group, Celts from Northern Ireland who became known as Scots, came into present-day Argyll, Kintyre, and the nearby islands, settling into their tiny kingdom of Dalriada. They spoke a different Celtic tongue than the existing tribes, and were loyal to Ireland.[9][10][11]

Around 500 A.D., a fresh "Scottish" group from Antrim in Ireland came to Kintyre, led by Fergus Mor, a chieftain of the Irish Gael, and his brothers Angus and Lorne.[12][13][14] Fergus Mor is traditionally called "the Founder of Scotland." It was they, supposedly, who brought the Stone of Scone with them, and the stone was certainly used in coronations from time immemorial.[15]

Theoretically, every Irish-Scottish clan can trace its roots back to Fergus Mor, but in our lineage so far, only two have claimed to: the MacAlpin Dynasty of Scottish kings (see *MacAlpin Dynasty*), and the Clan Donald (see *MacDonald Lineage*).

Now, the mythology would have us believe that Fergus Mor and his tiny band of Celts came over and somehow subjugated all the existing populations. The annals of the time did not bear this out. The tiny kingdom of Dalriada survived as its own entity but was often subjugated by its more powerful neighbors. The Bretons in Strathclyde often tried to oust them—except when they were allied with the Dalriadans in the struggle against the Angles.[16] In one memorable moment, all the northern kingdoms banded together against the Northumbrian king, Ecgfrid, who tried to subjugate them, but he was eventually defeated at the Battle of Nectansmere in 685.[17][18]

Instead of Dalriada being the driving force in the north, it was the Picts who became supreme in the early history of Scotland, particularly under two sons of a Pict also named Fergus. Angus and Constantine were very powerful warriors who not only united all of the Picts under them, but subjugated tiny Dalriada as well. Angus' victories were so massive, he began to trace the true beginnings of the kingdom of Scotland.[19] He subjugated Dalriada around 734 A.D. He died in 761.[20]

Subjugation in those days did not mean the total annihilation of the existing culture. Usually, the subjugated kingdom was allowed to continue as it had, simply paying a monetary tribute to the victorious king and usually allowing a Christian monastery to be founded within its precincts. Christianity had come to all four of the tribes of Scotland by the end of the 7th century, but they did not follow the Roman Orthodoxy, since their brand of Christianity had come from the Irish, who did not have close communication with Rome.[21]

After Angus, Constantine MacFergus continued his brother's gains. Dalriada seemed to have been all but obliterated during Constantine's reign, as the last known King of Dalriada, Doncorcin, died shortly after Constantine rose to power.[22] Constantine founded the monastery of Dunkeld in the area to consolidate his power.[23] Constantine died in 820 A.D.

In spite of this, it was from Dalriada, this tiny kingdom on the peninsula of Kintyre, that the reigning monarchs of the country of Scotland emerged. Fergus the Pict, father of Angus and Constantine, also had a daughter. This daughter married Eoganan, a king of Dalriada. They had Alpin, who also succeeded to the throne. Alpin begat Kenneth MacAlpin, who was the first king to be lord of Dalriada *and* the Picts, claiming the Pictish throne through his grandmother's lineage. It is then that the kingdom of Alba—modern day Perth, Fife, Stirling, Dumbarton, and Argyle—was born, and the core of what is now Scotland was founded (see *MacAlpin Dynasty*).[24]

During the reign of the pre-Kenneth MacAlpin Dalriadan kings, in the 8th and 9th century, when they were not fighting amongst themselves or against the Anglo-Saxons to the south, they were fighting the incursions of the Vikings, who gained ground in the Islands (Orkney, Shetland, Hebrides), and in the mainland counties of Caithness and Sutherland.[25] This clash with the Norsemen will be seen for many centuries, throughout the reigns of the MacAlpin Dynasty.

Records are sparse for these Dalriadic kings, but there is some history that we can trace.

Although there was cross-cultural exchange for years prior to 500 A.D., a large influx of Celtic Irish "Scots," led by Fergus Mor and his two brothers, Lorne and Angus, arrived to settle permanently. Fergus Mor's ancestry stretched back to **Conn of the Hundred Battles**, the High King in Tara in the 3rd century.[26]

Conn's great-grandson, **Cairbre Riada** of the Liffey, settled his followers in Munster, but famine forced him to move. They then settled in a small area around Dunseverick in the north of Ireland, between the Antrim mountains and the sea. This was known as "Dal-riada" or "Riada's Share." This was a small and narrow strip of land, but across the Irish Sea could be seen Kintyre and Lorne in Scotland.[27]

Cairbre Riada's son **Eochach Dubhlein** married a Pictish princess from Alba named Aelech[28], the daughter of King Ubdaire. This gave him property, relatives, and interests in both Ireland and Scotland. They had three sons, who each had an inheritance that stretched across the Irish Sea.[29]

Eochach Dubhlein's son **Colla Uais** aspired to the High Kingship of Tara, but was defeated and fled to his mother's people in Scotland, possibly in Colonsay. He and his brothers returned to Ireland and conquered a small kingdom called Oriel (or Oirghialla).[30]

Fergus Mor, Colla Uais's great-grandson, made the move to Scotland permanently, settling his people in Dunadd, Kintyre, Knapdale, Arran, and Bute, building the strongholds of Tarbert and Dunavertie.[31]

After Fergus died, the kingship passed to his son *Domangart*, then to Domangart's elder son Comgall, then to Domangart's younger son *Gabhran*, then to Comgall's son Conall.

At this time, Christianity was under attack by the pagan Picts and Anglo-Saxons, and Dalriada was the only Christian beachhead. Saint Columba came over from Ireland on a summons from Conall.[32] St. Columba successfully converted the Picts, securing peace on Dalriada's northern border.[33]

Conall and all of his sons were killed in a battle in Kintyre in 574, which led to a power struggle for the throne.[34]

After Conall's death, *Aedan* and his brother Eoghan, both fathered by King Gabhran but with different mothers, clashed for the throne. Eoghan was the favorite, but St. Columba interposed himself, claiming to have had a dream in which an angel told him that Aedan was the correct choice. By doing this, he was taking over the ancient Druidic role, where the Druid would choose a successor based on his visions.[35] [36]

St. Columba was a politically savvy monk, and he had his reasons for choosing Aedan over Eoghan. While Columba had secured peace with the northern Picts, the Breton kingdom of Strathclyde was another traditional enemy of Dalriada, and the Angles of Cumbria were another opposing force. Aedan, through his mother, was a grandson of a former king of Strathclyde and a nephew of the current king of Cumbria. Aedan's wife was the granddaughter of the current king of the Picts to the north. Aedan was also the sub-king of Manau in Gododdin, and had fought with distinction at the Battle of Ardderyd (a victory for the Christian factions), and had named his eldest son Arthur—the first Celtic prince to do so. For all of these reasons, Columba decided that Aedan's blood ties, ruling experience, and tested warrior status made him the better choice.[37]

Columba crowned Aedan in 574, and in 575 they both went to Ireland to settle a dispute with the Irish king, Baetan, who was Aedan's nominal overlord. However, Aedan didn't want to put his vast fleet at the disposal of Baetan, who was at the time ravaging all of his vassal's lands. The convention of Drum Ceatt decided that Aedan owed Baetan the soldiers due to an overlord, but that the fleet was his alone. For all intents and purposes, this made Alban Dalriada an independent kingdom.[38]

Aedan banded together with Strathclyde to oppose the Anglo-Saxons of Northumbria. He took as his second wife a princess of Strathclyde, to further strengthen the new Dalriadan-Breton alliance.[39]

In 580, Aedan led a seaborne expedition against the pirates of Orkney who were raiding into the Hebrides islands. In 582 he drove his one-time overlord Baetan out of the Isle of Man. In 583, the Anglo-Saxons attempted to take Gododdin, but Aedan defeated them in Stirlingshire.[40]

In 584, a renegade tribe of Picts invaded Gododdin, and Aedan caught up to them at Catterick. Aedan's men spent the night before the battle drinking, and they threw themselves recklessly upon the superior Pictish force. Aedan won the battle, but it was a devastating victory. He lost a large percentage of his men, and two of his sons—Eochaid and Arthur—died in the battle.[41]

In 603, Aedan once more rallied the troops of the coalition to defend against Aethelfrith, the Anglo-Saxon king of Northumbria. He barred their way at Degsaston (Dawstane in Liddesdale), but the Anglo-Saxons annihilated the Dalriadan coalition, also killing another son of Aedan, Domangart.[42]

After this loss, Aedan retreated to Kintyre, where he either died or abdicated in 605.[43]

The crown was taken by his son *Eochaid Buidh*, who reigned for 16 years before being overthrown and the kingdom plunged into a civil war.[44]

In 621, Eochaid Buidh's son *Domnall Breac* ("the Speckled") took over, and didn't have an easy reign. In 634, he warred with the Picts. In 637, he invaded Ulster in Ireland in support of an exiled kinsman named Congal Claen. The High King of Erin at the time was Domnall of the Ui Neill, thus Domnall Breac broke the long-standing alliance between his family and the family of St. Columba.[45]

The armies met at Mag Rath (Moyra), and Domnall Breac lost. Three of his brothers were killed, and he was captured and held in Ireland for a year. When he returned home in 638, he warred with the Picts again, and was defeated at Glendmairison. Finally, in 642, Domnall Breac was killed in a war with former ally Strathclyde at the battle of Strathcarron.[46]

Although Domnall's son *Domangart II* (d. 672) took over,[47] Dalriada ceased to exist as an organic whole, always being a subject state to other tribes.[48] After his death his son *Eochaid Roman Nose* came to the throne, but he was killed in 699[49] in a battle against the Clan Lorne. His wife was a Pictish princess, the sister of the Pictish king.[50]

The lineage we are following is the line of Gabhran, descendants of Fergus Mor. The descendants of Lorne, one of Fergus' brothers, also claimed the throne, and after Eochaid Roman Nose died, ruled from 677-723.[51]

In 723, *Eochaid III* reclaimed the throne for the line of Gabhran. He died ten years later in 733, and his son Aed Find was too young to rule. In 741, Dalriada was defeated and devastated by Angus mac Fergus of the Picts, mentioned above.[52] In 751, *Aed Find* recovered his inheritance, and reigned for 30 years. He is remembered as a lawgiver.[53]

His son *Fergus II* reigned for three years, and here the lineages of the MacAlpin dynasty and the MacDonald Clan split. Fergus II had two sons—*Eochaid IV*, who was the father of Alpin and grandfather of Kenneth MacAlpin; and Eacime, who became the local ruler of Argyll.[54] As Kenneth moved the seat of power east to Scone, the Argyll rulers and their people were isolated by the mountains of the Druim Alban, which kept them detached from all the dynastic struggles that took place later.[55]

Alpin, Eochaid IV's son,[56] fought the Picts, and was defeated and beheaded by them. Then the throne passed to his son *Kenneth MacAlpin*, and a new dynasty was born when he united the Scots and Picts in 843 A.D. (see *MacAlpin Dynasty*)[57] [58]

Many clans try to connect their origins to the early kings of Scotland, and one that has done so is the MacDonald clan (see *MacDonald Lineage*). As you can imagine, due to the sketchy record-keeping and massive destruction during the Viking raids, lists of the Kings of Dalriada are different from source to source, and it is often a matter of faith to believe who is the son of whom. That said, the MacDonalds claim a very specific traditional lineage to the Kings of Dalriada, and much of this list also applies to our

MacAlpin Dynasty lineage as well. To that end, I have copied this list from Ronald Williams' *The Lords of the Isles: The Clan Donald and the early Kingdom of the Scots*:

The Dalriadac Lineage[59]

as traced by the MacDonald tradition

Conn of the Hundred Battles	*High King in Tara (Ireland)*
Airt	*(Ireland)*
Cormac MacAirt	*(Ireland)*
Cairbre Riada	*Founder of Dalriadic tribe (Ireland)*
Eochach Dubhlein	*Married Aelach, dau. of Ubdaire, King in Alba/Scotland (Ireland)*
Colla Uais	*d. c. 337 (Ireland)*
Eochaidh	*(Ireland)*
Criomthan	*(Ireland)*
Erc	*d. c. 502 (Ireland)*
Fergus Mor	*First King of Dalriada, founder of Scotland*
Domangart	*King of Dalriada, d. c. 511*
Gabhran	*King of Dalriada, d. c. 560*
Aedan The Fair-haired	*King of Dalriada, d. 605*
Eochaidh Buidh	*King of Dalriada, d. 621*
Domnall Breac	*King of Dalriada, d. 642*
Domangart	*King of Dalriada, d. 672*
Eochaidh Roman Nose	*King of Dalriada, d. 699*
Eochaidh III	*King of Dalriada, d. 733*
Aed Find	*King of Dalriada, d. 772*
Fergus II	*King of Dalriada*
Eochaidh IV	*King of Dalriada*
Eacime – Fergus' 2nd son	*Ruler of Argyll, Ancestor of the Clan Donald*
Alpin	*King of Dalriada*
Kenneth MacAlpin	*First King of Scotland*

Also below is a list from E. William Robertson's book, *Scotland Under Her Early Kings, Part Two*.[60] I prefer to simply consider these people "traditional" or "legendary" ancestors—mythology rather than hard fact. That these people existed is certain (their names are historically proven), but the direct blood relationship is next to impossible to prove:

147

The Kings of Dalriada

Fergus Mor Mac Earca	d. 502
Domangart Mac Nissi	d. 505
Comgal Mac Domangart	d. 538
Gabhran Mac Domangart	d. 560
Conal Man Comgal	d. 574
Aidan Mac Gabhran	d. 606
Eocha Buidhe Mac Gabhran	d. 629
Conad Cer Mac Eocha	d. 629
Ferchar Mac Conad	
Donald Brec Mac Eocha	d. 642
Conal Crandomna Mac Eocha Dungal Donald Duin	d. 650
Domangart Mac Donald Brec	d. 673
Malduin Mac Conal	d. 689
Ferchar Fada	d. 697
Eocha Mac Domangart	
Aincellach Mac Ferchar	Expelled 698, died 719
Duncha Beg	d. 721
Selvach Mac Ferchar	Resigned 723, died 730
Dungal Mac Selvach	d. 733
Eocha Mac Eocha	d. 733
Muredach Mac Aincellach	Expelled 736
Eogan Mac Muredach	
Aodh Fin Mac Eocha	d. 778
Fergus Mac Eocha	d. 781
Doncorcin	d. 792
Selvach Mac Eogan	
Donald	
Conal	
Conal	
Constantine	
Angus	
Aodh	
Eoganan Mac Aodh	
Dungal Mac Selvach	
Alpin Mac Eoganan	
Kenneth Mac Alpin	

[1] Fitzroy Maclean, *A Concise History of Scotland*, (Thames & Hudson, New York, originally published 1970, this edition 1983) p. 10.

[2] Fitzroy Maclean, *A Concise History of Scotland*, (Thames & Hudson, New York, originally published 1970, this edition 1983) p. 13.

[3] E. William Robertson, *Scotland Under Her Early Kings: A History of the Kingdom to the Close of the 13th Century, Part One* (Edinburgh: Edmonston and Douglas, 1862), p. 1-2.

[4] Caroline Bingham, *Kings and Queens of Scotland* (orig. published 1976, Taplinger Publishing Co. this edition, 1985, Dorset Press) p. 3-4.

[5] Fitzroy Maclean, *A Concise History of Scotland*, (Thames & Hudson, New York, originally published 1970, this edition 1983) p. 13-14.

[6] Fitzroy Maclean, *A Concise History of Scotland*, (Thames & Hudson, New York, originally published 1970, this edition 1983) p. 14.

[7] Caroline Bingham, *Kings and Queens of Scotland* (originally published 1976, Taplinger Publishing Co. this edition, 1985, Dorset Press) p. 4.

[8] E. William Robertson, *Scotland Under Her Early Kings: A History of the Kingdom to the Close of the 13th Century, Part One* (Edinburgh: Edmonston and Douglas, 1862), p. 3.

[9] Ronald Williams, *The Lords of the Isles: The Clan Donald and the Early Kingdom of the Scots* (Chatto & Windus - The Hogarth Press, London, 1984) p. 25.

[10] Caroline Bingham, *Kings and Queens of Scotland* (orig. published 1976, Taplinger Publishing Co. this edition, 1985, Dorset Press) p. 4-5.

[11] Fitzroy Maclean, *A Concise History of Scotland*, (Thames & Hudson, New York, originally published 1970, this edition 1983) p. 14-15.

[12] Ronald Williams, *The Lords of the Isles: The Clan Donald and the Early Kingdom of the Scots* (Chatto & Windus - The Hogarth Press, London, 1984) p. 11.

[13] Caroline Bingham, *Kings and Queens of Scotland* (originally published 1976, Taplinger Publishing Co. this edition, 1985, Dorset Press) p. 5.

[14] Fitzroy Maclean, *A Concise History of Scotland*, (Thames & Hudson, New York, originally published 1970, this edition 1983) p. 18.

[15] Caroline Bingham, *Kings and Queens of Scotland* (originally published 1976, Taplinger Publishing Co. this edition, 1985, Dorset Press) p. 9.

[16] E. William Robertson, *Scotland Under Her Early Kings: A History of the Kingdom to the Close of the 13th Century, Part One* (Edinburgh: Edmonston and Douglas, 1862), p. 14.

[17] Fitzroy Maclean, *A Concise History of Scotland*, (Thames & Hudson, New York, originally published 1970, this edition 1983) p. 21.

[18] E. William Robertson, *Scotland Under Her Early Kings: A History of the Kingdom to the Close of the 13th Century, Part One* (Edinburgh: Edmonston and Douglas, 1862), p. 12.

[19] E. William Robertson, *Scotland Under Her Early Kings: A History of the Kingdom to the Close of the 13th Century, Part One* (Edinburgh: Edmonston and Douglas, 1862), p. 13.

[20] E. William Robertson, *Scotland Under Her Early Kings: A History of the Kingdom to the Close of the 13th Century, Part One* (Edinburgh: Edmonston and Douglas, 1862), p. 15, 19.

[21] Fitzroy Maclean, *A Concise History of Scotland*, (Thames & Hudson, New York, originally published 1970, this edition 1983) p. 20.

[22] E. William Robertson, *Scotland Under Her Early Kings: A History of the Kingdom to the Close of the 13th Century, Part One* (Edinburgh: Edmonston and Douglas, 1862), p. 19.

[23] E. William Robertson, *Scotland Under Her Early Kings: A History of the Kingdom to the Close of the 13th Century, Part One* (Edinburgh: Edmonston and Douglas, 1862), p. 21.

[24] Fitzroy Maclean, *A Concise History of Scotland*, (Thames & Hudson, New York, originally published 1970, this edition 1983) p. 20.

[25] Fitzroy Maclean, *A Concise History of Scotland*, (Thames & Hudson, New York, originally published 1970, this edition 1983) p. 21.

[26] Ronald Williams, *The Lords of the Isles: The Clan Donald and the Early Kingdom of the Scots* (Chatto & Windus - The Hogarth Press, London, 1984) p. 6.

[27] Ronald Williams, *The Lords of the Isles: The Clan Donald and the Early Kingdom of the Scots* (Chatto & Windus - The Hogarth Press, London, 1984) p. 6.

[28] Ronald Williams, *The Lords of the Isles: The Clan Donald and the Early Kingdom of the Scots* (Chatto & Windus - The Hogarth Press, London, 1984) p. 62.

[29] Ronald Williams, *The Lords of the Isles: The Clan Donald and the Early Kingdom of the Scots* (Chatto & Windus - The Hogarth Press, London, 1984) p. 6.

[30] Ronald Williams, *The Lords of the Isles: The Clan Donald and the Early Kingdom of the Scots* (Chatto & Windus - The Hogarth Press, London, 1984) p. 6.

[31] Ronald Williams, *The Lords of the Isles: The Clan Donald and the Early Kingdom of the Scots* (Chatto & Windus - The Hogarth Press, London, 1984) p. 11.

[32] Ronald Williams, *The Lords of the Isles: The Clan Donald and the Early Kingdom of the Scots* (Chatto & Windus - The Hogarth Press, London, 1984) p. 38-9.

[33] Ronald Williams, *The Lords of the Isles: The Clan Donald and the Early Kingdom of the Scots* (Chatto & Windus - The Hogarth Press, London, 1984) p. 41.

[34] Ronald Williams, *The Lords of the Isles: The Clan Donald and the Early Kingdom of the Scots* (Chatto & Windus - The Hogarth Press, London, 1984) p. 20.

[35] Ronald Williams, *The Lords of the Isles: The Clan Donald and the Early Kingdom of the Scots* (Chatto & Windus - The Hogarth Press, London, 1984) p. 42.

[36] Fitzroy Maclean, *A Concise History of Scotland*, (Thames & Hudson, New York, originally published 1970, this edition 1983) p. 19.

[37] Ronald Williams, *The Lords of the Isles: The Clan Donald and the Early Kingdom of the Scots* (Chatto & Windus - The Hogarth Press, London, 1984) p. 42-3.

[38] Ronald Williams, *The Lords of the Isles: The Clan Donald and the Early Kingdom of the Scots* (Chatto & Windus - The Hogarth Press, London, 1984) p. 43-4.

[39] Ronald Williams, *The Lords of the Isles: The Clan Donald and the Early Kingdom of the Scots* (Chatto & Windus - The Hogarth Press, London, 1984) p. 45.

[40] Ronald Williams, *The Lords of the Isles: The Clan Donald and the Early Kingdom of the Scots* (Chatto & Windus - The Hogarth Press, London, 1984) p. 45.

[41] Ronald Williams, *The Lords of the Isles: The Clan Donald and the Early Kingdom of the Scots* (Chatto & Windus - The Hogarth Press, London, 1984) p. 45-6.

[42] Ronald Williams, *The Lords of the Isles: The Clan Donald and the Early Kingdom of the Scots* (Chatto & Windus - The Hogarth Press, London, 1984) p. 46.

[43] Ronald Williams, *The Lords of the Isles: The Clan Donald and the Early Kingdom of the Scots* (Chatto & Windus - The Hogarth Press, London, 1984) p. 47.

[44] Ronald Williams, *The Lords of the Isles: The Clan Donald and the Early Kingdom of the Scots* (Chatto & Windus - The Hogarth Press, London, 1984) p. 55.

[45] Ronald Williams, *The Lords of the Isles: The Clan Donald and the Early Kingdom of the Scots* (Chatto & Windus - The Hogarth Press, London, 1984) p. 55.

[46] Ronald Williams, *The Lords of the Isles: The Clan Donald and the Early Kingdom of the Scots* (Chatto & Windus - The Hogarth Press, London, 1984) p. 55.

[47] Ronald Williams, *The Lords of the Isles: The Clan Donald and the Early Kingdom of the Scots* (Chatto & Windus - The Hogarth Press, London, 1984) p. 56.

[48] Ronald Williams, *The Lords of the Isles: The Clan Donald and the Early Kingdom of the Scots* (Chatto & Windus - The Hogarth Press, London, 1984) p. 55.

[49] Ronald Williams, *The Lords of the Isles: The Clan Donald and the Early Kingdom of the Scots* (Chatto & Windus - The Hogarth Press, London, 1984) p. 62.

[50] Ronald Williams, *The Lords of the Isles: The Clan Donald and the Early Kingdom of the Scots* (Chatto & Windus - The Hogarth Press, London, 1984) p. 56.

[51] Ronald Williams, *The Lords of the Isles: The Clan Donald and the Early Kingdom of the Scots* (Chatto & Windus - The Hogarth Press, London, 1984) p. 56.

[52] Ronald Williams, *The Lords of the Isles: The Clan Donald and the Early Kingdom of the Scots* (Chatto & Windus - The Hogarth Press, London, 1984) p. 56.

[53] Ronald Williams, *The Lords of the Isles: The Clan Donald and the Early Kingdom of the Scots* (Chatto & Windus - The Hogarth Press, London, 1984) p. 57.

[54] Ronald Williams, *The Lords of the Isles: The Clan Donald and the Early Kingdom of the Scots* (Chatto & Windus - The Hogarth Press, London, 1984) p. 62.

[55] Ronald Williams, *The Lords of the Isles: The Clan Donald and the Early Kingdom of the Scots* (Chatto & Windus - The Hogarth Press, London, 1984) p. 57.

[56] Ronald Williams, *The Lords of the Isles: The Clan Donald and the Early Kingdom of the Scots* (Chatto & Windus - The Hogarth Press, London, 1984) p. 62.

[57] Ronald Williams, *The Lords of the Isles: The Clan Donald and the Early Kingdom of the Scots* (Chatto & Windus - The Hogarth Press, London, 1984) p. 57.

[58] Caroline Bingham, *Kings and Queens of Scotland* (originally published 1976, Taplinger Publishing Co. this edition, 1985, Dorset Press) p. 6.

[59] Ronald Williams, *The Lords of the Isles: The Clan Donald and the Early Kingdom of the Scots* (Chatto & Windus - The Hogarth Press, London, 1984) p. 62.

[60] E. William Robertson, *Scotland Under Her Early Kings: A History of the Kingdom to the Close of the 13th Century, Part Two* (Edinburgh: Edmonston and Douglas, 1862), p. 186.

THE MACALPIN DYNASTY

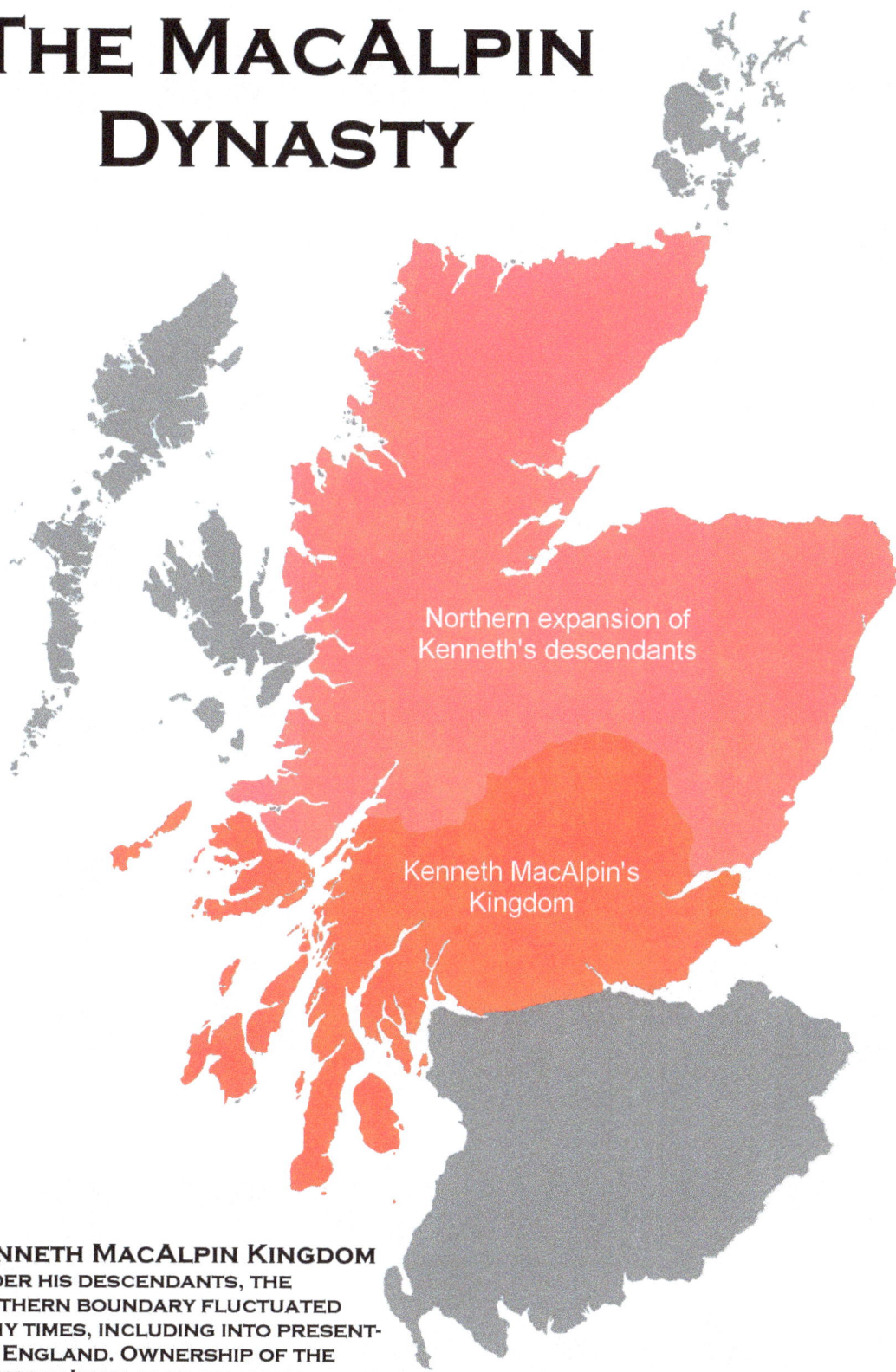

Northern expansion of
Kenneth's descendants

Kenneth MacAlpin's
Kingdom

KENNETH MACALPIN KINGDOM
UNDER HIS DESCENDANTS, THE
SOUTHERN BOUNDARY FLUCTUATED
MANY TIMES, INCLUDING INTO PRESENT-
DAY ENGLAND. OWNERSHIP OF THE
WESTERN ISLES ALSO CHANGED HANDS.

THE MACALPIN DYNASTY

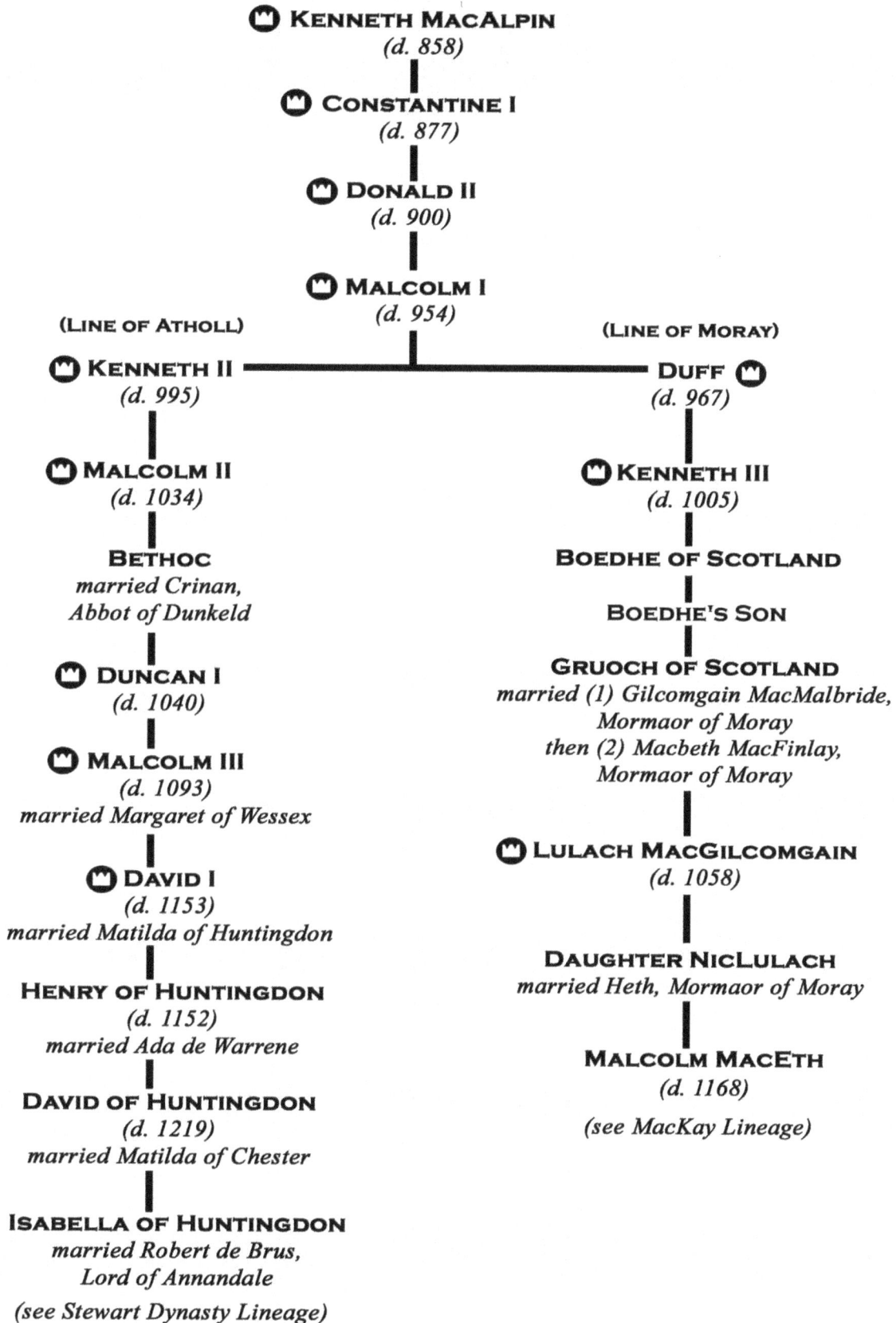

♔ **KENNETH MACALPIN**
(d. 858)

♔ **CONSTANTINE I**
(d. 877)

♔ **DONALD II**
(d. 900)

♔ **MALCOLM I**
(d. 954)

(LINE OF ATHOLL)   **(LINE OF MORAY)**

♔ **KENNETH II**   **DUFF** ♔
(d. 995)   *(d. 967)*

♔ **MALCOLM II**   ♔ **KENNETH III**
(d. 1034)   *(d. 1005)*

BETHOC   **BOEDHE OF SCOTLAND**
married Crinan,
Abbot of Dunkeld   **BOEDHE'S SON**

♔ **DUNCAN I**   **GRUOCH OF SCOTLAND**
(d. 1040)   *married (1) Gilcomgain MacMalbride,*
                                        Mormaor of Moray
                                        then (2) Macbeth MacFinlay,
♔ **MALCOLM III**   *Mormaor of Moray*
(d. 1093)
married Margaret of Wessex

                                        ♔ **LULACH MACGILCOMGAIN**
♔ **DAVID I**   *(d. 1058)*
(d. 1153)
married Matilda of Huntingdon

                                        DAUGHTER NICLULACH
HENRY OF HUNTINGDON   *married Heth, Mormaor of Moray*
(d. 1152)
married Ada de Warrene

                                        MALCOLM MACETH
DAVID OF HUNTINGDON   *(d. 1168)*
(d. 1219)
married Matilda of Chester   *(see MacKay Lineage)*

ISABELLA OF HUNTINGDON
married Robert de Brus,
Lord of Annandale

(see Stewart Dynasty Lineage)

THE MACALPIN DYNASTY

The ascension of Kenneth MacAlpin to the throne in 843 A.D. marked the beginning of a unified Scotland.[1] [2] [3] Almost 40 years before him, a dynasty of Gaelic-speaking Scots had gained power in the Pict kingdom—indeed, Constantine, King of the Picts, who defeated and subjugated Dalriada, was of Gaelic background. However, the Gaelic-Pictish hybrid dynasty fell in 839, when the entire royal family was killed in a battle against the Vikings. This left the way open for Kenneth.[4] Under him the Picts and the Dalriadans (Scots) were united into one kingdom. The unification of the areas of Fife, Atholl, and Fortreim under a single family made them unassailable, meaning permanent supremacy over the remaining provincial kings.[5]

Celtic government was, in a way, democratic. Their leaders, even kings and clan chiefs, were elected to their positions. They also believed in the balance of power. Every year, the Celts would elect two officials: one who was a military leader, and one who was a lawgiver. One person couldn't hold both positions at once.[6] This division of power could also be seen when a clan got too large—it would split into "septs" or sub-clans that would then elect their own leader and move to a new, but nearby, location. The power balance existed in every level of life, and could be seen in the perpetual strife between the Highlands and Lowlands of Scotland, which existed even at the time of the Picts.[7]

Another peculiarity of the Celtic system was the way the throne was passed down. They used the rule of tanistry. Any male of royal blood was eligible to be king. Usually, in order to try to stop bloodshed, the ruling king would appoint his successor (tanist) during his lifetime, and he would become "Second to the King." However, the throne usually did *not* pass from father to son; it usually passed from brother to brother, and then to the son of the eldest brother, and so on.[8] It was only gradually that the law of primogeniture became the norm, and power would pass from father to son in a direct line. Whoever came to the throne would ascend the sacred Stone of Scone, and be crowned by the principal bishop of the national church (first Druidic, later Christian, bishops).[9]

Kenneth MacAlpin founded a dynasty whose blood ran through all of the kings of Scotland, and still runs in the kings of England. In our direct family line, there are two branches of the MacAlpin dynasty: the Line of Atholl and the Line of Moray. The majority of the ruling house is the Line of Atholl, with the offshoot Line of Moray eventually begetting our MacKay lineage.

Kenneth I MacAlpin
(Cináed mac Alpin)
(d. 859)
(reigned 843-859)

Kenneth MacAlpin's claim to the throne came through his grandmother, as the Pictish laws of succession were matrilineal.[10] He began his rise to power in 840, after the last of the Pictish kings were slaughtered by the Danes. He helped protect Argyll (Dalriada) by bringing half-Gael, half-Norse Irishman Gofraid mac Fergusa to settle there.[11] Kenneth then raided into Pictland to the west, where he ran up against a family of four Pictish kings: Uurad mac Bargot (d. 842), Bridei (d. 842), Kineth (d. 843), and Drest (d. 848). With the death of Drest, Kenneth's position became secure. It may more accurately be said that Kenneth's rule of a united north began in 848.[12]

Kenneth united all the territory north of the Forth under his power, and moved the capital from Dunadd to Forteviot.[13] His reign was not without problems, because his kingdom was surrounded by his enemies: the Britons of Strathclyde, Danes, and Vikings. Kenneth overcame them all by sword and by diplomacy.[14]

In 849 A.D. he rebuilt the monastery of Dunkeld, which had been destroyed by Danes, and moved the relics of St. Columba from the sacred island of Iona to Dunkeld.[15 16 17 18]

He married his daughter to Cu, a Briton of Strathclyde. He was probably a king or at least royalty of that province, since Kenneth was giving his daughter in marriage to seal an alliance with Strathclyde.[19]

Kenneth had at least five children:

- *Constantine* – future King of Scotland
- Aed – future King of Scotland
- Maelmuire – married Irish King Aed Findliath [20]
- Daughter – married Cu (Rhun) of Strathclyde [21]
- Daughter – married Óláfr Hvitr, the Norse ruler of Dublin [22]

In 859, after a long and painful illness, Kenneth MacAlpin died [23] in his capital city of Forteviot,[24] and was buried on the isle of Iona.[25]

His brother **Donald I** succeeded him, reigning from 859-863. At the end of Donald's reign, Kenneth's son *Constantine* took the throne.

Constantine I
(Castantin mac Cináeda)
(d. 877)
(reigned 863-877)

Constantine I, crowned in 863, was most likely named after the Pict warrior, Constantine MacFergus, who would have been Kenneth's great-uncle.[26]

Constantine's biggest problem was the Viking attacks. During his reign, the Scandinavian kings Gorm, Eric, and Harald Harfager were consolidating their respective kingdoms of Denmark, Sweden and Norway, and they exiled any dissenters. As a result, nomadic Viking pirates roamed the northern seas, and Scotland was a good target for them.[27]

In 866, Norwegian Olave the Fair (Óláfr Hvitr) and Danish commander Ivar Ragnarsson teamed up and ravaged Scotland in the region bordering the Forth.[28] It was likely at this time that Constantine's sister was married to Óláfr, to keep him from coming back. In 870, Constantine was also implicated in turning Óláfr and Ivar onto raiding Strathclyde, and killing their captive King Arthgal of Strathclyde. This brought Cu, Constantine's sister's husband, to the throne of Strathclyde, making Scotland a little safer from war.[29] Óláfr and Ivar then raided into England and murdered the East Anglian King Edmund.[30]

In the meantime, Harald Harfager of Norway attacked the Orkney and Shetland Islands, because the Vikings hiding there kept returning to Norway to pillage. After Harald swept the islands clean, he set up a Jarldom (Earldom), and gave it to his friend Ragnvald (see *Norwegian Lineage*). Ragnvald didn't want it (he already had a Jarldom elsewhere), and gave it to his brother Sigurd. Normally, this would not have been a problem for King Constantine, because the islands weren't part of his kingdom.[31]

However, Sigurd teamed up with Thorstein the Red, son of a powerful king of the Hebrides. Together, they united their forces and invaded mainland Scotland, capturing all of modern-day Caithness and Sutherland (then, it was all called Caithness).[32]

In 875, Constantine faced a two-front war: Sigurd and Thorstein in the north, and the Dane Halfdan in Northumbria in the south. Caught in this pincer movement, Constantine did the only thing he could—he signed over all the northern provinces to Thorstein.[33]

But he betrayed the peace he had bought and killed Thorstein later that year. Sigurd had died in the initial invasion, and the death of Sigurd's son Guttorm returned control of the islands back to the independent Vikings, breaking Norse power in Scotland for the time. The Dane Halfdan was driven from Northumbria, and Constantine could breathe freely.[34]

Constantine had one known son, *Donald II*, future king of Scotland.

In 877, Constantine I was killed defending against a Norse incursion on the Fife coast. Some lore has him being captured by retreating Norsemen and executed in the terrible "spread-eagle" or "blood-eagle" torture in the Black Cave near Crail.[35] [36] [37]

Constantine's ceding of the northern provinces to the Norsemen came back to haunt his family after his death. The Highland Picts revolted against the power of the Kintyre kings, and for a time, the kingdom was ruled by a split that mirrored the old balance of power. In 878, **Aed**, son of Kenneth MacAlpin, was defeated and killed by **Cyric MacDungal** of the Highlands. Cyric became king of the north, and gave the south to **Eocha**, son of Cu, grandson of Kenneth, although Cyric was the real power behind both thrones.[38] Eocha died in 889, and *Donald II*, son of Constantine I, took the southern throne.[39]

Donald II
(Domnall mac Castantin)
(d. 900)
(reigned 889-900)

Donald II co-reigned with Cyric until Cyric's death in 896. Upon his death, no northern Pict came forward to claim the throne, so both areas once again were consolidated under one ruler, although the northern tribes still resented their southern overlords.[40] Another school of thought claims that Donald defeated and deposed both Eocha and Cyric in 889.[41]

Donald had a decisive victory over the Norsemen at Collin-on-Tay, although the date was unrecorded. Donald also moved the capital city to Scone.[42]

Donald had at least one son, *Malcolm I*, future king of Scotland.

In 900, Donald II died, killed in the province of Moray, in the town of Forres, while trying to reassert royal authority over the revolting north districts. His successor may have instigated the assassination, but there is no proof.[43] [44]

After Donald II's death, **Constantine II**, a son of Aed, took the throne. He ruled from 900-943. His main achievements were the defeat of the Norsemen in 904, which kept him safe from invasion, and putting his brother Donald on the Strathclyde throne, annexing that region to Scotland. In 943, already into his 80s, Constantine retired to the monastery of St. Andrews, and gave the throne to *Malcolm I*, son of Donald II.[45]

Malcolm I
(Máel Coluim mac Domnaill)
(d. 954)
(reigned 943-954)

Malcolm I took over in 943 when Constantine II retired to St. Andrews monastery.[46] Malcolm allied himself with King Edmund of England (see *Saxon Dynasty*),[47] and was given the province of Cumberland in return. Malcolm continued to consolidate Scottish control over the country south of the Forth.[48]

In 945, Olave Sitricson, a Norse friend of Constantine II, attacked Northumbria—and old Constantine II came out of retirement and joined Olave in conquering the province. Constantine returned to St. Andrews once Northumbria was in Olave's hands.[49]

In 952, Constantine died in St. Andrews. That same year, Malcolm allied with the Saxons and Britons to oppose the inroads of the Norsemen, but they failed to stop them. Eric Bloodaxe invaded Northumbria and expelled Olave Sitricson for the last time.[50]

Malcolm had at least two sons:

- Duff – future king of Scotland
- *Kenneth II* – future king of Scotland

In 954, Malcolm died, slain at Ulurn near Forres in Moray, perhaps in revenge by the Maerne men for their Mormaer (Earl) Cellach's death several years before.[51 52 53]

It is here that the Line of Atholl and the Line of Moray split, as both were founded by sons of Malcolm I.

Malcolm I was succeeded by a son of the Line of Aed, **Indulf** (954-962), who captured Edinburgh to extend Scotland's boundaries. Following Indulf was the eldest son of Malcolm I, **Duff** (962-967), founder of the Line of Moray. He was killed in Forres in Moray by agents of the Line of Atholl. Tradition says that his body was hidden under the bridge at Kinloss, and that the sun refused to shine until the king had a proper burial.[54]

Duff was followed by **Colin** (967-971), another Line of Aed, who died in battle against the Britons of Strathclyde in 971.[55] Colin's death brought *Kenneth II*, son of Malcolm I, and the Line of Atholl, to the throne.

Kenneth II
(Cináed mac Máel Coluim)
(d. 995)
(reigned 971-995)

Kenneth II took the throne in 971 with no opposition.[56] His reign saw the clashes of the Jarls of Orkney with the Scottish Mormaers of the north. Kenneth had at least one son, *Malcolm II*, future king of Scotland.

The Jarl Thorfinn Skull-Splitter (see *Norwegian Lineage*) died in 978, at the beginning of Kenneth's reign. Thorfinn had married Grelaud, the daughter of Duncan, Mormaer of Caithness, and left five sons to claim the Orkneys and the mainland.[57] One of his sons, Skuli, came to Kenneth II to ask for possession of Caithness by right of blood.[58] [59]

Kenneth either said yes or encouraged him to attack his brothers on Orkney to claim it. His brothers drove him back to Caithness and laid waste to the mainland province. This brought him into conflict with the powerful Mormaer of Moray, Malbride MacRory.[60] [61] Although the Orkney faction won, the Scots eventually wrested Caithness from Norse control sometime before 994.[62]

Since the Mormaers of Moray were occupied with Caithness problems, they caused no trouble for Kenneth II, allowing him to focus his attentions elsewhere. He invaded Strathclyde and England, finding plunder to reward his supporters. He also asserted his claim to Lothian and Cumberland. In 973 he supposedly met with English King Edgar (see *Saxon Dynasty*) in Chester, and Edgar acknowledged Kenneth's rights in exchange for peace in the north.[63] Robertson, in *Scotland Under Her Early Kings*, pointed out that Kenneth was busy elsewhere in 973, and theorized that this meeting never happened, but was added into the English chronicles in order to show Scotland as feudally subordinate to England.[64]

Opposition to Kenneth grew as he tried to secure the succession to his line by removing the rights of Duff's sons. Another thorn was his long-running feud with Cunthar, ruler of Angus and the Mearns.[65] Kenneth wanted to take over the kingdom of Angus, which had been a tributary to the Scottish crown for many years but had remained mostly independent. In Kenneth's time, the male line of the Mormaers of Angus died out. A nephew, a son of the woman Finella (Cunthar's daughter), was appointed, but Kenneth made up a pretext to execute him, thus annexing Angus to the crown.[66]

In 995, Kenneth was assassinated at Fettercairn in Kincardineshire, through the treachery of his immediate attendants, probably at the instigation of Finella.[67] [68]

After Kenneth II died, two more kings came to the throne: **Constantine III** (995-997) of the Line of Aed, and **Kenneth III** (997-1005) of the Line of Moray. Constantine III's death ended the Line of Aed. Kenneth III and his son were killed at Monaghvaird in Strathearn, and *Malcolm II*, Kenneth II's son, took the throne on 25 March 1005.[69] [70]

Malcolm II
(Máel Coluim mac Cináeda)
(d. 1034)
(reigned 1005-1034)

Malcolm II marked his ascension by attacking Northumbria in 1006, continuing the quest to bring Northumbria under Scottish control, but was defeated at Durham by Uchtred.[71][72]

Meanwhile, the north was heating up. Finlay MacRory, Mormaer of Moray and brother of Malbride MacRory, challenged Sigurd Hlodverson, the 11th Jarl of Orkney to battle (see *Norwegian Lineage*). Unfortunately for Finlay, Sigurd won. Given the continued tension between the throne and the Moray Mormaers, Malcolm II was happy that Sigurd won—so happy, in fact, that he gave his daughter Plantula to Sigurd in marriage.[73][74]

In 1009, Sigurd and Plantula had Thorfinn Sigurdson. When his father was killed in 1014, Malcolm immediately confirmed Thorfinn as the Earl of Caithness, securing Caithness to the Scottish throne.[75][76]

In 1018, Malcolm turned his attention back to Northumbria, and this time he defeated the Anglo-Saxons at Carham with the help of ally King Ywain of Strathclyde.[77][78] He was given the province of Lothian as a peace offering.[79][80] Also that year, King Ywain of Strathclyde died without children, and Malcolm placed his own grandson and heir, Duncan, on the throne.[81][82][83]

In 1031, Malcolm met with Canute, King of England, Denmark, and Norway, and promised loyalty to Canute in exchange for peace.[84][85]

In 1033, Malcolm continued the feud between his Line of Atholl and the Line of Moray. Kenneth III had a son named Boedhe, who died, and left a son whose name has been lost. But Malcolm wanted to make sure his Line of Atholl kept the crown, so he killed Boedhe's son.[86] Even though this was the extinction of the male line of Moray, Malcolm did not completely secure the line, because he left Gruoch, Boedhe's granddaughter, alive.[87][88]

On 25 November 1034, Malcolm was assassinated at Glamis in Moray.[89][90]

During Malcolm's reign, he had enlarged and consolidated his dominion, with Scotland reaching her permanent southern boundary. He had also secured the transmission of the throne to his own family.[91]

Malcolm also did away with untaxed tribal lands, bringing everyone under his authority. The powerful Mormaers of Scotland were creations of Malcolm and his father, and were revolutionary in their time. These Mormaers were dependent upon the king, answerable only to the king, but wealthy because they were in charge of collecting the king's taxes and they got to keep a cut.[92]

Malcolm also was likely the first Scottish king to create a truly stable court at Scone. Prior to Malcolm, all Scottish kings were on a constant royal progress through their kingdom, imposing their massive entourage on one locality after another. Wherever they stopped, the resources and wealth of the locality were drained, sometimes to the point of causing hardship and famine in their wake. Malcolm settled into a stationary court supported by the taxes of the lands, thereby freeing his subjects of this obligation.[93]

Malcolm II had no surviving son, but he had three daughters:[94] [95]

- **Bethoc** (sometimes called Beatrice) – his eldest daughter, so the line of Atholl went through her. She had married Crinan, the Abbot of Dunkeld, and they had a son named **Duncan**. He succeeded his grandfather to the throne with no opposition.[96]
- Donada – married Finlay (Finlaech) MacRory, Mormaer of Moray (mentioned above), and was the mother of Macbeth, future king of Scotland.[97]
- Plantula – married Jarl Sigurd Hlodverson of Orkney and had Thorfinn, Jarl of Orkney and Earl of Caithness (also mentioned above, and see *Norwegian Lineage*).[98]

Duncan I
(Donnchad mac Crinain)
(d. 1040)
(reigned 1034-1040)

Duncan I was born around 1001.[99] Duncan did not come to the Scottish throne unprepared. In 1018, in a move to bind the province of Strathclyde to the Scottish crown, Malcolm had placed Duncan on its vacant throne.[100] [101] Duncan was young when he came to the Strathclyde throne, and ambitious and aggressive. He was so aggressive, in fact, that he killed two possible rivals to the throne—one the day before his crowning, one the day after. He spared the life of the dim-witted Lulach, a mercy which would prove costly.[102] When he succeeded to the Scottish crown, the kingdoms of Scotia, Lothian, and Strathclyde were finally united into what we would recognize as Scotland.[103]

Duncan had two sons:

- **Malcolm III** – future king of Scotland
- Donald Ban – future king of Scotland

When Duncan came to the throne in 1034, all of the north—Caithness, Sutherland, and Orkney—was under the control of his cousin Thorfinn Sigurdson (see *Norwegian Lineage*).[104] This would seem ideal, keeping the lands in the family, and would seem like a recipe for peace.

However, the cousins didn't see eye to eye. Duncan demanded that Thorfinn pay the tribute of his dependency to the crown. Thorfinn countered by saying that his lands were all a gift from Malcolm II, and therefore not subject to the taxation of the crown.[105] [106]

Duncan had no time to deal with this himself, as he was trying to extend his southern border past Durham in Northumbria. He was unsuccessful, having been defeated at Durham in 1039.[107] [108] So, he appointed his general, Moddan, as the Earl of Caithness and sent him to wrest Caithness from Thorfinn by force. Thorfinn beat Moddan, and Duncan turned from the south to bring troops north to help in the fight.[109]

Duncan's fleet, with reinforcements, were driven from the Caithness shore, and landed in Moray to regroup, but Thorfinn followed him and defeated him in Moray.[110] [111] Duncan got stuck in Moray, and this was where his grandfather's actions caught up to him.

Malcolm had killed off the male Line of Moray, but left a daughter, Gruoch. She married Gilcomgan, who was the son of powerful Moray Mormaer Malbride MacRory. They had a son named Lulach—the same

Lulach who Duncan had spared when he took the throne of Strathclyde.[112] Gilcomgan died in 1029, and Gruoch married the current Mormaer of Moray—Macbeth MacFinlay. Macbeth was the son of Malcolm II's daughter Donada, and he coveted the crown in his own right, as well as championing his stepson, Lulach's, rights.[113] When Duncan got stranded in Moray, Macbeth saw his chance.

In 1040, at Macbeth's instigation, Duncan was assassinated near Elgin, in "the smith's bothy."[114][115][116][117][118] Other sources say Macbeth killed Duncan in battle at Pitgaveny near Elgin in Moray.[119][120][121] **Macbeth** took the throne. Macbeth seemed an able enough ruler, fighting off an attempt by Duncan's aged father, Crinan, and followers to overthrow him, killing Crinan in the battle.[122][123] Duncan's children were still infants, but it is unknown if they actually fled the country to England and the Western Isles as the myth suggests, or if they were simply raised by other nobles, much as Lulach of the Line of Moray was not forced to flee as a child. Current evidence indicates that they did in fact flee the country, as Edward the Confessor of England sent two expeditions into Scotland in 1046 and 1052 in support of the future king, Malcolm III.[124] Macbeth was killed in battle at Lumphanan in Aberdeen in 1058 by Malcolm III.[125][126] Macbeth's stepson, **Lulach,** took the throne for the Line of Moray.

Lulach was not a fit king. Often called Lulach the Simple, he didn't have what it took to keep the throne. After only a few months as king, he was betrayed and killed by his own kinsmen at Essie in Strathbogie, possibly at the behest of Malcolm III.[127][128]

Thus came the restoration of the Line of Atholl, in Duncan's son, *Malcolm III*.

Historically, Duncan I was considered the last of the House of Alpin, although the blood runs through the English monarchs to this day. Malcolm III began the line of the House of Canmore.[129]

Malcolm III Canmore
(Máel Coluim mac Donnchada)
(d. 1093)
(reigned 1058-1093)

Malcolm III took the throne for the Line of Atholl on 25 April 1058,[130][131][132] and it was never again taken by the Line of Moray, although the bad blood between them continued. Malcolm's nickname, Ceann Mór (Canmore), means Great Head or Great Chief.[133] He spent his years in exile in York, under the Scandinavian influence of the Anglo-Danish Earl Siward.[134][135]

In 1057, Malcolm's cousin Thorfinn Sigurdson died, and Malcolm married Thorfinn's widow, Ingibjorg, and they had sons:[136][137][138][139]

- Duncan II – future king of Scotland
- Donald

In 1059, Malcolm visited Edward the Confessor, Anglo-Saxon King of England. In 1061, he raided Northumbria.[140]

In England, William the Conqueror (see *Continental Dynasty*) invaded in 1066, wreaking havoc. In 1068, Edgar the Aethling, the rightful Saxon king of England, fled with his mother and two sisters to Scotland for refuge (see *Saxon Dynasty*).[141][142] Although Edgar made two attempts to retake England, William the

Conqueror enacted horrific vengeance upon the land in the face of Edgar's initial success, and Edgar never triumphed. [143]

In 1070, Malcolm III got into the fray, and he managed to take the province of Cumberland by force. In holding it, he protected it from William's vengeance. When the Earl of Northumbria attacked Malcolm's Cumberland, Malcolm destroyed Northumbria, massacring the people, burning the land, and taking the survivors as slaves. [144]

Between Malcolm and William's ravages, much of northern England became a wasteland, and famine gripped England. Many Northumbrians fled to Scotland in desperation. [145]

In 1070, Malcolm somehow had divested himself of first wife, Ingibjorg. It is unknown if she had died or if they were never married in the eyes of the church, but rather in what was known as a "hand-fast" marriage, something like our common-law marriage. At any rate, in 1070, Malcolm married Edgar the Aethling's sister Margaret of Wessex (see *Saxon Dynasty*). [146] [147] Margaret originally wanted to enter a nunnery like her sister Christina, but the advantages of the marriage were too obvious to pass up. Plus, Edgar was not really in a position to say no—if he did, his only ally might abandon him. This marriage may also have helped ease the immigration to Scotland of so many English. [148]

But William the Conqueror still wanted Scotland. In August 1072, he invaded Scotland and penetrated to Abernathy in Fife. There he met Malcolm, and they compromised in the Treaty of Abernathy. [149] William gave Malcolm 12 estates in England, and Malcolm agreed to pay tributary taxes on those estates to William. It was the custom of the time to give hostages to secure promises, and Malcolm gave his eldest son, Duncan, as hostage to William. [150] [151] [152] Since Malcolm could no longer protect him, Edgar fled to Flanders, then to France, where King Philip was an enemy of William the Conqueror. [153]

In 1073, Edgar the Aethling went to William and relinquished his rights to the throne. William accepted this, and gave him lands in Normandy, and a pension of a pound of silver a day. [154]

In 1077, Malcolm dashed the hopes the Moray Line might still have had of the throne. He crushed an uprising by Lulach's son Malsnechtan, although Malsnechtan was not killed—he died in 1085. [155]

Malcolm was friends with William the Conqueror's son Robert. In 1079, William was in Normandy in France, fighting against his son Robert. Robert called on Malcolm for help. In spite of his pledge of peace with William, Malcolm invaded England, attacking Northumbria. [156]

By 1080, Robert and William had made up, and William sent Robert into Scotland to avenge the Scottish invasion. [157] Robert was reluctant, so he met Malcolm at Falkirk and renewed the 1072 Treaty of Abernathy, but Malcolm had succeeded in pushing Scotland's southern frontier further south, to Newcastle-upon-Tyne. [158]

In 1087, William the Conqueror died, and Robert knighted and freed Malcolm's son Duncan from his hostage status. [159]

William's son William Rufus took the English throne, and in 1091 he expelled Edgar the Aethling from the lands given to him by William the Conqueror. Edgar fled to Scotland, and Malcolm took up arms to go into England. He wasn't doing it just for Edgar, but also because William Rufus had taken away the 12 estates

William I had ceded to him. Malcolm retreated when he heard that all England was ready to take up arms against him.[160]

William Rufus invaded Scotland but his army was weak, and Malcolm was eager to fight. Robert, William's brother and Malcolm's friend, intervened. They again renewed the 1072 Treaty of Abernathy. However, William Rufus never fulfilled any of his promises.[161] [162]

In 1092, Rufus took Cumberland by force from Malcolm. Malcolm insisted that the Treaty of Abernathy be met, and Rufus, ill and thinking he was going to die, agreed, asking Malcolm to meet him in Gloucester.[163]

On 24 August 1093, Malcolm arrived at Gloucester, but Rufus was no longer ill, and refused to see him. He said, "Talk to my barons, not to me." However, if Malcolm did that, then that would have been tantamount to admitting a feudal dependence on the English crown—basically making Scotland a part of England. So Malcolm refused.[164]

Malcolm returned to Scotland, raised an army, and invaded England, in spite of his wife, Margaret's, protestations.[165] [166] [167]

On 13 November 1093, Malcolm was killed by treachery on the banks of the river Alne.[168] His longtime friend Morel of Bamborough killed him[169] with a spearpoint through the eye.[170] [171] Malcolm's body was buried in an obscure grave at Tynemouth, until 20 years later when Alexander I returned it to Dunfermline. Malcolm's son Edward, eldest of his sons by Margaret, died of his wounds on 15 November, near Jedburgh. [172] [173]

A word about Malcolm's wife, Margaret of Wessex. She was very devout, and she became St. Margaret in 1251.[174] Her rite of canonization took place at Dunfermline Abbey, where she was buried on 19 June 1250.

She was about eight years old when she first arrived in England from Hungary, and as we have seen in the *Saxon Dynasty* chapter, she was highly intelligent and literate. She was a stern woman who believed in the "spare the rod, spoil the child" philosophy for her own brood. However, she was generous and always ready to give money and help the poor and needy.[175]

Margaret had a great impact on her semi-barbarous husband. He was likely illiterate, being mostly a warrior king, but she often turned his mind to matters other than war. She interested him in almsgiving, charity, and justice, which the king was barely concerned with until then. Her sons continued this interest. She taught her husband to spend his nights in prayer, rather than carousing with his buddies. Margaret also introduced pomp and ceremony to the court of Scotland, making a stylish royal court out of the spartan Dunfermline fortress.[176] She encouraged magnificence among her courtiers, too, and invited foreign traders to bring their wares. She began to change the Scottish king from a rude, semi-barbarous chieftain to a feudal monarch with knights and chivalry.[177]

Malcolm deferred to her in all matters of the Scottish church. Margaret had been raised in Hungary, where the western Church reform was newly established, and she found the Celtic Scottish church backward. She brought it into line with her church, the Roman Catholic Church.[178] She restored the sanctity of the Sabbath, regulated the start date of Lent, forbade the Celtic-rite mass, and deemed that Holy Communion should be taken by everyone.[179]

Margaret died on 16 November 1093, the day she learned of Malcolm's and her son's deaths.[180] [181]

The remains of Malcolm and Margaret, once housed in Dunfermline, have vanished. They were removed for safekeeping during one of the bloody uprisings during the Reformation. Their bodies were lost in Spain, while in the Church of St. Lawrence in the Escorial. Margaret's head, on the other hand, was housed for many years in the Scots College in Douay, France, but it disappeared during the French Revolution.[182]

Malcolm III and Margaret had six sons and two daughters, many of whom carried on the royal lineage:[183]

- Edward – died with his father
- Ethelred – became Abbot of Dunkeld, and died soon after
- Edmund – became co-king of Scotland with his uncle, Donald Ban, and died in an English cloister
- Edgar – became King of Scotland
- Alexander – became King of Scotland
- *David* (b.c. 1080)[184] – became King of Scotland
- Editha/Matilda/Good Queen Maud – married Henry I, King of England in 1100 (see *Continental Dynasty*)
- Mary – married Eustace, Count of Boulogne. Had a child, Matilda, who inherited Boulogne, which Matilda brought to her marriage to Stephen, who became king of England.

None of Malcolm's sons inherited the throne from him. Instead, his brother **Donald Ban** (Ban means "the fair" or "the white")[185] took over as **Donald III**, ruling first from November 1093 to May 1094. His crowning was partially the result of the "elective" element of Celtic kingship.[186] The nobles and the people wanted a king without Saxon blood (remember, Margaret was from England, and her children were therefore only half-Scottish), so they backed Donald Ban's ambition for the throne.[187]

Then Malcolm's eldest son by his first wife, Duncan, who lived in England, heard about Donald Ban's ascension and went to William Rufus for help. Duncan promised the unthinkable—that if Rufus would help him get the throne, Duncan would swear feudal fealty to Rufus. This would mean that Scotland would become a province of England, having to give money, food, and soldiers to the English king upon demand. Rufus jumped at the chance, and in 1094 Duncan, at the head of an English-Norman army, drove out Donald Ban and took the throne for himself.[188] [189]

Duncan II only reigned for a few months. His uncle Donald Ban schemed with Duncan's half-brother Edmund (one of Margaret's sons) to murder Duncan.[190] Duncan was killed at Mondynes on the banks of the Bervie on 12 November 1094, and **Donald Ban** returned to the throne, ruling from 1094-1097, splitting the kingdom with Edmund—Donald Ban ruled north of Forth-Clyde, Edmund, south.[191] [192] He exiled the remaining children of Malcolm, but it was of no use. Edgar the Aethling (then 42 years old) came out of Normandy to install his nephew, **Edgar,** on the Scottish throne.[193] [194] After successfully installing his nephew on the throne, Edgar the Aetheling went on Crusade, was caught up in an abortive attempt to overthrow Henry I in 1106, and eventually retired to his Hertfordshire estates, where he died sometime after 1125. Other versions on Edgar's installment say he bought English help by acknowledging King William Rufus of England as his feudal overlord.[195]

King Edgar, son of Malcolm III (1097-1107), brought some peace to Scotland. His brother Edmund, who had betrayed Duncan, was allowed to retreat to isolation in a priory in Somerset, England.[196] [197] In 1098, Magnus Olaveson sailed from Norway and ravaged the Scottish islands. Edgar readily admitted to Magnus' rights to the Hebrides, Kintyre, and Iona, although they reverted to their original owners in 1103, when

Magnus was killed in Ireland.[198] [199] [200] Because of Edgar's ceding of Iona, the sacred island and burial place of Scottish kings, Donald Ban was the last Scottish king buried there. In a way this was fitting, since he was the last of the purely Gaelic kings, with his nephews ushering in the new Scotto-Norman age in both their bloodline and their views.[201]

Edgar died on 8 January 1107, and bequeathed the throne to his brother David.[202] [203]

However, Edgar's brother **Alexander** didn't respect Edgar's wishes, and took the throne for himself. David threatened to use force to get the throne, unless Alexander gave David Scottish Cumbria. Alexander did, securing his crown.[204]

Alexander I's reign (1107-1124) brought major changes. First, he crushed the Mormaers of Moray when they moved against him.[205] Second, he witnessed the first collision between the secular and church powers in Scotland. Rome was trying to extend their temporal as well as spiritual powers, and Alexander was against the incursions of the English clergy trying to extend their power into Scotland.[206] [207]

Alexander tried to assimilate Scotland into the feudal monarchies of the contemporary age. He also tried to introduce the revised system of the Roman church to his clergy. Both met with limited success, but would be carried on under his successor.[208]

Alexander I married Sibylla, the illegitimate daughter of Henry I, King of England, (see *Continental Dynasty*), and Henry I married Alexander's sister Maude, thus any vassalage of Scotland to England seemed to have lapsed.[209] Alexander, however, had no heir.[210] [211] When Alexander died on 25 April 1124,[212] the kingdom passed to his brother *David*, and this was key in keeping Scotland whole. If Alexander had had a son to pass the crown to, David, who was a favorite of Henry I's English court, where his sister, Maud, was Queen, might have taken his province of Scottish Cumbria and become a fief of England.[213]

King David I and Earl Henry of Huntingdon
(David: d. 1153; Henry: 1114-1152)
(reigned 1124-1153)

Although Alexander kept him from the Scottish throne for many years, David I didn't waste his time while waiting. His sister Maud was married to English King Henry I, and David was a regular at the English royal court for some 25 years. Steeped in the feudal government of England, he became a feudal baron at heart.[214]

Prior to taking the throne, in 1113 he married Matilda de Senlis, the heiress of Waltheof, Earl of Northumberland,. David was her second husband. Her first husband became the Earl of Northumberland, and she bestowed the rest of her property on David, giving him the Honor of Huntingdon.[215] [216] [217]

Also in 1113, David founded the abbey at Selkirk in Cumbria. Like the rest of his family, he supported Church reform, and like his brother Alexander, he made sure that his Scottish bishops were free of English church influence.[218]

David and Matilda had only one child, *Henry*, born about 1114.[219] In an age of large families and high child mortality rates, it was rather ironic that this single child carried the bloodline forward to Robert the Bruce several generations later!

David was crowned 25 April 1124,[220] [221] [222] but he had misgivings. Unlike in England, there was no church involvement in the crowning, so he didn't feel he should. After so many years in England, his own Gaelic kingdom and culture seemed alien and barbarian to him.[223] Although he left the heart of Scotland in the hands of the powerful Gaelic lords, he did begin to bring in southern knights he trusted and grant them land—including Robert (I) de Brus (made Lord of Annandale) (see *De Brus Lineage*) and Walter FitzAlan, ancestor of the Stewarts (see *Stewart Lineage*).[224] [225]

David's reign was plagued by two conflicts—the civil war in England, and the revival of trouble in Moray.

Henry I of England declared Matilda (his daughter and former Empress Alicia of Germany) his heir, and had all of his barons swear their loyalty to her. David, since he held the fiefdom of Huntingdon in England, was among those who declared for Matilda, who was his niece (remember, Henry I's wife was David's sister).[226]

David spent a lot of time in England during the early part of his reign, because of the land he owned in England. Old enemies in Moray took advantage of his absence to stir up trouble.[227]

In 1125, Malcolm, the illegitimate son of David's brother Alexander I, rebelled.[228]

In 1128, David refounded the abbey at Dunfermline and granted land to the Bishoprics of Ross and Caithness.[229] [230]

In 1130, two brothers, Angus and Malcolm MacEth (see *MacKay Lineage*), who were King Lulach's grandsons, rose in arms to assert their claims.[231] Richard Oram says that this Malcolm was Malcolm son of Alexander I, not a brother of Angus, Earl of Moray, and that he was often conflated with a Malcolm MacEth who was active in the 1160s.[232]

Angus and Malcolm met David's constable Edward in battle at Stickathrow in Forfarshire, and lost. Angus was killed, but Malcolm escaped and continued to wage a guerilla war in the Highlands, rallying support from the northern chiefs, who were disgruntled by the Norman-English influence in David's court.[233]

But David had an answer to Malcolm's malcontents. In 1134, David rallied an *English* army from the northern counties in England, and they were so strong that the mere threat of them and their fleet scared Malcolm's men to turn on him and deliver him to David.[234] [235]

David imprisoned Malcolm in Roxburgh Castle, and declared the entire earldom of Moray forfeit to the Crown. Stripping land from those who would oppose him, he installed knights of English extraction and loyal Scots there. This was the death blow of the Moray family, although we see what became of the MacEth family in the chapter on the *MacKay Lineage*.[236]

No sooner did David settle things in Moray than England was in turmoil. On 1 December 1135, Henry I of England died. Although his daughter Matilda (see *Continental Dynasty*) was the presumptive heir, Henry's nephew Stephen declared himself king. Out of all those barons who swore to Henry that they would support Matilda, only one actually did. That one was David I, King of Scotland.[237]

On 5 February 1136, David and Stephen's armies met, but neither seemed to want an all-out conflict between the two countries. David didn't want to fight a war in which he was the only one on Matilda's side. Besides, even though Matilda was his niece, Stephen's wife was also David's niece, the daughter of his sister Mary.[238] So, David and Stephen made peace.[239] [240]

Stephen wanted David to take fiefdoms from him, which would have made him David's overlord. David was too savvy for that, but he accepted the fiefdoms of Carlisle and Doncaster in addition to Huntingdon on behalf of his son Henry, who was about 22 years old then. David also waived his claims to Northumberland, although this was to be reconsidered if Stephen ever gave out the earldom. David's son Henry, as an English fief owner and Earl of Huntingdon, returned to England with Stephen.[241] [242]

Later, Stephen somehow insulted Henry at court. David recalled his son to Scotland. Although Stephen repeatedly called Henry to fulfill his feudal obligations, David did not allow Henry to return south. In fact, in 1137, David insisted that Stephen make Henry Earl of Northumberland. Stephen refused, and David declared war on Stephen.[243] [244] [245]

The war raged during 1138, with the Scots laying waste to Northumberland, then Stephen laying waste to parts of Scotland, then David marching toward York. But the Yorkshiremen decided to fight for their lands, instead of holing up in their castles and allowing David to plunder and waste their lands. Among the York contingent was Robert de Brus (see *De Brus Lineage*), ancestor of Robert I Bruce, later King of Scotland. [246] [247]

On 22 August 1138, David's army moved to surprise the English, but they were discovered. Robert de Brus and Bernard de Balliol tried to broker a peace by offering Northumberland to Henry. David was inclined to accept, but his fiery chieftains persuaded him not to accept the peace.[248] [249] [250]

The Battle of Northallerton (also called the Battle of the Standard) commenced, but the Scots, outnumbered and out-armed, had lost their advantage of surprise.[251] Our Henry did himself proud, smashing through the English lines, and pursuing the fleeing English. However, in his absence, everything went wrong for the rest of the Scottish army.[252]

At this critical moment, when the Scots seemed to be winning, some English soldier raised a severed head above the battle and declared that David of Scotland was dead. David's army broke and fled. David, very much alive, refused to leave the field of battle until his bodyguards forced him to leave.[253]

Henry, returning to what he expected to be a Scottish victory, came upon the rout, and he and his men slipped away to rendezvous with the rest of the army at Carlisle three days after the battle. David, desperately worried about his only child, was greatly relieved to see Henry alive and well.[254]

In 1139, Henry and his cousin Queen Matilda (Stephen's wife) brokered a peace treaty.[255] Henry gained the earldom of Northumberland,[256] and swore feudal fealty for his English fiefs to Stephen. Again, Henry stayed with Stephen, becoming a favorite of his.[257]

Also in 1139, Henry married Ada de Warenne, daughter of Earl de Warenne.[258] Henry stayed with Stephen during the civil war, returning to Scotland in 1140, when the Earl of Chester tried to kill Henry.[259]

In 1141, Stephen was captured by Matilda's forces near Lincoln. David hurried to his niece's side, and escorted her to London to claim her throne. But the former Empress did not endear herself to her new citizens, and they ran her out of London. The Battle of Winchester was fought to free Stephen, and Matilda's forces were routed. David barely escaped with his life.[260]

With Stephen back on the throne and secure, peace between Scotland and England stood. There was a near-conflict in 1149, when there was a plot to place Empress Matilda's son Henry (the future Henry II of England) on the throne, but the conflict did not turn hot, with both armies drawing off without contest.[261] [262]

David was complicit in this plot to place Henry Plantagenet (see *Continental Dynasty*) on the throne, because it was David who knighted Henry at Carlisle. At this time, he extracted a promise from Henry that when king, Henry would respect the territorial status quo. However, Henry did not honor this, taking back the territories of Cumberland and Northumberland in 1157.[263] [264]

Through Henry of Huntingdon, the northern counties of England were secured to the Scottish crown, and this provided a buffer and neutrality with Stephen.[265]

Then, on 12 June 1152, Henry of Huntingdon died.[266] [267] David, heartbroken at losing his son, reacted quickly. He appointed Henry's oldest son, Malcolm, as heir to the throne, and Henry's second son, William, as the new Earl of Northumberland.[268]

Henry and Ada had six children:[269]

- Malcolm (b. 1141) – future King of Scotland
- William (b. 1142) – future King of Scotland
- *David (b. 1143)* – claimed the Honor of Huntingdon
- Ada
- Margaret
- Matilda

David's action to secure the throne and the northern counties was not premature. Less than a year later, David died, on 24 May 1153 at Carlisle.[270] [271] [272]

David I was the king who brought Scotland into the modern feudal world.[273] He ruled with a mixture of conciliation and authority, which helped him weld his diverse population into a more orderly government. He walked a tightrope between his native Scottish subjects and the Anglo-Norman subjects he brought with him. He did this by encouraging "free" foreign knights (many from Belgium) to settle in as barons of Scotland. These knights were loyal to his interests alone, serving as an armed bulwark between the other two factions. David also kept peace with his subjects by not riding roughshod over them. He respected their property rights but filled empty properties with foreign barons when the occasion arose.[274]

David also raised southern Scotland to prominence by establishing burghs (cities) and raising the burgher class (tradesmen, middle class) to respectable levels.[275] Prior to David, people who lived in cities could not be technically "free," because only people who owned a specific amount of property could be free, and tradesmen had no property outside the city walls. That is, they had no rights because they had no land. David changed that, establishing a free civil population within the walls. Many of the original burghers were foreign (mainly Flemish), and it took a long time for the native Scots to move into towns. The rise of the burgher class spread a common language throughout Scotland, and they tended to favor peace, order, and civilization, helping to stabilize the country.[276]

David did his bit for the landed peasants as well. David was known as a kind and warmhearted king, especially protective of the poor and defenseless people of his realm. One of the things he did was free the peasants of the burdens of their nobles. Like early kings, many nobles traveled a continuous progression through their territories at other people's expense, using up the resources of their underlings. David made the nobles build castles on their own lands, thus freeing the peasants of their overbearing lords.[277] David also instituted the practice of having written charters to prove ownership of land, and it was only at that time that written deeds became common in Scotland.[278]

David also instituted changes in the justice system, creating a jury of one's peers instead of trial by ordeal, or needing to find a certain number of people to testify on your behalf—a system that invariably had gone against unpopular people, regardless of their guilt or innocence.[279]

While David's mother, Margaret of Wessex, had begun making the Scottish royal court more stately, David continued that trend. When he took the throne, it was not considered an honor to be a courtier, with offices usually appointed to freemen rather than nobles. David, with his upbringing in the English court, changed that, bringing the pomp and circumstance of the feudal court to Scotland.[280]

He also tried to spread uniformity throughout the kingdom, instituting the first standardized weights and measures, and issuing the first Scottish coinage.[281]

One final place where David made significant reforms was the church. In his day, monasteries and abbeys were very powerful, but becoming corrupted with money, and their leaders were most often in hereditary positions held by powerful families of the area. David countered the power of the abbeys by founding more true, orthodox bishoprics in Scotland, including the sees of Glasgow, St. Andrews, Moray, and Dunkeld. The church, too, showed the split between the lines of Atholl and Moray, as St. Andrews and Dunkeld held sway in the south, and Moray in the north.[282]

David I's grandson, **Malcolm IV,** followed him to the throne, at the tender age of eleven.[283] Our line does not continue through the kings. Our line follows Henry's son *David*, who we will see throughout the reigns of his brothers Malcolm and William.

David, Earl of Huntingdon
(d. 1219)

When his brother Malcolm IV took the throne, young David wasn't much of a factor in politics. There was no record of him on governmental documents at all during Malcolm's reign. Remember, David's older brother William was the Earl of Northumberland, so David may not have held any sort of title at all during this time.

Malcolm IV's reign (1153-1165) saw a new uprising of the MacEth faction,[284] or more likely, Malcolm, son of King Alexander I's family. Malcolm MacEth/son of Alexander, imprisoned in Roxburgh castle, had a wife who was the sister of Somerled MacGillebride, the powerful Lord of the Isles (see *MacDonald Lineage*). Somerled wanted his nephew on the throne, and in 1156 he backed nephew Donald MacEth. However, Donald was captured in Galloway and imprisoned with his father, Malcolm, in Roxburgh Castle.[285][286]

Donald's capture seemed to have broken Malcolm's spirit. In 1157, Malcolm MacEth (see *MacKay Lineage*) came to terms with Malcolm IV and somehow purchased his own release. His son Donald was never heard from again. The exact terms of Malcolm's release have been lost, but both Malcolms were satisfied, as Malcolm MacEth never was a threat to the throne again.[287] [288]

Malcolm IV was often credited with the final expulsion of the Moraymen from their lands.[289] However, the historical evidence that a mass expulsion occurred is a little sketchy, and it was more likely a continuation of David I's policy of a gradual replacement of dissenters with loyal people. If the expulsion actually did occur, it may have been a result of whatever deal Malcolm MacEth made with the king.[290]

The only other major event of Malcolm IV's reign, in 1157, was that he resigned the three counties he held in England to King Henry II (see *Continental Dynasty*), to preserve the peace. Malcolm insisted upon keeping the Honor of Huntingdon, which was his family's by blood from their maternal line. Malcolm's brother William was no doubt the recipient of the Honor of Huntingdon at that time.[291] [292]

On 9 December 1165, Malcolm IV died at age 24.[293] His brother **William I the Lion** (1165-1214) took the throne, and our David came to the stage. When William gained the throne, he passed the Honor of Huntingdon to his younger brother David.

William's critical error in his reign came in 1173. He entered into a conspiracy with King Henry II of England's son, who promised William the northern counties if they were successful. William waged war on England, his brother David at his side, and was chased back into Scotland by the Yorkshire barons. William and a small force were surprised by the English, and King William was captured.[294] [295]

William's capture caused a revolt in Galloway, and a venting of animosity against the townsmen and burghers. David hurried back to Scotland to restore order and negotiate his brother, William's, release.[296]

William's release was arranged with crushing terms. Scotland became a feudal tributary of England, essentially giving up its independence. Also, the Scottish church became subordinate the English church. David gave himself as a hostage until the transfer of feudal power was complete, and then he turned over his own eldest son as a hostage to Henry II after his own release.[297] David also forfeited his own position as Earl of Huntingdon. On 10 August 1175, William formally pledged his liege fealty to Henry II of England.[298]

In 1181, the Highlands rose in revolt again, under the leadership of Donald Bane MacWilliam. William and David tried to engage him, but he retreated back into the rugged Highlands. William and David were content to leave him hiding in the hills.[299]

In 1185, Henry II of England gave Huntingdon back to William, and David was reinstated as Earl of Huntingdon.[300] William and David returned the favor by quelling a revolt in Galloway for Henry. They installed Roland as king, and made his older brother Duncan (the rightful heir) the first Earl of Carrick. Duncan was content with this, and became the great-grandfather of Robert I Bruce, King of Scotland (see *De Brus Lineage*).[301]

In 1187, Donald Bane MacWilliam rose again, this time with a significant following. But Roland of Galloway met him in battle and killed him.[302]

David likely participated in Richard the Lionheart's revolt against his father, Henry. David did carry the sword of state in Richard's first coronation, showing that he had a certain favored position with Richard. Once Richard took the throne, he needed money to go on Crusade. William, seeing his chance, gave

Richard money, but at a price. William bought back Scottish independence, ending the liege fealty that had crushed Scotland.[303]

Richard was held captive in the Holy Land after his Crusade. In the interim, King John (see *Continental Dynasty*) took over the throne. In 1194, Richard returned from captivity, and our David rallied to his side to dethrone John. Richard died in 1199, and John reclaimed the throne.[304]

In 1205, David of Huntingdon swore fealty to his 7-year-old nephew, Alexander. David never challenged either of his brothers for the throne, and, in supporting his nephew, he forfeited his own claims.[305]

King William of Scotland seemed unable to keep away from disastrous alliances with England. He and King John feinted at war several times, and finally reached a truce in 1209 that included William's daughters Margaret and Isabella going to England with John, so that John could marry them to the courtiers of his choice, at his discretion.[306] This was harsh, because royal children's marriages often solidify international and internal alliances, and leaving them in the hands of foreign monarchs could have significantly weakened William's bargaining power. This truce also sowed seeds of discord at home, because the Scots wanted fewer ties to England, rather than more.[307]

In 1211, William, David, and Alexander were nearly drowned in a flood in Perth.[308]

In 1212, another insurrection from the north roiled William's reign.[309] Godfrey MacWilliam, Donald Bane MacWilliam's son, revolted, and William turned to King John of England for help. John helped, but reserved the right to marry off young Alexander to the person of his choice in six years. Alexander returned to England with John.[310]

In 1213, Godfrey MacWilliam was defeated and killed.[311]

On 4 December 1214, William died.[312] David supported his nephew, as he promised, and **Alexander II** was crowned within 24 hours of his father's death.[313]

Alexander's coronation brought another uprising from the north, from the brother of Godfrey, Donald Bane MacWilliam (junior). With him was Kenneth MacEth, presumed to be the son of Donald MacEth, grandson of Malcolm MacEth, although some sources name him as a younger son of Malcolm. MacWilliam and Kenneth MacEth were killed in battle, and there ended the active revolts involving the MacEth/MacKay line.[314] See the *MacKay Lineage* for what happened next.

David, Earl of Huntingdon's story came to a close in 1219, when he died.[315] [316] David played a vital political role during William's reign, and was powerful in his own right. He held the Honor of Huntingdon, as well as lands in nine English counties. He also at various times was Earl of Garioch and Earl of Lennox, and held the Lordship of Strathbogie. Some legends say he followed Richard into the Second Crusade, but this is uncertain.[317]

David married Matilda, the sister of Randolph, Earl of Chester. They had seven children.[318] [319]

- David – predeceased his father
- Henry – predeceased his father
- John "the Scot" – inherited the Earldoms of Chester and Lincoln

- Margaret – married Alan of Galloway, and it is through her line that the Balliol family claimed the throne in Robert Bruce's time
- *Isabella* –married Robert de Brus (King Robert I's great-grandfather), thus establishing the Bruce claim to the throne
- Ada – married Henry de Hastings
- Matilda – did not marry

For the rest of our Scottish Royal Lineage, go to *The Stewart Dynasty* chapter. For more pre-Stewart Dynasty history, see the *De Brus Lineage* and the *Stewart Lineage* chapters.

[1] Ronald Williams, *The Lords of the Isles: The Clan Donald and the Early Kingdom of the Scots* (Chatto & Windus - The Hogarth Press, London, 1984) p. 57.

[2] John Cannon & Ralph Griffiths, *The Oxford Illustrated History of the British Monarchy* (2000 edition, Oxford University Press), p. 35.

[3] Caroline Bingham, *Kings and Queens of Scotland* (originally published 1976, Taplinger Publishing Co. this edition, 1985, Dorset Press) p. 6.

[4] Richard Oram (Ed.), *The Kings and Queens of Scotland* (Tempus Publishing Ltd., Stroud, Gloucestershire, England, 2001), p. 34.

[5] E. William Robertson, *Scotland Under Her Early Kings: A History of the Kingdom to the Close of the 13th Century, Part One* (Edinburgh: Edmonston and Douglas, 1862), p. 39.

[6] E. William Robertson, *Scotland Under Her Early Kings: A History of the Kingdom to the Close of the 13th Century, Part One* (Edinburgh: Edmonston and Douglas, 1862), p. 26-27.

[7] E. William Robertson, *Scotland Under Her Early Kings: A History of the Kingdom to the Close of the 13th Century, Part One* (Edinburgh: Edmonston and Douglas, 1862), p. 30.

[8] Caroline Bingham, *Kings and Queens of Scotland* (orig. published 1976, Taplinger Publishing Co. this edition, 1985, Dorset Press) p. 7-8.

[9] E. William Robertson, *Scotland Under Her Early Kings: A History of the Kingdom to the Close of the 13th Century, Part One* (Edinburgh: Edmonston and Douglas, 1862), p. 34-37.

[10] Caroline Bingham, *Kings and Queens of Scotland* (originally published 1976, Taplinger Publishing Co. this edition, 1985, Dorset Press) p. 6.

[11] Richard Oram (Ed.), *The Kings and Queens of Scotland* (Tempus Publishing Ltd., Stroud, Gloucestershire, England, 2001), p. 38.

[12] Richard Oram (Ed.), *The Kings and Queens of Scotland* (Tempus Publishing Ltd., Stroud, Gloucestershire, England, 2001), p. 36.

[13] Fitzroy Maclean, *A Concise History of Scotland* (First published 1970. This version published 2002. Thames & Hudson Ltd., London), p. 21.

[14] E. William Robertson, *Scotland Under Her Early Kings: A History of the Kingdom to the Close of the 13th Century, Part One* (Edinburgh: Edmonston and Douglas, 1862), p. 40.

[15] John Cannon & Ralph Griffiths, *The Oxford Illustrated History of the British Monarchy* (2000 edition, Oxford University Press), p. 35.

[16] Fitzroy Maclean, *A Concise History of Scotland* (First published 1970. This version published 2002. Thames & Hudson Ltd., London), p. 22.

[17] E. William Robertson, *Scotland Under Her Early Kings: A History of the Kingdom to the Close of the 13th Century, Part One* (Edinburgh: Edmonston and Douglas, 1862), p. 41.

[18] Caroline Bingham, *Kings and Queens of Scotland* (originally published 1976, Taplinger Publishing Co. this edition, 1985, Dorset Press) p. 9.

[19] E. William Robertson, *Scotland Under Her Early Kings: A History of the Kingdom to the Close of the 13th Century, Part One* (Edinburgh: Edmonston and Douglas, 1862), p. 41.

[20] Richard Oram (Ed.), *The Kings and Queens of Scotland* (Tempus Publishing Ltd., Stroud, Gloucestershire, England, 2001), p. 38.

[21] Richard Oram (Ed.), *The Kings and Queens of Scotland* (Tempus Publishing Ltd., Stroud, Gloucestershire, England, 2001), p. 39.

[22] Richard Oram (Ed.), *The Kings and Queens of Scotland* (Tempus Publishing Ltd., Stroud, Gloucestershire, England, 2001), p. 39.

[23] Fitzroy Maclean, *A Concise History of Scotland* (First published 1970. This version published 2002. Thames & Hudson Ltd., London), p. 22.

[24] E. William Robertson, *Scotland Under Her Early Kings: A History of the Kingdom to the Close of the 13th Century, Part One* (Edinburgh: Edmonston and Douglas, 1862), p. 41.

[25] John Cannon & Ralph Griffiths, *The Oxford Illustrated History of the British Monarchy* (2000 edition, Oxford University Press), p. 657.

[26] E. William Robertson, *Scotland Under Her Early Kings: A History of the Kingdom to the Close of the 13th Century, Part One* (Edinburgh: Edmonston and Douglas, 1862), p. 48.

[27] E. William Robertson, *Scotland Under Her Early Kings: A History of the Kingdom to the Close of the 13th Century, Part One* (Edinburgh: Edmonston and Douglas, 1862), p. 42.

[28] E. William Robertson, *Scotland Under Her Early Kings: A History of the Kingdom to the Close of the 13th Century, Part One* (Edinburgh: Edmonston and Douglas, 1862), p. 43.

[29] Richard Oram (Ed.), *The Kings and Queens of Scotland* (Tempus Publishing Ltd., Stroud, Gloucestershire, England, 2001), p. 39.

[30] E. William Robertson, *Scotland Under Her Early Kings: A History of the Kingdom to the Close of the 13th Century, Part One* (Edinburgh: Edmonston and Douglas, 1862), p. 43.

[31] E. William Robertson, *Scotland Under Her Early Kings: A History of the Kingdom to the Close of the 13th Century, Part One* (Edinburgh: Edmonston and Douglas, 1862), p. 45.

[32] E. William Robertson, *Scotland Under Her Early Kings: A History of the Kingdom to the Close of the 13th Century, Part One* (Edinburgh: Edmonston and Douglas, 1862), p. 45.

[33] E. William Robertson, *Scotland Under Her Early Kings: A History of the Kingdom to the Close of the 13th Century, Part One* (Edinburgh: Edmonston and Douglas, 1862), p. 46.

[34] E. William Robertson, *Scotland Under Her Early Kings: A History of the Kingdom to the Close of the 13th Century, Part One* (Edinburgh: Edmonston and Douglas, 1862), p. 47.

[35] James Grey, *Sutherland & Caithness in Saga-Time, or, The Jarls & The Freskyns* (Oliver & Boyd, Edinburgh, 1922), p. 18.

[36] John Cannon & Ralph Griffiths, *The Oxford Illustrated History of the British Monarchy* (2000 edition, Oxford University Press), Geneaolgies of Royal Lines Appendix.

[37] E. William Robertson, *Scotland Under Her Early Kings: A History of the Kingdom to the Close of the 13th Century, Part One* (Edinburgh: Edmonston and Douglas, 1862), p. 48.

[38] E. William Robertson, *Scotland Under Her Early Kings: A History of the Kingdom to the Close of the 13th Century, Part One* (Edinburgh: Edmonston and Douglas, 1862), p. 49-50.

[39] E. William Robertson, *Scotland Under Her Early Kings: A History of the Kingdom to the Close of the 13th Century, Part One* (Edinburgh: Edmonston and Douglas, 1862), p. 51.

[40] E. William Robertson, *Scotland Under Her Early Kings: A History of the Kingdom to the Close of the 13th Century, Part One* (Edinburgh: Edmonston and Douglas, 1862), p. 51.

[41] Richard Oram (Ed.), *The Kings and Queens of Scotland* (Tempus Publishing Ltd., Stroud, Gloucestershire, England, 2001), p. 40.

[42] E. William Robertson, *Scotland Under Her Early Kings: A History of the Kingdom to the Close of the 13th Century, Part One* (Edinburgh: Edmonston and Douglas, 1862), p. 51.

[43] E. William Robertson, *Scotland Under Her Early Kings: A History of the Kingdom to the Close of the 13th Century, Part One* (Edinburgh: Edmonston and Douglas, 1862), p. 52.

[44] Richard Oram (Ed.), *The Kings and Queens of Scotland* (Tempus Publishing Ltd., Stroud, Gloucestershire, England, 2001), p. 40-41.

[45] E. William Robertson, *Scotland Under Her Early Kings: A History of the Kingdom to the Close of the 13th Century, Part One* (Edinburgh: Edmonston and Douglas, 1862), p. 53-67.

[46] E. William Robertson, *Scotland Under Her Early Kings: A History of the Kingdom to the Close of the 13th Century, Part One* (Edinburgh: Edmonston and Douglas, 1862), p. 69.

[47] Richard Oram (Ed.), *The Kings and Queens of Scotland* (Tempus Publishing Ltd., Stroud, Gloucestershire, England, 2001), p. 43.

[48] E. William Robertson, *Scotland Under Her Early Kings: A History of the Kingdom to the Close of the 13th Century, Part One* (Edinburgh: Edmonston and Douglas, 1862), p. 72.

[49] E. William Robertson, *Scotland Under Her Early Kings: A History of the Kingdom to the Close of the 13th Century, Part One* (Edinburgh: Edmonston and Douglas, 1862), p. 73.

[50] E. William Robertson, *Scotland Under Her Early Kings: A History of the Kingdom to the Close of the 13th Century, Part One* (Edinburgh: Edmonston and Douglas, 1862), p. 73-74.

[51] John Cannon & Ralph Griffiths, *The Oxford Illustrated History of the British Monarchy* (2000 edition, Oxford University Press), Geneaolgies of Royal Lines Appendix.

[52] E. William Robertson, *Scotland Under Her Early Kings: A History of the Kingdom to the Close of the 13th Century, Part One* (Edinburgh: Edmonston and Douglas, 1862), p. 75.

[53] James Grey, *Sutherland & Caithness in Saga-Time, or, The Jarls & The Freskyns* (Oliver & Boyd, Edinburgh, 1922), p. 20.

[54] E. William Robertson, *Scotland Under Her Early Kings: A History of the Kingdom to the Close of the 13th Century, Part One* (Edinburgh: Edmonston and Douglas, 1862), p. 77.

[55] E. William Robertson, *Scotland Under Her Early Kings: A History of the Kingdom to the Close of the 13th Century, Part One* (Edinburgh: Edmonston and Douglas, 1862), p. 78.

[56] E. William Robertson, *Scotland Under Her Early Kings: A History of the Kingdom to the Close of the 13th Century, Part One* (Edinburgh: Edmonston and Douglas, 1862), p. 79.

[57] E. William Robertson, *Scotland Under Her Early Kings: A History of the Kingdom to the Close of the 13th Century, Part One* (Edinburgh: Edmonston and Douglas, 1862), p. 82.

[58] James Grey, *Sutherland & Caithness in Saga-Time, or, The Jarls & The Freskyns* (Oliver & Boyd, Edinburgh, 1922), p. 20.

[59] E. William Robertson, *Scotland Under Her Early Kings: A History of the Kingdom to the Close of the 13th Century, Part One* (Edinburgh: Edmonston and Douglas, 1862), p. 83.

[60] James Grey, *Sutherland & Caithness in Saga-Time, or, The Jarls & The Freskyns* (Oliver & Boyd, Edinburgh, 1922), p. 20.

[61] E. William Robertson, *Scotland Under Her Early Kings: A History of the Kingdom to the Close of the 13th Century, Part One* (Edinburgh: Edmonston and Douglas, 1862), p. 84.

[62] E. William Robertson, *Scotland Under Her Early Kings: A History of the Kingdom to the Close of the 13th Century, Part One* (Edinburgh: Edmonston and Douglas, 1862), p. 85.

[63] Richard Oram (Ed.), *The Kings and Queens of Scotland* (Tempus Publishing Ltd., Stroud, Gloucestershire, England, 2001), p. 44.

[64] E. William Robertson, *Scotland Under Her Early Kings: A History of the Kingdom to the Close of the 13th Century, Part One* (Edinburgh: Edmonston and Douglas, 1862), p. 91.

[65] Richard Oram (Ed.), *The Kings and Queens of Scotland* (Tempus Publishing Ltd., Stroud, Gloucestershire, England, 2001), p. 44.

[66] E. William Robertson, *Scotland Under Her Early Kings: A History of the Kingdom to the Close of the 13th Century, Part One* (Edinburgh: Edmonston and Douglas, 1862), p. 87.

[67] John Cannon & Ralph Griffiths, *The Oxford Illustrated History of the British Monarchy* (2000 edition, Oxford University Press), Geneaolgies of Royal Lines Appendix.

[68] E. William Robertson, *Scotland Under Her Early Kings: A History of the Kingdom to the Close of the 13th Century, Part One* (Edinburgh: Edmonston and Douglas, 1862), p. 89.

[69] E. William Robertson, *Scotland Under Her Early Kings: A History of the Kingdom to the Close of the 13th Century, Part One* (Edinburgh: Edmonston and Douglas, 1862), p. 91-92.

[70] John Cannon & Ralph Griffiths, *The Oxford Illustrated History of the British Monarchy* (2000 edition, Oxford University Press), List of Monarchs Appendix.

[71] John Cannon & Ralph Griffiths, *The Oxford Illustrated History of the British Monarchy* (2000 edition, Oxford University Press), p. 88.

[72] E. William Robertson, *Scotland Under Her Early Kings: A History of the Kingdom to the Close of the 13th Century, Part One* (Edinburgh: Edmonston and Douglas, 1862), p. 92.

[73] James Grey, *Sutherland & Caithness in Saga-Time, or, The Jarls & The Freskyns* (Oliver & Boyd, Edinburgh, 1922), p. 21, 26.

[74] E. William Robertson, *Scotland Under Her Early Kings: A History of the Kingdom to the Close of the 13th Century, Part One* (Edinburgh: Edmonston and Douglas, 1862), p. 93-94.

[75] James Grey, *Sutherland & Caithness in Saga-Time, or, The Jarls & The Freskyns* (Oliver & Boyd, Edinburgh, 1922), p. 27.

[76] E. William Robertson, *Scotland Under Her Early Kings: A History of the Kingdom to the Close of the 13th Century, Part One* (Edinburgh: Edmonston and Douglas, 1862), p. 95.

[77] John Cannon & Ralph Griffiths, *The Oxford Illustrated History of the British Monarchy* (2000 edition, Oxford University Press), p. 89.

[78] Richard Oram (Ed.), *The Kings and Queens of Scotland* (Tempus Publishing Ltd., Stroud, Gloucestershire, England, 2001), p. 46.

[79] E. William Robertson, *Scotland Under Her Early Kings: A History of the Kingdom to the Close of the 13th Century, Part One* (Edinburgh: Edmonston and Douglas, 1862), p. 95-96.

[80] Caroline Bingham, *Kings and Queens of Scotland* (originally published 1976, Taplinger Publishing Co. this edition, 1985, Dorset Press) p. 9.

[81] Fitzroy Maclean, *A Concise History of Scotland* (First published 1970. This version published 2002. Thames & Hudson Ltd., London), p. 22.

[82] E. William Robertson, *Scotland Under Her Early Kings: A History of the Kingdom to the Close of the 13th Century, Part One* (Edinburgh: Edmonston and Douglas, 1862), p. 99.

[83] E. William Robertson, *Scotland Under Her Early Kings: A History of the Kingdom to the Close of the 13th Century, Part One* (Edinburgh: Edmonston and Douglas, 1862), p. 99.

[84] John Cannon & Ralph Griffiths, *The Oxford Illustrated History of the British Monarchy* (2000 edition, Oxford University Press), p. 88.

[85] E. William Robertson, *Scotland Under Her Early Kings: A History of the Kingdom to the Close of the 13th Century, Part One* (Edinburgh: Edmonston and Douglas, 1862), p. 97.

[86] E. William Robertson, *Scotland Under Her Early Kings: A History of the Kingdom to the Close of the 13th Century, Part One* (Edinburgh: Edmonston and Douglas, 1862), p. 97.

[87] E. William Robertson, *Scotland Under Her Early Kings: A History of the Kingdom to the Close of the 13th Century, Part One* (Edinburgh: Edmonston and Douglas, 1862), p. 110.

[88] Richard Oram (Ed.), *The Kings and Queens of Scotland* (Tempus Publishing Ltd., Stroud, Gloucestershire, England, 2001), p. 47.

[89] John Cannon & Ralph Griffiths, *The Oxford Illustrated History of the British Monarchy* (2000 edition, Oxford University Press), Geneaolgies of Royal Lines Appendix; List of Monarchs Appendix.

[90] E. William Robertson, *Scotland Under Her Early Kings: A History of the Kingdom to the Close of the 13th Century, Part One* (Edinburgh: Edmonston and Douglas, 1862), p. 98.

[91] E. William Robertson, *Scotland Under Her Early Kings: A History of the Kingdom to the Close of the 13th Century, Part One* (Edinburgh: Edmonston and Douglas, 1862), p. 98.

[92] E. William Robertson, *Scotland Under Her Early Kings: A History of the Kingdom to the Close of the 13th Century, Part One* (Edinburgh: Edmonston and Douglas, 1862), p. 105-106.

[93] E. William Robertson, *Scotland Under Her Early Kings: A History of the Kingdom to the Close of the 13th Century, Part One* (Edinburgh: Edmonston and Douglas, 1862), p. 108-109.

[94] Ronald Williams, *The Lords of the Isles: The Clan Donald and the Early Kingdom of the Scots* (Chatto & Windus - The Hogarth Press, London, 1984) p. 59.

[95] E. William Robertson, *Scotland Under Her Early Kings: A History of the Kingdom to the Close of the 13th Century, Part One* (Edinburgh: Edmonston and Douglas, 1862), p. 111.

[96] Caroline Bingham, *Kings and Queens of Scotland* (orig. published 1976, Taplinger Publishing Co. this edition, 1985, Dorset Press) p. 13.

[97] Caroline Bingham, *Kings and Queens of Scotland* (orig. published 1976, Taplinger Publishing Co. this edition, 1985, Dorset Press) p. 13.

[98] Richard Oram (Ed.), *The Kings and Queens of Scotland* (Tempus Publishing Ltd., Stroud, Gloucestershire, England, 2001), p. 45.

[99] Caroline Bingham, *Kings and Queens of Scotland* (orig. published 1976, Taplinger Publishing Co. this edition, 1985, Dorset Press) p. 13.

[100] E. William Robertson, *Scotland Under Her Early Kings: A History of the Kingdom to the Close of the 13th Century, Part One* (Edinburgh: Edmonston and Douglas, 1862), p. 111.

[101] Caroline Bingham, *Kings and Queens of Scotland* (orig. published 1976, Taplinger Publishing Co. this edition, 1985, Dorset Press) p. 10.

[102] Ronald Williams, *The Lords of the Isles: The Clan Donald and the Early Kingdom of the Scots* (Chatto & Windus - The Hogarth Press, London, 1984) p. 59.

[103] Caroline Bingham, *Kings and Queens of Scotland* (orig. published 1976, Taplinger Publishing Co. this edition, 1985, Dorset Press) p. 10.

[104] E. William Robertson, *Scotland Under Her Early Kings: A History of the Kingdom to the Close of the 13th Century, Part One* (Edinburgh: Edmonston and Douglas, 1862), p. 113.

[105] Ronald Williams, *The Lords of the Isles: The Clan Donald and the Early Kingdom of the Scots* (Chatto & Windus - The Hogarth Press, London, 1984), p. 98.

[106] E. William Robertson, *Scotland Under Her Early Kings: A History of the Kingdom to the Close of the 13th Century, Part One* (Edinburgh: Edmonston and Douglas, 1862), p. 114.

[107] Richard Oram (Ed.), *The Kings and Queens of Scotland* (Tempus Publishing Ltd., Stroud, Gloucestershire, England, 2001), p. 47.

[108] E. William Robertson, *Scotland Under Her Early Kings: A History of the Kingdom to the Close of the 13th Century, Part One* (Edinburgh: Edmonston and Douglas, 1862), p. 114.

[109] James Grey, *Sutherland & Caithness in Saga-Time, or, The Jarls & The Freskyns* (Oliver & Boyd, Edinburgh, 1922), p. 29.

[110] Ronald Williams, *The Lords of the Isles: The Clan Donald and the Early Kingdom of the Scots* (Chatto & Windus - The Hogarth Press, London, 1984), p. 98.

[111] E. William Robertson, *Scotland Under Her Early Kings: A History of the Kingdom to the Close of the 13th Century, Part One* (Edinburgh: Edmonston and Douglas, 1862), p. 114-115.

[112] Caroline Bingham, *Kings and Queens of Scotland* (orig. published 1976, Taplinger Publishing Co. this edition, 1985, Dorset Press) p. 13.

[113] E. William Robertson, *Scotland Under Her Early Kings: A History of the Kingdom to the Close of the 13th Century, Part One* (Edinburgh: Edmonston and Douglas, 1862), p. 110-111.

[114] John Cannon & Ralph Griffiths, *The Oxford Illustrated History of the British Monarchy* (2000 edition, Oxford University Press), Geneaolgies of Royal Lines Appendix; List of Monarchs Appendix.

[115] E. William Robertson, *Scotland Under Her Early Kings: A History of the Kingdom to the Close of the 13th Century, Part One* (Edinburgh: Edmonston and Douglas, 1862), p. 116.

[116] Fitzroy Maclean, *A Concise History of Scotland* (First published 1970. This version, 2002. Thames & Hudson Ltd., London), p. 23.

[117] Ronald Williams, *The Lords of the Isles: The Clan Donald and the Early Kingdom of the Scots* (Chatto & Windus - The Hogarth Press, London, 1984), p. 59.

[118] James Grey, *Sutherland & Caithness in Saga-Time, or, The Jarls & The Freskyns* (Oliver & Boyd, Edinburgh, 1922), p. 29.

[119] Caroline Bingham, *Kings and Queens of Scotland* (orig. published 1976, Taplinger Publishing Co. this edition, 1985, Dorset Press) p. 14.

[120] Fitzroy Maclean, *A Concise History of Scotland* (First published 1970. This version, 2002. Thames & Hudson Ltd., London), p. 23.

[121] Richard Oram (Ed.), *The Kings and Queens of Scotland* (Tempus Publishing Ltd., Stroud, Gloucestershire, England, 2001), p. 48.

[122] E. William Robertson, *Scotland Under Her Early Kings: A History of the Kingdom to the Close of the 13th Century, Part One* (Edinburgh: Edmonston and Douglas, 1862), p. 122.

[123] Caroline Bingham, *Kings and Queens of Scotland* (orig. published 1976, Taplinger Publishing Co. this edition, 1985, Dorset Press) p. 14.

[124] Richard Oram (Ed.), *The Kings and Queens of Scotland* (Tempus Publishing Ltd., Stroud, Gloucestershire, England, 2001), p. 49-50.

[125] Caroline Bingham, *Kings and Queens of Scotland* (orig. published 1976, Taplinger Publishing Co. this edition, 1985, Dorset Press) p. 14.

[126] E. William Robertson, *Scotland Under Her Early Kings: A History of the Kingdom to the Close of the 13th Century, Part One* (Edinburgh: Edmonston and Douglas, 1862), p. 123.

[127] Caroline Bingham, *Kings and Queens of Scotland* (orig. published 1976, Taplinger Publishing Co. this edition, 1985, Dorset Press) p. 15.

[128] E. William Robertson, *Scotland Under Her Early Kings: A History of the Kingdom to the Close of the 13th Century, Part One* (Edinburgh: Edmonston and Douglas, 1862), p. 124.

[129] Richard Oram (Ed.), *The Kings and Queens of Scotland* (Tempus Publishing Ltd., Stroud, Gloucestershire, England, 2001), p. 50.

[130] John Cannon & Ralph Griffiths, *The Oxford Illustrated History of the British Monarchy* (2000 edition, Oxford University Press), List of Monarchs Appendix.

[131] E. William Robertson, *Scotland Under Her Early Kings: A History of the Kingdom to the Close of the 13th Century, Part One* (Edinburgh: Edmonston and Douglas, 1862), p. 125.

[132] Fitzroy Maclean, *A Concise History of Scotland* (First published 1970. This version, 2002. Thames & Hudson Ltd., London), p. 23.

[133] Caroline Bingham, *Kings and Queens of Scotland* (orig. published 1976, Taplinger Publishing Co. this edition, 1985, Dorset Press) p. 15.

[134] Caroline Bingham, *Kings and Queens of Scotland* (orig. published 1976, Taplinger Publishing Co. this edition, 1985, Dorset Press) p. 14.

[135] Richard Oram (Ed.), *The Kings and Queens of Scotland* (Tempus Publishing Ltd., Stroud, Gloucestershire, England, 2001), p. 53.

[136] John Cannon & Ralph Griffiths, *The Oxford Illustrated History of the British Monarchy* (2000 edition, Oxford University Press), Geneaolgies of Royal Lines Appendix.

[137] E. William Robertson, *Scotland Under Her Early Kings: A History of the Kingdom to the Close of the 13th Century, Part One* (Edinburgh: Edmonston and Douglas, 1862), p. 127.

[138] James Grey, *Sutherland & Caithness in Saga-Time, or, The Jarls & The Freskyns* (Oliver & Boyd, Edinburgh, 1922), p. 32.

[139] Caroline Bingham, *Kings and Queens of Scotland* (orig. published 1976, Taplinger Publishing Co. this edition, 1985, Dorset Press) p. 15.

[140] Richard Oram (Ed.), *The Kings and Queens of Scotland* (Tempus Publishing Ltd., Stroud, Gloucestershire, England, 2001), p. 53.

[141] Gabriel Ronay, *The Lost King of England: the East European adventures of Edward the Exile* (Woodbridge, Suffolk; Wolfeboro, N.H., USA: Boydell Press, 1989, ISBN 0-85115-541-3), p. 162.

[142] Caroline Bingham, *Kings and Queens of Scotland* (orig. published 1976, Taplinger Publishing Co. this edition, 1985, Dorset Press) p. 15.

[143] E. William Robertson, *Scotland Under Her Early Kings: A History of the Kingdom to the Close of the 13th Century, Part One* (Edinburgh: Edmonston and Douglas, 1862), p. 130-131.

[144] E. William Robertson, *Scotland Under Her Early Kings: A History of the Kingdom to the Close of the 13th Century, Part One* (Edinburgh: Edmonston and Douglas, 1862), p. 131-134.

[145] E. William Robertson, *Scotland Under Her Early Kings: A History of the Kingdom to the Close of the 13th Century, Part One* (Edinburgh: Edmonston and Douglas, 1862), p. 134.

[146] Ronald Williams, *The Lords of the Isles: The Clan Donald and the Early Kingdom of the Scots* (Chatto & Windus - The Hogarth Press, London, 1984) p. 60.

[147] Caroline Bingham, *Kings and Queens of Scotland* (orig. published 1976, Taplinger Publishing Co. this edition, 1985, Dorset Press) p. 15.

[148] E. William Robertson, *Scotland Under Her Early Kings: A History of the Kingdom to the Close of the 13th Century, Part One* (Edinburgh: Edmonston and Douglas, 1862), p. 135.

[149] Caroline Bingham, *Kings and Queens of Scotland* (orig. published 1976, Taplinger Publishing Co. this edition, 1985, Dorset Press) p. 17.

[150] Fitzroy Maclean, *A Concise History of Scotland* (First published 1970. This version, 2002. Thames & Hudson Ltd., London), p. 25.

[151] E. William Robertson, *Scotland Under Her Early Kings: A History of the Kingdom to the Close of the 13th Century, Part One* (Edinburgh: Edmonston and Douglas, 1862), p. 136-137.

[152] Caroline Bingham, *Kings and Queens of Scotland* (orig. published 1976, Taplinger Publishing Co. this edition, 1985, Dorset Press) p. 17.

[153] Gabriel Ronay, *The Lost King of England: the East European adventures of Edward the Exile* (Woodbridge, Suffolk; Wolfeboro, N.H., USA: Boydell Press, 1989, ISBN 0-85115-541-3), p. 166.

[154] Gabriel Ronay, *The Lost King of England: the East European adventures of Edward the Exile* (Woodbridge, Suffolk; Wolfeboro, N.H., USA: Boydell Press, 1989, ISBN 0-85115-541-3), p. 166.

[155] E. William Robertson, *Scotland Under Her Early Kings: A History of the Kingdom to the Close of the 13th Century, Part One* (Edinburgh: Edmonston and Douglas, 1862), p. 139.

[156] E. William Robertson, *Scotland Under Her Early Kings: A History of the Kingdom to the Close of the 13th Century, Part One* (Edinburgh: Edmonston and Douglas, 1862), p. 140.

[157] E. William Robertson, *Scotland Under Her Early Kings: A History of the Kingdom to the Close of the 13th Century, Part One* (Edinburgh: Edmonston and Douglas, 1862), p. 140.

[158] Richard Oram (Ed.), *The Kings and Queens of Scotland* (Tempus Publishing Ltd., Stroud, Gloucestershire, England, 2001), p. 54.

[159] E. William Robertson, *Scotland Under Her Early Kings: A History of the Kingdom to the Close of the 13th Century, Part One* (Edinburgh: Edmonston and Douglas, 1862), p. 141.

[160] E. William Robertson, *Scotland Under Her Early Kings: A History of the Kingdom to the Close of the 13th Century, Part One* (Edinburgh: Edmonston and Douglas, 1862), p. 141-142.

[161] E. William Robertson, *Scotland Under Her Early Kings: A History of the Kingdom to the Close of the 13th Century, Part One* (Edinburgh: Edmonston and Douglas, 1862), p. 142.

[162] Richard Oram (Ed.), *The Kings and Queens of Scotland* (Tempus Publishing Ltd., Stroud, Gloucestershire, England, 2001), p. 56.

[163] E. William Robertson, *Scotland Under Her Early Kings: A History of the Kingdom to the Close of the 13th Century, Part One* (Edinburgh: Edmonston and Douglas, 1862), p. 143.

[164] E. William Robertson, *Scotland Under Her Early Kings: A History of the Kingdom to the Close of the 13th Century, Part One* (Edinburgh: Edmonston and Douglas, 1862), p. 144-145.

[165] Fitzroy Maclean, *A Concise History of Scotland* (First published 1970. This version, 2002. Thames & Hudson Ltd., London), p. 25.

[166] E. William Robertson, *Scotland Under Her Early Kings: A History of the Kingdom to the Close of the 13th Century, Part One* (Edinburgh: Edmonston and Douglas, 1862), p. 145.

[167] Ronald Williams, *The Lords of the Isles: The Clan Donald and the Early Kingdom of the Scots* (Chatto & Windus - The Hogarth Press, London, 1984), p. 60.

[168] Caroline Bingham, *Kings and Queens of Scotland* (orig. published 1976, Taplinger Publishing Co. this edition, 1985, Dorset Press) p. 18.

[169] E. William Robertson, *Scotland Under Her Early Kings: A History of the Kingdom to the Close of the 13th Century, Part One* (Edinburgh: Edmonston and Douglas, 1862), p. 145.

[170] John Cannon & Ralph Griffiths, *The Oxford Illustrated History of the British Monarchy* (2000 edition, Oxford University Press), Geneaolgies of Royal Lines Appendix; List of Monarchs Appendix.

[171] E. William Robertson, *Scotland Under Her Early Kings: A History of the Kingdom to the Close of the 13th Century, Part One* (Edinburgh: Edmonston and Douglas, 1862), p. 146.

[172] John Cannon & Ralph Griffiths, *The Oxford Illustrated History of the British Monarchy* (2000 edition, Oxford University Press), p. 640.

[173] E. William Robertson, *Scotland Under Her Early Kings: A History of the Kingdom to the Close of the 13th Century, Part One* (Edinburgh: Edmonston and Douglas, 1862), p. 146.

[174] Caroline Bingham, *Kings and Queens of Scotland* (orig. published 1976, Taplinger Publishing Co. this edition, 1985, Dorset Press) p. 16.

[175] Gabriel Ronay, *The Lost King of England: the East European adventures of Edward the Exile* (Woodbridge, Suffolk; Wolfeboro, N.H., USA: Boydell Press, 1989, ISBN 0-85115-541-3), p. 176, 178.

[176] Caroline Bingham, *Kings and Queens of Scotland* (orig. published 1976, Taplinger Publishing Co. this edition, 1985, Dorset Press) p. 16.

[177] E. William Robertson, *Scotland Under Her Early Kings: A History of the Kingdom to the Close of the 13th Century, Part One* (Edinburgh: Edmonston and Douglas, 1862), p. 149-150.

[178] Caroline Bingham, *Kings and Queens of Scotland* (orig. published 1976, Taplinger Publishing Co. this edition, 1985, Dorset Press) p. 17.

[179] E. William Robertson, *Scotland Under Her Early Kings: A History of the Kingdom to the Close of the 13th Century, Part One* (Edinburgh: Edmonston and Douglas, 1862), p. 148-149.

[180] Caroline Bingham, *Kings and Queens of Scotland* (orig. published 1976, Taplinger Publishing Co. this edition, 1985, Dorset Press) p. 18.

[181] E. William Robertson, *Scotland Under Her Early Kings: A History of the Kingdom to the Close of the 13th Century, Part One* (Edinburgh: Edmonston and Douglas, 1862), p. 151.

[182] Gabriel Ronay, *The Lost King of England: the East European adventures of Edward the Exile* (Woodbridge, Suffolk; Wolfeboro, N.H., USA: Boydell Press, 1989, ISBN 0-85115-541-3), p. 181.

[183] E. William Robertson, *Scotland Under Her Early Kings: A History of the Kingdom to the Close of the 13th Century, Part One* (Edinburgh: Edmonston and Douglas, 1862), p. 151.

[184] Caroline Bingham, *Kings and Queens of Scotland* (orig. published 1976, Taplinger Publishing Co. this edition, 1985, Dorset Press) p. 22.

[185] Caroline Bingham, *Kings and Queens of Scotland* (orig. published 1976, Taplinger Publishing Co. this edition, 1985, Dorset Press) p. 18.

[186] Caroline Bingham, *Kings and Queens of Scotland* (orig. published 1976, Taplinger Publishing Co. this edition, 1985, Dorset Press) p. 18.

[187] E. William Robertson, *Scotland Under Her Early Kings: A History of the Kingdom to the Close of the 13th Century, Part One* (Edinburgh: Edmonston and Douglas, 1862), p. 156.

[188] Caroline Bingham, *Kings and Queens of Scotland* (orig. published 1976, Taplinger Publishing Co. this edition, 1985, Dorset Press) p. 19.

[189] E. William Robertson, *Scotland Under Her Early Kings: A History of the Kingdom to the Close of the 13th Century, Part One* (Edinburgh: Edmonston and Douglas, 1862), p. 157.

[190] Caroline Bingham, *Kings and Queens of Scotland* (orig. published 1976, Taplinger Publishing Co. this edition, 1985, Dorset Press) p. 19.

[191] Caroline Bingham, *Kings and Queens of Scotland* (orig. published 1976, Taplinger Publishing Co. this edition, 1985, Dorset Press) p. 19.

[192] E. William Robertson, *Scotland Under Her Early Kings: A History of the Kingdom to the Close of the 13th Century, Part One* (Edinburgh: Edmonston and Douglas, 1862), p. 158.

[193] E. William Robertson, *Scotland Under Her Early Kings: A History of the Kingdom to the Close of the 13th Century, Part One* (Edinburgh: Edmonston and Douglas, 1862), p. 159.

[194] Richard Oram (Ed.), *The Kings and Queens of Scotland* (Tempus Publishing Ltd., Stroud, Gloucestershire, England, 2001), p. 60.

[195] Caroline Bingham, *Kings and Queens of Scotland* (orig. published 1976, Taplinger Publishing Co. this edition, 1985, Dorset Press) p. 20.

[196] E. William Robertson, *Scotland Under Her Early Kings: A History of the Kingdom to the Close of the 13th Century, Part One* (Edinburgh: Edmonston and Douglas, 1862), p. 159.

[197] Caroline Bingham, *Kings and Queens of Scotland* (orig. published 1976, Taplinger Publishing Co. this edition, 1985, Dorset Press) p. 20.

[198] E. William Robertson, *Scotland Under Her Early Kings: A History of the Kingdom to the Close of the 13th Century, Part One* (Edinburgh: Edmonston and Douglas, 1862), p. 167, 169.

[199] Caroline Bingham, *Kings and Queens of Scotland* (orig. published 1976, Taplinger Publishing Co. this edition, 1985, Dorset Press) p. 20.

[200] Richard Oram (Ed.), *The Kings and Queens of Scotland* (Tempus Publishing Ltd., Stroud, Gloucestershire, England, 2001), p. 60-61.

[201] Richard Oram (Ed.), *The Kings and Queens of Scotland* (Tempus Publishing Ltd., Stroud, Gloucestershire, England, 2001), p. 59.

[202] E. William Robertson, *Scotland Under Her Early Kings: A History of the Kingdom to the Close of the 13th Century, Part One* (Edinburgh: Edmonston and Douglas, 1862), p. 170.

[203] Caroline Bingham, *Kings and Queens of Scotland* (orig. published 1976, Taplinger Publishing Co. this edition, 1985, Dorset Press) p. 20.

[204] E. William Robertson, *Scotland Under Her Early Kings: A History of the Kingdom to the Close of the 13th Century, Part One* (Edinburgh: Edmonston and Douglas, 1862), p. 171.

[205] E. William Robertson, *Scotland Under Her Early Kings: A History of the Kingdom to the Close of the 13th Century, Part One* (Edinburgh: Edmonston and Douglas, 1862), p. 172-173.

[206] E. William Robertson, *Scotland Under Her Early Kings: A History of the Kingdom to the Close of the 13th Century, Part One* (Edinburgh: Edmonston and Douglas, 1862), p. 174.

[207] Caroline Bingham, *Kings and Queens of Scotland* (orig. published 1976, Taplinger Publishing Co. this edition, 1985, Dorset Press) p. 21.

[208] E. William Robertson, *Scotland Under Her Early Kings: A History of the Kingdom to the Close of the 13th Century, Part One* (Edinburgh: Edmonston and Douglas, 1862), p. 183.

[209] Caroline Bingham, *Kings and Queens of Scotland* (orig. published 1976, Taplinger Publishing Co. this edition, 1985, Dorset Press) p. 20.

[210] Caroline Bingham, *Kings and Queens of Scotland* (orig. published 1976, Taplinger Publishing Co. this edition, 1985, Dorset Press) p. 20-21.

[211] E. William Robertson, *Scotland Under Her Early Kings: A History of the Kingdom to the Close of the 13th Century, Part One* (Edinburgh: Edmonston and Douglas, 1862), p. 182.

[212] E. William Robertson, *Scotland Under Her Early Kings: A History of the Kingdom to the Close of the 13th Century, Part One* (Edinburgh: Edmonston and Douglas, 1862), p. 183.

[213] E. William Robertson, *Scotland Under Her Early Kings: A History of the Kingdom to the Close of the 13th Century, Part One* (Edinburgh: Edmonston and Douglas, 1862), p. 183-184.

[214] E. William Robertson, *Scotland Under Her Early Kings: A History of the Kingdom to the Close of the 13th Century, Part One* (Edinburgh: Edmonston and Douglas, 1862). p. 187.

[215] John Cannon & Ralph Griffiths, *The Oxford Illustrated History of the British Monarchy* (2000 edition, Oxford University Press), p. 144; Geneaolgies of Royal Lines Appendix.

[216] E. William Robertson, *Scotland Under Her Early Kings: A History of the Kingdom to the Close of the 13th Century, Part One* (Edinburgh: Edmonston and Douglas, 1862), p. 187.

[217] Caroline Bingham, *Kings and Queens of Scotland* (orig. published 1976, Taplinger Publishing Co. this edition, 1985, Dorset Press) p. 22.

[218] Richard Oram (Ed.), *The Kings and Queens of Scotland* (Tempus Publishing Ltd., Stroud, Gloucestershire, England, 2001), p. 65.

[219] E. William Robertson, *Scotland Under Her Early Kings: A History of the Kingdom to the Close of the 13th Century, Part One* (Edinburgh: Edmonston and Douglas, 1862), p. 188.

[220] John Cannon & Ralph Griffiths, *The Oxford Illustrated History of the British Monarchy* (2000 edition, Oxford University Press), List of Monarchs Appendix.

[221] E. William Robertson, *Scotland Under Her Early Kings: A History of the Kingdom to the Close of the 13th Century, Part One* (Edinburgh: Edmonston and Douglas, 1862), p. 187.

[222] Fitzroy Maclean, *A Concise History of Scotland* (First published 1970. This version, 2002. Thames & Hudson Ltd., London), p. 27.

[223] Richard Oram (Ed.), *The Kings and Queens of Scotland* (Tempus Publishing Ltd., Stroud, Gloucestershire, England, 2001), p. 66.

[224] Agnes Mure MacKenzie, *The Rise of the Stewarts* (Oliver & Boyd, Ltd, Edinburgh. Originally printed 1935, this printing 1957.), p. 8.

[225] Richard Oram (Ed.), *The Kings and Queens of Scotland* (Tempus Publishing Ltd., Stroud, Gloucestershire, England, 2001), p. 67.

[226] E. William Robertson, *Scotland Under Her Early Kings: A History of the Kingdom to the Close of the 13th Century, Part One* (Edinburgh: Edmonston and Douglas, 1862). p. 188.

[227] E. William Robertson, *Scotland Under Her Early Kings: A History of the Kingdom to the Close of the 13th Century, Part One* (Edinburgh: Edmonston and Douglas, 1862). p. 189.

[228] Richard Oram (Ed.), *The Kings and Queens of Scotland* (Tempus Publishing Ltd., Stroud, Gloucestershire, England, 2001), p. 67.

[229] James Grey, *Sutherland & Caithness in Saga-Time, or, The Jarls & The Freskyns* (Oliver & Boyd, Edinburgh, 1922), p. 35.

[230] Fitzroy Maclean, *A Concise History of Scotland* (First published 1970. This version, 2002. Thames & Hudson Ltd., London), p. 29.

[231] E. William Robertson, *Scotland Under Her Early Kings: A History of the Kingdom to the Close of the 13th Century, Part One* (Edinburgh: Edmonston and Douglas, 1862), p. 189-190.

[232] Richard Oram (Ed.), *The Kings and Queens of Scotland* (Tempus Publishing Ltd., Stroud, Gloucestershire, England, 2001), p. 67.

[233] E. William Robertson, *Scotland Under Her Early Kings: A History of the Kingdom to the Close of the 13th Century, Part One* (Edinburgh: Edmonston and Douglas, 1862), p. 189-190.

[234] E. William Robertson, *Scotland Under Her Early Kings: A History of the Kingdom to the Close of the 13th Century, Part One* (Edinburgh: Edmonston and Douglas, 1862). p. 190-191.

[235] John Cannon & Ralph Griffiths, *The Oxford Illustrated History of the British Monarchy* (2000 edition, Oxford University Press), p. 144.

[236] E. William Robertson, *Scotland Under Her Early Kings: A History of the Kingdom to the Close of the 13th Century, Part One* (Edinburgh: Edmonston and Douglas, 1862), p. 190-191.

[237] E. William Robertson, *Scotland Under Her Early Kings: A History of the Kingdom to the Close of the 13th Century, Part One* (Edinburgh: Edmonston and Douglas, 1862). p. 191-192.

[238] Caroline Bingham, *Kings and Queens of Scotland* (orig. published 1976, Taplinger Publishing Co. this edition, 1985, Dorset Press) p. 22.

[239] Elizabeth Hallam, ed, *The Plantagenet Chronicles: Medieval Europe's most tempestuous family from Henry II and his wife Eleanor of Aquitaine to Richard the Lionheart and his scheming brother John seen through the eyes of their contemporaries.* (Weidenfeld & Nicolson, New York: 1986 (copyright held by Pheobe Phillips Editions)), p. 65.

[240] E. William Robertson, *Scotland Under Her Early Kings: A History of the Kingdom to the Close of the 13th Century, Part One* (Edinburgh: Edmonston and Douglas, 1862). p. 193.

[241] E. William Robertson, *Scotland Under Her Early Kings: A History of the Kingdom to the Close of the 13th Century, Part One* (Edinburgh: Edmonston and Douglas, 1862), p. 192-193.

[242] Fitzroy Maclean, *A Concise History of Scotland* (First published 1970. This version, 2002. Thames & Hudson Ltd., London), p. 30.

[243] John Cannon & Ralph Griffiths, *The Oxford Illustrated History of the British Monarchy* (2000 edition, Oxford University Press), p. 144.

[244] Fitzroy Maclean, *A Concise History of Scotland* (First published 1970. This version, 2002. Thames & Hudson Ltd., London), p. 30.

[245] E. William Robertson, *Scotland Under Her Early Kings: A History of the Kingdom to the Close of the 13th Century, Part One* (Edinburgh: Edmonston and Douglas, 1862). p. 194-195.

[246] E. William Robertson, *Scotland Under Her Early Kings: A History of the Kingdom to the Close of the 13th Century, Part One* (Edinburgh: Edmonston and Douglas, 1862), p. 200.

[247] Elizabeth Hallam, ed, *The Plantagenet Chronicles: Medieval Europe's most tempestuous family from Henry II and his wife Eleanor of Aquitaine to Richard the Lionheart and his scheming brother John seen through the eyes of their contemporaries.* (Weidenfeld & Nicolson, New York: 1986 (copyright held by Pheobe Phillips Editions)), p. 71

[248] John Cannon & Ralph Griffiths, *The Oxford Illustrated History of the British Monarchy* (2000 edition, Oxford University Press), p. 144.

[249] Fitzroy Maclean, *A Concise History of Scotland* (First published 1970. This version, 2002. Thames & Hudson Ltd., London), p. 30.

[250] E. William Robertson, *Scotland Under Her Early Kings: A History of the Kingdom to the Close of the 13th Century, Part One* (Edinburgh: Edmonston and Douglas, 1862). p. 203-204.

[251] Caroline Bingham, *Kings and Queens of Scotland* (orig. published 1976, Taplinger Publishing Co. this edition, 1985, Dorset Press) p. 22.

[252] E. William Robertson, *Scotland Under Her Early Kings: A History of the Kingdom to the Close of the 13th Century, Part One* (Edinburgh: Edmonston and Douglas, 1862), 204-207.

[253] E. William Robertson, *Scotland Under Her Early Kings: A History of the Kingdom to the Close of the 13th Century, Part One* (Edinburgh: Edmonston and Douglas, 1862), 204-207.

[254] E. William Robertson, *Scotland Under Her Early Kings: A History of the Kingdom to the Close of the 13th Century, Part One* (Edinburgh: Edmonston and Douglas, 1862), p. 209-210.

[255] John Cannon & Ralph Griffiths, *The Oxford Illustrated History of the British Monarchy* (2000 edition, Oxford University Press), p. 144.

[256] Caroline Bingham, *Kings and Queens of Scotland* (orig. published 1976, Taplinger Publishing Co. this edition, 1985, Dorset Press) p. 23.

[257] E. William Robertson, *Scotland Under Her Early Kings: A History of the Kingdom to the Close of the 13th Century, Part One* (Edinburgh: Edmonston and Douglas, 1862), p. 213-214.

[258] E. William Robertson, *Scotland Under Her Early Kings: A History of the Kingdom to the Close of the 13th Century, Part One* (Edinburgh: Edmonston and Douglas, 1862), p. 214.

[259] E. William Robertson, *Scotland Under Her Early Kings: A History of the Kingdom to the Close of the 13th Century, Part One* (Edinburgh: Edmonston and Douglas, 1862), p. 214-215.

[260] E. William Robertson, *Scotland Under Her Early Kings: A History of the Kingdom to the Close of the 13th Century, Part One* (Edinburgh: Edmonston and Douglas, 1862), p. 215-216.

[261] E. William Robertson, *Scotland Under Her Early Kings: A History of the Kingdom to the Close of the 13th Century, Part One* (Edinburgh: Edmonston and Douglas, 1862), p. 218-219.

[262] Elizabeth Hallam, ed, *The Plantagenet Chronicles: Medieval Europe's most tempestuous family from Henry II and his wife Eleanor of Aquitaine to Richard the Lionheart and his scheming brother John seen through the eyes of their contemporaries.* (Weidenfeld & Nicolson, New York: 1986 (copyright held by Pheobe Phillips Editions)), p. 78.

[263] E. William Robertson, *Scotland Under Her Early Kings: A History of the Kingdom to the Close of the 13th Century, Part One* (Edinburgh: Edmonston and Douglas, 1862), p. 218-219.

[264] Elizabeth Hallam, ed, *The Plantagenet Chronicles: Medieval Europe's most tempestuous family from Henry II and his wife Eleanor of Aquitaine to Richard the Lionheart and his scheming brother John seen through the eyes of their contemporaries.* (Weidenfeld & Nicolson, New York: 1986 (copyright held by Pheobe Phillips Editions)), p. 78.

[265] E. William Robertson, *Scotland Under Her Early Kings: A History of the Kingdom to the Close of the 13th Century, Part One* (Edinburgh: Edmonston and Douglas, 1862). p. 223.

[266] John Cannon & Ralph Griffiths, *The Oxford Illustrated History of the British Monarchy* (2000 edition, Oxford University Press), Geneaolgies of Royal Lines Appendix.

[267] Caroline Bingham, *Kings and Queens of Scotland* (orig. published 1976, Taplinger Publishing Co. this edition, 1985, Dorset Press) p. 25.

[268] E. William Robertson, *Scotland Under Her Early Kings: A History of the Kingdom to the Close of the 13th Century, Part One* (Edinburgh: Edmonston and Douglas, 1862). p. 226.

[269] E. William Robertson, *Scotland Under Her Early Kings: A History of the Kingdom to the Close of the 13th Century, Part One* (Edinburgh: Edmonston and Douglas, 1862), p. 225-226.

[270] John Cannon & Ralph Griffiths, *The Oxford Illustrated History of the British Monarchy* (2000 edition, Oxford University Press), p. 144; Geneaolgies of Royal Lines Appendix; List of Monarchs Appendix.

[271] E. William Robertson, *Scotland Under Her Early Kings: A History of the Kingdom to the Close of the 13th Century, Part One* (Edinburgh: Edmonston and Douglas, 1862), p. 227.

[272] Fitzroy Maclean, *A Concise History of Scotland* (First published 1970. This version, 2002. Thames & Hudson Ltd., London), p. 30.

[273] Caroline Bingham, *Kings and Queens of Scotland* (orig. published 1976, Taplinger Publishing Co. this edition, 1985, Dorset Press) p. 24.

[274] E. William Robertson, *Scotland Under Her Early Kings: A History of the Kingdom to the Close of the 13th Century, Part One* (Edinburgh: Edmonston and Douglas, 1862). p. 232.

[275] Caroline Bingham, *Kings and Queens of Scotland* (orig. published 1976, Taplinger Publishing Co. this edition, 1985, Dorset Press) p. 24.

[276] E. William Robertson, *Scotland Under Her Early Kings: A History of the Kingdom to the Close of the 13th Century, Part One* (Edinburgh: Edmonston and Douglas, 1862). p. 297-311.

[277] E. William Robertson, *Scotland Under Her Early Kings: A History of the Kingdom to the Close of the 13th Century, Part One* (Edinburgh: Edmonston and Douglas, 1862). p. 230-231.

[278] E. William Robertson, *Scotland Under Her Early Kings: A History of the Kingdom to the Close of the 13th Century, Part One* (Edinburgh: Edmonston and Douglas, 1862). p. 284.

[279] E. William Robertson, *Scotland Under Her Early Kings: A History of the Kingdom to the Close of the 13th Century, Part One* (Edinburgh: Edmonston and Douglas, 1862). p. 282.

[280] E. William Robertson, *Scotland Under Her Early Kings: A History of the Kingdom to the Close of the 13th Century, Part One* (Edinburgh: Edmonston and Douglas, 1862). p. 317-318.

[281] Caroline Bingham, *Kings and Queens of Scotland* (orig. published 1976, Taplinger Publishing Co. this edition, 1985, Dorset Press) p. 24.

[282] E. William Robertson, *Scotland Under Her Early Kings: A History of the Kingdom to the Close of the 13th Century, Part One* (Edinburgh: Edmonston and Douglas, 1862). p. 334-335.

[283] E. William Robertson, *Scotland Under Her Early Kings: A History of the Kingdom to the Close of the 13th Century, Part One* (Edinburgh: Edmonston and Douglas, 1862). p. 225, 345.

[284] Caroline Bingham, *Kings and Queens of Scotland* (orig. published 1976, Taplinger Publishing Co. this edition, 1985, Dorset Press) p. 26.

[285] E. William Robertson, *Scotland Under Her Early Kings: A History of the Kingdom to the Close of the 13th Century, Part One* (Edinburgh: Edmonston and Douglas, 1862). p. 345, 350.

[286] Ronald Williams, *The Lords of the Isles: The Clan Donald and the Early Kingdom of the Scots* (Chatto & Windus - The Hogarth Press, London, 1984) p. 121.

[287] Angus MacKay, *The Book of MacKay* (Edinburgh: Norman MacLeod, 1906), p. 26, 27.

[288] E. William Robertson, *Scotland Under Her Early Kings: A History of the Kingdom to the Close of the 13th Century, Part One* (Edinburgh: Edmonston and Douglas, 1862). p. 350-351.

[289] Caroline Bingham, *Kings and Queens of Scotland* (orig. published 1976, Taplinger Publishing Co. this edition, 1985, Dorset Press) p. 26.

[290] E. William Robertson, *Scotland Under Her Early Kings: A History of the Kingdom to the Close of the 13th Century, Part One* (Edinburgh: Edmonston and Douglas, 1862). p. 360-361.

[291] E. William Robertson, *Scotland Under Her Early Kings: A History of the Kingdom to the Close of the 13th Century, Part One* (Edinburgh: Edmonston and Douglas, 1862). p. 353.

[292] Caroline Bingham, *Kings and Queens of Scotland* (orig. published 1976, Taplinger Publishing Co. this edition, 1985, Dorset Press) p. 26.

[293] E. William Robertson, *Scotland Under Her Early Kings: A History of the Kingdom to the Close of the 13th Century, Part One* (Edinburgh: Edmonston and Douglas, 1862). p. 359.

[294] E. William Robertson, *Scotland Under Her Early Kings: A History of the Kingdom to the Close of the 13th Century, Part One* (Edinburgh: Edmonston and Douglas, 1862), p. 364.

[295] Caroline Bingham, *Kings and Queens of Scotland* (orig. published 1976, Taplinger Publishing Co. this edition, 1985, Dorset Press) p. 27.

[296] E. William Robertson, *Scotland Under Her Early Kings: A History of the Kingdom to the Close of the 13th Century, Part One* (Edinburgh: Edmonston and Douglas, 1862), p. 369, 371-372.

[297] E. William Robertson, *Scotland Under Her Early Kings: A History of the Kingdom to the Close of the 13th Century, Part One* (Edinburgh: Edmonston and Douglas, 1862), p. 372-373.

[298] E. William Robertson, *Scotland Under Her Early Kings: A History of the Kingdom to the Close of the 13th Century, Part One* (Edinburgh: Edmonston and Douglas, 1862), p. 375.

[299] E. William Robertson, *Scotland Under Her Early Kings: A History of the Kingdom to the Close of the 13th Century, Part One* (Edinburgh: Edmonston and Douglas, 1862), p. 385.

[300] E. William Robertson, *Scotland Under Her Early Kings: A History of the Kingdom to the Close of the 13th Century, Part One* (Edinburgh: Edmonston and Douglas, 1862), p. 386.

[301] E. William Robertson, *Scotland Under Her Early Kings: A History of the Kingdom to the Close of the 13th Century, Part One* (Edinburgh: Edmonston and Douglas, 1862), p. 389.

[302] Caroline Bingham, *Kings and Queens of Scotland* (orig. published 1976, Taplinger Publishing Co. this edition, 1985, Dorset Press) p. 28.

[303] E. William Robertson, *Scotland Under Her Early Kings: A History of the Kingdom to the Close of the 13th Century, Part One* (Edinburgh: Edmonston and Douglas, 1862), p. 396.

[304] E. William Robertson, *Scotland Under Her Early Kings: A History of the Kingdom to the Close of the 13th Century, Part One* (Edinburgh: Edmonston and Douglas, 1862), p. 397.

[305] E. William Robertson, *Scotland Under Her Early Kings: A History of the Kingdom to the Close of the 13th Century, Part One* (Edinburgh: Edmonston and Douglas, 1862), p. 414.

[306] Caroline Bingham, *Kings and Queens of Scotland* (orig. published 1976, Taplinger Publishing Co. this edition, 1985, Dorset Press) p. 28.

[307] E. William Robertson, *Scotland Under Her Early Kings: A History of the Kingdom to the Close of the 13th Century, Part One* (Edinburgh: Edmonston and Douglas, 1862), p. 423-425.

[308] E. William Robertson, *Scotland Under Her Early Kings: A History of the Kingdom to the Close of the 13th Century, Part One* (Edinburgh: Edmonston and Douglas, 1862), p. 425.

[309] Caroline Bingham, *Kings and Queens of Scotland* (orig. published 1976, Taplinger Publishing Co. this edition, 1985, Dorset Press) p. 28.

[310] E. William Robertson, *Scotland Under Her Early Kings: A History of the Kingdom to the Close of the 13th Century, Part One* (Edinburgh: Edmonston and Douglas, 1862), p. 425-429.

[311] E. William Robertson, *Scotland Under Her Early Kings: A History of the Kingdom to the Close of the 13th Century, Part One* (Edinburgh: Edmonston and Douglas, 1862), p. 430.

[312] E. William Robertson, *Scotland Under Her Early Kings: A History of the Kingdom to the Close of the 13th Century, Part One* (Edinburgh: Edmonston and Douglas, 1862), p. 433.

[313] E. William Robertson, *Scotland Under Her Early Kings: A History of the Kingdom to the Close of the Thirteenth Century, Part Two* (Edinburgh: Edmonston and Douglas, 1862), p. 1.

[314] E. William Robertson, *Scotland Under Her Early Kings: A History of the Kingdom to the Close of the Thirteenth Century, Part Two* (Edinburgh: Edmonston and Douglas, 1862), p. 3-4.

[315] John Cannon & Ralph Griffiths, *The Oxford Illustrated History of the British Monarchy* (2000 edition, Oxford University Press), Geneaolgies of Royal Lines Appendix.

[316] E. William Robertson, *Scotland Under Her Early Kings: A History of the Kingdom to the Close of the Thirteenth Century, Part Two* (Edinburgh: Edmonston and Douglas, 1862), p. 9.

[317] E. William Robertson, *Scotland Under Her Early Kings: A History of the Kingdom to the Close of the Thirteenth Century, Part Two* (Edinburgh: Edmonston and Douglas, 1862), p. 9.

[318] E. William Robertson, *Scotland Under Her Early Kings: A History of the Kingdom to the Close of the Thirteenth Century, Part Two* (Edinburgh: Edmonston and Douglas, 1862), p. 9-10.

[319] Ruth M. Blakely, *The Brus Family in England and Scotland, 1100-1295* (Boydell Press, Woodbridge, 2005), p. 73.

THE BRUCE & STEWART DYNASTY

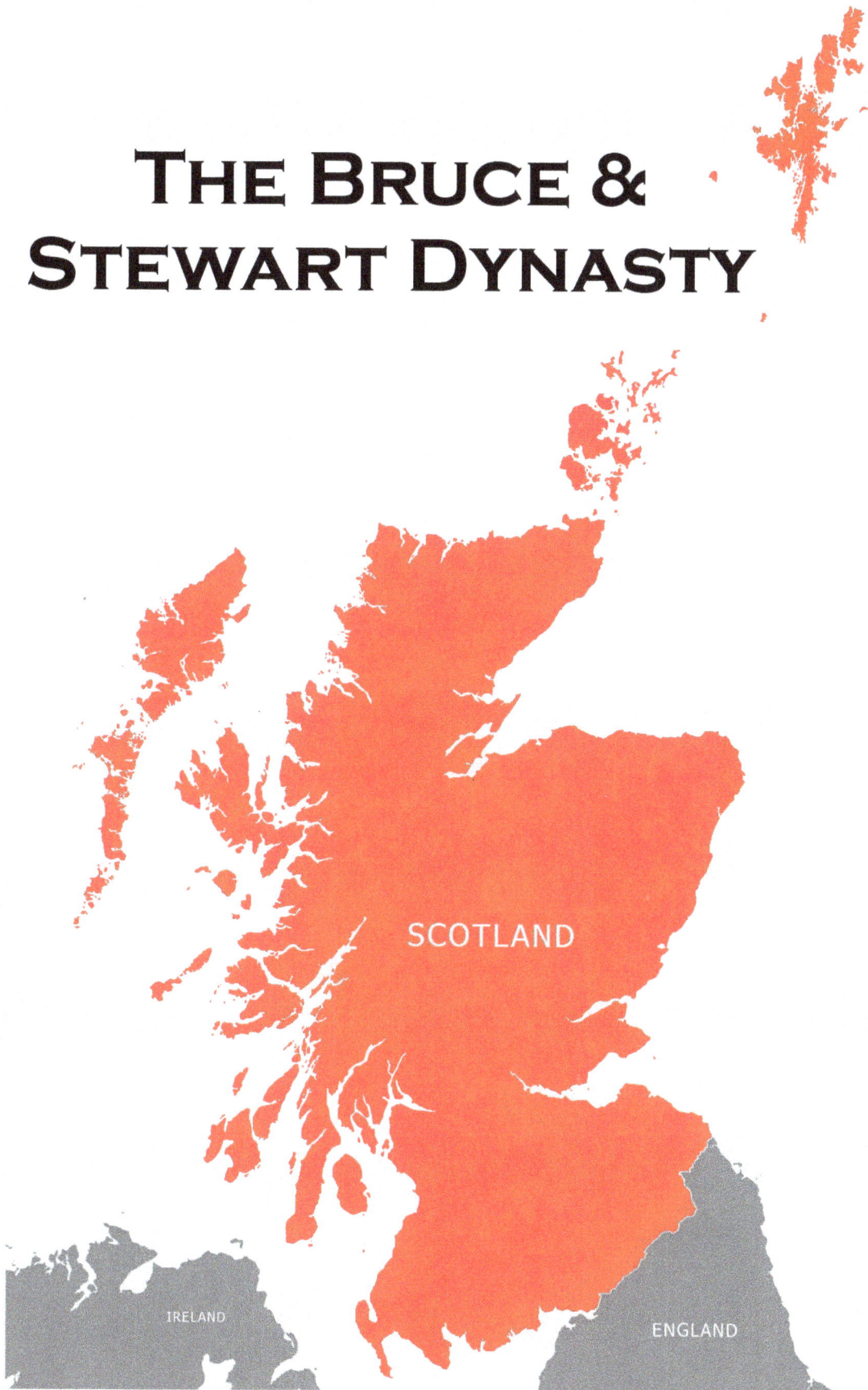

SCOTLAND

IRELAND

ENGLAND

THE STEWART DYNASTY

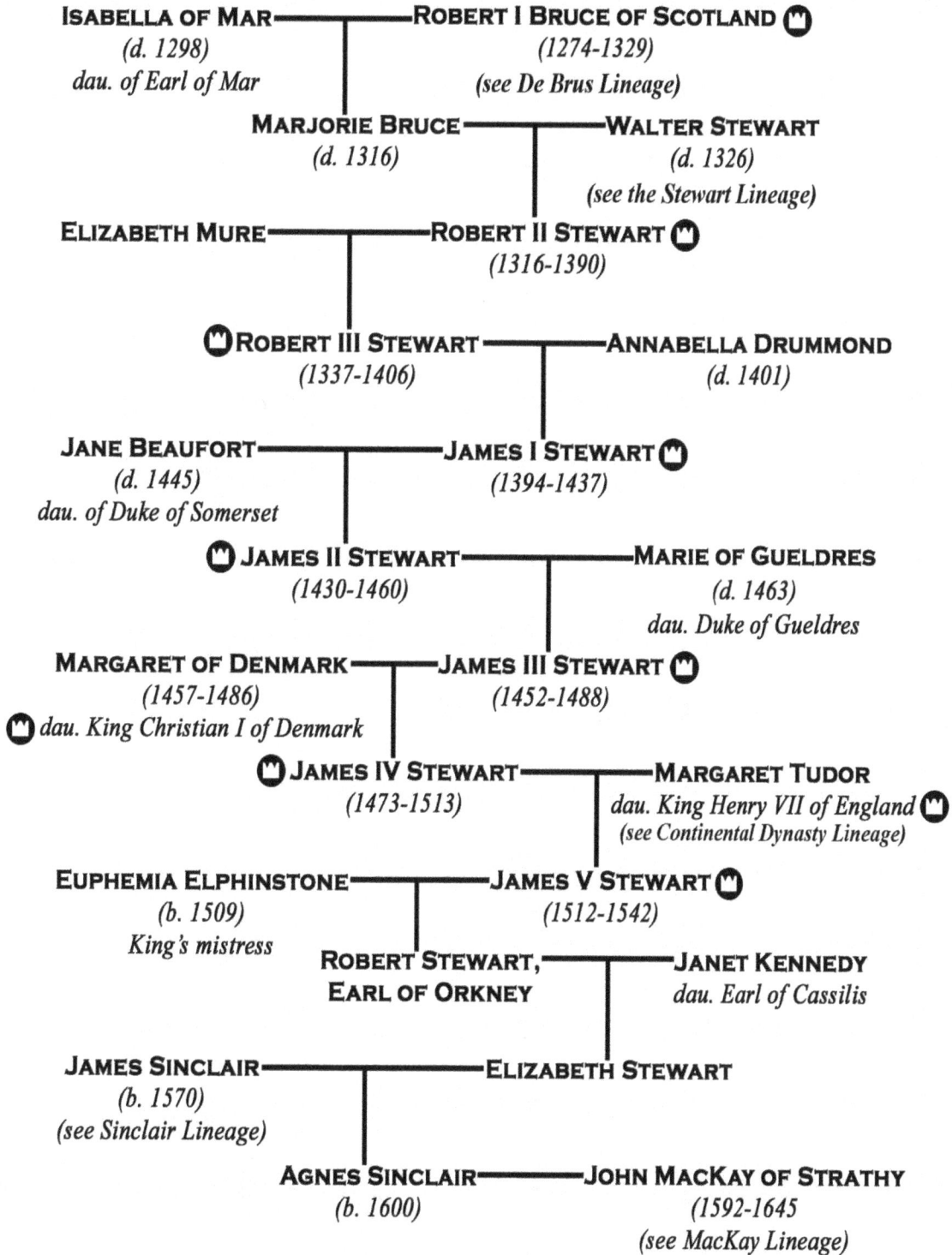

ISABELLA OF MAR —————— ROBERT I BRUCE OF SCOTLAND ♔
(d. 1298) *(1274-1329)*
dau. of Earl of Mar *(see De Brus Lineage)*

MARJORIE BRUCE —————— WALTER STEWART
(d. 1316) *(d. 1326)*
(see the Stewart Lineage)

ELIZABETH MURE —————— ROBERT II STEWART ♔
(1316-1390)

♔ ROBERT III STEWART —————— ANNABELLA DRUMMOND
(1337-1406) *(d. 1401)*

JANE BEAUFORT —————— JAMES I STEWART ♔
(d. 1445) *(1394-1437)*
dau. of Duke of Somerset

♔ JAMES II STEWART —————— MARIE OF GUELDRES
(1430-1460) *(d. 1463)*
dau. Duke of Gueldres

MARGARET OF DENMARK —————— JAMES III STEWART ♔
(1457-1486) *(1452-1488)*
♔ *dau. King Christian I of Denmark*

♔ JAMES IV STEWART —————— MARGARET TUDOR
(1473-1513) *dau. King Henry VII of England* ♔
(see Continental Dynasty Lineage)

EUPHEMIA ELPHINSTONE —————— JAMES V STEWART ♔
(b. 1509) *(1512-1542)*
King's mistress

ROBERT STEWART, —————— JANET KENNEDY
EARL OF ORKNEY *dau. Earl of Cassilis*

JAMES SINCLAIR —————— ELIZABETH STEWART
(b. 1570)
(see Sinclair Lineage)

AGNES SINCLAIR —————— JOHN MACKAY OF STRATHY
(b. 1600) *(1592-1645*
(see MacKay Lineage)

THE BRUCE AND STEWART DYNASTY

Although this is the Bruce and Stewart Royal Lineage chapter, it is necessary to fill in the blanks prior to getting to King Robert I Bruce. Also, although Stewart is often spelled Stuart, I am using the original spelling, since the change in spelling happened after James VI became James I of England.

We left off with our Scottish royalty (see *MacAlpin Dynasty*) when David, Earl of Huntingdon, died in 1219. His daughter Isabella had married Robert (IV) de Brus, King Robert I's great-grandfather. But there are 85 years between David of Huntingdon's death and King Robert's coronation, and much happened in Scotland between those times.

When David of Huntingdon died, his nephew King **Alexander II** was on the throne. Alexander put down insurrections in Galloway, Argyll, Moray, and Caithness during his reign. He also decided that the Hebrides Islands should belong to Scotland, not Norway, and massed an invasion. However, he died as the invasion was beginning, in 1249.[1] [2]

His son **Alexander III** took the throne and continued his father's raid against the Hebrides. In 1263, King Hakon of Norway returned the raid, skirmishing with Scotland. However, King Hakon was defeated at Largs in Ayrshire, and died on his way home. His successor, King Magnus, ceded the Hebrides Islands to Scotland in 1266, thus ending the Norwegian claim to them.[3] The Lords of the Islands (see *MacDonald Lineage*) ignored the Scottish monarch just as they had the Norwegian monarchs. Alexander's reign was peaceful and prosperous. He married the daughter of King Henry III of England, Margaret, in 1251, thus ensuring peace.[4] Alexander III died in 1286, with no direct heir to the throne—both his son and daughter had predeceased him. His only heir was his granddaughter, 3-year-old **Margaret of Norway**, daughter of King Eric of Norway and Alexander's daughter, Margaret. The then seven-year-old queen drowned off of Orkney on her way to Scotland. Her death ended the House of Dunkeld.[5]

This was the beginning of what is known in Scotland as The Great Cause.

After Queen Margaret, the Maid of Norway, died in 1290, thirteen people wanted the throne, but only two had a solid claim. John de Balliol was a third great-grandson of King David I of Scotland through his mother. Robert (V) de Brus (grandfather of Robert I) (see *De Brus Lineage*) was a second great-grandson of David. John was senior in primogeniture, but not in proximity of blood. Also, Robert had been named Alexander III's heir by the king while he was alive.[6] Both made their claim through the daughters of David of Huntingdon: John through Margaret, who married Alan of Galloway, and Robert through Isabella, who married Robert (IV) de Brus.[7] [8] [9]

John submitted the claim to Scottish auditors, with England's Edward I (see *Continental Dynasty*) as chief auditor, in an election at Berwick 6 June 1291. A decision was reached 17 November 1292 in favor of John. He was crowned 30 November 1292 at Scone. Prior to agreeing to arbitrate, Edward I insisted that all claimants recognize him as Lord Paramount of the realm, essentially their feudal overlord. They did.[10] [11]

Edward I treated King John as a feudal vassal, and John let him, and the Scots disliked it. The Scottish nobles took control of the government from King John at Stirling in July 1295, appointing a council of Guardians. This council concluded a treaty with France, which became known as the Auld Alliance.[12]

This led to the First Scottish War of Independence, because King Edward I of England was not happy with an alliance between England's two traditional enemies.

Edward I invaded Scotland, defeating the Scots at Dunbar 27 April 1296. King John was forced to abdicate 10 July 1296. As he left the country, Edward found the crown of Scotland in John's baggage, along with the Great Seal of Scotland, and a large sum of money. Edward ordered the crown given up to St. Thomas the Martyr. John kept the money, and Edward kept the Seal. On his way out of Scotland, Edward also took the Stone of Scone, making John the last Scottish King to be crowned upon it.[13] [14]

John lived the rest of his life under house arrest either in the Vatican or his estates in Picardy. He made no move to support his Scottish followers after 1302 and died in 1313.[15]

In Scotland, his supporters claimed he had abdicated under duress, and was still the rightful king. They rebelled against England in 1297 under William Wallace and Andrew de Moray, claiming to be acting on King John's behalf.[16]

King Robert I the Bruce
(1274-1329)
(reigned 1306-1329)

Before joining King Robert I, you may want to read his heritage, under the *De Brus Lineage* chapter.

Robert I Bruce was born 24 March 1274 at Turnberry Castle in Carrick in Ayrshire, Scotland.[17] [18] He was most likely fostered in the Western Isles, or Ulster, Ireland.[19] He had brothers Edward, Neil, Thomas, and Alexander, and a sister, Isabel. Robert probably took part in his grandfather's attacks on Comyn and Balliol interests in 1286-87. He also was probably present at Berwick for the debate over the Great Cause, which his grandfather lost to John Balliol. After the loss, Robert's grandfather resigned his Lordship of Annandale to Robert's father, and Robert's father gave Carrick to Robert as his own in 1292.[20] [21] Robert's grandfather died in 1295.[22] [23]

Robert probably traveled to Norway in 1292-93, to see his sister, Isabel, marry King Eric II of Norway—the same Eric who had been married to Margaret of Scotland, and the father of the Maid of Norway, young Queen Margaret.[24]

Robert was not always a staunch supporter of the Scottish monarchy. When King John Balliol was crowned at the expense of Robert's grandfather, he was not happy.[25]

When King John created the Auld Alliance with France, France asked Scotland to invade England, which King John did. However, King Edward I of England (see *Continental Dynasty*) invaded Scotland in return, only to be met by vassals paying him homage—including Robert Bruce. King John punished him for this by seizing all of Robert's Scottish lands and giving them to John's brother-in-law.[26]

During the First War for Scottish Independence, Robert fought on the English side, as did many other Scottish nobles.[27] While the English slaughtered the Scottish forces at Dunbar in 1296, Robert and the others supported England. Remember that many Anglo-Norman nobles held land in both England and Scotland, so their loyalties were divided.[28]

King John and his son Edward Balliol were captured at Dunbar, and King John abdicated, as seen above. King Edward I continued ravaging Scotland, capturing most of the main cities. In Berwick in August of 1296, two thousand Scottish nobles met with King Edward and recognized him as King of Scotland.[29] This was when King Edward took the Stone of Scone to England with him. He left behind English soldiers and English administrators.[30]

A year later, William Wallace rose against the English, and Robert Bruce supported him. No doubt, with King John Balliol out of the way, Robert saw his chance to forward his claim to the throne.[31] His attempt did not end well, as he surrendered to the English at Irvine in Ayrshire in July of 1297.[32] Robert may have been with Edward's army at the defeat of Wallace's Scots at Falkirk in July 1298, although researcher A.F. Murison says definitively he was not.[33] However, Edward turned on Robert and drove him back to the Scottish fold. [34]

In 1298, when William Wallace stepped down as Guardian of Scotland, Robert and his cousin John Comyn became joint Guardians.[35][36][37] But Comyn was a Balliol by blood, and thus an enemy of Robert, so that partnership fell apart in 1299.[38]

During the next six years, King Edward I (see *Continental Dynasty*) repeatedly invaded Scotland, and Robert swayed with the wind—sometimes supporting England, sometimes Scotland. In 1302, Robert reconciled with Edward I. In 1303-4 he fought on the English side, and even helped capture William Wallace. In April 1304, Robert's father died, and Robert inherited all the family lands in England and Scotland. His Scottish patriotism raised its head again as he stalled in giving King Edward siege engines for destroying Stirling Castle.[39] In 1304, Robert was the sheriff of Ayr and Lanark in Scotland, and an advisor at Westminster in England for the Scottish administration.[40][41][42]

All of Robert's vacillations did little to further his quest for the throne, as many people mistrusted him. His main rival to the throne, John Comyn, was seen as much more patriotic, and Robert decided he had to neutralize the threat.

In 1306, Robert lured John Comyn to Greyfriars' Church in Dumfries and murdered him on the altar. Another school of thought claims he met with Comyn simply to talk out their differences, and then killed him in a fit of rage.[43][44][45][46]

Whichever the truth, Comyn died, killed in a church. For this, Robert and the entire country of Scotland were excommunicated.[47] Robert realized that he now had no choice—he could either be a fugitive or the king. So he and his followers went to Scone and he was crowned king—first on 25 March 1306, then again on 27 March 1306, when Isabel, Countess of Buchan, arrived to officiate the coronation properly. However, he was a king without a kingdom, and he needed to fight England for one. [48][49][50]

Robert lost his first battle on 19 June 1306, at Methven, near Perth, and went into hiding.[51][52] He paid dearly for his new kingship; his lands were taken by King Edward I, (see *Continental Dynasty*) his brother Neil was killed, and his wife and daughter were imprisoned by Edward until 1314.[53] In raids in 1307, his brothers Thomas and Alexander were killed.[54][55]

In February of 1307, Robert made his way back into Scotland from his hideout in either the Western Isles or off the coast of Ulster, assisted by Angus Óg MacDonald (see *MacDonald Lineage*).[56][57] He came in through his own lands of Carrick, and started waging guerilla warfare on Edward.[58] In April he won at Glen Trool,[59] and in May he had a victory over the English at Loudoun Hill.[60][61][62][63] On 7 July 1307, King

Edward I died of dysentery at Burgh-by-Sands at the head of an army invading Scotland.[64] His successor, Edward II (see *Continental Dynasty*), abandoned Scotland.[65] Robert eventually secured most of Scotland north of the Forth and Clyde. A Parliament at St. Andrews on 16 March 1309 declared him the rightful heir of Alexander III, thus disinheriting the Balliol claim by saying the crown had been wrongfully given to John Balliol by Edward I.[66 67 68 69]

Robert was not just fighting Edward's English army—he was also fighting the Balliol/Comyn faction within Scotland. He was, in essence, fighting a civil war within an international one. After Edward I's death, Robert left his brother Edward in charge of the fighting in southwest Scotland, while he turned his attention to the north, to take on the Balliol/Comyn Scots. Robert never wasted troops occupying the strongholds he captured—he simply razed them to the ground and moved on.[70 71] He crushed Comyn resistance and took Aberdeen in August. In 1308 he defeated the MacDougalls on the west coast, then returned to the main war with England, clearing the many garrisons in southern Scotland of both English and Scottish enemies.[72 73] In 1313, Robert set a 12-month deadline for all his Scottish opponents to submit to him or face the consequences. By 1314, only Stirling Castle and the border strongholds remained in enemy hands.[74 75]

Edward II of England tried to relieve the troops holed up in Stirling Castle, and Robert crushed him in the Battle of Bannockburn in 23-24 June 1314. Although the Scots were badly outnumbered, the field at Bannockburn helped them. The field was marshy, accessible only by a narrow causeway. The Scots dug pits in the marsh in front of their lines, then hid them under brush.[76 77]

On the 23rd, Robert had a one-on-one duel with Henry de Bohun, and routed the small contingent he had led in. Robert proved to his own men that they could win even though the Scots were lightly armed and unmounted.[78]

On the 24th, the 25,000-man English army, compressed by the narrow causeway and their mounted soldiers unhorsed by the pits in the marsh, was destroyed by the mostly Celtic Scottish army.[79 80]

Robert used this victory to recover his wife and daughters from captivity, and ordered all of his Scottish opponents' lands forfeit to the Crown. He continued to raid in northern England, as there was no formal peace treaty between Edward II and himself, since the English still did not recognize him as the rightful king of Scotland.[81 82]

After Bannockburn, Robert decided he should be king of Ireland, too, so he sent his brother and heir, Edward, to conquer it in 1315. Edward had initial success in Ulster, but then got bogged down. Edward was killed at Dundalk in October 1318, ending Robert's Irish ambitions, and leaving Robert with no adult heir. His only heir was 2-year-old grandson Robert Stewart, son of Walter Stewart and Marjorie Bruce (see *Stewart Lineage*).[83]

In 1320, the Scottish nobility signed the Declaration of Arboath, often called the Scottish declaration of independence, which they sent to Pope John XXII, and asked for the church's recognition of their king.[84]

In 1323, there was finally an uneasy peace with Edward II of England (see *Continental Dynasty*).[85] On 5 March 1324, Robert's wife, Elizabeth, gave birth to twins—John and David. John, the elder, died, but David survived, thus giving Robert a direct heir to the throne.[86]

In 1326, Robert renewed a mutual defense alliance with France. In 1327, King Edward II was murdered by his wife. She, in the name of young King Edward III (see *Continental Dynasty*), sent an army against Robert, who promptly crushed it.[87] This was the final gasp of the First War of Scottish Independence.

The First War of Scottish Independence was ended in 1328 by the Treaty of Northampton, in which King Edward III of England formally acknowledged Scotland's independence and the legitimacy of the Bruce monarchy.[88][89][90] Also, Robert's young son David was married to King Edward III's sister. It was also during 1328 that Pope John XXII lifted the excommunication of Robert.[91][92] One other thing Robert had won from the Pope was the right to anoint the Scottish kings, thus making them equal in spiritual power to the English kings, who were always anointed. Robert's son David was the first of the anointed kings of Scotland.[93]

Robert Bruce married twice:[94]

First to Isobel of Mar, daughter of Donald, Earl of Mar, (d. c. 1298), with whom he had daughter:
- *Marjorie* – married Walter Stewart, 6th High Steward of Scotland [95][96]

Second to Elizabeth de Burgh, daughter of Richard, Earl of Ulster, who bore him:[97]
- Matilda[98]
- Margaret[99]
- John – died soon after birth, elder twin of David
- David (b. 5 March 1324) – the younger twin, succeeded his father[100][101][102]

On 7 June 1329, just as things seem settled, King Robert I Bruce died of a wasting disease at Cardross, leaving his five-year-old son as his heir.[103][104] Most of Robert was buried at Dunfermline Abbey, next to his second wife, although his organs were interred at St. Serf's Chapel near Dumbarton. His heart, however, was carried by Sir James Douglas on Crusade (as requested by Robert). Douglas was killed, but Robert's heart was returned and interred in Melrose Abbey on the Scottish-English border.[105][106][107][108]

Our line does not go through David, but through Robert's daughter by his first wife. Her name was *Marjorie*, and she married Walter Stewart, 6th High Steward of Scotland.[109][110][111] Their son, **Robert Stewart**, became King Robert II, the first Stewart on the throne.

King Robert II Stewart
(1316-1390)
(reigned 1329-1390)

If you haven't already, you may wish to read the pre-royal Stewart history in the *Stewart Lineage* chapter.

Robert II Stewart was born 2 March 1316, by Caesarian section after his mother, Marjorie, was killed by falling from a horse.[112] That is the popular story, but other sources say he was born in a more conventional manner, and his mother died in 1317.[113][114][115] He grew up on the Stewart family lands in Renfrew, Clydesdale, and the Gaelic-speaking Isle of Bute. [116] As with the Bruce Lords of Annandale, the office of High Steward was given to the FitzAlan family by King David I of Scotland, eventually supplanting the FitzAlan surname.

While infant Robert was heir to King Robert I Bruce in 1318-24,[117] and second in line behind David Bruce from 1326 on,[118] Robert Stewart was given new estates in Knapdale (Argyll), the Lothians, and Roxburghshire. His father Walter Stewart, 6th High Steward of Scotland, died 9 April 1327, and Robert became the 7th High Steward of Scotland at age 11.[119] [120]

But before we get to Robert as an adult, we have some history to cover. After King Robert the Bruce won the Battle of Bannockburn, he disinherited many of the Scottish nobles who had sided with Balliol (and therefore, the English), including our Malise III, Earl of Strathearn (see *Norwegian Lineage*).[121] Another disinherited earl, Henry Beaumont, Earl of Buchan, continually schemed to get his land back, with the backing of his other disinherited colleagues. They did this by cultivating relationships with England. When Robert I Bruce died in 1329 and Edward III of England (who was against the Treaty of Northampton that had conceded Scotland's independence) ended his minority, the time to act was upon them.

There was another claimant to the Scottish throne. Edward Balliol, son of deposed King John Balliol, still lived, and wanted the throne. He had many ties with the English court, and dispossessed Earl Henry Beaumont and his allies had fled to England for support, which King Edward III gave willingly. Henry Beaumont brought Edward Balliol back from the Continent, and with the unofficial support of Edward III, they took an English army to invade Scotland in summer 1332. Balliol had already sworn feudal allegiance to Edward III, meaning that if he won, Scotland would no longer be an independent nation.[122]
In 1331, after King Robert I Bruce's death, his eight-year-old son David was crowned **King David II Bruce**. Obviously, he was ill-equipped to deal with the stresses of war and revolt, so the country was in essence being run by his nephew, then 15-year-old Robert Stewart.[123] When Edward Balliol's army invaded, 10-year-old David and his wife, Joan, were sent to France for safety.[124] [125]

Balliol and his army won a decisive victory at Battle of Dupplin Moor,[126] and he was crowned at Scone 24 September 1332 by William Sinclair, Bishop of Dunkeld. His reign was not secure, and he traveled toward England to make further arrangements for his security with Edward III. He took refuge in Roxburgh Castle in November 1332, shadowed by troops of David II Bruce (under Robert Stewart's leadership).

While at Roxburgh, Edward Balliol wrote to Edward III (see *Continental Dynasty*), openly recognizing him as feudal overlord, and making major territorial concessions, making Balliol the subordinate client king of a dismembered Scotland.

In December 1332, Balliol's army was defeated by the Scots army in the Battle of Annan. Balliol barely escaped, and received the open help of Edward III, in violation of the Treaty of Northampton.

This began the Second War of Scottish Independence.

A re-armed Balliol entered Scotland at Berwick and defeated the Scots at the Battle of Halidon Hill 19 July 1333, where 17-year-old Robert Stewart led a division of the army.[127] The Battle at Halidon Hill left a great many of Scotland's leaders dead, and consequently political turmoil followed. This could explain why Robert was made a co-Regent of Scotland when he was not yet 18 years old.[128]

Balliol never really gained realm-wide authority, and after he ceded the promised territories of Scotland to Edward III in 1334, his popularity fell even further. During this time, Robert barely escaped by boat when his lands were overrun by Anglo-Balliol forces led by the Earl of Atholl.[129] He took refuge with Malcolm Fleming in Dumbarton. He crossed to Bute, where the men rose to support him. Robert allied with his cousins, the Campbells. They landed on the mainland in Argyll, and recovered the Renfrew, Cunningham, and Carrick castles.[130] Robert also recovered his lands in Clydesdale and southwest Scotland.[131] [132] As pro-Bruce forces grew stronger, Balliol's government fell apart, and in July 1334, he fled once more to England.

Although Edward III made several attempts to invade Scotland and secure his primacy (and Balliol's regency), they all failed, and by 1338, Balliol ruled Perth and little else. Most of his meager Scottish supporters had fallen away. In 1338 Balliol left Perth, never to return.

With help from France and other Scots, Robert took Perth in August 1339, [133] and took Stirling thereafter. By April 1341, he had recovered Edinburgh Castle, and all the territory north of that point.[134] [135]

King David II Bruce, about 18 years old, returned from France to take the throne in 1341.[136] Robert and David entered into a lifelong power struggle. Robert was older and always at court, and David could not simply remove him because Robert was his heir. Although David imprisoned Robert and his son in 1368 for a while, he was helpless to get rid of him completely. Robert used his influence to sabotage and limit David's power. He was able to do this because Robert's growing family owned a great deal of land, and he had numerous heirs.[137]

In 1346, David II invaded England in support of French King Philip (as part of the Hundred Years' War and the Auld Alliance). The Battle of Neville's Cross was a rout of the Scottish forces. Robert rallied those he could and retreated—a "desertion" that David never forgave.[138] [139] David was captured by the English at Neville's Cross. David remained a prisoner in England for 12 years.[140] During this time, Robert Stewart again took the regency and governed Scotland, possibly even purposely delaying David's release.[141]

Instead of using this capture to re-install Edward Balliol, Edward III (see *Continental Dynasty*) admitted to himself that Balliol would never be accepted by the Scots, and so realized David was the better asset. He grudgingly recognized the legitimacy of the Bruce dynasty.[142] [143]

By 1355, Scottish armies under the guidance of Robert Stewart had pushed the English and the Balliol supporters back from the borders and most of Galloway. Edward Balliol had had enough, especially since he had no heirs.[144]

On 20 January 1356, Balliol abdicated, making Edward III his heir to the Scottish throne. Edward III gained nothing by this since Balliol had no throne to give, but Balliol lived in Yorkshire on an annual pension from Edward III until his death in January 1364.[145]

The Second War of Scottish Independence officially ended in 1357, with the signing of the Treaty of Berwick. Under the terms of this treaty, David II was ransomed back to Scotland. He returned grudgingly to Scotland. He never really liked Scotland, having lived most of his life in the more lavish courts of France and England. Moreover, his ransom was a devastatingly high amount.[146] [147] David raised taxes heavily, which angered the people, and then began embezzling from his own ransom fund.

Furthermore, the childless David married Margaret Drummond, who was older and a widow. Robert had been formally named David's heir in May 1363. David's marriage completely enraged Robert and the other nobles, and David, under guise of his honeymoon, fled to England for some peace.[148] [149]

While there, David and Edward III ratified the Treaty of Westminster on 26 November 1363. This treaty stated that Edward would recognize David's kingship and remit the unpaid part of David's ransom, and

David agreed to name Edward's son Lionel, Duke of Clarence, as his heir. Since Lionel was not Edward's successor, this would enable Scotland to (nominally) remain a separate kingdom.[150] [151]

In 1369, David imprisoned Robert and his sons, at Queen Margaret's instigation, which nearly caused a civil war. John of the Isles, Archibald Campbell, and John of Lorne engaged in a pact threatening armed intervention if the Stewarts were not released. David annulled his marriage to Margaret and released and reconciled with Robert.[152]

On 22 February 1371, King David II Bruce died. The Scottish Parliament rejected Edward's son as heir, and crowned Robert Stewart as King Robert II Stewart. This ended the House of Bruce and began the House of Stewart. He was crowned at Scone on 26 March 1371,[153] [154] [155] but not without some controversy. William, Earl of Douglas, challenged him to a duel before Robert was confirmed at Scone, but Robert managed to buy his way out.[156]

Robert did not have a good reign as king, in spite of being such a brilliant High Steward. David's ransom had strangled the economy. Lawlessness prevailed, and the nobles brawled among themselves.

He began his rule well. By 1382, he had sidelined many of David's supporters, and gained control of most earldoms, many lordships, and key royal castles and offices. He also secured the succession through two Parliamentary Acts. The Acts of Succession in 1371 and 1373 designated that there be male heirs only— and that his first son, John, was to be the first heir—so there would be no queens who could marry and create a conflict about the succession with her husband's family.[157] [158]

Robert was a passive king, who preferred to spend his time in his own estates, rather than engaging in circuits of the country to enforce his laws and garner loyalty among the people. Part of this "lack of energy" as king could have been due to his severe ophthalmia (inflammation of the eyes), which handicapped him, because he was by all accounts an upright, intelligent, generous, tenderhearted, and courteous man.[159] This loose, decentralized type of kingship did not serve him well in crisis situations. His downfall would be his own sons.[160]

His son Alexander held Caithness and northern lands, and he was exploiting the north for his own gain and contributing to the lawlessness there, instead of helping to curb it. When Robert couldn't punish or control Alexander, Robert's eldest son, John, Earl of Carrick, staged a bloodless coup of his father at Holyrood in November of 1384. John had himself declared Lieutenant because of his father's incompetence.[161]

John decided to go to war with England. The Catholic Church was in schism at the time, with two popes; Robert and Scotland backed the French Pope, and England backed the Roman Pope. John attempted to invade England with a Scottish-French army, but failed. The nobles began criticizing his administration, and he, like Robert, was unable to control his brother, Alexander.[162]

John's strong ally, the Earl of Douglas, was killed in the battle of Otterburn in Northumberland, and John's brother Robert, Earl of Fife, saw his chance. He overthrew John in a coup on 1 December 1388. He proved no better at the job than John. He and Alexander engaged in a civil war in the north.[163]

With first wife Elizabeth Mure, daughter of Sir Adam Mure of Rowallan, Robert had:[164] [165] [166] [167]

- ***John (renamed Robert)*** – succeeded as king

- Walter – Earl of Fife
- Robert – Duke of Albany
- Alexander – Duke of Buchan
- Margaret – married John MacDonald, Lord of the Isles (see *MacDonald Lineage*)
- Marjorie – married John, Earl of Moray
- Elizabeth – married Thomas Hay
- Jean – married Sir John Lyon
- Isabella – married James, Earl of Douglas
- Two more daughters[168]

Initially, there was some question as to the legitimacy of his first family.[169] He had married Elizabeth in Ayrshire in 1336, one of the most terrible years of the war. A rushed affair, the marriage was accepted, but apparently, they overlooked something in the canon law that would have required a dispensation. Elizabeth and Robert were found to be kin in the fourth degree. The Pope did grant a retroactive dispensation, legitimizing their children, in December 1347.[170] [171]

With second wife Euphemia Ross:[172] [173]

- David – Earl of Strathearn
- Walter – Earl of Atholl
- Egidia – married Sir William Douglas
- Elizabeth/Katherine – married David, Earl of Crawford

He also had eight illegitimate sons:[174]

By mistress Lady Moran:
- John
- Thomas
- John

Three more by Marion Cardney, and at least two others.

King Robert II Stewart died on 13 May 1390[175] at age 74, at Dundonald Castle in Ayrshire,[176] [177] after completing one last circuit of northeastern Scotland in January 1390, which he was forced into by son Robert, Duke of Albany. King Robert was buried at the abbey of Scone, next to his second wife, who had died in the winter of 1387-88.[178] [179] [180]

His son ***John, Earl of Carrick, later renamed Robert***, succeeded him as king.

King Robert III Stewart
(c. 1337-1406)
(reigned 1390-1406)

Robert III Stewart was born around 1337, and his birth name was John. However, when he became king, "King John" held bitter memories of the Balliol struggle, so he changed to Robert. We have seen some of his activities in the biography of his father, and now we pick up with his crowning at Scone on 14 August 1390.[181] [182]

He was, like his father, gentle, kind, courteous, deeply religious, and dignified, but of broken health (Robert never fully recovered from getting kicked in the head by a horse in 1385),[183] [184] and a lack of vitality left him unable to cope with the turbulence of his nobles.[185]

His greatest enemy among the nobility was his brother Robert, Earl of Fife. Although King Robert III was unable to defend his and his sons' claims, his queen, Annabella, fought hard for them.[186]

In an attempt to placate his brother, Robert III named him Robert, Duke of Albany, in 1398, at the same time naming his own son David, Duke of Rothesay. This didn't ease the tensions, and in 1399 King Robert III was virtually deposed. Robert, Duke of Albany, and David, who was only 20 at the time, were named Regents.[187] [188] [189] [190]

David proved to be a wild and poor governor, and his father asked him to resign. He refused, and Robert III arrested him in 1401 (it is perhaps no coincidence that Queen Annabella died in 1401) and placed him in the custody of his brother Robert, Duke of Albany. Albany imprisoned him in the Falkland Palace, where David died in 1402. There was suspicion that Albany killed David, perhaps by starvation, but he was exonerated.[191] [192]

In spring of 1406, Robert III realized that his 12-year-old son and heir, *James*, was in danger (probably from his brother Albany), and tried to send him to France. James' ship was captured by English privateers off Flamborough Head, and he and Henry (III) St. Clair, Earl of Orkney (see *Sinclair Lineage*) were delivered to English King Henry IV as hostages.[193] [194] [195]

Robert married Annabella Drummond in the late 1360s, and they had seven children:[196] [197] [198]

- David – Duke of Rothesay, predeceased Robert
- Robert – died as a child
- *James* – succeeded his father
- Margaret – married Archibald, Earl of Douglas
- Mary – married George, Earl of Angus
- Elizabeth – married Sir James Douglas
- Egidia – died as a child

The shock of James' capture killed Robert III Stewart at Rothesay on 4 April 1406, and James was declared king.[199] [200] [201] Robert, years earlier, had declared to his wife that his epitaph should read: "Here lies the worst of kings and the saddest of men." [202] [203]

King James I Stewart
(1394-1437)
(reigned 1406-1437)

James I Stewart was born in July 1394, so he was about 12 when he was taken hostage by the English.[204] Although James was proclaimed king upon his father's death, the Regent of Scotland (James' uncle, Robert, Duke of Albany) decided that he would rather rule Scotland himself, and allowed young James to stay captive in England for the first 18 years of his rule.[205] During this time, the nobles consolidated their power in Scotland.[206]

During his captivity, James excelled at martial sports such as jousting, swordsmanship, and archery. He also became very learned, a good linguist, musician, singer, and poet, writing a poem called *The Kingis Quair (The King's Book).* The poem was about his falling in love at first sight with Joan Beaufort, Edward III's great-granddaughter, and the daughter of the Earl of Somerset.[207]

In 1424, at age 30, James' luck finally changed. The Regent died, and the English kings Henry IV and V died. James and Joan married on 12 February 1424[208] in St. Mary Overy, which is now Southwark Cathedral, on the Thames.[209] Together, the newlyweds returned to Scotland.[210]

James and Joan had eight children: [211]

- Alexander – James' twin, who died young
- *James* – Alexander's twin, who succeeded as king
- Margaret – married Louis XI, King of France
- Isabella – married Francis I, Duke of Brittany
- Jean – married the Earl of Angus
- Eleanor – married Sigismund, Archduke of Austria[212]
- Mary – married Wolfart von Borgelen, Count of Grand Pre
- Annabella – married first Louis, Count of Geneva, then George, Earl of Huntly

James was crowned again, this time at Scone, on 21 May 1424.[213] [214] Scotland was in bad shape on his arrival. The crown was weak, the nobles held inflated powers, the administration was in chaos, and poverty, pestilence, and lawlessness prevailed across the realm.[215]

James, determined that his rule would never be challenged again, executed the Earl of Albany's son Murdoch and his two sons in 1425.[216] He sent two of his stepmother, Euphemia's, descendants to England as hostages until James' ransom was paid in full.[217]

In 1428, James renewed the Auld Alliance with France and sent Scotsmen to fight along with King Charles VII and Joan of Arc.[218]

To add to James' troubles, the Highland chiefs were stirring. James arrested the chiefs, among them Angus Du MacKay, who was later set free when his son Neil Vass MacKay was delivered as hostage (see *MacKay Lineage*). James defeated the Highland allies, including Alexander MacDonald, Lord of the Isles, at Inverness.[219]

In 1431, Donald Balloch MacKay (see *MacKay Lineage*) met James' forces at Inverlochy. However, James himself took over, and later defeated Donald and pacified the Highlands once and for all.[220] [221]

Once peace was established, James enacted many much-needed reforms, earning the nickname *Rex Legifer*, the Lawgiver.[222] He greatly reformed the justice system, even providing for a public defender for those too poor to hire a lawyer.[223]

In wresting power from the nobles, James made enemies, chief among them the Earl of Atholl and an uncle of the Earl of Strathearn, relatives of the two men James had sent to England as hostages. On 20 February 1437, they forced their way into the Dominican Priory in Perth.[224] [225]

The ladies were readying the queen for bed, and James was already in his nightclothes, when they heard a disturbance. James ran to lock the door, but found that the lock had been intentionally broken, and the bar for the door was mysteriously missing. To make matters worse, there was not even a knife to fight with available in the room.[226]

James pried up the floorboards and jumped into the sewer vault beneath. There had been an exit from the vault to the tennis courts, however, just three days earlier James had ordered that exit blocked off because he kept losing his tennis balls down it. So, he was trapped in the vault.[227]

While there was still pounding on the door, the queen and her ladies replaced the floorboards and spread rushes on the floor to make it look undisturbed. To buy time, lady-in-waiting Katherine Douglas thrust her arm through the staples of the door (in lieu of the missing bar), and held it there until her arm broke. The men then rushed in, but found nothing. The queen, even at swordpoint, refused to tell them where James was.[228]

The men left, and if the ladies had just waited until help arrived (the castle was stirring by this time), all would have been well. However, they opened the sewer and tried to get James out. They made some noise in doing so, and the men rushed back into the room. Two men jumped into the vault with James, who was unarmed, and eventually killed him. He put up a fierce fight, though—a month later, when they were caught, they still had his grip marks on their throats, and James suffered fifteen wounds before he died.[229]

James I Stewart was buried at Charterhouse Monastery at Perth, which he had founded in 1429.[230][231]

His queen, Joan, wounded while trying to defend her husband, exacted savage and ingenious tortures on the murderers in revenge.[232][233]

In addition, she was a staunch defender of her young son, the newly crowned King James II Stewart. Shortly after his coronation, a man named Sir William Crichton tried to keep her from seeing James.[234]

Joan announced that she was going on a pilgrimage by sea to Whitekirk in Lothian from Edinburgh, which Crichton agreed to. Crichton did not agree to the smuggling of the king in his mother's luggage. The ship sailed up the Forth to Stirling Castle, which was held by Sir Alexander Livingstone of Callendar. Unfortunately for the queen, Livingstone had ambitions of his own, and turned on her.[235]

When the queen's only protector, Archibald Douglas, 5th Earl of Douglas, died in 1439, she quickly married Sir James Stewart, the "Black Knight" of Lorne. However, her new husband was not powerful enough to protect them, and on 3 August 1440, Livingstone arrested Joan, her husband, and her brother-in-law. She was imprisoned at Stirling, and brought before a council that was a trial in all but name.[236]

The queen was forced to come to terms with them, probably as a ransom for her husband and brother-in-law. She gave a formal pardon to Livingstone, she abandoned custody of her son, James, to Livingstone, she paid 4,000 merks for James' living expenses, she "lent" Livingstone her dowerhouse of Stirling Castle, she was never allowed to speak to her son alone, and Livingstone got to appoint her household.[237]

Joan was no longer a political force after this, but she lived six more years. She and her second husband had three sons:[238]

- John of Balconie (d. 1512) – Earl of Atholl
- James (d.c. 1500) – Earl of Buchan
- Andrew – Bishop of Moray

Joan died at Dunbar in 1445, upon getting the news that her husband was captured at sea by Flemish pirates. She was buried next to James I, her true love, in Charterhouse Monastery at Perth.[239][240]

We join James' son, James, after his crowning as *King James II Stewart*.

King James II Stewart
(1430-1460)
reigned 1437-1460)

James II Stewart was born 16 October 1430,[241][242] the one survivor of twin boys. He had a purple birthmark over half of his face, thus earning the nickname "James of the Fiery Face." [243]

He was six years old when he assumed the crown on 25 March 1437. [244] Unlike his predecessors, he was not crowned at Scone, but at Holyrood.[245][246] William Crichton served as his regent. To break the powerful grip the Earls of Douglas held, Crichton invited the young Earl of Douglas and his younger brother to dinner at Edinburgh Castle on 24 November 1440. They came, and Crichton kidnapped the 14-year-old Earl and his younger brother. King James, only nine, tried to protect the two boys, but instead was forced to preside over their mock trials and order their deaths. [247][248][249]

In 1449, at age 19, James took power himself. He was a good lawgiver, but he had to face a powerful alliance against the Crown—the Earl of Douglas, the Earl of Crawford, and John MacDonald, Lord of the Isles. They were parlaying with the English to gain power in Scotland.[250][251]

On 21 February 1452, James invited the Earl of Douglas to dinner at Stirling Castle.[252] Not learning from recent history, the earl arrived, and the king stabbed him to death, perhaps as strategy, perhaps in a fit of fury.[253][254][255]

This heightened the hostility, and in 1455 the king's forces and the Douglas forces clashed. James won, largely because of his superior gunnery. He beat the Douglas forces at Arkinholm, and the kingdom finally was at peace.[256][257]

James married Marie of Guelders, daughter of Arnold, Duke of Guelders,[258] and a sister of Philip, Duke of Burgundy, France. Marie was only sixteen when she came to Scotland on 18 June 1449. She and James married on 3 July 1449. [259][260]

They had six children: [261]

- *James* – succeeded to the throne
- David – Earl of Moray (died young)
- John (b. 1459) – Earl of Mar
- Alexander – Duke of Albany
- Mary – married Thomas Boyd, Earl of Arran, then Lord Hamilton
- Margaret

- Another daughter who died in infancy

With Scotland's affairs in order, James intervened in the English War of the Roses on the side of his mother's cousin, Henry VI, the last King of the House of Lancaster. On 3 August 1460, James II Stewart was killed at the Siege of Roxburgh Castle when a cannon blew up near him.[262] [263] A fragment of a Flemish cannon of his father's struck him in the groin and broke his thigh. He died almost immediately, at age 29. [264]

His queen took her nine-year-old son to Roxburgh and urged the generals to make the king's death an occasion of victory. The Scots stormed the castle and won.[265]

In 1460, James' son James was crowned *King James III of Scotland*.

King James III Stewart
(1451-1488)
(reigned 1460-1488)

James III Stewart was born 10 July 1451. [266] [267] He was crowned at Kelso Abbey near Roxburgh on 10 August 1460. [268] [269] He was nine years old when he became king, and so had a regent for the first nine years of his reign. He had the same regent problems as his father, as the nobles struggled for power over him and the throne.[270]

His mother, Queen Marie, still in her 20s, set herself up as Regent at first, as well as getting the guardianship secured to herself—apparently, she learned from her husband's young trials. However, her regency did not go well. Her attempts to make peace with England's Edward IV York (during the English War of the Roses) (see *Continental Dynasty*) made her unpopular (most of Scotland was backing the royal party of Henry VI). She was also accused of having Adam Hepburn as a lover, in addition to an old scandal of a similar nature with the Duke of Somerset. [271]

In July of 1462, the Estates (Parliament) decided she could no longer meddle in government affairs, although James could continue to live with her—as long as they maintained separate households. She died toward the end of 1463,[272] and was buried in Trinity College, which she founded. [273]

James' other regent, Bishop Kennedy, died 10 May 1465, leaving the 14-year-old king unprotected. [274] [275] In July 1466, James was kidnapped at Linlithgow by Lord Boyd of Kilmarnock and taken to Edinburgh. James was forced to publicly agree to the coup, and the Boyds enjoyed power until James came of age.[276]

On 13 July 1469, at Holyrood, [277] when he was 18, he married 13-year-old Margaret of Denmark, the daughter of King Christian I of Denmark.[278] At that time the king of Denmark was also the king of Norway and Sweden. He offered a very large dowry with his daughter, but had no cash to actually pay it. So, he gave the Norwegian islands of Orkney and Shetland to Scotland as security until it was paid.[279] The Islands are still part of Scotland today, in spite of several attempts by Norway to get them back over the years.[280] [281] During James' reign Scotland took its present shape: Berwick in the South was lost forever to England, Roxburgh was gained, the Western Isles were ceded to Scotland, and the Northern Isles were added. [282] James asserted his authority after his marriage, and the Boyds were either executed or exiled for their treason against him.[283]

James and Margaret had three children:[284]

- *James* – succeeded his father
- James – Marquis of Ormond, later Duke of Ross[285]
- John – Earl of Mar

James alienated his nobles, and was not interested in affairs of state, making no secret of his disgust for violence and martial arts.[286] James was a man of piety and a lover of the arts, particularly music and architecture.[287] He also had favorites in his court, most of whom were highly unpopular with the populace and nobility, with a strong suspicion of homosexuality.[288] In 1479, James imprisoned his two brothers: Alexander, Duke of Albany, and John, Earl of Mar.[289] John died in prison, but Alexander escaped and fled to England, to invade Scotland at the head of an English army.[290] [291] [292]

James went to meet him, but was waylaid by Archibald Douglas and brought to Edinburgh. Alexander captured Berwick, then retreated. James reassumed the throne upon his brother's retreat. James tried to reconcile with his brother, but it was no use, and in 1484 Alexander tried one more time to capture Scotland. Alexander was defeated at Lochmaben, and he fled to France, where he was killed in a tournament in 1485.[293] [294] [295]

Margaret of Denmark died in 1483, and in 1486 James petitioned to get her sainted, but it did not happen. She was devout, charitable, and devoted to her husband.[296]

By 1488, the nobles were fed up with James, and a new conspiracy arose, headed by Archibald Douglas and Colin Campbell, Earl of Argyll. They seized James' teenaged son James and declared him king instead of his unpopular father.[297] [298] [299]

King James III fled to Stirling, but when he reached the walled city, they expressed their displeasure by locking him out of his own capital.[300]

On 11 June 1488, James III Stewart and the opposing forces met at Sauchieburn. James' horse bolted, throwing him, and he was badly hurt and taken to a nearby building. He called for a priest. A passerby claimed he was a priest, but when he got to James he stabbed him to death as he lay helpless in the kitchen of Beaton's Mill near Bannockburn village.[301] [302] [303] He was buried beside his wife in the Abbey of Cambuskenneth. [304] [305] [306]

James' son became the uncontested *King James IV of Scotland*.

King James IV Stewart
(1473-1513)
(reigned 1488-1513)

James IV Stewart was born 17 March 1473.[307] [308] He was fifteen when he was forcibly made king by co-conspirators Douglas and Campbell, who reaped the rewards. Archibald Douglas became a de facto regent, and this period marked the beginning of the rapid rise to power of the Argyll Campbells. James was crowned on 26 June 1488 at Scone—the last Scottish king to be crowned there.[309] [310] [311]

James was remorseful for what had happened to his father, and his role, however unwilling, in it. He wore an iron chain around his waist for the rest of his life as penance.[312] [313] The chain didn't stop him from having many mistresses and illegitimate children, however.

James was a powerful king, not allowing his nobles to rule him. He defeated any rebellions against him, and restored order to his kingdom. It was during his reign that the Renaissance reached Scotland. Peace and prosperity contributed to this growth of learning and arts, and education grew more widespread.[314] He spoke eight languages (Latin, French, German, Italian, Flemish, Spanish, the Lowland vernacular of Scots-English, and the Highland vernacular of Gaelic).[315] He was a fan of learning and the arts, he was a superb horseman, and (unlike his father) excelled at martial sports.[316]

He created some problems for himself, however, in dealing with the Western Isles. James had frequently visited the Isles, starting in 1493. He returned twice in 1494, and in May of 1495, he was at Mingary Castle in Ardnamurchan. Just when the Islemen were beginning to trust him in 1498, he was convinced to revoke all the charters given to the Islemen, which they could only get back at a price. This arbitrary manner of dealing with them caused the first Isle uprising of James' monarchy. James returned to Kilkerran Castle in Kintyre in August of 1498, but few Islemen came to pay him homage. He left and never returned. [317] [318]

James was very popular with the ladies, having five children by four mistresses, including a son, Alexander, who became Archbishop of St. Andrews.[319] [320]

In 1496, James invaded England, supposedly on behalf of another Yorkist pretender to the English throne, but the people refused to restart the War of the Roses, and his invasion failed. English King Henry VII (see *Continental Dynasty*) made peace with James, offering his daughter's hand in marriage.[321] James didn't want to marry her at first, because he wanted to marry his mistress, Margaret Drummond. But Margaret died in 1500, possibly poisoned by enemies of the family.[322]

In 1501, James, then 28, agreed to marry Margaret Tudor (12 years old at the time), daughter of Henry VII, and signed a perpetual peace treaty with England.[323] [324] [325]

On 8 August 1503, James married Margaret Tudor (then 14) at Holyrood.[326] They had five children:[327]

- James (d. 1508)
- Arthur (d. 1510)
- *James* – succeeded his father
- Two others who died young

The Highlands still gave James headaches—royal power barely touched the Celtic patrimony there. Clans ruled all. James tried to visit the Highlands and Isles as a friend rather than an invader, something no other ruler had done. He also spoke Gaelic, which many rulers had not. However, this did not make the clans any more pliable. So, James tried to install feudal overlords.[328]

In 1503, Donald Dubh (Black Donald), son of Angus Óg and grandson of John, Lord of the Isles, rose up and burned Inverness. He was caught and imprisoned in 1506.[329]

James helped found the University of Aberdeen in 1494. He also passed the first compulsory education act, which required all major landholders to send their eldest son to school. In 1505, the College of Surgeons was founded in Edinburgh.[330] In 1507, the first printing press was brought to Scotland, with James' approval.[331] He also spent lavishly on building and improving his military artillery and building a large ship to further his naval ambitions. One of his other ambitions was to gather the European leaders into a crusade against the advancing Turks. This would have accomplished two things: stopped the Turkish advance, and kept the peace between England and France.[332] [333]

Because of the Auld Alliance, if France and England went to war, James would be caught in between. He was called Rex Pacificator—the Peace-Bringer. His efforts were in vain, however, because in 1511, the Pope, Spain, the Holy Roman Empire, and Venice, united in a Holy League against France—and King Henry VIII of England joined them.[334]

In 1513, the European war raged and France was in danger of being defeated and partitioned. Henry VIII threatened Scotland when James tried to diplomatically intervene. James responded by invading England.[335]

On 9 September 1513, James' army met the English in Northumberland at Flodden (the English call it the Battle of Branxton). The Scots were massacred in battle by the English (Iye Roy of our *MacKay Lineage* was there and survived[336]). King James IV, most of his nobles, most of his Highland chieftains, and the best young men of that generation were killed.[337] King James died of an arrow to the throat, and others who fell with him were the Bishop of Caithness, the Bishop of the Isles, 12 earls and 14 lords. Only four men of the Scottish peerage were left. As many as 10,000 men may have died, and all of the Scots' artillery was captured by the English.[338] [339]

King Henry VIII added to the disgrace by denying James burial, claiming he had been fighting against the Pope. No one knew what happened to him, which led to rumors that he lived and would return, like the legend of King Arthur, when his people were in their greatest need.[340] [341]

Another version stated that when Henry VIII refused James burial, the Pope gave a dispensation to allow James to be buried at St. Paul's. Henry did embalm the body, but did not comply with the burial. Instead, he left the corpse unburied at the Carthusian monastery at Sheen, wrapped in lead and stored among lumber. Many years later, workmen cut off the head of the by-then-unknown corpse, brought it home, then brought it to the sexton of Great St. Michael's, Wood Street, to bury it in the common charnel house. What became of the headless body is unknown.[342] A third version has the coffin being left at Sheen until the reign of Elizabeth I, when it was moved to Great St. Michaels.[343] Both the monastery and the church have long since been demolished and built over.

King James IV Stewart's death left Scotland in turmoil. His heir, **King James V**, was only about a year old at the time. The widow, Margaret Tudor, who acted as Regent, was not very competent, her brother Henry VIII, was aggressive toward the weakened Scotland, and the nobles began conspiring among themselves.[344]

King James V Stewart
(1512-1542)
(ruled 1513-1542)

James V Stewart was born 10 April 1512,[345] the only surviving legitimate child of James IV. He was only 17 months old when he was crowned king at Stirling on 21 September 1513, and the early years of his "reign" were filled with intrigue and danger.[346] [347]

In 1515, John, Duke of Albany, son of Alexander of Albany who had escaped imprisonment by James III, took over the regency of the young king.[348] Albany was French-educated and French speaking. By 1517, there were two political factions in Scotland. One, headed by Albany, was the National or French Party, and the other, headed by Margaret Tudor and her new husband, Archibald Douglas, Earl of Angus, was the English Party. The English Party plotted with King Henry VIII to kidnap James V (now five years old) and take him to England. They failed, and Margaret and Angus fled to England. Margaret returned to Scotland to support Albany and the French Party when she and her husband, Angus, had a falling out in 1521.[349]

By 1524, the Regent Duke of Albany had had enough of Henry VIII's intrigues and interference, and Margaret's wavering. He left Scotland and returned to France.[350]

In 1526, 14-year-old James V was declared fit to govern by his mother the regent. In fact, he was a prisoner of the Douglases (his stepfather, the Earl of Angus, was the head of the Douglas family).[351] [352]

In 1528, 16-year-old James escaped disguised as a groom, went to Stirling, and drove the Earl of Angus into England.[353] James then proceeded to make a truce with England, restore law and order, and even was conciliatory with the Highlanders.[354]

James was poorly educated compared to his predecessors, due to his stepfather's deliberate neglect. He was very handsome and loose with the ladies, but he did not inspire loyalty in his nobles. He ruled with an iron hand, relying on harsh discipline rather than persuasion. Although not popular with the nobles, he was popular with the common people, because he was a protector of the weak.[355]

Many of the rulers of other nations wanted James to marry into their families in order to secure the power of Scotland to them. On 1 January 1537, James married Madeline, the daughter of King Francois I of France, but she died six months later.[356] [357][358]

In 1538, James married another French bride, Mary de Guise-Lorraine. She bore him three children: [359] [360] [361] [362]

- James (1540-1541)
- Arthur (1541-1541)
- **Mary, Queen of Scots** (1542-1587) – succeeded James

In 1540, an uprising in the Isles—due to his arbitrary revocation of land grants[363]—caused James to make a circuit of the north, and he brought back many prisoners and hostages to ensure good behavior. The Lordship of the Isles was finally annexed to Scotland once and for all.[364]

The seeds of religious strife were planted when the Reformation entered Scotland. James believed the country's religion should be decided by the king, and he chose Catholicism over Protestantism. Although he gathered high taxes from the Catholic church, religious security was far from assured. And although he was an ally of the Pope, many of his nobles had embraced Protestantism.[365]

In 1542, Henry VIII invaded Scotland when the Irish offered James the crown of Ireland. Henry's true intent was to force Scotland to become Protestant, which James adamantly opposed.[366]

In response, James tried to invade England, but he was at odds with his nobles, and they refused to march. His feeble army was defeated by the English at Solway Moss on 24 November 1542.[367] [368]

Taken ill before Solway Moss, James died two weeks later, on 14 Dec 1542, at his palace of Falkland, upon hearing the news that the child his wife had born was a girl. It is said (although is likely a fabrication) that, remembering how the crown had come to the family through Marjorie Bruce, James' last words were, "It came with a lass and it will gang with a lass." [369] [370] [371] He was wrong, as his grandson, King James VI of Scotland, would also become King James I of England, uniting the thrones in 1603.

James V Stewart, like his father before him, was a tremendous womanizer, with numerous illegitimate children. One of James' mistresses was Euphemia Elphinstone, daughter of Lord Alexander Elphinstone (who died at Flodden), and Elizabeth Barlow (sometimes Berclay). Euphemia bore him a son, **Robert**.[372]

Robert Stewart, Earl of Orkney

James V's illegitimate son, Robert Stewart, was given the lease of the Orkney Islands on 26 May 1564.[373] He was made Earl of Orkney and Shetland in 1581.[374] He was not a well-loved earl. His son Patrick inherited the earldom, but was executed in 1614, and so the Stewart reign in the Isles ended.[375]

Robert married Lady Janet Kennedy[376] and they had a daughter, *Lady Elizabeth Stewart*.[377]

Elizabeth married James Sinclair, 1st of Murkle, who was the grandson of the 4th Earl of Caithness, George Sinclair (see *Sinclair Lineage*). They had:[378] [379]

- Sir James Sinclair
- Francis Sinclair
- *Agnes Sinclair* (b. 1600) – married John MacKay of Dirlot and Strathy (see *MacKay Lineage*)[380]
- Elizabeth Sinclair

Agnes, born in Murkle, Creich, Sutherland County, married *John MacKay*, 1st Chief of Strathy.[381] [382] Agnes and John MacKay are the fourth great-grandparents of Mary MacKay, wife of Hugh Campbell of Ayr. Please read the *MacKay Lineage* chapter to find out more about them and their descendants.

---

[1] Fitzroy Maclean, *A Concise History of Scotland* (First published 1970. This version published 2002. Thames & Hudson Ltd., London), p. 32.

[2] Caroline Bingham, *Kings and Queens of Scotland* (originally published 1976, Taplinger Publishing Co. this edition, 1985, Dorset Press) p. 30.

[3] Caroline Bingham, *Kings and Queens of Scotland* (originally published 1976, Taplinger Publishing Co. this edition, 1985, Dorset Press) p. 32.

[4] Caroline Bingham, *Kings and Queens of Scotland* (originally published 1976, Taplinger Publishing Co. this edition, 1985, Dorset Press) p. 30.

[5] Fitzroy Maclean, *A Concise History of Scotland* (First published 1970. This version, 2002. Thames & Hudson Ltd., London), p. 32-35.

[6] Caroline Bingham, *Kings and Queens of Scotland* (orig. published 1976, Taplinger Publishing Co. this edition, 1985, Dorset Press) p. 39-40.

[7] E. William Robertson, *Scotland Under Her Early Kings: A History of the Kingdom to the Close of the Thirteenth Century, Part Two* (Edinburgh: Edmonston and Douglas, 1862), p. 9-10.

[8] Ruth M. Blakely, *The Brus Family in England and Scotland, 1100-1295* (Boydell Press, Woodbridge, 2005), p. 73.

[9] Caroline Bingham, *Kings and Queens of Scotland* (originally published 1976, Taplinger Publishing Co. this edition, 1985, Dorset Press) p. 40.

[10] Fitzroy Maclean, *A Concise History of Scotland* (First published 1970. This version published 2002. Thames & Hudson Ltd., London), p. 35.

[11] Caroline Bingham, *Kings and Queens of Scotland* (orig. published 1976, Taplinger Publishing Co. this edition, 1985, Dorset Press) p. 40-41.

[12] Caroline Bingham, *Kings and Queens of Scotland* (orig. published 1976, Taplinger Publishing Co. this edition, 1985, Dorset Press) p. 42.

[13] A.F. Murison, *King Robert the Bruce* (Edinburgh, Oliphant, Anderson & Ferrier, 1899), p. 34.

[14] Caroline Bingham, *Kings and Queens of Scotland* (orig. published 1976, Taplinger Publishing Co. this edition, 1985, Dorset Press) p. 41-42.

[15] Caroline Bingham, *Kings and Queens of Scotland* (orig. published 1976, Taplinger Publishing Co. this edition, 1985, Dorset Press) p. 43.

[16] Caroline Bingham, *Kings and Queens of Scotland* (orig. published 1976, Taplinger Publishing Co. this edition, 1985, Dorset Press) p. 43.

[17] A.F. Murison, *King Robert the Bruce* (Edinburgh, Oliphant, Anderson & Ferrier, 1899), p. 18.

[18] John Cannon & Ralph Griffiths, *The Oxford Illustrated History of the British Monarchy* (2000 edition, Oxford University Press), Geneaolgies of Royal Lines Appendix; List of Monarchs Appendix.

[19] Richard Oram (Ed.), *The Kings and Queens of Scotland* (Tempus Publishing Ltd., Stroud, Gloucestershire, England, 2001), p. 116.

[20] A.F. Murison, *King Robert the Bruce* (Edinburgh, Oliphant, Anderson & Ferrier, 1899), p. 18.

[21] John Cannon & Ralph Griffiths, *The Oxford Illustrated History of the British Monarchy* (2000 edition, Oxford University Press), p. 220.

[22] A.F. Murison, *King Robert the Bruce* (Edinburgh, Oliphant, Anderson & Ferrier, 1899), p. 15.

[23] Richard Oram (Ed.), *The Kings and Queens of Scotland* (Tempus Publishing Ltd., Stroud, Gloucestershire, England, 2001), p. 117.

[24] Richard Oram (Ed.), *The Kings and Queens of Scotland* (Tempus Publishing Ltd., Stroud, Gloucestershire, England, 2001), p. 117.

[25] Caroline Bingham, *Kings and Queens of Scotland* (orig. published 1976, Taplinger Publishing Co. this edition, 1985, Dorset Press) p. 44.

[26] A.F. Murison, *King Robert the Bruce* (Edinburgh, Oliphant, Anderson & Ferrier, 1899), p. 18.

[27] A.F. Murison, *King Robert the Bruce* (Edinburgh, Oliphant, Anderson & Ferrier, 1899), p. 18.

[28] John Cannon & Ralph Griffiths, *The Oxford Illustrated History of the British Monarchy* (2000 edition, Oxford University Press), p. 220.

[29] A.F. Murison, *King Robert the Bruce* (Edinburgh, Oliphant, Anderson & Ferrier, 1899), p. 19.

[30] Richard Oram (Ed.), *The Kings and Queens of Scotland* (Tempus Publishing Ltd., Stroud, Gloucestershire, England, 2001), p. 115.

[31] Caroline Bingham, *Kings and Queens of Scotland* (orig. published 1976, Taplinger Publishing Co. this edition, 1985, Dorset Press) p. 44.

[32] A.F. Murison, *King Robert the Bruce* (Edinburgh, Oliphant, Anderson & Ferrier, 1899), p. 20.

[33] A.F. Murison, *King Robert the Bruce* (Edinburgh, Oliphant, Anderson & Ferrier, 1899), p. 21.

[34] Richard Oram (Ed.), *The Kings and Queens of Scotland* (Tempus Publishing Ltd., Stroud, Gloucestershire, England, 2001), p. 118.

[35] Caroline Bingham, *Kings and Queens of Scotland* (orig. published 1976, Taplinger Publishing Co. this edition, 1985, Dorset Press), p. 44.

[36] John Cannon & Ralph Griffiths, *The Oxford Illustrated History of the British Monarchy* (2000 edition, Oxford University Press), p. 220.

[37] A.F. Murison, *King Robert the Bruce* (Edinburgh, Oliphant, Anderson & Ferrier, 1899), p. 22.

[38] Ronald Williams, *The Lords of the Isles: The Clan Donald and the Early Kingdom of the Scots* (Chatto & Windus - The Hogarth Press, London, 1984) p. 151.

[39] Richard Oram (Ed.), *The Kings and Queens of Scotland* (Tempus Publishing Ltd., Stroud, Gloucestershire, England, 2001), p. 119.

[40] John Cannon & Ralph Griffiths, *The Oxford Illustrated History of the British Monarchy* (2000 edition, Oxford University Press), p. 220.

[41] A.F. Murison, *King Robert the Bruce* (Edinburgh, Oliphant, Anderson & Ferrier, 1899), p. 23.

[42] Richard Oram (Ed.), *The Kings and Queens of Scotland* (Tempus Publishing Ltd., Stroud, Gloucestershire, England, 2001), p. 120.

[43] Ronald Williams, *The Lords of the Isles: The Clan Donald and the Early Kingdom of the Scots* (Chatto & Windus - The Hogarth Press, London, 1984) p. 152.

[44] Caroline Bingham, *Kings and Queens of Scotland* (orig. published 1976, Taplinger Publishing Co. this edition, 1985, Dorset Press), p. 45.

[45] A.F. Murison, *King Robert the Bruce* (Edinburgh, Oliphant, Anderson & Ferrier, 1899), p. 28-33.

[46] Fitzroy Maclean, *A Concise History of Scotland* (First published 1970. This version published 2002. Thames & Hudson Ltd., London), p. 39.

[47] Ronald Williams, *The Lords of the Isles: The Clan Donald and the Early Kingdom of the Scots* (Chatto & Windus - The Hogarth Press, London, 1984) p. 152.

[48] Ronald Williams, *The Lords of the Isles: The Clan Donald and the Early Kingdom of the Scots* (Chatto & Windus - The Hogarth Press, London, 1984) p. 152.

[49] A.F. Murison, *King Robert the Bruce* (Edinburgh, Oliphant, Anderson & Ferrier, 1899), p. 34.

[50] Fitzroy Maclean, *A Concise History of Scotland* (First published 1970. This version published 2002. Thames & Hudson Ltd., London), p. 39.

[51] Ronald Williams, *The Lords of the Isles: The Clan Donald and the Early Kingdom of the Scots* (Chatto & Windus - The Hogarth Press, London, 1984) p. 153.

[52] A.F. Murison, *King Robert the Bruce* (Edinburgh, Oliphant, Anderson & Ferrier, 1899), p. 42.

[53] A.F. Murison, *King Robert the Bruce* (Edinburgh, Oliphant, Anderson & Ferrier, 1899), p. 46.

[54] Raymond Campbell Paterson, *The Lords of the Isles: A History of Clan Donald* (Birlinn Limited, Edinburgh, 2001), p. 20.

[55] A.F. Murison, *King Robert the Bruce* (Edinburgh, Oliphant, Anderson & Ferrier, 1899), p. 58.

[56] Ronald Williams, *The Lords of the Isles: The Clan Donald and the Early Kingdom of the Scots* (Chatto & Windus - The Hogarth Press, London, 1984) p. 154.

[57] Raymond Campbell Paterson, *The Lords of the Isles: A History of Clan Donald* (Birlinn Limited, Edinburgh, 2001), p. 21.

[58] A.F. Murison, *King Robert the Bruce* (Edinburgh, Oliphant, Anderson & Ferrier, 1899), p. 59.

[59] Ronald Williams, *The Lords of the Isles: The Clan Donald and the Early Kingdom of the Scots* (Chatto & Windus - The Hogarth Press, London, 1984) p. 155.

[60] Ronald Williams, *The Lords of the Isles: The Clan Donald and the Early Kingdom of the Scots* (Chatto & Windus - The Hogarth Press, London, 1984) p. 156.

[61] Caroline Bingham, *Kings and Queens of Scotland* (orig. published 1976, Taplinger Publishing Co. this edition, 1985, Dorset Press), p. 45.

[62] A.F. Murison, *King Robert the Bruce* (Edinburgh, Oliphant, Anderson & Ferrier, 1899), p. 61-62.

[63] Fitzroy Maclean, *A Concise History of Scotland* (First published 1970. This version published 2002. Thames & Hudson Ltd., London), p. 40.

[64] Ronald Williams, *The Lords of the Isles: The Clan Donald and the Early Kingdom of the Scots* (Chatto & Windus - The Hogarth Press, London, 1984) p. 156.

[65] A.F. Murison, *King Robert the Bruce* (Edinburgh, Oliphant, Anderson & Ferrier, 1899), p. 65.

[66] Ronald Williams, *The Lords of the Isles: The Clan Donald and the Early Kingdom of the Scots* (Chatto & Windus - The Hogarth Press, London, 1984) p. 157.

[67] A.F. Murison, *King Robert the Bruce* (Edinburgh, Oliphant, Anderson & Ferrier, 1899), p. 71.

[68] Fitzroy Maclean, *A Concise History of Scotland* (First published 1970. This version published 2002. Thames & Hudson Ltd., London), p. 41.

[69] Caroline Bingham, *Kings and Queens of Scotland* (orig. published 1976, Taplinger Publishing Co. this edition, 1985, Dorset Press) p. 45.

[70] A.F. Murison, *King Robert the Bruce* (Edinburgh, Oliphant, Anderson & Ferrier, 1899), p. 70.

[71] Richard Oram (Ed.), *The Kings and Queens of Scotland* (Tempus Publishing Ltd., Stroud, Gloucestershire, England, 2001), p. 122.

[72] Ronald Williams, *The Lords of the Isles: The Clan Donald and the Early Kingdom of the Scots* (Chatto & Windus - The Hogarth Press, London, 1984) p. 156-7.

[73] Raymond Campbell Paterson, *The Lords of the Isles: A History of Clan Donald* (Birlinn Limited, Edinburgh, 2001), p. 22.

[74] Caroline Bingham, *Kings and Queens of Scotland* (orig. published 1976, Taplinger Publishing Co. this edition, 1985, Dorset Press) p. 46.

[75] Richard Oram (Ed.), *The Kings and Queens of Scotland* (Tempus Publishing Ltd., Stroud, Gloucestershire, England, 2001), p. 123.

[76] Ronald Williams, *The Lords of the Isles: The Clan Donald and the Early Kingdom of the Scots* (Chatto & Windus - The Hogarth Press, London, 1984) p. 158.

[77] Fitzroy Maclean, *A Concise History of Scotland* (First published 1970. This version, 2002. Thames & Hudson Ltd., London), p. 41-43.

[78] Ronald Williams, *The Lords of the Isles: The Clan Donald and the Early Kingdom of the Scots* (Chatto & Windus - The Hogarth Press, London, 1984) p. 159.

[79] Ronald Williams, *The Lords of the Isles: The Clan Donald and the Early Kingdom of the Scots* (Chatto & Windus - The Hogarth Press, London, 1984) p. 160-1.

[80] A.F. Murison, *King Robert the Bruce* (Edinburgh, Oliphant, Anderson & Ferrier, 1899), p. 92-107.

[81] A.F. Murison, *King Robert the Bruce* (Edinburgh, Oliphant, Anderson & Ferrier, 1899), p. 108-110.

[82] Richard Oram (Ed.), *The Kings and Queens of Scotland* (Tempus Publishing Ltd., Stroud, Gloucestershire, England, 2001), p. 125.

[83] A.F. Murison, *King Robert the Bruce* (Edinburgh, Oliphant, Anderson & Ferrier, 1899), p. 110, 127.

[84] Caroline Bingham, *Kings and Queens of Scotland* (orig. published 1976, Taplinger Publishing Co. this edition, 1985, Dorset Press) p. 46.

[85] A.F. Murison, *King Robert the Bruce* (Edinburgh, Oliphant, Anderson & Ferrier, 1899), p. 141.

[86] Ronald Williams, *The Lords of the Isles: The Clan Donald and the Early Kingdom of the Scots* (Chatto & Windus - The Hogarth Press, London, 1984) p. 168.

[87] Ronald Williams, *The Lords of the Isles: The Clan Donald and the Early Kingdom of the Scots* (Chatto & Windus - The Hogarth Press, London, 1984) p. 168.

[88] Fitzroy Maclean, *A Concise History of Scotland* (First published 1970. This version published 2002. Thames & Hudson Ltd., London), p. 44.

[89] John Cannon & Ralph Griffiths, *The Oxford Illustrated History of the British Monarchy* (2000 edition, Oxford University Press), p. 220.

[90] Caroline Bingham, *Kings and Queens of Scotland* (orig. published 1976, Taplinger Publishing Co. this edition, 1985, Dorset Press) p. 47.

[91] Caroline Bingham, *Kings and Queens of Scotland* (orig. published 1976, Taplinger Publishing Co. this edition, 1985, Dorset Press), p. 47.

[92] A.F. Murison, *King Robert the Bruce* (Edinburgh, Oliphant, Anderson & Ferrier, 1899), p. 148.

[93] Caroline Bingham, *Kings and Queens of Scotland* (orig. published 1976, Taplinger Publishing Co. this edition, 1985, Dorset Press) p. 49.

[94] John Cannon & Ralph Griffiths, *The Oxford Illustrated History of the British Monarchy* (2000 edition, Oxford University Press), Geneaolgies of Royal Lines Appendix.

[95] A.F. Murison, *King Robert the Bruce* (Edinburgh, Oliphant, Anderson & Ferrier, 1899), p. 155.

[96] Caroline Bingham, *Kings and Queens of Scotland* (orig. published 1976, Taplinger Publishing Co. this edition, 1985, Dorset Press) p. 48.

[97] A.F. Murison, *King Robert the Bruce* (Edinburgh, Oliphant, Anderson & Ferrier, 1899), p. 155.

[98] A.F. Murison, *King Robert the Bruce* (Edinburgh, Oliphant, Anderson & Ferrier, 1899), p. 155.

[99] A.F. Murison, *King Robert the Bruce* (Edinburgh, Oliphant, Anderson & Ferrier, 1899), p. 155.

[100] Richard Oram (Ed.), *The Kings and Queens of Scotland* (Tempus Publishing Ltd., Stroud, Gloucestershire, England, 2001) p. 127.

[101] A.F. Murison, *King Robert the Bruce* (Edinburgh, Oliphant, Anderson & Ferrier, 1899), p. 155.

[102] Caroline Bingham, *Kings and Queens of Scotland* (orig. published 1976, Taplinger Publishing Co. this edition, 1985, Dorset Press) p. 48.

[103] Fitzroy Maclean, *A Concise History of Scotland* (First published 1970. This version, 2002. Thames & Hudson Ltd., London), p. 44.

[104] A.F. Murison, *King Robert the Bruce* (Edinburgh, Oliphant, Anderson & Ferrier, 1899), p. 149.

[105] Richard Oram (Ed.), *The Kings and Queens of Scotland* (Tempus Publishing Ltd., Stroud, Gloucestershire, England, 2001) p. 128-129.

[106] John Cannon & Ralph Griffiths, *The Oxford Illustrated History of the British Monarchy* (2000 edition, Oxford University Press), p. 640.

[107] A.F. Murison, *King Robert the Bruce* (Edinburgh, Oliphant, Anderson & Ferrier, 1899), p. 150.

[108] Caroline Bingham, *Kings and Queens of Scotland* (orig. published 1976, Taplinger Publishing Co. this edition, 1985, Dorset Press) p. 48.

[109] Richard Oram (Ed.), *The Kings and Queens of Scotland* (Tempus Publishing Ltd., Stroud, Gloucestershire, England, 2001),p. 142.

[110] Agnes Mure MacKenzie, *The Rise of the Stewarts* (Oliver & Boyd, Ltd, Edinburgh. Originally printed 1935, this printing 1957.), p. 15.

[111] Fitzroy Maclean, *A Concise History of Scotland* (First published 1970. This version, 2002. Thames & Hudson Ltd., London), p. 45.

[112] Caroline Bingham, *Kings and Queens of Scotland* (orig. published 1976, Taplinger Publishing Co. this edition, 1985, Dorset Press) p. 55.

[113] John Cannon & Ralph Griffiths, *The Oxford Illustrated History of the British Monarchy* (2000 edition, Oxford University Press), Geneaolgies of Royal Lines Appendix.

[114] Caroline Bingham, *Kings and Queens of Scotland* (orig. published 1976, Taplinger Publishing Co. this edition, 1985, Dorset Press), p. 55.

[115] Richard Oram (Ed.), *The Kings and Queens of Scotland* (Tempus Publishing Ltd., Stroud, Gloucestershire, England, 2001) p. 142.

[116] Richard Oram (Ed.), *The Kings and Queens of Scotland* (Tempus Publishing Ltd., Stroud, Gloucestershire, England, 2001) p. 142.

[117] John Cannon & Ralph Griffiths, *The Oxford Illustrated History of the British Monarchy* (2000 edition, Oxford University Press), p. 244.

[118] John Cannon & Ralph Griffiths, *The Oxford Illustrated History of the British Monarchy* (2000 edition, Oxford University Press), p. 244.

[119] Agnes Mure MacKenzie, *The Rise of the Stewarts* (Oliver & Boyd, Ltd, Edinburgh. Originally printed 1935, this printing 1957.), p. 16.

[120] John Cannon & Ralph Griffiths, *The Oxford Illustrated History of the British Monarchy* (2000 edition, Oxford University Press), Geneaolgies of Royal Lines Appendix.

[121] Caroline Bingham, *Kings and Queens of Scotland* (orig. published 1976, Taplinger Publishing Co. this edition, 1985, Dorset Press) p. 49.

[122] Caroline Bingham, *Kings and Queens of Scotland* (orig. published 1976, Taplinger Publishing Co. this edition, 1985, Dorset Press) p. 49.

[123] Caroline Bingham, *Kings and Queens of Scotland* (orig. published 1976, Taplinger Publishing Co. this edition, 1985, Dorset Press) p. 50.

[124] Caroline Bingham, *Kings and Queens of Scotland* (orig. published 1976, Taplinger Publishing Co. this edition, 1985, Dorset Press) p. 49.

[125] Fitzroy Maclean, *A Concise History of Scotland* (First published 1970. This version, 2002. Thames & Hudson Ltd., London), p. 46-47.

[126] Caroline Bingham, *Kings and Queens of Scotland* (orig. published 1976, Taplinger Publishing Co. this edition, 1985, Dorset Press) p. 49.

[127] Ronald Williams, *The Lords of the Isles: The Clan Donald and the Early Kingdom of the Scots* (Chatto & Windus - The Hogarth Press, London, 1984) p. 171.

[128] Fitzroy Maclean, *A Concise History of Scotland* (First published 1970. This version, 2002. Thames & Hudson Ltd., London), p. 46-47.

[129] Richard Oram (Ed.), *The Kings and Queens of Scotland* (Tempus Publishing Ltd., Stroud, Gloucestershire, England, 2001) p. 143.

[130] Agnes Mure MacKenzie, *The Rise of the Stewarts* (Oliver & Boyd, Ltd, Edinburgh. Originally printed 1935, this printing 1957.), p. 30.

[131] Richard Oram (Ed.), *The Kings and Queens of Scotland* (Tempus Publishing Ltd., Stroud, Gloucestershire, England, 2001) p. 143.

[132] Fitzroy Maclean, *A Concise History of Scotland* (First published 1970. This version, 2002. Thames & Hudson Ltd., London), p. 46-47.

[133] Fitzroy Maclean, *A Concise History of Scotland* (First published 1970. This version, 2002. Thames & Hudson Ltd., London), p. 47.

[134] Agnes Mure MacKenzie, *The Rise of the Stewarts* (Oliver & Boyd, Ltd, Edinburgh. Originally printed 1935, this printing 1957.), p. 34.

[135] Fitzroy Maclean, *A Concise History of Scotland* (First published 1970. This version, 2002. Thames & Hudson Ltd., London), p. 47.

[136] Fitzroy Maclean, *A Concise History of Scotland* (First published 1970. This version, 2002. Thames & Hudson Ltd., London), p. 47.

[137] Richard Oram (Ed.), *The Kings and Queens of Scotland* (Tempus Publishing Ltd., Stroud, Gloucestershire, England, 2001) p. 144.

[138] Agnes Mure MacKenzie, *The Rise of the Stewarts* (Oliver & Boyd, Ltd, Edinburgh. Originally printed 1935, this printing 1957.), p. 41.

[139] Caroline Bingham, *Kings and Queens of Scotland* (orig. published 1976, Taplinger Publishing Co. this edition, 1985, Dorset Press) p. 50.

[140] Fitzroy Maclean, *A Concise History of Scotland* (First published 1970. This version, 2002. Thames & Hudson Ltd., London), p. 47.

[141] Richard Oram (Ed.), *The Kings and Queens of Scotland* (Tempus Publishing Ltd., Stroud, Gloucestershire, England, 2001) p. 144.

[142] John Cannon & Ralph Griffiths, *The Oxford Illustrated History of the British Monarchy* (2000 edition, Oxford University Press), p. 251.

[143] Richard Oram (Ed.), *The Kings and Queens of Scotland* (Tempus Publishing Ltd., Stroud, Gloucestershire, England, 2001) p. 135.

[144] Fitzroy Maclean, *A Concise History of Scotland* (First published 1970. This version, 2002. Thames & Hudson Ltd., London), p. 47-48.

[145] Richard Oram (Ed.), *The Kings and Queens of Scotland* (Tempus Publishing Ltd., Stroud, Gloucestershire, England, 2001) p. 136.

[146] Fitzroy Maclean, *A Concise History of Scotland* (First published 1970. This version , 2002. Thames & Hudson Ltd., London), p. 48.

[147] Caroline Bingham, *Kings and Queens of Scotland* (orig. published 1976, Taplinger Publishing Co. this edition, 1985, Dorset Press) p. 50.

[148] Agnes Mure MacKenzie, *The Rise of the Stewarts* (Oliver & Boyd, Ltd, Edinburgh. Originally printed 1935, this printing 1957.), p. 52-53.

[149] John Cannon & Ralph Griffiths, *The Oxford Illustrated History of the British Monarchy* (2000 edition, Oxford University Press), p. 244.

[150] Agnes Mure MacKenzie, *The Rise of the Stewarts* (Oliver & Boyd, Ltd, Edinburgh. Originally printed 1935, this printing 1957.), p. 55.

[151] Fitzroy Maclean, *A Concise History of Scotland* (First published 1970. This version, 2002. Thames & Hudson Ltd., London), p. 48.

[152] Agnes Mure MacKenzie, *The Rise of the Stewarts* (Oliver & Boyd, Ltd, Edinburgh. Originally printed 1935, this printing 1957.), p. 58-59.

[153] Agnes Mure MacKenzie, *The Rise of the Stewarts* (Oliver & Boyd, Ltd, Edinburgh. Originally printed 1935, this printing 1957.), p. 60-61.

[154] Fitzroy Maclean, *A Concise History of Scotland* (First published 1970. This version, 2002. Thames & Hudson Ltd., London), p. 48.

[155] John Cannon & Ralph Griffiths, *The Oxford Illustrated History of the British Monarchy* (2000 edition, Oxford University Press), List of Monarchs Appendix.

[156] Richard Oram (Ed.), *The Kings and Queens of Scotland* (Tempus Publishing Ltd., Stroud, Gloucestershire, England, 2001) p. 144.

[157] Richard Oram (Ed.), *The Kings and Queens of Scotland* (Tempus Publishing Ltd., Stroud, Gloucestershire, England, 2001) p. 193.

[158] Caroline Bingham, *Kings and Queens of Scotland* (orig. published 1976, Taplinger Publishing Co. this edition, 1985, Dorset Press) p. 56.

[159] Agnes Mure MacKenzie, *The Rise of the Stewarts* (Oliver & Boyd, Ltd, Edinburgh. Originally printed 1935, this printing 1957.), p. 67.

[160] Richard Oram (Ed.), *The Kings and Queens of Scotland* (Tempus Publishing Ltd., Stroud, Gloucestershire, England, 2001) p. 193.

[161] Richard Oram (Ed.), *The Kings and Queens of Scotland* (Tempus Publishing Ltd., Stroud, Gloucestershire, England, 2001) p. 194.

[162] Richard Oram (Ed.), *The Kings and Queens of Scotland* (Tempus Publishing Ltd., Stroud, Gloucestershire, England, 2001) p. 194-195.

[163] Richard Oram (Ed.), *The Kings and Queens of Scotland* (Tempus Publishing Ltd., Stroud, Gloucestershire, England, 2001) p. 196.

[164] Richard Oram (Ed.), *The Kings and Queens of Scotland* (Tempus Publishing Ltd., Stroud, Gloucestershire, England, 2001) p. 144.

[165] Agnes Mure MacKenzie, *The Rise of the Stewarts* (Oliver & Boyd, Ltd, Edinburgh. Originally printed 1935, this printing 1957.), p. 43.

[166] John Cannon & Ralph Griffiths, *The Oxford Illustrated History of the British Monarchy* (2000 edition, Oxford University Press), Geneaolgies of Royal Lines Appendix.

[167] Caroline Bingham, *Kings and Queens of Scotland* (orig. published 1976, Taplinger Publishing Co. this edition, 1985, Dorset Press) p. 56.

[168] Richard Oram (Ed.), *The Kings and Queens of Scotland* (Tempus Publishing Ltd., Stroud, Gloucestershire, England, 2001) p. 144.

[169] Caroline Bingham, *Kings and Queens of Scotland* (orig. published 1976, Taplinger Publishing Co. this edition, 1985, Dorset Press), p. 56.

[170] Caroline Bingham, *Kings and Queens of Scotland* (orig. published 1976, Taplinger Publishing Co. this edition, 1985, Dorset Press), p. 56.

[171] John Cannon & Ralph Griffiths, *The Oxford Illustrated History of the British Monarchy* (2000 edition, Oxford University Press), p. 251.

[172] John Cannon & Ralph Griffiths, *The Oxford Illustrated History of the British Monarchy* (2000 edition, Oxford University Press), Geneaolgies of Royal Lines Appendix.

[173] Caroline Bingham, *Kings and Queens of Scotland* (orig. published 1976, Taplinger Publishing Co. this edition, 1985, Dorset Press) p. 56.

[174] Agnes Mure MacKenzie, *The Rise of the Stewarts* (Oliver & Boyd, Ltd, Edinburgh. Originally printed 1935, this printing 1957.), p. 65.

[175] Agnes Mure MacKenzie, *The Rise of the Stewarts* (Oliver & Boyd, Ltd, Edinburgh. Originally printed 1935, this printing 1957.), p. 77.

[176] Fitzroy Maclean, *A Concise History of Scotland* (First published 1970. This version, 2002. Thames & Hudson Ltd., London), p. 49.

[177] Caroline Bingham, *Kings and Queens of Scotland* (orig. published 1976, Taplinger Publishing Co. this edition, 1985, Dorset Press) p. 57.

[178] Richard Oram (Ed.), *The Kings and Queens of Scotland* (Tempus Publishing Ltd., Stroud, Gloucestershire, England, 2001) p. 196.

[179] Agnes Mure MacKenzie, *The Rise of the Stewarts* (Oliver & Boyd, Ltd, Edinburgh. Originally printed 1935, this printing 1957.), p. 77.

[180] John Cannon & Ralph Griffiths, *The Oxford Illustrated History of the British Monarchy* (2000 edition, Oxford University Press), p. 657.

[181] Agnes Mure MacKenzie, *The Rise of the Stewarts* (Oliver & Boyd, Ltd, Edinburgh. Originally printed 1935, this printing 1957.), p. 80.

[182] John Cannon & Ralph Griffiths, *The Oxford Illustrated History of the British Monarchy* (2000 edition, Oxford University Press), List of Monarchs Appendix.

[183] Fitzroy Maclean, *A Concise History of Scotland* (First published 1970. This version, 2002. Thames & Hudson Ltd., London), p. 49.

[184] Caroline Bingham, *Kings and Queens of Scotland* (orig. published 1976, Taplinger Publishing Co. this edition, 1985, Dorset Press) p. 57.

[185] Agnes Mure MacKenzie, *The Rise of the Stewarts* (Oliver & Boyd, Ltd, Edinburgh. Originally printed 1935, this printing 1957.), p. 80.

[186] Agnes Mure MacKenzie, *The Rise of the Stewarts* (Oliver & Boyd, Ltd, Edinburgh. Originally printed 1935, this printing 1957.), p. 81.

[187] Agnes Mure MacKenzie, *The Rise of the Stewarts* (Oliver & Boyd, Ltd, Edinburgh. Originally printed 1935, this printing 1957.), p. 89-90.

[188] Fitzroy Maclean, *A Concise History of Scotland* (First published 1970. This version, 2002. Thames & Hudson Ltd., London), p. 49.

[189] John Cannon & Ralph Griffiths, *The Oxford Illustrated History of the British Monarchy* (2000 edition, Oxford University Press), p. 251.

[190] Caroline Bingham, *Kings and Queens of Scotland* (orig. published 1976, Taplinger Publishing Co. this edition, 1985, Dorset Press) p. 58.

[191] Fitzroy Maclean, *A Concise History of Scotland* (First published 1970. This version, 2002. Thames & Hudson Ltd., London), p. 49.

[192] Caroline Bingham, *Kings and Queens of Scotland* (orig. published 1976, Taplinger Publishing Co. this edition, 1985, Dorset Press) p. 58.

[193] Agnes Mure MacKenzie, *The Rise of the Stewarts* (Oliver & Boyd, Ltd, Edinburgh. Originally printed 1935, this printing 1957.), p. 105.

[194] Fitzroy Maclean, *A Concise History of Scotland* (First published 1970. This version, 2002. Thames & Hudson Ltd., London), p. 50.

[195] Caroline Bingham, *Kings and Queens of Scotland* (orig. published 1976, Taplinger Publishing Co. this edition, 1985, Dorset Press) p. 59.

[196] Agnes Mure MacKenzie, *The Rise of the Stewarts* (Oliver & Boyd, Ltd, Edinburgh. Originally printed 1935, this printing 1957.), p. 81.

[197] Richard Oram (Ed.), *The Kings and Queens of Scotland* (Tempus Publishing Ltd., Stroud, Gloucestershire, England, 2001) p. 198.

[198] John Cannon & Ralph Griffiths, *The Oxford Illustrated History of the British Monarchy* (2000 edition, Oxford University Press), Geneaolgies of Royal Lines Appendix.

[199] Fitzroy Maclean, *A Concise History of Scotland* (First published 1970. This version, 2002. Thames & Hudson Ltd., London), p. 50.

[200] John Cannon & Ralph Griffiths, *The Oxford Illustrated History of the British Monarchy* (2000 edition, Oxford University Press), List of Monarchs Appendix.

[201] Caroline Bingham, *Kings and Queens of Scotland* (orig. published 1976, Taplinger Publishing Co. this edition, 1985, Dorset Press) p. 59.

[202] Agnes Mure MacKenzie, *The Rise of the Stewarts* (Oliver & Boyd, Ltd, Edinburgh. Originally printed 1935, this printing 1957.), p. 81.

[203] Caroline Bingham, *Kings and Queens of Scotland* (orig. published 1976, Taplinger Publishing Co. this edition, 1985, Dorset Press) p. 59.

[204] John Cannon & Ralph Griffiths, *The Oxford Illustrated History of the British Monarchy* (2000 edition, Oxford University Press), Geneaolgies of Royal Lines Appendix; List of Monarchs Appendix.

[205] Caroline Bingham, *Kings and Queens of Scotland* (orig. published 1976, Taplinger Publishing Co. this edition, 1985, Dorset Press), p. 59.

[206] Fitzroy Maclean, *A Concise History of Scotland* (First published 1970. This version, 2002. Thames & Hudson Ltd., London), p. 50.

[207] Caroline Bingham, *Kings and Queens of Scotland* (orig. published 1976, Taplinger Publishing Co. this edition, 1985, Dorset Press), p. 60.

[208] Agnes Mure MacKenzie, *The Rise of the Stewarts* (Oliver & Boyd, Ltd, Edinburgh. Originally printed 1935, this printing 1957.), p. 140.

[209] Caroline Bingham, *Kings and Queens of Scotland* (orig. published 1976, Taplinger Publishing Co. this edition, 1985, Dorset Press) p. 61.

[210] Fitzroy Maclean, *A Concise History of Scotland* (First published 1970. This version, 2002. Thames & Hudson Ltd., London), p. 54.

[211] Agnes Mure MacKenzie, *The Rise of the Stewarts* (Oliver & Boyd, Ltd, Edinburgh. Originally printed 1935, this printing 1957.), p. 171, 176, 184, 196-197.

[212] Richard Oram (Ed.), *The Kings and Queens of Scotland* (Tempus Publishing Ltd., Stroud, Gloucestershire, England, 2001) p. 208-209.

[213] Fitzroy Maclean, *A Concise History of Scotland* (First published 1970. This version, 2002. Thames & Hudson Ltd., London), p. 54.

[214] John Cannon & Ralph Griffiths, *The Oxford Illustrated History of the British Monarchy* (2000 edition, Oxford University Press), p. 263.

[215] Fitzroy Maclean, *A Concise History of Scotland* (First published 1970. This version, 2002. Thames & Hudson Ltd., London), p. 54.

[216] Fitzroy Maclean, *A Concise History of Scotland* (First published 1970. This version, 2002. Thames & Hudson Ltd., London), p. 54.

[217] Caroline Bingham, *Kings and Queens of Scotland* (orig. published 1976, Taplinger Publishing Co. this edition, 1985, Dorset Press), p. 61.

[218] Fitzroy Maclean, *A Concise History of Scotland* (First published 1970. This version, 2002. Thames & Hudson Ltd., London), p. 55.

[219] Fitzroy Maclean, *A Concise History of Scotland* (First published 1970. This version, 2002. Thames & Hudson Ltd., London), p. 55.

[220] Fitzroy Maclean, *A Concise History of Scotland* (First published 1970. This version, 2002. Thames & Hudson Ltd., London), p. 55.

[221] Caroline Bingham, *Kings and Queens of Scotland* (orig. published 1976, Taplinger Publishing Co. this edition, 1985, Dorset Press) p. 62.

[222] Fitzroy Maclean, *A Concise History of Scotland* (First published 1970. This version, 2002. Thames & Hudson Ltd., London), p. 56.

[223] Caroline Bingham, *Kings and Queens of Scotland* (orig. published 1976, Taplinger Publishing Co. this edition, 1985, Dorset Press), p. 62.

[224] Caroline Bingham, *Kings and Queens of Scotland* (orig. published 1976, Taplinger Publishing Co. this edition, 1985, Dorset Press), p. 62.

[225] Fitzroy Maclean, *A Concise History of Scotland* (First published 1970. This version, 2002. Thames & Hudson Ltd., London), p. 56.

[226] Agnes Mure MacKenzie, *The Rise of the Stewarts* (Oliver & Boyd, Ltd, Edinburgh. Originally printed 1935, this printing 1957.), p. 182.

[227] Agnes Mure MacKenzie, *The Rise of the Stewarts* (Oliver & Boyd, Ltd, Edinburgh. Originally printed 1935, this printing 1957.), p. 182.

[228] Agnes Mure MacKenzie, *The Rise of the Stewarts* (Oliver & Boyd, Ltd, Edinburgh. Originally printed 1935, this printing 1957.), p. 182.

[229] Agnes Mure MacKenzie, *The Rise of the Stewarts* (Oliver & Boyd, Ltd, Edinburgh. Orig. printed 1935, this printing 1957.), p. 182-183.

[230] Agnes Mure MacKenzie, *The Rise of the Stewarts* (Oliver & Boyd, Ltd, Edinburgh. Originally printed 1935, this printing 1957.), p. 184.

[231] John Cannon & Ralph Griffiths, *The Oxford Illustrated History of the British Monarchy* (2000 edition, Oxford University Press), p. 263.

[232] Fitzroy Maclean, *A Concise History of Scotland* (First published 1970. This version, 2002. Thames & Hudson Ltd., London), p. 56.

[233] Caroline Bingham, *Kings and Queens of Scotland* (orig. published 1976, Taplinger Publishing Co. this edition, 1985, Dorset Press) p. 62.

[234] Agnes Mure MacKenzie, *The Rise of the Stewarts* (Oliver & Boyd, Ltd, Edinburgh. Originally printed 1935, this printing 1957.), p. 188.

[235] Agnes Mure MacKenzie, *The Rise of the Stewarts* (Oliver & Boyd, Ltd, Edinburgh. Originally printed 1935, this printing 1957.), p. 189.

[236] Agnes Mure MacKenzie, *The Rise of the Stewarts* (Oliver & Boyd, Ltd, Edinburgh. Orig. printed 1935, this printing 1957.), p. 190-191.

[237] Agnes Mure MacKenzie, *The Rise of the Stewarts* (Oliver & Boyd, Ltd, Edinburgh. Originally printed 1935, this printing 1957.), p. 191.

[238] Agnes Mure MacKenzie, *The Rise of the Stewarts* (Oliver & Boyd, Ltd, Edinburgh. Originally printed 1935, this printing 1957.), p. 192.

[239] Agnes Mure MacKenzie, *The Rise of the Stewarts* (Oliver & Boyd, Ltd, Edinburgh. Originally printed 1935, this printing 1957.), p. 192.

[240] Caroline Bingham, *Kings and Queens of Scotland* (orig. published 1976, Taplinger Publishing Co. this edition, 1985, Dorset Press) p. 63.

[241] Agnes Mure MacKenzie, *The Rise of the Stewarts* (Oliver & Boyd, Ltd, Edinburgh. Originally printed 1935, this printing 1957.), p. 176.

[242] John Cannon & Ralph Griffiths, *The Oxford Illustrated History of the British Monarchy* (2000 edition, Oxford University Press), Geneaolgies of Royal Lines Appendix; List of Monarchs Appendix.

[243] Caroline Bingham, *Kings and Queens of Scotland* (orig. published 1976, Taplinger Publishing Co. this edition, 1985, Dorset Press), p. 63.

[244] Agnes Mure MacKenzie, *The Rise of the Stewarts* (Oliver & Boyd, Ltd, Edinburgh. Originally printed 1935, this printing 1957.), p. 185.

[245] Caroline Bingham, *Kings and Queens of Scotland* (orig. published 1976, Taplinger Publishing Co. this edition, 1985, Dorset Press), p. 63.

[246] John Cannon & Ralph Griffiths, *The Oxford Illustrated History of the British Monarchy* (2000 edition, Oxford University Press), p. 642, List of Monarchs Appendix.

[247] Agnes Mure MacKenzie, *The Rise of the Stewarts* (Oliver & Boyd, Ltd, Edinburgh. Originally printed 1935, this printing 1957.), p. 195.

[248] Fitzroy Maclean, *A Concise History of Scotland* (First published 1970. This version, 2002. Thames & Hudson Ltd., London), p. 57.

[249] Caroline Bingham, *Kings and Queens of Scotland* (orig. published 1976, Taplinger Publishing Co. this edition, 1985, Dorset Press) p. 64.

[250] Fitzroy Maclean, *A Concise History of Scotland* (First published 1970. This version, 2002. Thames & Hudson Ltd., London), p. 58.

[251] Caroline Bingham, *Kings and Queens of Scotland* (orig. published 1976, Taplinger Publishing Co. this edition, 1985, Dorset Press) p. 64.

[252] Agnes Mure MacKenzie, *The Rise of the Stewarts* (Oliver & Boyd, Ltd, Edinburgh. Originally printed 1935, this printing 1957.), p. 221.

[253] Fitzroy Maclean, *A Concise History of Scotland* (First published 1970. This version, 2002. Thames & Hudson Ltd., London), p. 59.

[254] John Cannon & Ralph Griffiths, *The Oxford Illustrated History of the British Monarchy* (2000 edition, Oxford University Press), p. 271.

[255] Caroline Bingham, *Kings and Queens of Scotland* (orig. published 1976, Taplinger Publishing Co. this edition, 1985, Dorset Press) p. 65.

[256] Fitzroy Maclean, *A Concise History of Scotland* (First published 1970. This version, 2002. Thames & Hudson Ltd., London), p. 60.

[257] Caroline Bingham, *Kings and Queens of Scotland* (orig. published 1976, Taplinger Publishing Co. this edition, 1985, Dorset Press) p. 65.

[258] Caroline Bingham, *Kings and Queens of Scotland* (orig. published 1976, Taplinger Publishing Co. this edition, 1985, Dorset Press) p. 64.

[259] Agnes Mure MacKenzie, *The Rise of the Stewarts* (Oliver & Boyd, Ltd, Edinburgh. Orig. printed 1935, this printing 1957.), p. 204-206.

[260] John Cannon & Ralph Griffiths, *The Oxford Illustrated History of the British Monarchy* (2000 edition, Oxford University Press), p. 271; Geneaolgies of Royal Lines Appendix.

[261] Agnes Mure MacKenzie, *The Rise of the Stewarts* (Oliver & Boyd, Ltd, Edinburgh. Originally printed 1935, this printing 1957.), p. 218, 239, 254, 273.

[262] Fitzroy Maclean, *A Concise History of Scotland* (First published 1970. This version, 2002. Thames & Hudson Ltd., London), p. 60.

[263] Caroline Bingham, *Kings and Queens of Scotland* (orig. published 1976, Taplinger Publishing Co. this edition, 1985, Dorset Press) p. 66.

[264] Agnes Mure MacKenzie, *The Rise of the Stewarts* (Oliver & Boyd, Ltd, Edinburgh. Originally printed 1935, this printing 1957.), p. 243.

[265] Caroline Bingham, *Kings and Queens of Scotland* (orig. published 1976, Taplinger Publishing Co. this edition, 1985, Dorset Press), p. 66.

[266] Agnes Mure MacKenzie, *The Rise of the Stewarts* (Oliver & Boyd, Ltd, Edinburgh. Originally printed 1935, this printing 1957.), p. 218.

[267] John Cannon & Ralph Griffiths, *The Oxford Illustrated History of the British Monarchy* (2000 edition, Oxford University Press), Geneaolgies of Royal Lines Appendix; List of Monarchs Appendix.

[268] Caroline Bingham, *Kings and Queens of Scotland* (orig. published 1976, Taplinger Publishing Co. this edition, 1985, Dorset Press), p. 66.

[269] John Cannon & Ralph Griffiths, *The Oxford Illustrated History of the British Monarchy* (2000 edition, Oxford University Press), p. 277; List of Monarchs Appendix.

[270] Fitzroy Maclean, *A Concise History of Scotland* (First published 1970. This version, 2002. Thames & Hudson Ltd., London), p. 61.

[271] Agnes Mure MacKenzie, *The Rise of the Stewarts* (Oliver & Boyd, Ltd, Edinburgh. Orig. printed 1935, this printing 1957.), p. 244-249.

[272] Caroline Bingham, *Kings and Queens of Scotland* (orig. published 1976, Taplinger Publishing Co. this edition, 1985, Dorset Press) p. 66.

[273] Agnes Mure MacKenzie, *The Rise of the Stewarts* (Oliver & Boyd, Ltd, Edinburgh. Originally printed 1935, this printing 1957.), p. 249.

[274] Agnes Mure MacKenzie, *The Rise of the Stewarts* (Oliver & Boyd, Ltd, Edinburgh. Originally printed 1935, this printing 1957.), p. 250.

[275] Fitzroy Maclean, *A Concise History of Scotland* (First published 1970. This version, 2002. Thames & Hudson Ltd., London), p. 61.

[276] Caroline Bingham, *Kings and Queens of Scotland* (orig. published 1976, Taplinger Publishing Co. this edition, 1985, Dorset Press), p. 66-7.

[277] Agnes Mure MacKenzie, *The Rise of the Stewarts* (Oliver & Boyd, Ltd, Edinburgh. Originally printed 1935, this printing 1957.), p. 257.

[278] John Cannon & Ralph Griffiths, *The Oxford Illustrated History of the British Monarchy* (2000 edition, Oxford University Press), Geneaolgies of Royal Lines Appendix.

[279] Caroline Bingham, *Kings and Queens of Scotland* (orig. published 1976, Taplinger Publishing Co. this edition, 1985, Dorset Press) p. 67.

[280] Fitzroy Maclean, *A Concise History of Scotland* (First published 1970. This version, 2002. Thames & Hudson Ltd., London), p. 61.

[281] John Cannon & Ralph Griffiths, *The Oxford Illustrated History of the British Monarchy* (2000 edition, Oxford University Press), p. 195.

[282] Agnes Mure MacKenzie, *The Rise of the Stewarts* (Oliver & Boyd, Ltd, Edinburgh. Originally printed 1935, this printing 1957.), p. 263.

[283] Fitzroy Maclean, *A Concise History of Scotland* (First published 1970. This version, 2002. Thames & Hudson Ltd., London), p. 61.

[284] Caroline Bingham, *Kings and Queens of Scotland* (orig. published 1976, Taplinger Publishing Co. this edition, 1985, Dorset Press) p. 67.

[285] Agnes Mure MacKenzie, *The Rise of the Stewarts* (Oliver & Boyd, Ltd, Edinburgh. Originally printed 1935, this printing 1957.), p. 263.

[286] Fitzroy Maclean, *A Concise History of Scotland* (First published 1970. This version, 2002. Thames & Hudson Ltd., London), p. 61.

[287] Caroline Bingham, *Kings and Queens of Scotland* (orig. published 1976, Taplinger Publishing Co. this edition, 1985, Dorset Press), p. 67.

[288] Caroline Bingham, *Kings and Queens of Scotland* (orig. published 1976, Taplinger Publishing Co. this edition, 1985, Dorset Press), p. 68.

[289] John Cannon & Ralph Griffiths, *The Oxford Illustrated History of the British Monarchy* (2000 edition, Oxford University Press), p. 277.

[290] Fitzroy Maclean, *A Concise History of Scotland* (First published 1970. This version, 2002. Thames & Hudson Ltd., London), p. 61.

[291] Caroline Bingham, *Kings and Queens of Scotland* (orig. published 1976, Taplinger Publishing Co. this edition, 1985, Dorset Press) p. 68.

[292] Agnes Mure MacKenzie, *The Rise of the Stewarts* (Oliver & Boyd, Ltd, Edinburgh. Orig. printed 1935, this printing 1957.), p. 274-276.

[293] Caroline Bingham, *Kings and Queens of Scotland* (orig. published 1976, Taplinger Publishing Co. this edition, 1985, Dorset Press), p. 69.

[294] Fitzroy Maclean, *A Concise History of Scotland* (First published 1970. This version, 2002. Thames & Hudson Ltd., London), p. 61-62.
[295] John Cannon & Ralph Griffiths, *The Oxford Illustrated History of the British Monarchy* (2000 edition, Oxford University Press), p. 277.
[296] Caroline Bingham, *Kings and Queens of Scotland* (orig. published 1976, Taplinger Publishing Co. this edition, 1985, Dorset Press), p. 67.
[297] Fitzroy Maclean, *A Concise History of Scotland* (First published 1970. This version, 2002. Thames & Hudson Ltd., London), p. 62.
[298] John Cannon & Ralph Griffiths, *The Oxford Illustrated History of the British Monarchy* (2000 edition, Oxford University Press), p. 277.
[299] Caroline Bingham, *Kings and Queens of Scotland* (orig. published 1976, Taplinger Publishing Co. this edition, 1985, Dorset Press) p. 70.
[300] Fitzroy Maclean, *A Concise History of Scotland* (First published 1970. This version, 2002. Thames & Hudson Ltd., London), p. 62.
[301] Agnes Mure MacKenzie, *The Rise of the Stewarts* (Oliver & Boyd, Ltd, Edinburgh. Originally printed 1935, this printing 1957.), p. 292.
[302] Fitzroy Maclean, *A Concise History of Scotland* (First published 1970. This version, 2002. Thames & Hudson Ltd., London), p. 62.
[303] John Cannon & Ralph Griffiths, *The Oxford Illustrated History of the British Monarchy* (2000 edition, Oxford University Press), Geneaolgies of Royal Lines Appendix; List of Monarchs Appendix.
[304] Caroline Bingham, *Kings and Queens of Scotland* (orig. published 1976, Taplinger Publishing Co. this edition, 1985, Dorset Press) p. 70-71.
[305] Agnes Mure MacKenzie, *The Rise of the Stewarts* (Oliver & Boyd, Ltd, Edinburgh. Originally printed 1935, this printing 1957.), p. 300.
[306] John Cannon & Ralph Griffiths, *The Oxford Illustrated History of the British Monarchy* (2000 edition, Oxford University Press), p. 657.
[307] Caroline Bingham, *Kings and Queens of Scotland* (orig. published 1976, Taplinger Publishing Co. this edition, 1985, Dorset Press), p. 70.
[308] John Cannon & Ralph Griffiths, *The Oxford Illustrated History of the British Monarchy* (2000 edition, Oxford University Press), Geneaolgies of Royal Lines Appendix; List of Monarchs Appendix.
[309] Agnes Mure MacKenzie, *The Rise of the Stewarts* (Oliver & Boyd, Ltd, Edinburgh. Originally printed 1935, this printing 1957.), p. 300.
[310] Fitzroy Maclean, *A Concise History of Scotland* (First published 1970. This version, 2002. Thames & Hudson Ltd., London), p. 63.
[311] John Cannon & Ralph Griffiths, *The Oxford Illustrated History of the British Monarchy* (2000 edition, Oxford University Press), List of Monarchs Appendix.
[312] Caroline Bingham, *Kings and Queens of Scotland* (orig. published 1976, Taplinger Publishing Co. this edition, 1985, Dorset Press), p. 71.
[313] Fitzroy Maclean, *A Concise History of Scotland* (First published 1970. This version, 2002. Thames & Hudson Ltd., London), p. 63.
[314] Fitzroy Maclean, *A Concise History of Scotland* (First published 1970. This version, 2002. Thames & Hudson Ltd., London), p. 63-64.
[315] Agnes Mure MacKenzie, *The Rise of the Stewarts* (Oliver & Boyd, Ltd, Edinburgh. Originally printed 1935, this printing 1957.), p. 295.
[316] Caroline Bingham, *Kings and Queens of Scotland* (orig. published 1976, Taplinger Publishing Co. this edition, 1985, Dorset Press), p. 71.
[317] Raymond Campbell Paterson, *The Lords of the Isles: A History of Clan Donald* (Birlinn Limited, Edinburgh, 2001), p. 57-59.
[318] Fitzroy Maclean, *A Concise History of Scotland* (First published 1970. This version, 2002. Thames & Hudson Ltd., London), p. 70.
[319] Caroline Bingham, *Kings and Queens of Scotland* (orig. published 1976, Taplinger Publishing Co. this edition, 1985, Dorset Press), p. 72.
[320] Richard Oram (Ed.), *The Kings and Queens of Scotland* (Tempus Publishing Ltd., Stroud, Gloucestershire, England, 2001), p. 235.
[321] John Cannon & Ralph Griffiths, *The Oxford Illustrated History of the British Monarchy* (2000 edition, Oxford University Press), p. 292.
[322] Caroline Bingham, *Kings and Queens of Scotland* (orig. published 1976, Taplinger Publishing Co. this edition, 1985, Dorset Press), p. 72-3.
[323] Fitzroy Maclean, *A Concise History of Scotland* (First published 1970. This version, 2002. Thames & Hudson Ltd., London), p. 73.
[324] Caroline Bingham, *Kings and Queens of Scotland* (orig. published 1976, Taplinger Publishing Co. this edition, 1985, Dorset Press) p. 73.
[325] John Cannon & Ralph Griffiths, *The Oxford Illustrated History of the British Monarchy* (2000 edition, Oxford University Press), p. 292.
[326] Fitzroy Maclean, *A Concise History of Scotland* (First published 1970. This version, 2002. Thames & Hudson Ltd., London), p. 73.
[327] John Cannon & Ralph Griffiths, *The Oxford Illustrated History of the British Monarchy* (2000 edition, Oxford University Press), p. 642; Geneaolgies of Royal Lines Appendix.
[328] Fitzroy Maclean, *A Concise History of Scotland* (First published 1970. This version, 2002. Thames & Hudson Ltd., London), p. 70.
[329] Fitzroy Maclean, *A Concise History of Scotland* (First published 1970. This version, 2002. Thames & Hudson Ltd., London), p. 70.
[330] Caroline Bingham, *Kings and Queens of Scotland* (orig. published 1976, Taplinger Publishing Co. this edition, 1985, Dorset Press) p. 73-74.
[331] Fitzroy Maclean, *A Concise History of Scotland* (First published 1970. This version, 2002. Thames & Hudson Ltd., London), p. 66.
[332] Caroline Bingham, *Kings and Queens of Scotland* (orig. published 1976, Taplinger Publishing Co. this edition, 1985, Dorset Press), p. 73-4.
[333] Fitzroy Maclean, *A Concise History of Scotland* (First published 1970. This version, 2002. Thames & Hudson Ltd., London), p. 71-72.
[334] Fitzroy Maclean, *A Concise History of Scotland* (First published 1970. This version, 2002. Thames & Hudson Ltd., London), p. 73.
[335] Fitzroy Maclean, *A Concise History of Scotland* (First published 1970. This version, 2002. Thames & Hudson Ltd., London), p. 74.
[336] Angus MacKay, *The Book of MacKay* (Edinburgh: Norman MacLeod, 1906), p. 76.
[337] Caroline Bingham, *Kings and Queens of Scotland* (orig. published 1976, Taplinger Publishing Co. this edition, 1985, Dorset Press) p. 75.
[338] Agnes Mure MacKenzie, *The Rise of the Stewarts* (Oliver & Boyd, Ltd, Edinburgh. Originally printed 1935, this printing 1957.), p. 379.
[339] Fitzroy Maclean, *A Concise History of Scotland* (First published 1970. This version, 2002. Thames & Hudson Ltd., London), p. 74-75.
[340] Caroline Bingham, *Kings and Queens of Scotland* (orig. published 1976, Taplinger Publishing Co. this edition, 1985, Dorset Press), p. 75.
[341] Fitzroy Maclean, *A Concise History of Scotland* (First published 1970. This version, 2002. Thames & Hudson Ltd., London), p. 75.
[342] Agnes Mure MacKenzie, *The Rise of the Stewarts* (Oliver & Boyd, Ltd, Edinburgh. Originally printed 1935, this printing 1957.), p. 384.
[343] John Cannon & Ralph Griffiths, *The Oxford Illustrated History of the British Monarchy* (2000 edition, Oxford University Press), p. 657.
[344] Fitzroy Maclean, *A Concise History of Scotland* (First published 1970. This version, 2002. Thames & Hudson Ltd., London), p. 75.
[345] John Cannon & Ralph Griffiths, *The Oxford Illustrated History of the British Monarchy* (2000 edition, Oxford University Press), p. 643; Geneaolgies of Royal Lines Appendix; List of Monarchs Appendix.
[346] Caroline Bingham, *Kings and Queens of Scotland* (orig. published 1976, Taplinger Publishing Co. this edition, 1985, Dorset Press), p. 75.
[347] John Cannon & Ralph Griffiths, *The Oxford Illustrated History of the British Monarchy* (2000 edition, Oxford University Press), List of Monarchs Appendix.
[348] Caroline Bingham, *Kings and Queens of Scotland* (orig. published 1976, Taplinger Publishing Co. this edition, 1985, Dorset Press) p. 76.
[349] Fitzroy Maclean, *A Concise History of Scotland* (First published 1970. This version, 2002. Thames & Hudson Ltd., London), p. 75-76.

[350] Fitzroy Maclean, *A Concise History of Scotland* (First published 1970. This version, 2002. Thames & Hudson Ltd., London), p. 76.

[351] Fitzroy Maclean, *A Concise History of Scotland* (First published 1970. This version, 2002. Thames & Hudson Ltd., London), p. 76.

[352] Caroline Bingham, *Kings and Queens of Scotland* (orig. published 1976, Taplinger Publishing Co. this edition, 1985, Dorset Press) p. 76-77.

[353] Caroline Bingham, *Kings and Queens of Scotland* (orig. published 1976, Taplinger Publishing Co. this edition, 1985, Dorset Press) p. 77.

[354] Fitzroy Maclean, *A Concise History of Scotland* (First published 1970. This version, 2002. Thames & Hudson Ltd., London), p. 76-77.

[355] Caroline Bingham, *Kings and Queens of Scotland* (orig. published 1976, Taplinger Publishing Co. this edition, 1985, Dorset Press) p. 77-78.

[356] Fitzroy Maclean, *A Concise History of Scotland* (First published 1970. This version, 2002. Thames & Hudson Ltd., London), p. 77.

[357] Caroline Bingham, *Kings and Queens of Scotland* (orig. published 1976, Taplinger Publishing Co. this edition, 1985, Dorset Press) p. 79.

[358] John Cannon & Ralph Griffiths, *The Oxford Illustrated History of the British Monarchy* (2000 edition, Oxford University Press), Geneaolgies of Royal Lines Appendix.

[359] Richard Oram (Ed.), *The Kings and Queens of Scotland* (Tempus Publishing Ltd., Stroud, Gloucestershire, England, 2001), p. 246.

[360] Fitzroy Maclean, *A Concise History of Scotland* (First published 1970. This version, 2002. Thames & Hudson Ltd., London), p. 78.

[361] Caroline Bingham, *Kings and Queens of Scotland* (orig. published 1976, Taplinger Publishing Co. this edition, 1985, Dorset Press) p. 79.

[362] John Cannon & Ralph Griffiths, *The Oxford Illustrated History of the British Monarchy* (2000 edition, Oxford University Press), Geneaolgies of Royal Lines Appendix.

[363] Raymond Campbell Paterson, *The Lords of the Isles: A History of Clan Donald* (Birlinn Limited, Edinburgh, 2001), p. 65.

[364] Caroline Bingham, *Kings and Queens of Scotland* (orig. published 1976, Taplinger Publishing Co. this edition, 1985, Dorset Press) p. 78.

[365] Caroline Bingham, *Kings and Queens of Scotland* (orig. published 1976, Taplinger Publishing Co. this edition, 1985, Dorset Press) p. 78-79.

[366] Fitzroy Maclean, *A Concise History of Scotland* (First published 1970. This version, 2002. Thames & Hudson Ltd., London), p. 78.

[367] Fitzroy Maclean, *A Concise History of Scotland* (First published 1970. This version, 2002. Thames & Hudson Ltd., London), p. 78.

[368] Caroline Bingham, *Kings and Queens of Scotland* (orig. published 1976, Taplinger Publishing Co. this edition, 1985, Dorset Press) p. 80.

[369] Fitzroy Maclean, *A Concise History of Scotland* (First published 1970. This version, 2002. Thames & Hudson Ltd., London), p. 78.

[370] Caroline Bingham, *Kings and Queens of Scotland* (orig. published 1976, Taplinger Publishing Co. this edition, 1985, Dorset Press) p. 80.

[371] John Cannon & Ralph Griffiths, *The Oxford Illustrated History of the British Monarchy* (2000 edition, Oxford University Press), Geneaolgies of Royal Lines Appendix.

[372] Orkney Family History Society, (Orkney Library and Archives; 44 Junction Rd., Kirkwall, Orkney, KW15 1AG, Scotland, UK), from Assistant Archivist Sarah Maclean.

[373] Roland William Saint-Clair, *Saint-Clairs of the Isles: A History of the Sea-Kings of Orkney and their Scottish Successors of the Sirname Sinclair* (Auckland, New Zealand, H. Brett, General Printer and Publisher, Shortland and Fort Streets 1898), p. 136.

[374] Roland William Saint-Clair, *Saint-Clairs of the Isles: A History of the Sea-Kings of Orkney and their Scottish Successors of the Sirname Sinclair* (Auckland, New Zealand, H. Brett, General Printer and Publisher, Shortland and Fort Streets 1898), p. 137.

[375] Roland William Saint-Clair, *Saint-Clairs of the Isles: A History of the Sea-Kings of Orkney and their Scottish Successors of the Sirname Sinclair* (Auckland, New Zealand, H. Brett, General Printer and Publisher, Shortland and Fort Streets 1898), p. 137.

[376] Charles Mosley, ed, *Burke's Peerage & Baronetage, 106th Edition* (Routledge; Slp edition (May 1, 1999), 2 volumes).

[377] Orkney Family History Society, (Orkney Library and Archives; 44 Junction Rd., Kirkwall, Orkney, KW15 1AG, Scotland, UK), from Assistant Archivist Sarah Maclean.

[378] Charles Mosley, ed, *Burke's Peerage & Baronetage, 106th Edition* (Routledge; Slp edition (May 1, 1999), 2 volumes).

[379] Angus MacKay, *The Book of MacKay* (Edinburgh: Norman MacLeod, 1906), p. 311.

[380] John Henderson, *Caithness Family History* (Edinburgh: David Douglas, 1884), p. 24.

[381] Charles Mosley, ed, *Burke's Peerage & Baronetage, 106th Edition* (Routledge; Slp edition (May 1, 1999), 2 volumes).

[382] Angus MacKay, *The Book of MacKay* (Edinburgh: Norman MacLeod, 1906), p. 311.

ENGLISH ROYALTY

THE SAXON DYNASTY

ENGLAND

WALES

THE KINGDOM OF WESSEX

THE SAXON KINGS BEGAN IN WESSEX,
BUT EVENTUALLY RULED ALL OF MODERN-
DAY ENGLAND.

THE SAXON DYNASTY

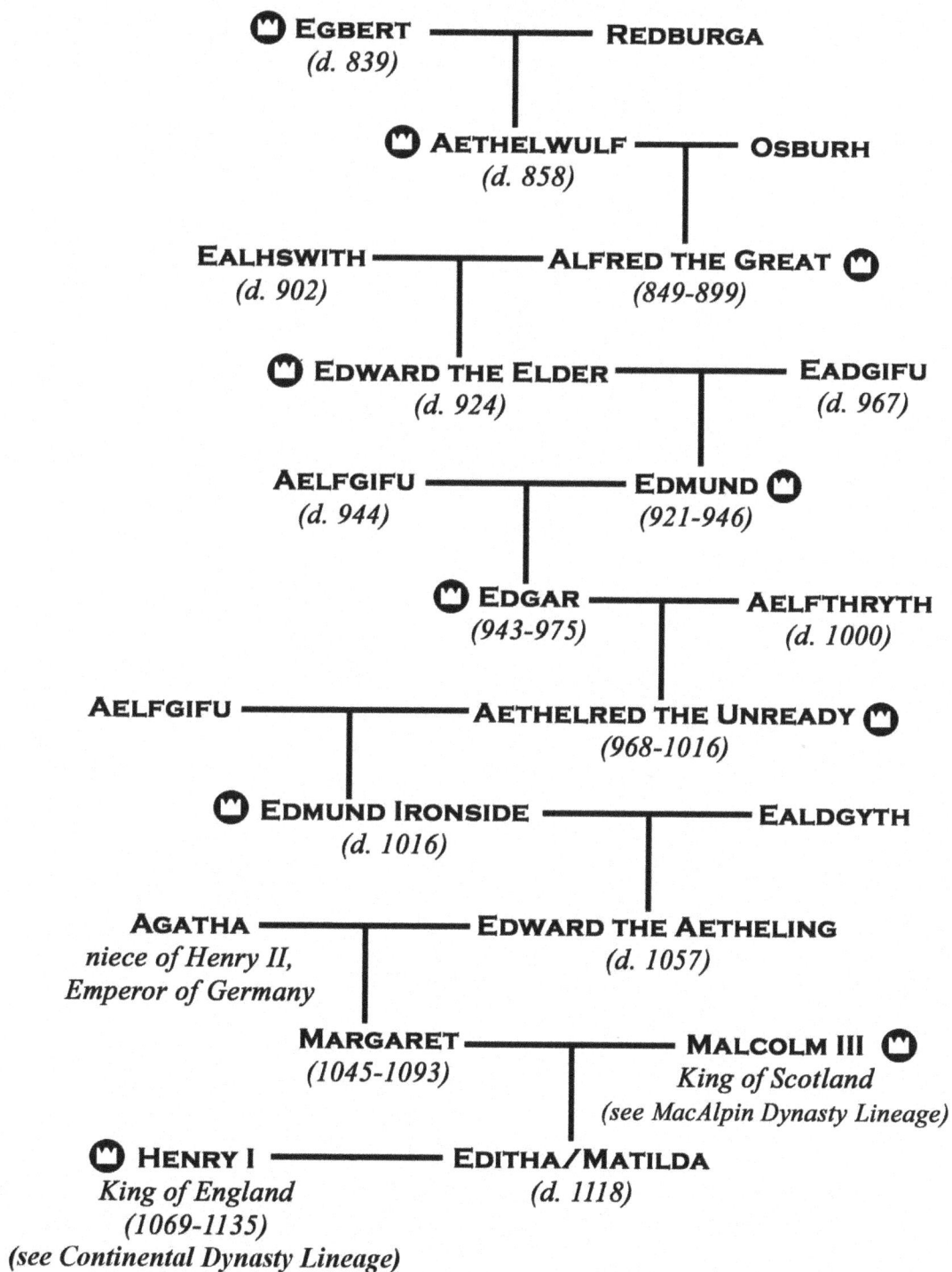

👑 **EGBERT**
(d. 839) —————————— **REDBURGA**

👑 **AETHELWULF**
(d. 858) —————————— **OSBURH**

EALHSWITH
(d. 902) —————————— **ALFRED THE GREAT** 👑
(849-899)

👑 **EDWARD THE ELDER**
(d. 924) —————————— **EADGIFU**
(d. 967)

AELFGIFU
(d. 944) —————————— **EDMUND** 👑
(921-946)

👑 **EDGAR**
(943-975) —————————— **AELFTHRYTH**
(d. 1000)

AELFGIFU —————————— **AETHELRED THE UNREADY** 👑
(968-1016)

👑 **EDMUND IRONSIDE**
(d. 1016) —————————— **EALDGYTH**

AGATHA
niece of Henry II,
Emperor of Germany —————————— **EDWARD THE AETHELING**
(d. 1057)

MARGARET
(1045-1093) —————————— **MALCOLM III** 👑
King of Scotland
(see MacAlpin Dynasty Lineage)

👑 **HENRY I** —————————— **EDITHA/MATILDA**
King of England
(1069-1135) *(d. 1118)*
(see Continental Dynasty Lineage)

THE SAXON DYNASTY

Long before William the Conqueror in 1066, there were kings who ruled virtually all of modern-day England. These rulers emerged from the kingdom of Wessex and stemmed from a single great family. But before we meet the first of these West Saxon kings, we need to establish some history.

After the Romans left Britain in 410 A.D., the Celts split into two factions. Vortigern wanted a Celtic revival with a native king, divesting themselves of Roman trappings. Ambrosius Aurelianus was the head of the Romanized Celtic gentry, and he wanted to keep many of the Roman ways.[1] Vortigern called upon Teutonic tribes from mainland Europe to help him fight Aurelianus, and that is how the Germanic tribes—Angles, Saxons, and Jutes—first got a foothold in Britain. They then went back to the continent and told their leaders about this island with rich resources and a good environment.[2]

The Germanic tribes invaded Britain in a coordinated attack meant to sweep away all resistance.[3] This attack was repelled, and they stayed away until 538 when Anglo-Saxon incursions resumed, not as a single unified battle plan, but in raids that nibbled the edges of the island and worked slowly inland from coastal toeholds.[4]

Now we move from England as a whole to the Kingdom of Wessex in particular. Wessex corresponded to the modern county of Wessex, in the southwest corner of England. Tradition holds that Wessex was founded in 495 by Cedric and his son Cynric, who were not West Saxons, as they had Breton, not Anglo-Saxon names.[5] It is said that the West Saxons, three shiploads, did not arrive in Wessex until 514. In 519, Cedric and Cynric took over the West Saxons' government and fought the native Britons, and from then on West Saxons ruled in Wessex.[6]

Egbert, King of Wessex
(d. 836)
(reigned 801-836)

Egbert's story began with a king named Cuthred, who ruled West Saxon (Wessex) until his death in 754. He was succeeded by Seabright, who was a terrible ruler. The Saxons had a tradition of the Council, or Witan, electing their kings, and they ousted Seabright in favor of Cynewulf. Seabright was killed. Some thirty years later, around 784, a kinsman of Seabright named Cyneard killed Cynewulf and was killed in return.[7]

Now the Witan had to choose a new king, and their choice was between Egbert and Beorhtric. Egbert was the son of Elmund, under-king of Kent, and the great-grandson of Ingild, brother to King Ina, one of the past over-kings (Bretwalda) of England.[8]

Beorhtric was chosen by the Witan, possibly because he was favored by neighboring King Offa of Mercia, a very powerful king. Egbert fled to Mercia for asylum, but Beorhtric sent to Offa to ask him to send Egbert back, and to arrange to marry Offa's daughter. When Offa seemed disposed to do as Beorhtric asked, Egbert fled to France, taking refuge in Charlemagne's court.[9]

For sixteen years Egbert learned from Charlemagne. He accompanied Charlemagne on many of his military campaigns, and he saw the administration of a great empire, learned the conduct of wars, followed the genius in military tactics, and enjoyed life in a brilliant court.[10]

In 800, Beorhtric's wife, Queen Eadburgha, poisoned him. Apparently, he had neglected her advice and company for that of a young ealderman named Warr. She poisoned Warr, but her husband drank from the same cup and died.[11]

Egbert returned to Wessex and was crowned king by the Witan. On the day of his coronation, a minor invasion of Wessex by Ethelmund of the Hwicce people (a Welsh tribe) occurred, but they were easily defeated.[12]

Egbert probably had ambitions to rule all of England from the start, but he took his time, planning and building up his army, particularly the cavalry, which he had seen used successfully by Charlemagne.[13]

In 813, he invaded Cornwall and subdued the Britons there. In 823 he had to do it all over again. Also in 823, a man named Beornwulf overthrew Cenwulf, the rightful king of Mercia (Offa had died in 796). Immediately after his coup, Beornwulf tried to invade Wessex, hoping to surprise Egbert while he was busy in Cornwall.[14]

He did surprise Egbert, but Egbert defeated Beornwulf soundly at Ellendun. After defeating the Mercians, Egbert decided to send his son Aethelwulf and a small army to Kent to demand submission from them. Kent surrendered, and Sussex and Essex also allied themselves with Wessex. Egbert then stoked an East Anglian revolt against Beornwulf of Mercia, in which Beornwulf was killed.[15]

Egbert had a strangely powerful army, in that his army would serve outside its native lands and for long periods of time. At this period in history, everything revolved around farms, and it was not unusual for an army to disperse as the harvest loomed and everyone went home to reap the crops. It was also very unusual for people to want to fight far from home, so for Egbert to have a cohesive army that served for long periods was an oddity, and one that no one can explain.[16]

In 827, Egbert finally conquered Mercia, deposing their king Wiglaf.[17] However, Egbert restored him to the throne as an under-king of Wessex in 828. In that same year, Egbert subdued North Wales.[18] He now ruled over all of England.

Then the Danes arrived, terrorizing the island. In 833, at Charmouth, Dover, 35 Danish ships landed. Egbert raced to the defense, but lost to the Danes, and he escaped in the night. He then called a council of nobles to strengthen the defenses of the kingdom.[19]

In 835, the Danes returned, and this time they brought an entire fleet—this was an all-out war, not a minor raid. The Danes joined with the Britons in Cornwall, and they faced Egbert together. Egbert met them at Hingston Down near Callington, and won resoundingly. The Danes escaped by sea, but the Cornwall Britons had nowhere to run.[20]

Egbert punished the Britons severely for their uprising and threatened to exterminate them all if there was any more trouble. He had seen Charlemagne destroy entire populations in his wars, so Egbert likely was not threatening idly.[21]

In 836, Egbert died. He had reigned for 37 years, and probably was in his 70s when he died, as he was likely in his 20s at the time he fled to Charlemagne.[22] This would put his birth somewhere around 763.

Egbert had married Redburga, and they had *Aethelwulf*, who succeeded his father.[23] Like all the Saxon kings of this period, he was a Christian of the Roman variety, unlike the Scottish kings who followed the unorthodox Christianity imported from Ireland.[24]

Aethelwulf, King of Wessex
(d. 858)
(reigned 836-858)

Aethelwulf was probably born around 801, after his father Egbert returned from his exile with Charlemagne. He was of age at Ellendun in 823 as he fought beside his father, and then was sent to Kent to secure their submission afterward.[25]

Unlike his father, Aethelwulf was by nature unwarlike, and leaned heavily toward the Church. Since he was the only son, or at least the only surviving son, of Egbert and Redburga, he became king in spite of his natural inclinations.[26]

When Aethelwulf went to Kent, he met with quick success, as seen above. Sussex, Essex, and Surrey also submitted to him. Egbert made his son under-king of these four provinces until 836, when Aethelwulf became King of Wessex. Aethelwulf installed his son Aethelstan as under-king there. Aethelstan was not the son of Aethelwulf's wife, Osburga, and so was either from an unknown first wife or was illegitimate.[27]

Aethelwulf married Osburga, daughter of Oslac, in 830.[28] Oslac was some type of servant of Aethelwulf's, but he traced his line back to the early Jutes, and was therefore of royal blood.

Aethelwulf and Osburga had four sons and at least one daughter.[29]

- Aethelbald – not only succeeded his father but married his widowed stepmother, Judith, daughter of Charles the Bald, King of the Franks
- Aethelberht – succeeded his brother
- Aethelred – succeeded his brother
- *Alfred the Great* – succeeded his brother
- Aethelswyth – married Burhred, King of Mercia in 853[30]

The Danes gave Aethelwulf no respite, but raided continuously for a number of years—all raids were met mostly successfully by the men of Wessex. In 837, the Danes were at Dorset and Southampton; in 838, they were in Lindsey, East Anglia, and Kent; in 839, they were in London, Canterbury, and Rochester; and in 840, Aethelwulf met 35 shiploads of Danes at Charmouth, but on that occasion, the Danes held the day.[31]

After five years of peace, the Danes returned. In 845, they attacked the Somerset coast, but Wessex prevailed. The West Saxons under Aethelwulf were efficient fighters with good armed organization. In 851, the Danes launched a two-pronged attack, from Devon near Plymouth and from Sandwich at Kent. The Kent battle was a sea battle, with under-king Aethelstan capturing nine Danish vessels. Aethelstan may have died soon after this battle, as he is never mentioned in the histories again.[32]

Meanwhile, 350 Danish ships attacked through London and moved into Surrey. If the number of ships was correct, then the Danes may have had about 10,000 men fighting in their army this time. Aethelwulf and his son Aethelbald met them at Aclea (Ockley) and won the battle. However, unlike after previous raids, the Danes did not retreat to their ships and sail away. This time, they wintered on English soil, at Thanet.[33]

In 853, the Kent and Surrey militias drove the Danes from Thanet, but again they wintered in England, this time on the Isle of Sheppey. The Saxons didn't seem to view them as much of a threat, however, since in 853 Aethelwulf and the King of Mercia went to subdue north Wales, and then in 854 Aethelwulf went to Rome for a year.[34]

Aethelwulf's preference for the Church was clear. Before going to Rome, he gave his English church money and lands as a gift. Once in Rome, he gave lavish gifts such as a gold crown and a jeweled sword. His youngest son, Alfred, accompanied him to Rome, even though the boy had been there already in 852.[35]

On his way home, he stayed at the Frankish king Charles the Bald's court. He was on very good terms with Charles, and they sealed their alliance by Aethelwulf's diplomatic marriage to Charles' daughter Judith— Aethelwulf was in his 50s and Judith was 13.[36][37]

The wedding took place at Charles' palace at Verberie on the river Oise. Unfortunately, the bishop crowned Judith as "Queen of Wessex." Saxon tradition held that there could be no Queen of Wessex, ever since Queen Eadburgha poisoned her husband King Beorhtric (Egbert's predecessor). Then Aethelwulf returned to Wessex.[38]

In his absence, Wessex had been ruled by a council of ministers, among them Aethelwulf's advisors, Bishop Swithun of Winchester (later a saint) and Bishop Ealstan of Sherborne, and his eldest son Aethelbald. While Aethelwulf was gone, the people had decided that they would rather have Aethelbald as their king. Ever a man of peace, Aethelwulf stepped down to avoid a civil war. He retired to Kent, once again ruling the four provinces he had ruled as a young man. He died in 858,[39][40] and was buried in Winchester Cathedral, Hampshire.[41]

Over the next eleven years, all three of Aethelwulf's older sons ruled the kingdom. Aethelbald, who had displaced his father, also married Aethelwulf's widow, Judith, then died a couple of years later in 860. His brother Aethelbert ruled until his death in 866, and then brother Aethelred ruled until he died in 871. This left the throne open for *Alfred*, soon to be Alfred the Great, the son no one expected to become king.[42]

Alfred the Great, King of Wessex
(849-899)
(reigned 871-899)

As the fourth son of the king, it was highly unlikely that Alfred would ever see the throne. More than likely, one of his elder brothers would inherit it, then have a family of his own to pass it to. Alfred's father, deprived of his own dreams of joining the Church, may have been grooming his youngest son for Church life. When Alfred was three, in 852, Aethelwulf sent him to Rome to be anointed in a baptism-like ritual. As we have when he was six he went with his father to Rome again.[43]

Alfred was born in Wantage, Wessex soon after Christmas in 849.[44][45] His home life was a happy one, and his mother, Osburga, was a lover of Saxon poetry and beautiful things—it was even possible that she could read. However, Alfred did not learn to read until he was 12, and was still learning Latin in his 30s.[46]

Aside from his two childhood trips to Rome, he also fought in battles with his elder brother King Aethelred. In 867, the Danes attacked Mercia. King Burhred, Alfred's brother-in-law, called on them for help, but by the time Wessex arrived, Burhred had made peace with the Danes.[47]

In 869 the Danes crushed Northumbria, East Anglia, and Mercia, and moved on Wessex. In 871, they camped at Reading fortress. King Aethelred and Alfred tried to besiege them but were run off the field. Four days later, they met the Danes at Ashdown.[48]

At Ashdown, Alfred showed the first signs of his greatness. His brother King Aethelred was meant to attack one group, Alfred another. But Aethelred was slow to come to battle, and Alfred grew impatient. He attacked without his brother, who joined him later with more troops. The Saxon forces won and massacred the Danes.[49]

Two weeks later, in a clash at Basing, the Danes won. Two months later, they met again, and although the Saxons seemed to be winning, the Danes prevailed. Aethelred died shortly after this battle, probably of his wounds,[50] and Alfred became king in April 871.[51][52]

The year 871 was a harrowing one for England. The Vikings were actually the first unifiers of England, overwhelming all the formerly strong Anglo-Saxon kingdoms that stood in their path.[53] The Danes, under the leadership of Ivar the Boneless (the Viking mastermind who killed King Edmund of East Anglia), simply destroyed everything. That was also the year Guthrum, Alfred's Danish nemesis, first came onto the scene, fighting alongside Ivar.[54] After Aethelred's death, Alfred made peace with the Danes, paying them off with a large sum of money, and the Danes retreated to London in 872.[55]

In 872, Alfred's brother-in-law King Burhred of Mercia was deposed by the Danes and fled to Rome where he died, thus depriving Alfred of an ally. Alfred's bribe to the Danes bought him almost five years of peace, during which time he further developed his "armed fleet," with which he successfully beat seven ships at sea in 875.[56]

The Danes returned in 876, taking the fortress Wareham in Wessex. Alfred trapped them inside, and they made a treaty, which the Danes promptly broke, with most escaping the fortress. Some Danes fled on horseback to Exeter, while some 4,000 escaped to the sea, where most drowned in a mist-induced shipwreck.[57]

Alfred chased the Danes into Exeter, cornered them, and once again struck a bargain with them. Then he escorted them back to Mercia, and returned home, the campaigning season done for the year.[58]

The season of war and plunder ended in the winter, so Alfred and his family retired to Chippenham for Christmas. However, the Danes (in a breach of the rules of war) attacked just after Twelfth Night (Epiphany) and took over the town. Alfred and his family barely escaped with their lives, while the Danes continued to plunder far and wide. Alfred and his men fled to the marshy moors of Somerset to regroup.[59]

Here is where Alfred gained his nickname "the Great;" he was the only English king to be titled "the Great." During the harsh winter, Alfred and his people fortified the Isle of Athelney, which was located in the Somerset marshes, and was inaccessible in the winter unless one knew the way. The Danes were content to keep him bottled up and watched him from the surrounding hills, particularly the Polden Hills. Alfred sallied out to raid and refresh his resources from time to time, but no major battles were fought.[60]

Still, Alfred's nemesis Guthrum knew it was just a matter of time before the weather improved and Alfred could threaten him. He also knew that Alfred's stronghold of Athelney could be reached by boat. So he decided to call for more men, and storm Athelney at the first opportunity.[61]

Guthrum's reinforcements, sailing upriver to meet him, stopped at a small fortress called Combwich. They intended to plunder it, but instead were surprised and massacred. Even worse, in the eyes of the superstitious Danes, their Raven banner was captured.[62]

Guthrum gathered his army on the Polden Hills, waiting. Alfred was done waiting. In May of 878,[63] at night, he and some men slipped out of Athelney, and gathered an army together in a place shielded by the forests of Selwood. In a swift march, he trapped the Danes on the ridges of the Polden Hills. Trapped by geography, the Danes were forced into a small area near Downend, where Alfred besieged them, and they surrendered.[64]

As part of the surrender, Alfred insisted that Guthrum be baptized, and he consented. The Danes all retreated back to East Anglia by 879. After this defeat, the Danes put down roots in East Anglia and were peaceful. Those who still wanted to fight went to France and devastated it instead. Peace reigned in Wessex until 885.[65]

In 885, the East Anglian Danes broke their treaty with Alfred, and began pillaging again. Alfred rescued Rochester from them, and defeated their 16-ship fleet with his own at the Stour River mouth. His ships then defeated an even larger fleet on the way home.[66]

In 886, Alfred recaptured London and signed a treaty with Guthrum demarcating the border between them at Watling Street, which extended Alfred's kingdom into territories he hadn't ruled before.[67] [68]

In 893, the Danish wars resumed in earnest. Alfred and the Dane Haesten clashed in the Weald in Kent. They skirmished to a stalemate in Devon, and the Danes broke into two groups. Alfred initially won the day at Farnham, but then the battle devolved into a stalemate, and Alfred's son Edward stalemated with the Danes on the Thames. The Danes regrouped at Benfleet in Essex.[69]

While Haesten was away from the camp, Edward stormed the Essex camp, destroyed it, and captured Haesten's wife and two sons. Alfred was a gentleman, and insisted on returning Haesten's family to him without demanding retribution of any kind.[70]

Haesten regrouped his Danes at Shoebury and went plundering. The English forces besieged them at Buttington on the Severn River, causing a desperate battle where the Danes managed to break out and flee back to Shoebury.[71]

Then the Danes descended on Chester, where Alfred again besieged them, this time using a scorched-earth policy to limit the resources the Danes could gain in their raids and sallies. The Danes raided into northern Wales instead, and escaped back to Shoebury.[72]

The year 894 brought a new Danish base, this time on the Lea River. Alfred found a place on the river to raise a water barrier and prevent the Danish ships from going in and out. The Danes went over land to Quatbridge (Bridgnorth), where they stayed all winter, but surrendered in the summer of 895.[73]

In the summer of 896, in one of those inexplicable moments when the Danes simply vanished from the scene, the Danish army dispersed. Those wanting a quiet life retired to East Anglia and Northumbria, and the rest turned on France to make their fortune.[74]

A few pirate raids along the south coast easily met by Alfred's fleet, were all the troubles Alfred had in the last four years of his reign.[75]

It may seem that Alfred did nothing but fight Danes for his entire reign, but that is not the case. If it were, his moniker, "the Great," might not have stuck, even though the magnitude of his defeat of the Danes cannot be overstated.

He was, possibly because of his father's early encouragement, a very religious man. He divided his time and his income devoutly—half to secular business, and half to the service of God.[76] During Alfred's reign, the Christian Church began a new campaign into the English territories. The Roman Catholic traditions established there were being threatened from the north by the Irish (unorthodox) Catholic ideas, and Rome wanted to advance and consolidate its hold on the island. This reform movement was supported by the king, as Church and State were very closely entwined in those days—the king was present at clerical synods, and bishops and clergy advised on secular matters.[77]

Although arrogant in his youth, Alfred matured into a thoughtful man who was only as ruthless as he needed to be. He also knew his limits. He never tried to annex all of the Danish-held territories, nor did he ever claim to be more than the "King of the West Saxons," even though every tribe bowed before him.[78]

Alfred, together with his son-in-law Ethelred, embarked upon raising the defenses of the country. Ethelred, alderman of Mercia and London, and husband of Alfred's daughter Aethelflaed, was a staunch and loyal backstop to Alfred in the lands he oversaw.[79]

Alfred fortified about 25 burghs, the greatest of which was London. Only after Alfred freed it from the Danes in 886 and strengthened it against future attacks did London begin to flourish into the major city it is today. Alfred wanted every district to have a fortified burgh, so when the highly mobile Danes attacked, the English would have places of refuge. Each burgh had its own permanent garrison, and the townspeople took great pride in defending their cities, often surprising the Danes with the ferocity of their fighting.[80]

Alfred was also a man of learning. He collected all of the codified laws in existence, as well as accepted common law, and created a new code of law for use throughout his kingdom. Among the revised laws: a limit to the blood-feud; a definition of the services a man must provide to his lord; a protection for Church personnel and property; and his laws contained a general bias toward protecting the weak and underprivileged from oppression by the strong. Alfred cleaned up the corrupt court system, insisting that the judges be fair and just in their rulings. When he found a dishonest judge, he gave him a choice: resign your position, or learn to read (thereby gaining wisdom and knowledge). Many chose to learn to read.[81]

Alfred was, as mentioned earlier, literate. He implemented a program for all sons of freemen with enough money to learn to read English—and if they were smart enough, Latin also. If carried out (and there's no reason to think it wasn't), then Wessex would have been the most literate country in Europe.[82]

Alfred insisted on writing in English, when at this time most documents were written in Latin. He himself (probably dictating to scribes), translated five books from Latin to English: Pope Gregory's *Pastoral Care*; Bede's *Ecclesiastical History*; St. Augustine's *Soliloquies*; Boethius' *Consolations of Philosophy*; and

Orosius' *History of the World*, to which Alfred added the discovery of the White Sea near the North Cape, which Alfred learned of from a Norse sea captain.[83]

Alfred also saved the *Anglo-Saxon Chronicles*. Alfred ordered a copy of this work, which in many cases is the only surviving history of the early Anglo-Saxon days, to be made and placed in all cathedrals and monasteries, and kept up to date by the monks.[84]

His family life seemed to have been a happy one. It was an odd characteristic of Egbert's descendants that the family was mostly harmonious—the siblings not only accepted the Council's decision as to who would become king, but actively supported that brother on the throne. [85] Alfred's wife Ealswith, daughter of Ethelred Mucel, Earl of Gaini, [86] [87] took no part in politics or public affairs, focusing on raising the children. She and her children accompanied Alfred into exile on the Isle of Athelney, suffering hardships with him, and she lost several children in infancy.[88]

Alfred and his wife Ealswith (d. 902) who married in 868 had:[89] [90] [91]

- Aethelflaed – married Ethelred, alderman of Mercia and London
- *Edward the Elder* – succeeded his father, was a warrior, not a scholar
- Ethelgeda – delicate and perhaps deformed, became the Abbess of Shaftesbury
- Aelfthryth – married Baldwin II, Count of Flanders. He was the son of Judith of France (stepmother and sister-in-law of Alfred) and her third husband.
- Ethelward – the youngest son, a lover of literature and scholarship. He was the Crown Prince, but died before his father, so his brother Edward succeeded Alfred.

Alfred the Great died 26 October 899, probably at Winchester. His exact cause of death was not known, but he had suffered his entire life from a debilitating disease. This disease attacked suddenly and painfully, even at his wedding feast, and could lay him low for days. So it is truly amazing that he accomplished all that he did.[92] [93] He was buried at Winchester Cathedral, Hampshire.[94]

In his will, he provided amply for his family, his advisors, the Church, and the needy He also did right by his nephews Ethelhelm and Ethelwald. These two sons of his brother Aethelred had been infants upon their father's death, and they had therefore been passed over in the line of succession in favor of Alfred. In his will, Alfred made certain that all of Aethelred's property went to the now-adult nephews. Alfred also decreed that all the bondsmen in his possession should be set free.

Edward the Elder, King of Wessex
(d. 924)
(reigned 899-924)

Edward the Elder was born around 870, and was eight or nine years old during the harrowing exile on Athelney—old enough to remember the hardships and difficulties. By 892, he was commanding a section of his father's army. It was Edward's men who caught up to the Danish raiders, laden with booty, at Farnham, routed them and besieged them on the Isle of Thorney in the Coln River. Having made his mark as a military man, it was only natural that when Alfred died in October 899, Edward was crowned king.[95] [96]

Not everyone was happy with this decision. Alfred's brother King Aethelred had left behind two sons, who were now of age. The elder, Ethelhelm, was content to let Edward rule, but the younger, Ethelwald, made trouble for the new king.[97]

Ethelwald took a band of men and occupied the royal estates of Wimborne and Twineham (Christchurch). Edward besieged them. Ethelwald made defiant threats, but then snuck away in the night, leaving his followers behind to face the king. If any further evidence of his character was needed, his wife (captured by Edward) was a consecrated nun Ethelwald had taken without the consent of the bishop or the king. Ethelwald himself escaped to Northumbria, where the Danes made him their king.[98]

This kingship didn't last long. In 901 Ethelwald appeared in Essex with a sizeable fleet. In 902, he enticed the Danes of East Anglia to rebel. He raided into Mercia and Wessex, then tried to depart. Edward pursued the raiders, but decided to let them go and sounded the retreat. Edward's Kentish men ignored the retreat and were surrounded by the Danes. A great battle followed, and Ethelwald was killed, ending his harassment of Edward.[99]

Following that battle, Edward and the Danes of Northumbria and East Anglia made peace at Yttingaford. This peace lasted until 909, when it was broken by Edward, although he was probably provoked by Danish raids. He attacked Northumbria and ravaged it for five weeks, until they made peace on his terms.[100]

In 910, it was Northumbria that broke the peace, sending a fleet south to Kent. Edward took a fleet of 100 ships to meet them, but the Danes bypassed him and plundered far and wide. Edward caught up to them at Tettenhall in Staffordshire, killing thousands and recapturing much of the plunder. Edward decided to drive the Danes from English soil once and for all.[101] [102]

In 911, Ethelred, Alfred's loyal and capable alderman of Mercia and London, died. His wife Aethelflaed, Alfred's daughter and Edward's sister, took the throne, becoming "The Lady of Mercia." In her, we met one of the more extraordinary ladies in history—a woman more than able to hold her own in a man's world.[103]

Edward and Aethelflaed joined forces, warring against the Danes. Edward apparently had no compunction about working with a woman. Together, the siblings expanded their father's strategy of building fortified burghs. Edward strengthened London, Oxford, and Chester, while Aethelflaed fortified Bridgnorth.[104]

Edward established new burghs in Hertford, using them as bases to launch attacks into Essex, where he built another burgh called Whitham. In Mercia, Aethelflaed embarked on a flurry of fortress-building to secure the realm. They proceeded to capture land in this step-by-step fashion: they built a fortress, took more land, built a fortress to hold the land, then advanced farther.[105]

In 914, a major Danish fleet from Brittany attacked into Wales. Aethelflaed's Mercian army defeated them. Edward's army joined and harassed the Danes until their tattered remains fled to Ireland. Edward and Aethelflaed then returned to their ongoing offensive with the eastern Danes.[106]

The Danes tried to fight, but they lacked coordination. Also, when a fortified town was not taken immediately, the Danes would break off the attack and go plundering. Alfred's children pressed the offensive, with success. Edward took Tempsford and killed most of the Danes within, including the East Anglian Danish king, while Aethelflaed engaged a Danish army at Derby. That autumn, the Northampton Danes surrendered. Edward took Huntingdon and Colchester, and the East Anglian Danes capitulated.[107]

In 918, Aethelflaed took Leicester without a fight, and the York Danes wanted to make peace with her. Unfortunately, on 12 June 918, she died, and Edward lost his most trusted and worthy ally.[108]

Upon her death, Edward hurried to Tamworth to forestall trouble over the succession, but the Mercians accepted him as their king. They wanted Aethelflaed's daughter Elfwina as regent, which Edward accepted. The next year, however, he removed her abruptly, maybe because she was involved in a possible conspiracy against him.[109] [110]

Edward completed the work of defeating the Danes. He gained security on the Welsh border when three kings of northern Wales paid homage to him. That enabled him to return to the Danish territories and the rest of the Danes gave up without a fight. It wasn't long before Danish soldiers began serving alongside English soldiers in the garrisons.[111]

Edward effectively was king of all England. Those territories he did not directly control allied themselves with him—English Northumbria, Strathclyde, and York. Even Scotland was on friendly terms with him.[112]

Edward was a prolific father. When a young man, he fell in love with a shepherd's daughter, Ecgwynn. They never married, but she lived at Alfred's court—Edward's son Aethelstan was Alfred's favorite grandson. Edward and Ecgwynn had: [113]

- Aethelstan – succeeded his father (in spite of the prohibition against bastards inheriting the throne)
- A daughter who married Sihtric, King of York

It was said that with his two legal wives he had 12 children, but only eight names have survived. Although Edward wasn't scholarly, he made sure his sons and daughters were properly educated. His daughters married into royal European families, and a few became nuns. Edward was not as devout as his father Alfred, but he did support the church financially and with his power.[114]

With first wife Aelfflaed (d. 902) he had: [115]

- Eadgifu – married first Charles the Simple, King of the Franks, then Herbert, Count of Meaux
- Aelfweard – died the same year as his father
- Eadhild – married Hugh, Duke of the Franks
- Eadgyth – married Otto I, Emperor of Germany
- Aelfgifu

And with second wife Eadgifu (d. 967), he had: [116]

- *Edmund* – succeeded his half-brother Aethelstan
- Eadred – succeeded Edmund
- Eadgifu – married Louis, Prince of Aquitaine

Edward the Elder died 17 July 924, at Farndon-on-Dee.[117] [118] He was buried at Winchester Cathedral, Hampshire.[119] His eldest son, **Aethelstan,** took the throne, and continued his father's policies. His most renowned feat was defeating the Danes at the Battle of Brunanburh. When he died, his half-brother *Edmund* became king.

Edmund I, King of Wessex and Mercia
(921-946)
(reigned 939-946)

Edmund I was only about three years old when his father died in 924. His eldest brother, Aethelstan, who became king, took care that Edmund and his brother Eadred were properly educated—another example of the startling solidarity found in Alfred's family line. When Edmund was only 16, he fought with Aethelstan in the Battle of Brunanburh, where the Wessex men defeated Olaf, an Irish Norseman who invaded England.[120] Covered in glory from his achievement there, Edmund was the obvious choice to become king when Aethelstan died two years later. In October 939, at the age of 18, Edmund was crowned King of Wessex and Mercia.[121] [122]

A mere two months into his reign, King Olaf Guthfrithson, king of the Irish Norse, invaded York, destroying and plundering the Midlands and Mercia. In 940, Edmund met them when they were on their way home, laden with plunder. Instead of a pitched battle, however, the Archbishops of Canterbury and York arranged a peace treaty that was decidedly not in King Edmund's favor, as King Olaf was allowed to retain control of the Danelaw territory (the modern East Midlands, and East Anglia).[123]

Edmund bided his time, and in 942 he attacked the Norsemen of York and won back all the territory he'd been forced to surrender. Happily, the Danes of the Danelaw welcomed Edmund. They had considered the York and Irish Norse to be oppressors. It must be remembered that the Danes and Norwegians were at war elsewhere, and that the Danes had enjoyed some autonomy under Aethelstan, so Edmund was much preferred.[124]

After this upheaval, two Norse claimants to the throne of York came to Edmund to settle their dispute. Before he would intervene, he insisted they both be baptized. Even after his intervention, no solution was reached, so Edmund marched into York and captured it for himself. This led to one of the claimants fleeing to the kingdom of Strathclyde and raiding from there, so in 946 Edmund invaded Strathclyde, which he then gave to Scottish King Malcolm I (see *MacAlpin Dynasty*) to seal an alliance of friendship with him.[125]

On St. Augustine Day (26 May) in 946, Edmund was feasting with his people. In the crowd, eating, he noticed a man named Leofa, who was a robber Edmund had banished six years before. Edmund attacked him from behind at the table, and Leofa reacted, stabbing the king in the heart. Edmund, only 25, died before he hit the ground. Leofa was torn limb from limb by the crowd.[126] [127]

Edmund was buried at Glastonbury Abbey, leaving two infant sons by wife Aelgifu:[128] [129]

- Eadwig – succeeded his uncle Eadred
- *Edgar* – succeeded his brother

Edmund I's brother **Eadred** succeeded to the throne. In 957, Edmund's older son, **Eadwig**, took the throne. A mere two years later, *Edgar* was crowned.

Edgar, King of England
(943-975)
(reigned 959-975)

Edmund's son Edgar, like many royal kinsmen, was raised in fosterage away from the court. Many were raised this way to protect them from intrigues and rivalries in the court. He grew up in Mercia, a sub-kingdom, raised by Athelstan "Half-King."[130]

Edgar was first a sub-king to his brother Eadwig, and set himself up as ruler of Mercia by 957.[131] [132] When Eadwig died in October 959, Edgar became king of all England.[133] [134]

Eadwig had banished one of his top aides, Dunstan, but Edgar reinstated him, and took much of his advice. Edgar made Dunstan Bishop of Worcester and later Bishop of London.[135]

Unlike his predecessors, there was almost no unrest during Edgar's reign. In 966 there was an Irish raid in Westmoreland, and in 969 there was some minor trouble in Thanet. Edgar was a strong king, and England's enemies didn't want to challenge him when there were easier pickings elsewhere.[136]

Edgar was also on good terms with his neighbors. Although he was less than five feet tall, he was powerfully built and a good fighter. There is a story that Scotland's King Kenneth II (see *MacAlpin Dynasty*), when visiting England, made a comment about his stature, whereupon Edgar challenged him to a duel. Kenneth backed down, apologizing, and Edgar accepted.[137]

In 973, there is an English story that Edgar had himself rowed by six kings in his barge on the river Dee.[138] While it is said that in 973 the Scottish King Kenneth II (see *MacAlpin Dynasty*) was brought under Edgar's overlordship, there is no mention of this in the history of Scotland as told by Scottish historians. Edgar supposedly went to Chester to receive the formal submission of the kings of Scotland, Strathclyde, and the Isles.[139] Robertson, in his book *Scotland Under Her Early Kings*, points out that there is no mention of this in contemporary sources and that, in fact, Kenneth was busy ravaging another part of the island during this supposed meeting in Chester.[140] In any event, it seems that this was more of pageant than homage, as the kings were all more allies than underlings of Edgar.[141]

Every year, Edgar sent his fleet around the island looking for pirates. Additionally, Edgar himself, along with his army patrolled the Roman roads, visiting the provinces and seeing that justice was done throughout the kingdom. He also reorganized the administration of England. He created the shires that still exist today, and divided them into hundreds, each with its own court. He updated the laws and enforced them vigorously. He gave extensive autonomy to the Danish districts (the Danelaw). He also encouraged the restoration of old monasteries and the founding of new ones, since the monks helped civilization flourish.[142]

During Edgar's reign, the reform movement of the Roman Catholic church saw its greatest glories. At this time, new bishoprics were created, Benedictine monasteries were reformed, and old monastic sites that had been reclaimed from the pagan Vikings were rededicated. King Edgar summoned a synod in Winchester around 970, which produced the Monastic Agreement (*Regularis Concordia*).[143]

In 973, Edgar underwent a lavish coronation ritual amid the Roman buildings of Bath. This highly religious ceremony was the culmination of the alliance between Church and State, and was masterminded by the Catholic reformers, particularly Dunstan.[144]

There is ample description of the coronation of himself and his queen, Aelfthryth—perhaps the first time a double coronation took place on the British Isles. Edgar was crowned on Whit Sunday in 973 at Bath, although most other coronations took place at Kingston-on-Thames. This coronation not only legitimized his claim to a large area of Britain, but it raised him to a priestly level as a Christian king. He had waited until he was thirty-one years old to be crowned—the age at which Rome "priested" people, and the age at which Christ began his public ministry. Edgar was decked out in the roses of martyrdom and the lilies of chastity. The ceremony stressed the king's semi-religious quality, according him divine protection, and laid on him an array of moral duties.[145]

The moral duties of the king were declared in an oath very similar, in spirit if not word, to the one still uttered by British monarchs today. The Saxon kings swore to defend and preserve the Church and Christian people, to ensure peace and order in their kingdom, and to assure justice and mercy in their judgments. Both the oath and the coronation rites remained virtually unchanged until the Norman conquest of 1066.[146]

Edgar married three times, plus he had a daughter, Edith, with an earl's daughter.

He and his first wife, Aethelflaed, had:[147]

- Edward the Martyr – succeeded his father and was murdered by servants of his stepmother, Aelfthryth

Edgar's second wife, Wulfthryth, had no children.[148]

Edgar's third wife, Aelfthryth, was the daughter of Ordgar, Earl of Devonshire.[149]

Edgar had heard her beauty was legendary, so he sent his trusted friend, Ethelwold, to check her out. Ethelwold fell for her, and told Edgar that she wasn't that pretty, and that Ethelwold should marry her instead. Edgar agreed. When Edgar found out about the deceit, he took Ethelwold out hunting in Harewood Forest, Hampshire, and killed him with a javelin.[150]

Aelfthryth, who had been very angry with Ethelwold when she found out she could have been the king's wife, happily married Edgar. This cold-hearted treatment of her first husband should have been a warning to Edgar, but it wasn't. She bore him two sons, the elder of whom died young. The other son was:

- ***Aethelred II the Unready*** – succeeded after the murder of his half-brother by his mother's servants[151]

Edgar was the first king to impose a truly imperial concept and control over the former kingdoms he now ruled. The language in his charters clearly implied a superiority over all Englishman, and his legislation was clearly intended to apply to all nationalities living in his lands, not just Anglo-Saxons. Englishmen, Britons, Vikings, and Danes were all supposed to enter into the English political sphere and the Catholic Church.[152]

Edgar died unexpectedly at age thirty-two, on 8 July 975.[153] Without him and his strong hand, the government collapsed.

Aethelred II the Unready, King of England
(965-1016)
(reigned 978-1016)

When his father, Edgar, died, Aethelred II the Unready was only 10 years old. He was Edgar's second son, and his much-older brother **Edward** was given the throne. Edward was an unpopular king while he lived, but the manner of his death gave him both the nickname Edward the Martyr and a polish of his reputation.[154]

Early stories do not name the culprit, but later stories name Aethelred's mother, Aelfthryth, as the instigator of Edward's murder. Supposedly, on 18 March 978, Edward visited Aelfthryth at her castle Corfe in Dorset while he was hunting in the area. She greeted him warmly and gave him a drink, then had her servant stab him in the back. He tried to escape, but died as his horse dragged him through the woods.[155]

Since kings were anointed by the church, the murder of one was a heinous crime, and a bad omen. The Saxons, Christian but still superstitious, told of Aelfthryth's riding in state to Edward's tomb, but her horse refusing to approach. Perhaps feeling the guilt, Aelfthryth retired to a nunnery at Wherwill in Harewood Forest. Aptly, it was the nunnery Edgar founded to repent of murdering her first husband. Aelfthryth spent the rest of her life in penance there.[156]

Aethelred, at age 14, was crowned in March 978, although he was not anointed as king until the Sunday a fortnight after Easter (9 May) in 979, at Kingston. That same year, there were bloody portends seen in the sky, and the Saxon people waited for the impending doom. This doomsday mindset probably affected the young king intensely—he may have felt that he was doomed to fail.[157] [158]

The Saxons didn't have long to wait for the doom to fall. In 980, the Danish attacks began again, with raids in Southampton, Thanet, and Cheshire. In 981, they were in Cornwall, Devon, and Wales. In 982, the Danes attacked Portland and London. And then they disappeared for about five years.[159]

In 987, Aethelred was 19 years old, and the Danes showed up in Watchet. In 988, they returned to Devon and Aethelred was further hampered by the death of his advisor Dunstan (not in battle). Through all of this raiding, Aethelred did nothing, allowing the Danes free rein. Then, in 991, the Danes sacked Ipswich, anchored in the Blackwater River, and camped on Northey Island. The local militia attacked the Danes. The Saxons had the upper hand and were winning when the Danes complained that they weren't fighting fairly. Giving way to this appeal to chivalry, the Saxons gave up their advantage and lost the battle.[160]

Aethelred held a conference and decided to pay a tribute to the Danes to stay away. It should be noted here that Aethelred's popular moniker, "the Unready," is a mistranslation of the Saxon. His nickname was actually "the Redless," which means "lacking in good counsel."[161]

Aethelred had other problems besides his youth and his poor advisors. Unlike many of his predecessors, his reign was beset with cowards and traitors. In 992, Alderman Elfric betrayed the English to the Danes, but somehow retained his power, only to betray them again in 1003 at Wilton.[162]

The Danish raids increased in 994, led by King Olaf Tryggvaon of Norway and Crown Prince Sweyn of Denmark. Aethelred bought peace again for £16,000. From 997 through 999, the Vikings stayed in England or Normandy at the end of the campaigning season, instead of going home.[163]

In 1000, Aethelred finally mounted a successful military campaign—against Strathclyde, a weak neighboring Breton kingdom.[164]

In 1001, the Danes were once again in Devonshire and Hampshire, but this time the price of peace was £24,000. Frustrated, on 13 November 1002, Aethelred committed the Massacre of St. Brice's Day. He ordered all Danes residing in England killed. Although this order was impossible to carry out particularly since there was a huge number of mixed-blood residents by then, it was tried. But even this cowardly act went wrong. One of the Danes murdered was Gunhilda, the sister of Sweyn, King of Denmark.[165]

Sweyn responded with massive raids in 1003, 1004, and 1005. The Danes devastated everything, and they moved across England at will. Aethelred was powerless to stop them, and retreated to an un-devastated part of England (Shropshire) for the winter. He once again paid off the Danes, this time with £30,000. Once again, he paid them off after the devastation was completed, instead of before.[166]

In 1008, Aethelred went to great expense to build a huge fleet to meet the Danes when they returned. However, a man stole 20 ships, and the 80 that pursued him were lost in a storm. Aethelred gave up the idea and retreated back to Wessex.[167]

In 1010, the Danes appeared in East Anglia. In 1011, they were in Kent at Canterbury, and they extorted £48,000 from Kent alone. In 1013, Sweyn of Denmark decided to make himself King of England as well. He attacked and swept across the country. Aethelred, aged 48, fled to Normandy.[168]

In 1014, Sweyn died, and his son Canute took over at Gainsborough. Aethelred saw his chance and returned to London, where he was surprisingly well received.[169] Part of this was the power of being a consecrated king. The sacredness of being a consecrated king made his claim secure. In his disastrous 34-year reign, no one had ever tried to remove him. Even during his exile, when his people were ruled by Sweyn the Dane, he was regarded by his people as the rightful king. When he returned from exile in 1014, he reiterated the royal oath in order to rally the people behind him.[170]

After rallying his people, he raised an army and managed to defeat Canute in the north. Canute escaped with his fleet and landed at Sandwich. Aethelred paid Canute £21,000 to leave him alone.[171]

As usual, this was a temporary fix. Canute returned in 1015, but ran into Aethelred's son Edmund Ironside, and was locked in an indecisive campaign when Aethelred died on 23 April 1016 in London.[172]

Aethelred was a tall, fair-haired, handsome man who liked soft living, drinking, feasting, and many women.[173] He married twice.

His first wife Aelfgifu bore him:[174]

- **Edmund II Ironside** – succeeded his father
- Eadwig

For his second wife, he chose Emma, the sister of Richard II, 4th Duke of Normandy. This was partly because of Normandy's Scandinavian origins, and Aethelred wanted to neutralize the Viking threat from at least one quarter. The two married in 1002.[175]

He and his second wife, Emma, had:[176]

- Edward the Confessor – eventually succeeded his half-brother
- Alfred
- Godgifu – married first Drew, Count of Mantes, then Eustace II, Count of Boulogne

Upon Aethelred II the Unready's death in 1016, his son ***Edmund Ironside***, already locked in battle with Canute, took the throne.

Edmund II Ironside, King of England
(d. 1016)
(reigned 23 April-30 Nov, 1016)

In 1015, Edmund II Ironside was involved in an intrigue that gained him a great deal of power and land. Edmund married the widow of a murdered thane, and then took possession of the land of two more murdered thanes. He was not implicated in the murders, just was opportunistic in the circumstances. Edmund was made king of "the Five Towns" of Derby, Leicester, Lincoln, Nottingham, Stamford, and their surrounding area.[177][178]

Then Canute returned and went plundering in Wessex. Edmund and his ally Alderman Edric raised an army and went to face Canute. Edric planned to betray Edmund to Canute, but Edmund found out and avoided the trap. Edric did manage to hand 40 ships over to Canute. At this time, Aethelred was ill at Corsham in north Wiltshire.[179]

Edmund tried to rally the army, but the people refused to fight unless Aethelred, their consecrated king, led them. However, Aethelred had lost his will to fight, and retreated to London. So Edmund took what troops he had and followed his father to London. He was there when Aethelred died on 23 April 1016.[180][181]

In the meantime, Canute was in Wessex. Upon Aethelred's death, the various Saxon councils elected two different kings—some wanted Edmund, but some wanted Canute.[182]

Edmund wrested his homeland of Wessex from Canute, but Canute took London, which Edmund had just left. Edmund and Canute met in indecisive battles at Penselwood in Somerset and Sherson in north Wiltshire. Then they met again at Danish-held London.[183]

Edmund won the battle, but suffered so many casualties that he had to retreat to Wessex to gather reinforcements. Canute tried to retake the newly liberated London, but the townspeople drove him off and he returned to Essex. Canute was met at Oxford by Edmund's reinforced army and was defeated.[184]

The treacherous Alderman Edric, who had been with Canute since his earlier betrayal of Edmund, fled Canute's side, and allied again with Edmund.[185]

On 18 October 1016,[186] Edmund met Canute at Ashingdon in Essex. However, Edric took his men off the field just as the battle was joined, and Edmund was routed. Fully half of England's nobility was killed, and Edmund fled to Gloucestershire as a fugitive.[187] Edmund suggested a duel, winner take all, but Canute declined. Apparently, the single combat did occur at a later time.[188]

Canute realized that he could not continue this deadlock with Edmund. The two kings met at Olney near Deerhurst and divided England.[189] The boundary was the Thames, with Edmund getting Wessex and Canute getting everything else.[190] They may have sworn brotherhood, and added a clause in the treaty that whoever died first, the other would inherit their portion of England.[191] The Danes returned to London for the winter. [192]

On 30 November 1016, Edmund II Ironside died. Contemporary accounts have him murdered in the privy, impaled in some horrific way (the method of skewering varies). Most suspicion for the murderer falls on Edric, either on his own or at Canute's suggestion.[193] [194]

Edric lived in Canute's court after betraying Edmund at Ashingdon. Rumors reached Canute that Edric's servants were responsible for Edmund's death. Edric himself seemed to back this up by boasting that he had removed Edmund to help Canute. Canute, not trusting Edric, could not stomach the murder of a fellow king, and had Edric killed.[195]

Edmund married Ealdgyth, the Swedish-born widow of murdered Earl Sigeferth, and had two sons:[196] [197]

- Edmund
- ***Edward the Aethling***

However, as neither son was of age, Wessex decided to elect **Canute** as their king, putting an end to the wars ravaging the country.

Edward the Aethling
(1016-1057)

Edward the Aethling was just a newborn baby when his father died. His brother, Edmund, was only a year old. Edmund Ironside's wife, Ealdgyth, was not present at his funeral, either because she was giving birth to Edward, or because she was already a prisoner of Canute.[198]

The newly elected King Canute of England decided to put his house in order. First, he married Emma, King Aethelred's widow, to secure the same political advantage Aethelred had. Emma had three children with Aethelred, one of whom was Edward the Confessor, a future king of England. Emma's children were sent into exile in Normandy.[199]

Then Canute had to deal with Edward Ironside's two sons. The most final solution was to murder them, but he did not want to do it in England—perhaps he was afraid of backlash from the people.[200] So, in 1017, he sent them to King Olof Skötkonung of Sweden, a relative of his, with a "letter of death." For some reason, the boys were instead left in Denmark with Earl Walgar, who raised and educated them as princes.[201]

The boys were secure there for quite some time, but in 1028 Canute faced a great deal of unrest in England. The people spoke of restoring the crown to the Anglo-Saxons, which meant one of the boys, or *aethelings* (royal children, particularly sons). Canute decided that they should be eliminated once and for all.[202]

A Danish baron in Canute's war council tipped off Walgar, the boys' guardian and tutor in Denmark. Walgar broke his loyalty to Canute and fled with the boys to the court of Sweden's King Anund Jacob.[203]

They could not stay there for long because Canute and his war fleet were in the Baltic area subjugating Norway, whose king had also fled to Sweden for refuge.[204]

Walgar would have liked to stay in the north so the boys could be in touch with England and active in the restoration movement. However, all of the north was currently under Canute's rule, and both the boys and Walgar were now targets of assassination from Canute.[205] The answer lay in Russia.

Kiev in Russia held many assets. First, it was Nordic in background, so the language and customs were familiar. Second, it had good communication with England. Third, King Anund Jacob of Sweden and Grand Duke Yaroslav of Kiev were brothers-in-law. And fourth, Yaroslav's wife, Ingegerd, was the half-sister of Ealdgyth, the boys' mother.[206]

The Russians gave them shelter, and Walgar left the boys there. Where he went and what happened to him is unknown, but this man risked everything to save these children who were not his own.[207] Edmund was about 14, Edward 13, when they arrived in Kiev. They quickly moved to Novgorod, which was Yaroslav's seat of power. The capital moved to Kiev in 1036.[208]

The boys grew up in the royal court. After living in Denmark virtually all their lives, they spoke Norse, as did the Russians, and they learned martial training from Norwegian and Swedish soldiers. The boys would have fought in the Russian army in their mid-teens, but their education was not just martial.[209]

Yaroslav loved books and learning, and he passed this to the boys. He was also a rabidly devout Greek Orthodox Christian, and probably pushed it heavily on the boys, who were likely Roman Catholic in upbringing. Yaroslav also gave them a wonderful example of what a ruler should be, in that he revised the laws of Russia to be more humane, just, and equally available to all.[210]

Yaroslav wanted to smash Canute's empire in order to give himself a foothold on the Baltic, and the best way to do that was to restore one of the boys to the throne of England.[211] To forward that plan, he wanted to tie the Holy Roman Emperor, Henry III of Germany, to him through marriage. Henry refused to marry Yaroslav's daughter, but sent his niece Agatha to Kiev with the returning Russian envoy in 1043.[212]

Meanwhile, events had moved on in England. Canute died, as had his successors Harold Harefoot and Harthacnut. In June of 1042, a Saxon king gained the throne—Emma and Aethelred's oldest son Edward the Confessor.[213] When this happened, the aethelings' hopes of a triumphant return to England faded, as they were now 27 and 26 years old.[214]

While living in Kiev, two other princes, also children although slightly younger than the British aethelings, arrived from Hungary. Hungary was in the middle of a war of succession, and Prince Andrew and Prince Levente, the rightful heirs, had been run out of the country. With circumstances so similar, it was inevitable that the four formed a close friendship.[215]

In 1046, the situation in Hungary had become unbearable. King Peter had turned tyrannical and to staff the church and state, he brought in Germans and Italians whom the king allowed to rape and pillage and oppress the people with impunity. The Hungarian people turned against him, and against the "foreign" church, and reverted to paganism. This pagan revolt turned horrifically bloody, and Andrew and Levente, now adults, were recalled by the nobles.[216]

Although the pagan revolt sickened Andrew and the aethelings, who were all devout Christians, Andrew had no choice but to allow the horrors of the purge to continue in order to keep the loyalty of his army. The aethelings went to Hungary with him, probably because of their fading hopes in England, and their deep friendship.[217] Andrew's brother was killed in the revolt, but Andrew was victorious on 15 April 1046, when Peter was killed.[218] Andrew was crowned by the four surviving bishops of Hungary (the rest were murdered in the revolt), and he forced the people to embrace Christianity again.[219]

For the aethelings, life in Hungary was good. They were richly rewarded by Andrew for their help, and as comrades-in-arms of the king, they were very popular. Their estates were most likely located near the village of Nadasd (now Mecseknádasd) in the Pecs district of the county Baranya.[220]

Edward was already married to Agatha, but Edmund was single. In 1047, he impregnated a royal princess and was forced to marry her. He died shortly thereafter, whether of murder or illness is not known, but local legend says he died of the pox. He left no children, so either the princess lost the baby, or the child did not reach adulthood.[221]

Edward's wife, Agatha, is something of a mystery. For a long time, the debate raged over who her parents were. The prevailing theory is that she was a daughter of Liudolf, Margrave of West-Friesland. Liudolf was the half-brother of Henry III, the Holy Roman Emperor, via their mother, Gisela of Swabia. Agatha was probably born around 1025, and Edward married her around 1044 in Kiev. They had:[222] [223]

- Edgar – designated as Edward the Confessor's heir
- *Margaret* – married Malcolm III of Scotland (see *MacAlpin Dynasty*)
- Christina – became the Abbess of Romsey

Agatha was a strong woman, and she raised her daughters Margaret and Christina very strictly. The mores of the Hungarian court were quite loose, and Agatha instilled her girls with a strong Catholic faith and high moral and ethical standards.[224]

Meanwhile, in England, Edward the Confessor was in a tough spot. He was a weak man politically and had no children. A powerful southern earl, Harold Godwinson, virtually ran the country. In 1051, Edward and William, 7th Duke of Normandy (see *Continental Dynasty*) had communicated, and supposedly Edward promised him the crown. Therefore, the succession was in a tug-of-war between Harold Godwinson and William of Normandy. In Edward the Confessor's eyes, Edward the Aethling represented a powerful compromise. Approved by the Council, with a legitimacy that couldn't be challenged, Edward the Aethling was seen as the way to keep the line of Alfred the Great on the throne.[225]

Edward the Confessor sent for Edward the Aethling in 1054, but the delegation, not being sure where Hungary was, went to the German court, where Emperor Henry III was expected to help them contact Edward.[226] The delegation could not have known that Henry held deep enmity toward Edward for his part in overthrowing Peter in Hungary. Henry stalled for a year or so, and then sent the delegation home with promises to "continue trying." It wasn't until after Henry's death that Edward was actually sent for.[227]

Edward and his family came to England in mid-August 1057. Edward was 41 years old, and his dream of being restored to the throne was finally coming true. The people welcomed him with wild joy, but there was treachery afoot. Soon after he arrived, his access to King Edward the Confessor was cut off, and before the end of August, Edward the Aethling was dead.[228] [229]

Although no one can say with certainty what happened to Edward, there had been no indication of illness prior to his death, so it was likely that he was poisoned. The most likely suspect was Harold Godwinson, whose supporters were in a position to both stop Edward from seeing the king and to slip him poison. William of Normandy's people were in no position to accomplish both these tasks.[230]

Edward the Confessor designated Edgar, who was only two years old at the time, as his successor. The king kept Agatha and the children at his court, and raised them like his own. Margaret and Christina were educated as princesses should be. Taught by Benedictine monks, they learned to read the sacred scriptures in Latin and to speak French, and they learned the finer points of needlework, deportment, and courtly customs. Edgar was also taught the art of war and knighthood.[231]

During their stay, another refugee prince arrived in King Edward's court: Malcolm III of Scotland, son of King Duncan, fleeing from Macbeth. Given the similarity in ages and circumstances, he and Edgar struck up a friendship that was to last well into adulthood.[232]

Meanwhile, Harold Godwinson tightened his grip on the government, and all of England prayed that Edward the Confessor would live long enough for Edgar to reach manhood.[233] On 5 January 1066, when Edgar was only 11, Edward the Confessor died.[234]

The Witan, or Anglo-Saxon council, would have preferred Edgar, but they were in a bind—a pre-teen could never hope to withstand the inevitable invasion from William of Normandy. They chose Harold as king. Harold made no move against Edgar, but Agatha worried for her son's safety.[235]

William of Normandy invaded, and Harold was killed at Hastings. The Witan then elected 12-year-old Edgar as their king, but the bishops of England refused to crown him, because the Pope wanted William on the throne. Lacking royal authority, and having two powerful earls abandon him and take their armies home, young Edgar was left with no choice but to surrender his kingdom to William.[236]

King William the Conqueror treated Edgar with surprising kindness. He kept his family at court, and gave Edgar an estate in Hertfordshire. However, many people were unhappy with the Norman rule, and more and more nobles fled to Scotland—to the court of King Malcolm III. In 1068, Edgar and family decided to join them.[237]

Agatha devised a crafty solution to get them out of the country without resistance from William. She told William that she wanted to take her family and return to Hungary. William, glad for this painless way to remove his adversary, agreed. However, Agatha set sail for Scotland instead.[238]

King Malcolm III, the formerly exiled prince in Edward the Confessor's court, welcomed them, espoused their cause, and fell in love with Margaret. **Margaret** eventually married Malcolm. For more information on her life with Malcolm and the ultimate fate of Edgar's claim to the English throne, see the *MacAlpin Dynasty* chapter.

---

[1] Ralph Whitlock, *The Warrior Kings of Saxon England* (Moonraker Press, 1977, Bradford-on-Avon, England), p. 8.
[2] Ralph Whitlock, *The Warrior Kings of Saxon England* (Moonraker Press, 1977, Bradford-on-Avon, England), p. 9.
[3] Ralph Whitlock, *The Warrior Kings of Saxon England* (Moonraker Press, 1977, Bradford-on-Avon, England), p. 10.
[4] Ralph Whitlock, *The Warrior Kings of Saxon England* (Moonraker Press, 1977, Bradford-on-Avon, England), p. 12.
[5] Ralph Whitlock, *The Warrior Kings of Saxon England* (Moonraker Press, 1977, Bradford-on-Avon, England), p. 17.

[6] Ralph Whitlock, *The Warrior Kings of Saxon England* (Moonraker Press, 1977, Bradford-on-Avon, England), p. 18.
[7] Ralph Whitlock, *The Warrior Kings of Saxon England* (Moonraker Press, 1977, Bradford-on-Avon, England), p. 39.
[8] Ralph Whitlock, *The Warrior Kings of Saxon England* (Moonraker Press, 1977, Bradford-on-Avon, England), p. 39.
[9] Ralph Whitlock, *The Warrior Kings of Saxon England* (Moonraker Press, 1977, Bradford-on-Avon, England), p. 40.
[10] Ralph Whitlock, *The Warrior Kings of Saxon England* (Moonraker Press, 1977, Bradford-on-Avon, England), p. 40.
[11] Ralph Whitlock, *The Warrior Kings of Saxon England* (Moonraker Press, 1977, Bradford-on-Avon, England), p. 40.
[12] Ralph Whitlock, *The Warrior Kings of Saxon England* (Moonraker Press, 1977, Bradford-on-Avon, England), p. 40.
[13] Ralph Whitlock, *The Warrior Kings of Saxon England* (Moonraker Press, 1977, Bradford-on-Avon, England), p. 41.
[14] Ralph Whitlock, *The Warrior Kings of Saxon England* (Moonraker Press, 1977, Bradford-on-Avon, England), p. 41.
[15] Ralph Whitlock, *The Warrior Kings of Saxon England* (Moonraker Press, 1977, Bradford-on-Avon, England), p. 42.
[16] Ralph Whitlock, *The Warrior Kings of Saxon England* (Moonraker Press, 1977, Bradford-on-Avon, England), p. 42.
[17] Ralph Whitlock, *The Warrior Kings of Saxon England* (Moonraker Press, 1977, Bradford-on-Avon, England), p. 42.
[18] Ralph Whitlock, *The Warrior Kings of Saxon England* (Moonraker Press, 1977, Bradford-on-Avon, England), p. 43.
[19] Ralph Whitlock, *The Warrior Kings of Saxon England* (Moonraker Press, 1977, Bradford-on-Avon, England), p. 43.
[20] Ralph Whitlock, *The Warrior Kings of Saxon England* (Moonraker Press, 1977, Bradford-on-Avon, England), p. 43.
[21] Ralph Whitlock, *The Warrior Kings of Saxon England* (Moonraker Press, 1977, Bradford-on-Avon, England), p. 44.
[22] Ralph Whitlock, *The Warrior Kings of Saxon England* (Moonraker Press, 1977, Bradford-on-Avon, England), p. 43.
[23] Ralph Whitlock, *The Warrior Kings of Saxon England* (Moonraker Press, 1977, Bradford-on-Avon, England), p. 55.
[24] John Cannon & Ralph Griffiths, *The Oxford Illustrated History of the British Monarchy* (2000 edition, Oxford University Press), Geneaolgies of Royal Lines Appendix.
[25] Ralph Whitlock, *The Warrior Kings of Saxon England* (Moonraker Press, 1977, Bradford-on-Avon, England), p. 55.
[26] Ralph Whitlock, *The Warrior Kings of Saxon England* (Moonraker Press, 1977, Bradford-on-Avon, England), p. 55.
[27] Ralph Whitlock, *The Warrior Kings of Saxon England* (Moonraker Press, 1977, Bradford-on-Avon, England), p. 57.
[28] John Cannon & Ralph Griffiths, *The Oxford Illustrated History of the British Monarchy* (2000 edition, Oxford University Press), Geneaolgies of Royal Lines Appendix.
[29] Ralph Whitlock, *The Warrior Kings of Saxon England* (Moonraker Press, 1977, Bradford-on-Avon, England), p. 57.
[30] Ralph Whitlock, *The Warrior Kings of Saxon England* (Moonraker Press, 1977, Bradford-on-Avon, England), p. 65.
[31] Ralph Whitlock, *The Warrior Kings of Saxon England* (Moonraker Press, 1977, Bradford-on-Avon, England), p. 58.
[32] Ralph Whitlock, *The Warrior Kings of Saxon England* (Moonraker Press, 1977, Bradford-on-Avon, England), p. 59.
[33] Ralph Whitlock, *The Warrior Kings of Saxon England* (Moonraker Press, 1977, Bradford-on-Avon, England), p. 59-60.
[34] Ralph Whitlock, *The Warrior Kings of Saxon England* (Moonraker Press, 1977, Bradford-on-Avon, England), p. 60.
[35] Ralph Whitlock, *The Warrior Kings of Saxon England* (Moonraker Press, 1977, Bradford-on-Avon, England), p. 61-62.
[36] Ralph Whitlock, *The Warrior Kings of Saxon England* (Moonraker Press, 1977, Bradford-on-Avon, England), p. 62.
[37] John Cannon & Ralph Griffiths, *The Oxford Illustrated History of the British Monarchy* (2000 edition, Oxford University Press), Geneaolgies of Royal Lines Appendix.
[38] Ralph Whitlock, *The Warrior Kings of Saxon England* (Moonraker Press, 1977, Bradford-on-Avon, England), p. 62.
[39] Ralph Whitlock, *The Warrior Kings of Saxon England* (Moonraker Press, 1977, Bradford-on-Avon, England), p. 62-63.
[40] John Cannon & Ralph Griffiths, *The Oxford Illustrated History of the British Monarchy* (2000 edition, Oxford University Press), Geneaolgies of Royal Lines Appendix.
[41] John Cannon & Ralph Griffiths, *The Oxford Illustrated History of the British Monarchy* (2000 edition, Oxford University Press), p. 656.
[42] Ralph Whitlock, *The Warrior Kings of Saxon England* (Moonraker Press, 1977, Bradford-on-Avon, England), p. 64-65.
[43] Ralph Whitlock, *The Warrior Kings of Saxon England* (Moonraker Press, 1977, Bradford-on-Avon, England), p. 62, 88.
[44] Ralph Whitlock, *The Warrior Kings of Saxon England* (Moonraker Press, 1977, Bradford-on-Avon, England), p. 98.
[45] John Cannon & Ralph Griffiths, *The Oxford Illustrated History of the British Monarchy* (2000 edition, Oxford University Press), p. 31; Geneaolgies of Royal Lines Appendix; List of Monarchs Appendix.
[46] Ralph Whitlock, *The Warrior Kings of Saxon England* (Moonraker Press, 1977, Bradford-on-Avon, England), p. 87, 89.
[47] Ralph Whitlock, *The Warrior Kings of Saxon England* (Moonraker Press, 1977, Bradford-on-Avon, England), p. 67.
[48] Ralph Whitlock, *The Warrior Kings of Saxon England* (Moonraker Press, 1977, Bradford-on-Avon, England), p. 69.
[49] Ralph Whitlock, *The Warrior Kings of Saxon England* (Moonraker Press, 1977, Bradford-on-Avon, England), p. 70.
[50] Ralph Whitlock, *The Warrior Kings of Saxon England* (Moonraker Press, 1977, Bradford-on-Avon, England), p. 70-71.
[51] Ralph Whitlock, *The Warrior Kings of Saxon England* (Moonraker Press, 1977, Bradford-on-Avon, England), p. 72.
[52] John Cannon & Ralph Griffiths, *The Oxford Illustrated History of the British Monarchy* (2000 edition, Oxford University Press), p. 31; List of Monarchs Appendix.
[53] John Cannon & Ralph Griffiths, *The Oxford Illustrated History of the British Monarchy* (2000 edition, Oxford University Press), p. 13.
[54] Ralph Whitlock, *The Warrior Kings of Saxon England* (Moonraker Press, 1977, Bradford-on-Avon, England), p. 70.
[55] Ralph Whitlock, *The Warrior Kings of Saxon England* (Moonraker Press, 1977, Bradford-on-Avon, England), p. 72-73.
[56] Ralph Whitlock, *The Warrior Kings of Saxon England* (Moonraker Press, 1977, Bradford-on-Avon, England), p. 73-74.
[57] Ralph Whitlock, *The Warrior Kings of Saxon England* (Moonraker Press, 1977, Bradford-on-Avon, England), p. 75.
[58] Ralph Whitlock, *The Warrior Kings of Saxon England* (Moonraker Press, 1977, Bradford-on-Avon, England), p. 76.
[59] Ralph Whitlock, *The Warrior Kings of Saxon England* (Moonraker Press, 1977, Bradford-on-Avon, England), p. 76.
[60] Ralph Whitlock, *The Warrior Kings of Saxon England* (Moonraker Press, 1977, Bradford-on-Avon, England), p. 79.
[61] Ralph Whitlock, *The Warrior Kings of Saxon England* (Moonraker Press, 1977, Bradford-on-Avon, England), p. 79.

[62] Ralph Whitlock, *The Warrior Kings of Saxon England* (Moonraker Press, 1977, Bradford-on-Avon, England), p. 79.

[63] John Cannon & Ralph Griffiths, *The Oxford Illustrated History of the British Monarchy* (2000 edition, Oxford University Press), p. 13, 31.

[64] Ralph Whitlock, *The Warrior Kings of Saxon England* (Moonraker Press, 1977, Bradford-on-Avon, England), p. 80.

[65] Ralph Whitlock, *The Warrior Kings of Saxon England* (Moonraker Press, 1977, Bradford-on-Avon, England), p. 81.

[66] Ralph Whitlock, *The Warrior Kings of Saxon England* (Moonraker Press, 1977, Bradford-on-Avon, England), p. 82.

[67] John Cannon & Ralph Griffiths, *The Oxford Illustrated History of the British Monarchy* (2000 edition, Oxford University Press), p. 31.

[68] Ralph Whitlock, *The Warrior Kings of Saxon England* (Moonraker Press, 1977, Bradford-on-Avon, England), p. 83.

[69] Ralph Whitlock, *The Warrior Kings of Saxon England* (Moonraker Press, 1977, Bradford-on-Avon, England), p. 82-83.

[70] Ralph Whitlock, *The Warrior Kings of Saxon England* (Moonraker Press, 1977, Bradford-on-Avon, England), p. 83.

[71] Ralph Whitlock, *The Warrior Kings of Saxon England* (Moonraker Press, 1977, Bradford-on-Avon, England), p. 84.

[72] Ralph Whitlock, *The Warrior Kings of Saxon England* (Moonraker Press, 1977, Bradford-on-Avon, England), p. 84.

[73] Ralph Whitlock, *The Warrior Kings of Saxon England* (Moonraker Press, 1977, Bradford-on-Avon, England), p. 84-85.

[74] Ralph Whitlock, *The Warrior Kings of Saxon England* (Moonraker Press, 1977, Bradford-on-Avon, England), p. 85.

[75] Ralph Whitlock, *The Warrior Kings of Saxon England* (Moonraker Press, 1977, Bradford-on-Avon, England), p. 85.

[76] Ralph Whitlock, *The Warrior Kings of Saxon England* (Moonraker Press, 1977, Bradford-on-Avon, England), p. 91, 97.

[77] John Cannon & Ralph Griffiths, *The Oxford Illustrated History of the British Monarchy* (2000 edition, Oxford University Press), p. 24.

[78] Ralph Whitlock, *The Warrior Kings of Saxon England* (Moonraker Press, 1977, Bradford-on-Avon, England), p. 90-91.

[79] Ralph Whitlock, *The Warrior Kings of Saxon England* (Moonraker Press, 1977, Bradford-on-Avon, England), p. 92.

[80] Ralph Whitlock, *The Warrior Kings of Saxon England* (Moonraker Press, 1977, Bradford-on-Avon, England), p. 92-93.

[81] Ralph Whitlock, *The Warrior Kings of Saxon England* (Moonraker Press, 1977, Bradford-on-Avon, England), p. 94.

[82] Ralph Whitlock, *The Warrior Kings of Saxon England* (Moonraker Press, 1977, Bradford-on-Avon, England), p. 95.

[83] Ralph Whitlock, *The Warrior Kings of Saxon England* (Moonraker Press, 1977, Bradford-on-Avon, England), p. 96.

[84] Ralph Whitlock, *The Warrior Kings of Saxon England* (Moonraker Press, 1977, Bradford-on-Avon, England), p. 97.

[85] Ralph Whitlock, *The Warrior Kings of Saxon England* (Moonraker Press, 1977, Bradford-on-Avon, England), p. 116.

[86] John Cannon & Ralph Griffiths, *The Oxford Illustrated History of the British Monarchy* (2000 edition, Oxford University Press), Geneaolgies of Royal Lines Appendix.

[87] Ralph Whitlock, *The Warrior Kings of Saxon England* (Moonraker Press, 1977, Bradford-on-Avon, England), p. 67.

[88] Ralph Whitlock, *The Warrior Kings of Saxon England* (Moonraker Press, 1977, Bradford-on-Avon, England), p. 97.

[89] Ralph Whitlock, *The Warrior Kings of Saxon England* (Moonraker Press, 1977, Bradford-on-Avon, England), p. 97-98.

[90] John Cannon & Ralph Griffiths, *The Oxford Illustrated History of the British Monarchy* (2000 edition, Oxford University Press), Geneaolgies of Royal Lines Appendix.

[91] Ralph Whitlock, *The Warrior Kings of Saxon England* (Moonraker Press, 1977, Bradford-on-Avon, England), p. 67.

[92] Ralph Whitlock, *The Warrior Kings of Saxon England* (Moonraker Press, 1977, Bradford-on-Avon, England), p. 98.

[93] John Cannon & Ralph Griffiths, *The Oxford Illustrated History of the British Monarchy* (2000 edition, Oxford University Press), Geneaolgies of Royal Lines Appendix; List of Monarchs Appendix.

[94] John Cannon & Ralph Griffiths, *The Oxford Illustrated History of the British Monarchy* (2000 edition, Oxford University Press), p. 656.

[95] John Cannon & Ralph Griffiths, *The Oxford Illustrated History of the British Monarchy* (2000 edition, Oxford University Press), List of Monarchs Appendix.

[96] Ralph Whitlock, *The Warrior Kings of Saxon England* (Moonraker Press, 1977, Bradford-on-Avon, England), p. 100.

[97] Ralph Whitlock, *The Warrior Kings of Saxon England* (Moonraker Press, 1977, Bradford-on-Avon, England), p. 101.

[98] Ralph Whitlock, *The Warrior Kings of Saxon England* (Moonraker Press, 1977, Bradford-on-Avon, England), p. 101.

[99] Ralph Whitlock, *The Warrior Kings of Saxon England* (Moonraker Press, 1977, Bradford-on-Avon, England), p. 101-102.

[100] Ralph Whitlock, *The Warrior Kings of Saxon England* (Moonraker Press, 1977, Bradford-on-Avon, England), p. 102.

[101] Ralph Whitlock, *The Warrior Kings of Saxon England* (Moonraker Press, 1977, Bradford-on-Avon, England), p. 102-103.

[102] John Cannon & Ralph Griffiths, *The Oxford Illustrated History of the British Monarchy* (2000 edition, Oxford University Press), p. 49.

[103] Ralph Whitlock, *The Warrior Kings of Saxon England* (Moonraker Press, 1977, Bradford-on-Avon, England), p. 103.

[104] Ralph Whitlock, *The Warrior Kings of Saxon England* (Moonraker Press, 1977, Bradford-on-Avon, England), p. 103.

[105] Ralph Whitlock, *The Warrior Kings of Saxon England* (Moonraker Press, 1977, Bradford-on-Avon, England), p. 103.

[106] Ralph Whitlock, *The Warrior Kings of Saxon England* (Moonraker Press, 1977, Bradford-on-Avon, England), p. 104.

[107] Ralph Whitlock, *The Warrior Kings of Saxon England* (Moonraker Press, 1977, Bradford-on-Avon, England), p. 105.

[108] Ralph Whitlock, *The Warrior Kings of Saxon England* (Moonraker Press, 1977, Bradford-on-Avon, England), p. 106.

[109] Ralph Whitlock, *The Warrior Kings of Saxon England* (Moonraker Press, 1977, Bradford-on-Avon, England), p. 106.

[110] John Cannon & Ralph Griffiths, *The Oxford Illustrated History of the British Monarchy* (2000 edition, Oxford University Press), p. 49.

[111] Ralph Whitlock, *The Warrior Kings of Saxon England* (Moonraker Press, 1977, Bradford-on-Avon, England), p. 106.

[112] Ralph Whitlock, *The Warrior Kings of Saxon England* (Moonraker Press, 1977, Bradford-on-Avon, England), p. 107.

[113] Ralph Whitlock, *The Warrior Kings of Saxon England* (Moonraker Press, 1977, Bradford-on-Avon, England), p. 107.

[114] Ralph Whitlock, *The Warrior Kings of Saxon England* (Moonraker Press, 1977, Bradford-on-Avon, England), p. 107-108.

[115] John Cannon & Ralph Griffiths, *The Oxford Illustrated History of the British Monarchy* (2000 edition, Oxford University Press), Geneaolgies of Royal Lines Appendix.

[116] John Cannon & Ralph Griffiths, *The Oxford Illustrated History of the British Monarchy* (2000 edition, Oxford University Press), Geneaolgies of Royal Lines Appendix.

[117] John Cannon & Ralph Griffiths, *The Oxford Illustrated History of the British Monarchy* (2000 edition, Oxford University Press), Geneaolgies of Royal Lines Appendix.

[118] Ralph Whitlock, *The Warrior Kings of Saxon England* (Moonraker Press, 1977, Bradford-on-Avon, England), p. 107.

[119] John Cannon & Ralph Griffiths, *The Oxford Illustrated History of the British Monarchy* (2000 edition, Oxford University Press), p. 656.

[120] Ralph Whitlock, *The Warrior Kings of Saxon England* (Moonraker Press, 1977, Bradford-on-Avon, England), p. 112, 117.

[121] Ralph Whitlock, *The Warrior Kings of Saxon England* (Moonraker Press, 1977, Bradford-on-Avon, England), p. 117.

[122] John Cannon & Ralph Griffiths, *The Oxford Illustrated History of the British Monarchy* (2000 edition, Oxford University Press), List of Monarchs Appendix.

[123] Ralph Whitlock, *The Warrior Kings of Saxon England* (Moonraker Press, 1977, Bradford-on-Avon, England), p. 117.

[124] Ralph Whitlock, *The Warrior Kings of Saxon England* (Moonraker Press, 1977, Bradford-on-Avon, England), p. 118.

[125] Ralph Whitlock, *The Warrior Kings of Saxon England* (Moonraker Press, 1977, Bradford-on-Avon, England), p. 118-119.

[126] Ralph Whitlock, *The Warrior Kings of Saxon England* (Moonraker Press, 1977, Bradford-on-Avon, England), p. 119.

[127] John Cannon & Ralph Griffiths, *The Oxford Illustrated History of the British Monarchy* (2000 edition, Oxford University Press), Geneaolgies of Royal Lines Appendix.

[128] Ralph Whitlock, *The Warrior Kings of Saxon England* (Moonraker Press, 1977, Bradford-on-Avon, England), p. 119.

[129] John Cannon & Ralph Griffiths, *The Oxford Illustrated History of the British Monarchy* (2000 edition, Oxford University Press), Geneaolgies of Royal Lines Appendix.

[130] John Cannon & Ralph Griffiths, *The Oxford Illustrated History of the British Monarchy* (2000 edition, Oxford University Press), p. 40.

[131] John Cannon & Ralph Griffiths, *The Oxford Illustrated History of the British Monarchy* (2000 edition, Oxford University Press), p. 17; 62.

[132] Ralph Whitlock, *The Warrior Kings of Saxon England* (Moonraker Press, 1977, Bradford-on-Avon, England), p. 124.

[133] John Cannon & Ralph Griffiths, *The Oxford Illustrated History of the British Monarchy* (2000 edition, Oxford University Press), p. 17; List of Monarchs Appendix.

[134] Ralph Whitlock, *The Warrior Kings of Saxon England* (Moonraker Press, 1977, Bradford-on-Avon, England), p. 124.

[135] Ralph Whitlock, *The Warrior Kings of Saxon England* (Moonraker Press, 1977, Bradford-on-Avon, England), p. 124.

[136] Ralph Whitlock, *The Warrior Kings of Saxon England* (Moonraker Press, 1977, Bradford-on-Avon, England), p. 125.

[137] Ralph Whitlock, *The Warrior Kings of Saxon England* (Moonraker Press, 1977, Bradford-on-Avon, England), p. 125.

[138] Ralph Whitlock, *The Warrior Kings of Saxon England* (Moonraker Press, 1977, Bradford-on-Avon, England), p. 126.

[139] John Cannon & Ralph Griffiths, *The Oxford Illustrated History of the British Monarchy* (2000 edition, Oxford University Press), p. 16.

[140] E. William Robertson, *Scotland Under Her Early Kings: A History of the Kingdom to the Close of the 13th Century, Part One* (Edinburgh: Edmonston and Douglas, 1862), p. 91.

[141] Ralph Whitlock, *The Warrior Kings of Saxon England* (Moonraker Press, 1977, Bradford-on-Avon, England), p. 126.

[142] Ralph Whitlock, *The Warrior Kings of Saxon England* (Moonraker Press, 1977, Bradford-on-Avon, England), p. 126.

[143] John Cannon & Ralph Griffiths, *The Oxford Illustrated History of the British Monarchy* (2000 edition, Oxford University Press), p. 24.

[144] Ralph Whitlock, *The Warrior Kings of Saxon England* (Moonraker Press, 1977, Bradford-on-Avon, England), p. 127.

[145] John Cannon & Ralph Griffiths, *The Oxford Illustrated History of the British Monarchy* (2000 edition, Oxford University Press), p. 30.

[146] John Cannon & Ralph Griffiths, *The Oxford Illustrated History of the British Monarchy* (2000 edition, Oxford University Press), p. 30.

[147] John Cannon & Ralph Griffiths, *The Oxford Illustrated History of the British Monarchy* (2000 edition, Oxford University Press), Geneaolgies of Royal Lines Appendix.

[148] John Cannon & Ralph Griffiths, *The Oxford Illustrated History of the British Monarchy* (2000 edition, Oxford University Press), Geneaolgies of Royal Lines Appendix.

[149] John Cannon & Ralph Griffiths, *The Oxford Illustrated History of the British Monarchy* (2000 edition, Oxford University Press), Geneaolgies of Royal Lines Appendix.

[150] Ralph Whitlock, *The Warrior Kings of Saxon England* (Moonraker Press, 1977, Bradford-on-Avon, England), p. 127-128.

[151] Ralph Whitlock, *The Warrior Kings of Saxon England* (Moonraker Press, 1977, Bradford-on-Avon, England), p. 129.

[152] John Cannon & Ralph Griffiths, *The Oxford Illustrated History of the British Monarchy* (2000 edition, Oxford University Press), p. 15-16.

[153] John Cannon & Ralph Griffiths, *The Oxford Illustrated History of the British Monarchy* (2000 edition, Oxford University Press), Geneaolgies of Royal Lines Appendix.

[154] Ralph Whitlock, *The Warrior Kings of Saxon England* (Moonraker Press, 1977, Bradford-on-Avon, England), p. 129-130.

[155] Ralph Whitlock, *The Warrior Kings of Saxon England* (Moonraker Press, 1977, Bradford-on-Avon, England), p. 130.

[156] Ralph Whitlock, *The Warrior Kings of Saxon England* (Moonraker Press, 1977, Bradford-on-Avon, England), p. 131.

[157] Ralph Whitlock, *The Warrior Kings of Saxon England* (Moonraker Press, 1977, Bradford-on-Avon, England), p. 131.

[158] John Cannon & Ralph Griffiths, *The Oxford Illustrated History of the British Monarchy* (2000 edition, Oxford University Press), List of Monarchs Appendix.

[159] Ralph Whitlock, *The Warrior Kings of Saxon England* (Moonraker Press, 1977, Bradford-on-Avon, England), p. 132.

[160] Ralph Whitlock, *The Warrior Kings of Saxon England* (Moonraker Press, 1977, Bradford-on-Avon, England), p. 133.

[161] Ralph Whitlock, *The Warrior Kings of Saxon England* (Moonraker Press, 1977, Bradford-on-Avon, England), p. 133.

[162] Ralph Whitlock, *The Warrior Kings of Saxon England* (Moonraker Press, 1977, Bradford-on-Avon, England), p. 134.

[163] Ralph Whitlock, *The Warrior Kings of Saxon England* (Moonraker Press, 1977, Bradford-on-Avon, England), p. 135.

[164] Ralph Whitlock, *The Warrior Kings of Saxon England* (Moonraker Press, 1977, Bradford-on-Avon, England), p. 136.

[165] Ralph Whitlock, *The Warrior Kings of Saxon England* (Moonraker Press, 1977, Bradford-on-Avon, England), p. 136.

[166] Ralph Whitlock, *The Warrior Kings of Saxon England* (Moonraker Press, 1977, Bradford-on-Avon, England), p. 136-137.

[167] Ralph Whitlock, *The Warrior Kings of Saxon England* (Moonraker Press, 1977, Bradford-on-Avon, England), p. 135.

[168] Ralph Whitlock, *The Warrior Kings of Saxon England* (Moonraker Press, 1977, Bradford-on-Avon, England), p. 137.

[169] Ralph Whitlock, *The Warrior Kings of Saxon England* (Moonraker Press, 1977, Bradford-on-Avon, England), p. 137-138.

[170] John Cannon & Ralph Griffiths, *The Oxford Illustrated History of the British Monarchy* (2000 edition, Oxford University Press), p. 30.

[171] Ralph Whitlock, *The Warrior Kings of Saxon England* (Moonraker Press, 1977, Bradford-on-Avon, England), p. 138.

[172] Ralph Whitlock, *The Warrior Kings of Saxon England* (Moonraker Press, 1977, Bradford-on-Avon, England), p. 138.

[173] Ralph Whitlock, *The Warrior Kings of Saxon England* (Moonraker Press, 1977, Bradford-on-Avon, England), p. 138.

[174] John Cannon & Ralph Griffiths, *The Oxford Illustrated History of the British Monarchy* (2000 edition, Oxford University Press), Geneaolgies of Royal Lines Appendix.

[175] John Cannon & Ralph Griffiths, *The Oxford Illustrated History of the British Monarchy* (2000 edition, Oxford University Press), p. 44.

[176] John Cannon & Ralph Griffiths, *The Oxford Illustrated History of the British Monarchy* (2000 edition, Oxford University Press), Geneaolgies of Royal Lines Appendix.

[177] Ralph Whitlock, *The Warrior Kings of Saxon England* (Moonraker Press, 1977, Bradford-on-Avon, England), p. 139.

[178] John Cannon & Ralph Griffiths, *The Oxford Illustrated History of the British Monarchy* (2000 edition, Oxford University Press), p. 75.

[179] Ralph Whitlock, *The Warrior Kings of Saxon England* (Moonraker Press, 1977, Bradford-on-Avon, England), p. 140.

[180] Ralph Whitlock, *The Warrior Kings of Saxon England* (Moonraker Press, 1977, Bradford-on-Avon, England), p. 140.

[181] John Cannon & Ralph Griffiths, *The Oxford Illustrated History of the British Monarchy* (2000 edition, Oxford University Press), List of Monarchs Appendix.

[182] Ralph Whitlock, *The Warrior Kings of Saxon England* (Moonraker Press, 1977, Bradford-on-Avon, England), p. 140.

[183] Ralph Whitlock, *The Warrior Kings of Saxon England* (Moonraker Press, 1977, Bradford-on-Avon, England), p. 140-141.

[184] Ralph Whitlock, *The Warrior Kings of Saxon England* (Moonraker Press, 1977, Bradford-on-Avon, England), p. 141.

[185] Ralph Whitlock, *The Warrior Kings of Saxon England* (Moonraker Press, 1977, Bradford-on-Avon, England), p. 142.

[186] Gabriel Ronay, *The Lost King of England: the East European adventures of Edward the Exile* (Woodbridge, Suffolk; Wolfeboro, N.H., USA: Boydell Press, 1989, ISBN 0-85115-541-3), p. 16.

[187] Ralph Whitlock, *The Warrior Kings of Saxon England* (Moonraker Press, 1977, Bradford-on-Avon, England), p. 142.

[188] Gabriel Ronay, *The Lost King of England: the East European adventures of Edward the Exile* (Woodbridge, Suffolk; Wolfeboro, N.H., USA: Boydell Press, 1989, ISBN 0-85115-541-3), p. 12.

[189] Gabriel Ronay, *The Lost King of England: the East European adventures of Edward the Exile* (Woodbridge, Suffolk; Wolfeboro, N.H., USA: Boydell Press, 1989, ISBN 0-85115-541-3), p. 17.

[190] Ralph Whitlock, *The Warrior Kings of Saxon England* (Moonraker Press, 1977, Bradford-on-Avon, England), p. 142.

[191] Gabriel Ronay, *The Lost King of England: the East European adventures of Edward the Exile* (Woodbridge, Suffolk; Wolfeboro, N.H., USA: Boydell Press, 1989, ISBN 0-85115-541-3), p. 17.

[192] Ralph Whitlock, *The Warrior Kings of Saxon England* (Moonraker Press, 1977, Bradford-on-Avon, England), p. 143.

[193] Gabriel Ronay, *The Lost King of England: the East European adventures of Edward the Exile* (Woodbridge, Suffolk; Wolfeboro, N.H., USA: Boydell Press, 1989, ISBN 0-85115-541-3), p. 22.

[194] John Cannon & Ralph Griffiths, *The Oxford Illustrated History of the British Monarchy* (2000 edition, Oxford University Press), Geneaolgies of Royal Lines Appendix; List of Monarchs Appendix.

[195] Ralph Whitlock, *The Warrior Kings of Saxon England* (Moonraker Press, 1977, Bradford-on-Avon, England), p. 143.

[196] John Cannon & Ralph Griffiths, *The Oxford Illustrated History of the British Monarchy* (2000 edition, Oxford University Press), Geneaolgies of Royal Lines Appendix.

[197] Gabriel Ronay, *The Lost King of England: the East European adventures of Edward the Exile* (Woodbridge, Suffolk; Wolfeboro, N.H., USA: Boydell Press, 1989, ISBN 0-85115-541-3), p. 24.

[198] Gabriel Ronay, *The Lost King of England: the East European adventures of Edward the Exile* (Woodbridge, Suffolk; Wolfeboro, N.H., USA: Boydell Press, 1989, ISBN 0-85115-541-3), p. 24.

[199] Gabriel Ronay, *The Lost King of England: the East European adventures of Edward the Exile* (Woodbridge, Suffolk; Wolfeboro, N.H., USA: Boydell Press, 1989, ISBN 0-85115-541-3), p. 25.

[200] Gabriel Ronay, *The Lost King of England: the East European adventures of Edward the Exile* (Woodbridge, Suffolk; Wolfeboro, N.H., USA: Boydell Press, 1989, ISBN 0-85115-541-3), p. 26.

[201] Gabriel Ronay, *The Lost King of England: the East European adventures of Edward the Exile* (Woodbridge, Suffolk; Wolfeboro, N.H., USA: Boydell Press, 1989, ISBN 0-85115-541-3), p. 28.

[202] Gabriel Ronay, *The Lost King of England: the East European adventures of Edward the Exile* (Woodbridge, Suffolk; Wolfeboro, N.H., USA: Boydell Press, 1989, ISBN 0-85115-541-3), p. 39.

[203] Gabriel Ronay, *The Lost King of England: the East European adventures of Edward the Exile* (Woodbridge, Suffolk; Wolfeboro, N.H., USA: Boydell Press, 1989, ISBN 0-85115-541-3), p. 40.

[204] Gabriel Ronay, *The Lost King of England: the East European adventures of Edward the Exile* (Woodbridge, Suffolk; Wolfeboro, N.H., USA: Boydell Press, 1989, ISBN 0-85115-541-3), p. 41.

[205] Gabriel Ronay, *The Lost King of England: the East European adventures of Edward the Exile* (Woodbridge, Suffolk; Wolfeboro, N.H., USA: Boydell Press, 1989, ISBN 0-85115-541-3), p. 43.

[206] Gabriel Ronay, *The Lost King of England: the East European adventures of Edward the Exile* (Woodbridge, Suffolk; Wolfeboro, N.H., USA: Boydell Press, 1989, ISBN 0-85115-541-3), p. 52-53.

[207] Gabriel Ronay, *The Lost King of England: the East European adventures of Edward the Exile* (Woodbridge, Suffolk; Wolfeboro, N.H., USA: Boydell Press, 1989, ISBN 0-85115-541-3), p. 62.

[208] Gabriel Ronay, *The Lost King of England: the East European adventures of Edward the Exile* (Woodbridge, Suffolk; Wolfeboro, N.H., USA: Boydell Press, 1989, ISBN 0-85115-541-3), p. 63.

[209] Gabriel Ronay, *The Lost King of England: the East European adventures of Edward the Exile* (Woodbridge, Suffolk; Wolfeboro, N.H., USA: Boydell Press, 1989, ISBN 0-85115-541-3), p. 64.

[210] Gabriel Ronay, *The Lost King of England: the East European adventures of Edward the Exile* (Woodbridge, Suffolk; Wolfeboro, N.H., USA: Boydell Press, 1989, ISBN 0-85115-541-3), p. 66.

[211] Gabriel Ronay, *The Lost King of England: the East European adventures of Edward the Exile* (Woodbridge, Suffolk; Wolfeboro, N.H., USA: Boydell Press, 1989, ISBN 0-85115-541-3), p. 69.

[212] Gabriel Ronay, *The Lost King of England: the East European adventures of Edward the Exile* (Woodbridge, Suffolk; Wolfeboro, N.H., USA: Boydell Press, 1989, ISBN 0-85115-541-3), p. 70.

[213] John Cannon & Ralph Griffiths, *The Oxford Illustrated History of the British Monarchy* (2000 edition, Oxford University Press), Geneaolgies of Royal Lines Appendix; List of Monarchs Appendix.

[214] Gabriel Ronay, *The Lost King of England: the East European adventures of Edward the Exile* (Woodbridge, Suffolk; Wolfeboro, N.H., USA: Boydell Press, 1989, ISBN 0-85115-541-3), p. 76.

[215] Gabriel Ronay, *The Lost King of England: the East European adventures of Edward the Exile* (Woodbridge, Suffolk; Wolfeboro, N.H., USA: Boydell Press, 1989, ISBN 0-85115-541-3), p. 76.

[216] Gabriel Ronay, *The Lost King of England: the East European adventures of Edward the Exile* (Woodbridge, Suffolk; Wolfeboro, N.H., USA: Boydell Press, 1989, ISBN 0-85115-541-3), p. 79.

[217] Gabriel Ronay, *The Lost King of England: the East European adventures of Edward the Exile* (Woodbridge, Suffolk; Wolfeboro, N.H., USA: Boydell Press, 1989, ISBN 0-85115-541-3), p. 82.

[218] Gabriel Ronay, *The Lost King of England: the East European adventures of Edward the Exile* (Woodbridge, Suffolk; Wolfeboro, N.H., USA: Boydell Press, 1989, ISBN 0-85115-541-3), p. 85.

[219] Gabriel Ronay, *The Lost King of England: the East European adventures of Edward the Exile* (Woodbridge, Suffolk; Wolfeboro, N.H., USA: Boydell Press, 1989, ISBN 0-85115-541-3), p. 86.

[220] Gabriel Ronay, *The Lost King of England: the East European adventures of Edward the Exile* (Woodbridge, Suffolk; Wolfeboro, N.H., USA: Boydell Press, 1989, ISBN 0-85115-541-3), p. 88, 91, 93.

[221] Gabriel Ronay, *The Lost King of England: the East European adventures of Edward the Exile* (Woodbridge, Suffolk; Wolfeboro, N.H., USA: Boydell Press, 1989, ISBN 0-85115-541-3), p. 108-109.

[222] Gabriel Ronay, *The Lost King of England: the East European adventures of Edward the Exile* (Woodbridge, Suffolk; Wolfeboro, N.H., USA: Boydell Press, 1989, ISBN 0-85115-541-3), p. 118-119.

[223] John Cannon & Ralph Griffiths, *The Oxford Illustrated History of the British Monarchy* (2000 edition, Oxford University Press), Geneaolgies of Royal Lines Appendix.

[224] Gabriel Ronay, *The Lost King of England: the East European adventures of Edward the Exile* (Woodbridge, Suffolk; Wolfeboro, N.H., USA: Boydell Press, 1989, ISBN 0-85115-541-3), p. 118.

[225] Gabriel Ronay, *The Lost King of England: the East European adventures of Edward the Exile* (Woodbridge, Suffolk; Wolfeboro, N.H., USA: Boydell Press, 1989, ISBN 0-85115-541-3), p. 130-131.

[226] Gabriel Ronay, *The Lost King of England: the East European adventures of Edward the Exile* (Woodbridge, Suffolk; Wolfeboro, N.H., USA: Boydell Press, 1989, ISBN 0-85115-541-3), p. 130.

[227] Gabriel Ronay, *The Lost King of England: the East European adventures of Edward the Exile* (Woodbridge, Suffolk; Wolfeboro, N.H., USA: Boydell Press, 1989, ISBN 0-85115-541-3), p. 135.

[228] Gabriel Ronay, *The Lost King of England: the East European adventures of Edward the Exile* (Woodbridge, Suffolk; Wolfeboro, N.H., USA: Boydell Press, 1989, ISBN 0-85115-541-3), p. 136-138.

[229] John Cannon & Ralph Griffiths, *The Oxford Illustrated History of the British Monarchy* (2000 edition, Oxford University Press), Geneaolgies of Royal Lines Appendix.

[230] Gabriel Ronay, *The Lost King of England: the East European adventures of Edward the Exile* (Woodbridge, Suffolk; Wolfeboro, N.H., USA: Boydell Press, 1989, ISBN 0-85115-541-3), p. 139, 141.

[231] Gabriel Ronay, *The Lost King of England: the East European adventures of Edward the Exile* (Woodbridge, Suffolk; Wolfeboro, N.H., USA: Boydell Press, 1989, ISBN 0-85115-541-3), p. 143.

[232] Gabriel Ronay, *The Lost King of England: the East European adventures of Edward the Exile* (Woodbridge, Suffolk; Wolfeboro, N.H., USA: Boydell Press, 1989, ISBN 0-85115-541-3), p. 144.

[233] Gabriel Ronay, *The Lost King of England: the East European adventures of Edward the Exile* (Woodbridge, Suffolk; Wolfeboro, N.H., USA: Boydell Press, 1989, ISBN 0-85115-541-3), p. 145.

[234] Gabriel Ronay, *The Lost King of England: the East European adventures of Edward the Exile* (Woodbridge, Suffolk; Wolfeboro, N.H., USA: Boydell Press, 1989, ISBN 0-85115-541-3), p. 148.

[235] Gabriel Ronay, *The Lost King of England: the East European adventures of Edward the Exile* (Woodbridge, Suffolk; Wolfeboro, N.H., USA: Boydell Press, 1989, ISBN 0-85115-541-3), p. 150, 152.

[236] Gabriel Ronay, *The Lost King of England: the East European adventures of Edward the Exile* (Woodbridge, Suffolk; Wolfeboro, N.H., USA: Boydell Press, 1989, ISBN 0-85115-541-3), p. 156-157.

[237] Gabriel Ronay, *The Lost King of England: the East European adventures of Edward the Exile* (Woodbridge, Suffolk; Wolfeboro, N.H., USA: Boydell Press, 1989, ISBN 0-85115-541-3), p. 162.

[238] Gabriel Ronay, *The Lost King of England: the East European adventures of Edward the Exile* (Woodbridge, Suffolk; Wolfeboro, N.H., USA: Boydell Press, 1989, ISBN 0-85115-541-3), p. 164.

THE CONTINENTAL DYNASTY

NORMANDY, PLANTAGENET, LANCASTER, YORK & TUDOR

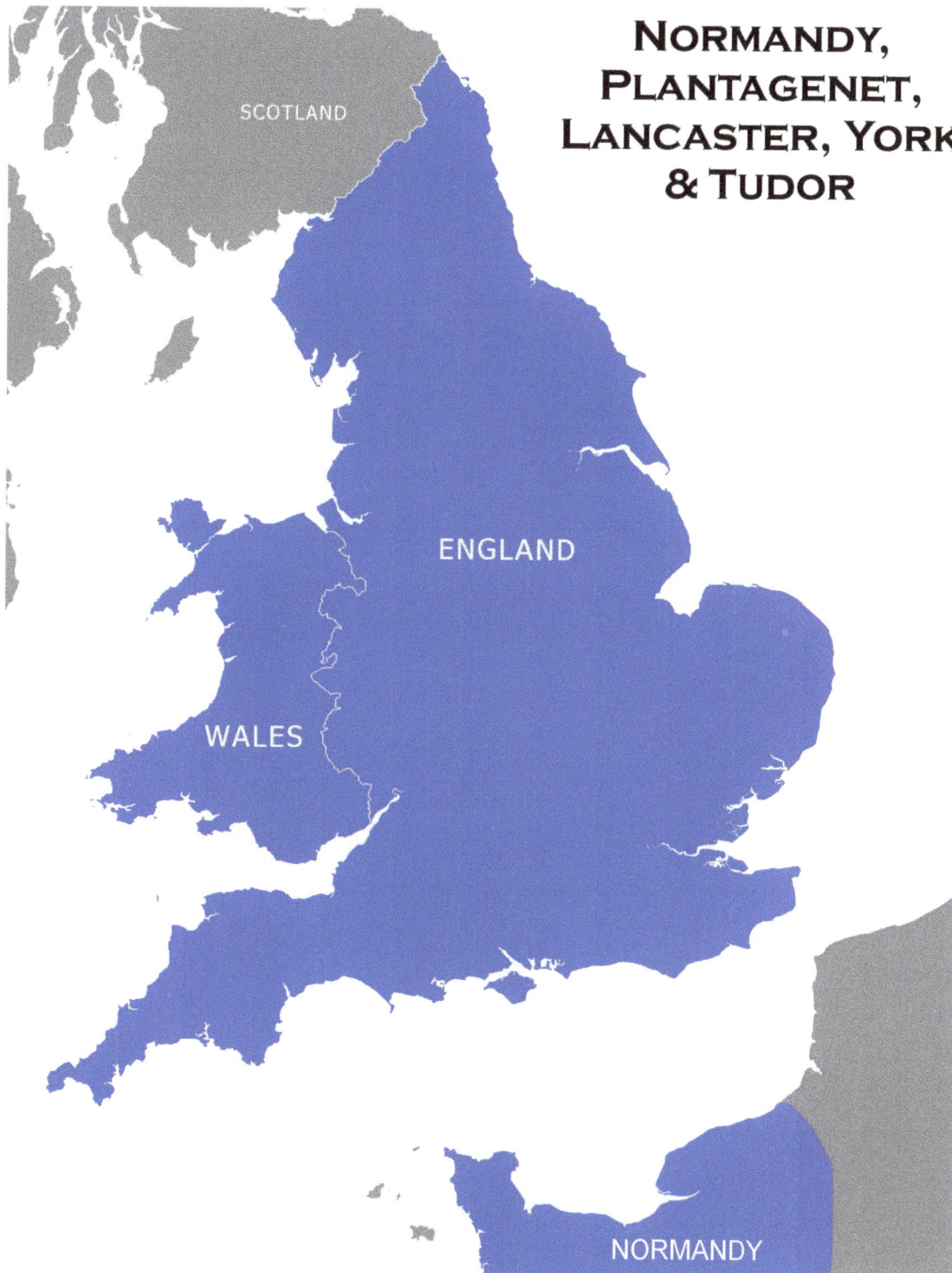

SCOTLAND

ENGLAND

WALES

NORMANDY

THE CONTINENTAL DYNASTY

WILLIAM THE CONQUEROR ———— **MATILDA OF FLANDERS**
(1027-1087)   *(d. 1083)*

HENRY I OF NORMANDY ———— **MATILDA OF SCOTLAND**
(1068-1135)   *(1080-1118)*
dau. of King Malcolm III of Scotland
(see MacAlpin Lineage)

GEOFFREY PLANTAGENET, COUNT OF ANJOU ———— **MATILDA OF NORMANDY**
(1113-1151)   *(1102-1167)*

HENRY II PLANTAGENET ———— **ELEANOR OF AQUITAINE**
(1133-1189)   *(d. 1204)*

ISABELLA OF ANGOULEME ———— **JOHN I PLANTAGENET**
(d. 1246)   *(1167-1216)*

HENRY III PLANTAGENET ———— **ELEANOR OF PROVENCE**
(1207-1272)   *(d. 1291)*

ELEANOR OF CASTILE ———— **EDWARD I PLANTAGENET**
(d. 1290)   *(1239-1307)*

EDWARD II PLANTAGENET ———— **ISABELLA OF FRANCE**
(1284-1327)   *(d. 1358)*
dau. King Philip IV of France

PHILIPPA OF HAINAULT ———— **EDWARD III PLANTAGENET**
(1369)   *(1312-1377)*
dau. Count William of Hainault

LIONEL PLANTAGENET, DUKE OF CLARENCE ———— **ELIZABETH DE BURGH, COUNTESS OF ULSTER**
(d. 1368)   *(d. 1363)*

EDMUND PLANTAGENET, DUKE OF YORK ———— **ISABELLA OF CASTILE**
dau. King Pedro of Castile

PHILIPPA PLANTAGENET, COUNTESS OF ULSTER ———— **EDMUND MORTIMER, EARL OF MARCH**
(d. 1382)

JOHN OF GAUNT, DUKE OF LANCASTER ———— **CATHERINE SWYNFORD**
(d. 1399)   *(d. 1403)*
his mistress, later his wife

ELEANOR HOLLAND OF KENT ———— **ROGER MORTIMER, EARL OF ULSTER** *(d. 1398)*
(d. 1405)

ANNE DE MORTIMER ———— **RICHARD OF CONISBURGH, EARL OF CAMBRIDGE**
(1390-1411)   *(1375-1415)*
dau. Earl of Ulster

JOHN BEAUFORT, EARL OF SOMERSET ———— **MARGARET DE HOLAND**
(d. 1410)   *dau. Earl Thomas of Kent*

JOHN BEAUFORT, DUKE OF SOMERSET ———— **MARGARET BEAUCHAMP OF BLETSO**
(d.1444)   *(d. 1482)*

RICHARD PLANTAGENET, DUKE OF YORK ———— **CECILY NEVILLE**
(1411-1460)   *(1415-1495)*

MARGARET BEAUFORT ———— **EDMUND TUDOR, EARL OF RICHMOND**
(1443-1509)   *(1430-1456)*
grandson King Charles VI of France

EDWARD IV YORK ———— **ELIZABETH WOODVILLE**
(1442-1483)   *(1437-1492)*
dau. Earl of Rivers

HENRY VII TUDOR ———— **ELIZABETH OF YORK**
(1457-1509)   *(1465-1503)*

MARGARET TUDOR
(1489-1541)
marr. King James IV of Scotland
(see Stewart Dynasty Lineage)

THE CONTINENTAL DYNASTY:
NORMANDY, PLANTAGENET, LANCASTER, YORK, AND TUDOR

Since our percentage of Continental English royal blood runs mainly through one marriage and is vanishingly small, I debated not including this chapter at all, but decided that since England is a part of Great Britain, I would. Similar marriages to Scottish kings from royal lines of Denmark, France, and Spain I have not pursued, as this book would be exceedingly long if I did. Royal families are well researched, and you may do so as you like.

For all that Scotland and England were enemies for hundreds of years, there were noble and royal connections made numerous times. There are at least four instances where English royalty married into our Scottish royal line:

King Malcolm III married Margaret of Wessex, the granddaughter of King Edmund Ironside, one of the last Saxon kings of England. She is also the great-granddaughter of King Olaf Skotkunung Eriksson of Sweden.[1] [2] (see *Saxon Dynasty* and *MacAlpin Dynasty*)

David of Huntingdon, himself the grandson of a king and brother to two others, married Matilda of Chester, the second great-granddaughter of King Henry I of England. Their great-great-grandson was King Robert the Bruce of Scotland.[3] [4] (see *MacAlpin Dynasty* and *Stewart Dynasty*)

King James I of Scotland married Joan Beaufort, who was the great-granddaughter of King Edward III of England, third great-granddaughter of King Edward I of England, and the fourth great-granddaughter of King Henry III of England.[5] [6] (see *Stewart Dynasty*)

Finally, the most important marriage was between *King James IV of Scotland* and Margaret Tudor.[7] [8] [9] Their grandson, King James VI of Scotland, inherited the English throne and united the kingdoms as King James the VI and I. (see *Stewart Dynasty*)

Margaret Tudor was a child of King Henry VII Tudor of England and Princess Elizabeth of York, combining blood from almost every house that ruled England. Because of this, her line traces all the way back to the very first Norman king, William the Conqueror.

King William I the Conqueror, Duke of Normandy
(c. 1027-1087)
(reigned 1066-1087)

When we left the chapter on the *Saxon Dynasty*, the age of Saxon rule was coming to an end. King Edward the Confessor held the throne, which passed to King Harold Godwinson upon Edward's death. Harold didn't get to enjoy his rule for very long, because the Normans invaded, with William the Conqueror at their head.

William I the Conqueror was born around 1027 out of wedlock to Robert "the Magnificent," the 6th Duke of Normandy (France), and Herleve of Falaise.[10] [11] Robert's lineage reached back to Rollo the Ganger, a Viking who was the 1st Duke of Normady—and who, tradition tells us, was the son of Ragnvald of Maeri, the 1st Norwegian Jarl of Orkney and Shetland.[12] [13] (see *Norwegian Lineage*)

Rollo, 1st Duke of Normandy, fathered William Longsword, 2nd Duke, who fathered Richard I the Fearless, 3rd Duke, who fathered Richard II the Good, 4th Duke, who fathered the 5th Duke, who died with no heirs. The dukedom passed to a second son of Richard II, Robert I the Magnificent, 6th Duke, and father of William the Conqueror. Much has been written about the Dukes of Normandy elsewhere, so I will not trace them here, for the sake of brevity.

When William's father, Robert, died in Turkey on his way home from Jerusalem in 1035, William became the 7th Duke of Normandy.[14][15] Not everyone was happy with an illegitimate son gaining the power, and his cousin Guy, Count of Burgundy, revolted. William went to King Henry I of France for help, and the king, grateful for the help William's father had given in raising him to the throne, rode with William into battle, and together they defeated Guy at Vel-es-Dunes near Caen.[16][17][18]

William was supposed to marry Matilda, daughter of Count Baldwin V of Flanders, in 1049 but Pope Leo IX prohibited the marriage, largely for political reasons. William ignored the pope, and he and Matilda married sometime prior to 1052. In 1059, Pope Nicholas II recognized their marriage. The Pope said that in return they must endow two abbeys. The couple endowed Saint-Etienne and La Trinite at Caens.[19] William and Matilda had ten known children:[20][21][22]

- Robert Curthose (c. 1050-1134) – 8th Duke of Normandy
- Richard (d. 1082) – Duke of Bernay
- William II Rufus (1060-1100) – King of England
- *Henry I* (1069-1135) – King of England
- Adela (d. 1137) – married Stephen, Count of Blois
- Agatha (d. 1079)
- Constance
- Cecelia/Cecily (d. 1126)
- Adeliza (d. 1113)
- Matilda

Possibly around 1051, King Edward the Confessor of England made William the heir to the English throne, as he had no children himself. While early chroniclers said William actually went to England, it was more likely that Edward's wishes were conveyed via messenger, because William was still heavily engaged in battles in that year and would not have been secure enough in his reign to leave Normandy.[23][24]

Also in 1051, Geoffrey Martel of Anjou rose to power and attacked the province of Maine, which lies between Anjou and Normandy. Geoffrey succeeded in capturing Maine's capital, Le Mans, after the death of Maine's count. William countered by marching south. Geoffrey withdrew for the moment, but this was the beginning of the struggle between Normandy and Anjou that ended only when the Plantagenets took the English throne from William's heirs.[25]

King Henry I of France grew uneasy with a strong Normandy rising to power. In 1054 he allied with Geoffrey of Anjou against William. Henry and Geoffrey marched from the south, while Henry's brother Odo marched from the east. William had never had to face pitched battle on two fronts. Odo's pillaging men were surprised and overwhelmed at Mortemer. The king and Geoffrey withdrew back to Anjou.[26]

King Henry and Geoffrey Martel tried once more in 1057 to invade Normandy. As they were fording the Dives at Varaville, Henry and Geoffrey were caught in the tides and routed with much slaughter. The king did not invade Normandy again.[27]

The king and William still had issues. In 1058, Henry and William clashed over the Vexin lands. William claimed the Vexin as his, passed down from his predecessors. Henry disputed this. The war raged until Henry died on 4 August 1060. William's other nemesis, Geoffrey Martel, died 14 November 1060, thus removing both of William's worst enemies.[28]

After 1060, William was secure in Normandy: Anjou was split by civil war, and William's father-in-law ruled France as regent for the young boy king, Philip I. William turned to building personal loyalties by divvying up forfeited lands to loyal nobles and tying as much knight-service to himself as he could. He participated vigorously in Church affairs, and was held in high regard by his Church—a valuable ally to have.[29]

All this set the stage for William of Normandy to strike at England in 1066.

In 1066, Harold Godwinson took the throne of England after Edward the Confessor died. Because Harold had (unwillingly) given homage to William as his overlord in 1064, Harold's seizing the throne in defiance of William's claim to it broke the feudal laws of the era. William asked Pope Alexander II for his verdict on Harold's actions, and the Pope gave his blessing to William's planned invasion; indeed, William invaded under a papal standard, making his invasion of England a "crusade" of sorts. Having the backing of the Pope would prove helpful in subduing English resentment later.[30]

September of 1066 was a fateful one for England. King Harold Godwinson was attacked near York by King Harald Haraldson of Norway, who thought he ought to be King of England because of his ties to Canute, the Viking King of England. Harold Godwinson defeated him at Stamford Bridge on 25 September, only to hear later that William had invaded at Hastings on 28 September. Harold hurried south, and on 14 October was defeated by William at Hastings.[31]

William then spent until Christmas Day "convincing" the rest of England that he really was the king.[32] After the towns capitulated to him, he was crowned King of England 25 December 1066 in Westminster Abbey.[33] [34]

From 1067 to 1071, William faced multiple uprisings throughout England, particularly in the north. William put down all revolts ruthlessly. Between York and Durham, he erased an entire generation, killing all the men and boys, burning food and homes, slaughtering animals, and generally devastating the land. Similar fates befell all the shires that revolted, although none near the magnitude of York-Durham.[35] [36] By 1071, William had had enough of rebellious English nobles and destroyed the English nobility, replacing them with Normans he could trust.[37]

In 1072, William invaded Scotland in retaliation for Malcolm III's support of Edgar the Aethling (see *Saxon Dynasty*) and Malcolm's subsequent ravaging of Lothian during the northern English uprisings. The war did not turn hot but instead resulted in the Treaty of Abernathy.[38] [39] [40]

With things settled in England, and much upheaval in his native Normandy, William returned to France, where he spent most of the rest of his life, only returning to England in 1075, 1080, 1082, and 1085.[41] Normandy was attacked by Anjou, by King Philip of France,[42] and by William's own son, Robert Curthose, who was impatient for power.[43] Robert and William eventually made up in 1080, but the reconciliation only lasted until 1083.[44]

Back in England, William ordered the Domesday Book created (1085-1086), to tally all the lands he owned in England and to figure out who owned what land, since there had been so much upheaval since 1066.[45] [46] He also faced a threat from Cnut IV of Denmark, who wanted the throne of England. Before battle was joined, Cnut IV was murdered, thus ending the last of the threats to William's power. On 1 August 1086, William received renewed oaths of fealty from all the major landowners in England, cementing his power.[47] [48]

Later in 1086, William returned to Normandy.[49] In August 1087, King Philip tried again to invade Normandy, but William met him and drove him out.[50] However, as he rode through the town of Mantes, William was seized with terrible internal pains. William retired to Saint-Gervais in Rouen to die. William lingered for several days and put his affairs in order. Although against his better judgment, he agreed to allow his rebellious son, Robert, to succeed to the Normandy dukedom. He designated his second surviving son, William Rufus, to be king of England and gave 5,000 pounds to his youngest son, Henry.[51]

William I the Conqueror died 9 September 1087,[52] and was buried in St. Stephen's in Caen, France.[53] His wife, Queen Matilda, had preceded him in death in November 1083.[54]

King Henry I of Normandy
(1068-1135)
(reigned 1100-1135)

William the Conqueror's son William Rufus became **King William II of England** upon his father's death. He ruled from 1087-1100. He extended and strengthened his control of England, and also became Duke of Normandy (in 1096) when his brother Robert Curthose went on Crusade. William was shot and killed (probably accidentally) in 1100 while hunting in New Forest and is buried in Winchester Cathedral.[55]

As William Rufus was childless, Henry I, the youngest of the Conqueror's sons, born in 1068, inherited England and Normandy. He was crowned King Henry I of England at Westminster Abby 5 August 1100.[56] [57]

Henry's brother Robert Curthose returned from Crusade, and was furious to find Henry in possession of Normandy. Robert wanted Normandy back (although he had pawned it to the English Crown to pay for his Crusade), and he believed that the English Crown should be his because he was older. At the Battle of Tinchebrai in Normandy, Henry defeated Robert and locked him in the Tower of London, where Robert died in 1134.[58]

In1112, 1117-18, 1124, and 1128, Henry was periodically fighting uprisings in Normandy—against his brother Robert's son and heir, William Clito, against Fulk of Anjou who wanted Maine, against Flanders, and against King Louis VI of France. He was also constantly taxing the people of England to pay for these wars, which they did not like at all, seeing their money go to fight in foreign places.[59]

In 1121, Henry founded the Reading Abbey at the behest of his sister Adela, who became a Clunic nun in widowhood. Adela was the Countess of Blois, and it was her son Stephen who would plunge England into civil war after Henry I's death, when Stephen disputed Henry's daughter Matilda's right to the throne.[60]

Wanting to secure the throne to his family, in 1126 Henry appointed his daughter Matilda to be his heir. He brought Matilda to England and had his barons swear fealty to her. She was the widow of German Emperor Henry V.[61]

Henry first married Maude of Scotland, daughter of King Malcolm III of Scotland (see *MacAlpin Lineage*).[62] [63] "Good Queen Maude" died in 1118 and was buried in Westminster Cathedral.[64] [65] They had:[66]

- William (1103-1120) – predeceased his father, drowned in the *White Ship* disaster[67]
- *Matilda* (1102-1167) – Empress of Germany, named heir to the English throne

His second marriage to Adele of Louvain, on 29 Jan 1211 in Windsor Castle, produced no children.[68] [69]

The website "The Peerage" attributes at least twenty-three other children with seven other women to Henry, but I will not list them here, as they do not play into our family history.

Henry I died in Lyons-la-Foret, Rouen, Normandy, France, on 1 December 1135,[70] [71] [72] [73] and was buried in the Reading Abbey he founded.[74]

Matilda of Normandy, Empress of Germany
(1102-1167)

Matilda of Normandy was only twelve in 1114 when she was sent to Germany to live in her future husband's court. She married Henry V, Emperor of Germany, and did not return to England until her husband's death in 1125.[75] [76]

As we read above, in 1126 she was made heir to her father, King Henry I of England. She left England again, however, when she married Geoffrey "the Fair" Plantagenet, 11th Count of Anjou in 1128.[77] [78] [79] This might have been an attempt to reconcile Anjou and Normandy, but it failed, as Geoffrey invaded Normandy four times, eventually being proclaimed Duke of Normandy in 1144.[80] [81] [82]

Matilda's marriage to Geoffrey was rocky, and she returned to England in 1131. She was unpleasantly surprised to find that Stephen of Blois, her first cousin, was very popular among the nobles and they would prefer that he take the throne when Henry I died.[83]

When Henry died in 1135, a prolonged war broke out between Stephen and Matilda. Although she held about half of England at one point, had the support of Scottish King David (see *MacAlpin Lineage*), and even had Stephen captured, she could not bring about the death blow to his reign. She was a harsh ruler, and was disliked even in the areas that supported her.[84]

Across the Channel, Geoffrey and Matilda mounted unsuccessful campaigns in Normandy in 1136, 1137, and 1138, seeking to wrest Normandy from King Stephen I of England. When in 1139 Matilda once again invaded England, Geoffrey attacked Normandy for a fourth time.[85]

Matilda's haughty personality was her worst enemy. In her brief moment of victory in 1141, after King Stephen was captured, she claimed the throne but alienated everyone she needed to keep on her side. She angered her two chief supporters, King David I of Scotland (her uncle), and Robert, Earl of Gloucester (her half-brother, who had invaded England with her in 1139). She also levied unreasonably heavy taxes on the people of London, who quickly turned from supporting her to reviling her, and eventually drove her out of the city.[86]

By 1148, Matilda of Normandy retired back to France, leaving the activity in England to her aggressive son, Henry Plantagenet. Matilda died in Rouen, France, in 1167. She was buried in Bec Abbey, but reinterred to Rouen Cathedral in 1846. Her epitaph is quoted as: "Here lies Henry's daughter, wife, and mother; great by birth—greater by marriage—but greatest by motherhood."[87]

Matilda had no children with her first husband, but with Geoffrey of Anjou she had:[88] [89] [90]

- ***Henry II*** (1133-1189) – King of England
- Geoffrey (d. 1158) – Count of Nantes
- William (d. 1164) – Count of Poitou

King Henry II Plantagenet
(1133-1189)
(reigned 1154-1189)

King Stephen's reign was short, and mostly filled with the strife of civil war. His wife died in 1151, and his son and heir died in 1153, leaving him sick and with no heir. Henry Plantagenet saw his chance, and forced Stephen into a treaty in 1153 where Stephen would remain king for life but Henry would be his heir. Stephen died in 1154.[91]

Born on 5 March 1133, Henry II Plantagenet's entrance into politics came at a young age. In 1142, when his mother Matilda was fighting Stephen, his father Geoffrey refused to send troops to help her—but he did send 9-year-old Henry to be used as a rallying point.[92] From that time on, things happened quickly for Henry. In 1148, his mother left her 15-year-old son in charge of the English war. In 1149 his great-uncle King David I of Scotland knighted him. In 1150, Henry's father Geoffrey made him ruler of Normandy, and in 1151 Geoffrey died and Henry became Count of Anjou at age eighteen.[93] [94] [95]

Henry married Eleanor of Aquitaine on 18 May 1152 in Poitiers Cathedral in Poitiers, France.[96] [97] [98] Eleanor brought the vast holdings of Aquitaine with her, which, when added to Normady and Anjou, made Henry more powerful in France than the French king. King Louis VII of France then attacked Henry, and was joined by Henry's younger brother Geoffrey, who was supposed to get Anjou upon his father's death, but Henry took it. Henry won the conflict and declared himself Duke of Aquitaine in 1153.[99]

A year later, on 19 December 1154, Henry was crowned King Henry II of England in Westminster Abbey.[100] He immediately issued a manifesto that promised the people the rights and customs they had enjoyed in King Henry I's time. Henry attempted to erase Stephen's reign, reclaiming land (including the northern lands lost to Scotland), castles, and authority, including claiming authority over the church.[101] [102] [103]

Like his Norman predecessors, King Henry spent a great deal of time in France. He left England for France in 1158, and stayed there until 1163, when trouble flared with Thomas Beckett.[104] While in France, he secured a strip of land between Normandy and the royal lands known as the Vexin, which had been a source of conflict between Normandy and the Kings of France for over a hundred years. The Vexin came to him as a dower from the marriage of his son Henry the Young King and Margaret, King Louis VII's daughter.[105]

Henry continued to acquire land. In 1165, Wales submitted to him; in 1166, Brittany, France became his; and in 1170 he became the overlord of Ireland, with the Pope's blessing.[106] Having all this land—England, Wales, Ireland, and almost half of France—required a strong political infrastructure, and Henry masterfully reformed the financial, legal, military, and judicial institutions to run effectively in his frequent absences.[107]

In an attempt to secure the succession peacefully, Henry had his eldest son, Henry the Young King, crowned in 1170,[108] and also wrote a will dividing up his lands. Henry the Young King got England, Normandy, and Anjou, Richard got Aquitaine, and Geoffrey got Brittany. Richard and Geoffrey were to be vassals of young Henry, and youngest son, John, got nothing in the will.[109] [110]

In 1171, the murder of Thomas Beckett threatened to end Henry's reign. Henry was excommunicated,[111] [112] and his sons and wife, Eleanor, conspired to revolt against him. Many of the barons who owned land on both sides of the Channel stood with Henry the Young King against his father.[113] [114] Henry II repented of the killing of Beckett,[115] [116] got reinstated to the church by the Pope,[117] [118] [119] and crushed the rebellion of his sons in 1174. Although Henry pardoned his sons, he kept his wife, Eleanor, under house arrest for the rest of his life.[120] [121]

To add to his power, Henry II captured King William the Lion of Scotland in 1174 and forced him to submit the whole of Scotland as a vassal state to England, as well as give the English church supremacy over the Scottish church. Had this state of affairs held, Scottish history would have been much different, but the Scottish church convinced the Pope to declare them independent of England, and William was able to buy back Scotland's independence when Henry's son Richard needed to raise money for his Crusade.[122]

Henry's sons squabbled when Richard of Aquitaine refused to become a vassal of Henry the Young King. Henry the Young King attacked Richard, but the conflict ended when young Henry died of a fever 11 June 1183 in Gascony, France.[123] [124]

Henry's son John was made King of Ireland in 1186, although he may have held that office as early as 1177. It was more of a ceremonial title, as there were plenty of kings in Ireland who refused to submit to the English overlords.[125]

In 1186, Henry's son Geoffrey died in Brittany, France. Only Henry's sons Richard and John were still living.[126]

In 1188, a complex war between Henry, Richard, and King Philip II Augustus of France began. First it was Henry vs. Richard, then Richard vs. Philip, then Henry and Richard vs. Philip, then Richard and Philip vs. Henry. While fighting in 1189, Henry became ill. He bequeathed Richard all the Plantagenet lands, including England.[127] [128]

Henry II Plantagenet died in 6 July 1189 in Chinon, France,[129] [130] [131] and was buried in the Abbey of Fontevrault in Anjou, France.[132] His wife, Eleanor of Aquitaine, died in Fontevrault, France, on 11 April 1204,[133] and was also buried in the Abbey there.[134] Henry and Eleanor had children:

- William (1153-1156) [135]
- Henry the Young King (1158-1183) [136] [137]
- Matilda (1156-1189) – married Henry the Lion, Duke of Saxony [138] [139] [140]

- Richard the Lionheart (1157-1199) – King of England [141] [142]
- Geoffrey (1158-1186) [143] [144]
- Eleanor (1161-1214) – married Alfonso VIII, King of Castile [145] [146]
- Joan/Joanna (1165-1199) – married William II, King of Sicily, then Raymond VI, Count of Toulouse [147] [148] [149]
- *John* (1167-1216) – King of England [150] [151]

King John Plantagenet
(1167-1216)
(reigned 1199-1216)

Henry II's son Richard inherited the English throne and ruled from 1189-1199. **King Richard I Lionheart's** reign was notable mostly for his absence. He was crowned 3 September 1189, then went on Crusade in 1190. For many reasons, he did not arrive home until 1194, when he found his brother John had usurped the throne. He kicked John out, got re-crowned in 1194, then promptly went to France to try and regain his lands there. He was killed in that effort in 1199.[152]

As the youngest of four sons of King Henry II, born on 24 December 1167, John Plantagenet's chances of becoming king of England were slim. His father made him King of Ireland, and in 1185-1186 John went to Ireland to enforce his rule. Unfortunately, he failed miserably and returned to England defeated.[153] [154]

John participated in his brother Richard's coronation, as did our ancestor David, Earl of Huntingdon (see *MacAlpin Dynasty*). Richard went on Crusade in 1191, and John made himself "rector" of England in Richard's absence. John granted London the right to municipal self-government that same year.[155] [156]

John overthrew Richard's chancellor, William Longchamp, who escaped to Normandy in October 1191. Once word reached England that Richard had been imprisoned by the Emperor of Germany (1193), John schemed to become king. He rallied support from the nobles and made a pact with France's King Philip II Augustus to exclude John's nephew Arthur (his brother Geoffrey's son) from any claim to the English throne.[157]

Unfortunately for John, Richard came back, and John begged his brother for forgiveness. In Normandy on 12 May 1194, Richard pardoned John for trying to usurp the throne. John finally obtained some power when he became Duke of Normandy 25 April 1199, although he had to fight to maintain his rule.[158]

Shortly thereafter, Richard died, and on 27 May 1199 John became King of England. England accepted him, but his French holdings were split: Normandy and Aquitaine accepted him, but Anjou, Maine, and Touraine wanted John's nephew, Arthur, for king. War naturally occurred, but John prevailed in 1200.[159] [160] [161]

John had married Isabella of Gloucester. They were second cousins, but the Pope gave his blessing. John enjoyed the lands and honors Isabella brought to the marriage, but once he was king, he hoped for a better match, and divorced Isabella on 20 June 1199. They had no children.[162]

John found a new bride, Isabella of Angoulme, daughter of the Count of Angoulme. He wanted her crowned as queen, so also had himself re-crowned at Westminster Abbey on 30 September 1200.[163] [164]

John spent most of his reign at war over land. In 1202, King Philip of France legally forfeited all of John's lands in France. This set off a war that raged for four years. John lost control of almost all of his French lands, then gained back some of them. He and Philip reached a truce in 1206 that lasted until 1214.[165] [166] [167]

John invaded Ireland again in 1210, this time with much success. The next year he conquered Wales, but the Welsh princes rose in 1212 and threw off John's rule.[168]

In 1214, John invaded France to try and regain his lost French lands, but instead lost badly and established a five-year truce with King Philip.[169] [170] [171]

At home, the nobles were angered at the high taxes and tyrannical government John instituted. Unrest grew, and to stave off civil war, John signed the Magna Carta in June of 1215, which established many rights of an individual against government that still stand today.[172] [173] [174]

In the end, civil war broke out anyway in November of 1215. The rebellious nobles called on King Philip of France to help them, so he sent his son Prince Louis to become king. King Alexander II of Scotland used this distraction to invade England, but John beat him back.[175] [176] [177]

Prince Louis invaded England 14 May 1216, but lost support along the way. When John died on 19 October 1216, the nobles had little appetite for continuing the war against 9-year-old King Henry III, and hostilities ceased. [178] [179] [180]

King John Plantagenet died in Newark, Nottinghamshire, on either the 18th or 19th of October 1216, and was buried in Worcester Cathedral.[181] [182]

John and second wife, Isabella, had five children:[183] [184] [185]

- *Henry III* (1207-1272) – King of England
- Richard (1209-1272) – Earl of Cornwall, King of Germany
- Joan (d. 1238) – married King Alexander II of Scotland
- Isabella (d. 1238) – married Emperor Frederick II of Germany
- Eleanor (d. 1275) – married Simon de Monfort, Earl of Leicester

King Henry III Plantagenet
(1207-1372)
(reigned 1216-1272)

Born 1 October 1207, in Winchester, Hampshire,[186] Henry III Plantagenet was only nine when he became king of England. Because Prince Louis of France was invading England as part of an English nobility uprising, Henry was hurriedly crowned on 28 October 1216 at Gloucester Cathedral in a ceremony of doubtful legality, as none of the correct officials or paraphernalia were used. However, the Papal legate presided, lending the Pope's authority to Henry's kingship.[187] [188] [189]

In the battles of Lincoln and Dover, the royalist forces (Henry's men) defeated the French army and set the stage for the Treaty of Kingston, which sent Louis of France home and ended hostilities.[190] [191] Both the judicial system and the Exchequer began functioning again, after all the years of upheaval.[192]

Henry had a second, proper, coronation at Westminster Cathedral in 1220, but still was not old enough to rule on his own.[193] In 1223, Pope Honorius III (technically England's feudal overlord thanks to King John) declared that sixteen-year-old Henry was old enough to control the kingdom. In reality, it wasn't until 1227 that Henry came into his own, proclaiming that all new charters must be issued under his seal, and demanding that all current landholders show proof of the validity of their claims. [194]

Henry, like his father, had military troubles in France and in England—often simultaneously. Henry went to war in France to try and reclaim Normandy and his other lands in 1230, 1242, and 1253, but failed.[195] [196] Finally, in 1259, he and King Louis IX of France signed the Treaty of Paris, which had Henry renounce his claims to all French lands except his Duke of Aquitaine lands, while acknowledging the French king as his feudal overlord. [197] [198] [199]

Henry had unrest at home as well. He appointed many French nobles (many his wife's kinfolk) to positions of power in England, and the English nobles resented this.[200] He also imposed heavy taxes to support his French wars and his attempt to have his son made King of Sicily.[201] The first uprising occurred in 1224, the next 1233, but both were put down quickly.[202] A larger and successful revolt of the nobles occurred in 1258, leading to the Provisions of Westminster in 1259, which laid out the reforms the nobles wanted.[203] [204] From 1261 through 1264, Henry did all he could to renege on the promised reforms, which led to a revolt in 1264, headed by Henry's brother-in-law, Simon de Montefort. Although Henry and his sons were captured in 1264, Simon was not able to rally support behind him, and Henry's son Edward escaped to lead the royalist forces. The future Edward I killed Simon in battle in 1265, and restored his father to full authority in 1266.[205] In 1267, the Statute of Marlborough restated the rights of the nobles, reaffirming the customs of the realm, the Magna Carta, and some of the Provisions of Westminster.[206] [207] [208]

While Henry, like his father, had repeated clashes with the English clergy over church authority, he did forbid any Inquisitions in England, saving the country from the terrors seen elsewhere in the world.[209]

Henry married Eleanor of Provence, daughter of Raimond Berenger, Count of Provence, and sister to the wife of King Louis IX of France,[210] [211] in 1236,[212] and they had children: [213] [214]

- *Edward I* (1239-1307) – King of England [215]
- Edmund "Crouchback" (1245-1296) – Earl of Leicester [216]
- Katherine (d. 1257)
- Margaret (d. 1275) – married Alexander III, King of Scotland
- Beatrice (d. 1275) – married John, Duke of Brittany

King Henry III Plantagenet died 16 November 1272 in Westminster Palace in London, and was buried in Westminster Abbey, which he had rebuilt in his lifetime.[217] His wife Eleanor died in 1291. [218]

King Edward I Plantagenet
(1239-1307)
(reigned 1272-1307)

King Edward I Plantagenet was born in July of 1239 at Westminster Palace in London.[219] [220] He spent most of his boyhood at Windsor,[221] and when he was fifteen years old, his father granted him lands in England, Wales, and Gascony, France.[222]

In 1264, the nobles rose against his father, Henry III, and Henry and his sons were captured at Lewes. Edward escaped, however, and returned the next year, killing the leader of the rebellion and ending it.[223] [224]

Like many of his time, Edward went on Crusade to Egypt and Syria from 1270-1274. His father died while he was away, and he was announced as King Edward I on 20 November 1272 at Westminster Abbey in London. He was formally crowned, also at Westminster, upon his return from Crusade in 1274.[225] [226]

It was under Edward's rule that Wales became tied to England. In 1283, Edward put down the final revolt of Llewellyn the Last, King of Wales, and made Wales a principality of England once and for all.[227] The English title "Prince of Wales" came into being when Edward I gave Wales to his heir, Edward II, and this title has belonged to the heir apparent ever since.[228] [229]

Edward enacted many laws defining rights, securing justice, and restoring order, but most of them also had an eye to strengthening royal authority. In 1290, he expelled all the Jews from England, since he saw himself as a Christian Crusader king. [230] Edward went to France from 1286-1289 to attend to his French lands. By 1297, the nobles and clerics were tired of high taxes and wars,[231] and they presented him with "Remonstrances," which Edward disliked.[232] [233]

Edward's main enemy was Scotland. He always wanted to get Scotland under English rule, and in 1292 he got his chance when he was asked to choose a new Scottish king from multiple contenders. He chose John Balliol, primarily because Balliol was willing to make Scotland a vassal state of England. Both Balliol and Edward underestimated the Scottish people, however.[234] [235]

The Scottish Wars of Independence broke out, and John Balliol abdicated 7 July 1296. William Wallace took up the cause and was executed by Edward in 1305 in London. Edward thought that would end things, but in 1306 the future King Robert the Bruce (see *Stewart Dynasty*) led a fresh uprising. [236] [237] Edward headed toward the Scottish border to meet Robert, but contracted dysentery and died on 7 July 1307 at Burgh-on-Sands, England, leaving his son to continue the struggle with Robert Bruce. [238] [239] [240] Edward was buried in Westminster Abbey in London.[241]

King Edward I Plantagenet married twice: first in 1254 to Eleanor of Castile, daughter of Alfonso X, King of Castile, in the monastery of Las Huelgas, Burgos, Castile, Spain,[242] then in 1299 to Margaret of France, daughter of Philip III, King of France,.[243] Eleanor died in 1290 in Nottinghamshire and was buried in Westminster Abbey.[244] [245] [246]

Edward and Eleanor had:[247] [248]

- Joan of Acre (d. 1307) – married first Gilbert de Clare, 6th Earl of Hertford, then Ralph de Monthermer
- Alfonso (d. 1284) – Earl of Chester
- *Edward II* (1284-1327) – became King of England
- Eleanor (d. 1298) – married Henry, Count of Bar
- Margaret – married John, Duke of Lorraine
- Elizabeth (1282-1316) – married Humphrey de Bohun, Earl of Hereford and Essex
- 7 other children, many of whom died in infancy

Edward and Margaret had:[249]

- Thomas of Botherton (d. 1338) – became 1st Earl of Norfolk
- Edmund of Woodstock (d. 1330) – became 1st Earl of Kent

King Edward II Plantagenet
(1284-1327)
(reigned 1307-1327)

Edward II Plantagenet was born on 25 April 1284 in Caernarvon Castle, Wales.[250] When he turned seventeen, his father, King Edward I, made him the first Prince of Wales, granting him the entire principality.[251] However, the king did not allow his son much experience in the running of the government, as Edward I was a paranoid man and didn't trust his friends or even his son.[252] [253]

When King Edward I died on his way to meet Robert the Bruce (see *Stewart Dynasty*) in the Scottish Wars, he left Edward II with a number of crises to deal with, including not just that war, but tension with France, and resentful nobles. King Edward II was crowned 8 July 1307, at Westminster.[254] In an attempt to placate the nobles, Edward chose to stress the king's obligations to his people, thus assuring the nobles that things would be different with him. [255]

In 1311, the nobles insisted he enact the Ordinances, which sought to limit royal power in finances and appointments—and to exile Peter Gavaston, a friend and favorite of Edward's. The nobles objected to the influence Gavaston had over Edward, and although there is no proof exactly what their relationship was, suspicion of a homosexual relationship played a role.[256]

Edward refused to exile Gavaston, and Gavaston was murdered in 1312, which made the two sides irreconcilable. The bad blood simmered for several more years, until Edward was decisively defeated by King Robert the Bruce at Bannockburn in 1314. This loss undermined Edward's credibility and his first cousin Thomas, 2nd Earl of Lancaster, seized power. However, Thomas was no better liked than Edward, so Edward wrested power back.[257] [258]

Full-blown civil war, led by Thomas, the Earl of Lancaster, erupted in 1321 and raged through 1322. Ultimately, Edward was victorious. He rescinded the Ordinances and executed Thomas, who had been captured at Boroughbridge in 1322.[259] [260]

Edward's victory did not end his problems. In 1326, Edward's wife, Isabella of France, and their fourteen-year-old son staged an uprising against him. Isabella and son Edward fled to her brother, the King of France, but he refused to protect her, so they went to Hainault. From there, Isabella allied with her lover Roger Mortimer and they attacked England.[261] [262]

The war lasted some months, and Edward II was captured by rebel forces in Wales on 16 November 1326.[263] His son became King Edward III 20 January 1327, when Edward II agreed to resign the throne to him.[264] After a failed attempt to rescue Edward II, the deposed king was murdered at Berkley Castle, Gloucestershire, England on 21 September 1327 (although some say it was natural causes, and others that he did not die there at all, but lived many more years in exile.) [265] Edward was buried in Gloucester Cathedral, Gloucestershire.[266] [267]

King Edward II Plantagenet had married Isabella of France (died 1358), daughter of Philip IV, King of France in 1308.[268] They had four children:[269]

- *Edward III* (1312-1377) – became King of England
- John of Eltham (d. 1336) – Earl of Cornwall
- Eleanor of Woodstock (d. 1335) – married Reinoud II of Guelders
- Joan of the Tower (d. 1362) – married King David II of Scotland

King Edward III Plantagenet
(1312-1377)
(reigned 1327-1377)

Edward III Plantagenet was born 13 November 1312 in Windsor Castle, England.[270] His tumultuous rise to early power was largely fueled by his mother, Isabella of France, and her lover Roger Mortimer, as Edward himself was only about fourteen at the time.[271]

King Edward III was crowned king 25 Jan 1327,[272] but the first three years of his reign saw his mother in the driver's seat. She concluded the Treaty of Northampton with Scotland, ending the First War of Scottish Independence and acknowledging Scotland's rights and the legitimacy of the Bruce monarchy.[273] [274] [275] The treaty was not popular with the English subjects, nor with Edward himself. In 1330, he overthrew his mother and Mortimer and took control.[276] [277]

Edward was obsessed with France, possibly believing he had a claim to the throne through his mother, whose father had been Philip IV, King of France.[278] [279] Also, the Plantagenets had wanted to recapture their old lands in France since King John had lost them. So Edward began the Hundred Years War in 1337.[280]

Edward's wars in France saw many victories but little actual land secured. The only territory he managed to capture and hold was Calais.[281] Still, his victories made the English happy, and he was popular because of them. In 1360, he signed the Treaty of Brétigny, which would have given him an enlarged Aquitaine with full sovereignty (not as a feudal fife of the French king) in exchange for giving up his claims to the throne. [282] Although he signed it, the treaty did not hold. [283] [284]

At home, he made nice with the nobles and the common folk, although many thought he was too preoccupied with chivalrous pursuits, such as his Order of the Garter, founded in 1328.[285] [286] He also harried southern Scotland, which he felt should be English, beating them at the Battle of Halidon Hill.[287] [288]

One of Edward's claims to fame was that he captured two kings in his battles. In 1346, his army captured King David II of Scotland at the battle of Neville's Cross while he himself was in England. This gave him a great deal of leverage over Scotland, and he demanded a crushing ransom for the king's return.[289] In 1360, Edward's son Edward, the Black Prince, captured King John of France at Poiters. This led to the Treaty of Brétigny, mentioned above.[290]

Back when his mother had been making war on her husband, she and Edward had lived in Hainault. While there, Edward agreed to marry Philippa of Hainault, daughter of William, Count of Hainault. They married in 1328.[291] When Philippa died in 1369, Edward withdrew from public life—he may have also suffered from senility.[292] His last years were sad times, as his son and heir, the Black Prince, died, and Parliament disapproved of his ministers.[293]

King Edward III died 21 June 1377 at Richmond Palace in Surrey. It is said that he died alone, his resources squandered by his mistress Alice Perrers and corrupt servants, and that at his passing Alice stole the rings from his fingers, and he had only a single priest to give him last rites.[294][295] He was buried in Westminster Abbey in London.[296]

Edward and Philippa had children:[297][298][299]

- Edward (1330-1376) – Prince of Wales, expected heir, but predeceased his father
- Lionel of Antwerp (1338-1368) – Duke of Clarence
- John of Gaunt (1340-1399) – 1st Duke of Lancaster
- *Edmund of Langley* (1341-1402) – Duke of York
- Thomas (d. 1397) – Duke of Gloucester
- Joan (d. 1348)
- Isabella (d. 1379) – married Engurrant de Coucy, Earl of Bedford
- Mary (d. 1362) – married John, Duke of Brittany
- Margaret (d. 1361) – married John of Hastings, Earl of Pembroke

King Edward III Plantagenet was succeeded by his grandson, son of Prince Edward, **King Richard II**.[300] Our line, however, temporarily leaves the kings, and goes through some younger sons. We actually have lines through three of Edward III's sons: Lionel of Antwerp, John of Gaunt, and Edmund of Langley. Edmund's is the shortest route, so I will follow that.

Edmund Plantagenet of Langley, 1st Duke of York
(1341-1402)

Edmund of Langley was the uncle of King Richard II, the son of Edmund's deceased brother Edward the Black Prince, and as such was favored with power and prestige. When Richard II traveled to Ireland in 1399 to quell the unrest there, he left Edmund in charge of England. Unfortunately for Edmund, this was the time Henry Bolingbroke decided to invade England and claim the crown. Henry was also Edmund's nephew, through his brother John of Gaunt.[301]

Henry landed in York, but Edmund delayed in the south of England as Henry made his way to Pontefract Castle with little opposition—in fact, many people joined his cause. Henry gained so much support that on 27 July 1399, Edmund switched sides at Berkeley Castle and helped Henry become King Henry IV.[302]

Edmund married Isabel of Castile, daughter of Pedro or Peter the Cruel, King of Castile. Isabel and Edmund had three children:[303]

- Edward of Norwich (d. 1415) – succeeded his father as 2nd Duke of York
- Constance of York (d. 1416) – married Thomas de la Spenser, 1st Earl of Gloucester
- *Richard of Conisburgh* (d. 1415) – created as Earl of Cambridge in 1414

After Isabel's death, Edmund married Joan de Holland, daughter of Thomas de Holland, 2nd Earl of Kent. Thomas fathered three daughters who married into the royal family: Joan, who married Edmund; Eleanor, who married Roger Mortimer and was great-grandmother of King Edward IV York of England; and Margaret, who married John Beaufort and was great-grandmother of King Henry VII Tudor of England.

Edmund and Joan had no children, and Edmund of Langley died in 1402.[304]

Richard Plantagenet of Conisburgh, 1st Earl of Cambridge
(d. 1415)

Richard of Conisburgh married Anne de Mortimer, who was the great-granddaughter of Edward III's son Lionel of Antwerp, 1st Duke of Clarence. Lionel had married Elizabeth de Burgh, 4th Countess of Ulster, and their daughter Philippa, 5th Countess of Ulster, married Edmund Mortimer, 3rd Earl of March. Philippa and Edmund's son, Roger Mortimer, 4th Earl of March, 6th Earl of Ulster, married Eleanor de Holland, who was herself the third great-granddaughter of King Henry III of England.[305] Roger and Eleanor had Anne de Mortimer.

Richard and Anne had two children:[306]

- Isabel (d. 1484) – married Henry Bourchier, 1st Earl of Essex
- *Richard* (d. 1460) – became 3rd Duke of York

Richard plotted to overthrow King Henry V in what was known as the Southampton Plot. Richard, Henry Scrope, 3rd Baron Scrope of Masham, and Sir Thomas Grey plotted to overthrow the king and replace him with Edmund Mortimer, 5th Earl of March. Mortimer descended from Lionel of Antwerp, the second surviving son of Edward III, and therefore had a superior claim to the throne than did Henry IV and V, both of whom descended from the younger son, John of Gaunt. Richard's son was to make the same claim when he tried to oust King Henry VI. Unfortunately, the Southampton conspirators seemed not to have confirmed that Mortimer was up for this, because it was Mortimer himself who exposed the plot to Henry V on 13 July 1415, just as Henry was set to sail to France as part of the Hundred Years' War. Richard of Conisburgh was caught, tried and beheaded on 5 August 1415 for treason in Southampton, Hampshire.[307] [308] [309] He is buried in the chapel of God's House in Southampton, Hampshire.

Richard Plantagenet, 2nd Earl of Cambridge, 3rd Duke of York
(d. 1460)

Richard became Earl of Cambridge from his father, but he also inherited his uncle Edward's land and titles when the 3rd Duke of York when Edward died without heirs at the battle of Agincourt.

Richard married Cecily Neville, who was the granddaughter of Edward III's son John of Gaunt.[310] John and Catherine Swynford, his mistress and later wife, had Joan Beaufort, who married Ralph Neville, 1st Earl of Westmoreland. Cecily was their daughter.

Richard and Cecily had twelve children, but only seven survived infancy:[311]

- Anne of York (d. 1476) – married Henry Holland, 3rd Duke of Exeter
- *Edward IV* (1442-1483) – became King of England
- Edmund (d. 1460) – 1st Earl of Rutland
- Elizabeth of York (d. c. 1504) – married John de la Pole, 2nd Duke of Suffolk
- Margaret of York – married Charles I the Bold, Duke of Burgundy
- George (d. 1478) – 1st Duke of Clarence

- Richard (1452-1485) – became Richard III, King of England

Richard, 3rd Duke of York, was heavily involved in the events leading up to the civil war known as the War of the Roses, the struggle between Richard and Edward IV's House of York and Henry VI's House of Lancaster. Richard, unhappy with the way Henry VI was ruling, claimed that he should rightfully be king. Henry VI was the descendant of John of Gaunt, Duke of Lancaster, King Edward III's third son, while Richard, through his mother, was descended from Lionel, Duke of Clarence, Edward III's second son.[312] Because England had no rules codifying the throne's succession, Richard was able to claim that a descendant from an elder son should take precedence over a descendant of a younger son.[313]

Richard marched on London in 1452, but the Earl of Somerset defeated him by trickery. In 1454, King Henry VI had a bout of insanity, and Richard was named Protector of the Realm and arrested Somerset. When Henry regained his senses in February of 1455, he dismissed Richard and freed Somerset. On 23 May 1455, Richard's Yorkist army defeated the king's army at St. Alban's, and Somerset was killed.[314]

While Henry would have allowed peace, his queen Margaret would not permit it. In the summer of 1459, she marched on Ludlow and routed the Yorkist army. Richard fled to Ireland, and his son Edward to Calais. The Yorkists did not stay down long and returned in 1460.[315]

Richard, Duke of York, captured Henry VI at Northampton in October 1460, and the king was forced to name Richard his heir. However, Margaret raised a new army against Richard and met him in the Battle of Wakefield in December 1460. Richard was killed and his son Edmund was executed. Shortly thereafter, on 4 March 1461, Richard's eldest son, Edward, took the throne as Edward IV, King of England.[316]

King Edward IV York
(1442-1483)
(reigned 1461-1470, 1471-1483)

Edward IV York was born on 28 April 1442, so he was eighteen when war broke out in 1460. He lost his father and his younger brother to the war, and Henry VI was rescued in 1461. But Edward did not give up, defeating the Lancastrian army at Mortimer's Cross in February 1461, and taking the throne on 4 March 1461, causing Henry, his wife, and his only son to flee to Scotland.[317] Henry made a foray into England in 1465, but was captured and put in the Tower of London in 1465.[318]

This did not settle things for Edward, though. Early supporters Richard, Earl of Warwick, and Edward's brother George, Duke of Clarence, turned against Edward, who eventually executed George for treason in 1478. When Edward refused to bow to their wishes, Warwick went to France and joined with the deposed Queen Margaret to restore Henry VI.[319]

Warwick and the queen successfully ousted Edward on 3 October 1470, and he fled to the Low Countries.[320] Edward didn't dally long and came back in force, defeating and killing Warwick in April 1471 at Barnegat, and killing Henry VI's son in battle at Tewksbury in May of that same year.[321] [322] Henry, his only heir gone, was deposed again on 11 April 1471, and was put to death on 21 May 1471.[323] [324]

One of the events that had caused resentment among the nobles was Edward's secret marriage to Elizabeth Woodville, daughter of Richard, Earl of Rivers, in 1464. Edward and Elizabeth had six children:[325] [326]

- Edward (1470-1483) – became Edward V, King of England, died in the Tower of London, possibly murdered by his uncle, King Richard III
- Richard (d. 1483) – disappeared into the Tower of London with his older brother, possibly murdered by his uncle, King Richard III
- ***Elizabeth of York*** (d. 1503) – married King Henry VII Tudor of England
- Cecily of England (d. 1507) – married John Welles, 1st Viscount Welles
- Anne of England (d. 1511) – married Thomas Howard, 3rd Duke of Norfolk
- Katherine of England (d. 1527) – married William Courtenay, 1st Earl of Devon

After his second coronation, Edward IV reigned another twelve years. He tried to invade France, but his allies deserted him, so he made peace with King Louis XI with the Treaty of Picquigny. He installed many reforms, tried to make the crown solvent, and was interested in foreign trade.[327] Although sometimes rocky, he gained some stability before his death from a fever on 9 April 1483 at Westminster. Unfortunately, things fell apart after his death.[328] [329] After the upheaval described below, the dowager Queen Elizabeth retired to Bermondsey Abbey, where she died in 1492. She was buried at Windsor next to her husband.[330]

When Edward IV York died, his son and heir was only twelve, and although recognized as king, he could not hold his power. Edward's brother Richard, Duke of Gloucester, who had been loyal to him throughout his reign, decided he should be king, instead of a child. Richard had Edward IV's two sons, King Edward V of England and Richard of Shrewsbury, Duke of York, put into the Tower of London. They never were seen again, and it is assumed they died or were murdered there around 1483, perhaps prior to Richard's coronation 26 June 1483.[331] Two skeletons found in the Tower in 1674 may be theirs.[332]

King Richard III's reign was short and fraught. His bloody ascent to the throne (he killed other rivals, not just the boy princes). His reliance on northerners turned the nobles against him and they turned to Henry Tudor, exiled in France, who also had a claim to the throne. Henry invaded England in 1485, and Richard III died fighting on 22 August 1485.[333]

King Henry VII Tudor
(1457-1509)
(reigned 1485-1509)

Henry VII Tudor was born on 28 January 1457 in Pembroke Castle, Pembrokeshire, Wales, after the death of his father, Edmund Tudor, 1st Earl of Richmond.[334] Henry's claim to the throne came from his mother, Lady Margaret Beaufort, who was a great-great-granddaughter of Edward III through Edward's son John of Gaunt and his mistress (later wife) Catherine Swynford.[335]

His early life was lived in Yorkist custody, but fought against Edward IV at Tewksbury, and when it was clear the Lancastrians had lost, fled to Brittany, France, where he lived from 1471-1484.[336] [337] His story might have ended there if Richard III had not usurped the throne of England and garnered the resentment of many of the nobles. This, plus the constant plotting of his mother, Margaret Beaufort, who had stayed in England to set things in place when Henry fled, caused the nobles to come to Henry and suggest that he replace Richard.[338]

Henry decided to do this, and agreed to marry Elizabeth of York, daughter of Edward VI (both Elizabeth and her mother approved of this)[339] and began calling himself the King of England in 1484. With the support of the French, he invaded England. His first attempt failed, but he tried again, landing on 7 March

1485 in Wales, where he had much support. He met Richard III's forces at Bosworth on 22 August 1485, and defeated and killed Richard. [340] [341]

Henry had himself legally declared king immediately upon his victory, but had a formal coronation on 30 October 1485. The Parliament also recognized him as their lawful sovereign. He married Elizabeth of York in 1486, and went on to have a successful reign.[342] [343] [344] He put down two pretenders to the English throne, resolved a conflict with Scotland caused by one of the imposters, quelled an uprising in Cornwall, rebuilt Richmond Palace in Surrey, and renovated the Chapel in Westminster Abbey.[345]

He and Elizabeth had four children:[346] [347]

- Arthur (1486-1502) – predeceased his father
- Henry (1491-1547) – became King Henry VIII of England
- *Margaret* (1489-1541) – first married King James IV of Scotland (see *Stewart Dynasty*), and second, Archibald, Earl of Angus
- Mary (1496-1533) – married Louis XII, King of France, and second Charles, Duke of Suffolk

Henry VII Tudor died on 21 April 1509 at Richmond Palace.[348] His wife Elizabeth had died in childbirth in 1503.[349] [350] Our line runs through their daughter Margaret, who married our ancestor King James IV of Scotland. See the *Stewart Dynasty* chapter for their story.

---

[1] Caroline Bingham, *Kings and Queens of Scotland* (originally published 1976, Taplinger Publishing Co. this edition, 1985, Dorset Press) p. 15.

[2] E. William Robertson, *Scotland Under Her Early Kings: A History of the Kingdom to the Close of the 13th Century, Part One* (Edinburgh: Edmonston and Douglas, 1862), p. 151.

[3] Ruth M. Blakely, *The Brus Family in England and Scotland, 1100-1295* (Boydell Press, Woodbridge, 2005), p. 73.

[4] E. William Robertson, *Scotland Under Her Early Kings: A History of the Kingdom to the Close of the Thirteenth Century, Part Two* (Edinburgh: Edmonston and Douglas, 1862), p. 9-10.

[5] Caroline Bingham, *Kings and Queens of Scotland* (orig. published 1976, Taplinger Publishing Co. this edition, 1985, Dorset Press), p. 60-61.

[6] Agnes Mure MacKenzie, *The Rise of the Stewarts* (Oliver & Boyd, Ltd, Edinburgh. Originally printed 1935, this printing 1957.), p. 140.

[7] Fitzroy Maclean, *A Concise History of Scotland* (First published 1970. This version published 2002. Thames & Hudson Ltd., London), p. 73.

[8] Caroline Bingham, *Kings and Queens of Scotland* (originally published 1976, Taplinger Publishing Co. this edition, 1985, Dorset Press) p. 73.

[9] John Cannon & Ralph Griffiths, *The Oxford Illustrated History of the British Monarchy* (2000 edition, Oxford University Press), p. 292.

[10] John Cannon & Ralph Griffiths, *The Oxford Illustrated History of the British Monarchy* (2000 edition, Oxford University Press), Geneaolgies of Royal Lines Appendix; List of Monarchs Appendix.

[11] Roland William Saint-Clair, *Saint-Clairs of the Isles: A History of the Sea-Kings of Orkney and their Scottish Successors of the Sirname Sinclair* (Auckland, New Zealand, H. Brett, General Printer and Publisher, Shortland and Fort Streets 1898), p. 16.

[12] James Grey, *Sutherland & Caithness in Saga-Time, or, The Jarls & The Freskyns* (Oliver & Boyd, Edinburgh, 1922), p. 19.

[13] Timothy Baker, *The Normans: The Men Who Made the English-Speaking World* (The Macmillan Company, New York: 1966), p. 10.

[14] John Cannon & Ralph Griffiths, *The Oxford Illustrated History of the British Monarchy* (2000 edition, Oxford University Press), Geneaolgies of Royal Lines Appendix.

[15] Timothy Baker, *The Normans: The Men Who Made the English-Speaking World* (The Macmillan Company, New York: 1966), p. 16.

[16] John Cannon & Ralph Griffiths, *The Oxford Illustrated History of the British Monarchy* (2000 edition, Oxford University Press), p. 117.

[17] Timothy Baker, *The Normans: The Men Who Made the English-Speaking World* (The Macmillan Company, New York: 1966), p. 17-18.

[18] Roland William Saint-Clair, *Saint-Clairs of the Isles: A History of the Sea-Kings of Orkney and their Scottish Successors of the Sirname Sinclair* (Auckland, New Zealand, H. Brett, General Printer and Publisher, Shortland and Fort Streets 1898), p. 17.

[19] Timothy Baker, *The Normans: The Men Who Made the English-Speaking World* (The Macmillan Company, New York: 1966), p. 89-90.

[20] Timothy Baker, *The Normans: The Men Who Made the English-Speaking World* (The Macmillan Company, New York: 1966), p. 133.

[21] John Cannon & Ralph Griffiths, *The Oxford Illustrated History of the British Monarchy* (2000 edition, Oxford University Press), Geneaolgies of Royal Lines Appendix.

[22] Dan Jones, *The Plantagenets: The Warrior Kings & Queens who made England* (New York, Viking, 2012), Genealogical Tree at Front.

[23] John Cannon & Ralph Griffiths, *The Oxford Illustrated History of the British Monarchy* (2000 edition, Oxford University Press), p. 117.

[24] Timothy Baker, *The Normans: The Men Who Made the English-Speaking World* (The Macmillan Company, New York: 1966), p. 82.

[25] Timothy Baker, *The Normans: The Men Who Made the English-Speaking World* (The Macmillan Company, New York: 1966), p. 88.

[26] Timothy Baker, *The Normans: The Men Who Made the English-Speaking World* (The Macmillan Company, New York: 1966), p. 89.

[27] Timothy Baker, *The Normans: The Men Who Made the English-Speaking World* (The Macmillan Company, New York: 1966), p. 89.

[28] Timothy Baker, *The Normans: The Men Who Made the English-Speaking World* (The Macmillan Company, New York: 1966), p. 89.

[29] Timothy Baker, *The Normans: The Men Who Made the English-Speaking World* (The Macmillan Company, New York: 1966), p. 90-91.

[30] Timothy Baker, *The Normans: The Men Who Made the English-Speaking World* (The Macmillan Company, New York: 1966), p. 99.

[31] Timothy Baker, *The Normans: The Men Who Made the English-Speaking World* (The Macmillan Company, New York: 1966), p. 104-111.

[32] Timothy Baker, *The Normans: The Men Who Made the English-Speaking World* (The Macmillan Company, New York: 1966), p. 115-117.

[33] John Cannon & Ralph Griffiths, *The Oxford Illustrated History of the British Monarchy* (2000 edition, Oxford University Press), List of Monarchs Appendix.

[34] Timothy Baker, *The Normans: The Men Who Made the English-Speaking World* (The Macmillan Company, New York: 1966), p. 116.

[35] Timothy Baker, *The Normans: The Men Who Made the English-Speaking World* (The Macmillan Company, New York: 1966), p. 120-121.

[36] M.T. Clanchy, *England and its Rulers: 1066-1272* (Blackwell Publishers; Oxford & Massachussetts; 1998 - 2nd Edition), p. 26.

[37] Timothy Baker, *The Normans: The Men Who Made the English-Speaking World* (The Macmillan Company, New York: 1966), p. 122.

[38] John Cannon & Ralph Griffiths, *The Oxford Illustrated History of the British Monarchy* (2000 edition, Oxford University Press), p. 117.

[39] Timothy Baker, *The Normans: The Men Who Made the English-Speaking World* (The Macmillan Company, New York: 1966), p. 125.

[40] M.T. Clanchy, *England and its Rulers: 1066-1272* (Blackwell Publishers; Oxford & Massachussetts; 1998 - 2nd Edition), p. 26.

[41] Timothy Baker, *The Normans: The Men Who Made the English-Speaking World* (The Macmillan Company, New York: 1966), p. 126.

[42] M.T. Clanchy, *England and its Rulers: 1066-1272* (Blackwell Publishers; Oxford & Massachussetts; 1998 - 2nd Edition), p. 26.

[43] Timothy Baker, *The Normans: The Men Who Made the English-Speaking World* (The Macmillan Company, New York: 1966), p. 127.

[44] Timothy Baker, *The Normans: The Men Who Made the English-Speaking World* (The Macmillan Company, New York: 1966), p. 127-128.

[45] John Cannon & Ralph Griffiths, *The Oxford Illustrated History of the British Monarchy* (2000 edition, Oxford University Press), p. 117.

[46] M.T. Clanchy, *England and its Rulers: 1066-1272* (Blackwell Publishers; Oxford & Massachussetts; 1998 - 2nd Edition), p. 37-40.

[47] Timothy Baker, *The Normans: The Men Who Made the English-Speaking World* (The Macmillan Company, New York: 1966), p. 128-129.

[48] John Cannon & Ralph Griffiths, *The Oxford Illustrated History of the British Monarchy* (2000 edition, Oxford University Press), p. 117.

[49] Timothy Baker, *The Normans: The Men Who Made the English-Speaking World* (The Macmillan Company, New York: 1966), p. 129.

[50] M.T. Clanchy, *England and its Rulers: 1066-1272* (Blackwell Publishers; Oxford & Massachussetts; 1998 - 2nd Edition), p. 26.

[51] Timothy Baker, *The Normans: The Men Who Made the English-Speaking World* (The Macmillan Company, New York: 1966), p. 130-131.

[52] John Cannon & Ralph Griffiths, *The Oxford Illustrated History of the British Monarchy* (2000 edition, Oxford University Press), p. 117; Geneaolgies of Royal Lines Appendix; List of Monarchs Appendix.

[53] Timothy Baker, *The Normans: The Men Who Made the English-Speaking World* (The Macmillan Company, New York: 1966), p. 131.

[54] Timothy Baker, *The Normans: The Men Who Made the English-Speaking World* (The Macmillan Company, New York: 1966), p. 128.

[55] John Cannon & Ralph Griffiths, *The Oxford Illustrated History of the British Monarchy* (2000 edition, Oxford University Press), p. 120.

[56] John Cannon & Ralph Griffiths, *The Oxford Illustrated History of the British Monarchy* (2000 edition, Oxford University Press), p. 122; List of Monarchs Appendix.

[57] M.T. Clanchy, *England and its Rulers: 1066-1272* (Blackwell Publishers; Oxford & Massachussetts; 1998 - 2nd Edition), p. 44-45.

[58] M.T. Clanchy, *England and its Rulers: 1066-1272* (Blackwell Publishers; Oxford & Massachussetts; 1998 - 2nd Edition), p. 41, 45.

[59] M.T. Clanchy, *England and its Rulers: 1066-1272* (Blackwell Publishers; Oxford & Massachussetts; 1998 - 2nd Edition), p. 45-47.

[60] M.T. Clanchy, *England and its Rulers: 1066-1272* (Blackwell Publishers; Oxford & Massachussetts; 1998 - 2nd Edition), p. 69-70.

[61] John Cannon & Ralph Griffiths, *The Oxford Illustrated History of the British Monarchy* (2000 edition, Oxford University Press), p. 131.

[62] Timothy Baker, *The Normans: The Men Who Made the English-Speaking World* (The Macmillan Company, New York: 1966), p. 133.

[63] John Cannon & Ralph Griffiths, *The Oxford Illustrated History of the British Monarchy* (2000 edition, Oxford University Press), Geneaolgies of Royal Lines Appendix.

[64] John Cannon & Ralph Griffiths, *The Oxford Illustrated History of the British Monarchy* (2000 edition, Oxford University Press), Geneaolgies of Royal Lines Appendix.

[65] Westminster Abbey.org website: http://www.westminster-abbey.org/our-history/royals/burials.

[66] Elizabeth Hallam, ed, *The Plantagenet Chronicles: Medieval Europe's most tempestuous family from Henry II and his wife Eleanor of Aquitaine to Richard the Lionheart and his scheming brother John seen through the eyes of their contemporaries.* (Weidenfeld & Nicolson, New York: 1986 (copyright held by Pheobe Phillips Editions)), p. 16.

[67] M.T. Clanchy, *England and its Rulers: 1066-1272* (Blackwell Publishers; Oxford & Massachussetts; 1998 - 2nd Edition), p. 46.

[68] John Cannon & Ralph Griffiths, *The Oxford Illustrated History of the British Monarchy* (2000 edition, Oxford University Press), p. 140; Geneaolgies of Royal Lines Appendix.

[69] Timothy Baker, *The Normans: The Men Who Made the English-Speaking World* (The Macmillan Company, New York: 1966), p. 133.

[70] John Cannon & Ralph Griffiths, *The Oxford Illustrated History of the British Monarchy* (2000 edition, Oxford University Press), Geneaolgies of Royal Lines Appendix; List of Monarchs Appendix.

[71] E. William Robertson, *Scotland Under Her Early Kings: A History of the Kingdom to the Close of the 13th Century, Part One* (Edinburgh: Edmonston and Douglas, 1862), p. 191.

[72] Timothy Baker, *The Normans: The Men Who Made the English-Speaking World* (The Macmillan Company, New York: 1966), p. 133.

[73] Elizabeth Hallam, ed, *The Plantagenet Chronicles: Medieval Europe's most tempestuous family from Henry II and his wife Eleanor of Aquitaine to Richard the Lionheart and his scheming brother John seen through the eyes of their contemporaries.* (Weidenfeld & Nicolson, New York: 1986 (copyright held by Pheobe Phillips Editions)), p. 60, 173.

[74] John Cannon & Ralph Griffiths, *The Oxford Illustrated History of the British Monarchy* (2000 edition, Oxford University Press), p. 167.

[75] Elizabeth Hallam, ed, *The Plantagenet Chronicles: Medieval Europe's most tempestuous family from Henry II and his wife Eleanor of Aquitaine to Richard the Lionheart and his scheming brother John seen through the eyes of their contemporaries.* (Weidenfeld & Nicolson, New York: 1986 (copyright held by Pheobe Phillips Editions)), p. 47.

[76] John Cannon & Ralph Griffiths, *The Oxford Illustrated History of the British Monarchy* (2000 edition, Oxford University Press), p. 138.

[77] M.T. Clanchy, *England and its Rulers: 1066-1272* (Blackwell Publishers; Oxford & Massachussetts; 1998 - 2nd Edition), p. 75.

[78] John Cannon & Ralph Griffiths, *The Oxford Illustrated History of the British Monarchy* (2000 edition, Oxford University Press), p. 131, 138; Geneaolgies of Royal Lines Appendix.

[79] Elizabeth Hallam, ed, *The Plantagenet Chronicles: Medieval Europe's most tempestuous family from Henry II and his wife Eleanor of Aquitaine to Richard the Lionheart and his scheming brother John seen through the eyes of their contemporaries.* (Weidenfeld & Nicolson, New York: 1986 (copyright held by Pheobe Phillips Editions)), p. 16, 43, 48.

[80] John Cannon & Ralph Griffiths, *The Oxford Illustrated History of the British Monarchy* (2000 edition, Oxford University Press), p. 138.

[81] M.T. Clanchy, *England and its Rulers: 1066-1272* (Blackwell Publishers; Oxford & Massachussetts; 1998 - 2nd Edition), p. 76.

[82] Elizabeth Hallam, ed, *The Plantagenet Chronicles: Medieval Europe's most tempestuous family from Henry II and his wife Eleanor of Aquitaine to Richard the Lionheart and his scheming brother John seen through the eyes of their contemporaries.* (Weidenfeld & Nicolson, New York: 1986 (copyright held by Pheobe Phillips Editions)), p. 45.

[83] John Cannon & Ralph Griffiths, *The Oxford Illustrated History of the British Monarchy* (2000 edition, Oxford University Press), p. 138.

[84] John Cannon & Ralph Griffiths, *The Oxford Illustrated History of the British Monarchy* (2000 edition, Oxford University Press), p. 138.

[85] Elizabeth Hallam, ed, *The Plantagenet Chronicles: Medieval Europe's most tempestuous family from Henry II and his wife Eleanor of Aquitaine to Richard the Lionheart and his scheming brother John seen through the eyes of their contemporaries.* (Weidenfeld & Nicolson, New York: 1986 (copyright held by Pheobe Phillips Editions)), p. 45.

[86] Elizabeth Hallam, ed, *The Plantagenet Chronicles: Medieval Europe's most tempestuous family from Henry II and his wife Eleanor of Aquitaine to Richard the Lionheart and his scheming brother John seen through the eyes of their contemporaries.* (Weidenfeld & Nicolson, New York: 1986 (copyright held by Pheobe Phillips Editions)), p. 47.

[87] John Cannon & Ralph Griffiths, *The Oxford Illustrated History of the British Monarchy* (2000 edition, Oxford University Press), p. 138.

[88] Elizabeth Hallam, ed, *The Plantagenet Chronicles: Medieval Europe's most tempestuous family from Henry II and his wife Eleanor of Aquitaine to Richard the Lionheart and his scheming brother John seen through the eyes of their contemporaries.* (Weidenfeld & Nicolson, New York: 1986 (copyright held by Pheobe Phillips Editions)), p. 16.

[89] John Cannon & Ralph Griffiths, *The Oxford Illustrated History of the British Monarchy* (2000 edition, Oxford University Press), Geneaolgies of Royal Lines Appendix; List of Monarchs Appendix.

[90] Dan Jones, *The Plantagenets: The Warrior Kings & Queens who made England* (New York, Viking, 2012), Genealogical Tree at Front.

[91] John Cannon & Ralph Griffiths, *The Oxford Illustrated History of the British Monarchy* (2000 edition, Oxford University Press), p. 138.

[92] M.T. Clanchy, *England and its Rulers: 1066-1272* (Blackwell Publishers; Oxford & Massachussetts; 1998 - 2nd Edition), p. 76.

[93] John Cannon & Ralph Griffiths, *The Oxford Illustrated History of the British Monarchy* (2000 edition, Oxford University Press), p. 87, 151.

[94] M.T. Clanchy, *England and its Rulers: 1066-1272* (Blackwell Publishers; Oxford & Massachussetts; 1998 - 2nd Edition), p. 77.

[95] Elizabeth Hallam, ed, *The Plantagenet Chronicles: Medieval Europe's most tempestuous family from Henry II and his wife Eleanor of Aquitaine to Richard the Lionheart and his scheming brother John seen through the eyes of their contemporaries.* (Weidenfeld & Nicolson, New York: 1986 (copyright held by Pheobe Phillips Editions)), p. 78, 81.

[96] John Cannon & Ralph Griffiths, *The Oxford Illustrated History of the British Monarchy* (2000 edition, Oxford University Press), p. 88, Geneaolgies of Royal Lines Appendix.

[97] M.T. Clanchy, *England and its Rulers: 1066-1272* (Blackwell Publishers; Oxford & Massachussetts; 1998 - 2nd Edition), p. 77.

[98] Elizabeth Hallam, ed, *The Plantagenet Chronicles: Medieval Europe's most tempestuous family from Henry II and his wife Eleanor of Aquitaine to Richard the Lionheart and his scheming brother John seen through the eyes of their contemporaries.* (Weidenfeld & Nicolson, New York: 1986 (copyright held by Pheobe Phillips Editions)), p. 81.

[99] Elizabeth Hallam, ed, *The Plantagenet Chronicles: Medieval Europe's most tempestuous family from Henry II and his wife Eleanor of Aquitaine to Richard the Lionheart and his scheming brother John seen through the eyes of their contemporaries.* (Weidenfeld & Nicolson, New York: 1986 (copyright held by Pheobe Phillips Editions)), p. 81, 97.

[100] John Cannon & Ralph Griffiths, *The Oxford Illustrated History of the British Monarchy* (2000 edition, Oxford University Press), p. 123, 151; List of Monarchs Appendix.

[101] M.T. Clanchy, *England and its Rulers: 1066-1272* (Blackwell Publishers; Oxford & Massachussetts; 1998 - 2nd Edition), p. 88.

[102] Elizabeth Hallam, ed, *The Plantagenet Chronicles: Medieval Europe's most tempestuous family from Henry II and his wife Eleanor of Aquitaine to Richard the Lionheart and his scheming brother John seen through the eyes of their contemporaries.* (Weidenfeld & Nicolson, New York: 1986 (copyright held by Pheobe Phillips Editions)), p. 93, 99.

[103] John Cannon & Ralph Griffiths, *The Oxford Illustrated History of the British Monarchy* (2000 edition, Oxford University Press), p. 89, 151.

[104] M.T. Clanchy, *England and its Rulers: 1066-1272* (Blackwell Publishers; Oxford & Massachussetts; 1998 - 2nd Edition), p. 88.

[105] Elizabeth Hallam, ed, *The Plantagenet Chronicles: Medieval Europe's most tempestuous family from Henry II and his wife Eleanor of Aquitaine to Richard the Lionheart and his scheming brother John seen through the eyes of their contemporaries.* (Weidenfeld & Nicolson, New York: 1986 (copyright held by Pheobe Phillips Editions)), p. 93.

[106] John Cannon & Ralph Griffiths, *The Oxford Illustrated History of the British Monarchy* (2000 edition, Oxford Univ. Press), p. 89, 99, 151.

[107] John Cannon & Ralph Griffiths, *The Oxford Illustrated History of the British Monarchy* (2000 edition, Oxford University Press), p. 151.

[108] M.T. Clanchy, *England and its Rulers: 1066-1272* (Blackwell Publishers; Oxford & Massachussetts; 1998 - 2nd Edition), p. 83.

[109] M.T. Clanchy, *England and its Rulers: 1066-1272* (Blackwell Publishers; Oxford & Massachussetts; 1998 - 2nd Edition), p. 78.

[110] Elizabeth Hallam, ed, *The Plantagenet Chronicles: Medieval Europe's most tempestuous family from Henry II and his wife Eleanor of Aquitaine to Richard the Lionheart and his scheming brother John seen through the eyes of their contemporaries.* (Weidenfeld & Nicolson, New York: 1986 (copyright held by Pheobe Phillips Editions)), p. 93.

[111] Elizabeth Hallam, ed, *The Plantagenet Chronicles: Medieval Europe's most tempestuous family from Henry II and his wife Eleanor of Aquitaine to Richard the Lionheart and his scheming brother John seen through the eyes of their contemporaries.* (Weidenfeld & Nicolson, New York: 1986 (copyright held by Pheobe Phillips Editions)), p. 121.

[112] John Cannon & Ralph Griffiths, *The Oxford Illustrated History of the British Monarchy* (2000 edition, Oxford University Press), p. 106.

[113] M.T. Clanchy, *England and its Rulers: 1066-1272* (Blackwell Publishers; Oxford & Massachussetts; 1998 - 2nd Edition), p. 84.

[114] Elizabeth Hallam, ed, *The Plantagenet Chronicles: Medieval Europe's most tempestuous family from Henry II and his wife Eleanor of Aquitaine to Richard the Lionheart and his scheming brother John seen through the eyes of their contemporaries.* (Weidenfeld & Nicolson, New York: 1986 (copyright held by Pheobe Phillips Editions)), p. 113, 125.

[115] M.T. Clanchy, *England and its Rulers: 1066-1272* (Blackwell Publishers; Oxford & Massachussetts; 1998 - 2nd Edition), p. 93.

[116] Elizabeth Hallam, ed, *The Plantagenet Chronicles: Medieval Europe's most tempestuous family from Henry II and his wife Eleanor of Aquitaine to Richard the Lionheart and his scheming brother John seen through the eyes of their contemporaries.* (Weidenfeld & Nicolson, New York: 1986 (copyright held by Pheobe Phillips Editions)), p. 119, 130.

[117] John Cannon & Ralph Griffiths, *The Oxford Illustrated History of the British Monarchy* (2000 edition, Oxford University Press), p. 106.

[118] M.T. Clanchy, *England and its Rulers: 1066-1272* (Blackwell Publishers; Oxford & Massachussetts; 1998 - 2nd Edition), p. 92.

[119] Elizabeth Hallam, ed, *The Plantagenet Chronicles: Medieval Europe's most tempestuous family from Henry II and his wife Eleanor of Aquitaine to Richard the Lionheart and his scheming brother John seen through the eyes of their contemporaries.* (Weidenfeld & Nicolson, New York: 1986 (copyright held by Pheobe Phillips Editions)), p. 122.

[120] M.T. Clanchy, *England and its Rulers: 1066-1272* (Blackwell Publishers; Oxford & Massachussetts; 1998 - 2nd Edition), p. 93.

[121] Elizabeth Hallam, ed, *The Plantagenet Chronicles: Medieval Europe's most tempestuous family from Henry II and his wife Eleanor of Aquitaine to Richard the Lionheart and his scheming brother John seen through the eyes of their contemporaries.* (Weidenfeld & Nicolson, New York: 1986 (copyright held by Pheobe Phillips Editions)), p. 101, 136.

[122] Elizabeth Hallam, ed, *The Plantagenet Chronicles: Medieval Europe's most tempestuous family from Henry II and his wife Eleanor of Aquitaine to Richard the Lionheart and his scheming brother John seen through the eyes of their contemporaries.* (Weidenfeld & Nicolson, New York: 1986 (copyright held by Pheobe Phillips Editions)), p. 140.

[123] M.T. Clanchy, *England and its Rulers: 1066-1272* (Blackwell Publishers; Oxford & Massachussetts; 1998 - 2nd Edition), p. 93.

[124] Elizabeth Hallam, ed, *The Plantagenet Chronicles: Medieval Europe's most tempestuous family from Henry II and his wife Eleanor of Aquitaine to Richard the Lionheart and his scheming brother John seen through the eyes of their contemporaries.* (Weidenfeld & Nicolson, New York: 1986 (copyright held by Pheobe Phillips Editions)), p. 172.

[125] John Cannon & Ralph Griffiths, *The Oxford Illustrated History of the British Monarchy* (2000 edition, Oxford University Press), p. 99.

[126] Elizabeth Hallam, ed, *The Plantagenet Chronicles: Medieval Europe's most tempestuous family from Henry II and his wife Eleanor of Aquitaine to Richard the Lionheart and his scheming brother John seen through the eyes of their contemporaries.* (Weidenfeld & Nicolson, New York: 1986 (copyright held by Pheobe Phillips Editions)), p. 178.

[127] Elizabeth Hallam, ed, *The Plantagenet Chronicles: Medieval Europe's most tempestuous family from Henry II and his wife Eleanor of Aquitaine to Richard the Lionheart and his scheming brother John seen through the eyes of their contemporaries.* (Weidenfeld & Nicolson, New York: 1986 (copyright held by Pheobe Phillips Editions)), p. 185-193.

[128] M.T. Clanchy, *England and its Rulers: 1066-1272* (Blackwell Publishers; Oxford & Massachussetts; 1998 - 2nd Edition), p. 94.

[129] John Cannon & Ralph Griffiths, *The Oxford Illustrated History of the British Monarchy* (2000 edition, Oxford University Press), p. 89, 151; Geneaolgies of Royal Lines Appendix; List of Monarchs Appendix.

[130] M.T. Clanchy, *England and its Rulers: 1066-1272* (Blackwell Publishers; Oxford & Massachussetts; 1998 - 2nd Edition), p. 77.

[131] Elizabeth Hallam, ed, *The Plantagenet Chronicles: Medieval Europe's most tempestuous family from Henry II and his wife Eleanor of Aquitaine to Richard the Lionheart and his scheming brother John seen through the eyes of their contemporaries.* (Weidenfeld & Nicolson, New York: 1986 (copyright held by Pheobe Phillips Editions)), p. 193.

[132] John Cannon & Ralph Griffiths, *The Oxford Illustrated History of the British Monarchy* (2000 edition, Oxford Univ. Press), p. 88, 167, 652.

[133] John Cannon & Ralph Griffiths, *The Oxford Illustrated History of the British Monarchy* (2000 edition, Oxford University Press), Geneaolgies of Royal Lines Appendix.

[134] John Cannon & Ralph Griffiths, *The Oxford Illustrated History of the British Monarchy* (2000 edition, Oxford Univ. Press), p. 88, 167, 652.

[135] John Cannon & Ralph Griffiths, *The Oxford Illustrated History of the British Monarchy* (2000 edition, Oxford Univ. Press), p. 141, 163.

[136] Elizabeth Hallam, ed, *The Plantagenet Chronicles: Medieval Europe's most tempestuous family from Henry II and his wife Eleanor of Aquitaine to Richard the Lionheart and his scheming brother John seen through the eyes of their contemporaries.* (Weidenfeld & Nicolson, New York: 1986 (copyright held by Pheobe Phillips Editions)), p. 102, 125, 172.

[137] John Cannon & Ralph Griffiths, *The Oxford Illustrated History of the British Monarchy* (2000 edition, Oxford University Press), Geneaolgies of Royal Lines Appendix.

[138] Elizabeth Hallam, ed, *The Plantagenet Chronicles: Medieval Europe's most tempestuous family from Henry II and his wife Eleanor of Aquitaine to Richard the Lionheart and his scheming brother John seen through the eyes of their contemporaries.* (Weidenfeld & Nicolson, New York: 1986 (copyright held by Pheobe Phillips Editions)), p. 113.

[139] John Cannon & Ralph Griffiths, *The Oxford Illustrated History of the British Monarchy* (2000 edition, Oxford University Press), Geneaolgies of Royal Lines Appendix.

[140] M.T. Clanchy, *England and its Rulers: 1066-1272* (Blackwell Publishers; Oxford & Massachussetts; 1998 - 2nd Edition), p. 94.

[141] John Cannon & Ralph Griffiths, *The Oxford Illustrated History of the British Monarchy* (2000 edition, Oxford University Press), Geneaolgies of Royal Lines Appendix.

[142] Elizabeth Hallam, ed, *The Plantagenet Chronicles: Medieval Europe's most tempestuous family from Henry II and his wife Eleanor of Aquitaine to Richard the Lionheart and his scheming brother John seen through the eyes of their contemporaries.* (Weidenfeld & Nicolson, New York: 1986 (copyright held by Pheobe Phillips Editions)), p. 16.

[143] John Cannon & Ralph Griffiths, *The Oxford Illustrated History of the British Monarchy* (2000 edition, Oxford University Press), Geneaolgies of Royal Lines Appendix.

[144] Elizabeth Hallam, ed, *The Plantagenet Chronicles: Medieval Europe's most tempestuous family from Henry II and his wife Eleanor of Aquitaine to Richard the Lionheart and his scheming brother John seen through the eyes of their contemporaries.* (Weidenfeld & Nicolson, New York: 1986 (copyright held by Pheobe Phillips Editions)), p. 125, 178, 300.

[145] John Cannon & Ralph Griffiths, *The Oxford Illustrated History of the British Monarchy* (2000 edition, Oxford University Press), Geneaolgies of Royal Lines Appendix.

[146] Elizabeth Hallam, ed, *The Plantagenet Chronicles: Medieval Europe's most tempestuous family from Henry II and his wife Eleanor of Aquitaine to Richard the Lionheart and his scheming brother John seen through the eyes of their contemporaries.* (Weidenfeld & Nicolson, New York: 1986 (copyright held by Pheobe Phillips Editions)), p. 17.

[147] John Cannon & Ralph Griffiths, *The Oxford Illustrated History of the British Monarchy* (2000 edition, Oxford University Press), Geneaolgies of Royal Lines Appendix.

[148] Elizabeth Hallam, ed, *The Plantagenet Chronicles: Medieval Europe's most tempestuous family from Henry II and his wife Eleanor of Aquitaine to Richard the Lionheart and his scheming brother John seen through the eyes of their contemporaries.* (Weidenfeld & Nicolson, New York: 1986 (copyright held by Pheobe Phillips Editions)), p. 17.

[149] M.T. Clanchy, *England and its Rulers: 1066-1272* (Blackwell Publishers; Oxford & Massachussetts; 1998 - 2nd Edition), p. 94.

[150] John Cannon & Ralph Griffiths, *The Oxford Illustrated History of the British Monarchy* (2000 edition, Oxford University Press), Geneaolgies of Royal Lines Appendix; List of Monarchs Appendix.

[151] Elizabeth Hallam, ed, *The Plantagenet Chronicles: Medieval Europe's most tempestuous family from Henry II and his wife Eleanor of Aquitaine to Richard the Lionheart and his scheming brother John seen through the eyes of their contemporaries.* (Weidenfeld & Nicolson, New York: 1986 (copyright held by Pheobe Phillips Editions)), p. 17, 125, 265.

[152] John Cannon & Ralph Griffiths, *The Oxford Illustrated History of the British Monarchy* (2000 edition, Oxford University Press), p. 159.

[153] Elizabeth Hallam, ed, *The Plantagenet Chronicles: Medieval Europe's most tempestuous family from Henry II and his wife Eleanor of Aquitaine to Richard the Lionheart and his scheming brother John seen through the eyes of their contemporaries.* (Weidenfeld & Nicolson, New York: 1986 (copyright held by Pheobe Phillips Editions)), p. 294.

[154] John Cannon & Ralph Griffiths, *The Oxford Illustrated History of the British Monarchy* (2000 edition, Oxford University Press), p. 174.

[155] Elizabeth Hallam, ed, *The Plantagenet Chronicles: Medieval Europe's most tempestuous family from Henry II and his wife Eleanor of Aquitaine to Richard the Lionheart and his scheming brother John seen through the eyes of their contemporaries.* (Weidenfeld & Nicolson, New York: 1986 (copyright held by Pheobe Phillips Editions)), p. 200, 297.

[156] M.T. Clanchy, *England and its Rulers: 1066-1272* (Blackwell Publishers; Oxford & Massachussetts; 1998 - 2nd Edition), p. 97.

[157] Elizabeth Hallam, ed, *The Plantagenet Chronicles: Medieval Europe's most tempestuous family from Henry II and his wife Eleanor of Aquitaine to Richard the Lionheart and his scheming brother John seen through the eyes of their contemporaries.* (Weidenfeld & Nicolson, New York: 1986 (copyright held by Pheobe Phillips Editions)), p. 221, 226.

[158] Elizabeth Hallam, ed, *The Plantagenet Chronicles: Medieval Europe's most tempestuous family from Henry II and his wife Eleanor of Aquitaine to Richard the Lionheart and his scheming brother John seen through the eyes of their contemporaries.* (Weidenfeld & Nicolson, New York: 1986 (copyright held by Pheobe Phillips Editions)), p. 232, 259.

[159] John Cannon & Ralph Griffiths, *The Oxford Illustrated History of the British Monarchy* (2000 edition, Oxford University Press), p. 90; List of Monarchs Appendix.

[160] Elizabeth Hallam, ed, *The Plantagenet Chronicles: Medieval Europe's most tempestuous family from Henry II and his wife Eleanor of Aquitaine to Richard the Lionheart and his scheming brother John seen through the eyes of their contemporaries.* (Weidenfeld & Nicolson, New York: 1986 (copyright held by Pheobe Phillips Editions)), p. 259, 262.

[161] M.T. Clanchy, *England and its Rulers: 1066-1272* (Blackwell Publishers; Oxford & Massachussetts; 1998 - 2nd Edition), p. 132.

[162] Elizabeth Hallam, ed, *The Plantagenet Chronicles: Medieval Europe's most tempestuous family from Henry II and his wife Eleanor of Aquitaine to Richard the Lionheart and his scheming brother John seen through the eyes of their contemporaries.* (Weidenfeld & Nicolson, New York: 1986 (copyright held by Pheobe Phillips Editions)), p. 204, 263, 259.

[163] John Cannon & Ralph Griffiths, *The Oxford Illustrated History of the British Monarchy* (2000 edition, Oxford University Press), p. 140.

[164] Elizabeth Hallam, ed, *The Plantagenet Chronicles: Medieval Europe's most tempestuous family from Henry II and his wife Eleanor of Aquitaine to Richard the Lionheart and his scheming brother John seen through the eyes of their contemporaries.* (Weidenfeld & Nicolson, New York: 1986 (copyright held by Pheobe Phillips Editions)), p. 264.

[165] M.T. Clanchy, *England and its Rulers: 1066-1272* (Blackwell Publishers; Oxford & Massachussetts; 1998 - 2nd Edition), p. 133-134.

[166] Elizabeth Hallam, ed, *The Plantagenet Chronicles: Medieval Europe's most tempestuous family from Henry II and his wife Eleanor of Aquitaine to Richard the Lionheart and his scheming brother John seen through the eyes of their contemporaries.* (Weidenfeld & Nicolson, New York: 1986 (copyright held by Pheobe Phillips Editions)), p. 261-282.

[167] John Cannon & Ralph Griffiths, *The Oxford Illustrated History of the British Monarchy* (2000 edition, Oxford University Press), p. 90.

[168] Elizabeth Hallam, ed, *The Plantagenet Chronicles: Medieval Europe's most tempestuous family from Henry II and his wife Eleanor of Aquitaine to Richard the Lionheart and his scheming brother John seen through the eyes of their contemporaries.* (Weidenfeld & Nicolson, New York: 1986 (copyright held by Pheobe Phillips Editions)), p. 292-293, 295-296.

[169] John Cannon & Ralph Griffiths, *The Oxford Illustrated History of the British Monarchy* (2000 edition, Oxford University Press), p. 90, 174.

[170] M.T. Clanchy, *England and its Rulers: 1066-1272* (Blackwell Publishers; Oxford & Massachussetts; 1998 - 2nd Edition), p. 135.

[171] Elizabeth Hallam, ed, *The Plantagenet Chronicles: Medieval Europe's most tempestuous family from Henry II and his wife Eleanor of Aquitaine to Richard the Lionheart and his scheming brother John seen through the eyes of their contemporaries.* (Weidenfeld & Nicolson, New York: 1986 (copyright held by Pheobe Phillips Editions)), p. 261, 305-6.

[172] John Cannon & Ralph Griffiths, *The Oxford Illustrated History of the British Monarchy* (2000 edition, Oxford University Press), p. 174.

[173] Elizabeth Hallam, ed, *The Plantagenet Chronicles: Medieval Europe's most tempestuous family from Henry II and his wife Eleanor of Aquitaine to Richard the Lionheart and his scheming brother John seen through the eyes of their contemporaries.* (Weidenfeld & Nicolson, New York: 1986 (copyright held by Pheobe Phillips Editions)), p. 312, 315.

[174] M.T. Clanchy, *England and its Rulers: 1066-1272* (Blackwell Publishers; Oxford & Massachussetts; 1998 - 2nd Edition), p. 136.

[175] Elizabeth Hallam, ed, *The Plantagenet Chronicles: Medieval Europe's most tempestuous family from Henry II and his wife Eleanor of Aquitaine to Richard the Lionheart and his scheming brother John seen through the eyes of their contemporaries.* (Weidenfeld & Nicolson, New York: 1986 (copyright held by Pheobe Phillips Editions)), p. 316-317, 321.

[176] John Cannon & Ralph Griffiths, *The Oxford Illustrated History of the British Monarchy* (2000 edition, Oxford University Press), p. 92, 174.

[177] M.T. Clanchy, *England and its Rulers: 1066-1272* (Blackwell Publishers; Oxford & Massachussetts; 1998 - 2nd Edition), p. 136.

[178] Elizabeth Hallam, ed, *The Plantagenet Chronicles: Medieval Europe's most tempestuous family from Henry II and his wife Eleanor of Aquitaine to Richard the Lionheart and his scheming brother John seen through the eyes of their contemporaries.* (Weidenfeld & Nicolson, New York: 1986 (copyright held by Pheobe Phillips Editions)), p. 317, 321.

[179] John Cannon & Ralph Griffiths, *The Oxford Illustrated History of the British Monarchy* (2000 edition, Oxford University Press), p. 92, 174.

[180] M.T. Clanchy, *England and its Rulers: 1066-1272* (Blackwell Publishers; Oxford & Massachussetts; 1998 - 2nd Edition), p. 136.

[181] Elizabeth Hallam, ed, *The Plantagenet Chronicles: Medieval Europe's most tempestuous family from Henry II and his wife Eleanor of Aquitaine to Richard the Lionheart and his scheming brother John seen through the eyes of their contemporaries.* (Weidenfeld & Nicolson, New York: 1986 (copyright held by Pheobe Phillips Editions)), p. 321.

[182] John Cannon & Ralph Griffiths, *The Oxford Illustrated History of the British Monarchy* (2000 edition, Oxford University Press), List of Monarchs Appendix.

[183] M.T. Clanchy, *England and its Rulers: 1066-1272* (Blackwell Publishers; Oxford & Massachussetts; 1998 - 2nd Edition), p. 132-3, 240.

[184] Elizabeth Hallam, ed, *The Plantagenet Chronicles: Medieval Europe's most tempestuous family from Henry II and his wife Eleanor of Aquitaine to Richard the Lionheart and his scheming brother John seen through the eyes of their contemporaries.* (Weidenfeld & Nicolson, New York: 1986 (copyright held by Pheobe Phillips Editions)), p. 17, 263.

[185] Dan Jones, *The Plantagenets: The Warrior Kings & Queens who made England* (New York, Viking, 2012), Genealogical Tree at Front.

[186] John Cannon & Ralph Griffiths, *The Oxford Illustrated History of the British Monarchy* (2000 edition, Oxford University Press), p. 648; Geneaolgies of Royal Lines Appendix; List of Monarchs Appendix.

[187] M.T. Clanchy, *England and its Rulers: 1066-1272* (Blackwell Publishers; Oxford & Massachussetts; 1998 - 2nd Edition), p. 143-4.

[188] John Cannon & Ralph Griffiths, *The Oxford Illustrated History of the British Monarchy* (2000 edition, Oxford University Press), p. 189; List of Monarchs Appendix.

[189] Antonia Fraser, Editor, *The Lives of the Kings & Queens of England* (Berkley, University of California Press, 1998, Weidenfield & Nicholson), p. 72.

[190] M.T. Clanchy, *England and its Rulers: 1066-1272* (Blackwell Publishers; Oxford & Massachussetts; 1998 - 2nd Edition), p. 145.

[191] John Cannon & Ralph Griffiths, *The Oxford Illustrated History of the British Monarchy* (2000 edition, Oxford University Press), p. 189.

[192] M.T. Clanchy, *England and its Rulers: 1066-1272* (Blackwell Publishers; Oxford & Massachussetts; 1998 - 2nd Edition), p. 148.

[193] John Cannon & Ralph Griffiths, *The Oxford Illustrated History of the British Monarchy* (2000 edition, Oxford University Press), p. 189.

[194] M.T. Clanchy, *England and its Rulers: 1066-1272* (Blackwell Publishers; Oxford & Massachussetts; 1998 - 2nd Edition), p. 147.

[195] John Cannon & Ralph Griffiths, *The Oxford Illustrated History of the British Monarchy* (2000 edition, Oxford University Press), p. 189.

[196] M.T. Clanchy, *England and its Rulers: 1066-1272* (Blackwell Publishers; Oxford & Massachussetts; 1998 - 2nd Edition), p. 165.

[197] Antonia Fraser, Editor, *The Lives of the Kings & Queens of England* (Berkley, University of California Press, 1998, Weidenfield & Nicholson), p. 75.

[198] John Cannon & Ralph Griffiths, *The Oxford Illustrated History of the British Monarchy* (2000 edition, Oxford University Press), p. 189.

[199] M.T. Clanchy, *England and its Rulers: 1066-1272* (Blackwell Publishers; Oxford & Massachussetts; 1998 - 2nd Edition), p. 198.

[200] Antonia Fraser, Editor, *The Lives of the Kings & Queens of England* (Berkley, University of California Press, 1998, Weidenfield & Nicholson), p. 74.

[201] M.T. Clanchy, *England and its Rulers: 1066-1272* (Blackwell Publishers; Oxford & Massachussetts; 1998 - 2nd Edition), p. 169-172.

[202] M.T. Clanchy, *England and its Rulers: 1066-1272* (Blackwell Publishers; Oxford & Massachussetts; 1998 - 2nd Edition), p. 147, 157.

[203] John Cannon & Ralph Griffiths, *The Oxford Illustrated History of the British Monarchy* (2000 edition, Oxford Univ. Press), p. 189, 208.

[204] M.T. Clanchy, *England and its Rulers: 1066-1272* (Blackwell Publishers; Oxford & Massachussetts; 1998 - 2nd Edition), p. 190, 196-197.

[205] M.C. Scott Moncrieff, *Kings & Queens of England* (London, Blanford Press Ltd., 1966), p. 35.

[206] John Cannon & Ralph Griffiths, *The Oxford Illustrated History of the British Monarchy* (2000 edition, Oxford University Press), p. 189.

[207] M.T. Clanchy, *England and its Rulers: 1066-1272* (Blackwell Publishers; Oxford & Massachussetts; 1998 - 2nd Ed.), p. 190-191, 195, 198.

[208] Antonia Fraser, Editor, *The Lives of the Kings & Queens of England* (Berkley, University of California Press, 1998, Weidenfield & Nicholson), p. 78.

[209] M.T. Clanchy, *England and its Rulers: 1066-1272* (Blackwell Publishers; Oxford & Massachussetts; 1998 - 2nd Edition), p. 160-161.

[210] M.T. Clanchy, *England and its Rulers: 1066-1272* (Blackwell Publishers; Oxford & Massachussetts; 1998 - 2nd Edition), p. 241.

[211] M.C. Scott Moncrieff, *Kings & Queens of England* (London, Blanford Press Ltd., 1966), p. 34.

[212] Antonia Fraser, Editor, *The Lives of the Kings & Queens of England* (Berkley, University of California Press, 1998, Weidenfield & Nicholson), p. 74.

[213] John Cannon & Ralph Griffiths, *The Oxford Illustrated History of the British Monarchy* (2000 edition, Oxford University Press), p. 189; Geneaolgies of Royal Lines Appendix.

[214] Dan Jones, *The Plantagenets: The Warrior Kings & Queens who made England* (New York, Viking, 2012), Genealogical Tree at Front.

[215] Elizabeth Hallam, ed, *The Plantagenet Chronicles: Medieval Europe's most tempestuous family from Henry II and his wife Eleanor of Aquitaine to Richard the Lionheart and his scheming brother John seen through the eyes of their contemporaries*. (Weidenfeld & Nicolson, New York: 1986 (copyright held by Pheobe Phillips Editions)), p. 17.

[216] M.T. Clanchy, *England and its Rulers: 1066-1272* (Blackwell Publishers; Oxford & Massachussetts; 1998 - 2nd Edition), p. 169.

[217] Antonia Fraser, Editor, *The Lives of the Kings & Queens of England* (Berkley, University of California Press, 1998, Weidenfield & Nicholson), p. 77-78.

[218] John Cannon & Ralph Griffiths, *The Oxford Illustrated History of the British Monarchy* (2000 edition, Oxford University Press), p. 292, 651; Geneaolgies of Royal Lines Appendix; List of Monarchs Appendix.

[219] John Cannon & Ralph Griffiths, *The Oxford Illustrated History of the British Monarchy* (2000 edition, Oxford University Press), p. 223; Geneaolgies of Royal Lines Appendix; List of Monarchs Appendix.

[220] Antonia Fraser, Editor, *The Lives of the Kings & Queens of England* (Berkley, University of California Press, 1998, Weidenfield & Nicholson), p. 79.

[221] M.C. Scott Moncrieff, *Kings & Queens of England* (London, Blanford Press Ltd., 1966), p. 37.

[222] John Cannon & Ralph Griffiths, *The Oxford Illustrated History of the British Monarchy* (2000 edition, Oxford University Press), p. 207.

[223] M.T. Clanchy, *England and its Rulers: 1066-1272* (Blackwell Publishers; Oxford & Massachussetts; 1998 - 2nd Edition), p. 190-1.

[224] John Cannon & Ralph Griffiths, *The Oxford Illustrated History of the British Monarchy* (2000 edition, Oxford University Press), p. 189.

[225] John Cannon & Ralph Griffiths, *The Oxford Illustrated History of the British Monarchy* (2000 edition, Oxford University Press), List of Monarchs Appendix.

[226] M.T. Clanchy, *England and its Rulers: 1066-1272* (Blackwell Publishers; Oxford & Massachussetts; 1998 - 2nd Edition), p. 212.

[227] Antonia Fraser, Editor, *The Lives of the Kings & Queens of England* (Berkley, University of California Press, 1998, Weidenfield & Nicholson), p. 84.

[228] John Cannon & Ralph Griffiths, *The Oxford Illustrated History of the British Monarchy* (2000 edition, Oxford University Press), p. 207.

[229] M.T. Clanchy, *England and its Rulers: 1066-1272* (Blackwell Publishers; Oxford & Massachussetts; 1998 - 2nd Edition), p. 206, 217, 219.

[230] Antonia Fraser, Editor, *The Lives of the Kings & Queens of England* (Berkley, University of California Press, 1998, Weidenfield & Nicholson), p. 84-85.

[231] M.C. Scott Moncrieff, *Kings & Queens of England* (London, Blanford Press Ltd., 1966), p. 37.

[232] John Cannon & Ralph Griffiths, *The Oxford Illustrated History of the British Monarchy* (2000 edition, Oxford University Press), p. 207.

[233] M.T. Clanchy, *England and its Rulers: 1066-1272* (Blackwell Publishers; Oxford & Massachussetts; 1998 - 2nd Edition), p. 208.

[234] John Cannon & Ralph Griffiths, *The Oxford Illustrated History of the British Monarchy* (2000 edition, Oxford University Press), p. 207.

[235] M.T. Clanchy, *England and its Rulers: 1066-1272* (Blackwell Publishers; Oxford & Massachussetts; 1998 - 2nd Edition), p. 222-3.

[236] M.T. Clanchy, *England and its Rulers: 1066-1272* (Blackwell Publishers; Oxford & Massachussetts; 1998 - 2nd Edition), p. 223-224.

[237] Ronald Williams, *The Lords of the Isles: The Clan Donald and the Early Kingdom of the Scots* (Chatto & Windus - The Hogarth Press, London, 1984), p. 147-148.

[238] John Cannon & Ralph Griffiths, *The Oxford Illustrated History of the British Monarchy* (2000 edition, Oxford University Press), Geneaolgies of Royal Lines Appendix; List of Monarchs Appendix.

[239] Antonia Fraser, Editor, *The Lives of the Kings & Queens of England* (Berkley, University of California Press, 1998, Weidenfield & Nicholson), p. 86.

[240] Ronald Williams, *The Lords of the Isles: The Clan Donald and the Early Kingdom of the Scots* (Chatto & Windus - The Hogarth Press, London, 1984), p. 156.

[241] Westminster Abbey.org website: http://www.westminster-abbey.org/our-history/royals/burials.

[242] Antonia Fraser, Editor, *The Lives of the Kings & Queens of England* (Berkley, University of California Press, 1998, Weidenfield & Nicholson), p. 79.

[243] John Cannon & Ralph Griffiths, *The Oxford Illustrated History of the British Monarchy* (2000 edition, Oxford University Press), p. 238; Geneaolgies of Royal Lines Appendix.

[244] John Cannon & Ralph Griffiths, *The Oxford Illustrated History of the British Monarchy* (2000 edition, Oxford University Press), Geneaolgies of Royal Lines Appendix.

[245] Westminster Abbey.org website: http://www.westminster-abbey.org/our-history/royals/burials.

[246] Antonia Fraser, Editor, *The Lives of the Kings & Queens of England* (Berkley, University of California Press, 1998, Weidenfield & Nicholson), p. 79.

[247] Dan Jones, *The Plantagenets: The Warrior Kings & Queens who made England* (New York, Viking, 2012), Genealogical Tree at Front.

[248] Antonia Fraser, Editor, *The Lives of the Kings & Queens of England* (Berkley, University of California Press, 1998, Weidenfield & Nicholson), p. 70-71.

[249] Dan Jones, *The Plantagenets: The Warrior Kings & Queens who made England* (New York, Viking, 2012), Genealogical Tree at Front.

[250] John Cannon & Ralph Griffiths, *The Oxford Illustrated History of the British Monarchy* (2000 edition, Oxford University Press), p. 223; Geneaolgies of Royal Lines Appendix; List of Monarchs Appendix.

[251] M.C. Scott Moncrieff, *Kings & Queens of England* (London, Blanford Press Ltd., 1966), p. 39.

[252] M.T. Clanchy, *England and its Rulers: 1066-1272* (Blackwell Publishers; Oxford & Massachussetts; 1998 - 2nd Edition), p. 217.

[253] John Cannon & Ralph Griffiths, *The Oxford Illustrated History of the British Monarchy* (2000 edition, Oxford University Press), p. 216.

[254] John Cannon & Ralph Griffiths, *The Oxford Illustrated History of the British Monarchy* (2000 edition, Oxford University Press), List of Monarchs Appendix.

[255] John Cannon & Ralph Griffiths, *The Oxford Illustrated History of the British Monarchy* (2000 edition, Oxford University Press), p. 216.

[256] John Cannon & Ralph Griffiths, *The Oxford Illustrated History of the British Monarchy* (2000 edition, Oxford University Press), p. 216.

[257] John Cannon & Ralph Griffiths, *The Oxford Illustrated History of the British Monarchy* (2000 edition, Oxford University Press), p. 216.

[258] M.C. Scott Moncrieff, *Kings & Queens of England* (London, Blanford Press Ltd., 1966), p. 39.

[259] John Cannon & Ralph Griffiths, *The Oxford Illustrated History of the British Monarchy* (2000 edition, Oxford University Press), p. 216.

[260] Antonia Fraser, Editor, *The Lives of the Kings & Queens of England* (Berkley, University of California Press, 1998, Weidenfield & Nicholson), p. 92.

[261] John Cannon & Ralph Griffiths, *The Oxford Illustrated History of the British Monarchy* (2000 edition, Oxford Univ. Press), p. 216, 238.

[262] Antonia Fraser, Editor, *The Lives of the Kings & Queens of England* (Berkley, University of California Press, 1998, Weidenfield & Nicholson), p. 92.

[263] John Cannon & Ralph Griffiths, *The Oxford Illustrated History of the British Monarchy* (2000 edition, Oxford University Press), p. 216.

[264] John Cannon & Ralph Griffiths, *The Oxford Illustrated History of the British Monarchy* (2000 edition, Oxford University Press), p. 208; List of Monarchs Appendix.

[265] M.C. Scott Moncrieff, *Kings & Queens of England* (London, Blanford Press Ltd., 1966), p. 39.

[266] John Cannon & Ralph Griffiths, *The Oxford Illustrated History of the British Monarchy* (2000 edition, Oxford University Press), p. 216, 210, 653, Geneaolgies of Royal Lines Appendix; List of Monarchs Appendix.

[267] Antonia Fraser, Editor, *The Lives of the Kings & Queens of England* (Berkley, University of California Press, 1998, Weidenfield & Nicholson), p. 93.

[268] John Cannon & Ralph Griffiths, *The Oxford Illustrated History of the British Monarchy* (2000 edition, Oxford University Press), p. 238; Geneaolgies of Royal Lines Appendix.

[269] Dan Jones, *The Plantagenets: The Warrior Kings & Queens who made England* (New York, Viking, 2012), Genealogical Tree at Front.

[270] John Cannon & Ralph Griffiths, *The Oxford Illustrated History of the British Monarchy* (2000 edition, Oxford University Press), p. 223; Geneaolgies of Royal Lines Appendix; List of Monarchs Appendix.

[271] Antonia Fraser, Editor, *The Lives of the Kings & Queens of England* (Berkley, University of California Press, 1998, Weidenfield & Nicholson), p. 94.

[272] John Cannon & Ralph Griffiths, *The Oxford Illustrated History of the British Monarchy* (2000 edition, Oxford University Press), List of Monarchs Appendix.

[273] Fitzroy Maclean, *A Concise History of Scotland* (First published 1970. This version, 2002. Thames & Hudson Ltd., London), p. 44.

[274] John Cannon & Ralph Griffiths, *The Oxford Illustrated History of the British Monarchy* (2000 edition, Oxford Univ. Press), p. 220, 225.

[275] Antonia Fraser, Editor, *The Lives of the Kings & Queens of England* (Berkley, University of California Press, 1998, Weidenfield & Nicholson), p. 98.

[276] John Cannon & Ralph Griffiths, *The Oxford Illustrated History of the British Monarchy* (2000 edition, Oxford University Press), p. 225.

[277] Antonia Fraser, Editor, *The Lives of the Kings & Queens of England* (Berkley, University of California Press, 1998, Weidenfield & Nicholson), p. 94.

[278] M.C. Scott Moncrieff, *Kings & Queens of England* (London, Blanford Press Ltd., 1966), p. 46.

[279] Antonia Fraser, Editor, *The Lives of the Kings & Queens of England* (Berkley, University of California Press, 1998, Weidenfield & Nicholson), p. 99.

[280] John Cannon & Ralph Griffiths, *The Oxford Illustrated History of the British Monarchy* (2000 edition, Oxford University Press), p. 225.

[281] Antonia Fraser, Editor, *The Lives of the Kings & Queens of England* (Berkley, University of California Press, 1998, Weidenfield & Nicholson), p. 99-100.

[282] Antonia Fraser, Editor, *The Lives of the Kings & Queens of England* (Berkley, University of California Press, 1998, Weidenfield & Nicholson), p. 102.

[283] M.C. Scott Moncrieff, *Kings & Queens of England* (London, Blanford Press Ltd., 1966), p. 47.

[284] John Cannon & Ralph Griffiths, *The Oxford Illustrated History of the British Monarchy* (2000 edition, Oxford University Press), p. 225.

[285] M.C. Scott Moncrieff, *Kings & Queens of England* (London, Blanford Press Ltd., 1966), p. 46.

[286] Antonia Fraser, Editor, *The Lives of the Kings & Queens of England* (Berkley, University of California Press, 1998, Weidenfield & Nicholson), p. 98.

[287] John Cannon & Ralph Griffiths, *The Oxford Illustrated History of the British Monarchy* (2000 edition, Oxford University Press), p. 225.

[288] Antonia Fraser, Editor, *The Lives of the Kings & Queens of England* (Berkley, University of California Press, 1998, Weidenfield & Nicholson), p. 98.

[289] Antonia Fraser, Editor, *The Lives of the Kings & Queens of England* (Berkley, University of California Press, 1998, Weidenfield & Nicholson), p. 100.

[290] Antonia Fraser, Editor, *The Lives of the Kings & Queens of England* (Berkley, University of California Press, 1998, Weidenfield & Nicholson), p. 102.

[291] John Cannon & Ralph Griffiths, *The Oxford Illustrated History of the British Monarchy* (2000 edition, Oxford University Press), p. 225; Geneaolgies of Royal Lines Appendix.

[292] M.C. Scott Moncrieff, *Kings & Queens of England* (London, Blanford Press Ltd., 1966), p. 47.

[293] John Cannon & Ralph Griffiths, *The Oxford Illustrated History of the British Monarchy* (2000 edition, Oxford University Press), p. 225.

[294] John Cannon & Ralph Griffiths, *The Oxford Illustrated History of the British Monarchy* (2000 edition, Oxford University Press), p. 225, 644; Geneaolgies of Royal Lines Appendix; List of Monarchs Appendix.

[295] M.C. Scott Moncrieff, *Kings & Queens of England* (London, Blanford Press Ltd., 1966), p. 48.

[296] Westminster Abbey.org website: http://www.westminster-abbey.org/our-history/royals/burials.

[297] John Cannon & Ralph Griffiths, *The Oxford Illustrated History of the British Monarchy* (2000 edition, Oxford University Press), Geneaolgies of Royal Lines Appendix.

[298] Dan Jones, *The Plantagenets: The Warrior Kings & Queens who made England* (New York, Viking, 2012), Genealogical Tree at Front.

[299] Antonia Fraser, Editor, *The Lives of the Kings & Queens of England* (Berkley, University of California Press, 1998, Weidenfield & Nicholson), p. 70-71.

[300] John Cannon & Ralph Griffiths, *The Oxford Illustrated History of the British Monarchy* (2000 edition, Oxford University Press), Geneaolgies of Royal Lines Appendix; List of Monarchs Appendix.

[301] Antonia Fraser, Editor, *The Lives of the Kings & Queens of England* (Berkley, University of California Press, 1998, Weidenfield & Nicholson), p. 111.

[302] Antonia Fraser, Editor, *The Lives of the Kings & Queens of England* (Berkley, University of California Press, 1998, Weidenfield & Nicholson), p. 117.

[303] John Cannon & Ralph Griffiths, *The Oxford Illustrated History of the British Monarchy* (2000 edition, Oxford University Press), Geneaolgies of Royal Lines Appendix.

[304] John Cannon & Ralph Griffiths, *The Oxford Illustrated History of the British Monarchy* (2000 edition, Oxford University Press), Geneaolgies of Royal Lines Appendix.

[305] John Cannon & Ralph Griffiths, *The Oxford Illustrated History of the British Monarchy* (2000 edition, Oxford University Press), Geneaolgies of Royal Lines Appendix.

[306] John Cannon & Ralph Griffiths, *The Oxford Illustrated History of the British Monarchy* (2000 edition, Oxford University Press), Geneaolgies of Royal Lines Appendix.

[307] John Cannon & Ralph Griffiths, *The Oxford Illustrated History of the British Monarchy* (2000 edition, Oxford University Press), Geneaolgies of Royal Lines Appendix.

[308] Douglas Richardson, *Magna Carta Ancestry: A Study in Colonial and Medieval Families*, ed. Kimball G. Everingham (2nd Edition, 2011, Salt Lake City), p. 193-196.

[309] T.B. Pugh, *Henry V and the Southampton Plot of 1415* (1988, Alan Sutton), p.104.

[310] John Cannon & Ralph Griffiths, *The Oxford Illustrated History of the British Monarchy* (2000 edition, Oxford University Press), Geneaolgies of Royal Lines Appendix.

[311] John Cannon & Ralph Griffiths, *The Oxford Illustrated History of the British Monarchy* (2000 edition, Oxford University Press), Geneaolgies of Royal Lines Appendix.

[312] Antonia Fraser, Editor, *The Lives of the Kings & Queens of England* (Berkley, University of California Press, 1998, Weidenfield & Nicholson), p. 132.

[313] John Cannon & Ralph Griffiths, *The Oxford Illustrated History of the British Monarchy* (2000 edition, Oxford University Press), p. 214.

[314] Antonia Fraser, Editor, *The Lives of the Kings & Queens of England* (Berkley, University of California Press, 1998, Weidenfield & Nicholson), p. 132-133.

[315] Antonia Fraser, Editor, *The Lives of the Kings & Queens of England* (Berkley, University of California Press, 1998, Weidenfield & Nicholson), p. 135.

[316] John Cannon & Ralph Griffiths, *The Oxford Illustrated History of the British Monarchy* (2000 edition, Oxford University Press), p. 267, 290, Geneaolgies of Royal Lines Appendix; List of Monarchs Appendix.

[317] Antonia Fraser, Editor, *The Lives of the Kings & Queens of England* (Berkley, University of California Press, 1998, Weidenfield & Nicholson), p. 135.

[318] John Cannon & Ralph Griffiths, *The Oxford Illustrated History of the British Monarchy* (2000 edition, Oxford University Press), p. 267, 290, List of Monarchs Appendix

[319] John Cannon & Ralph Griffiths, *The Oxford Illustrated History of the British Monarchy* (2000 edition, Oxford University Press), p. 290.

[320] Antonia Fraser, Editor, *The Lives of the Kings & Queens of England* (Berkley, University of California Press, 1998, Weidenfield & Nicholson), p. 146.

[321] M.C. Scott Moncrieff, *Kings & Queens of England* (London, Blanford Press Ltd., 1966), p. 56.

[322] Antonia Fraser, Editor, *The Lives of the Kings & Queens of England* (Berkley, University of California Press, 1998, Weidenfield & Nicholson), p. 146, 148.

[323] John Cannon & Ralph Griffiths, *The Oxford Illustrated History of the British Monarchy* (2000 edition, Oxford University Press), p. 267, 290, List of Monarchs Appendix.

[324] Antonia Fraser, Editor, *The Lives of the Kings & Queens of England* (Berkley, University of California Press, 1998, Weidenfield & Nicholson), p. 148.

[325] M.C. Scott Moncrieff, *Kings & Queens of England* (London, Blanford Press Ltd., 1966), p. 57.

[326] John Cannon & Ralph Griffiths, *The Oxford Illustrated History of the British Monarchy* (2000 edition, Oxford University Press), p. 290, Geneaolgies of Royal Lines Appendix.

[327] Antonia Fraser, Editor, *The Lives of the Kings & Queens of England* (Berkley, University of California Press, 1998, Weidenfield & Nicholson), p. 148, 142.

[328] John Cannon & Ralph Griffiths, *The Oxford Illustrated History of the British Monarchy* (2000 edition, Oxford University Press), p. 290, List of Monarchs Appendix

[329] Antonia Fraser, Editor, *The Lives of the Kings & Queens of England* (Berkley, University of California Press, 1998, Weidenfield & Nicholson), p. 149.

[330] Antonia Fraser, Editor, *The Lives of the Kings & Queens of England* (Berkley, University of California Press, 1998, Weidenfield & Nicholson), p. 165.

[331] M.C. Scott Moncrieff, *Kings & Queens of England* (London, Blanford Press Ltd., 1966), p. 58.

[332] John Cannon & Ralph Griffiths, *The Oxford Illustrated History of the British Monarchy* (2000 edition, Oxford University Press), p. 294, Geneaolgies of Royal Lines Appendix.

[333] John Cannon & Ralph Griffiths, *The Oxford Illustrated History of the British Monarchy* (2000 edition, Oxford University Press), p. 294, List of Monarchs Appendix.

[334] Antonia Fraser, Editor, *The Lives of the Kings & Queens of England* (Berkley, University of California Press, 1998, Weidenfield & Nicholson), p. 162.

[335] John Cannon & Ralph Griffiths, *The Oxford Illustrated History of the British Monarchy* (2000 edition, Oxford University Press), p. 295, List of Monarchs Appendix.

[336] M.C. Scott Moncrieff, *Kings & Queens of England* (London, Blanford Press Ltd., 1966), p. 57.

[337] Antonia Fraser, Editor, *The Lives of the Kings & Queens of England* (Berkley, University of California Press, 1998, Weidenfield & Nicholson), p. 162.

[338] John Cannon & Ralph Griffiths, *The Oxford Illustrated History of the British Monarchy* (2000 edition, Oxford University Press), p. 295.

[339] M.C. Scott Moncrieff, *Kings & Queens of England* (London, Blanford Press Ltd., 1966), p. 59.

[340] John Cannon & Ralph Griffiths, *The Oxford Illustrated History of the British Monarchy* (2000 edition, Oxford University Press), p. 295.

[341] M.C. Scott Moncrieff, *Kings & Queens of England* (London, Blanford Press Ltd., 1966), p. 60.

[342] John Cannon & Ralph Griffiths, *The Oxford Illustrated History of the British Monarchy* (2000 edition, Oxford University Press), p. 295, List of Monarchs Appendix.

[343] M.C. Scott Moncrieff, *Kings & Queens of England* (London, Blanford Press Ltd., 1966), p. 66.

[344] Antonia Fraser, Editor, *The Lives of the Kings & Queens of England* (Berkley, University of California Press, 1998, Weidenfield & Nicholson), p. 165.

[345] Antonia Fraser, Editor, *The Lives of the Kings & Queens of England* (Berkley, University of California Press, 1998, Weidenfield & Nicholson), p. 168.

[346] John Cannon & Ralph Griffiths, *The Oxford Illustrated History of the British Monarchy* (2000 edition, Oxford University Press), Geneaolgies of Royal Lines Appendix.

[347] Antonia Fraser, Editor, *The Lives of the Kings & Queens of England* (Berkley, University of California Press, 1998, Weidenfield & Nicholson), p. 166.

[348] M.C. Scott Moncrieff, *Kings & Queens of England* (London, Blanford Press Ltd., 1966), p. 67.

[349] John Cannon & Ralph Griffiths, *The Oxford Illustrated History of the British Monarchy* (2000 edition, Oxford University Press), p. 295, List of Monarchs Appendix.

[350] Antonia Fraser, Editor, *The Lives of the Kings & Queens of England* (Berkley, University of California Press, 1998, Weidenfield & Nicholson), p. 166.

INDEXES

NAME INDEX

Scotland, father of Duncan I, King of
Scotland), 157, 158
Kings of Dalriada
Aed Find, 146
Aedan, 145, 146
Alpin, 146
Domangart, 145
Domangart II, 146
Domnall Breac, 146
Eacime, founder of Clan MacDonald,
146
Eochaid Buidh, 146
Eochaid III, 146
Eochaid IV, 146
Eochaid Roman Nose, 146
Fergus II, 146
Fergus Mor, 143, 144
Gabhran, 145
Irish Ancestors
Cairbre Riada of the Liffey, 144
Colla Uais, 144
Conn of the Hundred Battles, High
King of Tara, 144
Eochach Dubhlein, 144
MacAlpin Dynasty
Bethoc (dau. Malcolm II, King of
Scotland, wife of Crinan, Abbot of
Dunkeld), 157
Constantine I, 79, 80, 152, 153
David I, 29, 32, 63, 64, 86, 94, 126,
127, 137, 161, 162, 163, 164, 165,
166, 235, 236
David, Earl of Huntingdon, 130, 165,
166, 167, 168, 179, 231, 238
Donada (dau. Malcolm II, King of
Scotland, wife of Finlay MacRory,
Mormaor of Moray), 157, 158
Donald II, 153, 154
Duncan I, 83, 157, 158
Gruoch (dau. Boedhe, wife of Macbeth,
Mormaor of Moray, future King of
Scotland), 156, 157
Henry, Earl of Huntingdon, 127, 162,
164, 165
Isabella (dau. David, Earl of
Huntingdon, wife of Robert (IV) de

Brus, Lord of Annandale), 129, 130,
169, 179
Kenneth I MacAlpin, 146, 151, 152
Kenneth II, 154, 155, 216
Lulach, 29, 64, 157, 158
Macbeth, 157, 158
Malcolm I, 153, 154, 215
Malcolm II, 82, 83, 155, 156, 157
Malcolm III, 84, 157, 158, 159, 160,
161, 223, 224, 231, 233, 235
Maud (dau. Malcolm III, King of
Scotland, wife of Henry I, King of
England), 161, 162, 235
Plantula (dau. Malcolm II, King of
Scotland, wife of Sigurd Hlodverson,
11th of Orkney), 82, 156, 157
Stewart Dynasty
Agnes (wife of John MacKay, 1st of
Strathy), 44, 120, 197
Bruce, Marjorie (dau. Robert I Bruce,
King of Scotland, wife of Sir Walter
Stewart, 6th High Steward of
Scotland), 140, 183, 197
Elizabeth (dau. Robert Stewart, Earl of
Orkney, wife of James Sinclair, 1st
of Murkle), 44, 120, 197
James I, 34, 114, 115, 188, 189, 190,
231
James II, 189, 190, 191, 192
James III, 36, 115, 116, 191, 192, 193
James IV, 36, 37, 49, 116, 117, 193,
194, 195, 231, 248
James V, 38, 39, 120, 194, 195, 197
Margaret (dau Robert II, King of
Scotland, wife of John MacDonald,
1st Lord of the Isles), 34, 71, 72, 187
Robert I Bruce, 32, 68, 69, 70, 97, 98,
111, 133, 138, 139, 140, 180, 181,
182, 183, 184, 231, 241, 242
Robert II, 69, 71, 99, 140, 183, 184,
185, 186, 187
Robert III, 113, 114, 186, 187, 188
Robert Stewart, Earl of Orkney, 120,
197

Sinclair

PLACE INDEX

Place Index

2352 31st, 16
248-10 Depew, 7
31-58 36th, 7
967 Lawncrest, 15

WALES
  Gwynedd
    Caernarvon
      Caernarvon Castle, 242

CHURCH & CEMETERY INDEX

CHURCHES

www.ingramcontent.com/pod-product-compliance
Lightning Source LLC
Chambersburg PA
CBHW080617030426
42336CB00018B/2994